Innocence & Experience:
Essays & Conversations on Children's Literature

INNOCENCE & EXPERIENCE:

Essays & Conversations on Children's Literature

Compiled and Edited by
Barbara Harrison and Gregory Maguire
from Programs Presented at
Simmons College Center for the Study of
Children's Literature
Boston, Massachusetts

LOTHROP, LEE & SHEPARD BOOKS • NEW YORK

First Edition 1 2 3 4 5 6 7 8 9 10

Library of Congress Cataloging in Publication Data
Innocence and experience.
    Includes bibliography and index. 1. Children's literature—History and criticism. I. Harrison, Barbara. II. Maguire, Gregory. III. Simmons College. Center for the Study of Children's Literature. PN1009.A1I495 1987   809'.89282   86-10344
                    ISBN 0-688-06123-0

COPYRIGHT NOTICES AND ACKNOWLEDGMENTS

"The Third Eye" by Mollie Hunter. Copyright © 1987 by Maureen Mollie Hunter McIlwraith.

"Between a Peach and the Universe" by E. L. Konigsburg. Copyright © 1987 by E. L. Konigsburg.

"How I Found *The Treasure*" by Uri Shulevitz. Copyright © 1987 by Uri Shulevitz.

Grateful acknowledgment is made for permission to reprint essays:

Agathon Press, Inc., for "Translation and Internationalism in Children's Literature" by Marianne Carus. *Children's Literature in Education*, 1980, 11:4, 171–179.

ChLA Quarterly, for "Archilles in Altjira" by Alan Garner and "Picture Books as Literature" by Sonia Landes.

The Horn Book Magazine, Inc., for "Nahum Tarune's Book" by Susan Cooper, copyright © 1980 by Susan Cooper; portions of "From Our Correspondent in Utopia" by Fritz Eichenberg, copyright © 1980 by Fritz Eichenberg; "Bilingual Children" by Norma Farber; "Rememory" by Virginia Hamilton, copyright © 1981 by Virginia Hamilton; "Do I Dare Disturb the Universe" by Madeleine L'Engle, copyright © 1983 by Madeleine L'Engle; "Bones in the Sand" by Penelope Lively, copyright © 1981 by Penelope Lively; "Rememory: An Introduction" by Gregory Maguire; "Sounds in the Heart" by Katherine Paterson, copyright © 1981 by Katherine Paterson.

" 'Go and Catch a Falling Star': What *Is* a Good Children's Book?" by Ethel Heins. *Theory Into Practice*, 1982, Vol. 21, No. 4, pp. 247–253. Copyright 1982, College of Education, The Ohio State University.

"What Has Happened to the 'All-White' World of Children's Books?" by Rudine Sims, copyright © 1983, Phi Delta Kappan, Inc.

"Literary Criticism and Children's Books" by Paul Heins, copyright © 1981 by Paul Heins. Originally published in *Quarterly Journal of the Library of Congress*, Fall 1981.

Marcia Brown, "The Lotus Blossom—Or Whodunit?" from *Lotus Seeds*. Copyright © 1986 Marcia Brown. Reprinted with permission of Charles Scribner's Sons.

"Howl like the Wolves" by Barbara Harrison. *Children's Literature*, Vol. 15, edited by Francelia Butler et al. Yale University Press, 1987. Reprinted by permission of Yale University Press.

Grateful acknowledgment is made for permission to reprint copyrighted materials:

"Compass" excerpted from the book *Jorge Luis Borges, Selected Poems 1923–1967*. Edited, with an Introduction and Notes, by Norman Thomas di Giovanni. English Translation, Copyright © 1968, 1969, 1970, 1971, 1972 by Emecé Editores, S.A., and Norman Thomas di Giovanni. Introduction and Notes, Copyright © 1972 by Norman Thomas di Giovanni. Original Spanish Texts, Copyright © 1954, 1958, 1960, 1964, 1966, 1967, 1969 by Emecé Editores, S.A., Buenos Aires. Reprinted by permission of Delacorte Press/Seymour Lawrence.

The Literary Trustees of Walter de la Mare and The Society of Authors as their representative are acknowledged for permission to reprint "The Dream Voyage" by Walter de la Mare.

Excerpt from *The Odyssey*, Homerus. Translated by Robert Fitzgerald. Doubleday, 1961. By permission of the publisher.

The part title illustration for Part VI is from *William Blake: Songs of Innocence*, illustrated by Ellen Raskin (Doubleday, 1966), and is used by permission of the publisher.

"The White Deer," from *The Gold of the Tigers: Selected Later Poems by Jorge Luis Borges*, translated by Alastair Reid. English translation copyright © 1976, 1977 by Alastair Reid. Reprinted by permission of the publisher, E. P. Dutton, a division of NAL Penguin Inc.

Excerpt from "Little Gidding" in *Four Quartets* by T. S. Eliot, copyright 1943 by T. S. Eliot; renewed 1971 by Esme Valerie Eliot. Reprinted by permission of Harcourt Brace Jovanovich, Inc.

Excerpts from "The Love Song of J. Alfred Prufrock" in *Collected Poems 1909–1962* by T. S. Eliot, copyright 1936 by Harcourt Brace Jovanovich, Inc.; copyright © 1963, 1964 by T. S. Eliot. Reprinted by permission of the publisher.

Excerpt from "The Rum Tum Tugger" in *Old Possum's Book of Practical Cats*, copyright 1939 by T. S. Eliot; renewed 1967 by Esme Valerie Eliot. Reprinted by permission of Harcourt Brace Jovanovich, Inc.

Text of "Marie Lucille" from *Bronzeville Boys and Girls* by Gwendolyn Brooks. Copyright © 1956 by Gwendolyn Brooks Blakely. Reprinted by permission of Harper & Row, Publishers, Inc.

Excerpt from *The Odyssey of Homer: A Modern Translation* by Richmond A. Lattimore. Copyright © 1965, 1967 by Richmond A. Lattimore. Reprinted by permission of Harper & Row, Publishers, Inc.

"Mother to Son." Copyright 1926 by Alfred A. Knopf, Inc. and renewed 1954 by Langston Hughes. Reprinted from *Selected Poems of Langston Hughes* by Langston Hughes, by permission of Alfred A. Knopf, Inc.

The part title illustration for Part V is from *The Magician* by Uri Shulevitz. Copyright © 1973 by Uri Shulevitz. Reproduced by permission of Macmillan Publishing Company.

"On Translating Eugene Onegin" by Vladimir Nabokov. Reprinted by permission of Dimitri Nabokov as trustee of Article 3B Trust under the Will of Vladimir Nabokov.

The part title illustration for Part II by Alice and Martin Provensen is used courtesy of the National Geographic Society.

Excerpt from "Musee des Beaux Arts" from *The English Auden: Poems, Essays and Dramatic Writings, 1927–1939* by W. H. Auden, edited by Edward Mendelson. Copyright 1940, renewed 1968 by W. H. Auden. Used by permission of Random House, Inc.

Contents

Contents   ix

Acknowledgments

We would like to thank the contributors to this volume for their enormous generosity and unstinting friendship through the years. All of the selections have been donated by their authors to benefit graduate study in children's literature; proceeds from the sale of the book will provide scholarship assistance.

We are very grateful to Ethel Heins, Paul Heins, and Betty Levin, who took the book to heart early in its evolution and contributed essays, chapter introductions, boundless enthusiasm, and support. In addition, Betty Levin accepted the difficult challenge of creating a single tapestry—"The Perilous Realms: A Colloquy"—from literally hundreds of pages of transcripts. And with the deft eyes of an accomplished editor and critic, Ethel Heins provided much judicious advice and editorial assistance. We would like to acknowledge her help and express our admiration and gratitude.

It is a pleasure to recognize the commitment of the many apologists for children's literature—parents, teachers, school and public librarians, aspiring writers and illustrators—who have joined us in our quests and investigations. We would like to thank students and graduates of the Center and advisory board members, who have shaped the program from its inception and contributed so generously to this book; we also warmly thank the faculty members whose spirits continue to invigorate our work and who have contributed ideas, essays, and encouragement to the book—Nancy Bond, Ginny Moore Kruse, Sonia Landes, John Langstaff, Jane Langton, Jill Paton Walsh, Joan M. Tieman, John Rowe Townsend, and Kate Waters. We are grateful to Virginia Haviland, former head of the Children's Book Center of the Library of Congress, for her encouragement and to the National Endowment for the Humanities for financial assistance in the early years of the program. We are also grateful to Ginny Golodetz, Vas Vrettos, and Maggie Stern-Terris, who have been supportive in countless ways.

The firm, sure hand of our publisher Dorothy Briley is apparent in the book; we are profoundly indebted to her for her commitment to our work and for her support and affirmation. To Dinah Stevenson, executive editor at Lothrop, we would like to offer a special thanks for everything she has done to make the book a reality.

Invaluable aid in the transcription of tapes and the preparation of the manuscript was given by Cathie Mercier, Lucy Loveridge, Barbara Lowe, and Martha Vaughan; we are appreciative of the technical skill of Brian Anastasi and Helen Snively and are particularly indebted to Faith Smith for her professional expertise in copy editing. Cathie Mercier organized much of the work, attending to endless detail, always with grace and good humor.

These acknowledgments would not be complete without an expression of gratitude to Simmons College for providing the environment in which the Center for the Study of Children's Literature could grow and develop. This book truly would not have been possible without the support and cooperation of the College, its faculty, staff, and officers.

In January 1977, during the ceremony at the Boston Athenaeum announcing the establishment of the Center, and on various occasions through the years, David McCord recited a poem highlighting our central concern—the child:

> Blessed Lord, what it is to be young:
> To be of, to be for, be among—
> Be enchanted, enthralled,
> Be the caller, the called,
> The singer, the song, and the sung.

Our work has been emboldened by these words. We would like to thank him and everyone who, through the years, heralded the child's voice in all its infinite variety, and celebrated the child as portrayed in literature—the child embattled and triumphant in a world awesome in its inertia and age-old patterns as well as in its aspirations and promise.

Introduction

In the realms of innocence and of experience, the voyager is at times like a comic and frail Diogenes with lantern in hand, asking each person he or she meets, What is your conception of innocence? And your conception of experience? Is innocence ecstasy? Experience wretchedness? Is one made of nightmare, and one of dream? Are innocence and experience stages through which we pass? Is childhood innocence, and old age experience? Or are they states in which we exist simultaneously in childhood and in old age? Are we bent by experience as is Edward Tulliver in George Eliot's *The Mill on the Floss,* who cries out, "I'm a tree as is broke, a tree as is broke . . . this world is too many for me"? Or are we ennobled by it? Are innocence and experience both divine songs?

For more than a decade an extraordinary number of talented people—among them, British and American authors, illustrators, publishers, educators, and librarians—have met at the Center for the Study of Children's Literature at Simmons College in Boston to discuss such questions in the context of childhood, literature, and society. A small nucleus of these people was employed by the College, teaching graduate courses in children's literature and meeting in spontaneous seminars often lasting late into the night.

The lectures, informal colloquies, and conversations in this book are gathered from programs beginning in 1975 with a summer institute. Some of the selections are formal lectures, some are informal talks, and a few are composite pieces reconstructed from various remarks, interviews, and presentations. Our guiding principle has been to reflect as truly as possible the nature of the investigative process that has defined our work. The contributors offer refreshing observations about memory and the creative process, the power of language and what it means to make language accessible to children, the qualifying differences between realism and fantasy and between writing for children and writing for adults. The speakers give insights into moral courage and heroism in children's fiction, quests and mythic patterns, the significance of the child's early experiences with literature, and the primacy of poem, story, and picture. The essays and conversations have much to say about childhood and literature in the context of William Blake's two contrary states of the human soul.

Although the visionary Blake and his *Songs of Innocence and of Experience* are the imaginative force in the work of the Center, other allusions appear and reappear in the talks and conversations—like the benevolent spirits of poets whose works are part of the landscape of theme and topic that we have examined: references to T. S. Eliot's "The Love Song of J. Alfred Prufrock" and to C. P. Cavafy's "Ithaka." T. S. Eliot's lines "Do I dare/Disturb the universe?" provide a framework for considering moral concerns in children's literature, while Cavafy's "Ithaka" speaks to the nature of the journey rendered into children's fiction—to Odysseus's question asked from the point of view of the child protagonist, "What in the long run will befall me?" Through the years the informing critical question that has accompanied our investigation of children's literature is inspired by F. R. Leavis: How significant are the works, not only in form and structure, but "in terms of the human awareness they promote; awareness of the possibilities of life"?

The talks engage us in matters that go beyond the common round; they dispel a number of myths about childhood and children's literature; and in an era when respect for the humanities is at a low ebb and when illiteracy exists in staggering proportions, they offer new perceptions of the value of the arts and humanities to children; in fact they share many interesting perspectives. Nina Bawden says that "a story can often mean more to a child, do more for him, in fact, than a novel may do for an adult." In recalling her own childhood reading experiences, she says, "I could see that the authors of some of the stories were cleverer than the adults I knew, and, what was more important, thought as I did, agreed with me." Clearly, Nina Bawden values what she is doing; she takes childhood seriously and asks us to do the same.

In the painting *Puberty* Edvard Munch depicts a young girl sitting at the edge of a bed, her arms concealing her nakedness, her legs tightly drawn together, her feet on the floor. Rising from the bed, a dark shadow hovers behind the child. A nascent awareness of sexuality and death emerges in this portrait, which could be called Innocence and Experience. Innocence is unacquainted with shadow and death; it exists before experience, and it is vulnerable.

F. L. Lucas, too, sheds light on the tension and duality between innocence and experience. In explaining the meaning of tragedy, Lucas states:

> By tragedy, I think, we imply also something fundamentally true to life. It need not be the whole truth, but it must be true. Twice at the theater I can remember having felt in the midst of a play, "Yes, this is the very essence of Tragedy": once, in Turgenev's *A Month in the Country*, where the slow disillusionment of years is crowded into one agonized scene and a girl frozen into a woman before our eyes. Were the truth and the beauty of it less perfect, we should feel it less keenly; were they less perfect, we might feel it more keenly than we could bear. As it is, we mutter, "How unbearable!"—and yet, yes, that is how it happens, the inevitable change that comes on all of us, made visible here as never before. This is life. This is growing up. How appallingly—how fascinatingly true!

Lucas implies that life is a tragic experience, that growing up inevitably involves change and often moments of disillusionment—some decidedly greater than others—which can become, over time, a crescendo of despair.

Yes, experience has the capacity to diminish, but it also has the capacity to ennoble. It can be disillusioning and even tragic, but not necessarily either one—although because of it we are not the same person we were a moment before. Something has happened—a change, an awakening, an understanding. It can be what happens to Bridie McShane in Mollie Hunter's *A Sound of Chariots* when she is overcome for the first time with the "great and terrible yearning for something she could not name and which she knew she would never reach." It can be what happens to Ged in Ursula Le Guin's *A Wizard of Earthsea* when he realizes the enormous evil that he has unleashed through hubris. In his autobiographical writing—*In My Father's Court*, published for adults, and *A Day of Pleasure*, for children—Isaac Bashevis Singer describes his childhood universe at 10 Krochmalna Street in Warsaw, in a treeless Polish ghetto with an outhouse in the courtyard occupied by rats and mice; and yet, as he stands on his balcony—a young boy on the holy Sabbath in his satin gabardine and his velvet hat—he contemplates:

> How vast this world, and how rich in all kinds of people and strange happenings! And how high was the sky above the rooftops! And how deep the earth beneath the flagstones! And why did men and women love each other? And where was God, who was constantly spoken of in our house? I was amazed, delighted, entranced. I felt that I must solve this riddle, I alone, with my own understanding.

Galvanized and energized by experience, the child as well as the adult, in W. H. Auden's words, "is obliged at every moment to transcend what it was a moment before."

In terms of the kind of tragic experience that F. L. Lucas writes about, in literature for the young we see moments of slow disillusionment in varying degrees of intensity. Rarely do we see the colossal moments—the absolute crowding together of years of disillusionment into one agonized scene such as Lucas describes, of a girl frozen into a woman before our eyes.

Through the years I have said in a number of different contexts—and the idea is borne out in the essays in this book—that the demands of writing literature for children are as exacting as in the experience of childhood itself. Adults who hold tenaciously to the myth that childhood is an idyllic, carefree state respond to children's literature as they might to a child— amicably, but as if it were merely cute or silly. The myth is without basis. It belies human experience and art.

Our personal and collective pasts, as Penelope Lively reminds us, are both retrievable and irretrievable; and the bond that unites people writing for children, and that is reflected in these essays, is their enormous and impressive commitment to memory and their stunning ability to give it shape and to transform it into story. Every one of them dispels the commonly held notion of childhood as a splendid golden age without grief and sorrow, blessed by the gods. They are unabashed in their honesty. Few would choose to be children again.

Children's literature is a growing and evolving branch of literature nearing the spring of its life, says Peter Dickinson. Children's books are "quite an important branch on the ramified tree of art—a very vigorous and leafy branch at the moment, too: While a lot of other more regarded branches have gone half bare or full of strange rots, ours is still strong enough to hang a swing on." Few people would disagree. The broad view of "an ailing adult literature in contrast to a thriving literature for children" is held by John Rowe Townsend; and although he does not make excessive claims for children's literature, he at least wants to set the record straight. Isaac Bashevis Singer lends support to Townsend's view; Singer says that he came to writing for children "because he saw in the child a last refuge from a literature gone berserk and ready for suicide."

Many of the authors, among them Penelope Lively, Peter Dickinson, Isabelle Holland, Jane Langton, Paula Fox, and Nina Bawden, write for both children and adults, and they make some illuminating observations about language and meaning and the qualifying differences between writing for children and writing for adults. The challenge to most children's writers is to achieve a lucid and pure prose style. About *Carrie's War* Nina Bawden says, "I was trying to say a number of rather complicated things about living and growing up, and I wanted to say them as simply as possible." Alan Garner says, "My experience, over twenty-seven years, is that richness of content varies inversely with complexity of language. The more simply I write, the more I can say. The more open the prose as the result of clarity, the more room there is for you, the reader, to bring something of yourself to the act of translating the story from subjectivity to your own." Clearly, to write simply is not to write condescendingly.

"With so many perils besetting us in the real world," says Lloyd Alexander, "it seems quixotic to worry about the world of literature." And yet Alexander and others provide ample evidence that many intelligent people are worrying about it and choosing to spend their lives as authors, illustrators, scholars, teachers, librarians, and promoters of books—raising public consciousness of children's books and knowledge of the inextricable and vital connection between literature and language.

One of the predicaments of the human condition that arises sporadically and is apparent in the final decades of the twentieth century is life's tendency to escape us. It seems that this elusiveness increases as does our technocracy. And although along with young Emily in Thornton Wilder's *Our Town*, we cannot—and probably wouldn't want to even if we could—realize life "every, every minute," we sense that we need to realize a few more minutes than we do. But to realize anything—a droplet of water on a leaf, or tears in the eyes of a friend—we must be able to apprehend it and re-create it in our minds. Against the titans Time and Death we are all poor, frail creatures, and our power lies in the depth of our compassion and in our abilities to imagine each other in ourselves.

In children's literature there is often a mediator. The reading experience becomes a brilliant configuration reminiscent of the head of the constellation Perseus in the northern sky—an almost perfect triangle: at one angle the book, at another the child, and at the third the adult. Just as it is hard to imagine that an adult can read George Eliot's *Middlemarch* without being concerned about heroic longings and possibilities, it is difficult to imagine that a child—with or without an adult mediator—can read Dr. Seuss's *Horton Hatches the Egg* without being concerned about loyalty and trust. Or Ivan Southall's *Josh* without feeling deeply what it means to come of age. Much of children's literature, in fact, is large in theme and in tone. The complex dilemma that great literature places before the world in a variety of ways is also voiced by Alice: "Who in the world am I? Ah, *that's* the great puzzle!" The earlier we are prompted to ask such questions, the greater the bulwark we can create against life's elusiveness or against the loss of memory in our seductively hurried world.

Place and circumstance shape our attitudes and realities; to be located in New England means to be partially shaped by that period in literary history called the "flowering of New England." Along with Blake, Eliot, and Cavafy, the spirit of transcendentalism reflected in Jane Langton's essay has animated the work of the Center since its inception. Through the years many students have made pilgrimages from the Back Bay fens to Concord to walk in the steps of some literary giants—Hawthorne, Emerson, Alcott, Thoreau; to visit the Thoreau Lyceum, the Alcotts' Orchard House, and Bronson Alcott's adjacent School of Philosophy; and to meet on the sprawling lawn of the Langtons' historic farmhouse in Lincoln, a stone's throw from Walden Pond.

As we have examined the dimensions of childhood experience in children's literature, we have addressed a variety of questions. How do children portrayed in literature come to know themselves and their worlds? What are their conflicts and fears, their nightmares and dreams? What causes them anguish, and what causes them joy? When are they victimized, and when are they victorious? What are their songs of innocence and their songs of experience? During these years, as we met in courses and in special programs, we were also reaffirming the essential value of what we were doing, realizing that we had at our fingertips the basis of our literacy. It is scarcely frivolous or quixotic to be concerned about children's literature, for nowhere are childhood's mysteries more faithfully or scrupulously rendered.

BARBARA HARRISON

It takes Odysseus ten years of travel to reach his home at Ithaca. The cautious narrator of "The Love Song of J. Alfred Prufrock," growing old, may still hear the mermaids singing. And William Blake reveals that "Old John, with white hair, / Doth laugh away care" on the Echoing Green. We look at the examples of these dissimilar and irregular travelers and wonder what patterns emerge about the voyage from innocence to experience. Of all places it is portrayed, the voyage may be most evocatively and incisively depicted by poetry and myth, but it is still impossible to chart.

Children, the most intrepid of travelers, are irregular beings. They do not glide as gracefully from innocence to experience as nineteenth-century Romantics and their descendants would suggest. Children are never wholly innocent nor experienced, just as those two "contrary states of the human soul," as Blake calls them, are not entirely synonymous with joy and pain or with ignorance and knowledge. The aim of this book is to comment on childhood, creativity, and literature for the young; it does so by eschewing a concentration on developmental stages of childhood in favor of an appreciation, admittedly less convenient from a clinical point of view, of the irregularity of human nature.

As soon as children are old enough, they scorn the easy schematizing that may, in some respects, describe them but which they know intuitively can never define them. To overhear that one is "going through *that* phase" is as contemptuous and demeaning to a nine-year-old as it is to a grown person. Children know what adults often forget or overlook: that children are children and never the perfect specimen Child. For the sake of dialectics we who work with children sometimes use that convenient shorthand, but it is a temptation to be resisted.

One instructor began a graduate seminar by bringing in fistfuls of pictures of children she knew and naming the children out loud. She had studio portraits of infants, grade school class photos, and Polaroid snapshots; the kids were toothy, intent, mischievous, bored. The instructor described them as siblings, friends, enemies, or indifferent to each other. The crop at hand included devotees of Prince and Sting, addicts of "The Far Side" and Care Bears.

They were not to be confused with the children who had taken in stride Michael Jackson, or the Muppets, or Batman and Robin, or Barbie and Ken. No more were they identical to Victorian or Regency children. These were not The Child, marching through the ages. They were an irregular and wholly specific group of individuals—they shared some interests, some fears, some needs and passions, and even some literature with children of another year—but they lived blissfully apart, uninterested in serving as anyone's paradigm.

If they were The Child, then perhaps the path from innocence to experience would be easier to chart. But maps and schemes of any sort can never be specific enough, sure enough. People will always differ as to what song the Sirens sing and where Scylla and Charybdis are most likely to be lurking. In just the way that children find their own heroes, their metaphors, their values, they also seek their own way through the thorny woods and across the troubled seas.

Children's encounters with literature may serve them in a way that is different from their encounters with myth and ritual and faith, and yet again different from their life experiences. In twentieth-century life the power of the well-told tale has not been entirely dissipated, and books for children—from the picture book on up to the young adult novel—are a primary repository of some of the most important stories of our polyglot culture. In an age when a limited diet for hundreds of millions of Americans daily is prescribed through the medium of TV, there is more nourishment, more privacy, and—best yet—more freedom of selection to be had in children's reading. Because it is personal and powerful, reading can help weather children into an individuality which will help them to weather that which is *impersonal* and powerful.

There is a famous Thurber cartoon of a well-educated gentleman standing on a chair in an art gallery and peering at a painting through a monocle. The caption recounts the comment of one observer to another: "He knows all about art, but he doesn't know what he likes." It is one of the axioms of the field of children's literature that children fit into the opposite camp: they care little about value and aesthetic content, but they are devoted to what they love. One must treat that axiom, like any other, a bit gingerly; yet it may be safe to suppose that children, unaware of sorting out life from art, come to their literature unabashed. Young children clutch their dog-eared copies of picture books with reverence. One child I know built herself a house every washday, with picture books borrowed from the library. Another child, older than that, read his way through a complete wartime set of Hardy Boys books, ripping strips of margin out of every page and chewing the pulpy yellow paper as he went. Equally as intense is Ann Schlee's recollection, included in Part IV, of a young woman's almost desperate appreciation of a very middle-quality novel. It is in part the thousand and one ways in which a book can be ingested that make questions about quality so knotty and the relationship of reading to understanding so personal and provocative.

There is a tendency to think of children's literature as being a dynamic cultural force whose heyday has sadly passed. Changing reading patterns in America, declining scores in national literacy studies, and the continuing rush of commercialization in every aspect of our lives may make us wistful for what seem like the quieter times of the past. The sentimental picture of pallid Edwardian children in lengthy convalescences, living in their minds while their bodies could not be allowed to stir, seems to have little to do with the violent dangers and satisfactions of modern urban life. Yet, one may be reminded that when Eleanor Farjeon talks of the real little bookroom of her childhood, she is as clearly talking about the attics and bookrooms of the mind, which, while not so celebrated today, continue to exist in the lives of children. It is there that children make sense of what they know. Dorothy Butler recounts her five-year-old grandson playing at being a deep-sea diver with a fairy godmother. Although the culture may at times fail them, children are not born jaded or without arms; this sort of imaginative play has never disappeared from the world.

In a collection whose subtitle includes the word *conversations*, one may expect to find—in addition to several introductions—a fair amount of disagreement, contradiction, and rebuttal. The seventy-odd contributors do not speak with a single voice, no more than myriad children can become The Child. It is safe to say, however, that the contributors share a fundamental and unswerving interest in the good story, how it comes about, what it means to them and to children. Contributors to this book and children value the skepticism of the great travelers on the road from innocence to experience. They do not always rely on accepted rites of passage, on prescribed ritual or hallowed convention for their fund of wisdom. Prufrock may still hear the mermaids; Old John may laugh despite his age. Odysseus, straight from the Trojan War, must live a childhood again on his voyages back to Ithaca. So do we all, charting for ourselves as we go, and taking heart in the conversations and stories of our companions on the road.

GREGORY MAGUIRE

I

Rememory

Early New England gravestone rubbing (18th century)
Logo for "Rememory"
Simmons College Colloquium, 1981

Introduction

GREGORY MAGUIRE

William Butler Yeats began the work entitled *Reveries over Childhood and Youth* with these words: "My first memories are fragmentary and isolated and contemporaneous, as though one remembered some first moments of the Seven Days." His childhood seemed to him so distant as nearly to suggest not just the beginning of *his* time but the beginning of time itself. And so, in the Romantic tradition Yeats—at least initially—associated childhood memories with a sense of lost grandeur, a sense of original and archaic splendor. Yeats's childhood, like the Seven Days of Creation, was over and done with and distinctly unrepeatable.

Yet, that childhood, like the Seven Days of Creation, had been filled with wonders, agonizingly mysterious, brilliantly peopled. And Yeats came into a second creation as a writer, a poet, an interpreter of history, and a zealous merchant of myth. His works may be said to be profoundly and primarily concerned with creating a memory.

Is it any wonder that we view childhood with bedeviled fascination? For although we are beyond it, we can still see it in evidence—inside us, slyly influencing how we act as adults; outside us, cavorting noisily in schools, in streets, and in our homes. The mocking proof of childhood is all around us, not mysteriously suggested, like afterlife, nor impossible to conjecture, like before-life. It is a territory from which we've been exiled. We may be grateful for the exile; and whether we view childhood in the Romantic sense as a state of unearthly innocence or in an earlier, puritanical sense as a state of sinful rudeness to be chastened into grace—or in any other sense—we are uniformly barred from it still. We speculate on our childhoods, however; we want to recall our pasts, suspecting that in our childhoods and in the memories of our childhoods lie images, perceptions, realizations, and clues that can and will illuminate the present.

Just as it is clearly a logical pursuit for us as adults to recall our own

3

childhoods to help inform our present selves, so, too, is it a common and understandable pursuit for people interested in the work of an author to turn to the author's childhood for clues as to how the first creation, the childhood, begot the second, the works themselves.

Of course, an author's childhood and an author's recollection of his or her childhood may be two separate things. Lucy Boston reminds us in the foreword of her memoir *Perverse and Foolish* that memory is a "known cheat"; yet, however historically inaccurate a memory might be, it is still wide and potent and worthy of examination. What the mind chooses to retain indicates a great deal. The mind may be faulty as a repository of precise data, but it is faultless as a prop room, a costume department, a storyboard, and an editorial office.

In his *Confessions*, Augustine speaks of the vast potential for creation when he writes, "And I come into these fields and spacious palaces of my memory, where are the treasures of innumerable images of every kind of thing conveyed into it by the senses . . . and all this I do within, in the huge court of my memory. For there I have in readiness even the heavens and the earth and the sea. . . . There also I meet with myself." There is a cosmos within the memory, Augustine suggests, and that cosmos is at once like and unlike the experiences which helped shape it.

It may be that the very small person, still young in years and wondrously afflicted with childhood, being so near to the beginnings of the heavens and the earth and of experience, has little or no need to translate these beginnings, to reinterpret or to record them. When the child does begin to imitate life—in play, in crayon masterpieces, in private singsong arias—it may be said that the Wordsworthian clouds of glory begin to disperse. It may be that as the child puts his hand to the story, the drawing, or the act, he is making a mark to indicate time, to signify a point in the passing of the endless Seven Days and the coming of the rush of life. That point of recognition of time's relentless advance may be for many people that point at which artistic urges coalesce and begin to exert pressure.

It is Rilke's suggestion that a flood of experience and perceptions and realizations, transformed into memory, constitutes the necessary ingredients for the act of creating successful verse, and that these forces need not—cannot, in fact—be evident but must be internal, silent, and nameless. With such a remark we could close our investigation as quickly as we have opened it, not daring to interfere with the mechanisms of creativity, not wanting to expose to light that which must remain in deep, unapproached quiet in order to function. Every person and every artist has memories; how one uses them is one's own affair.

There is, however, an added concern, which has to do with the children who will read the books the authors write. A complicated set of considerations arises. How does the adult artist, compelled to communicate with children on many levels, select a vocabulary of images and concerns that the child can understand? To what extent does memory of the author's childhood inform or impede the author? What does the adult author, firmly beyond childhood, intend to convey about time and memory to the child who will have little sense of these things? Are books written for children inherently about childhood?

Concerns such as these have been raised at Simmons College conferences and graduate courses for ten years—perhaps most notably at a 1981 colloquium, "Rememory," on the use of memory in the writing of fiction for children. The word is Virginia Hamilton's, and her talk leads off the section. In a sense, all writers for children, in ways obvious and subtle, rely on the secret core of personal history and its effect on the creative imagination for a touchstone, an ignescent road-marker.

I suspect that a deep and abiding memory of our own childhoods has been part of the impetus for us as adults to concern ourselves with books for children. A sense of responsibility and a love for children, yes; an urge to encourage and assist and sometimes instruct, yes; a strong desire to entertain, certainly; but I think all of these philanthropic motivations are related to our memories, apparent or hidden, of that time in life when we could not quite believe that we would be forcibly evicted from the trying and tremendous paradise about us.

Ah, Sweet Rememory!

VIRGINIA HAMILTON

Rememory is a "reword" out of my past. It is not poetic license but a volunteer, like a self-sown seed come forth unbidden. A given. I was fourteen, and I met a dashing fellow who told me he wasn't much on names, but he had a perfect rememory of my smile ("Haven't I seen you somewhere before?") . . . *Rememory* stayed with me through the years; I don't know what happened to the dude-with-a-line. Fortunately, I was able to use rememory as a device for indicating a change in the time frame in *Arilla Sun Down.*

There were a number of words back then that I got wrong quite on my own—words I'd seen in print but never heard spoken. I used what I considered long, sophisticated words principally on my mother, to impress her with my maturity. A favorite one was de-ter-min-ED, hard accent on the last syllable, as in, "Mom, I'm de-ter-min-ED to stay out until twelve; all the other girls are allowed to." Whereupon, Mother informed me that as long as I was de-ter-min-ED, *she* was de-TER-mined I would be home by eleven.

Thereafter, I was careful to look up the pronunciations of peculiar-looking words. How I cringed that I might have fractured *amiable* or *amicable* had I not made use of the dictionary. Looking things up, I discovered *rememory* wasn't a word. Of course, it should be. If one recalls or remembers something remarkable, such as a high compliment from a jiving dude, then one must need use one's rememory in order to do so. Therefore, I take it upon myself to define this reword for the sake of *réchauffé*: Rememory: An exquisitely textured recollection, real or imagined, which is otherwise indescribable.

Which brings me around again to Mother. The local PBS radio station and its zealous young reporter discovered my going-on-eighty-nine, feisty mother. The station was preparing programming devoted to Underground Railroad history in Ohio, which—I suppose—it intended to use for a decade of Black History months. Mother was to give a commentary, of whatever length she desired, on the escape of her father and his mother from slavery.

I was present for the interview. Mother looked like the canary who had had the cat for lunch. The reporter suddenly reminded me of that sincere folk-collector fellow, called the Dude, who visited the Higgins family in *M. C. Higgins, the Great;* each generation, in or out of fiction, has its faithful compilers. Mother kept her eyes on the tape machine as she began; it was clear to me she didn't trust a small black box with about six keys to take down her every word. And at last, she asked the reporter to play it back so she coud hear how she sounded. When he did, sure enough, there she was.

"That's not *me*," Mother announced.

"Of course, it's you; who else would it be?" I said. But I understood what she was getting at. She meant it didn't sound like her in every which way, the same as I don't sound quite like me when I stand before an audience. Mother was not used to hearing herself as chronicler, utilizing unlikely tones and rhythms in order to reveal the action. There were cadences and inflections that had to have been similar to her father's speech peculiarities when first he told about the incredible journey that took him north across the Ohio River to freedom. She definitely didn't sound like Mother. And what she had to say wasn't what I'd heard before. We had spent lots of time, over the years, going into family history.

The reporter fellow must have been thanking his lucky stars. It was clear he considered Mother a great *find*. Anyone could see his excitement—eyes shining, gasps escaping him. Mother always knew she was a find. She gave a glance at me with a look of reproach, I thought. The fact that I hadn't laid bare the spectacular information she was freely giving away to a perfect stranger served me right, the look seemed to say, and there was a lesson in that.

Well, I am for the most part a fiction writer. I use from the source, but I *create* my characters. Mother *is* a character. After all these years she'd been waiting to reveal herself. All that rememory! Real and imagined places and times—thank goodness the young man came along and got it all.

Place and time are at the heart of the fiction I write. The place being a minuscule, unlikely piece of southern Ohio, where I was born. The time is the period of my early life that is transformed and heightened to uniqueness through the creative process. Or it is the memory of my life or my mother's memory of her life as told to me, revised by me toward rememory; or it is that of her mother's and her grandmother's and of old friends'. Time and place are bound together, a solid sensation in the present and past of that which has been accomplished.

Subject matter is for me derived from intimate and shared places of the hometown and the hometown's parade of life and all that is known, remembered, and imagined throughout time therefrom. Home is where I find the emotional landscape for my own spiritual growth and the geographical location for the fictions. Time and place become almost mythical. I suffer through them as I imagine, historically, others have suffered through them. The progress of a people across the hopescape of America gives to my writing a sense of continuity and a narrative source.

Which brings me to a kind of source that is narrative and a way of talking. Going down an open field from where I live to Mother's house. At a certain hour in late day, the ancient hedgerow marking the west property line is backlighted by the slanting sun, and great old Osage hedge trees are a mystery of glowing depths and sparkles. I slip quietly inside the house from the back door. I find Mother in the "front room" talking with my Aunt Sarah Perry. They greet me kindly enough, but I am young; I can wait. They must get back to their talking in the quiet semidark that holds past and present like loops of an invisible bow. I settle back in an easy chair redone in deep plush velvet.

Aunt Sarah Perry is in her late sixties and troubled by arthritis. Mother likes to pretend she's ninety and is troubled by nothing. They are discussing Mother's sister, Aunt Leah, who is seventy-two. These ages are not relevant, for they see one another as they were in their prime. Aunt Leah, being the "Auntie Mame" of Mother's Perry clan, carries on as if she were as free as a bird. This ruffles Mother's feathers; probably because at her advanced age she considers any sudden movement a personal affront. Aunt Leah continually flies off to distant places, buying one-way tickets only.

"Why only one-way?" I asked, captured in the overwrought chair.

"Leah never knows how long she will stay somewhere," said Aunt Sarah Perry.

"Because she never knows when to come home, you mean," said Mother. "Sarah, you are too polite. Leah won't leave until she's told."

"Where is she going?" I thought to ask.

"To Kansas City to spend the summer," answered Aunt Sarah. "You know, Early Lee is out there." (Early Lee is my second cousin.)

"And if Early asks her to leave early," said Mother, aware of the play with words, "she will go on to Germany."

I was startled by the lack of transition and dared ask, "Who's in Germany?"

"Some people she once knew," said Aunt Sarah, smiling her sweet, shy smile.

"Who won't know she's coming," said Mother, "until she arrives."

"She'll stay in Germany or Kansas City until summer's over," explained Aunt Sarah.

"Leah never could take the summers in this town." Mother sniffed. "Sarah, you remember the first time she got married, it was summer?" Aunt Leah is somewhat overextended when it comes to marriage.

"It does get hot here," I thought to say. "But surely it won't be as hot as it gets in Kansas City."

"Virginia, it's not the heat," said Aunt Sarah Perry. "It's the spiders. Leah says they come in the house where it's cool and wait until nightfall to get on her pillow and in her slippers. She can't stand the thought of them crawling in her ears and her hair."

I shuddered in sympathy.

"And in her slippers," Mother added, sounding disgusted.

I had to smile, knowing Aunt Leah well enough to have figured out how carefully she must have combed her vivid imagination to come up with an explanation that had *style*—as a reason for escaping a stifling village in its steamiest season.

Suddenly, I wondered what sort of children they had been—Aunt Sarah Perry, Mother, and Aunt Leah. Yet I felt moved to leave this question unanswered as shadows deepened around my mother and my aunt. Both were comfortable on the Autumn Gold couch. Their heads were thrown back as they created light and time, past and people, with just their talking.

I am a teller of tales, in part, because of the informal way I learned from Mother and her relatives of passing the time, which they also utilize for transmitting information, for entertainment, and for putting their own flesh and blood in the proper perspective. The Perrys are interesting talkers. They began as farmers who had been fugitives from injustice. Acquiring land and homes, place and time, was to them the final payment in the cause of freedom. After long days, a long history in the fields, they talked their way into new states of mind. They could appreciate a good story in the companionship of one another, not only as entertainment but as a way to mark their progress. Stories, talking, grew and changed into a kind of folk history of timely incidents. And these developed in lines of force that had beginnings, middles, and endings—a certain style. True memory might lapse, and creativity come into play. It was the same creativity and versatility that had helped the first African survive on the American continent. An uncle of mine told the most astonishing lies. An aunt whispered in perfect rememory the incident of Blind Martha and how she found her way down the dusty road to the spot where the log cabin had stood in which she had been born. The day Uncle Saunders was killed, all of the ivy fell from the Pasony house. Pasonys were neighbors, quiet and shrewd. But they could not save the ivy.

There's the story I remember always knowing, about my Grandpaw Levi Perry and how his hand burned shut from a fire in the gunpowder mill where he worked. And from the time that his life and mine coincided, his hand was a fist with burn scars hidden in the tightly shut palm. I would lace my fingers over his closed fist when I was a child, and he would lift me up and up, swing me around and around—to my enormous delight. Ever after, the raised black fist became for me both myth and history, and they were mine. Grandpaw Perry was John Henry and High John de Conquer. He was power—the fugitive, the self-made, the closed fist in which I knew there was kept magic. Oh, but the rememory!

What is transformed from myth, history, and family narrative in my own fictions is not a play-pretty to be held in the hands of children. My fictions for young people derive from the progress of Black adults and their children across the American hopescape. Occasionally, they are light-hearted; often, they are speculative, symbolic and dark, and brooding. The people are always uneasy because the ideological difference they feel from the majority is directly derived from heritage. In the background of much of my writing is the dream of freedom tantalizingly out of reach. Echoes of long-past times serve to feed my imagination. They may sound of African dreams, family truths, and even speculations on the future. All of it grows from my own experience in some way. The writer will uncover ways of expressing the source and essence of living which belong to her, alone.

In my daily professional life I see myself as a woman working at a complicated job. The way I approach the job changes, consistent with the changes going on inside me, as a woman moving through time. I keep that vision of the writer which I started with—that of the humble crusader locked in the garret room. The writer up there suffers for life, creating all-purpose prose with bruised, delicate hands. The works of crusading sociologists, such as Lincoln Steffens, Jacob Riis, Shirley Graham, and W. E. B. Du Bois, made an indelible impression on me. No wonder, then, that there is something of the social reformer in the back of my mind while I work.

The job—laboring through a fiction from the beginning to the end—takes from eight to fifteen months. I never lack for beginnings of fictions. But what I find I need is the process for uncovering the art form that will transform ideas into coherent fictions. The challenge is to deal with the revelation that there is no way of knowing beforehand how a fiction is to be written. I discover how it's done only by writing it; and when it's finished, I am able to say, "Ah, so that's the way!"

The fictionist's occupation is the only one I know in which acquired knowledge cannot be applied. What is learned concerning the writing of a single novel is hopelessly inadequate in writing the next—or any others, for that matter. Each book is like a new system that must be uncovered. It is not precisely created, as we sometimes like to believe. All of it is inside, but hidden. In order to begin, one must find the system of it each time. I find the system and the way through. If a concept occurs to me, so must its creative development follow. Therein lie instinct and intuition. Solving must be the natural tendency of writers. And yet, to paraphrase T. S. Eliot, between the idea and the reality falls the shadow. In the shadow, then, the woman working lives. In the shadow, life is very long and worth the time it takes. In the shadow I recall, reconstruct. I create. I am the shadow.

I begin with a fairly clear concept of story, only to have the characters who must live it take it over. They become individuals who change and shape plot according to their needs. Created characters express their power of intent on the page. I may not alter the intentions to suit myself. In the early books I tended to exaggerate the physical traits and quirks of the characters in order to control what they might do. Zeely Tayber was six-and-a-half feet tall and thin as a beanpole. Mr. Pluto from *The House of Dies Drear* was lame and looked like the devil with green eyes. Junior Brown from *The Planet of Junior Brown* was in danger of drowning in his own fat. Grotesqueries were my props, my crutches, which I didn't need. The characters did whatever they wanted, anyway. The fact that Pluto looked like the devil did not stop him from sitting in the first pew at church, and Junior Brown climbed over the rocks of the Hudson River, despite his weight.

In later books emotions and the way characters act upon them tend to reveal who they are from the beginning. Jack Sun Run from *Arilla*, bare-chested and golden, riding his horse, is a still-shot—an old sepia print—and a revelation of his commitment to being Amerind. I concentrate on the emotions all of us share, and I use the most comfortable milieu or vantage from which to reveal them. These fictions may involve folk wisdom and superstition, since I am interested in archetypes and archaic heritage. Black-being may be significant to a story, and it may not be. I enjoy having the freedom to make that decision.

In the fantasy books of the Justice cycle, race has nothing whatever to do with plot and the outcome for the characters. The powers of extrasensory perception, telepathy, and telekinesis the children have are not meant to be peculiarities. They represent a majestic change in the human race. We find that Justice and her identical twin brothers, in *Justice and Her Brothers, Dustland,* and *The Gathering,* have unleashed new gene information, which provides them with psychic powers, allowing them to extend themselves into an extraordinary future where things are not as they seem. With their friend Dorian Jefferson they travel through time as a unit, and only as a unit are they able to return to the present. The fictions depend for effect on the weirdness of location or setting and on the increasing strangeness of the characters. A golden animal, Miacis, roams, talks, and telepaths; a band of wild children communicate through song; winged Slaker beings search for an end to Dustland and their despair; a cyborg, Celester, and a stupendous computer, Colossus, go about saving civilization.

There is not a formal way such speculative fiction should be written. But it does assume the individual will pit himself or herself against a world or worlds that have grown cold and impersonal. I write all fantasy, from *Jahdu* to *Justice*, to bring the power of magic into a world that seems increasingly lacking in the marvelous. There enters into my work a sense of melancholy, however, which has its origin in Black history and life in America. It is often an inherent quality of the writing and inseparable from the lives of the characters. It pervades the fictional hopescape with the reality that Black life is at once better and worse than it has ever been. Better for some, worse for most. This is not bitterness; it is truth.

The challenge for the fictionist is to deal with the truth through youth literature with an evolvement of a fiction of compassion, hope, and humor. There is no question that the young should appreciate and share the truth. For it is not merely subject matter that occasionally turns grim. It is the history of a people and their life at present. What can be shared of it is its depiction as serious entertainment through the art of writing.

Within the heritage and history are boundless possibilities for creative writing. There begins a literature that indicates a people's range and unique capacity for living. But it is not accomplished as simply as other kinds of writing with less historical grounding. On the surface the stories are straightforward. And young people are capable of varied reading levels and of several degrees of difficulty when given the opportunity. My own books don't have to be understood in a hard and fast sense. Certainly, they don't need to be *taught* in elementary and junior high school. The best way to read fiction is to open the mind and enjoy.

Bones in the Sand

PENELOPE LIVELY

All writing is the expression of experience. Each writer's experience is different; every response to experience is different. Those of us who are writing for children, though, have a special problem; we are writing for people whose experience is limited in a special way—it is brief. We cannot make a basic assumption about the reader's sense of the passage of time and of his or her own place in a chronological scheme. When I write a novel for adults, I am addressing my contemporaries in a special sense—those who live in the same country of the imagination. Children live in another country; and although it is one we have all passed through, to pass beyond it is to have lost, irretrievably, I believe, its language and its beliefs. We have lost the sense of a continuous present and have moved into an awareness of what has been and what is yet to be and of our own situation in relation to time—both personal time as the context of a life and collective time, history.

I am eight, I think. Or nine. I am in Egypt standing in a desert. There is a war on, offstage. I know this because armored cars and lorries pass from time to time—this is the road to the distant front in Libya—and the sand is studded with rusting petrol cans and old tires, the rubbish of an army. I am looking at a shallow depression in the sand. Within the depression, curled like a fetus, is the delicate structure of a skeleton: backbone, ribs, leg bones, the tracery of a hand. A person. A once-person. This person, I am told, lived here thousands of years ago. Thousands. We have come to this spot in the desert to be shown this person by someone called an archaeologist, who is digging all this up in order to know about it, while above us in a hard blue sky the RAF planes chug toward Tripoli, and somewhere over the sand dunes there is the distant thump of an explosion.

I am thirteen. It is 1946. I stand in Cheapside, in the heart of the City of

13

London. Saint Paul's Cathedral is just behind me, and I can see the spires of other city churches—Saint Mary-le-Bow, Saint James Garlickhithe, Saint Nicholas Cole Abbey. I can hear blackbirds and thrushes; I could pick myself a bunch of wildflowers—willow herb and ragwort and oxeye daisies. All around, there is a sea of rubble, but organized rubble out of which you can pick the lines of streets and buildings, of alleys, of courtyards. The bombs have stripped the landscape down to its origins: the medieval street plan, the exposed bastions of the Roman wall. Time is lying there in front of me, but I cannot make head nor tail of it. I am an ignorant child, a refugee of a kind, who has spent only a year in this cold northern country which, nevertheless, is apparently home. I have never been to school or read any history. I do not know if these Romans they are talking about are the same Romans I heard of in Egypt, and if so, what were they doing up here? But something happens to me, standing there in the rubble, looking at old walls. I am excited; I am lifted out of the prison of my own head and glimpse something larger. Imagination reaches out.

Awareness of the past, it seems to me, is an achievement of the imagination. In my own case it was prompted first by this kind of experience—a response to the physical world, a perception of things not understood but recognized, a child's amazed vision of the layered world. Subsequently, what seems now like a quasi-mystical experience was overlaid by knowledge, and I'm all for knowledge, too, but I think that the two go hand in hand. You can know about the past but not sense the reality of the past; indeed, a great deal of present concern with the past obscures its immediacy. I think of television's treatment of the past as entertainment—in drama, in documentaries, too. Of the ways in which physical reconstruction of the past distorts it—the mannered look of historical sites, the textbook presentation of vanished landscapes. To be confronted with the authenticity of the past, to be jolted into understanding that the past is true, people must see it in context: the Roman bricks of Cheapside laid bare by a German bomb, the shape of a human being etched into the desert sands.

And what does this have to do with the children's writer? A great deal, a very great deal. The past may well be entertaining, but it is not entertainment; it is a serious matter. And I am thinking not just of the collective past but of the past with which I have been much more concerned in my own books—the personal past of which we are each composed and of which we are so aware as adults but so much less so as children. And the writer, of all people, is a Freudian being, drawing on hidden resources—the well of experience—in ways of which I suspect many of us are sometimes barely even aware. The use of this experience in children's fiction is our theme: how we translate something personal into something general, how—using the knowledge and language of an adult—

to strike a chord in children so that they recognize, without ever having been there, the wider country into which we are inviting them.

I don't know exactly how to do this, but I think I know how to try. Refusing to patronize; refusing to be didactic; refusing to allow the book to become a vehicle for other things such as social or moral instruction, historical information, or possibly well-meaning but irrelevant urges to persuade the young to come to terms with life, whatever that may mean. I have never come to terms with life, and I wouldn't wish anyone else to do so. If fiction is to help at all in the process of living, it is by illuminating its conflicts and its ambiguities. We read to find out more about what it is like to be a human being, not to be told how to be one. And one of the things we can do for children, in books, is just that—expand their vision of a world that is too often rooted both in place and in time.

Let us here make a distinction between memory and the past, two quite different things. When I write fiction, I am concerned with memory; if I were concerned with the past, I would write history. What I am trying to do is translate into fictional terms that marvelous process of recollection interspersed with oblivion that goes on inside our own heads. History is another matter altogether; history is linear and chronological and public. Memory is none of these things. "Things remembered can be intimately felt," David Lowenthal has said in *The Past is Another Country*. "Things learned historically simply gain our assent. The remembered past is a living spectacle, the historical past is dead. . . . historical awareness requires social organization." And hence the dependence of the novelist on the operation of memory—not only for creative inspiration but for artistic effect. The pictures in our own heads are the ones that have the immediacy to reach out to others, given our skill to transform them into imageries that go beyond those that are merely personal; and, here, we are concerned with the intricacies of language and of literary reference. Memory is the novelist's raw material; history is the landscape in which to place it.

In both of those childhood anecdotes with which I started, the Second World War was present—off-center, lurking, instrumental. I am preoccupied, both as a person and as a novelist, with the relationship between private and public life—the way in which we are, each one of us, the children of circumstance, played with by the cruelties and kindnesses of random fate, bound up with a historical process that few people feel they can influence or alter. I have tried to explore this theme most in my novels for adults, but I would want to use it also in writing for children, though pehaps in a rather different way. This, to digress for a moment, is one of the fascinations of writing both for children and for adults: the subtle and sometimes half-conscious way in which you find yourself adjusting tone and mood according to the audience, although the theme may remain the same. In *The Ghost of Thomas Kempe* I was trying—through the medium of what I hope is an entirely lighthearted story—to suggest to the child reader something of the palimpsest quality both of people and of places, those layerings of memory of which both are composed. And, also, the interlocking of people with place and time—that you and I are, inescapably, set against this or that backcloth, that our lives run for their short span against the greater continuity of history. Even if you are eight or nine or thirteen and as ignorant as sin, you can grasp that astonishing idea and be enlarged by it. Whether it is a comfort or a distress is another matter, but it is an idea you spend the rest of your life trying to resolve; it goes hand in hand with the other torment of rejoicing in the physical world and not knowing whether its permanence and its indifference are a solace or an outrage.

I've always tried to tether a book for children firmly and precisely to a physical world and hence have made liberal use of the landscape of my own country in writing children's books; it has prompted many of the stories and been an integral part of them. *Thomas Kempe* is set in the kind of gray limestone Cotswold village in which I have lived for the last fifteen years and where time is jumbled in every street and in every building, so that sixteenth-century cottages sprout television aerials and a medieval barn bears graffiti celebrating distant football teams. *A Stitch in Time* was conceived on an afternoon in Lynn Regis, while I was sitting on a beach famous for its fossils, picking up a chunk of the blue Lias stone through which streamed the ghostly outlines of ammonites and belemnites. "To be certain there is a past we must at least see some of its traces"; to see is to believe, and especially so for children, for whom the borderline between fact and fantasy is even more shadowy than for the rest of us. Suspension of disbelief is a natural part of childhood; what is real and what is imagined, what happens and what does not, are hardly divided. It is only later that we are supposed to be sure of these distinctions.

Children are natural fantasists; they have an elasticity of imagination that most of us lose in adult life. What literature can do is nourish that imagination and give it something on which to feed and flourish and fly off on its own discoveries and adventures. I've chosen to present the possibilities of memory to children in terms of fantasy because, for the writer, this seems to offer an infinite scope; the sky is the limit, there are no holds barred, and the only limitations are your own. Which is one of the reasons why I find writing for children so liberating. I don't mean that writing adult novels does not have liberations as well, but a children's book offers peculiar literary freedoms. You can enter a different world, almost literally.

And that being said, I have to say with the same breath that I do not believe it is possible for an adult to recover the vision of childhood. You write for children, as an adult, with the expanded understanding of experience, and there is no way in which this understanding can be shed. Jorge Luis Borges, the South American writer, bases one of his essays on

Heraclitus's saying about the impossibility of revisiting the same river twice—the onlooker is as unstable, as impermanent, as the flow of water—which could be an image of the irretrievable nature of our own past selves. And the memory of these selves is itself colored by subsequent wisdoms; those pictures in the mind that seem so static are actually changed at each recovery. What I thought was thus, was in fact otherwise, given what I now know; the scene that appears so fixed and definite is subject to subtle changes each time one revisits it in the mind. I once tried to express in fictional terms the fragmented and selective nature of memory in a book called *Going Back*. The narrator remembers a crucial incident from her own childhood, and the narrative is interspersed with passages in the present tense representing the pictures-in-the-mind aspect of memory—a piece of stylistic adventurism that may or may not work. But I found, when I began to think about the book, that in order to breathe life into it I had to make direct use of my own memory. Not in an autobiographical sense but in a visual one; the snapshot passages had to be of my own world, and, accordingly, I used my grandmother's house and garden in West Somerset, which have been familiar to me all my life. There was a double advantage; not only was the landscape a real one, real and vivid to me, but in describing it, I was using that very function of memory that I was trying to suggest in the book—the fragmented, dreamy, preserved quality of selective recollections. It is a process that can be effectively suggested by cinema, with the one large and crucial reservation that cinema can never do what words can do—that is, leave an area of maneuver to the reader. The camera defines; the greater power of language is that it suggests.

And this is where words and the act of reading are of such importance to children. A child cannot receive a book in a passive state; an act of participation is required. However lumpen, reluctant, uncomprehending, or even hostile the reader, the imagination is aroused in some way. I rather like the idea of the hostile reader, especially the hostile child reader—a scowling, restless figure who would rather be doing something else, driven to the book, maybe, as a last resort on a tedious Tuesday afternoon. Resisting stubbornly and yet, up to a point, unavailingly because whatever the book and however ineffectual its impact, the imagination is forced into a response of some kind. And, of course, the author's hope and prayer is to share with the reader some of the imaginative excitement that went into creation and—more than that—to contribute to a small extent to the child reader's expanding imaginative landscape. When the operation of memory is a theme, it has always seemed that the most powerful way to suggest it is in terms of imagery: those three-dimensional experiences in which something said is tethered forever to its background, to sounds and sights, to a vanished scene. A majestic literary subject, of course, along with the enshrinement of memory in objects—Proust's *madeleine*, the landscape of Wordsworth's *Prelude*.

I'd like at this point to turn to another aspect of the fictional use of memory, one which is curiously difficult to suggest to children. I mean what has been called the interval of forgetting, the way in which past sensation, past experience, is summoned back by its relation to the present, perhaps after a period of total oblivion. When something seen or heard jolts us into a recollection we didn't know we had. This is something we all know about as we grow older; children less so; and again it is a service of fiction to point this out, to suggest the force and value of something the reader may have experienced without ever having recognized its significance. Distance interprets events and, similarly, memory enhances emotion. As Virginia Woolf said in her diary: "The past is beautiful because one never fully realises an emotion at the time. It expands later, and thus we don't have complete emotions about the present, only about the past. That is why we dwell on the past." I would ally with the vividness of recollection the refined pleasures—and fears, I suppose—of anticipation. There is a curious sense in which we never live at our fullest in the present; the worlds of heightened consciousness are the past and the future. Now is less real than then.

For the writer there is an extension to this way in which memory performs, and that is what I think of as the digestion of memory. I write short stories for adults; for some odd reason I've never been able to manage short stories for children. A number of these have derived from experiences of my own twenty years or more ago; at the time the experiences seemed quite without significance. Years later, I have been able to see them in another light and use them as the vehicle for a story illuminating something that was in no way apparent to me at the time. When I was fourteen or fifteen, I went out shooting rabbits with a boy my own age; when the episode was discovered by the aunt with whom I was staying, I was aware of and shamed by the blistering disapproval of the household. They were passionate animal lovers; I took their contempt for a condemnation of the slaughter and was humiliated and ashamed. Only years and years later, as the scene returned—what was said, the allusions, and the language—did I realize that the issue was quite different. The boy was socially unacceptable, and I had transgressed against conventions of behavior that were not apparent to a lonely ex–colonial schoolgirl. The death of the rabbit never came into it. And this, of course, is the great strength of the short story as a literary form; it gives the writer the opportunity to make a point that could not or should not be expanded into a novel but that may have quite as much impact and significance. And memory serves the short-story writer ideally, but it has to be this kind of digested memory. There is even a sense in which you recognize the conception of a story—it snaps into the head at the moment of overhearing a scrap of conversation or of observing some incident—but you know at the same time that the thing must be allowed to marinate in the head for months and quite possibly years before you dare commit it to paper. Raw, it will not do; it has to be interpreted by the passage of time.

I was making a stern distinction, earlier, between memory and history and saying that as a novelist I was concerned with the former. I have a mistrust of the historical novel, with one or two shining exceptions. Nevertheless, I think the children's writer has a role to play in generating awareness of the past; what I am wary of is the danger of didacticism—the awful shadow that looms over us all, the legacy of the nineteenth century. It dies hard, and it survives best not only in the novel of social relevance but in the fatal note of instruction that creeps into so many stories dealing with the past, even an immediate past. And at that point the life goes out of them. The child is being told what is what—or rather what was what; he is not being offered that far more exciting and stimulating liberation of finding out for himself. To stimulate historical curiosity you have first to persuade people—of any age—of the reality of the past, which is far more difficult or subtle than telling them how things were done then. Or how you think they were done. Because that is the other truth I would want to get across to children—the notion that history itself is fluid, that it is not received opinion but a matter of debate and discussion and interpretation. Plenty of educational systems never suggest this; I arrived at university to discover it with amazement.

I prefer my own history straight—as debated among historians. And when I want the flavor of the past, I would go not to historical novels but to survivals—to diaries and letters and documents. I don't want the interference of the novelist; the past is quite capable of speaking for itself. Museums and art galleries, pictures and architecture, the palimpsest of the landscape—whether green fields or city streets. One of the excitements for the first-time British visitor to the United States is the shock of recognition; here is a world strange and yet familiar, a mirror-world in which you are offered your own past, but a past that has undergone a sea change in which style has been both preserved and translated, so that a church spire or the design of a chair are the same but elegantly different. There is something oddly moving about it, as though you looked into the face of a stranger and saw the shadow of your own. And nothing prepares you for the impact of this; the impressions accumulated from photographs, movies, and books are all irrelevant before the extraordinary enlightenment of reality. It is one of those heady moments when the past becomes true. All the books, all the historical discussions lose significance at the first sight of New England; this is the point at which you *know* the seventeenth century happened.

But this is an irresponsible statement. It suggests a disregard for knowledge and a mystical response to the physical world which I would be the first to condemn. We have to relate ourselves to the landscapes through which we move; this is a principal theme of literature, whether it be prose or poetry, and for good reason. The early nineteenth century saw it as a question of spiritual enhancement and conferred a kind of divinity on solitude and the external qualities of a natural world. And romanticism survives nicely, in travel brochures and television documentaries and in the hunger for that remote country retreat. But I am thinking of a different accord with surroundings—an accord that seems to come from, ideally, a marriage between that moment of insight of which I spoke and the knowledge, the bare ordinary facts, from which it derives. Anyone who has crossed the Atlantic can see that the spire of a New England church resembles the spire of a Wren church in the City of London; to relate that observation to some familiarity with the history of European religious persecution is to illuminate both the sight and the knowledge. To understand what you are looking at is to extract new meaning from the visual world. We move through the natural world of mountain and river, of spider's web and roadside flower, and the man-made world of church spires and the road itself. We do indeed need to relate ourselves to the indifferences of the physical world, but we need even more to relate to our own past and our future within it. We need to place ourselves within this confusing scenery; we need anchors beyond the context of our own lives as well as within them. The indifference of the natural world has to be accepted; the relics of our own passage through it are another matter. People cannot be unresponsive to them, and their presence is charged with an emotional impact that the natural world does not have. We do not look at a building in the same way we look at a sunset, although we might say of both that they are beautiful and make us feel uplifted. The man-made landscape has a human relevance; we need it differently. Children, perhaps, need it most of all. The question is one of escape from isolation of the mind, that kind of retarded and therefore dangerous mentality that cannot make the imaginative leap into the experience of others—intellectual egotism.

All of which may seem a rather heavy-handed way of saying that it is vastly more stimulating to be informed than to be ignorant. And we are, after all, concerned with children, who can't be anything other than ignorant. But, as a novelist, I am not in the education business; the alleviation of ignorance in that sense is not my concern. What I am bothered about is that children should come to see that knowing about things is a right as well as an obligation. That they should see that awareness of the past and the force of memory are adjuncts to living, that they are going to have a better time with them than without them. And I don't think this is something learned in the classroom—which is where we children's writers come in. We are concerned with suggestion, not with instruction. I think again of that hostile reader slumped over the book on a wet Tuesday, convinced in his soul that books are a load of rubbish, turning the pages over, involved despite himself, suggestible in ways he hardly realizes. The power of words. No wonder people burn books.

I've tried to make a distinction between the processes of memory and an informed response to the past. At the same time, I'm well aware that there is a sense in which the two are interdependent. Certainly, the writer who is concerned with either will be concerned with both and preoccupied with how to express both in fictional terms. To go back to that child standing in the desert staring down at the skeleton in the sand—the revelation that there is a collective past is the revelation also that the collective past is composed of myriad private pasts, that the pursuit of social memory is matched by the need for personal memory. Let us have a final look at what the writer concerned with memory is trying to do and why memory is in such a special sense the material of the novelist.

This writer tries to turn private matters into forms that will be universal. What each of us actually remembers is too personal to be communicable; what the writer has to do is interpret experience and relate it in language accessible to all. It is the extraction from private memory of those elements of privacy that would alienate others; the writer's recollection must become the reader's experience. *Then* for one person is turned into *now* for many; the picture in the mind is shared.

And this is done only by the writer transmitting to the reader that sense of having been there in person, of having seen with those eyes and stood in that landscape. It is the extra dimension given to those novels that draw on experience as much as on imagination, and it is also the closest bond between writer and reader. The one thing we all share is the capacity to remember; the novelist tries to convey the significance and the power of that capacity in fictional terms, to make universal stories out of the particular story that we each carry in our own head. At its grandest this theme is the most compelling in all literature; it is the means whereby we, as writers for children, hope to introduce them to larger and more exciting worlds—to talk about what it is like to be a human being.

Sounds in the Heart

KATHERINE PATERSON

Several years ago I read an article about writing for children in which the writer said that her qualification for writing for children lay in her photographic memory. She had never forgotten anything that had happened to her as a child, and therefore she could write meaningfully for children. I have typically forgotten who the writer was and where the article appeared, and the only reason I remember the statement at all is that it made me resolve all over again not to read any more articles on the qualifications needed to be a writer for children.

Indeed, as I was writing *Jacob Have I Loved*, I was carrying on a running quarrel with Louise Bradshaw. I wanted to write the book in the third person because I knew perfectly well that no one—well, no one I knew—could remember her past in the kind of detail that Louise was pretending to. I was very nervous about this since I know I have a poor memory for specific events. When I am called upon to tell about something from my past, I find myself wondering, midstory, how much of what I seem to be remembering actually occurred. Gilly Hopkins would probably say that I lie a lot, but I assure you that I do not lie intentionally. I seem incapable, however, of separating the bare facts from my constantly enlarging perception of those facts. It is part of what makes me a writer of fiction, for a writer of fiction is never content with mere fact but must somehow find a pattern, a meaning, in events.

Of course, this is what Louise Bradshaw has done from the vantage point of age. She has scooped out a hunk of her youth and molded it into a story. The differences between writing a story and simply relating past events is that a story, in order to be acceptable, must have shape and meaning. It is the old idea that art is the bringing of order out of chaos, and it is interesting to me how much I crave that order. Recently, I read Elizabeth Hardwick's *Sleepless Nights*. On the front of the jacket it is called

22

a novel. On the back it is called "subtle . . . beautiful . . . extraordinary . . . haunting"; "daring"; "miraculous and almost perfect." For a change, I have little argument with the back of the book. It may very well be called subtle, beautiful, extraordinary, haunting, daring, miraculous, and almost perfect. But it ain't no novel. At least it is not what I would ever call a novel. Perhaps there is order in the book, but if there is, it is far too subtle for me. I find no shape to the memories set down in this book, and I put it down deeply dissatisfied.

I believe it is the job of the novelist to shape human experience so that a reader might be able to find not only order but meaning in the story. It seems to me, also, that the way a writer shapes human experience depends to a great extent on her history—all those forces, most of which she had nothing to do with, that made her what she is. In speaking of those forces, we are speaking of our human heritage, our particular family history, and our individual past experience. These are the memories that we call up consciously or unconsciously as we write.

Among the many Chinese and Japanese ideographs for our word *idea* is one which combines the character for *sound* with the character for *heart*— the heart being the seat of the intelligence as well as of emotion. Thus, an idea is something that makes a sound in the heart. Now, if you want to change *idea* into a verb that means *to remember*, you do so by adding an extra symbol for *heart*. In preparing to talk of the relation of memory to writing, I tried to ask myself as objectively as I could: What are the sounds that I hear in my deepest heart? What causes me to shape human experience in the way that I do?

If I tell you that I was born in China of Southern Presbyterian missionary parents, I have already given away the three chief clues to my tribal memory.

Let me start at the end and work backward through the description. Missionary parents. I have discovered as I have gone out into the world that most people do not regard missionary work as a respectable occupation. And I'm sure that many of us "mish kids" would argue whether having been born one was a plus or a minus for the living of this life. There is no way to escape a certain peculiarity of personality. But all that comes later. For the most basic and most lasting gift of this parentage was a total identification with the children of Israel. The stories of the Bible were read to us, not to make us good but to tell us who we were. It seems a bit strange to me, as I look back, that my feeling of kinship was not with the early Christian church but with the Hebrew people. In fact, it was years later, after considerable study of Paul's Epistles, that I had to come to the conclusion that *gentile*, after all, was not a dirty word.

It was still hard for me to accept as fact that my blood ancestors were gentiles and were until fairly recently painting themselves blue and running around naked. My real ancestors left Ur of the Chaldees with Abraham and wandered in the wilderness with Moses. Add to this strong biblical heritage the interpretation of it by Calvin, Knox, and the Westminster divines, and you have got one sure foundation beneath your feet. Again, it was amazing to me to learn that to most people Calvinism seems like the foundation garments which ladies of my mother's generation used to wear—squeezing all the breath out of you and poking into you every step you take. This, of course, was not my experience. For if the Bible told me who I was, my Presbyterian tradition told me why I was.

"What is the chief end of man?" the Westminster catechism asks in its very first question; and we could all answer before we could read: "Man's chief end is to glorify God and enjoy him forever." Again, many people outside this tradition have a very different view of the Calvinist position. They think of it more like a slogan that was on a T-shirt our son John used to own. This one had four monkeys: "Hear no evil, see no evil, speak no evil, have no fun." Other people contend to the contrary that Presbyterians see nothing but evil—from original sin to total depravity—dragging guilt through the world as Marley's ghost dragged his chains. Still others can't understand why Presbyterians, who profess to believe in divine predestination in which everything depends on God, spend their lives working as if everything depended on them. I haven't the time, and you haven't the patience for me to pursue this line of thought in much more detail, but I bring it up because I am trying to discover what this heritage has to do with what I write.

The other day someone was telling me of an article he had read about a recent discovery of galaxies ten billion light-years from Earth, and it reminded me of something a former theology professor of mine said last year. He had just survived a heart attack and bypass surgery. "People are always asking me if I believe in the next world. Why," he said, "I can hardly believe in this one."

Those of us, you see, who were raised in this tradition know how puny we are. It is not our ability to understand or believe or remember that ultimately matters. That will come and go. But the truth we have drunk in with our mother's milk is that the one who flung the stars in their courses does not forget his children. A friend asked me how I dared to go into Louise's loss of faith. Wasn't I afraid that I would lose my own along the way? But I know that I am always carrying about within myself faith and unfaith, obedience and rebellion, trust and fear. When I write with the eyes of hope, it is not my own ability to believe that I am writing about but the biblical affirmation that God is faithful—justice and righteousness will prevail. In the words of one of my spiritual fathers, the Roman Catholic priest and poet Gerard Manley Hopkins: "Because the Holy Ghost over the bent / World broods with warm breast and with ah! bright wings."

I am also a child of another heritage that will seem strange to most of you. Let me illustrate. A man I met at a party had just taken his son to Gettysburg and had found a fascinating detail of history there. He learned, while at the site of Pickett's charge, that the Union officer who had repulsed the charge and therefore saved the day and perhaps the Union was George Custer. "So, you see," he said, "Custer did have his moment of glory."

Now this story did not have the effect he intended. The teller did not realize that I had been raised on the story of my grandfather's two older brothers who died in the War Between the States. (We even called the war by a different name where I came from.) One of these brothers was a cavalry officer under Pickett and was mortally wounded in that desperate, heroic charge. (Here again, with a different heritage it might be called suicidal or insane.)

There is a very romantic (once more from our point of view) story connected with my uncle's death. As he lay dying, a young Union chaplain came to him and asked if there was anything he could do. My uncle asked him to take the Confederate flags and two brass buttons from his uniform and send them to his father and his sweetheart in Georgia. He was able to tell the chaplain his name—Goetchius—but he died before he could give the chaplain his address. For years the chaplain carried the flags and buttons in his pocket, unable to forget the dying man's request but unable to fulfill it. Twenty years later, he was traveling on a ferryboat in Georgia and heard one of the Black ferrymen address an elderly passenger as "Marse Goetchius." He approached the man and asked him if he had a relative who took part in Pickett's charge. The man was my great-grandfather, whose son had been missing in action all those years. Together he and the chaplain traveled to Pennsylvania. They located the trench grave because the corn grew taller and greener along it, and—I was told as a child—they identified my uncle's body by his dental work. My great-grandfather took his son's remains home to Georgia. My mother remembered my uncle's sweetheart, who was, of course, no longer young when my mother knew her. She always reminded my mother and her sisters that she should have been their aunt. She never married and, I was told, treasured those two brass buttons until she died.

Now it doesn't matter that I know it would have been tragic if our nation had become two nations, one slave and one free. It doesn't matter that I think that the holding of slaves is an abomination before God and that to regard any other human being as inferior to oneself is a grievous sin. Somehow, there is still something in me that sees the glory in my uncle's death and not in Custer's triumph. The image of the saintly, larger-than-life Robert E. Lee in defeat will forever seem more magnificent than that of Ulysses S. What's-his-name in victory.

One of the things I was told never to forget as a child, and haven't, is that I have been kissed by Maude Henderson. (In my own defense, I should like to have it in the record that I spent an enormous effort in my childhood wriggling out from under kisses. Missionary children are fair game for any maudlin matron.) The significance of this particular kiss, however, is that when Maude Henderson was a little girl, her father, one of the landed Virginia gentry, was a close friend of Robert E. Lee's and a fellow vestryman in the Episcopal church in Lexington. The General used to give little Maude rides on his horse. (I was sure that meant Traveller, but I have no proof for those of you who prefer your history straight.) Coming home together from a vestry meeting one evening, the General stopped by the Hendersons' house to speak to his friend's wife, and as he was leaving, he stooped down and gave little Maude a kiss. Then he went home, sat down at his own supper table, and slipped into unconsciousness. Miss Maude explained to us that the General's widow had told her she must always remember that although many people had kissed the General before he died, she was the last person on earth whom *he* had kissed. And my brother and sisters and I were to remember that she in turn had kissed us. This would be sappier than it sounds (if that is possible), except that Maude Henderson is one of the genuine heroes of my life. But more about her later.

I want to make one probably obvious point about this part of my heritage, which is that since 1865 we white Southerners have been suckers for a losing cause. Struggle dashed to defeat by inexorable might is somehow more glorious than mere success. I, for example, cannot escape the notion that those years when I was writing doggedly and publishing nothing were far more honorable than these last few years. This heritage explains, of course, why I was drawn to the Heike clan rather than to the Genji when I read Japanese history. And then, too, the Japanese tend to romanticize the person who struggles but is in the end brought down.

This brings me to the third sound in my heart—the music of the East. Among my earliest memories are those of a Chinese woman who lived very close to us. When I was four years old, it was my habit every day to walk to Mrs. Loo's house precisely at her lunchtime. One day as I was going out on my usual jaunt, my mother said to me, in what I'm sure she thought was a joking manner, "If you keep on eating so much Chinese food, you might turn into a little Chinese girl." Her remark bothered me: I didn't really want to give up the parents I had. But it didn't bother me enough to keep me from going to Mrs. Loo's for lunch. Today, I still discover that when I am happy and want to celebrate, I will cook Japanese food; but when I hit bottom and need all the comfort life can afford, it is Chinese food that I crave. This is a very physical heritage of smell and sight and touch, because they are my earliest impressions.

Chinese was my first language, although I quickly became bilingual. When I was five, we were refugeed to the United States for the first time, and even though we returned to China the following year, only my father got back to our home in Hwaian. The rest of us lived among foreigners, so my fluency in Chinese disappeared. I have forgotten Chinese almost entirely, but I believe and I hope it is still there, bred into my bones along with steamed pork dumplings.

I spend a lot of time trying to explain to people that China and Japan are two different countries with different languages, histories, and cultures, although I cannot but feel that those early years in China prepared me in a unique way to live in Japan.

My father was raised a farmer in the Shenandoah Valley of Virginia. His people never owned slaves, although they were farming the valley before the revolutionary war. They were a combination of German peasant and Scotch-Irish rock, fiercely independent, glorying in God and in their own strong backs. My father went from Washington and Lee University to join the French as an ambulance driver before America entered the First World War. He left his right leg in France and brought home a croix de guerre and a dose of toxic gas. He was, I believe, as ideally suited as any Westerner to go to China. He was intelligent, hard-working, almost fearless, absolutely stoical, and amazingly humble, with the same wonderful sense of humor found in many Chinese. Not only was he capable of learning the language and enduring the hardships of his chosen life, but also he was incapable of seeing himself in the role of Great White Deliverer.

We lived, unlike most foreigners of that era, in a Chinese house in a school complex where all our neighbors were Chinese. My father's co-worker and closest friend was the first son of a first son, a well-born man and a recognized scholar. He chose to become a Christian pastor. He and my father traveled together, riding donkeys from village to village, sleeping on the straw in flea-ridden pigsties because they were the best accommodation some friendly farmer could offer. Where there was famine—as there too often was—they went with food, and where there was plague or disease, they went with medicine. Mr. Lee disappeared in the first Communist purges in 1949, and my father still grieves for him.

What this meant for me was that when I went to Japan many years later, I had, through no virtue of my own, an attitude toward the Orient that most Westerners, especially the Americans I met there, seemed to lack. I knew that I had come to a civilization far older than my own, to a language that after a lifetime of study I would still be just beginning to grasp, to a people whose sense of beauty I could only hope to appreciate but never to duplicate.

Against these convictions, there was, of course, a fear. The only Japanese I had known as a child were enemy soldiers. What made it possible for me to go to Japan at all was a close friend I had in graduate school, a Japanese woman pastor who persuaded me that despite the war I would find a home in Japan if I would give the Japanese people a chance. And she was right. In the course of four years I was set fully free from my deep, childish hatred. I truly loved Japan, and one of the most heartwarming compliments I ever received came from a Japanese man I worked with who said to me one day that someone had told him I had been born in China. Was that true? I assured him it was. "I knew it," he said. "I've always known there was something Oriental about you."

How, then, has this affected how and what I write? The setting of my first three novels is the most obvious result. But there are other things, some of which I can identify and some which I cannot. One thing living in Japan did for me was to make me feel that what is left out of a work of art is as important as, if not more important than, what is put in. (As Virginia Buckley, my editor, will testify, I tend from time to time to eliminate to the point of obscurity, but the principle is a good one.) I am also a great lover of form. As a writer, I seek freedom within a form. I rather doubt that I am capable of truly experimental art. And form for me has something to do with the order woven into the universe.

A friend of mine who had lived in Japan for a number of years was preparing to return to the States, and at her farewell party a young student said to her, "You must tell them the truth about us." "What do you want me to say?" she asked. "Tell them that we have four seasons," he replied. Now if you know anything about the Japanese, you know that this is not an idle request. The sound that rings deepest in the Japanese heart is not Sony or Mitsubishi or even Honda, but spring, summer, fall, and winter. Every time I change the season in a novel, I remember that I have lived in this rhythm. I have known the glory of spring as seen in the cherry blossoms, which so quickly fade and fall to the earth, reminding us that life, too, is fleeting, but that the seasons continue, the earth turns, and an order greater than our single lives prevails.

As I was trying somehow to pull together this talk, it came to revolve, to my surprise, around Maude Henderson, the woman who as a little girl had been kissed by Robert E. Lee. The reason I knew Maude Henderson was not that she came from Lexington, Virginia, where my father's people have lived for more than two hundred years. Her family was wealthy and Episcopalian; mine was solvent and Presbyterian. Maude Henderson and my parents became friends in Shanghai. Miss Maude left her elegant Virginia home to become a deaconess in the Episcopal church. She went out to China at about the turn of the century, and there in the poorest section of Shanghai she opened a home for abandoned baby girls. She was their mother in every way and stayed in that home for forty-nine years. Her teeth fell out, as did most of her hair. When Japanese soldiers pillaging the city appeared at her door, demanding her girls, she stood there, all of five feet tall, and would not move. They would have to kill her first, she said. They didn't kill her. Even after December 1941, when they were arresting all Americans and determined that she must be arrested, they made it house arrest—her own house with her present generation of girls.

In 1949 she was forced out of China, and for the first time in fifty years she came back to Virginia. We were living in West Virginia at the time, and she got on a bus and came to see us. My mother was a wonderful cook, and Miss Maude loved every bite. "I've only got one tooth left," she told us, "but it's all right. The doctor says it's my sweet one." She had then only the barest suggestion of white hair under her deaconess's cap, and her face looked exactly as though it had been shriveled like dried apple, but from deep among the wrinkles, her blue eyes shone with humor and delight. I find in Maude Henderson the convergence of all my heritages. I will never forget her. And the fact that she kissed me will sound and resound in my deepest heart.

A Writer's Journey

ELEANOR CAMERON

When I was a child, our home on a hillside in Berkeley had a vast view of cities, bay, and ocean; directly in front of our western windows stood the Golden Gate through which San Francisco Bay and the Pacific interchange their waters. The Japanese Current, curving down across the Northern Pacific, determines the weather of our coast, and when warm inland air meets cold air rising from that current, fog results. Many mornings during the summer I would stand at our windows and look out over a sea of billowing white turned salmon by the rays of the rising sun. Through this rolling sea, which I could easily imagine to be the real sea out there beyond the Golden Gate, would gradually begin to be visible the little houses and trees and city center of Berkeley. Then, here and there, patches of the dark waters of the bay appeared, with ferries and steam boats and tugs plying back and forth and, later still, the minute buildings of San Francisco, tiered in steps by the hills, their windows flashing.

My child's eyes, at home at least, always rested on the bay, with the sea beyond, San Francisco to the left, and the hills of Marin County to the right, the silhouette of an Indian maiden lying along their summits. There was for me, then, always a sense of calm, enormous distances over water, here at the edge of the continent, of the view being endless whenever the vagaries of weather allowed. For in those days it *was* only the weather— clouds of rain or the clean, cool fog—that intervened before man's steely indifference to the earth and its waters had determined that from Berkeley, more often than otherwise, you could not see even San Francisco, let alone the Pacific, because of the filth in the air.

There is no doubt in my mind that my love of looking out on this particular meeting of land and water (which I did not realize then would mean so much to me in my later writing) caused me to suffer acutely for over thirty years in Los Angeles, locked in its noisy, smog-ridden interior.

Because of my childhood, I am certain, I was determined that as soon as possible my husband and I would escape to the sea. Our flight hasn't ended as I'd pictured it, with a solitudinous beach at our door or one of the cliff edges of the Big Sur, where the sea would be our world and our outlook. We are in a forest lying along the coast, and although there are houses around us, at least I can hear the sea at night not ten minutes' walk away, a continuous uproar when the tide is in, and I can hear the seals barking on the seal rocks. With C. S. Lewis I can say, "And the sea! I cannot bear to live too far away from it . . . whether hidden or in sight, still it dominates the general impression of nature's face, lending its own crisp flavor to the winds and its own subtle magic to the horizons, even when they conceal it!"

Our horizons are the tall, shaggy Monterey pines. When I walk by the sea's edge, I look back at the long, somber facade of blackish green, the forest wall. Some days it is half-hidden in mist, but on clear evenings the blackish green is washed over with a velvety lavender in the almost level rays of the molten ball slipping into the sea, then with muted copper from the radiance, called the afterglow, that lights up the whole western sky about fifteen or twenty minutes after the sun is gone.

I turn toward the ocean road from the beach; the sky is green, and the lights along the shore are beginning to come on, "the honey lights of home," the blind poet called them in the *Odyssey*, the lights Odysseus saw when, after ten years of wandering, he drew near to Ithaca at last.

We speak of blind Homer, but there is a mystery in this. Was he actually blind? How could he have been when the *Odyssey* is filled with such precise and vivid descriptions, not static, but filled with the kind of life and movement that bears evidence of the personal experience involved? For instance, Richmond Lattimore's translation says of Odysseus's ship that

> as in a field four stallions drawing
> a chariot all break together at the
> stroke of the whiplash,
> and lifting high their feet lightly
> beat out their path, so
> the stern of this ship would lift and
> the creaming wave behind her
> boiled again in the thunderous crash
> of the sea. She ran on
> very steady and never wavering; even
> the falcon,
> that hawk that flies lightest of
> winged creatures, could not have
> paced her,

> so lightly did she run on her way
> and cut through the sea's waves.

Passages evoking sense of place in the *Iliad* are seen to be formulaic, but those in the *Odyssey* are peculiar to the style of one man. George Steiner tells us in his *Language and Silence,* in one of the most fascinating essays I have ever read, that it is quite possible that the group of devotees known after Homer's time as the *Homeridae,* the bardic guild, spoke of their idol as being blind to keep secret the fact that he had been technically illiterate so that he had had to dictate his poems to scribes.

What is the answer? Can it be that both epics are by one man? Steiner believes that they are; that the Homer we know, the poet who, even to this day, shapes many of the forms of our Western imagination, was the compiler of the *Iliad* but in his old age was the creator of the *Odyssey.* In his youth, having sailed upon and minutely observed the seas in numberless moods, the look of hundreds of sheer headlands rising behind him, beaches with their "laundered pebbles"—as he puts it—steep promontories, and white cities, he wrote the *Iliad* with the ruthless mind of the young. In his old age he dictated the *Odyssey* out of imagination, out of his memory of places and the looks of them, while turning back to the *Iliad* "in order," says Steiner, "to compare its vision of human conduct with that of his own experience," looking back "across a wide distance of the soul [there's a journey, if you like!] with nostalgia and smiling doubt" because of all he had learned in the intervening years.

If Homer did, indeed, in the *Odyssey,* look back from blind old age to the seeing years of youth, what a powerful memory the man had. With what individuality, with what a piercing and passionate vision did he put into words the sights he recalled as the place for his last great epic, seeing most clearly in his mind's eye everything he described in his own unique fashion, although he might repeat certain adjectives on certain occasions to describe an object or a person, "the wine-dark water" or "gray-eyed Athene."

Steiner says of Homer's characters in the *Iliad* that they "are of a rich simplicity and move in a clear light" but that Odysseus is "elusive as fire." Richmond Lattimore says of the *Odyssey* that it is "a brilliant series of adventures linked and fused by character."

And place pervades all.

I have told more than once how much place means to me in the books I have lived with year after year and read again and again, place not as backdrop or as a background to be worked up or largely ignored or even dismissed entirely in order to get on with the action. Place, for me, must be loved and known; it *gives rise* to the book and its characters so that the sense of it could never come if its place meant nothing, if I had not experienced it aesthetically and emotionally.

In this talk I shall speak of journeys I have taken physically, aesthetically, and in the mind; from childhood place to one never absorbed into my writing life; from an adult novel *The Unheard Music* to *The Court of the Stone Children*, and from the Literature Department of the Los Angeles Public Library to *The Green and Burning Tree*.

I was sixteen when I experienced my uprooting from Berkeley, the wrenching from my own place when I was just beginning to be aware of how much that place meant to me. Is such an uprooting, which many a writer has been subject to in a far more traumatic way than I, good for one's art or bad? Possibly good, because then one writes out of loneliness and unhappiness and longing for that place and the people one has left behind in ways not possible if one lives in it. For me, at least, memory of what has been lost is a better creator of vivid place than happy satisfaction in being in it, if there is to be a cutting edge to whatever emotions are aroused in one's protagonists and to whatever influence place has over them, coloring their moods and, therefore, very often directing their actions.

I know, of course, that there are innumerable instances disproving a notion of what seems to work for me. Think of Proust and Emily Dickinson; no need for journeyings there. "My mind to me a kingdom is." Who wrote that? Emily herself? Shakespeare? I had to look it up—Edward Dyer, and I'd never even heard of him.

> My mind to me a kingdom is;
>   Such present joys therein I find,
> That it excels all other bliss
>   That earth affords or grows by kind. . . .

Virginia Woolf, living in London, wrote *Mrs. Dalloway*, a superb evocation of that city. Both Eudora Welty and Flannery O'Connor, living in their own towns in the South all their lives, have written classic short stories of the South. E. B. White wrote *Charlotte's Web* while living right on his farm in North Brooklin, Maine, where he'd ached to be all those years in New York. Lucy Boston has lived in her cherished Norman manor house— Green Knowe—and gone on writing about it ever since she first bought it and had all the later excrescences torn away to reveal the ancient, original structure. Yellow Springs, Ohio, was where Virginia Hamilton was born and where she has lived for the greater part of her life. And it is—as Marilyn Apseloff has put it in her essay "Creative Geography in the Ohio Novels of Virginia Hamilton"—the inspiration for the settings of most of her fictions, while "creative geography" within Yellow Springs marks their differences, one from the other, bringing forth different characters and situations.

But Virginia Woolf wrote a better novel than *Mrs. Dalloway* in *To the*

Lighthouse, about a much-loved childhood summer place in Cornwall opposite the Godrevy Lighthouse, when she was many miles and years away from the scene. Katherine Mansfield wrote her finest and artistically most truthful short stories about her childhood home in New Zealand—"Prelude," "At the Bay," and a handful of others—when she was in France, ill much of the time and unhappy. Colette's "My Mother's House" and "Sido," about her adored mother and her childhood home in Saint-Saveur in Burgundy, were written in Paris in the midst of an unhappy marriage. Perhaps, because of this and because of a longing to return to that particular aura which her mother had always created ("the earthly paradise," as Colette thought of it afterward), these collections of short pieces are written with a peculiar luminosity and remain for many as well as for myself the purest and most satisfying of her works. Richard Adams has said of *Watership Down* that when he was a child he lived in a big house just outside Newbury in three acres of garden, and that Sandleford Warren, where his novel begins, was just across the fields from the bottom of it. Now, he says, the house has been torn down and the garden destroyed, and in its place are twenty-two little dwellings. "In a way I'm Fiver," Adams has said, "and it's my warren that's been destroyed. . . . When Holly describes the bulldozer that destroyed the field, so that it wasn't the same place anymore, I feel this most bitterly." Adams loved that garden "passionately," and he's never been back because he doesn't think he could bear it. All he could do to ease his sorrow was to write about it.

The whole matter, certainly, is a very personal one. Natalie Babbitt told me once that she does not write from the inside out at all, as those do to whom place means so much, but from the outside in, getting an idea and then creating place and characters to flesh it out. For her, apparently, the journey either to or away from some special, loved place does not signify in her writing as far as intensity of feeling is concerned.

Louise Bogan, the poet, in a biography by Elizabeth Frank, is quoted as saying, "The initial mystery that attends any journey is: how did the traveler reach his starting point in the first place?" No doubt the journey for the writer goes back to the very beginning of his life, and if we take inheritance into consideration, before that. But as for preparing to write a particular book, the start of my own journey toward *The Unheard Music*, a library novel, began long before the writing. It began not only because of love of the place I had grown up in and an intense longing to return to it but because of a sensitivity and devotion to the old Carnegie public library in Berkeley, which I discovered when I was five—so great a devotion that I howled with grief when told that I could not at that age have a card of my own. I even remember how I was dressed. As for the novel's form, it began to materialize, I can only think, with my reading of Woolf's *Mrs. Dalloway*. For my own novel adopts the idea of all the action taking place within twenty-four hours and going down and back in time within those hours in the lives of my multiple protagonists, here again using her technique. No danger there. But the *sound* of Virginia Woolf was a far more serious matter. It was almost my nemesis.

There is something touching now, when I look back on it, in the fact that I could not endure to write a single fictional sentence if it failed to give me the evocation of Woolf's sentences. Many a young artist has been devoted in this way to Cézanne or Renoir, Picasso or Degas or Monet—held captive before developing a style of his own. Roger Fry's paintings, for the most part, never really got over looking like Cézanne's. As for writers, both Margery Fisher and John Rowe Townsend have commented on the echoings of Woolf in Jill Paton Walsh's *Goldengrove*. But they are echoings only, and as Townsend said, Paton Walsh is always her own woman.

In my own case, I might have remained stuck in the Woolf rut if it had not been for a plain-spoken friend who said, after the publication of *Unheard Music,* that if I wanted to go on writing, I could not go on echoing a genius. He was quite right—I admitted that—but there seemed nothing I could do about it. I knew that I must break out of this echoing, and yet every time I tried and then read over what I had written, I felt wrenched and wretched, unable to go further, even though I knew what I wanted to say. The pain continued as if I had an ulcer. I tried to find my own voice, but what *was* that voice? Anything I wrote in a style other than one echoing Woolf sounded to my ear unendurably clumsy and awkward; anything in the Woolf style, satisfying.

It would seem sensible to say that if one has an idea, one will usually have enough words to express it. And yet it isn't solely a matter of having enough words, but of finding the satisfying way peculiar to the individual writer. I believe that style, in its simplest definition, is sound—the sound of self. It arises out of the whole concept of the work, from the very pulse-beat of the writer and all that has gone to make him, so that it is sometimes difficult to decide definitely where technique and style have their firm boundary lines.

It was my young son who saved me. He asked me to write a certain kind of story, and as if my unconscious wanted to please him, it offered me the story overnight. Because you cannot write a space fantasy for children in the stream-of-consciousness style of Woolf's early novels, and because I was at once, as if I belonged there, inside a nine-year-old boy, looking at the world through his eyes, experiencing his desires and astonishments and sorrows and delights, I at last escaped Woolf. I wonder if I could have done it in any other way than by being compelled, through this sudden, unconscious response, to write a story that children could enjoy.

But this new voice, this new sound for me, as I heard it in my first books for children, wasn't one I could be wholly satisfied with, even though it was right for those books, because it wasn't expressing all I was capable of saying, *if* I could find a voice to encompass a greater territory of emotion and meaning. I had explored a territory as I wanted to explore it in the novel for adults, but in another's voice. Now I had to get back to that wider expanse in my own voice. And it was Frances Clarke Sayers, then a teacher of children's literature at UCLA, who—by asking me to speak on fantasy and therefore strictly to compose my thoughts on the subject—caused a change in the course of my writer's journey. For I discovered, in working on that talk, that the practice of literary criticism, which demands a searching-out of the precise reasons for one's reactions to a piece of writing, offered a different kind of mental invigoration from novel writing, one which I thoroughly enjoyed.

Years before, I had discovered that reading literary criticism was a peculiar pleasure. When I worked as a clerk for six years in the Literature Department of the Los Angeles Public Library, it was one of my jobs to cut out reviews of books that would be bought by our department. These I folded up and filed for public reference, a deadly task except that I found myself reading with absorption (but quickly and guiltily) reviews of certain books I wanted to dig into on my own for some reason I couldn't have explained clearly to anyone because at that time I was only at the end of my teens.

But it was not until thirty-five years afterward, in the late 1960s, that I discovered that I myself wanted to enter the field of literary criticism, although I certainly didn't think of it in such specific terms. It never occurred to me to reflect on my lack of training and therefore to take a course in the subject. I'd been reading for years the critical essays of Edmund Wilson, Alfred Kazin, Philip Rahv, Virginia Woolf, David Daiches, and Herbert Read, among others. At the same time I'd been soaking myself in what I most enjoyed in children's books—for pure pleasure and not because I had any purpose in mind. And suddenly I became consumed with the idea of combining these two absorptions in order to discover whether an application of what I'd learned of criticism in adult books might lead to fascinating discoveries in children's books. It did indeed, and proved to be one of the richest intellectual adventures of my life. Not an easy one, nor one entered into lightly, but it turned out to be a watershed in the course of writing fiction, for I discovered later that I had taught myself far more than I would ever have dreamed possible.

For one thing, I found, when I went back to fiction, that a complete change in my point of view regarding the book I'd had it in mind to write next had somehow taken place. The handling as I'd envisioned it before *Tree* was no longer possible, and the subject matter took on far greater depth. Nothing less than an entirely different conception and approach would satisfy, because I wanted now, rather than simply to tell a diverting story, to get back a little closer to the adult novel writing I'd broken away from and therefore to use certain emotional crises and discoveries I'd experienced.

Using emotional crises and discoveries, however, brings me to Louise Bogan's biography again. She said of the poet's use of his own life, and I quote her words as being just as valuable with reference to the novelist's: "The poet represses the outright narrative of his life. He absorbs it, along with life itself. The repressed becomes the poem. Actually, I have written down my experience in the closest detail. But the rough and vulgar facts are not there." By "vulgar," she of course means the precise autobiographical facts, for note that she has written her "experience," not her "life." The writer uses his experience of key situations rooted in the texture of his whole attitude toward life, these situations being for him his "usable past," uniquely usable because, for some reason buried in the unconscious, they are fertile. Situations, in this respect, are like usable places—mysterious in their ability to arouse the writer's creative response.

In *A Room Made of Windows* I used my experience of having to accept into the family someone I was intensely jealous of and of having to acknowledge, if not willingly accept, that my mother was not created solely for my own convenience and pleasure and that she had an existence and needs apart from those interlacing my own. I have called the book partly autobiographical because the situation was mine, because I was Julia (a child trying to be a writer) as I have not been my other protagonists, and because I knew various people in the book. But I never had an Aunt Alex and an Uncle Hugh, who play a large part within the sequence of four novels. I never knew a Rhiannon Moore who turned out to be central to *Room*, and I never had a brother—I was an only child. Most of the things that happened in the novel never happened to me, and I wish that as a child I had thought to have a *Book of Strangenesses*, for Julia's contemplation of the absolutely extraordinary quality of day-to-day life was mine.

> "Strangenesses," said Julia. "Of *course!*" Some days there were so many she couldn't put them all down, yet here was Paul, who lived in Canada and who'd gone camping in the Canadian Rockies where there were glaciers that had been lying in the clefts of peaks for maybe a thousand years, he had told them, and who'd seen with his own eyes bear and elk and moose and mountain lions, saying maybe everything wasn't ordinary after all, just as if he thought everything was. And here she had envied him!

Another entry has directly to do with journey, the life journey as affected by interplay with others, and our own and their characteristic reactions inextricably linked or locking. Julia is looking back in wonderment over a curious train of events:

> "Everything is strange," she wrote. . . . . *"everything."* Because if she had never had a dream, she would never have written "The Mask," and if she hadn't written "The Mask," she would never have gone out to mail it, and if she hadn't gone out to mail it at the same time Mrs. Moore went to mail her letter and Mr. Kellerman went out to get some air, she and Mrs. Moore might not have become friends. And if they hadn't become friends, then Mrs. Moore wouldn't have given Julia the key to her house so that Julia could go in and water the plants, and if Julia hadn't had the key to be forgetful about and leave in the lock of the door, Ken would never have got in and played his trick. And if he hadn't got in, he wouldn't have been blamed for stealing Mrs. Moore's jewels, and his father would never have beaten him the way he did, and he wouldn't have run away to Canada, and Mrs. Kellerman would never have decided to go too.
>
> "It almost looks as if your dream," said Greg, "will have caused Ken and Addie and Mrs. Kellerman all to go to Canada."

In *The Court of the Stone Children* it was the experience of finding myself— after that high view out toward the Golden Gate and the ocean—in the heart of Los Angeles boxed into one of those blind little apartments, furnished with the kind of dirty scrim curtains and dusty overstuffed furniture impregnated with the smell of other people's cooking, that one must rent after a financial crisis has occurred during a depression, the family has lost its home, and the journey must be taken to another beginning. But nothing that happened in *Court* ever happened to me, outside of my strong sense of the past, my "museum feeling," and a love of the de Young Museum in San Francisco, transformed into an imagined French Museum in a location purely imagined. It was the situation I knew—the shock of that awful little apartment and the desperate determination to get out of it.

In the novel Nina, because of her father's ill health and consequent loss of livelihood, has come with her parents to San Francisco where her father has found work, when all her life she has lived in the little town of Silverspring in the foothills of the Sierra Nevada Mountains. About the loss of one's own place, I wrote the following passage:

Still in the dark, she went to the window and looked out through the rain to a narrow slit of lighted city, shining between the roofs of stores. "A crack of view," she said aloud. . . . And she would never have imagined, until she saw it, that people could exist without the sight of green through their windows, without sky, sometimes with nothing but a wall.

Someone came into the bedroom door, and by his step she knew it to be her father. He came over and his arms went around her; his chin rested on the top of her head. "We'll find a place," he said. "Don't you worry, Squirrel, we'll find one—some little house." . . .

"How can we?" demanded Nina, her throat tight and burning so that the question could scarcely get through. "What is there to find that we'd want? A *house*!". . . What they had to find, Nina kept saying, was some sort of special apartment, with a view of trees.

"Squirrel, Squirrel, you're like a bonfire, blazing and crackling. Your fury never dies down—"

"But it can't, it can't," and she twisted round to face him. "Dad, don't *let* this place do. Don't get *used* to it. Hate it—*keep* hating it! It's the only way out."

Regarding the life journey, Nina's parents, when they could no longer stay in Silverspring, are like Kath's mother in South Angela, Ohio, in *To the Green Mountains*. For she finds, after the death of Tiss, the black woman, which she feels she has unwittingly caused, that she can no longer stay on at the hotel. She says,

"I have experiences, and I've always known when each one has come to an end. For me, they're like plants. They grow and come to flower, and die. And this one, here at the hotel, has died. I can't do anything more with it. It's finished."

And so in the end they get on the train, perhaps the very same one that caused Tiss's death.

They pass the road to Uncle Paul's that . . . [Kath] had not seen since that late golden afternoon when the shadows of trees were drawn long across the landscape, and the pony cart was being swept, as if fatefully marked out for destruction, into the path of the approaching train as it

hurtled toward them under the overarching sky in which
swallows were skimming, sketching out, with swift strokes
of their arrow-shaped bodies, intricate designs against the
untroubled blue and calling to each other with plaintive
cries. Now it is early morning and the shadows of trees are
drawn long in the opposite direction across the shorn
fields as the train bears them away and away, out into the
rolling open countryside to which they will never return.

There's a discovery I've made on my writer's journey—that if a book is
somehow meant to be, if the situation, the place, the characters, the mood
are, for some inexplicable reason, right for each other and for me, moments
will be found most naturally within the flow of events for evoking in some
way or another the expression of a particular outlook on life. This will
emerge inevitably through the action and voices of the characters and
never through bald speeches by the writer. I don't have to fight for or hunt
for these places, or force them. They seem to belong just where they weave
themselves in. My struggle is always with expression and often in
determining the most effective sequence of events.

I see several themes expressed in that outlook: an intense awareness of the
natural world, of wars, of the complexities of the phenomena of time and of
dreams, but above all another theme, expressed very strongly in *Mountains*,
although I hadn't realized this at the time of writing. It comes through in the
voice of Uncle Tede, not Kath's real uncle but a dear friend of hers. He is a
man who has lived with his two unmarried sisters Maud and Hattie all his
life, and to the domineering, demanding sister he finally bursts out,

> "I'll tell you what, Maud, you're an oppressor and a
> blamer. You oppress both me an' Hat, an' you're always
> blamin' us for something. Somebody's always got to take
> the blame in your view, so you figure God's made in your
> image an' likeness. You're a life killer, instead of a life
> giver, an' I swear if one o' you has got to kick the bucket
> before me, I hope it'll be Hat can stay on for a while,
> because she's warm and loving, not sharp and fault-
> finding like you. An' if I have to take *care* o' one o' you, I
> pray to God it'll be Hat, because I'd wait on that woman
> hand an' foot for all the caring she's given me all these
> years, but I swear I'd grudge every dish I lifted for you. I
> swear I'd be tempted to light out like Clayton did if I had
> to live in that house alone with you, an' I don't doubt but
> what I'd do it. Because without Hat to lighten my days, I
> don't think I could make it."

The strange thing is that I put "facing a fact until it divides you through the heart and marrow like a sword"—words of Alfred Kazin's—at the beginning of the book as expressive of the theme. And only after the book was published did I discover that, revealed through the actions of five couples, one member of whom in each case was tyrannizing the other, my theme was actually "Thou shalt not try to possess another." This admonishment I've always thought should be an eleventh commandment.

Like Julia, looking back over the events of the preceding few months of her life and seeing how, in the linkage of events, one led to the next, so I've looked back in this talk to discover links in my own journey. And in doing so I see now, for the first time, an unexpected repetition woven through the entirety—a repetition closely related to attempted possession. Only it is the opposite—resistance to it, escape from enclosure, from being boxed in by anything or anybody. It is there in *Room* and in *Julia and the Hand of God*; in *Court*, in *Mountains*, and in *Beyond Silence*.

And so, it would seem, all these years I have been telling myself stories about the efforts of my characters to attain freedom, sometimes across space, sometimes across time, sometimes of the mind. Just as I saw for the first time, in writing a talk on dreams, art, and the unconscious, that lostness in the protagonists' dreams is a thread running through my novels, so I see now how the idea of escape from enclosure, either physical or spiritual, has haunted me, as it has haunted Mary Norton in her tales of the Borrowers.

I read four of the Borrowers books to my mother during her last illness. She had been reading the autobiography of a Russian woman who had undergone capture and imprisonment and brutal treatment, a tragic account which I wondered how my mother could endure, considering the condition under which she was reading it and her own awareness of the impending end of her life's journey. I therefore chose Mary Norton's fantasies because I wanted to take her as far from the world of Russian prisons as I could.

And yet, when I'd finished reading, a curious parallel struck me, a parallel which reinforces the truth that the finest fantasies are never escape reading, something shallow and merely amusing. On the back flap of *The Borrowers Avenged*, Mary Norton says that the original idea for the Borrowers came from her childhood fascination with playing out elaborate games with small painted china dolls on the floor of her home. In an article by Philippa Pearce, however, Mary Norton, a shortsighted child, described how she would turn "sideways to the close bank, the tree-roots, and the tangled grasses" so that "moss, fern stalks, sorrel stems created the *mise en scène* for a jungle drama." Here would be a conception relating the vulnerability of insects under the devastating hands and feet of giants to that of a race of tiny humanlike creatures scurrying for their lives, and I suddenly perceived something I'd never perceived before, something underlying.

For when I come to think of it, *The Borrowers* and its four sequels are in their own light and touching way exactly as much about terror and persecution and the longing for freedom of movement as are *The Diary of Anne Frank* and Johanna Reiss's *The Upstairs Room*. The poles-apart difference, of course, between these accounts of enforced hiding during World War II and Mary Norton's books is that the latter's are fantasy and that, throughout, there is a constant play of the most delectable and elusive humor which permeates her stories as though it were their atmosphere. Yet what we chiefly feel is a great fear and loneliness, as if the little creatures sense that all other Borrower families, outside of the two we learn about, have been killed or died off long ago. And the two that remain are desperately trying to keep up their courage while their first concern is to remain hidden, invisible, undetected. To be seen is for them, just as it was for Anne Frank and Johanna Reiss, the fatal and final disaster. Whether Mary Norton has ever realized the parallel between her Borrowers and the refugees of war, I do not know, but certainly it is there.

What strikes me about Mary Norton's writer's journey is the fact that she started out (after *Bed-knob and Broomstick*) with what proved to be a classic in her own time and continued to produce classics with each new addition to the series, ending triumphantly after twenty-one years with a fifth in the sequence. And each book is as perfectly conceived and written as the others.

This is what makes the writer's journey—or any artist's, for that matter—exhilarating. One never knows what will emerge from the unconscious, memories that, surprisingly enough, begin coalescing into a pattern, only dimly perceived at first. But before long, for some mysterious reason, this pattern begins taking on the kind of substance and detail that tell the writer that another novel, not necessarily of the past, is in the process of coming into being. It is something to be grateful for because it can be devastating to see nothing in the offing. I remember Lloyd Alexander saying, when I congratulated him on his latest book, "Oh, but I haven't an idea what to do next. It's terrible—I'm utterly barren and it frightens me!" He had not the faintest notion that *The First Two Lives of Lukas-Kasha* would appear within the next two years, not to speak of the Westmark trilogy during the four after that. There are seven lines near the end of Cafavy's poem "Ithaka" that particularly move me:

> Always have Ithaka in your mind.
> Your arrival there is your destiny,
> But do not hurry the journey;
> Better if it lasts for years,

> And you are old when you anchor at the island,
> Wealthy with all you have acquired on the way.
> Do not expect further riches from Ithaka.

These lines are so many-layered in meaning that they remind me of certain ones near the end of *A Room Made of Windows*, having specifically to do with writing. Julia and her mother are speaking of Julia's father, an unpublished writer in his lifetime, who was killed in the war before his final story was accepted, and of Daddy Chandler, the old man who, in the attic room next to Julia's, had been writing his autobiography, knowing that in all likelihood it would never see print. Mrs. Redfern says of both instances:

> "When your father was lost in his work, the way Daddy Chandler was lost in his, he wouldn't have exchanged his life for any other. Those were the happy times, even though it's a battle to write what one truly sees and feels. It was the work itself that counted above everything else, and not what would happen to it. And that's the way it was with Daddy. He knew he'd die before he could see his book sent off. But he had to keep going because he was reliving the past, calling it up all around him right there in his attic, and it was the great pleasure of his days to wake every morning and know that he could go on struggling to shape the past on paper as near his heart's desire as he possibly could. That's what meant most to him—the doing of it."

Ah, yes, you will say, but you mustn't fool either yourself or us. You know perfectly well that your reader finishes the novel, completes it, by losing himself in it, identifying with it, visualizing it, hearing it in his mind and imagination. Without the reader making *his* journey into your mental and imaginative world, what is the use of your own? To which I answer, I know, I know! And I *do* have a sense of audience. I never write for myself alone and not for children at all, as a good many writers have claimed to do, while promptly sending their manuscripts off to the children's departments of publishing houses and confessing afterward in interviews and articles (undoubtedly not realizing the contradiction) that they have used certain words or approaches rather than others so that the children would understand. And I have even written an essay, "The Sense of Audience." But I wrote those words of mine near the end of *Room* almost fifteen years ago, and how many times have I thought since then that, yes, *there* is the real paradise, the writing of the book, thorny though it may be, to quote

Barbara Willard's phrase "the thorny paradise." It is a phrase Edward Blishen borrowed as the title of a collection of essays on writing because it is so precise a description of the writer's state of being while undergoing the effort to grasp his conception.

As we sit at our desks, struggling to bring that conception into existence, we are always trying—if we are serious and not working simply for money and attention—to make ourselves worthy of the vision, no matter how modest the accomplishment. There, for me at least, lies the mingled hardship and true joy of writing, of the journey taken.

On Imagination

JOAN AIKEN

I am going to divide this talk into two halves—the first about my own imaginative progress and the second about the use and value of imagination and how it can be developed.

It may seem a solipsistic approach to start with my own childhood, but this is something I do know about. And an advantage is that it falls into four clearly defined stages. From the second stage, when I learned to read and write, the enlargement, if any, of my imagination can be measured to some extent by what I was writing, because I wrote a lot, from the age of five on.

First a brief synopsis of family history. My father, the American poet Conrad Aiken, came to England in 1921 with my mother and elder brother and sister (who are twelve and seven years older than I). They spent a cold, unhappy winter in London furnished rooms and then moved to a cottage in Winchelsea, Sussex, which seemed to them like paradise. Just before my birth in 1924, they moved five miles away to a bigger house in the small town of Rye, down the street from where Henry James had lived and died in 1916. So there were lots of literary and romantic associations.

Jeake's House, where I was born, was, and is, beautiful—a high stone house, built in the seventeenth century as a granary, in a steep, narrow cobbled street. It is four stories high; the downstairs rooms are paneled, and the upper rooms are all sorts of queer shapes. And there is a marvelous smell of ancient wood, weathered by sun and sea wind. From the top windows you can see the sea across the marsh, three miles off. Rye is a stunningly beautiful little town, an old harbor, unbelievably ancient and picturesque. On the debit side, Jeake's House was cold, cavernous, and hard to run; my mother and two subsequent stepmothers complained of that. Also, at the time of my birth and for the next thirty years, my father was finding it extremely hard to make a living.

I lived with my father for only two years. In the fall of 1926 he went to Boston to look for ways of earning money, returned briefly for Christmas, and then went back. And that was the last I saw of him till I was nine. So I have no early memories of him, although I'm told he used to carry me about as a baby to look at the Japanese prints on the walls.

The fact that my parents' relationship was on the point of splitting up powerfully affected my first four years. My mother, in her early thirties, was very unhappy. In 1927 Conrad wrote about her to a friend, "Jessie is in an indescribable agony." They had been married sixteen years and although she later said of her second marriage, "It was like sunshine after storm," I'm certain she loved Conrad to the end of her life. She was unable to feed me as a baby and told me how she used to walk with me in her arms, up and down for hours in the large studio where Conrad worked by day and my cot was put at night. I have a kind of subliminal memory of that. I still dream about that room—I did while writing this talk—although it is over thirty years since my father sold the house.

After Conrad had gone, when I was about three, I can remember my elder brother anxiously asking, "Are you sad, Mama?" when she was silent at mealtimes, and her invariable answer "No, just pensive." Probably she was wondering how to support three children in a foreign country— she was Canadian—with no money and a husband who wanted to marry somebody else.

My father himself, of course, had had a very unhappy, disrupted childhood. When he was twelve, *his* father, a doctor in Savannah, Georgia, shot his wife and then himself; the four children were adopted by different relations, and my father was separated from his siblings. For the first forty years of his life, he entertained fears that we, his children, might be mentally unstable, or that he might, in a sudden brainstorm, murder his wife and us. He kept a diary about this, paralleling his life with that of his father.

Anyway, my memories of my first four years, in Jeake's House, wholly lack any memory of Conrad. But they are full of a strange, melancholy, haunted beauty, not unlike the atmosphere of an Edgar Allan Poe story. My elder siblings adored Rye, where they went to day schools. Jessie, our mother, put family life absolutely above all else—she had been one of a family of eight—and took care that we had plenty of beach picnics, trips to bluebell woods, blackberry picking, birthday cakes, and Christmas festivities. And from my brother and sister I received a kind of mirror-glimmer of my father's imagination. He had been in the habit of telling them marvelous stories. One, a long serial called *The Jewel Seed*, had been written down by my brother in several tiny notebooks. The story was full of djinns and Chinese magic and the ghost of Samuel Jeake, the astrologer who had built our house. My brother and sister played imaginative games with me, of the kind I'm sure Conrad must have played with them. One was about an invisible friend, Gladiolus—they were always teasingly kidnapping her.

I had not learned to read by the time we left Rye, so my book memories from that time are all of books that were read aloud to me: *Peter Rabbit*, the *Just So Stories*, and *Pinocchio*; then Jean de Bosschère's Flemish tales *Beasts and Men*, containing a tremendously powerful story, "Balten and the Wolf" (which also influenced Freud's patient, the Wolf Man); and Walter de la Mare's poems *Peacock Pie*. I still know many of those poems by heart. Many were a little frightening. The theme of a ghostly visitor recurs: "Some one came knocking / at my wee, small door" and another on the same theme about a cobbler, "I saw an eye at the keyhole, Susie!" Many of them are concerned with disappearance or loss; people vanish, children get stolen, articles are lost: "Has anyone seen my Mopser, a comely dog is he." "Poor little Lucy / by some mischance, / lost her shoe / as she did dance." An even more worrying one was "Do, diddle di do, / Poor Jim Jay / got stuck fast / in Yesterday."

Poor Jim Jay got stuck fast in my father's subconscious, too; I found a reference to him in a letter from that period. The fact that many of the de la Mare poems were concerned with anxiety and loss must have connected, in my mind, with the anxiety and fear of loss pressing on my mother. She was also, at that time, attempting to write a novel, which never got finished. I think parents' unfulfilled ambitions often come out strongly in their children, and there is no question of my mother's intense pride and delight when, subsequently, both my sister and I began producing books.

Besides reading aloud to us—she was reading *The Cloister and the Hearth* to my elder brother and sister, and I listened, too, avidly—my mother sang to us. We had a book of English folk songs, and we used to gather round the piano and sing them. About a dozen of these songs are rooted in my memory with the same intensity as the de la Mare poems, although I haven't seen the book since childhood. First, there was "The Raggle-Taggle Gypsies," another example of sorrow and loss, for the lady runs off with the Gypsies and, although the lord goes after her, we don't hear that he finds her. The next, "Lord Randal," was even sadder and more sinister; the hero is poisoned by his sweetheart, heaven knows why: "I'm sick to my heart, / and I fain would lie down." There was an ostensibly cheerful one about a tailor and a mouse; it went to a rattling tune, but the mouse died, and the tailor baked him in a pie. Then there was "Cock a doodle doo, / My dame has lost her shoe. / My master's lost his fiddling stick, / and doesn't know what to do." A Freudian ballad if ever there was one. We sang a song about an outlandish knight from the north country, who courts the heroine for her dowry and then abandons her. It had a haunting tune and was very sad. And there was a really terrifying song about an old lady who, coming home from market, falls asleep by the highway. A peddler cuts off her petticoats, and when she wakes she cries, "Lawk a mercy, this is none of I!" Worse, when she gets home, her dog doesn't recognize her. That song appalled me; I used to wake at night and wonder what in the world the old woman did next. Its scene for me is indelibly set on the highway between Winchelsea and Rye.

The point I'm making here isn't that such songs are unsuitable for or should be kept away from small children. I loved them dearly. But, picking up my mother's vibrations, I suppose I was in a state to notice the grimmer aspects of them, which another child—or I, at another stage of development—would have missed. I was a painfully shy, home-oriented child; apparently, if taken out to tea in somebody else's house, I used to cry and howl until I was safe at home again.

In 1928, when I was four, Conrad came back to England briefly, to arrange for a divorce. I didn't see him. For Christmas that year he gave me and my sister Edward Lear's *Nonsense Songs and Stories.* Out of that beautiful book the poems that stuck in my mind were "The Jumblies," with the haunting refrain, "Far and few, far and few, / are the lands where the Jumblies live," and, saddest of all, "The Dong with a Luminous Nose"; "Then, through the vast and gloomy dark, / There moves what seems a fiery spark, / A lonely spark with silvery rays, / Piercing the coal-black night" and "While ever he seeks, but seeks in vain / To meet with his Jumbly Girl again."

Thinking through these songs and poems, an exercise I hadn't done for years, I was struck by how many of them did seem, in fact, to have connections with my later writing: "Lord Randal" with a thriller, *The Crystal Crow,* in which the hero is poisoned by his sister; "The Old Woman and the Pedlar" with a thriller in which the heroine loses her identity; "Cock a Doodle Doo" with my children's book *Midnight Is a Place,* in which the main characters lose everything and a violinist loses the use of his fiddling hand; the wolf story with my book *The Wolves of Willoughby Chase.* Farfetched, maybe, but I believe it's in that early period that the most lasting influences are laid down.

In 1929 all this anxiety and sadness was resolved; my parents were divorced, both remarried, and my mother went to live with my stepfather, the English writer Martin Armstrong, in a tiny house in a rural setting in Sutton, at the other end of Sussex. For us children it was great grief to leave Jeake's House. And, sadder still, my elder brother and sister had to go to boarding schools, for in the village to which we had moved, there was only a tiny elementary school. So, although my mother's troubles, except continuing financial worry, were over, my brother's and sister's continued; both my brother and my sister were unhappy at their schools, my sister desperately so. John soon went on to university, where he was happy, but Jane stayed at her school six years and was wretched. Holidays were oases, but she used to cry, steadily, for the two days before going back each term. I hated the days when my elders went off, more and more as I grew older. And I was aware of their sadness that the times they were at home were now so brief.

Life at Sutton, however, was happy, serene, and civilized. The place was beautiful—unspoiled country all around. We had known my stepfather for years; he was a family friend (indeed, visiting Jeake's House the night I was born). He made no attempt to be a father to us but was friendly and entertaining. My mother taught me lessons herself because she didn't trust the village school, and I immediately learned to read.

Also, for two years I had a friend, our maid. Even low-income families had maids in the thirties. Alice was fourteen and had just left the village school. Domestic service was the only career for country girls, so she came to work for us—it was her first job. My mother taught her cooking and the niceties of housework, and every afternoon she took me for a walk. I told her about the books I was reading—Andrew Lang's fairy books and Kipling's *Jungle Books*—and she lent me a book she had won as a school prize, *The Golden Key*, by George MacDonald. She also told me about the films she saw every week, riding her bike five miles to a tin shack in Petworth, the town where I now live. Between us, Alice and I concocted a huge fantasy world. She told me that if I buried certain flowers and other objects in the garden and wished hard enough, I would grow wings overnight. I tried several times, but it never worked.

During my first four years in Rye my principal experiences had been beauty, mystery, anxiety, and the fear of loss. At Sutton with Alice I discovered the concept of heroic friendship. All the stories from films she told me were about gallant comrades, who generally came to tragic ends. These were mostly World War I films: *Journey's End; Tell England; The Dawn Patrol*, in which the hero, or hero's friend, was always "going over the top" and not returning. I can remember the names of some of those heroes— Courtney, Stanhope, Ivan, Stephen—they had almost godlike associations. We lived imaginary lives as male characters from those films. Alice also told me about Tarzan, and we had a whole mythology in which she was Tarzan and I was Mowgli from *The Jungle Books*. Under her influence I assembled an army of imaginary characters culled from reading—the Three Musketeers, characters from the Arthur Ransome books, Robin Hood, Ivanhoe, heroes and gods from Greek myths—all in my army, which Alice christened The Mischiefs. I made a catalogue of them, all assembled into companies ready to defend an imaginary country, the Island of Seny. Alice and I, although I was six and she was fourteen, were more truly coevals than I was at that time with my brother and sister. I loved them devotedly and would do anything for them, but I was on my best behavior in their presence; I felt I had to propitiate them by inventing tales of my exploits while they were away at boarding school, pretending to be more interesting than I was. But I felt comfortable with Alice.

Sad to tell, that happy period soon ended. At seven I visited cousins in the north of England, and when I came back—bursting to tell Alice that in the house where I had stayed there was a monkey, a real monkey, kept as a pet—I found that she had gone. Much later, I learned that she had had a breakdown. I am somewhat haunted by the thought that all that freewheeling imaginative life may have been harmful to her.

For my fifth birthday I had bought myself a fat writing pad in which to put down poems and stories. As soon as I began to read, I began to write. I have that book still, and all its successors. At the start I was writing in disjoined script and could not spell such words as *unusual* or *demon* or *pattern*. My mother took the liberty of occasionally underlining a spelling mistake, but I was affronted by this and asked her to stop. Lessons were one thing. But this was *my* book.

When I was six, my father returned to England, to Jeake's House, for which he paid my mother rent (this is what paid for our schooling), and my older siblings used to visit him for ten days in each school holiday. When I was nine, I began doing that, too. I was startled, on seeing Conrad again, to find how much he resembled my brother. Reentering Jeake's House was also a very powerful experience. I had remembered it with the intensely detailed memory of childhood, but it had become unreal to me—a magical place. Now it was real again, exactly as before, except that my mother had removed the furniture that was hers. Also, all our children's books and belongings were at Sutton. Three or four children's books accidentally remained behind and acquired great importance because they were all that was left. Conrad never laid in any children's books for us to read; I expect he thought it would be better for us to grapple with adult books. So *Hans Brinker*, *The Call of the Wild*, *White Fang*, and *Vice Versa* got read over and over. Other reading matter was all of English literature and the modern poetry in Conrad's extensive library, from which we could pick at will, and he made suggestions—Vachel Lindsay, whom I adored, and Alfred Kreymborg and Hilda Doolittle.

Conrad always, however, sent us beautiful and original books for birthdays and Christmas. To me he frequently gave books by child writers—Daisy Ashford, Mimpsy Rhys, and Patience Abbe, who wrote *Around the World in Eleven Years*. I assume this was a kind of nudge to me to think about getting into print—a nudge which I was wholly incapable of responding to. I admired Daisy Ashford but could not imitate her.

I'm now coming to the point about the difference between my parents' attitudes to my writing. Both, certainly, were keen on my becoming a writer and took my youthful efforts seriously—more seriously than, in themselves, they deserved. Nothing I wrote was either original or striking.

I have seen far better stories and poems by children. What was to be taken seriously, I suppose, was my perseverance.

There was a complete contrast between the time spent at Sutton and the time spent at Rye. At Sutton I had an orderly timetable—lessons learned in the morning, work done by myself in the evening, various tasks about the house. (We had given up having a maid.) There was ample spare time and masses of books—all those of my brother and sister, Martin's and my mother's books—and I did read for several hours every day. But if my mother saw a child idling around at loose ends, she would instantly find some task that needed doing. She read aloud a great deal—Dickens or Scott or the Brontës or the Bible—and we held long conversations while we did jobs in the kitchen or took walks.

Whereas at Rye, with my father, there were long blank periods. Later in life, Conrad remarked to a colleague that he had never been a good father, hadn't attempted to be. What he *was* good at, he claimed, was inspiring children. If by inspiring he meant leaving one alone in a state of creative boredom, he certainly did that. He made no concessions to the fact that we visited only for a few days. Well, poor man, he had his living to earn. Now I know how hard the life of a writer can be. He would retire to his study, and long hours would pass in which there was nothing much to do. If my brother and sister were at Rye with me, we would walk to the beach three miles off to hunt for shells; when I was alone there, I wrote poetry. Conrad gave me a fat exercise book which I kept at Jeake's House and added to on each visit.

So I have these parallel notebooks, the one I kept at Sutton and the one I kept at Rye. When my father's papers were sold to the Huntington Library after his death, my childish poetry notebook was among them; so I am greatly indebted to Mr. Daniel Woodward, the librarian, who kindly had all my youthful efforts photocopied and sent me the copies. I hadn't seen them for forty years or so and was hoping they would be better than the poems I wrote at Sutton, but on the whole they were amazingly flat and dull. What they did do, quite plainly, was reflect my attitude to Conrad.

He and I were shy of each other and found it hard to converse. We had been separated too much; we had too few points of contact. He had taken pains to stimulate the imaginations of my brother and sister; he told them stories and encouraged their interest in wildflowers and shells and the beauty of words. I expect he thought that I, by the age of nine, was too old for stories. And I was tongue-tied in his presence, although I loved him. Sometimes, of course, if not too worried about money, he could be wonderful company, making jokes and puns, being funny about the neighbors, with a whole hagiology of cats, to which he was devoted. If a cat was at hand, we had something to talk about.

When I was in my forties, and later, by which time I had of course gone through various stages of filial rebellion and was again on very happy terms with Conrad, I heard him speak many times of the importance of stimulating children's imagination or, indeed, poetic imagination of any kind. But I can't honestly recall any instances of his doing so with me, apart from giving me volumes of poetry and Keats's letters and the plays of Webster. What he did do was keep me constantly aware that writing was a hard, serious pursuit.

The poems I wrote at Rye were, therefore, angled to his eye in hopes of amusing him and winning his approval. I would write facetious lines about a next-door neighbor with whom Conrad conducted a feud.

> What is that I hear, coming up the shady
> Side of Mermaid Street? Why, it is a lady
> It's Mrs. Perugini, Perugini's wife
> Flee and scat and scatter! Run for your life!

and about her cat, which Conrad had christened Lady Precious Stream because it led such a protected existence.

> He glowers from under bushes and his eyes seem quite
>   on fire
> His garden is protected by five feet of chicken wire
> He is a sort of idol; so it would surely seem
> And now I have no more to say of Lady Precious Stream.

I didn't have to win my mother's approval; with her, as with Alice, I was always at ease. So, while at Sutton, I was writing nature poetry.

> The thunder cracks and the lightning flies
> With fierce wild points of light
> From peak to peak of the trembling skies
> All through the screaming night.

My mother was pragmatic in her approach to my writing. When giving me dictation, she nearly always chose poetry; I have reams from *The Oxford Book of English Verse*, written down in careful copperplate, which got poetic language and verse forms very thoroughly into my head. And many of her casual remarks were pungent and memorable in themselves. "Look at the squirrel, how he suddenly stops and strikes an attitude," she would say, and I would write a poem about the squirrel.

> The squirrel with his rodent face
> And brittle thistlefeather grace

> Goes soaring up from bough to bough
> His tail a helm, his nose a prow . . .
> Squirrel with airy fancy scorning
> The iron calm of Sunday morning
> You lack the speed to get away
> Upon the final judgment day.

Or my mother, coming into the kitchen, would exclaim, "I dropped a pea in the larder—that sounds like the first line of a poem!" and I would scoot upstairs to the tiny writing-desk that I shared with my sister and write:

> I dropped a pea in the larder
> Swift in the cool wet dark
> I heard it land on the sweating bricks
> And roll to a corner. Hark!
> What noise was that by the egg vat?
> (The shapes of great dishes loom
> Like ghosts in earthenware, waiting
> Hid in the silent room)

My mother was a direct teacher and believed in learning by imitation. "Write a poem like Wordsworth, like Chaucer, like Swinburne; write a sonnet, write a villanelle," she would suggest, and I would produce accordingly.

Conrad made no such suggestions. But he gave me *The Oxford Book of French Verse* when I was fifteen, remarking that very few people could translate poetry well. I had one bash at Verlaine, "In the old park, empty, lonely / Two shapes passed by, two spectres only . . ." and decided that I was not among the few who could do it. The poems I wrote at Rye were more and more influenced by those of Conrad, although mine were on a more mundane level.

> Down in the park is an apple-tree
> Blossoming coral and white
> The blossoms are drifting and blowing around it
> Like speckles of light . . .

(Then two nursemaids come and sit on the seat under the apple tree and talk.)

> They chatter and gossip and giggle there
> Not noticing how, round the seat

> The blossoms are piling in swift-growing hummocks
> And hiding their feet.

This has the rhythm from some of the stanzas in his poem "Priapus and the Pool."

Conrad never told me made-up stories. But he did, of course, tell his dreams, and they were amazing; I have never, anywhere, encountered anybody who had such extraordinary dreams. I have often used my own dreams in stories, but they are just not in the same league with Conrad's. He used, too, to tell me real stories about his childhood in Savannah; as I grew older, these grew grimmer. Of course, from the age of seven on, I also avidly read his poems and short stories, dovetailing them in, as best I could, with what I knew of him, and these, I'm sure, influenced me quite as much as his spoken remarks.

Children grow, according to psychologists, in two spurts: One spurt ends at five; there is a period of latency and incubation and then another spurt around puberty. Because of the solitary circumstances of my own childhood up to the age of twelve, I can't help feeling that my latent period lasted until I was about eighteen. I found relating to other people extremely difficult. During that time I was using my imagination not to create, but as a means of defense; to help me hope, to keep me afloat. It was not until my thirties that I learned how to make my imagination *work* for me—that I discovered how to delve into it and make it rearrange reality, how to fetch out those haunting fears and mysteriously beautiful memories from before the age of five, which I think are sometimes recognized in my work by other people making connections with kindred experiences of their own.

There are various popular misconceptions about imagination. Many people have a somewhat patronizing attitude toward it—as if it were an odd, unnecessary attribute, rather atavistic, like being able to move your ears. "You have such a wonderful imagination," such people say politely to writers and quickly change the subject as if it embarrassed them. I suppose Freud was responsible for this attitude; he said fantasy was an escape from real life, and this theory has conditioned popular thought for almost a century. I think Freud was wrong and did much harm in this regard; fortunately, many of his successors think so, too.

Melanie Klein said that creative activity reduces mental stress, both in depression and in schizoid cases when life appears futile and meaningless. Jerome L. Singer, in *The Child's World of Make Believe*, pointed out that the low-fantasy child reveals much action and little thought, whereas the high-fantasy child is more highly structured and creative and tends to be verbally, rather than physically, aggressive. In other words, if your imagination is working well, you are able to do more interesting things and are not so likely to be bad-tempered. Coleridge wrote, "Much is effected by works of imagination;—that they carry the mind out of self, and show the possible of the good and the great in the human character."

Creativity seems to have little to do with intelligence or IQ tests. But creative people do rate highly in terms of dominance, self-acceptance, responsibility, self-control, tolerance, and mental efficiency. Creative people show up well in tests that require a perceptive appreciation and appraisal of the needs of others—that is to say, they are socially and emotionally sensitive. Presumably because they have the habit of observation. But creativity is only one product of imagination.

In *The Uses of Enchantment* Bruno Bettelheim says that children under stress are able to battle through their problems only if they can fantasize about future achievements—even if in an exaggerated and improbable way: "If a child is for some reason unable to imagine his future optimistically, arrest of development sets in." And Bettelheim tells a story of an autistic child, who on emerging from withdrawal was asked for a definition of good parents; the child said, "They hope for you." They do your hoping for you when you can't do it for yourself. So what does imagination do? It helps you to hope. Without hope you are done for.

The imaginations of very small children are sharply divided. Before we acquire the flexibility of language, there are bound to be some rather crude distinctions. Mother is either an angel of goodness or a malevolent persecutor. The use of imagination is necessary as a medium, like oil in painting, to moderate these images and make them manageable. Absolute trust, after all, is just as risky as total mistrust. If Othello hadn't idealized Desdemona, he would have been more reasonable about the handkerchief. Jung believed that dreams regulate our existence, and I go along with that idea. I notice that my own dreams are powerfully on my side: If I am lonely, they become full of good company; if I'm working on a book, they often start to deal with my invented characters and grow particularly lively and significant. People deprived of dreams become mentally ill; and what are dreams but our subconscious helpfully spreading out our imagination in such a way that we can take a look at it?

Imagination is not the same as fancy: imagination is a leap to new ground, and fancy merely a decoration of existing material. Imagination is needed in industry—to produce articles that consumers will want to buy, to devise new occupations for workers whose jobs have become obsolete, to render dull tasks interesting. (Remember the sisters in *Little Women*, hemming sheets, pretending they were continents?—a practical use of imagination.) Medicine, architecture, town planning, teaching, physics, law—it's impossible to think of an area where imagination is not needed. It is emphatically needed in world affairs; who but a person completely lacking in imagination could make serious plans for a nuclear war? Our trouble is that, as with so many faculties, we have turned over our imaginations to the professionals: doctors, gurus, computer programmers, scientists, film directors. Instead of using our own gifts, we watch "The Day After" or "When the Wind Blows"; instead of attempting to think out future prospects for ourselves, we wait until somebody like Jonathan Schell does it for us.

Herbert Read said: "Art, at the dawn of human culture, was a key to survival—a sharpening of faculties essential to the struggle for existence." We need to keep our faculties sharpened, just as much now as at the dawn of culture. We need imagination for our own protection. Art—which is other people's imaginations—helps us to look at reality in unaccustomed ways and learn to adjust to other people's viewpoints. When the impressionists held their first show, the public kicked up a great fuss, but, by and by, they began to understand this new vision—really began to see things in a new way. No doubt there were the same reactions when perspective was first discovered.

People are alarmed or shocked when their basic trusts are disrupted. Darwin, Galileo, Ibsen, Shaw—all the innovators outraged public opinion. It is imagination, the extended use of the mind, that helps us grow accustomed to revolutions, to revolutionary ideas. Curiosity and adaptability are qualities that help us survive.

So how can we cultivate our imaginations? More important, how can we cultivate this faculty in our children? Or, at the very least, not deaden it? I think this cultivation very important, indeed—perhaps crucial to the human race. Seriously, I believe there should be imagination classes in every school, which teach children to use their own wits to amuse themselves, to keep themselves hopeful, to solve apparently insoluble problems, to try to get inside other people's personalities, to envisage other periods of time, other places, other states of being. Children should be taught to carry speculations to infinity, to play games with concepts such as height, speed, power, and memory.

How have great artists set about sharpening their imaginations? Leonardo advised painters to study damp-stained walls and unevenly colored stones and see landscapes in them; in other words, to make use of *anything* that is not the obvious subject, to use one thing as a metaphor for another.

Training the imagination takes time and energy. Most adults keep their imagination at low-level voltage a lot of the time. In a way, we have to; otherwise, life would be too grim. We are so bombarded with news from outside; unlike our ancestors, who knew only what was happening in their own cities, we know, all the time, what is happening in the whole *world*. We see on television that a city has been bombed continuously for twelve hours, a ship sunk with a thousand men on board; we see one brief shot of a crumbling building or an overturned hull. But do we make the mental effort to comprehend what actually happened to even one of the thousand men on that ship in some dark, red-hot place below decks? And yet we should do this; given the privilege and responsibility of knowing about the whole world, we should be prepared to take on the imaginative effort, too. It is lack of imagination that tosses the cigarette out of the car window and starts the forest fire.

The use of imagination makes a difference—like the difference between an adult taking a walk, and a child. The adult just marches along; the child leaves nothing unexplored, climbs over each doorstep, runs up every bank, looks through the stems of every hedge. Children explore because they instinctively know they don't yet have a fund of experience to draw on.

How can we help children retain this curiosity, this urge to explore? To use their minds flexibly and inductively, to stretch out and grab concepts that may seem just out of reach? I'm sure that, for a start, we should revise our methods of reading instruction. If reading becomes a bore, mental death is on the way. Children taught to read by tedious mechanical means rapidly learn to skim over the dull text without bothering to delve into its implications—which in time will make them prey to propaganda and to assertions based on scanty evidence, or none. Mass entertainment is produced on the assumption that everything must be understood by everybody, reducing all to its lowest common denominator. Once stories were written for one local group, and all the richness could come from local or personal allusions. Now, because of mass distribution, the writer is obliged to write for the whole world, which in many ways means that he is writing for nobody.

The imaginations of young children are developed by play. Here's a passage of Victor Hugo's *Les Misérables* that beautifully demonstrates children's imaginative play.

> They had seized the cat, and Eponine was saying, "This . . . is my little daughter, and I am a lady; you will call on me and look at it. By degrees you will see its whiskers and that will surprise you, then you will see its ears and tail, and that will surprise you too, and you will say to me, 'Oh, my goodness!' and I shall answer, 'Yes, Madame, it is a child I have like that; little children are so, at present.' "

This passage contains the whole germinative process of play turning into literature.

What kinds of stories particularly stimulate children's imaginations? Open-ended tales do, of course, such as the story of foolish wishes, which comes in various forms: "The Golden Touch," "The Three Wishes," or "The Fisherman and His Wife." Children are impressed by this kind of story because they begin to see where it is going—that the result arises from choice and that there could have been other choices. Of great value, I think, are stories that actually demonstrate how imagination can be used to help in difficulties. There's a beautiful Canadian Indian folktale, ''The Boy Who Was Saved by Thoughts,'' about a boy carried off by an eagle to a cliff top, whose mother sends him dreams suggesting how he can escape. I suppose the mother is the tribal unconscious, showing the boy what his conscious mind was slow to grasp—as Richard Wagner supplied himself with his Rhine theme in a dream.

I don't think that wildly imaginative works are needed to start children's own imaginations working; a book such as *Charlotte's Web*, just a step beyond the ordinary, makes a better springboard than way-out fantasy or science fiction. Imagination does not have to deal with the supernatural; imaginative use of everyday material is just as valuable, or more so. When I say that children's imaginations should be stimulated, I don't mean that children should be encouraged to think about bug-eyed monsters and vampires and giant, man-eating rats, but that they should acquire the habit of thinking about familiar things in an unaccustomed way. If a child on a boring car ride can while away the time by thinking of forty different ways to use a teapot, that's a much more satisfactory use of his mind than reading a comic.

As a child I was remarkably lucky. I lived among people who encouraged me to write and were interested in what I produced; much more, I was with people whose talk and pursuits were stimulating so that along the way I picked up all kinds of ideas not necessarily meant for my ears. Despite all these advantages, however, I didn't produce any particularly original writing until my late teens. I was no infant prodigy. I wanted to be a writer, and I kept practicing, but my early work was in no way distinguished. So what does this suggest about imagination in general?

We mustn't look for any instant outcome from the things we do for our children; the results may take years to make their appearance. The imagination may have gone underground, as it did in my case; it may be doing useful work in producing supportive dreams or hidden mental activity. So the fact that a child doesn't paint remarkable or fantastic pictures, write stunningly evocative poetry, create pots or sculptures or three-volume novels does not by any means indicate poverty of imagination. The effects of imagination may not be immediately apparent. But its importance—its life-and-death importance—and the need for its encouragement and cultivation are things that I believe cannot be overemphasized. And we must not forget, not for a minute, that *everything* we do affects our children, is affecting them right now, at this particular moment, and it is our duty to keep this in mind all the time.

Travel Notes

LLOYD ALEXANDER

Most of us, on our journey, go no-frills economy. But we get postcards from other travelers who have ventured before us: views of country churchyards, daffodils, Grecian urns, nightingales, birch trees. A windmill, from Don Quixote. A specimen of unusual insect life, sent by Gregor Samsa. A raft on the Mississippi—best wishes from Huck and Jim. Greetings from Paradise. From the Inferno. From the rabbit hole.

The messages vary. Don't eat the lotuses. Exact change required on the ferry across the Styx. The best of times, the worst of times. All the world's a stage. All happy families are alike. Beware the Jabberwock. I only am escaped alone to tell thee.

C. P. Cavafy writes to us:

> As you set out on the voyage to Ithaka
> Pray that your journey be long,
> Filled with adventures, filled with wisdom.
> Do not fear the Laistrygonians and the Cyclops
> And furious Poseidon.

To which adds Lemuel Gulliver: "A traveller's chief aim should be to make men wiser and better, and to improve their minds by the bad as well as the good example of what they deliver concerning foreign places."

A commendable purpose. Travelers' tales, though, are notorious for enhancing the facts. They rank with fish stories and autobiographies, a few notches above political speeches. Mark Twain, that most reliable of pilots, who spoke as much truth as any of us have courage to bear, claimed superiority over George Washington. "He couldn't tell a lie," says Mark Twain. "I can."

We are entitled to ask if these tales have any credibility. They are not laboratory reports or discoveries of science, awesome and enlightening as those may be. They are not official communiqués, which seldom have more than a nodding acquaintance with veracity. They are not history, an altogether different order of fantasy. The messages of literature come from flesh-and-blood creatures like ourselves. They have been there ahead of us. They know the territory.

I believe their messages are the most accurate we will ever get. They are true. As a fairy tale is true. As mythology is true. "Myths are among the subtlest and most direct languages of experience," writes George Steiner. "They re-enact moments of signal truth or crisis in the human condition." And from Elizabeth Cook: "The inherent greatness of myth and fairy tale is a poetic greatness. . . . extended lyrical images of unchanging human predicaments and strong, unchanging hopes and fears, loves and hatreds."

My purpose, however, is not to explore the great cosmologies, but the small ones; and to suggest that art is a process whereby life becomes myth, and myth becomes life. The great mythologies may be embedded in the collective unconscious, if indeed there is such a thing. The small ones are embedded in our childhood, in our families—a home-style, do-it-yourself variety. As a very articulate and engaging Jungian analyst, Dr. James Hillman, points out, family figures, family deeds can take on larger-than-life proportions.

Certainly in my family we had no shortage of mythology and legend. For example, the saga of my Uncle Roy, who in youth fell from a sycamore tree and had to have his head operated on. To me, that sycamore loomed as large as the cosmic ash tree, Yggdrasil, its roots and branches binding earth, heaven, and hell. And my uncle, transfigured by his ordeal, ranked with every hero who, from the very jaws of death, came back nobler and wiser. He subsequently found employment with the Pennsylvania Railroad.

I could recount the expulsion of my parents from their West Philadelphia Eden, barred forever by an angel—or landlord—brandishing a flaming lease. In point of fact, the analogy doesn't hold up. My mother would have paid no attention to a talking reptile. My father's temptation did not take the form of a piece of fruit. He worshiped at the shrine of the goddess Fortuna, also known as Dow Jones. Still, I could cast his creditors in the role of the Eumenides.

The Romans had their lares and penates. We, too, had a sacred object— my Aunt Belle's gall bladder. This was a numinous entity; venerated, spoken of in hushed voices; capricious, with a life of its own; enigmatic, its behavior a subject of constant discussion and oracular interpretation. When it was, at last, found and removed, it nevertheless occupied a place in our thoughts, its absence as much felt as its presence. It allowed me a later insight into the nature of the Holy Grail.

Happily, this mythopoeic process continues. I have heard my daughter describe to her own family, in convincing detail, incidents I know never happened quite that way or never happened at all. I wouldn't dream of interfering and spoiling a good story with boring facts. I only hope her children will develop the same devotion to accuracy that their grandfather has.

For my part, I might evoke Jacob's years of servitude with Laban, although my goal was not the hand of Rachel (I was already married) but something more elusive than the Grail or my aunt's gall bladder—namely, the pursuit of that *ignis fatuus*, literary publication. While I did labor seven years before one of my ambitious undertakings was actually printed, Laban—my departmental supervisor—and I parted company before that, when he discovered me writing a novel instead of a brochure on industrial lubricants.

It would have been poetic justice had that fatal novel become a best-seller. But even I shrink from tormenting truth beyond endurance, so I must admit: It did not. The manuscript went unpublished, as its author went unemployed. Not poetic justice, but at least a measure of aesthetic symmetry. And I did gain a profound understanding of the myth of Sisyphus.

We can all provide other examples of domestic micromythology, the difference being that writers turn theirs into novels or poems. Which is only a roundabout way of stating the obvious: Artists, one way or another, draw from their own lives, from their own experiences, external or internal. Painters—Van Gogh, Rembrandt, and so many others—have given us their portraits showing themselves at a moment of crisis or self-comprehension. In music, Beethoven titles a movement of his Quartet in A Minor, opus 132, "Song of thanksgiving to the Deity by a convalescent." In *Art of Fugue*, Bach spells out his name in the emerging, developing theme as a means of symbolizing his own spiritual journey. When it breaks off in midphrase, we can almost see the pen drop from his hand. And there are many other instances.

Literary examples abound, from Dostoevsky to James Joyce, from Dickens to Marcel Proust, too familiar, too numerous to detail. But Flaubert's famous line *"Madame Bovary, c'est moi"* means a great deal more than absorption with a character. The creative process is subtler than that; it is both transformative and synthesizing.

It's a simple idea, although many talk-show hosts apparently have some difficulty grasping it. The hapless author, who usually comes on after the trained orangutan, is usually asked: "Did you actually do all those things your heroine [or hero] did?" If that were the case, heaven help all writers—with the possible exception of Jackie Collins. They'd have neither time nor energy to write. I, for one, doubt that I would have strength, cunning, or courage to survive ten minutes in any of my own fictional worlds. It is not uncommon to find the hale and hearty, outdoor type of author concerned with the dissection of subtle sensitivities, while the ninety-pound dishrag rejoices in derring-do.

This, I think, is more than Walter Mittyism or the attraction of opposites, although such elements may be present. We are dealing as much with inner life as with outer life; with metaphor, which is another way of saying, with a kind of mythology.

The advice—wise advice—given young writers is "write what you know." Not accidentally are so many first novels thinly veiled autobiographies. This, unfortunately, does not automatically make them good novels.

Writers are not always trustworthy critics of their own works. Discussing their merits, they are inevitably self-serving; as for their shortcomings, they can always rely on their friends to point them out. So I will only say that the novel which sent me to the unemployment line dealt with life among the old Philadelphia aristocracy. I should also mention that I had never met an old Philadelphia aristocrat, or a young one. The equally disastrous manuscripts that followed were much alike in subject matter. Only when I finally despaired of writing about inhabitants of the elegant Main Line and drew on the less-than-elegant denizens of my own unstately home did I succeed in having a novel published.

Yes, "write what you know" is sound advice. But we also need to understand that we know many things, more than we suppose. Our work lies in discovering what they are, in discovering what matters to us. Not what we think should matter to us—literature is not civic duty—but what *really* matters to us, on the level of our bone marrow. Otherwise, we have good journalism but not necessarily good art.

As I've said elsewhere, coming finally to write fantasy for young people was, for me, the most creative and liberating experience. And, I believe, precisely for this reason: It was a form that allowed me not only to say what I most wanted to say, but also to find—to my surprise—what I never before realized I wanted to say.

I'm reluctant to theorize. Whenever I come up with what seems a good theory, I can think of any number of exceptions. The only thing to do about the exceptions is what any sensible theoretician does—ignore them. So, I'll suggest only a very general principle. Whether we use the metaphor of a voyage, whether we draw from the common heritage of mythology, we deal from strength when we connect our writing to our own vital centers. All the clever devices of fiction are no more than clever devices unless we bring to them some part of ourselves. To bring a work to life, we give some portion of our own life. This is no guarantee the work will be good. We can do everything right in principle and have everything come out wrong in practice. Yet, it's possible for a flawed work of art to be more interesting than a perfect work of nonart.

As for the exceptions: By any standard of literary excellence, there are books—and some of them I dearly love—that are perfectly awful. Yet they move us deeply. Whatever else we may say about them, they work. For one quick example: I doubt that anyone would commend Edgar Rice Burroughs as one of our great literary stylists. Even so, *Tarzan of the Apes* has grown to mythic proportion. This is not the occasion to explain such phenomena, nor do we have to explain them. They exist. They become part of our popular culture, part of our national consciousness. Perhaps all we can say is that their creators builded better than they knew.

Nevertheless, I think artists prefer the personal over the impersonal. Impersonal art may well be a contradiction in terms. I don't mean that art must be a confessional or an exercise in narcissism. Self-expression is not the same as self-impression. Small prefixes make large differences. I would also suggest that none of the humanities are impersonal. The discoveries of science may be objective, neutral; but the directions and motivations, the priorities of investigation, the changing modes of scientific thought reflect social context and individual mind-sets. Scientists aren't Olympians. The Olympians themselves behave more like humans than divinities.

I doubt that any human activity is truly impersonal. Is teaching, for example, impersonal? I think not. For I make a distinction between teaching and instruction, as I make a distinction between education and schooling. Schooling centers around institutional discipline. With education, there's the risk we might actually learn something.

We are, however, limited by our humanity. That is, we can only give what we have, what we are, and what we may have picked up along the road.

When Cavafy sets his poem "Ithaka" in terms of Odysseus and his voyage, with all a poet's instincts he chooses one of the strongest evocations in our culture. The journey—the pattern of departure, challenge, and return—is at the heart of our mythology; ancient, eternally renewed.

Robert Graves called the *Odyssey*, masquerading as an epic, the first Greek novel. When Odysseus names himself *Oudeis*—Nobody—he might well have named himself Everybody. He was, of course, too wily to do that, or he'd never have escaped the Cyclops.

For us, the journey is a central fact of our lives. Having set out on it, like it or not we have to keep on—to be heroic in spite of ourselves. Sometimes our most courageous act is to get up in the morning. Cavafy tells us:

> Pray that your journey be long.
> May there be many summer mornings
> When with pleasure and joy
> You will come upon harbors seen for the first time.

> May you linger at Phoenician trading posts
> And get precious things—
> Mother of pearl and coral, amber and ebony.

Marvelous souvenirs. But we can't keep them. They become valuable only when given away. This is not to say that we have gained nothing:

> Ithaka gave you the splendid journey;
> Without her you would not have set forth.

I hope the postcards we send back are of some use to those who have only started on their own journey; if not useful, at least pleasurable. Earlier, I asked if we could trust those messages. I should have asked, Can we trust art? We not only can, but I think we must. I see no better defense of our fragile humanity. Without it, we have no compass, no maps, in a world that seems enchanted with the idea of destroying itself. Art is not necrophilic; it is biophilic.

Having dutifully quoted so many other writers, I hope to be forgiven if I quote one more. At the end of *The Smith, The Weaver, and the Harper*, Menwy the harper tells the gray-cloaked horseman:

> I see you for what you are, Lord of Death. And I fear you, as all men do. For all that, you are a weak and pitiful king. You can destroy, but never build. You are less than the humblest creature, the frailest blade of grass. For these live, and every moment of their lives is a triumph over you. Your kingdom is dust; only the silent ending of things, never the beginnings.
>
> At that, Menwy took his harp and began to play a joyful melody. Hearing it, the horseman's face tightened in rage; he drew his sword from its sheath and with all his might he struck at the bard.
>
> But the blow missed its mark and instead struck the harp, shattering it to bits. Menwy, however, flung aside the pieces, and laughed in defiance, calling out:
>
> "You fail, Death-Lord! You destroy the instrument but not its music. With all your power, you have gained only a broken shell."
>
> In that moment, when the harp had been silenced, arose the song of birds, the chiming of brooks, the humming of wind through grass and leaves; and all those

voices took up the strands of melody, more beautiful than before.

And the Lord of Death fled in terror of life.

The messages art sends us, however, are always unfinished, with few answers; and these, at best, are very sketchy. It does not give us all the answers. It cannot give us all the answers. We should be glad of that.

Given all the answers, we would be obliged to stop looking for them.

Through the Dark Wood

NINA BAWDEN

My son Nicholas has had a hard time in the last twelve years or so. He has been diagnosed as schizophrenic; his crippling illness, and the pain and distress it has caused him, has been painful and distressing for his family, too—for me and my husband, my parents, his brother and sister. One night, a couple of years ago, I had a dream. My son was a little boy again, the fair, happy child who had once been so open and eager and loving. I was holding his hand and we were running together along a seashore, skipping with joy and laughing together.

I don't pretend to understand this dream. A kind of nostalgic, wish-fulfillment fantasy, perhaps, in which I was going back to a time before his troubles began, when he was still small enough for me to protect him and put things right for him. But I know that when I woke up the next morning, the dream was still with me, clear in my mind, and although nothing about his situation had changed, I felt different about it from the way I had felt before I went to sleep. I had been particularly despairing about him the evening before, about my inability to help him. Nothing was outwardly changed by the dream. It hadn't put back the clock, there had been no miracle, and he was still a grown man with great difficulties that I and my husband, his stepfather, could only help him with marginally. But something had happened to *me*. I felt in a curious way very much *stronger*, as if this dream-reminder of a time when my boy had been little and I had been a confident mother, able to smooth out his childish troubles and look cheerfully toward his future, had made me better able to cope with the present.

Normally, one expects one's children to take on responsibility for their own lives as they grow older. The dream had told me that this cannot always happen, that there are some burdens one can never lay down. I knew this intellectually, of course. What the dream had done—*has* done,

66

rather, since the effect is still with me—was to make me accept the situation, take it into my life as no rational argument could have done and, by facing the truth without dodging or denying it, to turn defeat into a kind of victory. And it was as important, therefore, as any outside, observable happening. Dreams and thoughts are as much a part of reality as what we say and do. This dream has changed my attitude toward my son in a way that I cannot really describe, nor is my changed attitude toward him much to the point in this context. I am using it as an example. The mysterious life of the subconscious and the workings of the imagination are fundamental to human existence. One could not give a truthful account of a life without including them, nor write a realistic story for adults or children without recognizing their vital importance.

What adults have to learn painfully—or relearn—children know instinctively. My goddaughter had an imaginary friend called William, a bad little boy who used to play with matches and refused to eat certain foods that she didn't much care for. William lived with her family for a number of years, an unseen presence at mealtimes and a rather untidy and destructive person to have round the house. He broke things occasionally, stole from his mother's purse, hated the dentist, and was rude to his teachers. Being a free spirit, unfettered by awkward adult demands for "good" behavior, he could be as "bad" as he liked—and, indeed, my goddaughter often expressed her disapproval of him. "William thinks *old* grown-ups are smelly. He doesn't like kissing them. I think that's rather unkind and rude of him, don't you?"

William was a neat way of explaining one or two problems of this kind and also, to some extent, helped her to explain to herself contradictions and impulses that she was aware of—and perhaps alarmed by—in her own character.

Imaginary friends are very common in childhood, a simple example of how children can lead double lives without any difficulty. Children rely on their imaginations, need symbolic ideas and images, because so much happens both within them and around them that they find hard to understand. "Realistic" explanations given by "sensible" adults are often incomprehensible, and if a child doesn't understand the answer to one of his questions, he will simply assume that the adult has not understood it. Lacking the power of abstract reasoning, he needs to interpret the world in some other way.

Fairy stories, as Bruno Bettelheim has told us, can be helpful for this purpose. They express deep truths but in an easily understandable way. Both good and evil are present, but in a fairy story a child can understand the struggle between the two without feeling threatened as he might be by a realistic story set in his own environment. An angry giant is more bearable than an angry grown-up. The heroes and heroines of fairy stories are usually small, poor, and helpless, as all children are; and for a child to see a giant of uncertain temper being given his comeuppance, as in "Jack and the Beanstalk," is agreeably comforting. But I think that although Bettelheim puts his argument most eloquently and movingly in *The Uses of Enchantment*, he does tend to overstate his argument for the supremacy of the fairy story over all other kinds of imaginative fiction. The fact is, myths and fairy tales contain certain motifs that crop up everywhere, in fantasies, dreams, and delusions—archetypal ideas that many writers, even many writers of so-called realistic fiction, use naturally and instinctively.

Here is a simple example from my children's book *The Robbers*. I wanted to write about a boy who was unusually innocent, a kind of Candide looking at the world with fresh eyes and making his own judgments about it. To do this he had to have an exceptionally secure and protected upbringing. Since I didn't want to make this point too laboriously, I started the story with the sentence "All his life, Philip had lived in a castle"—a kind of shorthand that I hoped would make his situation immediately apparent. The castle is a linguistic clue that children can easily recognize, and Philip's journey away from it, into the dangers and delights of urban society—the real world, in fact—is a way of presenting the classic theme of the adventure-quest: how the young child sets off on the journey all children must take, toward independence and self-awareness, learning as he goes how to cope with the demands of living. I don't take any credit for that first sentence, by the way; I simply woke up one morning with it in my head, as if it had formed there while I was sleeping, and knew that it was the best way to begin this particular story. And it may be of some significance that this was shortly after I had had my happy dream about my son who had once been safe in *his* childhood's "castle."

A lot of discussion about children's literature suffers from pompous inflation. But I don't think it is pompous to say that a story can often mean more to a child, *do* more for him, in fact, than a novel may do for an adult. Children are not less intelligent than we are, but they lack experience. Stories that operate on a number of levels—which is only to say all *good* stories—help them to understand their own nature, the confusion they may be feeling about the conflicting impulses and emotions they are aware of within themselves, and help them to understand the world they are growing up into. Fiction can be a bridge between the child and his future as well as a guide to his present.

When I was young, it certainly seemed to me that I learned more about the real world from stories than I did from my parents and teachers. This may have been partly because my family are much given to secrecy. I was twenty-five before I learned that I had a half sister, living not many miles away, and rising fifty before I found out that my grandfather, my father's father, was not a man called George Mabey, a lighterman on the Thames, as I had always been told, but an Italian ship's cook called Achille Benati—a much more romantic ancestor altogether. My father's mother had been married to a George Mabey, but he died long before my father was born. My grandmother kept a lodging house for seamen in London, in the East India Dock Road—a very superior one, taking no one below the rank of first mate. Whether a ship's cook qualified for a room in this establishment I don't know, but Achille Benati married my grandmother a month before my father was born and then, some years later, deserted her.

My father, who had been christened Mario Angelo Benati, decided, when he was eleven years old and leaving school to be apprenticed to an engineering shop in the docks, to take his mother's first husband's name and called himself Charles Mabey. I suppose he felt ashamed of his real father's defection and preferred his children not to know of it. I don't know. But I do know that it was my mother who decided that we should not be told about our half sister, my father's daughter by his first wife who had died shortly after the baby was born. When my mother and father were married, my mother looked after her stepdaughter for a while, but there were family complications and jealousies of an obscure and passionate kind and, finally, shortly after I was born, my half sister was sent to live with some cousins. My father took her away in a taxi, she remembers, and gave her a box of chocolates to comfort her. Chocolates were always his answer whenever he was faced with females in distress. For many years afterward, twenty-five years, she knew that I and my brothers existed, was given photographs of us by my father, but we knew nothing about her existence.

This family habit of keeping skeletons locked up in cupboards might deter me from starting my autobiography—who knows what revelations the next twenty-five years may bring?—but it provided fertile soil for a novelist. Whispers surrounded me in my childhood; voices fell when I entered a room; meaningful glances were exchanged between the grown-ups. Their world was obviously full of secrets that were dangerous for me to know. "Never ask your father to show you his birth certificate," my mother once hissed at me—God knows why, since the idea of asking such a strange thing had never occurred to me. I imagine that she must have quarreled with him and was taking it out on me the way parents do. But the effect of this kind of remark was to make me realize that the adult world contained many questions that I could not expect my parents, or indeed any grown-up, to answer or explain.

I turned to books for the answers. Not to fairy tales—I came too late to Grimm, and I disliked Hans Andersen because of the cruel and morbid streak in some of his stories that frightened me. I didn't much care for fairies or witches, and, except for Beatrix Potter and Kenneth Grahame, authors who wrote about talking animals seemed mildly insane to me. But my grandmother, my *other* grandmother, my mother's mother, had a shelf of Victorian children's novels that she had won as Sunday School prizes— among them *Little Lord Fauntleroy, Tom Sawyer, Huckleberry Finn*—and I learned from them and from the novels of Dickens when I was a bit older that a great many exciting things went on in the world. People died, murdered each other, went to prison, lost all their money. That there was no outward sign of these interesting goings-on in our family or in our street didn't deceive me. People kept themselves to themselves in our poor but respectable suburb; lace curtains at their windows, chains on their front doors. Of course, they wouldn't want their neighbors to know what they were up to!

To put the record straight, I began to make up tales about our neighbors—excellent stories of death and disaster—and told them to my friends. And, encouraged by their eager, wide-eyed response, I turned, somewhat unwisely, to inventing alarming situations of a more personal kind. I told my best friend that I had heard her mother and father talking in their garden one day, planning to abandon her and her three sisters. Not a very original plot, of course, but few plots are really original. It is all in the telling, and I must have told this tale well enough to frighten her badly. Her mother heard her crying in bed one night and asked her what was the matter. Then her mother told my mother the wicked thing I had done, and I became known as a liar, which seemed most unfair to me; I had only been trying to entertain her with a good, scary story, and I thought she ought to have known this perfectly well.

Stories, I insisted, weren't lies. They might not be true in the way that school history books were true—I was still young enough to believe *that* hoary old fallacy—but they were true in a different way. They told you true things about what people did, what they thought, how they behaved, and why.

As you may imagine, I didn't win that particular argument. At least I didn't win it then, and perhaps I have been trying to prove it to my mother ever since. But as far as I was concerned, I was right. The stories I read helped me to solve some of the riddles that puzzled me, to understand the secret passions that I sensed were raging about me. And since all art is subversive and, as Marcuse has said, gives individuals a chance to realize their own "images of liberation," they gave me confidence in myself as a person. For one thing, I could see that the authors of some of the stories were cleverer than the adults I knew and, more important, thought as I did and agreed with me. I chuckled to myself with sly pleasure as I realized that most of these authors were on my side, wonderful allies for a small child who was always engaged, as I seemed to be, in a series of battles with my parents and teachers. They made me feel less lonely because they told me that other people thought and felt as I did, were angry, resentful, willful, and jealous—all the things my mother said that a nice little girl shouldn't be. They helped me, in fact, to understand my own inner processes; and I think, when I started to write for children, I wanted to do for them what the novels of Dickens and Mark Twain and the books in my grandmother's house—her Victorian Sunday School prizes—had long ago done for me. I wanted to set my stories in an emotional landscape that children would recognize as very much like their own, even if the physical or social backgrounds were different.

After all, Shakespeare is still relevant today. Many families have their own King Lear. One evening last winter I watched a performance of *Hamlet* put on by the Young Vic Theatre Company in London for an audience largely composed of young people in their early teens. There were a few school groups, but most of the seats were filled by the local kids that this particular theater—near the National Theatre on the South Bank but not part of it—does its best to attract with lively productions, cheap prices, and an informal coffee bar. For most of them, *Hamlet* was not a school text but a piece of new, living theater, a story they'd not heard before. And for me it was fascinating to be sitting among them—it made me realize afresh what a good play it is. So good that there was no shuffling or whispering throughout the performance except for one remark made by a husky boy just in front of me. He turned to his girl and said, about Hamlet's mother, "Bloody cow, ain't she? Just like me Mum." A long way from Elsinore—but he had made the jump easily and responded quite naturally to the emotional truth of the play.

And, although I don't set myself up to be Shakespeare, this is the kind of response I hope for when I write my novels for children. To give them a chance to recognize something of their own feelings—about themselves, their parents, their friends—and their own situation as a kind of subject race, always at the mercy of the adults who mostly run their lives for them.

Albert, the older boy in *Carrie's War*, says, "It's a fearful *handicap* being a child. . . . you can never make anything happen"; and when I was young, I felt this very strongly. I knew what I thought and even more what I felt, but it seemed to me that my opinions were always being swept aside, as if they were of no value, and my feelings disregarded. This may not have been true, or not always true, but I have fierce memories of feeling angry and oppressed, of being talked down to or laughed at when I said something "quaint," not taken seriously.

And children need to be taken seriously. Even difficult things can be explained if you take the trouble to look at how they see things, which is different from the way adults see things sometimes. A child whose parents are being divorced, like my bad-tempered small heroine in *The Runaway Summer*, doesn't want to be told how his or her parents feel, how much Mummy and Daddy still love them, and unctuous things of that kind. They want to know practical things like where they are going to live, whether they will be able to take their new bicycles, what is going to happen to *them*.

I had said something of this in my early, adult novels—in the ones, that is, that had children in them—but I assumed that in a children's book there would be no need to say it explicitly because my readers would know it, after all. So when I began my first children's book, although I knew there would have to be some differences in the way I told my tale—the plot would have to be stronger, move faster—I hoped to incorporate in it the same kind of depth of ideas and character that all good novels should have. There would have to be adventures, of course, because all children love adventures, but it should be possible, I thought, to use the exciting events of the narrative to make my readers think about other aspects of life, about other people. *The Witch's Daughter*, for example, is a straightforward adventure story of a fairly conventional kind: a group of children on a Scottish island get tangled up with some sinister jewel thieves and find hidden treasure. But one of the children is blind, and one is a witch's daughter—a rather odd, wild little girl, an orphan who is tormented by the local children and has never been to school. A lot of readers who wrote to me about this book were fascinated by these two characters, seeing—it seemed—in the blindness of the one and in the strange wildness of the other a kind of echo, or mirror image, of the feelings they sometimes had: feelings of being lonely, different from other people, cut off, set apart. And their letters showed me that my adventure story had been realistic in the way I had wanted it to be—true to the inner, imaginative experience which is such a large part of most people's lives.

I was pleased that my books seemed to give pleasure, and the plots bounced along well enough and were fun to construct, but I wanted to write for children in a less contrived way, so that the situations and adventures rose more naturally out of the characters and their background. The difficulty seemed to be that although children like to read about adventures, in real life they seldom have them—they rarely catch jewel thieves or find hidden treasure.

I solved the problem, I think, in a novel called *Squib*. That is the name that a group of children give to a pale, silent little boy they sometimes see in the park, who, they later discover, is locked up in a ruined tower in the grounds of an old people's home. This child, Squib—who never speaks until right at the end of the book—is being badly treated by a careless and stupid relation. A cruelly abused child, in fact. I didn't want to write about him directly because it seemed to me that a clear view of his situation would be too distressing for children or, at least, too bewildering. The action and the excitement of the story lie, in fact, in the fantasies that the different children make up to explain what is happening to this sad child.

The little ones tell each other that he has been caught by a witch and is being fattened up for her supper. (They have clearly been reading "Hansel and Gretel"!) An older boy believes Squib has been kidnapped and is being held for ransom. And a girl dreams that he is her young, drowned brother come back. When Squib is eventually rescued by the timely intervention of adults, this particular girl realizes that the story of Squib is, as she tells herself, "something more frightening than a hundred old witches." And so it is, of course. The cruel treatment of children by the adults who are supposed to take care of them is one of the ultimate terrors of childhood. But although I used this theme later in an adult novel called *Anna Apparent*, it never could be, used straightforwardly, a suitable one for a children's book. Or not for children of the age that I write for.

Nor would the unhappiness some children suffered in World War II be suitable if one wrote about it explicitly, as one might write for adults. (I am not speaking here about the kind of horrors that happened in Europe, only about the pain of separation and loss that the luckier children of my country had to endure.) *Carrie's War* is based on my own wartime experience. Carrie, who is twelve, and her brother, Nick, who is younger, are sent away from London as the bombs start to fall, just as my brother and I were sent away. They leave the city in a darkened train, not knowing where they are going, with labels round their necks as if they are parcels. (I remember when we asked our teacher why we had to have labels, she said, very briskly, that if the train was bombed and we were killed, they might be helpful to identify our bodies.) Carrie and Nick arrive (as my brother and I did) in a Welsh mining village and are lined up by their school teachers so that the local people can come and pick them over and choose the children they like the look of best. Carrie is certain that no one will choose her and her brother. Nick has been sick on the train and looks dreadful. Why should anyone want a boy who looks as if he might be ill, and a nuisance. She says, "Why don't you smile and look nice."

This was a frightening situation for Carrie, as it had been for me, and as I guessed it could be for the children who read about it—evoking not only the fear of being separated from parents but also the additional fear of never seeing them again. I didn't want to underline this too heavily, and so I used some of the devices of fairy tales to make my points clear at a level a child would understand instinctively, without too much explanation. When someone does choose them, it is little Miss Evans, Auntie Lou, who looks like a bright-eyed red squirrel—a "good creature" as in the old fairy tales. Her brother, Councillor Samuel Isaac Evans, on the other hand, is quite a dreadful man—an ogre, is how young Nick thinks of him. But like a proper fairy-tale ogre he has his small weaknesses. His false teeth don't fit. And just as Jack defeats the giant by cunning and guile, Nick defeats Mr. Evans by being just that little bit smarter.

Children, faced with something that is too complicated and fearsome for their comprehension, handle it by using the abstractions of myth. Just as in the landscape of myths and fairy tales, evil and good inhabit human form and must be accepted as they are, in times like 1939, children (and some adults, too) will accept the fact that, in this example, all Germans are one indivisible mass of evil and Britain and the Allies are good. Having settled this huge and difficult problem in their own minds in this way, Carrie and Nick have to learn how to live alone among strangers and grow up without the help and certain love of their parents, in the shadow of a war that is always there, if only as a dark cloud on the horizon.

The framework of the book (although, as I will explain in a minute, I didn't realize this when I wrote it) is a kind of archetypal tale, beginning and ending with a journey through a dark wood. It opens like this:

> Carrie had often dreamed about coming back. In her dreams she was twelve years old again, short, scratched legs in red socks and scuffed sandals, walking along the narrow, dirt path at the side of the railway line to where it plunged down, off the high ridge, through the Druid's Grove. The yew trees in the Grove were dark green and so old that they had grown twisted and lumpy, like arthritic fingers. And in Carrie's dreams, the fingers reached out for her, plucking at her hair and her skirt as she ran. She was always running by the end of this dream, running away from the house, uphill towards the railway line.
>
> But when she did come back, with her own children, the railway line had been closed. The sleepers had been taken up and the flat, stony top of the ridge was so overgrown with blackberries and wild rose and hazelnut bushes that it was like pushing through a forgotten forest in a fairy tale. The tangled wood round Sleeping Beauty's castle. Pulling off the sticky brambles that clung to their jeans, Carrie's children said, "No one's been here for hundreds of years. . . . a million, billion, *trillion.*"

Carrie is taking her children back to the mining village where she grew up in the war, to a house called Druid's Bottom, where she had been happy and which is important to her for other reasons, too. Mr. Evans, the Ogre, used to have a dying sister who lived in this house with a housekeeper called Hepzibah. The place is an old farm and can be reached only by walking along the side of the railway line and going down through a wood which is, so local people say, not a place to go after dark because it is full of the old religion still. Going down through this wood the first time is a terrifying experience for Carrie: fingers of trees clutching at her, and a sense of something silently waiting. "Not a ghost—nothing so simple. Whatever it was had no name. Something old and huge and nameless."

And even years later, when she is grown, she is still afraid. She has to go through the wood which is now even more overgrown, almost impenetrable, before the story can be finished, the loose ends tidied up, and everything made plain.

When I wrote the book, I didn't know exactly what I was doing. I only knew that I was trying to say a number of rather complicated things about living and growing up and that I wanted to say them as simply as possible. And this journey through a dark wood is something that quite a young child can comprehend. He may not be able to put it into words—and, indeed, if you put it into words for him, he would not understand them— but he knows, all the same, that the dark wood is himself, the mysterious world of his unconscious mind and that, like the brave knights of old, he has to get through it if he is to prove himself, to find his identity. It is the dark wood that Dante writes of at the beginning of *The Divine Comedy*, the dark wood that we all remember from childhood and still visit in dreams.

It is quite important that I didn't know that I had used an ancient image until I had finished *Carrie's War* and a lecturer in English pointed it out to me. It means that in spite of the fact that there are certain elements of what some people might call fantasy in the book, it is still, on *my* terms, a realistic novel. I had written instinctively about the dark wood, and my instincts, which spring from my inner life, are after all part of me, and a vital part. They are what Jung, the great philosopher, calls "existent thoughts which are part of our wholeness." Which is to say, we may not be entirely "such stuff as dreams are made on," but we cannot write truthfully about the human experience without recognizing that instincts and dreams—the images that come to us naturally, springing out of our unconscious minds—are a large part of our reality.

NOTE

This was written in 1980. Nicholas Bawden disappeared in November 1982 and his body was recovered from the River Thames in February 1983.

Nahum Tarune's Book

SUSAN COOPER

From a place halfway between innocence and experience, here is the beginning of a story.

In my rovings and ramblings as a boy I had often skirted the old stone house in the hollow. But my first clear remembrance of it is of a hot summer's day. I had climbed to the crest of a hill till then unknown to me, and stood there, hot and breathless in the bright slippery grass, looking down on its grey walls and chimneys as if out of a dream. And as if out of a dream already familiar to me.

My real intention in setting out from home that morning had been to get to a place called East Dene. My mother had often spoken to me of East Dene—of its trees and waters and green pastures, and the rare birds and flowers to be found there. Ages ago, she had told me, an ancestor of our family had dwelt in this place. But she smiled a little strangely when I asked her to take me there. "All in good time, my dear," she whispered into my ear, "all in very good time! Just follow your small nose." What kind of time, I wondered, was *very good time?* And *follow my nose*— how far? Such reflections indeed only made me the more anxious to be gone.

Early that morning, then, I had started out when the dew was still sparkling, and the night mists had but just lifted. But my young legs soon tired of the steep, boulder-strown hills, the chalky ravines, and burning sun, and having, as I say, come into view of the house in the valley, I went no further. Instead, I sat down on the hot turf—the

> sweet smell of thyme in the air, a few harebells nodding
> around me—and stared, down and down.

My title is "Nahum Tarune's Book," and anyone who recognizes that name will also recognize the passage above. The rest of you may wonder what on earth I am up to. Who is Nahum Tarune? An eighteenth-century preacher? A leathery old Maine fisherman? Perhaps an Elizabethan composer, some obscure acquaintance of John Dowland?

None of these. Nahum Tarune belongs in fact to one of the most remarkable books in the English language: Walter de la Mare's anthology of verse, *Come Hither.* I've had my copy of this wonder for thirty years and must have turned to it at least as many times each year—sometimes for solace, sometimes for sunlight, always with an emotion that I have never quite been able to define. *Come Hither* is my talisman, my haunting: a distillation of the mysterious quality that sings out of all the books to which I've responded most deeply all my life—and that I dearly hope, as a writer, I might someday, somehow, be able to catch. But the quality is as evanescent as a rainbow; it will never stay to be examined. It's a kind of magic, but not from books which are necessarily *about* magic—not at all. What is it?

I don't know, but it's high time I tried to find out.

To begin at the beginning: *Come Hither* is magical not simply because it's a wonderfully far-ranging collection of verse put together by a very remarkable poet, but because it has an introduction and a set of notes half as long again as the verse. That doesn't sound very promising, I grant you. But the notes are no ordinary notes. They are the musings of a full and most agile mind, which wanders over hill and dale instead of keeping to the narrow path of scholarship. You read, for instance, an early poem which is a kind of general wassail, entitled "Bring Us in Good Ale"—and you find as a note to it the engaging information that in 1512 the two young sons of the Earl of Northumberland were allowed for their daily breakfast "Half a Loif of houshold Brede, a Manchet, a Dysch of butter, a Pece of Saltfish, a Dysch of Sproits or iii White herrynge"—and eight mugs of ale.

Or there's the note to Chaucer's lines about the month of May, when, as you will remember, "the foules singe / And . . . the floures ginnen for to springe." This transports de la Mare into five pages of beautifully random reflections about flowers, including the observation that Shakespeare never mentions foxgloves once in all his plays—though he names the rose fifty-seven times and the violet eighteen. The reason turns out to be that foxgloves dislike limestone and are rarely found in South Warwickshire. So that, says our editor, "it is possible . . . that Shakespeare when a child never saw a foxglove . . . and it is what we see early in life that comes back easiest later." (It is, indeed. And it is, I suspect, the root of what I'm talking about.)

Now, I don't know about you, but when I was reading scholarly editions of this and that at university, I was never blessed with footnotes like those. I love the idea of finding out, gratis and with total irrelevance, that Shakespeare never saw a foxglove (after all, think what he might have done with it in *A Midsummer Night's Dream*), and that two small boys had eight mugs of ale and a manchet for breakfast in 1512. As a result I can even report to you, from *The Oxford English Dictionary*, that a manchet is "a small loaf or roll of the finest wheaten bread."

Let me go back to the introduction of *Come Hither*, which is called "The Story of This Book." The boy, Simon, set out to find East Dene and instead came upon a house in a valley, at which he stared, down and down. And then he went down, to the house. Its name was inscribed in faded letters on the gateway: THRAE. It was an old, old house with embrasured windows, a round stone tower with a twirling weathervane, and a great overgrown garden. And an old lady lived there, called Miss Taroone.

Our boy came back to visit it again and again, growing bolder and going closer each time, and at length he met Miss Taroone and came to know her house with its multitude of rooms. He heard that she had once lived on another more ancient family estate called Sure Vine. He learned of some villages nearby called the Ten Laps, and was told that there was indeed a way to East Dene from this house—he would come to a Wall and would have to climb over.

But instead of going hunting for East Dene, he stayed to explore Miss Taroone's house. She was a strange, aloof old lady. The story goes on: "She never said anything affectionate; she never lost her temper. I never saw her show any pity or meanness or revenge. 'Well, Simon,' she would say . . . 'you are always welcome. Have a good look about you. Don't waste your time here. Even when all is said, you will not see too much of me and mine. . . . Sleeping, waking; waking, sleeping, Simon'; she said, 'sing while you can.' "

Then Miss Taroone told the boy about Nahum Tarune: Mr. Nahum. He was never quite sure of Mr. Nahum's relationship to her, but only that she had raised and taught him and that he had grown up in this house. One day she took Simon to the round room at the very top of the old stone tower, Nahum's room, and left him free to look at everything in it. It was the kind of marvelous room that you find described in books quite often, so often that I suspect every writer secretly hankers after it—or perhaps it's an image of the inside of any artist's mind. It was not unlike Merlin's room in *The Sword in the Stone*, full of

> odd-shaped coloured shells, fragments of quartz, thunder-
> bolts and fossils; skins of brilliant birds; outlandish shoes;
> heads, faces, masks of stone, wood, glass, wax, and metal;

pots, images, glass shapes, and what not; lanterns and bells; bits of harness and ornament and weapons. There were, besides, two or three ships of different rigs in glass cases, and one in a green bottle; peculiar tools, little machines; silent clocks, instruments of music, skulls and bones of beasts, frowsy bunches of linen or silk queerly marked, and a mummied cat (I think). And partly concealed, as I twisted my head, there, dangling in an alcove, I caught sight of a full-length skeleton, one hollow eye-hole concealed by a curtain looped to the floor from the ceiling.

Every inch of space on the walls, in this cluttered room, was covered in pictures painted by the absent Mr. Nahum. Some were of Thrae, some painted in foreign parts; many were from his mind. " 'He has,' said Miss Taroone, 'his two worlds.' " Over and over, Simon would stare at the pictures, never quite understanding why each had a name and Roman numerals on the back—as, for instance, "BLAKE: CXLVII." Then one day, in one of the many bookcases in the room, he found a certain book.

It was "an enormous, thick, home-made-looking volume covered in a greenish shagreen or shark-skin. Scrawled in ungainly capitals on the strip of vellum pasted to the back of this book was its title: THEOTHER-WORLDE." Simon—or Walter de la Mare—tells us that the book was full of rhymes and poems, some with Mr. Nahum's thoughts on them jotted in the margin, or a piece of prose bearing on a particular poem. Some had illuminated capitals, some were queerly spelled, some had names and numbers which linked with the pictures on the walls. Day after day the boy read them, as they took his fancy, and he learned to hear the music of the words and to see those pictures in them which were not on the walls.

And he began to realize that even when Mr. Nahum's pictures were about real things and places and people, they were still only of the places and people that the words made for him in his mind. He had, that is, to *imagine* all they told. So what he read remained as a single clear remembrance, as if his imagination had carried him away, like a magic carpet, into another world. He realized that Mr. Nahum had chosen only those poems which carried away his own imagination like that. And since they called to Simon's imagination, too, as the fowler's whistle calls to the wild duck, he sat down to copy them out and to make his own book.

So this inconsequential but unforgettable story leads to the collection of verse and prose which is *Come Hither,* the book which has haunted me, as reader and writer, since I was fourteen years old. And de la Mare's struggle to describe the *kind* of poems that he found in Nahum Tarune's book is my struggle to find out precisely what the quality is, in this book and others, which carries me so deeply into delight.

We never meet Nahum Tarune in the story of *Come Hither*, but he is all of us. Walter de la Mare has been playing with words. Nahum: human. Tarune: nature. Nahum Tarune is human nature. I don't really have the right kind of mind for anagrams, crossword puzzles, or word games, and I find allegory a very tiresome form; the more ingenious and convoluted, the more tiresome it becomes. But here, being biased I suppose, I find the parallels so deliberately clear that they have both charm and power. Thrae is the Earth, spelled, in effect, backward; Miss Taroone is Nature (Mother Nature, if you like); Sure Vine is the Universe; the villages called the Ten Laps are the Planets; and the ancestral home East Dene is Destiny.

It doesn't matter, all this; it doesn't affect the nature of what de la Mare is doing. But it does perhaps add a dimension to the way in which Miss Taroone speaks to the small boy she persists in calling Simon (or, perhaps, as a thoughtful friend of mine suggests, "my son"). " 'Remember,' she says, 'that, like Nahum, you are as old as the hills, which neither spend nor waste time, but dwell in it for ages, as if it were light or sunshine. Some day perhaps Nahum will shake himself free of Thrae altogether. I don't *know*, myself, Simon. This house is enough for me, and what I remember of Sure Vine, compared with which Thrae is but the smallest of bubbles in a large glass.' "

In the images of this story—in the old house set in its broad valley, with misted mountains all around and beyond them a glimpse of the sea, and in Nahum Tarune's great book that has in it all the best reading of a lifetime— I find something like a beckoning phrase of music, which sounds all too rarely but is wonderful to hear. Once upon a time I put such a phrase into a book of my own, as a recurrent herald of enchantment. Perhaps it was part of the *Come Hither* haunting.

What is it, the hearing of this music, the sense of being bewitched? It's not a matter simply of recognizing greatness or great talent. It isn't, as the jargon has it, a value judgment. It's subjective, idiosyncratic; perhaps it has something to do with form. I have that kind of gut response to a late Mozart symphony rather than to a Bach concerto grosso; to a Turner or a Renoir rather than to the formalities of the Flemish school. My appreciation of each, that is, is different—just as one finds different kinds of pleasure in reading different kinds of books. The appeal of a biography is different from that of a lyric poem; the appeal of a so-called realistic novel different from that of a so-called fantasy.

I say "so-called" because I've never been happy with either classification; classifying means drawing lines, and I find it hard to draw a line between any one novel and another. That magical shiver of response—I can't justify it by genre. I remember feeling it certainly from the moment the children in *The Five Children and It* first come upon the Psammead, the ancient living creature suddenly emerging from the sand after its thousand years of sleep, and certainly from the moment Kay Harker in *The Box of Delights* first meets the old man Cole Hawlings and is given that dreadful, thrilling message, "The wolves are running." But I remember it, too, from the cocky malice of Alan Breck in *Kidnapped* or from a biography in which Lord Nelson, ordered to retreat, put the telescope to his blind eye and remarked airily, "I do not see the signal." Any line that's drawn has to be instantly trampled down.

That shiver, that *frisson*, when I was growing up, came from legend, myth, and fairy tale and from a great deal of verse. My mother and my schools between them, thank God, sent poetry ringing through my head to leave most powerful echoes. I can't really tell you how many of the novels I read were "fantasies." There was most of Kipling—but the sum included his "realistic" short stories as well as *The Jungle Books; Kim* as well as *Puck of Pook's Hill*. (But perhaps *Kim* is a fantasy? Perhaps *any* novel is a fantasy, in the last analysis.) There was Elizabeth Goudge's *Henrietta's House*, if any of you remember it. There was Masefield, of course, and E. Nesbit, but Dickens and Jack London as well—and Arthur Ransome, whose books are certainly fantasies in their convenient and magical abolition of grown-ups. I was born too early for most of the overt fantasy that children read—or adults analyze—today. I never chanced to read George MacDonald; Tolkien didn't write the Lord of the Rings until I was an undergraduate; and it was only after I'd written five fantasies of my own that I took off on a deliberate orgy of reading the masters of the last twenty-five years: Alan Garner, William Mayne, Lucy Boston, Ursula Le Guin, C. S. Lewis, and the rest. Mind you, books like *Earthfasts, The Children of Green Knowe*, and *The Owl Service* produce that same stab of joy whatever age the reader may be.

But for me, when young and growing, that lovely shock came primarily from three things which are not "books" at all: from poetry, as I've said; from radio, which was at its peak as an imaginative medium in England when I was between ten and fifteen years old; and, above all, from the theater. My mother tells me that I was first taken to the theater when I was about three—to that Christmas institution in England known as the pantomime. I sat there enchanted, she says, not a whit puzzled by our transvestite tradition in which the hero of a pantomime is played by a strapping girl and the hero's mother by a large hairy man. And when it was all over and the curtain came down, I sat unmoving in my seat, and I howled and howled. All the others left on their legs, but they had to carry me out. I couldn't believe that this wonderful, magical new world, in which I had been totally absorbed, had vanished away. I wanted to bring it back again. I suppose I've been trying to bring it back again, in one way or another, ever since.

It's horribly elusive, this same kind of sensation one has from certain books, poems, and works of art. Only the symptoms are easy to describe.

The hair prickles on the back of the neck, and there is a hollowness in the throat and at the pit of the stomach—a great excitement that is a mixture of astonishment and delight. It's a little like catching sight unexpectedly of someone with whom you are very much in love. And the delight when it swamps you is full of echoes, carrying you away, as de la Mare said, "as if into another world."

The expectation of this, the hope of it in spite of all previous disappointments, is something that possesses me, always, in that moment which is one of the most powerful I know: when you are sitting in a theater before a performance, and the lights go down, and there is a hushed, murmuring expectancy, before the curtain—if there is one—goes up. It never fails to bewitch me, even if the play to come is one I've seen ten times before—just as a book or a poem can bring the same delight even if you've read it ten times before. I'm hoping always, I suppose, that when the curtain does go up, I shall find again the same joy that I found and lost, and mourned so embarrassingly, when I was three. And now and again, I do.

Why is the feeling so much intensified in the theater? It must be because, given the right playwright, the right actors, and the right director—all linked together by a rare and peculiar kind of chemistry—that special delighting quality comes totally alive to a degree possible nowhere else. The fantasy is made real. The other world is *there*, before your eyes. You are caught up, while the play lasts, in a waking dream.

For, of course, a dream, a particular kind of marvelous glowing dream that may come only once or twice in a lifetime, is the epitome of the whole thing. It's small wonder that mystics, blessed with a dream so ecstatic that they call it a vision, feel that they have had a glimpse of Heaven. Out of that part of the mind that is not sleeping there can come an image so powerful that it is an experience—odd and meaningless in itself, but always leaving a very strong visual impression and a sensation of intense joy.

I had one of those dreams three or four years ago, for no reason at all. I dreamed that I was high up on the roof of a building in a great city; roofs and towers and pinnacles stretched all around me, all of them golden, glittering in the light of a newly risen sun. In just one direction, instead of the shining gold, there seemed to lie a wide park with tall, spreading green trees rising out of an early morning mist, like islands out of a white sea.

I knew in my dream that I wanted very much to go down, toward the park, toward the trees. I looked about me on the roof but could see no way down. Then I reached out and touched a golden balustrade that ran round the edge of my roof; and the part that I touched fell away and became a kind of ladder, unfolding as it fell, the sound ringing out musically over the silent city: clang, clang, clang. I looked at it rather nervously, I remember, and then I took a deep breath and climbed down; and from the ladder I reached a sloping roof with crosswise ridges that gave purchase for the feet. And I went down that roof and came to a great sweeping stone stairway, gray and sparkling like granite, and I ran down the stairs faster and faster, toward the trees.

Then I woke up, without, of course, having accomplished anything in the dream—but with a feeling of such wonder and excitement that I lay there smiling for a while and then got up and found a pencil and paper and wrote it all down. I half expected to find the paper full of gibberish in the morning, but there was the dream: recorded, real.

I was working on a book at the time, and a few weeks later I came to a point in my story where two of my characters were to find themselves in a magical place called the Lost Land. That was an image—the Atlantis myth, I suppose—that had haunted me ever since I was very young. But I had no picture of it in my mind. I sent my two characters on their way there, but I had no idea what they would find when they arrived. Then I remembered the dream, and I put it into the book; put my two boys up on that strange golden roof high in the golden city, to come down from it as I had come down. And they did, and found all manner of things when they reached the trees.

The dream seemed to me to fit naturally there, but I haven't the least idea whether it really did. I never read the reviews of my books, through cowardice or arrogance or perhaps both, so I don't know whether some critic said that my golden city was a strikingly original concept or whether another decried it as ludicrous and irrelevant. Perhaps nobody said anything about it at all. I rather hope so—that would mean that the image did fit.

The image. It seems always to be an image of one kind or another, that sparks off this reaction of fierce delight. And images are the language of the poetic imagination. Perhaps that's the key to my slippery puzzle—for the poetic imagination is not limited to writing verse. I've known, as you have, undeniable poets who never wrote a rhyme or a metrical line in their lives. It's a quality of certain creative minds. Robert Bolt, in the introduction to his play *A Man for All Seasons*, reflected on the fact that he had used poetic imagery in the writing of it and that nobody had noticed. "I comfort myself with the thought," he said, "that it's the nature of imagery to work, in performance at any rate, unconsciously. But if, as I think, a play is more like a poem than a straight narration, still less a demonstration or lecture, then imagery ought to be important. It's perhaps necessary to add that by a poem I mean something tough and precise, not something dreamy."

And tough and precise is what, to go back to our beginning, the best books read by children have to be. That audience will settle for nothing less. A dream itself, while it's happening, is almost always singularly tough and precise, though incomplete. Certainly those words apply to every book I've mentioned, in this stumbling attempt to ferret out the roots of delight. The story is tough, the language is precise, and the whole work is clothed—noticeably or not—in imagery.

Lucy Boston once wrote, "I believe children, even the youngest, love good language, and that they see, feel, understand and communicate more, not less, than grownups. Therefore I never write down to them, but try to evoke that new, brilliant awareness that is their world."

"That new, brilliant awareness"—only the poetic imagination can bring it back. The freshness of a child's vision of the world is what every artist strives to retain. That's what we're all after, painters and poets and composers and the authors of certain kinds of books. If we can capture it, if we can make our audience catch its breath, create that great stillness that comes over a visible audience at moments of pure theater—if we can do that just a few times in our lives, then we've done what we were put here to do. And the whole life of an artist, it seems to me, is captured at the end of Walter de la Mare's story of *Come Hither*. Perhaps that, in the end, is the reason why this story, like others of the same magical kind, can carry away the longing, striving adult just as it does the unwitting, rejoicing child. Listen now to the music, and the metaphor.

The small boy Simon falls asleep one night over Nahum Tarune's book, and he wakes in the gray morning light in the tower room, amongst all the pages and pictures and strange outlandish objects, with an "indescribable despair and anxiety—almost terror even" at the rushing thought of his own ignorance and unimportance. "I thought," he says, "of Miss Taroone, of Mr. Nahum, of the life before me, and everything yet to do. And a sullen misery swept up in me at these reflections. And . . . I wished from the bottom of my heart that I had never come to this house."

But then the sun rose, and in the light, everything that had seemed strange became familiar; and he stood up and stretched.

> To this day I see the marvellous countryside of that morning with its hills and low thick mists and woodlands stretched like a painted scene beneath the windows—and that finger of light from the risen Sun presently piercing across the dark air, and as if by a miracle causing birds and water to awake and sing and shine. . . . I was but just awake, and so too was the world itself, and ever is. And somewhere—Wall or no Wall—was my mother's East Dene. . . .
>
> In a while I crept softly downstairs, let myself out, and ran off into the morning. Having climbed the hill from which I had first stared down upon Thrae, I stopped for a moment to recover my breath, and looked back.

The gilding sun-rays beat low upon the house in the valley. All was still, wondrous, calm. For a moment my heart misgave me at this farewell. The next, in sheer excitement—the cold sweet air, the height, the morning, a few keen beckoning stars—I broke into a kind of Indian war-dance in the thin dewy grass, and then, with a last wave of my hand, like Mr. Nahum himself, I set off at a sharp walk on the journey that has not yet come to an end.

II

Mythic Patterns

Introduction

PAUL HEINS

In many ways these essays reflect the critical point of view of the Center for the Study of Children's Literature: the consideration and appreciation of children's books in the context of all literature. This method obviously owes much to that of Northrop Frye, which examines literary works in the light of related literary works. The title of this section is an allusion to a course given at the Center, "Mythic Patterns in Children's Literature," which traces and correlates what appear to be an astonishingly universal series of motifs extending from the text of the Sumerian epic *Gilgamesh* through biblical narratives, Greek mythology, and medieval epics and sagas to folktales of the world. It is not a course in modern scientific folklore but an experiencing of the repeated patterns of traditional story-telling. And, finally, these essays also reflect the accomplishments of various institutes held at the Center, institutes based on allusive literary material which became the subject of the fruitful discussion of many children's books. Some of the papers were the outcome of the exploration of the possibilities inherent in two remarkable institutes: "Do I Dare Disturb the Universe?" based on a line from T. S. Eliot's "The Love Song of J. Alfred Prufrock," and "Ithaka and Other Journeys," based on a poem of the same name by the modern Greek poet C. P. Cavafy.

The selections that follow are really concerned with literary patterns and their variations; and if from one point of view *pattern* means *convention*—or at best *tradition*—then considered a little more deeply, myth itself is pattern indeed and requires further examination. In most translations of Aristotle's *Poetics*, the word *plot* is used to convey the meaning of the word μῦθος, the Greek root of our word *myth*. To do the word full justice, one must perceive and actually feel the relationship between *plot* and *myth*. In other words, one must realize that the mythic power of plot and the narrative power of myth work at the same time to carry along both story and meaning. In his essay "The Life Journey" John Rowe Townsend makes the point that "the most profound themes can be explored by way of story."

Most of the essayists represented are writers of fiction. They have thought critically about language and books and have themselves molded narratives; and what they present here are explorations of their concepts—of life as well as of their books, of experiences as well as of craftsmanship. Natalie Babbitt examines fantasy in terms of Joseph Campbell's concept of the hero, based on the distinguishable phases of separation, adventure, and return. Betty Levin tells and analyzes a simple barnyard tale in terms of parallel events and characterizations found in far-ranging books for young people. Peter Dickinson considers tradition and innovation in terms of a time journey. And reminding us that for "each generation, the *Iliad* must be told anew," Alan Garner comes to the conclusion that "to live as a human being is in itself a religious act"; and Jill Paton Walsh embarks on an intellectual journey of mythic investigation.

Of the fifty or more allusions to books and authors in these essays, more than half pertain to adult literature. The unpremeditated cross-references to these books and authors give the highly individualistic discussions a binding force even though as a group they were not invoked to bolster a critical theory. Every contribution offers a fresh point of view on some of the essential aspects of children's literature. Thus, each survey creates another mythic pattern or voyage; and each writer may be said, as Wordsworth said of Sir Isaac Newton, to be "voyaging through strange seas of thought."

The Burden of the Past

PETER DICKINSON

This talk is fundamentally about time and art, which you may think a large theme for an audience mainly interested in children's books. On the other hand, our very interest in children's books means—or ought to mean—that we think of them as quite an important branch on the ramified tree of art— a very vigorous and leafy branch at the moment, too. While a lot of other more highly regarded branches have gone half bare or full of strange rots, ours is still strong enough to hang a swing on. And as a matter of fact, I shall get around in the end to children's books and the child reader, and how the whole question affects both us and that reader in quite practical ways.

Let's start with the McLeod of Barra. Barra is a tiny island, the southernmost of the Outer Hebrides, the last crumb from the great table of Europe that hasn't been swept away by the broom-strokes of the Atlantic Ocean. Barra has a natural harbor, a pretty little bay with a rock at the center, and on that rock the McLeods of Barra built their own miniature castle. It is still there for tourists to look at, partly ruined, idyllic, peaceful, but so small and remote from the wars of the world that it is inevitably a little absurd. The absurdity was even greater three hundred years ago, for in those days the McLeod of Barra had a splendid custom. He would come into his miniature hall and sit down to his evening meal with his two dozen retainers ranged at the trestles before him and his own trumpeter and his own herald behind him; and when he had eaten his fill, the trumpeter would blow a clumsy fanfare and the herald would bawl out in Gaelic, "The McLeod of Barra has finished his meal, and the princes of the rest of the world may now sit down to dine!"

Take this as a metaphor or an allegory. As a writer I am the Laird of Barra, part, but only just part, of the great rich continent of art, a crumb fallen from the feast and waiting for the ocean of time to sweep me and my works away. And yet to myself I am the center of that continent, and all the princes of literature must wait while I ponder the flavor of an adjective. There is a further paradox here. The attitude is absurd, but because of its absurdity, it works. If the McLeod of Barra had sat down and gobbled his meal and gone away without waiting for his trumpeter to blow his fanfare and his herald to bawl his boast, who would now know his name? Yet here we are, talking about him three hundred years after his death, when who knows how many more prestigious rulers are mere names in the indexes of unopened books?

This is one of the themes I want to talk about—survival through time. But I want to consider it not so much from the point of view of the artist who has brought it off as from that of two other groups: the later artists who have to do their work with this survival in their midst; and the much larger society of art consumers to whom these survivals are permanent features in the landscape of the mind—trees, as it were, which were already full-grown when they themselves first opened their eyes and will still be there for the most part when they finally close them. The art consumers simply have to live with these trees, but the later artists have to farm and garden around them.

I think anyone who is remotely interested in art is at least vaguely aware of this business. When we read an ancient love song, a fragment found on some crumbling papyrus, which, despite the garblings of translation and the generalized static of the centuries, still transmits its message to us, we are moved because it speaks to us not only of love but of our shared humanity with all dead lovers. Of course, not all of us are so moved. Some may be indifferent, some actively irritated.

When I go into schools, I sometimes play a game on this theme with the children. I ask them to imagine that they are an unsuccessful songwriter. Late one evening they are slogging away at yet another lyric which has somehow lost its bounce between the bathroom and the typewriter, when—zowie—there is the devil standing beside their chair, making them an offer. In exchange for their immortal soul they can write one truly successful song, and this year there are two models on offer. They can write an instant success that will sell its ten million copies, sweep the world for a year, and never be heard of again. Or else they can have a colossal win in the football pools, which makes them as much money as the instant success would have done; and at the same time they can write a song that nobody notices at the moment but simply goes on being sung, like "Greensleeves," generation after generation, although nobody actually remembers who wrote it. Shall we give it a go? You understand the rules? The devil offers you the choice of instant fame or anonymous immortality. Hands up, those who choose to have their glory now. And those who would rather eke it out through the generations.

And now let's alter the rules a bit. The devil has, of course, been cheating you. The first part of the offer is still the same—that's the sort of thing the devil can be relied on for; he's trusting in instant fame to be your moral ruination. But the second half is not what you thought. Oh yes, your song will still be sung, generation after generation, but only by a very few people, only in one place—in a remote harbor—that might even be Barra itself; it will be the song which the wives of fishermen sing when they are mending nets. They will teach their daughters to sing it, and they in turn will pass it on, so the devil will remain true to his promise, after his fashion; but the song you have written will not be "Greensleeves" or anything like it. Does this change your mind?

You might be interested to know that in England, at any rate, the voting is about fifty-fifty on the first part of the game, but there are seldom more than three or four who would still choose to conquer time in the mouths of a handful of women sitting round a peat fire and mending nets.

I've always been interested in these questions, but my interest was sharpened and made more complex a couple of years ago when I was asked by my publisher if I would like to write a collection of stories from the Old Testament. My first instinct was to say no. I thought the whole idea boring—not because I thought the stories themselves boring but for the typical writer's reason that it had already been done so often. That it had usually been done rather badly made no difference—if anything it made it harder to think of myself doing any better. But then I had an idea that altered my whole attitude to the proposal.

One of the problems about telling Bible stories is that of context. The Bible has been a living book for so many generations, and it has been seen through so many different visions, adapted to particular ways of thinking by so many minds, that it has almost entirely become its own context. The events in it seem to take place somehow out of time, in a different set of dimensions, a sort of generalized vague, hot landscape called the Holy Land. But for the people who originally told the stories, it was not like that at all. The events had taken place among the very rocks where their goats browsed, and long after the events themselves were past, the context remained the same. Not only could a particular field at Beth-Shemesh be pointed out as the place where the Ark of the Covenant had rested when the Philistines sent it back to Israel, but a particular custom, a particular habit of thought, could be justified and passed on by this story of a deed of Joshua or that of a quarrel between the sons of Jacob. The stories themselves had the substance and actuality almost of tactile objects, so much so that when eventually they were written down and codified by priests who wished to draw from them a particular set of inferences—a whole world view central to the faith—there were still inconvenient elements which didn't fit that picture but had to be left in because their solidity was too great merely to wish away.

And before that writing down, through how many mouths and ears must the stories have threaded almost unaltered? In some cases it is possible to do rough calculations. The crossing of the Red Sea—or at least the definite event which few scholars now doubt gave rise to the story in Exodus—must have taken place very approximately in 1300 B.C. Shortly after that, the Song of Miriam came into existence. All we have of the song now are the words which King James's Bible translates "Sing ye to the Lord, for he hath triumphed gloriously; the horse and his rider hath he thrown into the sea." For something like four hundred years these words were passed on, probably as a central element in an annual ritual of thanksgiving, until they were written down shortly after the time of Solomon in the earliest of the documents which were collated several hundred years later still to make the book of Exodus.

Think of that in terms of our own history. It means that the tradition must have lasted, mouth to mouth, since before the *Mayflower* sailed.

Well, my idea was that if I were to make the imaginative leap and tell these stories as they might have been told during those four hundred years—and tell them not just as stories but as things used for definite purposes in a particular culture and context; if I were to choose here and there among the many, many mouths that might—must—have told them, then I would be able to do something different from other collections of Old Testament stories. Not different for the sake of my own vanity but different for the sake of the stories themselves. (If you want to see how I made out, you'll have to get hold of a copy of *City of Gold* and read it.)

I've told you this to explain why, more and more as I wrote, I became almost oppressed by the length and power of the traditions that were needed to keep the stories alive, particularly because it is remarkable how few of them seem to have been told as stories, for their own sake. By a story told for its own sake, I mean something like "Snow White" or the Oedipus cycle, stories which in themselves have such a powerful shape and plot line that anyone who hears them will remember them and want to pass them on. Most of the Bible stories aren't like that. They have power all right—sometimes almost appalling power—but its sources lie outside them, in what I have called the context, in the positive need of a people to tell and hear them. What, I kept wondering, could it be like to live in such a context? More particularly, what could it be like for the artist to work in such a context—in a world where the inflection of every note in a marriage song, the shape and color of every stitch in an embroidered hanging, must be what they were because that was how they always had been and always would be?

We live in a culture almost diametrically opposite. We have what I think of as the Athenian mentality. Do you remember when Paul in his missionary journeys came to Athens, which then appeared—at least to itself—to be the center of the civilized universe, the author of the Acts of the Apostles explains that he had to preach a different kind of sermon there from his usual style? I quote: "For all the Athenians and strangers which were there spent their time in nothing else, but either to tell, or to hear some new thing."

This is our world, isn't it? The world in which the single word *new* is still the most potent weapon in the advertiser's armory. The world in which one season's fashion is so dominant while it lasts that even big and serious causes get taken up and dropped again like so much junk jewelry. In a world ruled by fashion, by the rage for the new, it is almost impossible to be serious. To make way for the new, the old must be dumped like garbage, regardless of how many years of useful life it may have in it. But even as each new and shiny notion is installed on the emptied shelf-space of our minds, we are half aware that in another season all this stuff will also be old and need to be chucked out to make space for yet newer newnesses. So we content ourselves with thinking disposable thoughts, admiring disposable arts, conducting our lives by disposable ethics, worshiping disposable gods.

What on earth has this to do with children's books? Quite a bit, I think, if you believe that books help to shape a child's view of the world and her expectations of it, not simply by what they contain but also by what they are. I'll get around to that, but first, to keep things tidy, I want to talk about the position of the artist, the writer, in what I have called an Athenian world.

I said earlier that I found it hard to imagine what it was like to be an artist in a world where nothing changed; I do know what it's like to be a writer in a world where everything is compelled to keep changing, and although at least it's possible to write in a world like ours, there are dissatisfactions which mirror those of merely living in such a world. First, of course, there is the process whereby disposable junk seems to breed like yeast in a vat. Every year there seems to be more of everything. We're in a deep recession in England, which, because of cuts in government spending, has affected the publishing trade. Do the publishers respond by producing fewer books? Not a bit of it. Just as a dying apple tree seems to foretell its own demise and in a desperate effort to reproduce its stock bears innumerable tiny apples, so our publishers respond to the threat of economic extinction by producing innumerable books. If you believe, as I do, that practically all books that are any good are going to get published, whatever the state of the trade, and that in any case these represent only a small proportion of all books published, then it follows that all the extra books published in the desperate search for a winner are rubbish. To publish a book in such circumstances is to publish an autumn leaf in a forest. Scarcely has it fallen, scarcely has the wanderer in that forest had one moment to take in its particular vein pattern and coloring, when fresh leaf-fall has snowed it under and it is lost.

That's a purely practical consideration for one writer in our Athenian world. There is a vaguer but more important one which I find hard to formulate. It has to do with our need for a tradition both to work from and to work against. The fact that I have been deriding the cult of the new doesn't mean I'm not aware of the need of the artist to feel that everything he produces is somehow different from anything that anyone has done before. I know this in my own work. It's a peculiar and thrilling feeling to step onto what you know to be new ground. But at the same time you don't go deliberately searching for the new; it has to happen—and happen, somehow, when it is ready for you. The deliberate search for the new leads only to the phony. It is like a script conference for a disaster movie, say: "We've done volcanoes; we've done earthquakes. Tidal waves? Yeah, done that. Apartment block holocausts, yeah. Plague rats, yeah. Airplanes, liners, subs, nuclear power stations, all done. Oh God, there must be something! Hey! What about an ice age? The coming of the glaciers! Too slow? Can't someone think of a way of getting us some quick glaciers?"

You can tell almost at a glance the books that have been written as a result of the writer having that kind of script conference in his head. The reason why these books won't do has, I believe, a connection with the concept of tradition. It is tradition itself that defines the new. Think of the serious writers of a country being, as it were, a grazing herd moving across a prairie. They keep loosely together. It is the outliers who find the fresh pasture, but still they are merely outliers, not fully separated from the herd. They don't go bounding off into the distance to look at every far green patch because if they do, they are no use to the herd as a whole. The herd must keep roughly together, or it will perish.

Tradition is a necessary restraint, like the invisible boundary of the herd. The boundary moves. It is the outliers of the herd, the artists who are breaking new ground, who cause it to move, but it is the invisible boundary itself which defines what that new ground can be.

But at the same time, of course, the necessity to stay with the herd is a restraint. Tradition itself can be vexing. When I started to think coherently about this talk, I gave it the provisional title "The Burden of the Past," because often the burden is what the writer is most conscious of when he thinks actively about the past. Earlier I likened the existence of the great old works of literature to trees in a landscape, around which modern writers had to farm or garden. I have three such trees in my own garden, marvelous great beeches in their prime, getting on for a hundred and fifty years old. I'm very glad they're there, really, but at the same time I'm perpetually irritated that almost nothing will grow beneath them.

Now, at last, we come back to children's books. The writer of children's books is less burdened by the past than writers in most other fields. This is partly because children's literature is a comparatively young branch on the tree of art—we are still at the stage where there seems almost endless fresh pasture for the herd to explore. We are still near the springtime of our art. There are, it is true, a few great, dead writers to daunt us by their achievements—Mark Twain, Robert Louis Stevenson, Rudyard Kipling, E. Nesbit are the ones I would name—but they are, on the whole, benevolent ghosts. To resume my metaphor about the trees in the landscape, the shade beneath their branches seems somehow not so dense as that beneath the branches of, say, Charles Dickens. Various and interesting things can still be persuaded to grow there.

But mainly, I believe, we owe this feeling that the tradition is not yet burdensome to the nature of our audience. Suppose you were to say that the normal cycle of an art is for it to begin in a world of minimum change, in the conservatism of biblical times, and to move at greater or lesser speed toward the Athenian model of constant change for change's sake; you might also argue that what we recognize as great art tends to be produced in spasmodic eruptions somewhere toward the middle of the process, while the fresh ground is still there to find, while the herd is on the move but at the same time still has a strong compulsion to keep itself roughly together.

Now, in a sense, children are permanently at this stage. They have the urge to explore and experiment, but they also have a deep need to know where they belong. You must have watched a very small child playing while its mother sits on a park bench. The child will explore and venture but always within a definite limit. It is as though it were attached to its mother by an elastic cord of a fixed length and tension, which every few minutes, as it reaches the outer limit of its range, whisks it back to the mother, ostensibly so that the child can show her a leaf it's picked up or complain about some bump but really just reassure itself that its mother is still at the center of its range.

That's only another metaphor, of course. I'm not saying that children who have reached the reading age remain that unadventurous—they can be intellectually very daring indeed. What I am saying is that when a book suddenly rages through the minds of the children of a nation, as if it were a highly infectious disease, you'll often find out that despite its apparent novelty it's in some ways much more traditional than many apparently more ordinary books. *Watership Down* is a case in point. It's an immensely artful book, written with conscious brilliance and elaboration, with the various episodes in the plot carefully echoing those of Virgil's *Aeneid*. That's not the sort of traditionalism I'm talking about, although the values which drove Richard Adams to write it in that way are, indeed, highly traditional and literary ones. But what you might call the moral tenor of the book is also traditional, the Victorian boy's adventure story—*The Coral Island* rather than *Treasure Island*—inculcating, throughout, the virtues of the imperial officer class and teaching smaller lessons in natural history by the wayside.

Another element in children's books that makes for traditionalism is partly negative; the comparative lack of sophistication on the part of the audience means that there's not much point in attempting the wilder forms of experimental writing. The reader isn't interested in any of that for its own sake. If the book you are writing actually demands experiment, the child reader will go along with you quite comfortably; but she won't take much interest in novelty for the pleasure of novelty. And on the more positive side, the fact that the primary object of a children's book is to tell a story, and stories tend to have a particular shape and architecture, means that a particular set of virtues is more or less imposed on the whole field— the tradition is there, whether we like it or not. It is as though the very lie of the land more or less compelled our grazing herd to keep its cohesion.

So is all well? Can one actually say that the almost accidental traditionalism of children's writing makes a usefully stable platform in the shift and drift of our Athenian society? Perhaps one can, but it's still a very small platform, and soon abandoned. I think something can be done by people like you and me to enlarge it, to provide a more permanent center of stability based partly in the world of books, for the child who in a few years' time is going to have to start making some kind of sense of an adult life. We can help that child acquire a sense of the mysterious nature of time itself.

We tend to forget that there is a provincialism of time as well as of place. The provincialism of place exists when a citizen of, say, Squaw's Neck, Idaho, judges the moral and aesthetic standards of the universe by those prevailing in Squaw's Neck. The provincialism of time exists when the citizen inhabiting the locality known as 1980 judges the moral and aesthetic standards of the universe of past and future by those prevailing in 1980. In this sense the citizen of New York is probably more provincial than the citizen of Squaw's Neck; and Paris, France, simply because it prides itself on being the world capital of cultural and intellectual fashion, is probably the most provincial city in the world.

Does this matter? Is the child of the Athenian age any the worse for being brought up to regard the moment he lives in as all there is? Surely, yes, just as the child of the biblical age may be worse off for regarding the moment he lives in as being essentially the same as all other ages. They are both worse off in two ways—first, internally, in a lack of a sense of the richness that spreads through time; and second, externally, in a lack of feel for the years before and after that positively lowers their chances of survival— almost as though they lived on the seashore and tried to ignore the movement of the tides. Some of the saddest people among us now seem to me to be those ex-flower children, whose whole philosophy—if you can call it that—was based on a belief that it is possible to live in the moment. I am quite sure a sense of time, a respect for it, whether embodied in slowly changing tradition or in other ways, is one of the most valuable intellectual gifts one can give to one's children.

I must correct that. One cannot give it. One can only help them to acquire it. How?

Certainly not by taking them off to computerized history centers where they can listen to the Gettysburg oration through headphones. What have headphones to do with Abraham Lincoln? This sort of thing is an attempt to give, at its most superficial and useless. The glossy gift-wrapping is a more powerful mind-conditioner than the gift itself.

Nor should one rely on the unassisted reading of historical novels or old books. It is very easy to treat ideas of or about the past as one nowadays treats old farm implements. You varnish them and hang them on the wall. A butter churn so varnished and displayed gives you very little real feel for the people who made and used it. You want to try making some butter in it—preferably before dawn on a sleety February morning. So with ideas and with those far vaguer but often more important areas of mixed thought and feeling one might call notions.

To take a very simple example. If a child were to pick up a copy of H. G. Wells's *The War of the Worlds* and simply start to read it as though it were written yesterday, she might very well feel it was tame stuff compared with *Dune* or *Star Wars*. I think, even so, she might carry on reading it, not quite knowing why, only dimly feeling that there was a kind of excitement, unconnected with the plot, that throbbed through every line—the excitement, as you and I know, of breakthrough, of the artist moving into new pasture.

But suppose the same child can make the imaginative leap to reading *The War of the Worlds* as people read it when it was yesterday—then it is *Star Wars* that will begin to seem less substantial. She will not only have got more out of the book by way of fun and stimulus, but the nature of a whole field of modern thought will have been made clearer by the knowledge of how its seed came to be sown.

It is the same with moral judgments. Suppose you are an ardent feminist. You wish your own children, or the children you teach, to march in your army. To my mind one of the best gifts you can give them is an understanding of the nature of your enemies. A *sympathetic* understanding, what's more. Unless you can grasp what it is like to feel and think as they do, you will never defeat them. I disagree with the viewpoint, for instance, of Bob Dixon in *Catching Them Young*, a stimulating book on race, sex, and class published in Britain in 1977. Writing about the Little Women series, he says:

These books are competently written and skillfully constructed. The values and attitudes so untiringly put forward in them, however, leave a lot to be desired. I can
never see much in the argument which "makes allowance"
for the period when a book was written. If books are read
now—and these are certainly very widely read indeed—
then surely we have to apply contemporary standards in
evaluating them.

This seems to me entirely mistaken. However valiant a fighter you may be
in the war for the rights of women, however much you march shoulder to
shoulder with Jo, you will get nowhere until you understand what it is like
to view the world with Meg's eyes and to sense it with her fingertips. To
fight without that knowledge is to conduct your war without knowing
whether your enemies are going to bomb you with napalm or shoot at you
with bows and arrows. Emotionally, it is a losing strategy.

I am prepared to take an extreme view about all this. To move from the
field of social injustice to the field of pure horror, recall the Bulldog
Drummond stories by a writer of thrillers called Sapper. The earlier books
are badly written, but somehow compulsively readable, and scattered
throughout with anti-Semitic asides. I can remember the headmaster of my
preparatory school reading them aloud to us after chapel on Sunday
evenings. The whole school, seventy of us, would sit around and listen in
silence for an hour, loving it. He was a good man, an excellent schoolmas-
ter, and we adored him. So anti-Semitism was part of the air we breathed—
and not only us, at our almost apelike level of consciousness. Virginia
Woolf, for instance, would lard her talk with casually anti-Semitic snip-
ing—and she was married to a Jew. I would say that during the thirties the
consciousness of Europe was pervaded by an unspoken feeling that we
would all be better off without the Jews. And then, appallingly, an attempt
was made to see that our dream came true, and we were in the nightmare.

This must not be forgotten. It must not be forgotten that what happened
in the Holocaust was done by humans to other humans. But it must also
not be forgotten that it happened in a context; that, in a sense, dear old
Dick Harris—bluff, genial, ginger-eyebrowed—reading to his room of
ten-year-olds in the Sunday evening calm, was also a scene of horror. To
read about the Holocaust as though it were something that happened
outside the context of its time is to begin to think of it as something that
had somehow happened on a different planet, a kind of counter-Earth, and
could not happen again here.

In their trivial way books like the unspeakable Sapper's actually help
build this feeling for the context. Provided, always provided, that the child
who reads them is, so to speak, inoculated against infection, is given,

almost as a magic amulet, a grasp of how one year succeeds another and how deep our roots really lie in the ever-accumulating drift of time.

I've been talking about old books—and the same thoughts apply in a way to historical novels—because the arguments are clearer. But all good fiction is full of the sense of time. In every book where the author has full imaginative grip of his material—even where that material is something as wholly contemporary as, say, the story of a boy getting into and then safely out of some street gang which turns out to be less glamorous on the inside than it had seemed from outside—that imaginative grip will grasp a section of time. The characters, streets, houses of the book will be what they are now because of what they've been before. There is no need actually to tell the reader any of this past; but he must be convinced that the past is there, fully imagined, so that if the author had wanted to tell him, it would have come out on the page as solid as anything in the apparent present of the story line. If that conviction is lacking, then all the inventions of the book will be no more substantial than the paper on which it is printed. However glamorous it may seem in other ways, the book will still be rubbish. Fashionable rubbish.

Time is the enemy of fashion. Fashion is a fidgety but fundamentally idle monster. Fashion takes valuable resources and turns them into hula hoops. Fashion takes honorable causes and turns them into cultural chitchat. Where you and I are in a position to influence what books children read, the ones we should regard with suspicion are the books that make the currently acceptable noises. We should regard with deep scepticism, if not positive hostility, those which claim to be on our own side in any cause we may value. It is the nature of all causes to try to force our vision of the world into the simple images and lines of a cartoon, and this week's cartoon is next week's fish-wrapping.

But most of all, it seems to me, any influence we have—and, God knows, it's not much—must lie in the way we think and read ourselves. We are ourselves, after all, part, a major part, of our children's context. They can see and sense time, and not merely the ravages of time, in us. That, it seems to me, is a gift we can all truly give: an acceptance of, a delight in, the movement of the years, the wavelike succession of the generations. We should adopt, not only for our own sake but also for theirs, a view of the world in which the passing moment is not all there is—in which time, both past and future, is on our side.

The Universe and Old MacDonald

BETTY LEVIN

Once upon a time Old MacDonald had a farm, ee-yi, ee-yi, oh. And on that farm there was a duck, a plain brown mallard duck. Every morning Old MacDonald opened the duck pen, and the duck, with all the other ducks in the flock, led her babies down to the pond. "She taught them how to swim and dive. She taught them how to walk in a line, to come when they were called, and to keep a safe distance from bikes and scooters and other things with wheels." Every evening she brought the ducklings back to the pen to be safe from raccoons and owls and nighthawks. But in the daytime they were always in some danger, and when a crow or hawk flew near, the duck would call, and all her babies would scuttle around and under her for protection. Their mother warned them about the dangers. "You may go into the fields or down the lane," she warned them, "but don't go into Mr. MacDonald's garden. Now run along and don't get into mischief."

But there was one duckling who was full of " 'satiable curtiosity, and that means he asked ever so many questions." One fine morning he asked a new question that he had never asked before. "What does the turtle have for dinner?" Well, there was a great snapping turtle who had just moved to the pond. Unlike Peter Rabbit, who was simply sent to bed without any supper and given camomile tea while Flopsy, Mopsy, and Cotton-tail had bread and milk and blackberries; unlike the elephant's child, who simply got a trunk out of his encounter with the crocodile, this little duckling was snapped up and eaten.

The plain brown mallard duck screamed her other ducklings out of the pond; then she charged after the turtle, which weighed eleven times as much as she did.

Snapping turtles are extraordinary creatures. They have beaked jaws that open incredibly wide and can, if big enough, hold or break a man's arm. Not only that, their skin is extremely tough, their shell hard and shaped to allow great flexibility and speed. Their feet are powerful grippers, too, with long curved talons. And they are so primitive that their tiny brains make them difficult to kill. They have ganglia, or nerve centers, distributed through their bodies, and these serve as additional brains. If you cut off a snapping turtle's head, the jaws will continue to be active and lethal for several hours, and the headless body will be capable of moving a considerable distance and inflicting serious damage on its prey or adversary.

It wasn't long before the snapping turtle grabbed the mallard duck. The fight was so fierce that it brought the farmer on the run. Old MacDonald didn't see the turtle but guessed what was dragging the duck, flapping and screaming, across the pond and then, inexorably, beneath the water.

Now, no sensible person risks attack from a snapper to save a plain brown mallard duck, just one of many in the flock. Every farmer knows you lose some, and you win some, all the time. But Old MacDonald didn't have time to react sensibly. This farmer reached the pond just as the duck disappeared into the churned-up water, and this farmer plunged in and swept through the mud and bubbles with both hands until they came in contact with the duck and pulled her out of the clamped jaws of the turtle. Old MacDonald was very lucky indeed that the turtle had a large mouthful of duck. Most of one side of the duck under her wing was gone; her leg was wrenched around backward and stuck straight out behind her.

Now what? Remember, this is a farmer. A farmer lives close to nature and experiences birth and death all the time. Old MacDonald squelched out of the muddy water, holding the duck in both hands, wings pressed to her sides against the gaping wound. She was nearly drowned, nearly dead from shock and loss of blood. The farmer could set her down and let her die, or dispatch her quickly to put her out of her misery. But a voice inside the farmer cried, " 'Do *away* with it? You mean *kill* it?' " The farmer told this voice to control itself. " 'Control myself,' " yelled the voice inside the farmer, " 'this is a matter of life and death, and you talk about *controlling* myself.' "

Well, like Mr. Arable, the farmer listened to the child's voice and carried the duck to the house, doctored it, set it in a box under a heat lamp, and went out to get the remaining ducklings back to the safe duck yard. That took awhile. When Old MacDonald returned to the duck, she was cold as stone, her eyes were closed, and she was shaken by spasms like death throes. Old MacDonald went back to the duck pen, picked up three of the ducklings, and brought them to the mother duck in the box under the heat lamp. And watched.

As soon as the ducklings were with their mother, they began to peep anxiously, desperately. The duck, moribund in one instant, was transformed in the next. She began to speak to them in those soft murmuring sounds all brooding fowl utter to their young. And she scootched over onto her injured side to raise her good wing and tuck the babies under it. And began to live.

Now that may be the end of one story, but it is only the beginning of another, which I'm going to finish telling in a little while. But first let's look at what has been told so far, and by whom. There's been a bit of *Make Way for Ducklings,* of *The Tale of Peter Rabbit,* of "The Elephant's Child" from the *Just So Stories,* and of *Charlotte's Web.* The narrative has not been altered to include these bits, but you will have noticed that the point of view has had to change. We have moved from farmer and ordinary duck to naughty duckling, to heroic duck, to foolish farmer, and to defender of the weak. And as this story progresses, there will be further shifts in viewpoint, until you may well ask, "Whose universe is this, anyway?"

A good question. *The* question, or, as Riddley Walker would say, the Heart of the Would.

Because every decision and action is appended to that question. Although child psychologists tell us that children see the world with themselves at its center, we know that they can respond to literature which suggests otherwise. Even if the Zuckerman barnyard in *Charlotte's Web* is seen as a microcosmic universe, its center isn't easily fixed. The reader may begin with the child Fern, the heroine and listener; but then the reader moves on. To Wilbur, innocent and anxious; to Charlotte and her life-giving web which is also, importantly, a killing web. In this book people take action and appear to be in charge of their lives (or, anyhow, the life of a runty pig), until the animals themselves take charge, each according to its nature and supernature. Who disturbs the universe? Fern, charging in to rescue Wilbur from the ax? Wilbur himself, striving to overcome the ordinary fate of a farm pig? ("Wilbur burst into tears. 'I don't *want* to die,' he moaned. 'I want to stay alive, right here in my comfortable manure pile with all my friends. I want to breathe the beautiful air and lie in the beautiful sun. . . . I don't want to die!' screamed Wilbur, throwing himself to the ground.") Or was it Charlotte, who tells Wilbur, " 'I was never more serious in my life. I am not going to let you die, Wilbur' "?

I think that on one level, very much a child's level, all three of these characters dare to disturb the universe. But on a deeper level, the author's inmost Heart of the Wood, none of them can disturb the universe, not really. The pig is born and for a while lives, and for a while more is famous, is "SOME PIG." But the world goes on—Fern to the Ferris wheel, Charlotte to dust. And when the novelty wears off, Wilbur's future is not all that certain. I think this is a powerful and consuming idea for the child-centered world of the storybook, especially when it comes through as perspective, not explicit message.

The other side of the coin is equally true, of course—that we cannot help

disturbing the universe. It's what Ged tells Arren in *The Farthest Shore:*
" 'When that rock is lifted, the earth is lighter, the hand that bears it
heavier. When it is thrown, the circuits of the stars respond, and where it
strikes or falls the universe is changed.' " It is the tension between these
opposites that sets the predicament of choice and action for the protagonist
in most fiction. The responsibility and dilemma of the children's writer is
to show the protagonist taking charge and pressing past the easy or passive
development while at the same time showing some effectiveness on the
part of the individual. E. B. White uses this tension in *Charlotte's Web* by
creating and sustaining a balance between action and the universe.

If you read White's story for adults "Death of a Pig," you will clearly see
his recognition of the different needs of children and adults. In the adult
story the assumed point of departure is the same as in *Charlotte's Web*,
though more explicit:

> The scheme of buying a spring pig in blossomtime, feed-
> ing it through summer and fall, and butchering it when the
> solid cold weather arrives is a familiar scheme to me and
> follows an antique pattern. It is a tragedy enacted on most
> farms with perfect fidelity to the original script. The murder,
> being premeditated, is in the first degree but is quick and
> skillful, and the smoked bacon and ham provide a ceremo-
> nial ending whose fitness is seldom questioned.
>
> Once in a while something slips . . . and the whole
> performance stumbles and halts. My pig simply failed to
> show up for a meal. The alarm spread rapidly. The classic
> outline of the tragedy was lost. I found myself cast
> suddenly in the role of pig's friend and physician—a
> farcical character with an enema bag for a prop. I had a
> presentiment, the very first afternoon, that the play would
> never regain its balance and that my sympathies were now
> wholly with the pig. This was slapstick—the sort of dra-
> matic treatment that instantly appealed to my old dachs-
> hund, Fred, who joined the vigil, held the bag, and, when
> all was over, presided at the interment. When we slid the
> body into the grave, we both were shaken to the core. The
> loss we felt was not the loss of ham but the loss of pig. He
> had evidently become precious to me, not that he repre-
> sented a distant nourishment in a hungry time, but that he
> had suffered in a suffering world.

White then goes on to piece out the narrative. It is a tragicomedy, full of
prodigious and futile human endeavor and laced with strong animal

cynicism. On it goes, painful and hilarious, to the pig's death and burial, from which the author had to drag Fred away by the same rope he'd used to drag the carcass to the grave:

> . . . although he weighed far less than the pig, was harder to drag, being possessed of the vital spark. . . . I have written this account in penitence and in grief, as a man who failed to raise his pig, and to explain my deviation from the classic course of so many raised pigs. The grave in the woods is unmarked, but Fred can direct the mourner to it unerringly and with immense good will, and I know he and I shall often revisit it, singly and together, on flagless memorial days of our own choosing.

A wonderful story in its own right. While almost all adults love *Charlotte's Web*, only occasional children may enjoy "Death of a Pig," for there is no hero in the story, no suspense or hope—only trying, caring, and failing. Charlotte herself accomplishes what White would have done if he could have. Instead, he brings the pig to life in the character of Wilbur. Where Charlotte spun her web, White spins a yarn; he, too, sets his words in it where they count. It is the same old story of life and death, love and commitment, freshly told—a miracle.

The relationship between humankind and nature, the kind and extent of control over the natural world or the universe that is at the core of so much children's literature, has concerned storytellers and mythmakers since long before words like *ecology* came into use. The Celtic god Bres, defeated in battle, bargained for his life with promises of a harvest in every quarter. The Druids considered and rejected his offer. It was sufficient, they said, for the season to run its course, for the land to rest before sending forth new life. Icarus, flying like a bird to escape from Crete, overreached; he flew so close to the sun that the wax melted and the feathers dropped from his manmade wings. His story has been told, painted, and written. In Auden's "Musée des Beaux Arts," we have a double perspective—the Dutch master's and the modern poet's.

> In Brueghel's *Icarus*, for instance: how everything turns away
> . Quite leisurely from the disaster; the ploughman may
> Have heard the splash, the forsaken cry,
> But for him it was not an important failure; the sun shone
> As it had to on the white legs disappearing into the green
> Water; and the expensive delicate ship that must have seen
> Something amazing, a boy falling out of the sky,
> Had somewhere to get to and sailed calmly on.

The same old story.

As I continue mine, I am going to touch base now and then with children's books most of you know and with a few older ones you are less likely to know. The familiar stories illumine the extent and variety of viewpoints and answers to the question of disturbing the universe. The older stories lend perspective to the idea of perspective in children's literature.

Now, Old MacDonald had been transformed in an instant into Fern Arable. That is, the farmer rescued the duck from the terrible jaws of the snapping turtle. Some, or most, of you may identify with that person; you realize that in a rash moment you, too, could become the child Fern. Children, who know all about that impulse, are not likely to consider what follows. The farmer has to, for no farmer is likely to zip off to the animal hospital to incur vet fees for a plain brown mallard duck, one of many.

But if the farmer has failed to wring the duck's neck in the first instance, there's going to be some time and effort devoted to keeping the duck on the mend. Even if the farmer only thinks that it makes sense to keep the old bird going until her ducklings are old enough to be on their own, that constitutes a commitment to the life of one plain mallard duck with a gaping hole in her side and a twisted, useless leg.

It was the child Fern inside the farmer that began the reversal of the normal outcome of an encounter between a duck and a snapping turtle. It was something in the farmer and something in the duck, which fiercely attacked and pursued the predator and drove it away from the remaining ducklings. Something in the duck that is programmed by genes and hormones, and yet is perceived as brave and magnificent. Beyond that, the return to life is triggered by the peeping ducklings. Genes again; hormones, for sure. More than half dead, the mother duck lives for her babies as before she would have died for them. And Old MacDonald and most adults and all kids are thrilled by this creature, this life. Like E. B. White, the farmer ends up grinding tiny granules of antibiotic to feed to the duck with an eyedropper and is consequently late for chores and behind schedule for days.

Some would say the farmer is living in harmony with nature. This is an arguable viewpoint. It is my belief that however close to nature Old MacDonald may be, almost every act of farming disturbs the universe. Every weed pulled to make room for the lettuce and peas changes the natural order of things, even without the use of pesticides and herbicides. The farmer actively alters the environment. Old MacDonald may live in harmony with the elements, but at every stage of preparing and tilling the soil and cultivating seeded crops and selectively breeding livestock, the farmer is striving to control the natural world. And that has been so since people gave up hunting and gathering food and settled down to grow it for themselves and their animals.

But look what happens in the next chapter of my story. Mother duck is sitting not so pretty, but doing her thing and slowly healing. She is the object of everyone's admiration. All the other ducks, as if by some mysterious communications system, have from that day forth stayed away from the pond. Mother duck and babies are kept apart from the others, who nevertheless have known since the duckling was eaten that danger lurks in that pond.

Old MacDonald has to deal with the snapping turtle or give up the ducks. So the hunt begins. Only, first, the quest; Old MacDonald must not only locate the enemy but find the right weapon for vanquishing it. Now the farmer's inner voice is no longer Fern's. Maybe it is Taran who speaks from the farmer's heart. Taran, eager and impatient to fulfill the hero's mighty task.

Old MacDonald waits with rifle in hand. And waits. But snapping turtles do not often show their great hooked beaks; they surface just long enough to take in air and sink back into the mud to wait for the next victim. MacDonald–Taran baits a big fishhook, casts it, and waits some more. The farmer learns how to build a turtle trap out of chicken wire and pine boughs. But the snapper is as elusive as ever. The Taran part of Old MacDonald continues the quest and learns, as Taran does in Prydain, that alone a person accomplishes very little. So MacDonald–Taran seeks the help of a wise hermit who knows all the secrets of fishing and trapping. The hermit exacts a promise: If the farmer will bring him the turtle for soup, he will make a hook which cannot fail. As Lloyd Alexander tells us, nothing is ever given for nothing.

The hook is baited exactly according to the hermit's orders; it is attached to a long, strong wire with just enough weight and with flotation consisting of a plaster cider jug and a child's yellow plastic bathtub ducky. Old MacDonald swings back to cast the lot onto the pond. And is stopped. Stopped by the farm dog standing so close behind that the flying hook would get him first. Who can say why the dog takes that moment to place himself there, disturbing the hero's universe?

Perhaps it is the beginning of another story. It could be "A White Heron," by Sarah Orne Jewett, from *The Country of the Pointed Firs*. There is a solitary child, Sylvie, who watches and listens to the forest creatures and climbs a great tall fir to see the rare white heron. There is an appealing young man, a hunter, who seeks that bird. The story tells how Sylvie diverts him from his quarry. Barbara Cooney portrays the tension and purity of the story in her beautiful, illustrated version for children.

So now the dog has diverted Old MacDonald, and most effectively. For the cast of hook, line, and floats having been aborted, the hook has struck the farmer's hand and embedded itself there. The hero marches off to the local hospital, clutching all that weaponry that has pierced the hand, and with it the yellow plastic bathtub ducky. Not very dignified. It is a comeuppance appropriate to an early nineteenth-century cautionary tale about pride, about overstepping oneself—and even possibly about cruelty to animals.

Eventually, though, all obstacles are overcome, and the weapon is properly cast, its position noted. The next day Old MacDonald–Taran finds the cider jug and yellow ducky in another part of the pond. The farmer draws in the line and pulls to the edge of the pond a huge and fearsome snapping turtle. But victory is not so easy. Now half helpless because of the stitched and bandaged hand, the farmer must call on a neighbor, who comes with rifle and ax to deal the death blow.

The handicapped farmer cannot be equated with one-armed Drem in Rosemary Sutcliff's *Warrior Scarlet*, seeking his wolf kill to establish his place as a man of his tribe. For one thing, the tribal imperative is absent. For another, the handicap is not of the magnitude of a permanently useless hand, nor are the consequences of this kill so dire. We may see Taran in Old MacDonald, and before that Fern, but if we insinuate the character of Drem into this person and this circumstance, we reduce it to mock-heroics. The farthest we can take this fancy is to say that the farmer, like Taran, must temper glory with dependence.

But the creature will not die. Two bullets in the head, and its great jaws snap and seize the rifle; the barrel cannot be pried loose. So the ax must be wielded. Yet even this weapon proves unequal to the awesome power of the turtle. The first ax stroke glances off the sinewy neck. And now the snapper raises its taloned forelegs and covers its eyes. The gesture strikes to the farmer's heart, the axis tilts, and the universe is altered once more.

If Taran is there, if Bilbo Baggins is there, pity will stir in the hero, and the enemy's life will be spared. Compassion is the stuff of which children's heroes are made.

Or perhaps the story itself has shifted with the turtle's genetically programmed gesture, which the reader sees as beseeching. If so, the issue is not even mercy from the would-be murderer, Old MacDonald. The issue is the turtle, is life and death. Dragon it is, but not the slimy, treacherous devourer of innocent ducklings, the maimer of devoted mother ducks. This dragon trying to cover its eyes with its terrible claws is Le Guin's marvelous dragon. "It did not move. It might have been crouching there for hours, or for years, or for centuries. It was carven of iron, shaped from rock—but the eyes, the eyes he dared not look into, the eyes like oil coiling on water, like yellow smoke behind glass, the opaque, profound, and yellow eyes watched." Or, beheaded, the great Orm Embar of Earthsea, the dying dragon who declares in the Old Speech: " 'The sense has gone out of things. There is a hole in the world and the sea is running out of it. The light is running out. We will be left in the dry land. There will be no more speaking, and no more dying.' "

Who dares disturb the universe? Not Fern. Not even Taran anymore. Just Old MacDonald, finishing the job and not relishing it very much.

But a kind of equilibrium is restored in the disturbed universe. On the farm normal life resumes. All the waterfowl return to the pond. Within a day. How did they discern that the dragon was vanquished and their habitat made safe once again? They are not especially clever, mallard ducks. Perhaps like the farm dog, like Sylvie and Fern and, eventually, Taran, like Orm Embar and Ged and Riddley Walker, they have the *first knowing.*

The dead turtle is admired much as the maimed duck was. Before he is made into soup (according to tradition, the promise is kept), he is weighed and surrounded by a circle of farmers, all of whom have turtle stories of their own, tales of loss and sorrow, of peril and risk, struggle and conquest, respect and awe. One tried to deal with a forty pounder which bit a two-by-four in half. Another lost a black Angus calf to a brute of a turtle in the swamp. The stories ring as true as "Death of a Pig." They will be retold and passed along and remembered as myth. Thus the turtle becomes dragon, the farmer dragon-slayer.

The writer for children is keenly aware of the shifting relationship between responsibility and action. " 'You don't really suppose, do you,' " says Gandalf to Bilbo Baggins in *The Hobbit,* " 'that all your adventures and escapes were managed by mere luck, just for your sole benefit? You are a very fine person, Mr. Baggins, and I am very fond of you; but you are only quite a little fellow in a wide world after all!' " Children need heroes. They need stories about people taking charge of their lives and finding life beyond the self. They also need Gandalf's reminder, or Baloo's maxim, "But the jungle is large and the Cub he is small. Let him think and be still."

Old MacDonald is now left with a duck that can barely stand. The deformed leg seems likely to freeze come winter since she can't draw it under her. But farmers are busy this time of year, and there's no pressing need to deal with her just now. Her remaining babies are thriving. She even manages to lead them to the pond, although by evening she is too exhausted to make the trek back with the others. She lets the farmer know where she can be found; her vocal chords are undamaged. Old MacDonald gets into the habit of scooping her up along the way. Having summoned help, she allows this handling, flattening herself and waiting. "All right, Gimpy," Old MacDonald tells her, carrying her to safety.

"Gimpy." Without realizing it, Old MacDonald has bestowed a name on the duck. Which changes everything. It's a whole new ball game now. Naming establishes relationships and rights. Remember the foundling boy in William Mayne's *A Year and a Day.* Sara and Becca, who found him, are told that he is a changeling and will be gone in a year and a day. A changeling can belong to no one, but they are attached to him, and he possesses them. He is given a proper name. "Adam was happy that night, and Mother thought it was because he knew he had a home with them now, even though she knew he could not really understand what had happened to him." When he dies, the girls, who loved him and could not keep him, "knew that he was with them still in some way. . . . 'It is the first whole year I remember,' said Sara. 'We are a year older now.' 'A year and a day,' said Becca."

These two children took in the foundling, cared for him, and when the time came, let him go. They and their parents did dare to disturb their disapproving community, but their village is not the universe. They sensed the larger world, the connection with things beyond their door and their understanding.

For the plain brown mallard duck, the time for dying has not yet come. Winter frostbite, a new season of ducklings which she allows another duck to foster and lead to and from the pond, a gradual weakening. And round again through the next winter. A long hard winter. It must have looked to her as if spring would never come. The way Mary Call Luther felt in *Where the Lilies Bloom* when she despaired of spring ever returning to Trial Valley. "Only a miracle could bring it. It's such an old story, spring. . . . It had to come to an end sometime. This is probably the year for it." But Mary Call also thought of spring as a "wondrous necessity." And so it is, a miracle and a necessity.

Mary Call was right, too, about its being such an old story. It has preoccupied children's writers since the beginning of real fiction for the young. Even as long ago as 1847 in Frederick Marryat's *The Children of the New Forest,* an immensely popular historical adventure story in which an old forester taught the children of the manor to live in respectful balance with the wildlife they hunted and the food they found and grew. Marryat's view was nonetheless grounded on the solid assumption of the primacy of man in the universe. After all, didn't God give men and women "dominion over the fish of the sea, and over the fowl of the air, and over every living thing that moveth upon the earth"? And didn't He command man and woman to "replenish the earth, and subdue it"?

In Marryat's last book for young people, *The Little Savage,* the theme of man and nature dominates the story of man's inhumanity to man. It is only after the shipwrecked boy learns how to live in harmony with the wild creatures that he becomes something more than a savage. Marryat seemed to be saying that civilized man may be more bestial than any wild beast living according to its nature. An odd book for its time, deeply felt.

In the 1880s, after Darwin and sweeping changes in thinking about man and nature, another children's writer, Juliana Ewing, imbued many of her stories with a sense of place and humanity's relationship with the natural world. The following passage from *The Story of a Short Life* describes the establishment of an army camp near the child hero's home:

> Take a highwayman's heath.
>
> Destroy every vestige of life with fire and axe, from the pine that has longest been a landmark, to the smallest beetle in smoking moss. Burn acres of purple and pink heather, and pare away the young bracken that springs verdant from its ashes.
>
> Let flame consume the perfumed gorse in all its glory, and not spare the broom, whose more exquisite yellow atones for its lack of fragrance. In this common ruin be every lesser flower involved; blue beds of speedwell by the wayfarer's path—the daintier milkwort, and rougher red rattle, down to the very dodder that clasps the heather, let them perish, and the face of Dame Nature be utterly blackened! Then:
>
> Shave the heath as bare as the back of your hand, and if you have felled every tree, and left not so much as a tussock of grass or a scarlet toadstool to break the force of the winds; then shall the winds come, from the east and from the west, from the north and from the south, and shall raise on your shaven heath clouds of sand that would not discredit a desert in the heart of Africa.
>
> By some such recipe the ground was prepared for that Camp of Instruction at Asholt. . . . Then a due portion of this sandy oasis in a wilderness of beauty was mapped out into lines, with military precision, and on these were built rows of little wooden huts, which were painted a neat and useful black.

This for children in 1880. A little under a century later, such physical transformation stands for more than environmental change. In Penelope Lively's *The House in Norham Gardens*, Clare envisions the New Guinea village after great-grandfather and westernization. "She came out of the bamboo and into the clearing where the village had been. But the huts had gone. In their place were neat ranks of small concrete bungalows." Here an entire culture has been disturbed, its universe unalterably changed.

On a more lyrical note Ewing wrote of an opposite impact of people on the land, of a child's power to alter nature *and* human nature. *Mary's Meadow* tells of a lovely field where the children play until their father and the neighboring squire, who owns the meadow, argue and "go to law." When Mary reads a book by a naturalist who digs up wild flowers where they grow in profusion and transplants them in barren places, she is inspired. "Some books put things into your head with a sort of rush, and now it suddenly rushed into mine—*That's what I'll be!* I'll take seeds and cuttings and offshoots from our garden and set them in waste-places and hedges and fields, and I'll make an earthly paradise of Mary's Meadow." Eventually, the squire catches her there as she is planting double cowslips. He accuses her of digging up his flowers, and it takes a whole season for him to discover the new double cowslips. By then the child and her flowers have reformed him; he is cured of his possessiveness and misuse of the land.

When, in the following generation, Frances Hodgson Burnett wrote *The Secret Garden*, a book that seems strongly derivative of *Mary's Meadow*, the view shifted. The love and care of growing things in the garden still function as a vital link between the child and the outside world. But while Dickon has one foot in the wild and one in domestic cultivation, Mary and Colin thrive only when their garden grows and thrives. Nature for them is indeed subdued, and it is contained within the high garden wall.

This view of nature tamed and limited seems to have prevailed in children's books through the early decades of this century. Of course, there are notable exceptions, like Kipling's *Jungle Books*, especially when the elephants rampage through the village and the jungle takes over, obliterating every sign of habitation and cultivation. Exceptions aside, it was a long distance and a long time to Lucy Boston's cherished garden at Green Knowe, where, despite the efforts and skills of Mrs. Oldknow and Boggis, the gardener, the spring floods overrun the place and once, for a brief time, the garden becomes the sanctuary for the magnificent and pitiable Hanno. Green Knowe cannot hide a gorilla. He is a force of nature, like the river bursting its banks and invading all that is peaceful and tidy and beautiful.

For a while Hanno, like the flood, will leave his mark on the place; he will leave his mark in Ping's heart forever. Who disturbs this universe? It all depends. Mrs. Oldknow and Boggis do continually, although their disturbance is periodically interrupted, if not disturbed, by conditions beyond their control. The zoo people who wrenched the gorilla from his world. Hanno himself, not only uprooting vegetation as he would do in his own habitat, but destroying much more than he ever would have done in the jungle. And little Ping most certainly does in his attempt to set things right. There is no solution for Hanno any more than there is for the tribes-people in New Guinea—no returning to a time before the disturbance.

For disturbance, it seems, is inevitable whether or not we exercise forethought. And forethought may stop more people in their tracks than Hamlet. " 'It's the same as chess,' " says Julia's brother Greg in *A Room Made of Windows*. " 'Every single move affects what all the other pieces can do. Every move determines the end in a way no ordinary player can see.

But a chess master can. I wonder if there are life masters. I wouldn't want to be a life master—I couldn't stand it. I should think it would be impossible to do anything. You wouldn't have the courage.' "

The alternative to disturbing the universe is, of course, not a real alternative. To do nothing, to choose passivity, is not only dull, it is unnatural. And to be unnatural is to disturb the natural world. It is, thank goodness, in our nature to be the child Fern, to be Drem pressing on against almost impossible odds, or Buddy Clark, in *The Planet of Junior Brown*, determined to overcome the plight of the homeless. They are heroes and heroines not because they succeed but because they strive.

" 'I wouldn't want to be a life master,' " says Greg. " 'I couldn't stand it. I should think it would be impossible to do anything. You wouldn't have the courage.' " He's right, of course, just as Riddley Walker is right when he discovers why you have to act and where courage comes from.

> You myt think you can jus go here and there doing nothing. Happening nothing. You cant tho you bleeding cant. You put your self on any road and some thing wil show its self to you. Wanting to happen. Waiting to happen. You myt say, 'I dont want to know.' But 1ce its showt its self to you you *wil* know wont you. You cant not know no mor. There it is and working in you. You myt try to put a farness be twean you and it only you cant becaws youre carrying it inside you. The waiting to happen aint out there where it ben no mor its inside you.

These two statements about the human condition are about the making of every hero and heroine I have mentioned. Leonard Woolf has remarked on "the importance of truth and the impossibility of absolute truth." I think the relationship between the fictional hero or heroine and the universe is poised, like Woolf's position, between conditions as important and as impossible as truth itself.

The fictional lives in children's literature, those of Fern or Sylvie or Drem, of Taran or Ged, of Ping or Clare or Mary Call Luther, and even of Orm Embar or Hanno or Charlotte, are in all of us, or we could not feel with them and for them as we do. "You put your self on any road," says Riddley Walker, "and some thing wil show its self to you." You put yourself in any book, and that is a road, too. "Wanting to happen. Waiting to happen." And the child who takes that road to Fern or Wilbur or Charlotte, or to all three together, "cant not know no mor," because Fern or Wilbur or Charlotte is inside the child now.

Old MacDonald did not suffer from a split or multiple personality. The farmer, like everyone else, came equipped with the potential to become any of those characters. It's up to the singer of the song or the teller of the tale to decide which role fits the story and its meaning. And it's up to the listener or reader to recognize a part of himself or herself—and perhaps a new self—in Old MacDonald.

Or else to pass Old MacDonald by. For in the last chapter, the axis tilts one more time, and it is the plain brown mallard duck whose song I sing or whose tale I tell.

This spring she hatched out seven ducklings. It is harder for her to brood them now, for her good leg barely supports her and her rigid, twisted leg interferes with her balance. She has trouble protecting her babies; some of the ducklings have been trampled and killed. Sooner or later something will get her, too. Either that, or she'll just spread her wings in exhaustion and collapse. If what E. B. White calls the "vital spark" is dimming by the time the farmer scoops her up, she will be carried to the duck pen anyhow, because that is what she expects from Old MacDonald; it is her due.

Nothing more will be done for her, even though she has been a survivor, a heroine, and a tyrant and is still hauntingly appealing. So this ends as her story just as she is leaving it. Now I can fully appreciate why E. B. White, who wrote one story called "Death of a Pig" for adults, wrote another for children, which he had to call *Charlotte's Web*. Like Charlotte living and dying according to her nature and all nature, the plain brown mallard duck, weak and failing, emerges as the pivotal and enduring theme. One duck among many but as unforgettable as a particular spider, "in a class by herself."

Achilles in Altjira

ALAN GARNER

I am speaking here as the conscious result of events set in motion one day in October 1950 by a remarkable man. Eric James, Lord James of Rusholme, was High Master of Manchester Grammar School throughout the seven years of my time there: a remarkable man and a remarkable school, which instills the concept of excellence, in the absolute and for its own sake. I have not achieved such excellence, but at least I know that it exists, and I was equipped by that school to seek it out. Eric James's special contribution was that he, a chemist, impressed on me, a classical linguist, that without him science would continue, but without me and my companions Western culture would be at risk. I can remember the room, the window, the desk, the swirl of his gown as he turned and said to me (only because I was the boy in his line of sight!) that for each generation the *Iliad* must be told anew. The moment is so clear because it was the first realization that privilege is service before it is power; that humility is the requirement of pride. Without that realization, I should not have found the temerity proper to the will to write.

Today I want to discuss written language, as an art rather than as a science; and for the purpose of the discussion I shall take *art* to mean the fabrication whereby reality may be the more clearly revealed and defined.

A prime material of art is paradox, in that paradox links two valid yet mutually exclusive systems that we need if we are to comprehend reality; paradox links intuition and analytical thought. Paradox, the integration of the irrational and logic, engages both emotion and intellect without committing an outrage on either; and, for me, literature is justified only so long as it keeps a sense of paradox central to its form. Therefore, I speak for imaginative writing, not for the didactic; for ambivalence, not for instruction. When language serves dogma, then literature, denied the paradox, is lost.

Two questions the writer has to answer before he can write are: What is the story? What words can tell it? The answers to the questions are the matter of my argument, and, I shall suggest, in order to fulfill what the answers require, the writer must employ and combine two human qualities that are not commonly used together in harmony—a sense of the numinous, and a rational mind. The revelation and definition of reality by art is an act of translation. It is translation, by the agency of the writer and the instrument of story, across the gap between reality and the reader.

What is the story? The story is the medium through which the writer interprets reality, but it is not reality itself. The story is a symbol, which makes a unity of the elements, hitherto seen as separate, that combine uniquely in the writer's vision.

What words can tell it? The words are the language, the medium through which the story is made plain; and unless the language is apt, the story will not translate, for the final translator is not the writer but the reader. To read also is to create.

Language shifts continually; it changes through space and through time. The problem is more easily understood where the language has to translate over chasms of space and time, for then the gap between story and reader, which is always present, is plain to see. Eric James made me aware of the challenge when he said, "For each generation, the *Iliad* must be told anew."

Μῆνιν ἄειδε, θεά, Πηληϊάδεω Ἀχιλῆος
οὐλομένην, ἣ μυρί᾽ Ἀχαιοῖς ἄλγε᾽ ἔθηκε,
πολλὰς δ᾽ ἰφθίμους ψυχὰς ῎Αϊδι προΐαψεν
ἡρώων, αὐτοὺς δὲ ἑλώρια τεῦχε κύνεσσιν
οἰωνοῖσί τε πᾶσι, Διὸς δ᾽ ἐτελείετο βουλή,
ἐξ οὗ δὴ τὰ πρῶτα διαστήτην ἐρίσαντε
Ἀτρεΐδης τε ἄναξ ἀνδρῶν καὶ δῖος Ἀχιλλεύς.

That is the opening of the *Iliad* as Homer told it. Quite clearly, we have to find other words if we are to tell the story. Here are some:

The Wrath of Peleus' Son, the direful Spring
Of all the Grecian Woes, o Goddess, sing!
That Wrath which hurl'd to Pluto's gloomy Reign
The Souls of mighty Chiefs untimely slain;
Whose Limbs unbury'd on the naked Shore
Devouring Dogs and hungry Vultures tore.
Since Great Achilles and Atrides strove,
Such was the Sov'reign Doom, and such the Will of Jove.

And so Alexander Pope in the year 1715.

There we may have an example of a generation's voice. But Pope encapsulates another theme of my argument—the duty of translation. I am not talking about the mechanical transposition of words but about what those words express: the culture of an epoch viewed through the subjectivity of an individual. Words are more than the packing of a dictionary. They evoke mood as well as dispense fact.

For instance, my impression when reading Plato is that of drinking cold, fresh water. To me, Aeschylus is blood and darkness. And Homer is leather, oak, the secrets of the smith; Man; God; Fury; above all, magic and wonder in the world of Chaos and the logic of Dream. I see little of that in Pope's immaculate couplets. His *Iliad* is the *Iliad* Homer might have written if he had been an eighteenth-century gentleman of polite society in England. That is not quite the same thing as giving a generation its voice. The difference is important. Pope's duty was to translate to polite society of the eighteenth century the heart and mind of Homer, and that he did not do. Instead, the Greek poet was dressed as an Englishman.

Homer raises another issue that Pope illustrates by his failure. What is a writer to do when his text is not a written one? For where Pope wrote, Homer sang. His was an oral art, in which memory and improvisation were talents that are not used by the deliberate, self-correcting, word-by-word progress of ink over paper. The word in the air is not the same word on the page. The storyteller meets the same intractable problem now in a different guise—in the writing of dialogue, which is never the mere transcription of a tape recording.

The chasm between literate Pope and preliterate Homer is valuable because we can see it. But the chasm is always there for every writer, always too wide, and the translator's bridge too slender. For the translator, the storyteller, there are the questions: What is the story? What words can tell it? And we must add a question for ourselves: What does the story require of the teller? That is, what skills has the writer to deploy?

I would suggest that, since the function of language is to communicate, the writer must at least start from a shared ground with the reader. The place for worthwhile experiment to begin is in the middle of the mainstream. Linguistic and cultural crafts must be not so much simplified thereby as integrated. It is not enough to know. It is not enough to feel. The disciplines of heart and head, emotion and intellect, must run true together—the heart, to remain open to the potential of our humanity; the head, to control, select, focus, and give form to the expression of that potential. A third necessity, after heart and head, is that the writer should have authority—not the authority of a reputation but the authority of experience. Without that experience his judgment is suspect, his necessary iconoclasm a mischief. In order to control the vision, the gift, the work, or whatever term we care to use, the writer is required to harness an untrammeled receptivity to a strict intellectual vigor. It is not necessary to be able to analyze what one is doing, as I am attempting now. Indeed, for some it may be inhibiting; but for others, such analysis is a positive knowledge, leading to a refinement of technique and thereby achievement.

Already we have a picture of a dynamic union of opposites; heart and head, emotion and intellect—not the one subservient to the other, but integrated. It is the tension of the paradox, and the paradox must be active within the writer.

To turn what I am saying into less of an abstraction, I shall make the questions personal. What is my story? What words can tell it?

The words for me must be English words, and a strength of English is its ability to draw for enrichment on both Germanic and Romance vocabularies. The English themselves have no clear view of this. We tend to assume (because they come late in our infant learning) that words of Romance origin are intrinsically superior to those of Germanic. Certainly, when I look at my own primary school essays, it is the use of the Romance word that has won for me the teacher's approving tick. But in evolved English the assumption is wrong. The two roots have become responsible for separate jobs. We use the Germanic when we want to be direct, close, honest: such words as *love, warm, come, go, hate, thank, fear*. The Romance words are used when we want to keep feeling at a distance, so that we may articulate with precision: *amity, exacerbate, propinquity, evacuate, obloquy, gratitude, presentiment*. Romance, with its distancing effect and polysyllabic intricacies, can also conceal, so that the result is not ambivalence but opacity. Extreme cases are to be found in political and military gobbledygook, which is the product of having Madison Avenue allied to death. Here, death itself is called "zero survivability situation"; explosion, "energetic disassembly"; and we do not see human flesh in the phrase "maximize harassment and interdiction," which means "wipe out."

Romance is rodent, nibbled on the lips. Germanic is resonant, from the belly. It is also simple, and through its simplicity, ambivalent; the paradox again.

A more general aspect of English is that vowels may be seen to represent emotion and consonants to represent thought. We are able to communicate our feelings in speech without consonants and to understand a written statement when the vowels are omitted. The head defines the heart, and together they make the integrated word.

A large vocabulary is another characteristic of English. English contains some four hundred and ninety thousand words plus another three hundred thousand technical terms—more than three-quarters of a million fragments of Babel. But, of these, it is currently estimated that no one person uses more than sixty thousand words; that is, the most fluent English speakers use less than an eighth of the language. My own vocabulary is about thirty-three thousand words—7 percent of what is available to me.

British children, by the age of five, use about two thousand words; by the age of nine, six thousand (or eight thousand, if encouraged to read). By the age of twelve the child will have a vocabulary of twelve thousand words, which is that of half the adult population of all ages. Twelve thousand words: 2.4 percent of the language is spoken by 75 percent of the population. These are rough figures, but even an approximation does not hide the discrepancy.

The function of language is to communicate. How, then, can I, with a vocabulary nearly three times bigger than that of three quarters of my fellows, choose the words that we have in common? The question is unreal. I pose it in order to draw attention to the nature of imaginative writing.

My experience, over twenty-seven years, is that richness of content varies inversely with complexity of language. The more simply I write, the more I can say. The more open the prose as the result of clarity, the more room there is for you, the reader, to bring something of yourself to the act of translating the story from my subjectivity to your own. It is here that reading becomes a creative act. The reason why I have no dilemma over choosing the one shared word in three is that the vocabulary I use in writing is almost identical to the twelve thousand words of children and of most adults. They are the words of conversation rather than of intellectual debate; concrete rather than abstract; natural rather than imposed; Germanic rather than Romance.

Through a preference for the simple and the ambivalent and the clear, the relatively sophisticated mind arrives at a choice of vocabulary that coincides with that of the relatively less sophisticated mind. It is in the deployment of the word that the difference and the sophistication lie. And by deployment, by cunning, I am able to choose words, in addition, that are not shared and to place them without confusion and with implicit meaning, so that they are scarcely noticed, but the reader is enriched. It is a beauty of English. Yet I could be critical. English, for all its power, has mislaid its soul. English, despite my fluency, is a language not my own.

To make sense of what I mean, it is necessary for me to explain a little of my background, which is a background still common to many children in Britain today.

I come from a line of working-class rural craftsmen in Cheshire. I was not the first of my family to show intelligence, but I was the first to benefit from the Education Act of 1944, which enabled me to go to the school with the highest academic standards in the country, Manchester Grammar School, and from there to Oxford University.

Manchester Grammar School had, at that time, no English department. English as a main subject was for the few who could not master the literature of a foreign tongue. My ability lay in Latin and Greek. When I came to peer at English from the disdainful heights of the Acropolis, I saw only a verbal pulp. No writing after *The Tempest* had much to say to me. I was not surprised. Modern English, I would have said if I had thought about it, was a partial creole of Latin, and little more. My true discovery of English began some time after I had started to write.

I was reading, voluntarily, the text of *Sir Gawain and the Green Knight*, and I wondered why there were so many footnotes. My grandfather was an unlettered smith, but he would not have needed all these footnotes if a native speaker had read the poem to him aloud.

> a little on a lande / a lawe as hit were;
> A balg berg bi a bonke / the brimme besyde.
> Bi a fors of a flode / that ferked there.

This was no Latin creole. This was what I knew as "talking broad." I had had my mouth washed out with carbolic soap for speaking this way at school when I was five years old.

> Hit hade a hole on the ende / and on ayther syde,
> And ouergrowen with gresse / in glodes aywhere,
> And al was holwe inwith / nobbut an oulde cave,
> Or a crevisse of an olde cragge.

Every generation needs its voice, but here I was, at home in the fourteenth century, reading a language that I did not find foreign, whereas the English of later centuries was alien, empty. Something had gone wrong.

I realized that I had been taught (if only by default) to suppress, and even to deride, my primary native tongue. Standard, received English had been imposed on me, and I had clung to it, so that I could be educated and could use that education. Gain had been bought with loss.

This sense of loss, I found later, had been expressed, albeit patronizingly, long before I could feel sorry for myself. Roger Wilbraham, a landed gentleman of the eighteenth century, read a paper before the Society of Antiquaries on May 8, 1817, in which he made a plea for the compilation of what he called Provincial Glossaries. Provincial Glossaries,

> "accompanied by an explanation of the sense in which
> each of them still continues to be used in the districts to

which they belong, would be of essential service in explaining many obscure terms in our early poets, the true
meaning of which, although it may have puzzled and
bewildered the most acute and learned of our Commenta-
tors, would perhaps be perfectly intelligible to a Cheshire
clown."

Years after my surprised reading of *Sir Gawain and the Green Knight*,
Professor Ralph Elliott of the Australian National University told me that I
could be the first writer in six hundred years to emerge from the same
linguistic stock as the Gawain poet and to draw on the same landscapes for
its expression. Then I felt humbled and, above all, responsible; responsible
for both my dialects and for their feeding. I saw, too, why little in English
literature after *The Tempest* had said anything to me. It was an aspect of the
Age of Reason that had committed the nuisance, and the nuisance was not
only linguistic but social.

When the English, through Puritanism, tried to clarify their theology,
they demystified the church and also cut themselves off from their national
soul; and a culture that wounds its soul is in danger. The English
disintegrated heart from head and set about building a new order from
materials foreign in space and time—the classical Mediterranean.

Just as I would claim that the English language benefits from its Romance
and Germanic roots, so I would claim that all language is fed from the roots
that are social. But those roots were incidentally denied us by the sweep of
the Puritan revolution. No distinction was made. Our folk memory was
dubbed a heresy. The ancient world was the pattern for men of letters, and
the written word spoke in terms of that pattern. Education in the
humanities was education in Latin and Greek. English style came from the
library, not from the land; and the effect, despite the Romantic movement,
has continued to this day.

Yet many British children share the experience of being born into one
dialect and growing into another, and since the Education Act of 1944 we
have had an increased flow of ability from the working class into the arts.
The result has been singularly depressing. We discovered our riches, so
long abused—and we abused them further by reacting against the precepts
of discipline inherent in classical art as mindlessly as the Puritan revolution
had suppressed our dreams.

Generally speaking, among the newly educated, the historical inability
of the working class to invest time and effort without an immediate return
has joined with the historical opportunism of the middle class and has
produced a disdain for controlled and structured form. Excellence is not
pursued. We are in a phase without direction, the heart ruling the head. It

is most noticeable in theater and in television, where surface brilliance is mistaken for substance, and verbal maundering is held to be reality. It is the wages of universal partial education. Now, to be cultured, it is enough to be vulgar. Little is integrated. We are still reduced.

The whole rationale, which I have done no more than touch on here, was laid before me when I read *Sir Gawain and the Green Knight*. The irony was savage. I had been educated to articulate precisely what that education had cost. But I was fortunate. I had a lifeline. I could get back.

The physical immobility of my family was the lifeline. My family is so rooted that it ignores social classification by others. On one square mile of Cheshire hillside, Alderley Edge, the Garners *are*. We know our place. And this sense of fusion with a land rescued me.

The education that had made me a stranger to my own people, yet had shown me no acceptable alternative, did increase my understanding of the hill. The awareness of place that was my birthright was increased by the opening of my mind to the physical sciences and to the metaphors of stability and change that were given by the hill. Until I came to terms with the paradox, I was denied, and I myself denied, the people. But those people had their analogue in the land, and toward that root I began to move the stem of the intellect grown hydroponically in the academic hothouse. The process has taken twenty-seven years so far, and my writing is the result.

It is a writing prompted by a feeling of outrage—personal, social, political, and linguistic. Yet if any of this were to show overtly on the page, it would defeat itself. My job is to tell stories.

To summarize: I have said that a story is a symbol; that all storytelling is translation; that English is rich in its linguistic inheritance but that for historical reasons there is a social and cultural imbalance, which has limited the spectrum available to the arts. I have also said that many British children become, in effect, bilingual. It may be instructive, or at least entertaining, to illustrate what I mean.

My primary tongue, which I share with several million other people, I would call northwest Mercian. My secondary tongue is standard English, which is a dialect of the seat of power, London. Both are valid. Both can be described. Standard English, because of its dominance, has the greater number of abstract words. Northwest Mercian is the more concrete, with little of the Romance in its vocabulary, and native speakers think of it as debased, "talking broad," while English purists treat it as a barbarism. There are differences between the dialects; but they are little more than differences. Neither is wholly superior to the other.

In the sixteenth century English achieved an elegance of Germanic and Romance integration that it has not captured since. We respond instinctively to its excellence. The Bible had the good fortune to be translated into this excellence, and the debility of English thereafter is plotted in all subsequent failures to improve on that text. Here is a short passage from the Bible, and its equivalent in northwest Mercian:

> And Boaz said unto her, At mealtime come thou hither, and eat of the bread, and dip thy morsel in the vinegar. And she sat beside the reapers: and she reached her parched corn, and she did eat, and was sufficed, and left.
> And when she had risen up to glean, Boaz commanded his young men, saying, Let her glean even among the sheaves and reproach her not:
> And let fall some handfuls of purpose for her, and leave them, that she may glean them, and rebuke her not.
> So she gleaned in the field until even, and beat out that she had gleaned; and it was about an ephah of barley.

Northwest Mercian:

> Un Boaz sed to ur, Ut baggintaym, thay kum eyur, un av sum o'th'bred, un dip thi bit u' meet i'th' alliger. Un oo sat ursel dayn usayd u'th' reepers; un oo raut ur parcht kuurn, un oo et it, un ad ur filt, un went uwee.
> Un wen oo wuz gotten up fer t' songger, Boaz gy'en aurders t' iz yungg yooths, sez ay, Lerrer songger reyt umungg th' kivvers, un dunner yay skuwl er.
> Un let faw sum antlz u'purpus fer er, un leeuv um fer er fer t' leez um, un dunner sneep er.
> So ur songgert in th' felt ter th' neet, un oo bumpt wor oo songgert, un it koom ter ubayt too mishur u' barley.

The language of *Sir Gawain and the Green Knight* is still spoken in the northwest of England today, but it has no voice in modern literature. The detriment works both ways. Modern literature does not feed from its soil. Northwest Mercian is not illiterate nor preliterate; it has been rendered nonliterate and nonfunctional. I have just demonstrated its failure to communicate anything other than an emotion.

It would be retrogressive, a negation, if I were to try to impose northwest Mercian on the speakers of standard English, and I should deservedly fail. Writer and language are involved in the process of history, and in history standard English has become dominant over all other regional dialects, of which northwest Mercian is but one. How, then, can I feed the two, to both of which I must own?

The answer is seen only with hindsight. Each step has appeared at the time to be simple expediency, in order to tell a story. One image, though, has remained—the awareness of standing between two cultures represented by two dialects: the concrete, direct culture from which I was removed and to which I could not return, even if I would; and the culture of abstract, conceptual thought which had no root in me, but in which I have grown and which I cherish. It was self-awareness without self-pity, but full of violence. I knew that I had to hold on to that violence and, somehow, by channeling them through me, make the negative energies positive.

All my writing has been fueled by the instinctive drive to speak with a true and northern voice integrated with the language of literary fluency, because I need both if I am to span my story. It was instinctive, not conscious, and I have only recently become aware enough to define the niceties.

First efforts were crude and embarrassing—a debased phonetic dialogue in the nineteenth-century manner. Such awkwardness gets in the way, translates nothing. Phonetic spelling condescends. Phonetic spelling is not good enough in its representation of the speakers. It is ugly to look at, bespattered with apostrophes. It is a sign of a writer alienated from his subject and linguistically unschooled. Worst of all, in my writing and in that of others, the result is to reduce demotic culture to a mockery; to make of fair speech mere rustic conversation; to render quaint, at best, the people we should serve. The place for phonetics, I would suggest, is not the novel.

Dialect vocabulary may be used to enrich a text, but it should be used sparingly, with the greatest precision, with deployment and cunning; otherwise, the balance is tipped through the absurd to the obscure. The art is to create the illusion of demotic rather than to record it. The quality of northwest Mercian and of all dialects, including standard English, is not in the individual words but in the cadence, in the music of it all.

So what words can tell my story?

The words are the language, heart and head—a language at once idiosyncratic and universal, in the full growth of the disciplined mind, fed from a deep root. To employ one without the other is to be fluent with nothing to say, or to have everything to say and no adequate means of saying it. Yet, for historical reasons, those are the only alternatives for the artist in Britain today, unless he or she, consciously or unconsciously, wages total war—by which I mean total life—on the divisive forces within the individual and within society.

The conflict of the paradox must consume but not destroy. It must be grasped until, leached of hurt, it is a clear and positive force, matched to an equal clarity of prose. It must become rage—rage *for*, not rage *against*. That way, although there is no guarantee, a new language may result that is neither false nor sentimental, that can stand without risk of degradation, without loss of ambivalence, and be at all times complete. Twenty-seven years have not given me that language, but at least I feel that I know some of its qualities and where to look for them in myself.

Here is a tentative example, from *The Aimer Gate*. It describes, as did the earlier passage from the Bible, a harvest field:

> The men stood in a line, at the field edge, facing the hill, Ozzie on the outside, and began their swing. It was a slow swing . . . back and to, against the hill they walked. They walked and swung, hips forward, letting the weight cut. It was as if they were walking in a yellow water before them. Each blade came up in time with each blade, at Ozzie's march, for if they ever got out of time, the blades would cut flesh and bone.
>
> Behind each man the corn swarf lay like silk in the light of poppies. And the women gathered the swarf by armfuls, spun bants of straw and tied armfuls into sheaves, stacked sheaves into kivvers. Six sheaves stood to a kivver, and the kivvers must stand till the church bells had rung over them three times. Three weeks to harvest—but first was the getting.

Standard English and northwest Mercian are there combined in syntax, vocabulary, and cadence. They speak for me, as the head to the heart, as the consonant to the vowel, as Romance to Germanic, as the stem to the root.

From such are the words formed. Now what else is the story? To answer that question I have to draw on the work of the late Professor Mircea Eliade, in whose clarity of discourse I have often found my apprehensions to be articulately defined.

The story that the writer must tell is no less than the truth. At the beginning I took *art* to mean the fabrication whereby reality may be the more clearly revealed. Now I would equate *truth* with that same reality.

A true story is religious, as drama is religious. Any other fiction is didacticism, instruction rather than revelation, and not what I am talking about. *Religious,* too, is a quarrelsome word. For me, *religion* describes that area of human concern for, and involvement with, the question of our being within the cosmos. The concern and involvement are often stated through the imagery of a god, or gods, or ghosts, or ancestors, but not necessarily so. Therefore, I would consider humanism, for instance, and atheism to be religious activities.

The function of the storyteller is to relate the truth in a manner that is simple, to integrate without reduction, for it is rarely possible to declare the truth as it is, because the universe presents itself as a mystery. We have to find parables; we have to tell stories to unriddle the world.

It is yet another paradox. Language in itself, no matter how finely worked, will not speak the truth. What we feel most deeply, we cannot say in words. At such levels only images connect, and hence story becomes symbol.

A symbol is not a replica of an objective fact. It is not responsive to reductive analytical rationalism. A symbol is always religious and always multivalent. It has the capacity to integrate several meanings simultaneously, the unity between which is not evident on the plane of experience. This capacity to reveal a multitude of united meanings has a consequence. The symbol can reveal a perspective in which diverse realities may be integrated without reduction, so that the symbolism of the moon, for example, reveals a unity between the lunar rhythms, water, women, death and resurrection, horses, ravens, madness, the weaver's craft, and human destiny—which includes the Apollo space missions. All that is not an act of reason, but it is of story. Here is a dimension where paradox is resolved; for story itself is myth, and myth is truth.

> In the beginning, the earth was a desolate plain, without hills or rivers, lying in darkness. The sun, the moon and the stars were still under the earth. Above the earth was Wallanganda, and beneath everything, in a waterhole, was Ungud.
>
> Ungud stirred. And the sun, and the moon and the stars rose to Wallanganda. Ungud moved. And with every movement the world was made: hills, rivers and sea, and life was woken. And all this Ungud did "altijirana nambakala," "from his own Dreaming"; that is, from his own Eternity.
>
> The life that Ungud woke was eternal, but lacked physical form. This life became both animals and men. And these, the Ancestors, were given shapes and emerged onto the face of the new earth. And the place where each Ancestor emerged is sacred for ever.

That is a synthesis of a pan-Australian myth. From myth came the totemism of the aboriginal Australian and an awareness that amounts to symbiosis with the land. For the Australian the Ancestor exists simultaneously under the earth; in ritual objects; in places such as rocks, hills, springs, waterfalls; as "spirit children" waiting between death and rebirth; and, most significantly, as the man in whom he is incarnate. It is a world view close to the one I discovered for myself as a child of my family on Alderley Edge.

Through the mediation of myth, the aboriginal Australian has not only a religious nobility of thought but, coincident with the "real" earth, a mystical earth, a mystical geography, a mystical time, a mystical history, and, through the individual, a mystical and personal responsibility for the universe.

Ritual initiation of the individual is the assumption by the individual of this knowledge and responsibility. When an aboriginal Australian boy is initiated into manhood, the sacred places of his people are visited, the sacred rites performed, to help the boy to remember. For this boy, this reincarnated Ancestor, has to recall the primordial time and his own most remote deeds. Through initiation, the novice discovers that he has been here already, in the Beginning, Altjira, the Dreamtime. It is a Second Coming. It is a Holy Communion. To learn is to remember.

In Greek the word is *anamnesis* and was first expounded to us by a father of Western philosophy and, therefore, of our own thought structures, Plato. There are many differences between the Australian *altjira* and Greek *anamnesis,* but both are spiritual activities: philosophy for the Greek, life itself for the Australian.

I am not advocating a rejection of sophisticated values in favor of primitive animism. I am a rationalist, schooled in the classical Mediterranean languages and an inheritor of two thousand five hundred years of Western thought. I need Manchester Grammar School just as much as I need Alderley Edge.

My concern, in writing and in life, is that by developing our greatness, the intellect, we should not lose the other greatness, our capacity to Dream. The two can be integrated. Achilles can walk in Altjira; indeed, he must. He has such a lot to remember.

Not least of the memories is that to live as a human being is in itself a religious act.

That is why the stories must be told. It is why Eric James had such a catalytic effect upon one of his sixth formers—and so justified his function as a chemist, after all.

Mythic Journeys

PAUL   HEINS

Mythic journeys is an ambiguous term since it may mean journeys encountered in mythology, or journeys with a mythological purpose, or even accounts of voyages casually including mythical elements. Cavafy's poem "Ithaka" is allusive in its imagery and is best understood against the background of the *Odyssey*; but unless one means that Cavafy's personal point of view is a myth, then any personal point of view can become a myth, and thus the term *mythic journeys* becomes watered down by too much generalization. We must limit the use of the term to apply to collective belief and remember that what we call myth was originally religion.

The proportion of myth in ancient narratives telling of journeys is therefore variable. Odysseus's visit to Hades to consult with the spirit of the prophet Tiresias is obviously mythical, but according to the French classical scholar Victor Bérard, the itinerary of Odysseus was modeled on that of the actual routes followed by Phoenician navigators, who sailed across the Mediterranean before the ancient Greeks did. On the other hand, in the Sumerian epic *Gilgamesh*, which was also preserved in later Mesopotamian writings, the partially divine hero-protagonist makes three journeys, each one in the form of a quest. Gilgamesh seeks out and destroys the monster Humbaba; in his search of immortality he goes beyond the bounds of the known world to consult with Utnapishtim, whose story parallels in many ways the biblical account of Noah and the Flood; and he visits the underworld, the world of the dead, to speak to the spirit of his friend Enkidu.

Accounts of ancient journeys, then, can incorporate both realistic and mythical elements, and if there is some metaphysical goal in mind, such as Gilgamesh's search for immortality or the quest of the Holy Grail in the Arthurian legends, the journey may be termed a mythic journey; otherwise, it is a series of adventures with mythic trimmings. The story of Jason and the quest of the Golden Fleece, for example, is essentially an adventure story with the geographical ambience of the Black Sea rather than that of the Mediterranean, plus a number of mythic details.

Cavafy's Ithaka is not Odysseus's Ithaca. Cavafy is not in a hurry to get home. With him, Ithaka is merely a metaphor for homecoming, which can be extended to create a further metaphor for the good, an end attained, completion—the very end of life itself. It makes one think of Stevenson's epitaph "Home is the sailor, home from sea," in which life is envisioned as a voyage. It also makes one think of the word *home* in the song sung in Shakespeare's *Cymbeline*.

> Fear no more the heat o' the sun,
>   Nor the furious winter's rages;
> Thou thy worldly task has done,
>   Home art gone, and ta'en thy wages.

But Cavafy is not lugubrious. He hopes that the journey of life will be long and full of adventures, wisdom, pleasures, and joy.

He is not concerned with monsters and outraged divinities and considers them as self-induced in an individual's imagination.

> You will not meet the Laistrygonians and the Cyclops
> And raging Poseidon
> If you do not carry them in your soul.

At this point I should like to digress for a moment and say something about the Laistrygonians. I never have trouble with the Cyclops and Poseidon because the part they play in the *Odyssey* is perfectly clear. But it is a bit puzzling to find another set of cannibalistic monsters so soon after Odysseus's account of his adventure in Polyphemus's cave.

So each time I read the *Odyssey*, I have to check the facts. The wife of Antiphates the Laistrygonian was a "mountainous woman," Antiphates ate one of Odysseus's men "for his dinner," and the other giants—really ogres—were "busy spearing my people like fish and collecting them to make their loathsome meal" (T. E. Shaw translation). The content of the episode obviously preserves some traditional material, but the two unrelated cannibalistic situations are not so effective from the point of view of inducing horror as, let us say, the appearance of Grendel's mother soon after the death of her son.

Of course, Odysseus really wanted to go home. Although Homer was obviously appealing to the age-old human desire to hear of unusual, strange, and even harrowing adventures, the poet carefully molded his story and made it clear early in the poem that Odysseus preferred returning to Ithaca and his family to remaining on Calypso's enchanting island. As early as lines 57 to 59 of the first book of the *Odyssey*, Athene makes it clear in the council of the Olympian gods that Odysseus "only wishes to see one day the chimney smoke rising from his home" (translated from the French of Victor Bérard). Or to put it in the words of T. E. Shaw's translation, "Odysseus is so sick with longing to see if it were but the smoke of his home spiring up."

Odysseus and the *Odyssey*, however, have continued to live beyond their time and have interwoven themselves into the images and stories of later writers and poets. In one famous instance, the poet preserved the Homeric point of view and intention. The French Renaissance writer Joachim du Bellay, serving in the French diplomatic service in Rome, wrote a sonnet, published in 1558, deploring his exile. It begins, "Heureux qui, comme Ulysse, a fait un beau voyage." The first eight lines, the octave, beautifully reflect the original Homeric imagery and intention. Here is a rather free translation:

Happy is the man who like Ulysses has completed a successful journey,
Or like the man who brought back the golden fleece
And then returns, full of experience and wisdom,
To live with his family for the rest of his life.
When shall I see, alas, smoke rising from the chimneys of my little village
And in what season shall I see the enclosure of my simple house,
Which to me is not only my possession but much more?

In molding a narrative or a poem, however, a writer may make use of various possibilities based on the concepts and experiences of differing eras or personalities. In the *Odyssey* itself, there is actually a hint of another kind of adventure of Odysseus. When he encounters the spirit of the prophet Tiresias, he is advised to "go forth under your shapely oar till you come to a people who know not the sea. . . ."; they will say that he bears "a winnowing fan. . . ." "At the last, amidst a happy folk, shall your own death come to you, softly, far from the salt sea, and make an end of one utterly weary of slipping downward into old age." We have already considered how these words influenced Cavafy's concepts in "Ithaka," but it is interesting to note that during the Middle Ages Dante already had individual ideas about Ulysses.

In the twenty-sixth canto of the *Inferno*, the medieval poet tells a strange story about the ancient hero. He recounts how Ulysses sailed west beyond Gibraltar and south below the Equator:

> neither fondness for my son, nor reverence for
> my aged father, nor the due love that should
> have cheered Penelope,
>
> could conquer in me the ardour that I had to
> gain experience of the world, and of human
> vice and worth.

The episode, which is said to have been an invention of Dante's, furnished Tennyson with the theme for his poem entitled "Ulysses."

Earlier in the nineteenth century Keats had proclaimed:

> Ever let the Fancy roam,
> Pleasure never is at home,

but Tennyson in his dramatic monologue reveals a deadly serious determined Ulysses, who makes leaving home a moral imperative, a heroism of determination and will.

> It little profits that an idle king,
> By this still hearth, among these barren crags,
> Matched with an agèd wife, I mete and dole
> Unequal laws unto a savage race,
> That hoard, and sleep, and feed, and know not me.
> I cannot rest from travel; I will drink
> Life to the lees.
>   * * *
>   I am become a name;
> For always roaming with a hungry heart
> Much have I seen and known, cities of men
> And manners, climates, councils, governments
>   * * *
> I am part of all that I have met;
>   * * *
> How dull it is to pause, to make an end,
> To rust unburnished, not to shine in use!

He desired "To follow knowledge like a sinking star,/Beyond the utmost bound of human thought," and ends "strong in will/To strive, to seek, to find, and not to yield."

As in Cavafy's poem, Tennyson's verses encapsulate the themes of knowledge and experience, but the pleasures of sensuous perfumes are definitely lacking. The nineteenth-century British cultural temperament of

Tennyson reveals itself as more akin to that of the hero Beowulf than to that of Odysseus; for the ancient Greek hero certainly accepted his emotions and his pleasures as they came to him.

If Odysseus's character invited speculation and alteration after his original portrayal in the epic poem devoted to him, since Shakespeare's day translators of the *Odyssey* have been faithful to the original. But in versions told and retold for children, the narrations generally depart from the plan—one might say the architectural plan—of Homer's poem. This disparity of telling was very skillfully analyzed and commented on by Lillian Smith in the chapter entitled "Heroes of Epic and Saga" in her critically astute discussion of children's literature, *The Unreluctant Years*. She states, "Some of these versions lack any resemblance to Homer's poem except to give an outline of the events of the story. The best versions attempt to convey the dignity of Greek epic poetry and the classic feeling for the need of noble words to express noble deeds." She comments on Charles Lamb's *The Adventures of Ulysses* and says the following about Alfred Church's *The Odyssey for Boys and Girls:* "The interpolation of the story of Telemachus in the middle of the adventures of Odysseus slows the dramatic swiftness of events and breaks the unity of Homer's plan of *The Odyssey*. It is true, however, that the adventure with the Cyclops provides an arresting opening for the story which arouses the immediate interest of children to the further adventures of Odysseus."

Of Padraic Colum's *The Children's Homer* she says that it follows "the sequence of events as Homer tells them, but instead of having Telemachus return to Ithaca on learning of his father's captivity on Calypso's island, Colum holds him in Sparta to hear the whole story of the Trojan War as told in Homer's *Iliad*."

Two later versions, not considered by Lillian Smith, show similar rearrangements of Homer. Barbara Picard's *The Odyssey of Homer* is divided into three parts: (1) Odysseus sails for Ithaca, (2) Telemachus seeks tidings of his father, and (3) Odysseus in Ithaca. Bernard Evslin's *Greeks Bearing Gifts* recounts the epics of Achilles and Ulysses as separate stories. Ulysses's story appears in two parts—his adventures and his return home—but the author invents and interpolates an episode in which an enchanted crow tells Odysseus what has happened in Ithaca during the hero's absence.

Although it is true—as suggested by Lillian Smith—that to begin Odysseus's story with his remarkable and uncanny adventures is an effective way of arousing the interest of a reader, especially that of a young reader, the actual structure and arrangement of Homer's poem has a definite meaning. It falls into three discernible portions. First, while Odysseus is being detained on Calypso's island, Telemachus is involved in his own journey—a quest to discover some information about his long-

missing father. Second, Odysseus leaves Calypso's island, completes the
rest of his adventurous journey, and tells of his earlier adventures in the
form of a flashback while at the Phaeacian court. Third, Odysseus and
Telemachus complete their individual journeys to Ithaca and open the way
for the solution of their domestic problems. The very structure of the
Odyssey stresses the fact that Odysseus wanted to go home and that he was
wanted at home. The content is a skillfully maintained balance between the
trials and tribulations of a family—on the one hand—and, on the other, the
marvelous adventures of the protagonist.

It is obvious, however, that when ancient journey tales and poems
become stories for children to hear and read, they have to be remodeled
and remolded to suit their audience, to make them immediately attractive
to the young reader. I shall now try to show how this kind of remodeling
has been successfully accomplished by presenting portions from three epic
poems which have been transformed into noteworthy children's books.

First, a selection from the ninth book of the *Odyssey* (translated from the
French of Victor Bérard), an episode that has been referred to more than
once in the course of this institute: Odysseus and his men in the cave of the
Cyclops. It tells how Odysseus blinded Polyphemus and vividly demonstrates Homer's power in presenting realistic details.

> I spoke, but without pity he answered me: "Very well! I
> shall eat No-man last of all—after his friends. They will
> come first; that's the present I'm giving you, my guest."
>
> Then he turned around and lay on his back. Soon we
> saw him turn his enormous neck; and sleep, the invincible
> conqueror, came over him. But from his throat he threw up
> wine and human flesh, and he belched, the drunkard.
>
> I seized the pointed stake, which I had heated beneath
> the ash heap, and spoke to my men, encouraging them.
> What if one of them, seized by fear, had abandoned me?
>
> When the olive stake was about to burst into flame—as
> green as it still was, one could already see a terrifying
> glow—I drew it from the fire and carried it as I ran. My
> men huddled around me, and a god inspired them with
> sudden audacity. They raised the stake and stuck its point
> into the corner of his eye. From above I pressed and turned
> it. You have doubtless seen a drill pierce the timber of a
> ship. . . . Thus in his eye we held and turned our fiery
> point, and his eye bubbled around the burning. Eyelid and
> eyebrow were mere vapors surrounding the flaming eye-
> ball. . . . When a master metalworker plunges a great axe
> or an adze into a basin of cold water to temper the metal,

the iron hisses and cries. Thus in his eye our olive staff whistled and cried.

This is how Alfred Church condensed the passage in *Stories from Homer:* The language is simple, the movement of the sentences is swift, and the reteller has retained enough of the concreteness of the original to make his retelling feel like Homer, although one is inclined to believe that Church was cleaning up the passage to make it suitable for young readers.

> And he said, "My gift shall be that I will eat thee last of all thy company."
> And as he spoke he fell back in a drunken sleep. Then Ulysses bade his comrades be of good courage, for the time was come when they should be delivered. And they thrust the stake of olive wood into the fire till it was ready, green as it was, to burst into flame and they thrust it into the monster's eye; for he had but one eye, and that in the midst of his forehead, with the eyebrow below it. And Ulysses leaned with all his force upon the stake, and thrust it in with might and main. And the burning wood hissed in the eye, just as red-hot iron hisses in the water when a man seeks to temper steel for a sword.

I have already referred to an epic that is older than the *Odyssey*—the Mesopotamian story *Gilgamesh,* which tells of the journey of the semidivine hero engaged in a quest to find immortality. I shall first quote from Bernarda Bryson's retelling. Gilgamesh has finally found his ancestor Utnapishtim, the prototype of Noah in the book of Genesis, and a rare kind of man—one who has attained immortality.

> Listen to me, O Utnapishtim! I had a friend dearer to me than a brother. Day and night we went together; together we roamed over the wild steppes and through the forests, hunting and wrestling with wild animals. Together we demolished the monster Humbaba that daily threatened our city; together we killed the Bull of Heaven that had been sent against us to destroy us. Everywhere we walked together, sharing all dangers and delights. Then death came to Enkidu: the fate of mortal men overtook him!

When one examines a translation of the original poem as it was found on damaged clay tables and supplemented with bits and pieces from various sources, one realizes how a modern reteller must be genuinely creative to

make the ancient narrative not only understandable but acceptable to the
modern reader, especially to the young reader.

> . . .
> . . . "animal
> . . . not like
> . . . before me
> . . . [one who] roams the steppe,
> [chased] the panther of the steppe,
> . . . *etc.*
> we climbed the mountain,
> captured the Bull of Heaven and killed him,
> [brought Humbaba to grief], who lives in the cedar forest;
> [entering the mountain gates we slew] lions;
> [my friend whom I love dearly underwent with me all hardships.]"

The third selection I have chosen is from *Beowulf*; the translator Kevin
Crossley-Holland, who made a complete translation of the Anglo-Saxon
epic, also prepared a retelling for young readers in a striking format with
powerful illustrations by Charles Keeping. *Beowulf* is a quest poem: the
hero-protagonist makes his journey to rid the Danish king's hall of the
murderous incursions of the monster Grendel. One of the episodes from
the original poem described Beowulf's sea voyage to Denmark.

> Foaming at the prow and most like a sea-bird,
> the boat sped over the waves, urged on by the wind;
> until next day, at about the expected time,
> so far had the curved prow come
> that the travelers sighted land,
> shining cliffs, steep hills,
> broad headlands. So did they cross the sea;
> their journey was at an end. Then the Geats
> disembarked, lost no time in tying up
> the boat—their corselets clanked;
> the warriors gave thanks to God
> for their safe passage over the sea.

The retelling has not only been reduced in length, but the material has
been compressed—as in Alfred Church's retelling of Homer—and aims at
a powerful simplicity.

> The great sea-bird rode over the breakers. And as soon
> as the Geats hoisted a sail, a bleached sea-garment, the

boat foamed at the prow and surged over the waves, urged
on by the wind.

After that day and the night that darkened it, the
warriors sighted shining cliffs, steep headlands—the
shores of Denmark.

I am sure that from time to time some of you will reread Cavafy's
"Ithaka" to see how it fits into what you have been reading. I am still
astonished at the last line: "You will understand by then the meaning of
Ithakas." The plural *Ithakas* can be puzzling or even confusing in its
context. But for us who are interested in reading and literature, the
meaning should be clear enough. Each work of literature we explore is
another Ithaka. Some Ithakas are unprepossessing, and others we come
upon the first time with pleasure and joy.

The Life Journey

JOHN ROWE TOWNSEND

"Old and young, we are all on our last cruise." My quotation comes from Robert Louis Stevenson's *Virginibus Puerisque*—a work that has given us many splendid quotations, including one that is better known than mine: "To travel hopefully is a better thing than to arrive."

There are, I think, two principal emblems of life. One of these is the river. We emerge from the womb as spring from hillside; we tumble swiftly and briskly through the foothills of youth; we expand and slow down into our graver middle age; and eventually we run out through the sands of time to the universal destination. The poet Algernon Charles Swinburne saw this final analogy as a comforting one:

> From too much love of living,
> From hope and fear set free,
> We thank with brief thanksgiving
> Whatever gods may be
> That no man lives for ever,
> That dead men rise up never;
> That even the weariest river
> Winds somewhere safe to sea.

The river as a representation of the pattern of life has occurred from time to time in books on the children's list; for instance, Ernest Thompson Seton, back in 1904, telling the life story of a bear, paralleled its course with the course of a river, using chapter heads such as "The Freshet," "Roaring in the Canyon," "The Ford," "The Deepening Torrent," "The Cataract," and so on. And there is an interesting small touch in Philippa Pearce's *Tom's Midnight Garden*, when Tom is looking out from the walled garden which, as the writer said, represents the sheltered security of early childhood, at the extensive and tempting landscape of adult life beyond. The chapter in which this incident occurs is headed "The River to the Sea." Certainly a river is prominent in this landscape, but why to the sea, since the sea plays no part in *Tom's Midnight Garden?* I can tell you—and I am not speculating—that the answer lies precisely in Philippa Pearce's awareness of the river as emblem of life. To the sea is where the river goes.

If time allowed, the analogy could be pursued further. It is, for instance, a commonplace observation that some of the force of *Huckleberry Finn* comes from the identification of the river with the course of human life.

The other great emblem of life is the journey. Unless our life comes to an untimely end, it can obviously be likened to a long journey, embarked upon with hope and having its ups and downs, its joys and sorrows, its successes and failures, its times of exhilaration, and its times of despair. And however great or however insignificant we are, the conclusion of the journey is the same.

> And all that beauty, all that wealth e'er gave,
> Awaits alike th'inevitable hour:
> The paths of glory lead but to the grave.

So wrote Thomas Gray in the famous *Elegy.* To speak of the life journey is to speak also of death, for without death the phrase would have no meaning. And to contemplate death is never pleasant or easy. "Ni le soleil ni la mort," said La Rochefoucauld, "ne se peut regarder fixement." We cannot look steadily at the sun or at death.

I have often said, and have put in writing, that serious fiction—whatever its genre, whatever its period, whatever its ambience—is concerned in the end with the human heart, human relationships, the human predicament. The human predicament essentially is that of being mortal, of being in a world in which life, health, and happiness are all precarious. Naturally, we hope that our children's lives will be joyful, but we know that they are in the human predicament from the moment they are born. They may be confronted at any time by life itself, with mortality, suffering, disease, or dreadful accident.

Fortunately, in our advanced societies, a great many children do not experience the worst possibilities. They arrive in late childhood, in adolescence, at the stage at which one asks the difficult questions: Who am I? What am I here for? What do I have it in me to be and to do? They face Plato's question: How then should a person live? And I will rephrase and thereby slightly change it for my present purpose. What shape do I wish my life to take? Where is *my* life journey to lead me?

I do not think it is the task of writers for young people to tell their readers what to do with their lives. But there are some subjects that are of great and special interest to young people and that can be explored through fiction, and this is one of them. If you have a life journey to make, you not only want to consider the possibilities, you need to get a sense of what a lifetime *is*, of the size and scale of the landscape on which you are entering.

In her Library of Congress lecture "The Lords of Time" in 1978, Jill Paton Walsh observed that "change and time are the true ecology of the human soul. We are immersed in them utterly, and they sweep us toward our projected end. Like an author at the beginning of a book, we know what the projected end will be; like his, our task is to find a trajectory which will make sense of the end by finding the action of which that end is the appropriate conclusion." We want, in fact, to find a meaningful and satisfying pattern for our lives—and not only our outward lives but also our inward or, if you like, our spiritual lives.

And Penelope Lively wrote:

> Children need to sense that we live in a permanent world that reaches away, behind and ahead of us, and that the span of a lifetime is something to be wondered at, and thought about, and that—above all—people evolve during their own lives. People are never complete, as it were, but knowledge expands and contracts, opinions harden and soften, and people end up as a curious, irrational blend of experience and memory. Children have to be told about these things because they haven't had time to see how life works on them, or to see how it works on other people. They haven't yet seen the process, as we have seen it on the faces of friends and relatives. They can't yet place themselves in a wider framework of time and space than *today* and *here*. But they have to, if they are not to grow up enclosed in their own personalities.

The sense of life as a journey through time, of the completed life as a pattern in time, and of the way people change with the passage of time, is very evident in Penelope Lively's own novels. It's her main preoccupation, I think, in her adult fiction as well as in her children's books. Probably her best-known children's book is *The Ghost of Thomas Kempe*, of which the young hero is a boy called James Harrison. I find the time perspective particularly intriguing in James's relationship with Arnold, the boy who stayed in his house a hundred years before.

Arnold, of course, has long been dead, but James has read about him in an old diary and feels that he is a kindred spirit. He'd have liked to go fishing and rambling the countryside with Arnold. He thinks of Arnold as he was described in the diary, a boy of his own age. Then toward the end of the book he finds a portrait of Arnold as the benefactor of the local school. "The bewhiskered face of an elderly man looked out at him: waterfalls of hair threatened to engulf his features, moustache, sideburns, beard, flowing down to a high cravat, stopping short of the watch-chain stretched across a substantial stomach." He looks "for all the world like a benevolent walrus." James muses upon him. "Mister Arnold Luckett. A person with a gold watch-chain, giving money and things to schools. An important man. A serious man. James Harrison. Mister James Harrison." And James finds that old Mrs. Verity remembers Arnold as "an old gentleman who used to come down from London every year. Very fond of Ledsham he was—he used to spend his holidays here as a boy, I think."

On two or three such occasions, Penelope Lively has children becoming conscious of their own futures, contemplating the strange prospect of themselves changing, becoming adult, growing old—contemplating, in fact, the life journey on which they are setting out. Maria, in *A Stitch in Time*, ponders the thought of "mysterious and interesting future Marias, larger and older, doing things one could barely picture." And Clare, in *The House in Norham Gardens*, a girl of fourteen living with two aged aunts, also tries to project herself forward in time to meet the unknown future woman with her own name and face; but "she walked away, the woman, a stranger, familiar and yet unreachable. The only thing you could know about her for certain was that all this would be part of her: this room, this conversation, the aunts."

The sense of continuity through time of people, families, crafts, is an outstanding feature, too, of Alan Garner's Stone Book quartet—perhaps *the* outstanding feature and what the quartet is all about. The place is a village, solid and stable in contrast to the flow of human life that goes on in it. And the way time is dealt with is extremely ingenious. These four short books deal with the events of only one day each, a total of four days, yet they span five generations, as persons who are young in one book reappear, older, in another.

There is a specific reference in the Stone Book quartet to the life journey, and that is the title of the third book of the quartet, *The Aimer Gate*. It is a title that has baffled many people. It means, I believe, in the dialect of its corner of England, "the more direct way"; and the key character in this book is Uncle Charlie, a World War I soldier, who does not appear again in the quartet. The irresistible implication is that he has taken the aimer gate, the shorter route, to the end of the human journey.

Time awareness can often be felt as a vibration, as something in the air of a book. Such vibrations are strong, for instance, in Virginia Hamilton's *M. C. Higgins, the Great*. The Higgins family lives on Sarah's Mountain, named for Great-grandmother Sarah who came there more than a century before, an escaping slave with her baby in her arms. The main event of the story is M.C.'s realization, after illusory imaginings of escape, that he belongs to the mountain and the mountain to him, and his setting to work to build a wall to stop the spoil-bank that threatens it.

Time is fluid in this novel; sometimes M.C. and his father Jones can feel that Sarah is still there on the mountain.

> Times, in the heat of the day. When you are not thinking much on nothing. When you are resting quiet. Trees, dusty-still. You can hear Sarah a-laboring up the mountain, the baby, whimpering. . . . She climbs eternal. Just to remind us that she hold claim to me and to you and each one of us on her mountain.

Earlier, M.C., gazing out in a trance, has "sensed Sarah moving through undergrowth up the mountainside. As if past were present. As if he were a ghost, waiting, and she, the living." And earlier still, M.C. has "pretended" to be in the future:

> Mama and Daddy in the ground. . . . The kids, grown old, too, and died. I lived longer than each of them. I'm old now but I can still get around. Never did leave the mountain. None of the others did, either. But buried here. Ghosts. Just like Great-grandmother Sarah and the other old ones who really did pass away long ago.

Although the outward and visible events of *M. C. Higgins, the Great* take place within quite a brief period, it holds within it the life journeys not only of M.C. but also of his forebears—life journeys that are completed in one place and are none the worse for that.

A novel of which the life journey, seen in journey terms, is the specific subject is *What About Tomorrow*, by the Australian writer Ivan Southall. It is not as well known as, in my view, it deserves to be, so perhaps I should say something about it for the benefit of those to whom it may not be familiar. It is about a boy called Sam, and, intermittently, it is about a man called Sam—the same Sam.

In the year 1931 the young Sam, aged fourteen, collides with a streetcar while he is on his bicycle, delivering newspapers. The bike is smashed up, and that is a disaster; no bike means no job, and times are hard. The prospects are so horrifying that Sam runs away from home.

The main bulk of the book tells of Sam's journeyings, over an area not very large and not very far from Melbourne, during the next few days. He suffers various hardships and discomforts; he gets help from a young married woman, from a farmer in a beat-up truck, from a girl minding a country store. He falls in love, in quick succession, with three different girls—Rose, the young married woman who gives him breakfast; Sally, the daughter of the farmer; and Mary, who is the girl in the country store. At the end he's still on the road. But interspersed with this account, and crucial to the novel, are brief forward flashes to World War II, with Sam, a flying-boat captain on his last mission, in which he gets killed.

The journey of the young Sam, obviously, is a journey into adult life. During one of the forward flashes Sam, the pilot, looks back on Sam, aged fourteen, and thinks: "So then you were a boy with a man's job to do. Growing up if you're a boy is a man's job at any time. But dying's the job for now, and that's just got to be the job for a full-grown man." So we don't only see young Sam in a microcosm of growing up; we see what he is growing up *toward*, and what he is growing up toward is death in war. There's an ingenious confluence of the book's two streams at the end, when it becomes clear that Mary in the store, the last of the three girls encountered by young Sam, is the one the mature Sam has gone back to and married. His last words, as he's dying in the seaplane, are to her: "Oh, Mary," Sam cried, "I have to leave you behind"; and, "Oh Mary," Sam cried, "till I die."

In reading *What About Tomorrow*, it is hard to escape a sense of the futility of growing up to be killed, as thousands of young men grew up to be killed in World War II. Yet, as I said in my essay on Ivan Southall in *A Sounding of Storytellers*, it would be wrong to see this as a testament of despair. Sam's is a sadly shortened life journey, and his death is part of the enormous tragedy of a generation, and yet we know that Sam has lived and loved and (as the forward flashes tell us) has married the girl who mattered and has begotten a child. It is an achieved journey, short as it is.

Actually, to present the whole of a person's life journey, if it's a full life span from cradle to grave, is not an easy thing for a novel to do; it has difficulty, within present conventions, in covering that amount of ground. Nor does a full life span often offer a *shape* that will have fictional impact. But, as in the Southall book just mentioned, there are ways in which concentration can be achieved and much implied in little.

Consider the situation where a life journey, or the journey together of two or a few people, is going to be short and is *known* to be going to be short. Isn't it possible that there will be a condensation into a brief time of what would normally be the slow development of a relationship? Does this not indeed happen quite often in life—in wartime, for instance, or in any of a number of sets of circumstances where people are thrown together temporarily?

I have always been fascinated by the relationship—usually a love relationship—which has only a little time in which to flower but which does its best to flower nonetheless. I have attempted to deal with this in more than one of my own books—especially in *The Summer People*, which is about a teenage boy and girl who play a game of house together in a cottage on a crumbling cliff, in the summer of 1939. Nothing can last, and they know it; the summer will end, the cottage will go down the cliff, and in a few days or weeks Britain will be at war with Hitler's Germany. They are never going to see each other again. But in the little time they have, their relationship does flower. It is, I should add, an innocent relationship. This is a story about love, not about teenage sex; and in 1939 young people could be and often were sexually innocent.

Incidentally, *The Summer People* ends with a chapter telling you what became of the characters afterward. This is an old-fashioned device but one which as an author I rather like, perhaps because I like it as a reader. If fictional characters have achieved reality for me, I want to know what happened to them *after* the last page. I think the interest we take in fictional people, provided they've convinced us, is very similar to the interest we take in actual people we know; and there is a full and natural curiosity about "what became of So-and-so?" which we all express repeatedly in our lives but which modern fiction tends not to provide for.

I don't think it was mere adherence to a formula that caused so many of the old fairy tales to end with "and they lived happily ever after." It was a proper sense of audience; the hearer wanted to know. You could even say it was a proper sense of story; the story was not complete without it. I, for one, have always been delighted to know that when the woodcutter's son married the princess, or the prince married the goose-girl, they duly inherited the kingdom, ruled well and wisely, lived long and happily together, and had sons and daughters. In terms of the metaphor we've been using, the life journey was joyful; the river ran a pleasant, long, and tranquil course to an acceptably distant sea. What more could one wish than that?

Let me now look at a fictional variation on the theme of the life journey that I find particularly interesting. I have spoken of the river as an emblem of life, and I quoted the Swinburne poem which says that even the weariest river winds somewhere safe to sea. But what if it didn't? What if there were a river that went on flowing without cease and never got to sea at all? The last two books I wish to discuss, Natalie Babbitt's *Tuck Everlasting* and Ursula Le Guin's *The Farthest Shore*, are concerned with immortality in the sense of the indefinite prolongation of life on this earth: What would it imply, and if it were possible, would it be worth having? What would it mean if, instead of being on what Stevenson called your last cruise, you could cruise forever on that endless river?

Actually, immortality in this sense does not usually get a good press. Nobody suggests that the Wandering Jew was—or is—a happy man. Ghosts are generally shown as longing to be put at rest. The most powerful fictional portrayal of such immortality that I can bring to mind is that of the Struldbruggs in "A Voyage to Laputa," part of Swift's *Gulliver's Travels*. Gulliver, on hearing about them, thinks at first how wonderful it would be to live forever, acquiring learning and wisdom. But then he finds out what it is actually like. The Struldbruggs, when they grow old,

> had not only all the follies and infirmities of other old men, but many more which arose from the dreadful prospect of never dying. They were not only opinionative, peevish, covetous, morose, vain, talkative, but uncapable of friendship, and dead to all natural affection, which never descended below their grandchildren. Envy and impotent desires are their prevailing passions.

That is only part of the plight of the Struldbruggs. No wonder that whenever they see a funeral, they lament and repine that others are gone to a harbor of rest to which they themselves can never hope to arrive.

Tuck Everlasting offers a less gruesome and, indeed, a more logical portrayal of immortality, although its verdict is the same as Swift's. Immortality does not necessarily imply getting older and older and older. In *Tuck Everlasting* it comes from drinking at a certain tiny spring, and it means remaining forever at the point in life that one has then reached. The Tucks, a memorable family, "plain as salt," have done just that. Should the young protagonist Winnie do the same?

It is as pointless to argue that immortality is not possible as it would be to argue that there is no such thing as a flying horse. We may note, however, that *Tuck Everlasting* is at the naturalistic end of fantasy; that is, it's the kind of fantasy that makes just one change in the natural order of things and allows everything else to follow naturally from that, in contrast to the kind of fantasy like that of Tolkien or Le Guin, which creates a world of its own and is full of constant invention.

The story is simply told; this really *is* a book for children, but the theme is a large one. If immortality were to become possible, it would present enormous, probably insuperable moral and practical problems for society. And would it be a good thing for the individual? Mr. Tuck puts to Winnie, as clearly as it can be put, the case against it. Here as a reminder is a small part of his exposition. They are in a little boat, and Tuck has told her how the water they are on flows down to the ocean, is sucked up to form clouds, then falls as rain, and the process continues.

> It's a wheel, Winnie. Everything's a wheel, turning and turning, never stopping. The frogs is part of it, and the bugs, and the fish, and the wood thrush, too. And people.

But never the same ones. Always coming in new, always
growing and changing, and always moving on. That's the
way it's supposed to be. That's the way it *is* . . . Being part
of the whole thing, that's the blessing. But it's passing us
by, us Tucks. Living's heavy work, but off to one side, the
way *we* are, it's useless, too. It don't make sense. If I
knowed how to climb back on the wheel, I'd do it in a
minute. So you can't call it living, what we got. We just *are*,
we just *be*, like rocks beside the road.

Winnie, as we know, has the option of remaining forever at any age she
likes, and, indeed, the eternally young Jesse Tuck wants her to wait until
she's the right age for him and then make herself immortal. But Winnie
never does drink the spring water, and when the Tucks come back many
years later, they find that she has died in the ordinary way. Mr. Tuck says,
approvingly, " 'Good girl.' " There's no doubt that this course has the
author's approval, and when we've read the book, it has ours. The
arguments against indefinite prolongation of the individual life are overwhelming from the point of view of society and, indeed, of the creation at
large. And yet and yet, it is often possible for individuals to benefit from
something that does not benefit society as a whole; and although the
message is so clear, can we be sure it would really be easy to make this
choice if we had the option? If we were promised that, unlike the
Struldbruggs, we could keep ourselves alive, active, healthy, in full
possession of our wits and our senses forever and ever, can we as
individuals be sure we would not be tempted?

It is possible to feel that the right answer is made just a little too easy in
Tuck Everlasting. It is also possible, however, to say that ultimately the
argument of this book is one of reconciliation with our own mortality; there
is comfort to be drawn from it. And *Tuck Everlasting* has an underlying
quietness and dignity about it that comes from its cool, controlled, and
beautifully limpid writing.

In Ursula Le Guin's *The Farthest Shore* the achievement of immortality by
one immensely clever, evil man is presented as the most spectacular
manifestation of something wider than itself: a disastrous derangement of
the natural order of things—of the great Equilibrium with which it is
perilous to tamper. The result is the loss of wisdom, of wizardry, of ancient
skill and craft and husbandry, of belief, of the will to live and act. It is in
fact de-Creation; an embodiment of the author's theme that "death is the
price we pay for our life, and for all life."

For the individual, Cob, the defeat of death means the loss of all that has
value in life. His condition is that of a Struldbrugg, or worse. When the
hero Ged forces him to appear in the flesh, he lifts up his face and "there

was no comeliness left in it, only ruin, old age that had outlived old age. The mouth was withered, the sockets of the eyes were empty and had long been empty." By his action Cob had opened "a door that had been shut from the beginning of time." We are shown the door as a physical thing that Ged closes by a great act of power; and to Cob he says, "I would give you life if I could, Cob. But I cannot. . . . But I can give you death."

Coming from Earthsea to our own world, we do not need to think for long in order to perceive that we have more immediate routes to disaster than the indefinite extension of human life. The knowledge of how to bomb or pollute humanity into extinction has been released upon us. There are those who, for the present, control it, and we hope desperately that they will not let it loose on the world. Before the bomb there were dark places enough, ranging back from Auschwitz and Buchenwald through countless cruelties of battlefield and jail and torture chamber; but never before did the ultimate darkness gape so wide as it does now. So *The Farthest Shore*, and indeed the whole Earthsea saga, is engaged with the human predicament as deeply as fiction can be, although it speaks in the language of myth and symbol.

It should be no surprise to find children's books that are fully engaged in this way. The most profound themes can be explored by way of story, and modes of telling that are accessible to the young mind can have infinite resonances.

I have spoken at other times about the hero journey; I am speaking now about the life journey. It must have occurred to you, as it soon did to me, that these are vastly overlapping categories. The life journey *is* a hero journey. Although we may not feel very heroic, we are all embarked on the heroic quest, to live lives that have meaning for ourselves and for others. We are on our individual Odysseys, our personal roads of trials. We have had our adventures, and we shall have more, but we shall come to Ithaca at last. We know where Ithaca is. We know what Ithaca means. But although we cannot forget what Stevenson expressed so pithily—we are indeed on our last cruise—we can remember, too, the key words of the Cavafy poem: Ithaka has given us our lovely journey.

Fantasy and the Classic Hero

NATALIE BABBITT

I thought I might take advantage of this opportunity to register a complaint about, and also to celebrate, a certain common inheritance of ours—yours and mine. Did you realize that all of us writers and readers of fantasy are in a trap and have always been in a trap—and that there's no escape? I didn't realize it myself until a few years ago. Oh, there were hints. For instance, I often wondered why it seemed so essential to take the young heroes of my stories away from their bed and board and send them out alone into the world to have their adventures. It was very hard, and *is* very hard, to keep on inventing reasonable excuses for separating them from their parents. You can't go on forever making orphans of them—it's tiresome, and it doesn't always make sense. But beyond grumbling over this single problem, I didn't recognize the trap for what it was until one day in 1972.

I had been working for nearly a year on a story which refused to be good. It was about a group of people staying at a lakeside summer hotel, whose lives were all stalled in one way or another. They had lost their dreams and hopes and were not enjoying themselves very much. Each one had the physical characteristics of a different animal and a name to match (Eunice Woolsey Merino, for instance, was a woman who was a lot like a sheep), but each had forgotten how to accept and enjoy life on the simple, innocent level of young animals or, if you will, children. In the course of the story, each was turned into the animal he most resembled and was carried off by a character called the Animal Man—who himself had turned into a stork— to a small, abandoned island just offshore from the hotel. Here, when they were all assembled, they remembered their childhood and their dreams and were refreshed into a happier, more hopeful view of the future.

I couldn't make the story work, but it seemed, nevertheless, to be such a good idea—the whole notion of rebirth by means of a stork and a magic island set apart from the world where one could recapture one's innocence and joy and then come back to the real world restored to one's physical self but refreshed and renewed. It seemed like a very original idea, and I had solved the separation problem for its child hero by giving her a trip to the hotel with an aunt who was keeping her while her mother had a new baby. Birth again! The fact that the story was ultimately a failure is beside the point here. The key thing is the excitement I felt over its ingredients: the magic island, the stork who carried people there, the whole idea of renewal and return.

During the same period I had been reading Roald Dahl's *James and the Giant Peach*, urged on me by one of my children. It was a splendid story, I thought, but there was something the matter with the way it ended. I couldn't figure out exactly what bothered me though, and since I was working on my own troublesome story, I forgot about *James*.

Then, on a fateful day in 1972, a student of mine gave me a book she had been reading in a philosophy class. It was called *Hero with a Thousand Faces*, and its author was a man named Joseph Campbell. My student was very excited about the book, and spurred by her excitement, I sat down and began to flip through its pages. As I did so, my eye lit on a few lines at the end of the first chapter:

> This first stage of the mythological journey—which we have designated the "call to adventure"—signifies that destiny has summoned the hero and transferred his spiritual center of gravity from within the pale of his society to a zone unknown. This fateful region of both treasure and danger may be variously represented: as a distant land, a forest, a kingdom underground, beneath the waves, or above the sky, a secret island, lofty mountaintop, or profound dream state.

I was dumbfounded. What had I done? Had I somehow forgotten a story I had once read that had a secret island in it exactly like mine? An unknown zone to which a character was summoned? Was I an unwitting plagiarist? So I began to read the book in earnest, and that is how I discovered, to my delight and annoyance, the trap I mentioned a moment ago.

There's no point in trying to explain in any detail what *Hero with a Thousand Faces* has to say. It is a dense, scholarly work which has finally more to do with religion, and particularly Buddhism, than it does with the writing of fantasy. There are large portions which *I*, at least, had great difficulty in following. And it never even mentions children's literature except for the classic fairy tales. But the gist is simple enough, and that I will try to outline for you so that you will see the trap and be sympathetic.

Hero with a Thousand Faces shows that the fantasy hero and his adventures are universal to all cultures,* and the ancient path he follows, although it leaves room for certain variations of detail, is mainly unalterable and inescapable. In Campbell's own words: "The standard path of the mythological adventure of the hero is . . . separation—initiation—return." Once you understand the pattern, you see it everywhere in fairy tales, folktales, and children's fantasy literature, as well as in classical myth. As I trace it for you, I'll use for examples *Peter Pan*, *The Wizard of Oz* (Baum's version, not Hollywood's), and *Alice's Adventures in Wonderland*. This will help in seeing how the pattern emerges.

The hero's story begins with a call to adventure, usually from a character of some sort which Campbell calls the herald. The herald can be ugly or beautiful, frightening or attractive or curious, but whatever form he takes, he summons the hero to cross a threshold—from the real world into mystery, from life into death, from the waking state into dream. For Campbell these are all one and the same threshold.

For Alice the herald is the White Rabbit, and she leaves her sister's side to follow him down the rabbit hole. For Wendy and Michael and John, Peter Pan is the herald. For Dorothy the herald takes the nonhuman form of a cyclone.

"Once having crossed the threshold," says Campbell, "the hero moves in a dream landscape where he must survive a succession of trials." But he will be assisted by some kind of protective figure who will give him charms to help him in his struggles.

For Alice there are a number of protective figures, but the Caterpillar is the most obvious—he gives her the hint about the sides of the mushroom which will eventually make it possible for her to get through the tiny door into the beautiful garden. For Wendy and her brothers, Peter Pan, in addition to being the herald, is the protector. For Dorothy it is the Good Witch of the North who starts her on her way and provides the charm, the mark of a kiss on her forehead. And Dorothy has beside her throughout the story the very protective Scarecrow, Tin Woodman, and Cowardly Lion.

If it weren't for these protective figures or devices, which Campbell calls symbols of "the benign, protecting power of destiny," the hero would never be able to survive the trials of his or her adventures to come. And although in every story the trials are different, they all represent, according to Campbell, a coming face-to-face with the confusions, terrors, and pains hidden in our subconscious mind that stand between us and the achievement of spiritual perfection.

This concept can best be described, where children's literature is concerned, as the lesson the hero must learn before he can become an adult. That lesson takes many forms. In *Alice's Adventures in Wonderland* it is very difficult to see clearly at all; for although Alice's adventures are full of trials, there is no overt lesson beyond that of the exposure of the adult world as one full of foolishness, inanity, and strident egotism. But for Wendy and her brothers the lesson *is* clear: When the time comes to grow up, it's best to do it and leave childhood behind. And for Dorothy the lesson is equally clear, although Hollywood and Baum spell it out differently: We can control our own destiny if we want to. As Russell MacFall says in *To Please a Child,* his biography of Baum, "What we want, [Baum] the moralist whispers, is within us; we need only to look for it to find it. What we strive for has been ours all the time."

Having survived the trials and learned the lesson, the hero is then free to return to the real world or the waking state or life—however you wish to define it—to recross the threshold, bringing with him his new knowledge. In classical myth this knowledge, what the hero has learned in that other place, may be used to enlighten the world. But sometimes the knowledge, or "boon" as Campbell calls it, is too difficult or too bizarre to be understood by ordinary people. "How [can the hero] communicate," he says, "to people who insist on the exclusive evidence of their senses, the message of the all-generating void? Why attempt to make plausible, or even interesting, to men and women consumed with passion, the experience of transcendental bliss?"

On her return Dorothy makes no attempt to explain Oz to Auntie Em, and even in Hollywood's version, although she does try, the people around her don't believe her, and she soon gives up the effort. Wendy and Michael and John are likewise silent, although their mother, Mrs. Darling, would have understood Never-Never-Land very well indeed. Alice, on the other hand, gets around the problem quite easily: She calls her adventures a dream, and as we all know, anything can happen in dreams. Tolkien has said that *Alice in Wonderland* is not a true fantasy since it dismisses the adventures in this way. He claims that in true fantasy the world across the threshold is as real on its own level as the everyday world we inhabit and continually coexists with it. But Campbell would say, I think, that it doesn't matter that Alice calls her adventures a dream; for him dreams, myth, and fantasy are all the same world, all using the same symbols for the same ends.

Where does this pattern of the classic hero's path leave the writer of fantasy? Once Campbell had laid it out for me, I could understand why I was trapped into separating my child heroes from their parents. I was following a route laid down thousands of years ago. It was strong in my subconscious, even though I didn't know it. Adventure means exposure, danger, and growth, and there can be very little of these if parents are around. They have to be done away with, kept out of sight, left behind, if anything interesting is going to happen. They belong to one reality, while the adventure belongs to another. And on top of that they are symbols of overprotection and can retard development. The hero cannot grow if he or she is shielded from the very elements that create growth. So acceptance of the call to adventure represents the great rite of separation, the cutting of the apron strings.

One does not have to cross the threshold into adventure and danger all alone. Hansel and Gretel have each other. In *Charlie and the Chocolate Factory* Charlie Bucket takes along his grandfather. Sometimes, as in *The Wizard of Oz*, the hero will take an animal along. But the hero never takes a parent along. The apron strings, which are a symbol of the umbilical cord, are severed forever when the call to adventure is answered.

After this, the hero's path is clear. He has his trials, survives them, receives his "boon" or learns his lesson, and then returns to the real world. And seeing this final step, I knew at once why the ending of *James and the Giant Peach* was disturbing to me: James goes to a magic world, crosses his threshold, and stays there rather than returning. This ending is a violation of the pattern—a remaining in the dream state, the death state, a rejection of the notion of rebirth. In myth, in dream, in fantasy, if you are the hero, you must go home again. In every case home, though safer, is less attractive than the other world. Kansas, compared to Oz, is a wasteland. London, compared to Never-Never-Land, is dull. And sitting under a tree with your sister is far less exciting than being in Wonderland. Nevertheless, if you are the hero, home is where you have to go.

Campbell would say that all of us know the pattern well without having to be taught. We were born with a subconscious understanding of it, and everything that happens in our lives reinforces it. But for most of us, certainly for me, it remains subconscious until it is somehow exposed. I've told you that *Hero with a Thousand Faces* is a dense, scholarly work. I can't keep much of its wealth of detail in my head for long at a time. I read it first in 1972 and then again last year. In between I wrote several stories, including one called *Tuck Everlasting*. Imagine my chagrin on coming across the following passage during my most recent reading, one I must have read in the chapter dealing with that first step, the call to adventure: "Typical of the circumstances of the call are the dark forest, the great tree, the babbling spring, and the loathly, underestimated appearance of the carrier of the power of destiny."

Some of you may have read *Tuck Everlasting*. If so, you will recall my own dark forest, great tree, babbling spring, and loathly carrier, or herald, Winnie Foster's toad. I had a letter from a child recently asking me why I put a toad into the story. How can I give a simple answer? The toad is there because my subconscious told me I had to supply my hero with a herald? But that is the only true answer.

It is annoying in the extreme to find that one's work, struggled with for so long and finally finished after trying and discarding numberless bits of detail, can be found to have been summed up—parts of it, anyway—by a scholar years before one even began, and described as "typical." I knew my ash tree and spring were ancient symbols of immortality, and I used them for that very reason; but I didn't know, consciously, that for this story they were representing any kind of threshold. And I certainly didn't like to think of them as preordained and typical. I didn't and don't like to think that I have so little freedom of choice, that the pattern with all of its elements laid out is so deeply instilled in me that it leads me without my knowing I am being led.

Still, we have to come to the conclusion that all fantasy stories are fundamentally alike. Their patterns are immutable, and as writers we must follow them willy-nilly or suffer the consequences of a plot line gone askew. It is annoying, but it is miraculous, too. We are trapped, but it is a kind of confinement that joins us together in a brotherhood, writers and readers alike—here, everywhere, and on back to our shared prehistoric ancestors. For the questions have never changed, and the answers are always the same.

The common questions, put simply, seem to be: Who am I? How did I get here? What is the meaning of life? Can I make my way through it alone? Must death be the final end? We all begin, after all, in the same way: We are protected by our parents for a time, and then we are thrust out into the world without them. Sometimes, there are happy ceremonies to mark this thrusting out—ceremonies like Bar Mitzvahs or graduations. Sometimes the event is unceremonious and harsh. But it must take place if we are to grow. Still, the world is dangerous for all, and most of us are afraid as we head out into it alone. We wonder if we are strong enough. But we face our trials as bravely as we can, and most of us, fortunately, can say to ourselves, as the theme song of the old Mary Tyler Moore show says to *its* hero (for TV shows are no more exempt from the pattern than other fiction): "You're going to make it after all." We all must follow the mythic hero's path, and his experiences have for centuries served as a guide for us, whether we realize it or not.

Throughout the struggle, however, no matter how successful we are, we still fear the ultimate separation, death. In myths and fairy tales the heroes seldom die a literal death within the bounds of the story. But their happy endings are not denials of death. The happy ending, says Campbell, is "to be read, not as a contradiction, but as a transcendence of the universal tragedy of man." In myth and fairy tale, death is dealt with symbolically. Snow White and Sleeping Beauty are both awakened from their long sleeps—in fact, resurrected—by the kiss of a prince and are carried off to the typical fairy-tale heaven of a castle, where it is possible to live happily ever after. This was, for me, a new way to understand "happily ever after": It means, simply, going to a well-deserved heaven after death. The prevailing pattern, then, is not so very different from that of the story of Jesus Christ and his own trials, death, and resurrection. In much of children's literature this last step to the hero's final reward will take place, as I have said, beyond the scope of the story; but the reader knows that some kind of heaven waits for the hero. He has completed his trials successfully and has earned that final reward. For my own Tuck family the final reward is withheld, but Winnie, the standard hero, achieves it fully.

So this is the full round of the hero's path of separation, adventure, and return. To see a very modern hero, look at Max, in Maurice Sendak's *Where the Wild Things Are*. For him the call to adventure is brought about by his own daring disobedience, and he responds by setting sail in his little boat and crossing the threshold from reality into mystery. Protected from total exposure by the wolf suit he wears, which is for him as much a charm as the kiss of the Good Witch of the North is for Dorothy, he confronts and eventually controls the monsters of his subconscious. This accomplished, he is free to go home again and accept his mother's love.

I've already mentioned *Peter Pan*. But Peter is more complex than Max. He is both the herald and a hero himself, who has refused to take the final step and return to the real world, to adulthood, and eventually to death. Instead, he chooses to remain forever in Never-Never-Land, having the same adventures over and over again, and he tries hard to persuade Wendy and the Lost Boys to do the same. Barrie makes it clear, however, that there is a heavy price to pay for refusing to return: One forfeits all rights to putting one's learned lessons, or "boons," to work in the real world. To remain a child, although it has its own great charms, nevertheless means that one will remain immature, ignorant, powerless, and unfulfilled.

Campbell points out that the return is sometimes refused in myth and folklore. James refuses it in *James and the Giant Peach*. "The full round . . .," says Campbell, "requires that the hero [come back into] the kingdom of humanity, where the boon may redound to the renewing of the community, the nation, the planet, or the ten thousand worlds." And when the hero refuses to complete the round, he has, in fact, chosen to withdraw from his own humanity.

One could go on and on with examples. It would be difficult to name a single fantasy or fairy tale where the pattern or some major portion of it does not prevail. Whether the call to adventure is heralded by Pinocchio's Cat and Fox or Charlie Bucket's golden ticket or the appearance of Mary Poppins, there will be a herald of some sort, always. Whether the threshold is Alice's rabbit hole or the desert surrounding Oz or the wardrobe in the Narnia series, there will be a threshold, always. Whether the protective charm is as simple as Cinderella's fairy godmother or as complex as the usual youngest son's usual three objects given him by the usual hag he encounters on the road, there will always be some kind of protective charm. Adventures and trials will always be present, for they not only form the conflict and suspense of the story, but, more important, they represent the struggle to learn the necessary lesson and achieve the mastery of one's own fears. As for coming home again, when it happens, there is a completion of the round and a feeling of satisfaction. And where there is a refusal to return, there is the suggestion that for the particular hero of the particular story, reality is not worth returning to. For most heroes, however, the ending will be happy.

Why, if the patterns of fantasy are so unchangeable, do writers of fantasy not get tired of it? Well, I for one *do* get tired of it and sometimes wish for more elbowroom to explore my ideas. The trouble is, I believe in the pattern. It's the only kind of story line that seems to make any kind of sense, finally. And that means that I believe in happy endings. Modern adult fiction, and much of what we call teenage fiction, cannot entirely escape the pattern of the classic hero; the difference is that in much of this type of fiction, the hero will refuse the call in the first place, or he will cross the threshold only to be defeated in his trials or to opt for remaining in that other world. For instance, consider the principal difference between the movies *Star Wars* and *Close Encounters of the Third Kind*. *Star Wars* is a classic fantasy with the hero's round intact. *Close Encounters* is a modern study: The hero, after struggling through most of the story merely to answer the call to adventure, crosses the threshold only at the end, and the implication is that the round, which took so long to begin, will never be completed— the hero will not come home again.

For me, and for all writers devoted to fantasy as a means of exploring ideas, the total round of the hero's path is vitally important. Without it we cannot tell stories that satisfy us. And I think that as long as the basic, simple questions are asked, there will always be a place for us in the world of fiction. Fantasy will continue to answer those questions symbolically at some level and in some place that is always unexplained and yet universally understood. To carry on in that tradition, to take the hero through his round and bring him home again, over and over, is an ancient and honorable exercise that will never lose its vitality or its value. It has always existed somewhere in literature, whether recited around a prehistoric campfire or in a cottage in the medieval Black Forest; whether in the religions of ancient Greece, or in those of Wales or Norway or the American Indian; whether in a trilogy by Tolkien or in the fantasy literature of modern children. I hope that in these practical times, with their new and urgent practical problems, you will agree with me that while we must, with realistic fiction, define and redefine for our children our rapidly changing physical world, we also have an obligation to serve the needs of their ancient, searching, universal souls.

Disturbing the Universe

JILL PATON WALSH

In an Institute called "Do I Dare Disturb the Universe?" and concerned, under however portentous a banner, to consider children's books, I thought the participants would certainly consider *daring* and *disturbances* sufficiently, and that I myself therefore would take as my subject the leftover, bottom-of-the-bottle one—the universe, no less.

Time was when the universe had a beginning, thus: "In the beginning God created the heaven and the earth. And the earth was without form, and void; and darkness was upon the face of the deep. . . . And God said, Let there be light: and there was light. . . . and God saw that it was good."

Or was it perhaps like this?

> Ymir was the father of all living things. Once when he was asleep it happened that he became bathed in sweat. Under his left arm were formed a man and a woman, both giants like him. At the same time the ice continuing to melt, gave forth a cow, Audumla, the wet nurse of the giants. . . . The cow licked blocks of ice, and was nourished by the salt which they contained. Now in thus licking the ice which melted under the warm tongue she brought to light the body of a living being whose name was Buri. Buri had a son, Bor, who married one of the giant's daughters. With her he fathered three Gods, Odin, Vili, and Ve, these three sons of giant race immediately killed Ymir. From his flesh they made the land, and from his blood the sea. From his bones the gods made mountains, and from his hair the trees. They took his skull, and raising it upon four pillars made of it the vault of the heavens. In the vault they placed sparks of fire, thus creating the moon, the stars, the sun.

The sun travelled across the sky, and warmed the earth, and soon there appeared the first green blades of grass.

Or, perhaps, like this?

> Thus spoke Ahura Mazda to the holy Zarathustra: I have created the universe where none existed; if I had not made it the entire world would have gone towards the Airjana Vaeja. In opposition to this world, which is all life, Angra Mainyu created another which is all death, where there are only two months of summer, and where winter is ten months long, months which so chill the world that even summer is icy; cold is the root of all evil.
>
> Then I created Ghaon, the abode of Sughdra, the most delightful place on earth. It is sown with roses; there the birds with ruby plumage are born.
>
> Angra Mainyu then created insects which are noxious to plants and animals.
>
> Then I founded the holy and sublime city of Muru, and into it Angra Mainyu introduced lies and evil counsel.
>
> Then I created Bashdi, the enchanting, where surrounded by lush pastures a hundred thousand banners fly, and Angra Mainyu sent wild beasts there, to devour the cattle that serve for man's use. Afterwards I created Haroju, the city of rich palaces. Angra Mainyu caused sloth to be born there, and soon the city was poverty stricken. Afterwards I created Nissa, the city of prayer, and into it Angra Mainyu insinuated the doubt which gnaws at faith. Thus each of the marvels I have given men for their welfare has been counteracted by a gift from Angra Mainyu. It is to him the earth owes the evil instincts which infest it. It is he who established the criminal usage of burning or burying the dead, and all the misfortunes which ravage the race of mankind.

However it was, when the universe had a creator, it was full of spiritual power and, indeed, of spiritual beings, God or gods, who could be called to account for things.

Let me remind you, for example, of the first proof of the existence of God formulated by Thomas Aquinas. It is a matter of common experience, he asserted, that things move. Nothing, however, moves unless it is moved by some other thing. A javelin, for example, does not move unless it is moved by the hand of the thrower. But the chain of events in which each thing that moves is moved by some other thing cannot proceed to infinity; there must somewhere be something which moves other things but is itself not moved—a prime mover—"and this all men understand to be God."

Let us ignore Thomas Aquinas's theology for a moment and look at his mechanics, derived from Aristotle. This starts from the common-sense view that the natural state of things is for objects to be at rest. Any movement, or continuation of movement, requires an explanation. Much ingenuity was needed over javelins, which continue to move after they have left the thrower's hand. Since no longer moved by the thrower, they must be moved by something else; otherwise they could not, as they demonstrably do, continue in flight.

The great conceptual revolution that marks the beginning of modern thought was brought about by Galileo and Newton, who started with a different idea of the norm. While any deviation from the norm still requires explanation, the problem of javelins is neatly turned over. If it is normal for objects to continue moving in a straight line, it is not the flight of the javelins that needs explanation but their eventual falling to the ground and lying at rest. The explanation, of course, being the law of gravity.

Let me underline a little the peculiar nature of the medieval universe, which required for its operation the constant labor of unseen hands, and supernatural forces. Such a universe was already half open to the spirits, the intelligences, who supported the flight path of the javelin and turned the very spheres about their orbits.

It was the modern law of motion that helped, in the seventeenth century, to drive the spirits out of the world and open its workings to the curiosity of the human mind. Already in the fourteenth century Jean Buridan pointed out that alternative theories might remove the need for intelligences and noted that there was no authority for them in the Bible, and only a little later Nicholas of Oresme proposed that God might have set the universe running like a mighty clock and then *gone away.*

The whole direction of Western thought has been toward the despiritualization of explanations—as, for example, of the flight of javelins. Once we see that objects continue in a straight line unless acted upon by a force, we no longer need "intelligences" to propel missiles or to roll the planets in their courses, and the spirits lose their attraction for us the moment we need them no longer. This principle was, like so many other things, enunciated clearly by a Greek of the Hippocratic school. "Men call epilepsy a divine affliction," he said, "because they do not understand it. But if men called all things divine which they do not understand, there would be no end of divinities."

Let me offer you, then, in grotesquely simplified form, a prospectus of human images of the universe; I mean, for the moment, the physical universe. In the beginning the universe was a theater for the actions of the divine. Everything that happened was an act of God or, possibly, of the devil. And the universe was to have an end. Interestingly enough, the three beginnings I quoted to you were to have three different ends. The familiar one—the Bible—was to have a judgment day, a great settling of accounts between good and evil. The Norse one, with a cow licking creation out of ice, envisaged a great final battle between good and evil gods, with the best human beings enlisted to help the good, and the good destined to lose. Finally, the Zoroastrian world picture, full of conflict between good and evil, likewise imagined a final battle in which the good finally triumph.

Then, in the dawn of science, we reach the idea of the universe as a machine. God becomes a clockmaker. He does not turn the wheels with an ever-present hand. The universe has the regularity and predictability of a machine, and a machine's neutrality. We do not appeal to it, pray to it, offer sacrifices or make covenants to persuade it to vary or to change its motion. Instead, we apply our wits to understanding and predicting it.

Finally, in modern times the arbitrary and personal reenter the universe. Taught by Einstein, we have learned that we do, after all, influence the ticking and whirring of the cosmic clock; that human limitations enter into every measurement and observation that we make; that we disturb the universe in every attempt we make to understand it. The light beam down a microscope disturbs what it illuminates; seen, it is not what it would have been unseen. Our presence and our position modify everything we think we know. We have even discovered some things which we cannot, in principle, ever know. We cannot ever discover, about a single subatomic particle, both its mass and its velocity. Either one, but never, till the end of time, *both*. And it is important to realize that this is not a fact about subatomic particles. It is a fact about human beings doing physics about subatomic particles. This principle of modern science is well named the uncertainty principle.

Let me now point out to you how useful the immanent divinities once were to us in considering the moral universe and, especially, the question of human responsibility. Consider, for example, this:

"Lord of the earthquake," replied Zeus the Cloud-compeller, "you have read my mind aright, and know why I have summoned this gathering. They [the Greeks and Trojans] do concern me, even in their destruction. Nevertheless, I propose to stay here and seat myself in some Olympian glen from which I can enjoy the spectacle. The rest of you have my permission to join the Trojans and Achaeans, and to give your help to either side as your sympathies dictate. For if Achilles is allowed to fight the

Trojans without interference they will not for a moment
hold that fiery spirit. Even before they used to tremble and
run at the sight of him; and now that he has been
embittered by the loss of his friend, I am afraid he may
cheat Destiny, and storm the walls of Troy." Up to the
moment when the gods came down among men, the
Achaeans carried all before them. . . . but the scene
changed when the Olympians reached the battlefield.

Or this:

And the Lord said unto Satan, whence comest thou?
Then Satan answered the Lord, and said, From going to
and fro in the earth, and from walking up and down in it.
And the Lord said unto Satan, Hast thou considered my
servant Job, that there is none like him in the earth, a
perfect and an upright man, one that feareth God and
escheweth evil? Then Satan answered the Lord, and said,
Doth Job fear God for naught? Has thou not made a hedge
about him, and about his house, and about all that he hath
on every side? Thou has blessed the work of his hands,
and his substance is increased in the land. But put forth
thy hand now and touch all that he hath, and he will curse
thee to thy face. And the Lord said to Satan, Behold, all
that he hath is in thy power.

We may well find the first quotation childish: "We were doing all right
until Apollo pitched in on their side" sounds more like an excuse to us than
a serious moral explanation. With the second passage we are right in the
main area of difficulty for the Western moral universe—the problem of evil.
The news that God did not actually harass Job himself but merely gave the
devil permission to do it, by way of scoring points in a debate, will not
greatly reassure us. For anyone who believes in an omnipotent deity of
total benignity, evil is certainly a scandal, a stumbling block. The argument—a long-standing one of great authority in our culture—that God, in
his omnipotence, is not really to blame for evil, but that man, in his
helplessness, is to blame because of the sin of Adam or because of more
recent sins, reveals a guilt-making, self-accusing attitude, and is little better
than the argument that it was the devil's doing; little better, that is, at
extricating us from the intellectual problem. For in our humble dealings
with one another, in our mundane common laws, we know how to allocate
responsibility in a situation where, for example, a parent has allowed a

child to inflict terrible damage on itself; or one in which the owner of a vicious dog has let it loose on the neighborhood.

Here is God's reason, his excuse if you like, for harassing Job:

> Where wast thou when I laid the foundations of the earth? Declare, if thou hast understanding. Who hath laid the measures thereof, if thou knowest? or who has stretched the line upon it? Whereupon are the foundations thereof fastened? or who laid the corner stone thereof? When the morning stars sang together, and all the sons of God shouted for joy? Or who shut up the sea with doors, when it brake forth, as if it had issued out of the womb? When I made a cloud the garment thereof, and thick darkness a swaddling band for it . . . And said, Hitherto shalt thou come, but no further, and here shall thy proud waves be stayed?

There has surely never been so poetical a statement of man's insignificance and ignorance; but as a moral argument in explanation of God's unfairness to Job, what this amounts to is "I'm bigger than you."

I am now ready to point out to you that the progress of moral universes echoes the progress of physical ones. First, as in the passages quoted above, from the *Iliad* and from Job, our moral actions and our fortunes are, like the early flight of javelins, moderated to an amazing extent by the intervention of the divine. The divine have their own motives. It is very difficult to reconcile this world picture with any serious degree of human responsibility, or even human free will. It is even harder, if you think that everything that happens in the universe is someone's doing, to exonerate the authorities and continue to believe that God is both all-powerful and all-good. It is hard, but it has been and still is managed by many people.

The divine remained intimately in play in the moral universe for roughly as long as it continued to propel javelins—until sometime in the seventeenth century in European cultures. For example, in 1640 an English jury recorded a verdict on the death of a man who had been struck by lightning while continuing to plow during a thunderstorm. His companion had taken shelter under a tree. The jury did not consider the man had been careless of his own safety. They found as the cause of death the "Immediate Providence of God." And, of course, if God was out to get you, it was useless to try to save yourself. Bubonic plague, to take another example, was unable to spread of itself; it was not only futile but blasphemous to stop visiting the sick or to flee the infected towns to avoid it; if God did not wish to strike you, you would be safe anywhere. In the Great Plague of London the king had to threaten the church to make sure that it did not preach against the sanitary precautions being taken by the civic authorities!

And then in the next century we are suddenly well into a different era. God has laid down the ground rules and withdrawn. People seek to understand a mechanical cause of diseases; Ben Franklin flies a kite into the Immediate Providence of God by way of investigating lightning, and the thing is to study the mechanical movements of the universe and act rationally for our own good. God is a gentlemanly and benign proprietor, and his greatest gift to his tenants is not grace, but reason.

That this was a more profitable line of thinking, we can be sure. Sufficient witness to this fact are the comfort, safety, triumphant medicine, fine bridges, telephones, computers, and the rational, democratic societies with orderly laws that were achieved when we stopped blaming God for things and began to exert ourselves to understand the universe and do what we could. It was a more profitable line of thinking, but it has not proved sufficient. For just as we have understood now that the nature of the observer conditions the observation, we also know now in the moral field that the nature of the actor conditions our actions. There are many things we can do, physically—like feeding all the hungry in the world or abolishing leprosy, war, or prejudice, the difficulty with which is a difficulty that lies within ourselves. We can do a vast quantity of good that remains undone, and we cannot be sure that we will forever restrain ourselves from blowing up our tiny planet and putting a permanent end to that universe which we call the universe of discourse.

It is time we saw that the uncertainty principle applies as much to the moral as to the physical universe.

For we can know the universe only in our own descriptions of it. Some descriptions may be better than others, as Newton's astronomy was better and clearer and accounted accurately for more observations than Ptolemy's. But they are not really all assimilable into one another. When you have heard all three of the creation stories with which we began, you will probably not believe any of them in the way in which a person might who had heard only one. Religious and moral beliefs, and even beliefs in physics—like belief that the world is flat, to take an extreme example—can and do survive in the presence of widespread dissent and disbelief; but they do not survive unchanged. Believing what everyone all around you also believes and takes for granted, and believing something in the presence of others who dissent, are two different kinds of faith; and in an open, Western, democratic, and contemporary society only the second kind is possible.

It is open to you, of course, to say that different systems of belief are all really attempts at describing the same god, as it is open to physicists to say that Newtonian mechanics still stand in the age of Einstein, being a special case, valid in certain circumstances. But when we consider moral schema, this maneuver is harder. Can one say that Christian forgiveness of one's enemies and Aztec immolation of their living hearts are attempts, really, at the same morality? Or that Antigone's view of the imperative duty to bury the dead and the view that burying and burning the dead are abominable practices introduced to the world by the god of evil are really the same? People were once prepared to burn alive those who disagreed with them about the nature of the moral universe, even by quite small degrees of disagreement, but there is now no attitude less useful than certainty such as that.

The gods have departed, more or less, and so has the marvelous clockwork machinery, and what is left is ourselves. We stand where God once stood, at the center of explanations. If someone has blundered, we have only ourselves to blame; but on the other hand, we can stop accepting responsibility beyond our powers, which is really a metaphysical form of taxation without representation! We are not fully free and fully capable, and the human condition, let alone the circumstances and characters of each of us, was not chosen by us. I believe we should work on the problem of evil the same kind of inversion that Newton's mechanics worked on the flight of javelins; we should see that it is not evil that needs accounting for, but good. Not the polio virus, but the Salk vaccine. Not human selfishness, but human altruism. This inversion has the merit of turning our thoughts in the direction of matters that really are amenable to thinking. The problem of evil has been around since the dawn of thought, and we have got nowhere with it; famine may be a difficult problem, but is surely an easier one to solve.

In a universe that evolved over mind-baffling ages of time, which, having no beginning we can identify, moves toward no particular end but is endlessly transformed and modified; in a world in which God has become only one possible explanation among many others, may we then do exactly what we like—and in writing for children, is this what we should tell them?

I am among those modern consciousnesses who believe that we may act without fear of hell or hope of heaven, but not without regard to the consequences. And considering the consequences of human actions—their physical, moral, social, and psychological consequences—considering what, if God asks nothing of us, we may yet ask of one another, is complicated and hard. Hell may be a fiction, but hell on earth—as we well know—is not; and heaven there may be none, but happiness is sometimes found. We cannot tell the whole truth because any account of the universe we contrive is too partial, too subjective, too provisional to deserve so grand a word; and we must remember that our children, like ourselves, must live in a world full of others who disagree. Believers and disbelievers rub shoulders in every generation and, we must hope, will keep faith with their own universes while refraining from burning the adherents of others.

We can neither know the whole truth nor convey it to children, but we can and must consider the consequences of our voluntary actions and teach those younger than ourselves, as far as is in our power, to do likewise. And for considering consequences, especially moral consequences, story is the major tool of thought, as measurement is for geometry, number for physics, and logic for philosophy. In the beginning was the word. The making and breaking of patterns of explanation—storytelling—is to our species what swimming is to fish or flight to birds. In the beginning the word was with God; all explanations, physical and moral, rested on the divine. And now for all storytellers, even those whose patterns of explanation are strictly human, the word has not lost a superhuman power to connect young and old, writer and reader; to connect us with each other and with the causes and consequences of what we do.

The word is with us, now. And can there be anything more important to do with it than to fashion with it what sense we can about the universe we find ourselves in, and start to tell a story to our children?

III

Fantasy:
The Perilous Realm

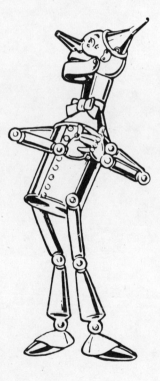

Drawing by W. W. Denslow from *The Wonderful Wizard of Oz* (1900)
Logo for "Elements of Popularity in Literature for Children"
Simmons College Summer Institute, 1981

Introduction

BETTY LEVIN

Many of the fantasy writers represented in Part III have not heard or read each other's lectures. Their fiction spans the whole breadth of this genre—in concept, subject, and style. Yet, the conditions they address and the concerns they reflect bring them into astonishing harmony. The sources and illustrations for their ideas—Joseph Campbell and Charles Dickens, Narnia and the rabbit hole, Charlotte and the face of a spider, world myths and the natural world—stand as variations on a primary theme.

Before them, setting the stage for the consideration of fantasy at the beginning of the nineteenth century, Coleridge asserted, "The imagination is the distinguishing characteristic of man as a progressive being." Some decades later, Ruskin declared that as "every fairy tale worth recording at all is the remnant of a tradition possessing true historical value," children should be encouraged to "read down its utmost depth." Soon other serious writers, especially writers for children, were expanding this view and expressing their own convictions. Juliana Ewing, who wrote some of the finest juvenile fiction of her century, remarked that "there are ideas and types, occurring in the myths of all countries, which are common properties. . . . Like Proverbs and Parables . . . [fairy tales and folktales] deal with first principles. . . . They treat, not of a corner of the nursery or a playground, but of the world at large, and life in perspective; of forces visible and invisible; of Life, Death, and Immortality."

Small wonder that by the end of the nineteenth century the term *fairy tale* had become inadequate; it could not contain the great mythopoeic works of George MacDonald and the fantasies of Lewis Carroll and Rudyard Kipling. By the time George MacDonald published *The Fantastic Imagination* in 1893, fantasy as a literary genre had gained full acceptance. MacDonald's study connects nineteenth-century thought with the critical works of twentieth-century children's writers like J. R. R. Tolkien and C. S. Lewis and, more recently, Ursula Le Guin. And now they connect with those whose views and experience appear here.

In the contemplation of fantasy, the common themes are realism, meaning, conviction, and moral framework. Variations stress a sense of place and of time, the reiteration of narrative patterns, the limits imposed on the writer by the use of the supernatural, and the release fantasy allows.

H. M. Hoover tells us that fantasy has to make sense. Lloyd Alexander believes that "in its conception, and in its deep substructures, the fantasy world must, if anything, be more carefully rationalized than the real world. . . . The writer may populate his world with all manner of imaginary creatures, human or otherwise. But within that world . . . their fantastic condition must speak to our real one." Jan Mark points out that "although all fiction derives from a known constant, from a certain truth, the truth with which a writer begins may not ultimately be the one he presents to the reader."

Some of these writers, like Zilpha Keatley Snyder, create alternative worlds where they must work out every detail. In writing the three Green-sky fantasies, she tells us, she "even knew . . . what the plumbing was like."

For others, a sense of place is equated with a sense of nature. Laurence Yep informs us, "Fantasyland isn't some faraway special place. It's right around you, right now." H. M. Hoover says, "If you simply look around you, you will see the most wondrous creatures, and they're all of this Earth. . . . The fact remains that no matter how science fiction we get, the most glorious spacecraft we'll ever know is Earth." Jane Langton asks us to stand "a hair's breadth aside" to see the extraordinary in the ordinary. And Susan Cooper remarks that, like nature, magic is all around us.

Some regard our connection with the past as part of our primary world. Natalie Babbitt believes in the monomyth that joins all peoples in all times. For her, "fantasy, which covers things larger than life, must follow the complete round. The hero must return. The happy ending, according to Campbell, is not a denial of life but a going beyond." And Jane Yolen agrees. She sees writing as patterned on Campbell's definition of the hero journey, a journey that is "fundamentally inward." Susan Cooper, who suggests that fantasy writers are "creative dreamers," shares that view.

But Babbitt maintains that "true fantasy is not so much invented as it is distilled and interpreted—from impressions that go far back into prehistory . . . [and] are common to us all. . . . True fantasy . . . aims to define the universe." "And fantasy offers a system of symbols everyone of every age understands; it enriches and simplifies our lives and makes them bearable." Jane Langton, on the other hand, shows us *the thing itself*. "In *Charlotte's Web*," she tells us, "the miraculous rebirth of springtime . . . is embodied in the emergence of a new generation of spiders from Charlotte's egg sac. . . . The spiders stand for nothing but themselves. They *are* the spring. In the absence of allegory the purity of the thing itself is revealed." Hoover, whose science fiction is so different from Langton's fantasy, would agree; she, too, looks upon a spider with wonder, although her vision comes through the perspective of an electron microscope.

Lloyd Alexander proposes that "staying alive and relatively sane on the downhill slope of the twentieth century is a precarious occupation," and that "the profession of literature is equally hazardous. . . . Writers who believe in what they do, however, will continue to write . . . because the act of creation in a world seemingly bent on its own destruction is the only thing that makes any sense." He speaks for all these writers and for all literature. Jan Mark's planet in *The Ennead* supports inhabitants who cling to life in a barren world; they cannot respond to or learn from the telling of a myth because they no longer know what a story is. They are beyond help, but we are not. Lloyd Alexander reminds us that "with so many perils besetting us in the real world, it seems quixotic to worry about the world of literature. But the world of literature—which is the world of ideas, attitudes, and emotions—is no less real than this island planet we're obliged to live on."

"A Hair's Breadth Aside"

JANE LANGTON

On the afternoon of December 11, 1855, Henry Thoreau threaded the tangle of Holden Swamp near the Sudbury River and looked at the thicket of black alders and blueberry and thought about the pine grosbeaks that would soon be warbling in the wintry woods and fields.

> I had a vision . . . of these birds as I stood in the swamps. I saw this familiar—too *familiar*—fact at a different angle, and I was charmed and haunted by it. But I could only attain to be thrilled and enchanted, as by the sound of a strain of music dying away. I had seen into paradisaic regions, with their air and sky, and I was no longer wholly or merely a denizen of this vulgar earth. . . . It is only necessary to behold thus the least fact or phenomenon, however familiar, from a point a hair's breadth aside from our habitual path or routine, to be overcome, enchanted by its beauty and significance. . . . To perceive freshly, with fresh senses, is to be inspired. . . . It is a wonderful fact that I should be affected, and thus deeply and powerfully, more than by aught else in all my experience,—that this fruit should be borne in me, sprung from a seed finer than the spores of fungi, floated from other atmospheres! finer than the dust caught in the sails of vessels a thousand miles from land!

It happens to all of us, this experience of being transfixed by nature. A graceful tree, the spotted fur of a dog, the sky in some moment of ineffable purity will catch us by the throat, and we will fumble for words to express our delight. We will certainly fail to find any as subtle as Thoreau's when he stood in the thicket of blueberry, looking at the bare landscape, thinking of winter birds.

He was standing, he said, "a hair's breadth aside." For the moment he had separated himself from the daily routine of life on Concord's Milldam, from his customary work of surveying for the local farmers around town, from the tasks that interested him that particular week—sawing wheels from a pine log to transport his boat, bringing up wood from the bottom of the river. His eyes were open wider than usual, he was seeing in a new way, and he was sharply aware of the beauty of something he had seen a hundred times before—lesser redpolls and pine grosbeaks in the snow. Their significance seemed overwhelming, more important than anything else, more affecting than *aught else in all my experience.*

Henry Thoreau did not write stories. He certainly did not invent fantastic fictional adventures for children. But some writers of fantasy for young people have seen the natural world in the same enchanted way and have translated it into their books.

One thinks of Rudyard Kipling's reverence for wild nature in *The Jungle Books,* whose creatures obey natural law, whose talk is of stalking prey and of escaping enemies—as in the hunting verse of the wolf pack: "Feet that make no noise; eyes that can see in the dark; ears that can hear the winds in their lairs, and sharp white teeth, all these things are the marks of our brothers." Kipling takes pains to depict each beast in its natural setting in all its wild splendor: "The sea is full of fire on summer nights . . . and each seal leaves a wake like burning oil behind him and a flaming flash when he jumps, and the waves break in great phosphorescent streaks and swirls."

But for most British writers of fantasy for young people, the landscape and its wild creatures are not enough. Britain is old, and its countryside is fertile with history, with myth and legend. Kipling himself, in *Puck of Pook's Hill,* produces Puck from among the alders, and three men from times that are gone emerge from the bank of the stream, from the stand of broom on the hillside, to tell stories of old England. The soil itself is charged with its real and fabled past.

And in the work of many other British writers there is the same thick intertwining of field and forest with myth and history—in the stories of Kenneth Grahame, E. Nesbit, Lucy Boston, Susan Cooper, Alan Garner, William Mayne. American writers who set their books in Great Britain have also dug into British soil to bring history to life on ancient ground—Nancy Bond in Wales, Betty Levin in Ireland and in Orkney.

But when American writers set their fantasy adventures on this side of the Atlantic, they have less history to draw on. No mythical heroes wait to be called out of primeval American oak trees; the ground is not rich with the bones of dead kings. It is bald of mythology, bare of folk tale. Its open fields are not marked by standing stones. When Stuart Little goes questing for Margalo, he is not seeking the Holy Grail nor the great god Pan, but only what is beautiful and good. When in *Charlotte's Web* the spider writes magical messages with her silk, her miracle is only at one remove from that of an ordinary spider, which can create a perfect round web in an hour of hard work. Charlotte's fantastic feat helps us to stand "a hair's breadth aside" and see the daily magic of spiders and spiderwebs and the immense mystery of earth itself. E. B. White's *Charlotte's Web* is not merely a story about talking pigs and spiders. Rather, it celebrates the wonder of life and the sadness of death and the mystery of the eternal cycle that goes on and on, bringing lambs and pigs and rats and spiders and children into the barn—that "warm delicious cellar, with the garrulous geese, the changing seasons, the heat of the sun, the passage of swallows, the nearness of rats, the sameness of sheep, the love of spiders, the smell of manure, and the glory of everything." And it celebrates all these glorious things without the help of metaphor. The miraculous rebirth of springtime, for example, is embodied in the emergence of a new generation of spiders from Charlotte's egg sac rather than in some Green Knight from medieval romance. The spiders stand for nothing but themselves. They *are* the spring. In the absence of allegory the purity of the thing itself is revealed.

I hope I will be forgiven for tossing my own books into the same pile with the journals of Thoreau and Kipling's *Jungle Books* and E. B. White's *Charlotte's Web*. In the series of stories that begins with *The Diamond in the Window* and ends with *The Fragile Flag*, the fantastic adventures of my child characters often set them "a hair's breadth aside" from ordinary life in order that they may see it freshly on their return. When in one adventure Edward's senses are taken away from him, leaving him nearly blind, nearly deaf, nearly dumb, he is filled with joy at his recovery, exulting in physical powers he had barely noticed before, the miraculous senses that were his birthright: "He felt all alive-alive-o, as if his nose could hear, his eyes could smell, his ears could taste, his mouth could see . . . Someone was calling his name . . . The sound . . . fell on Eddy's ear and twisted around inside his eardrum and vibrated in his brain. He had never heard anything so wonderful."

And in *The Fledgling*, after young Georgie's miraculous flights with the Goose Prince are all finished, she discovers that his parting gift of a little rubber ball is really an image of the earth itself—"turning slowly and majestically in the immense and impalpable night. The blue surface of the ball was streaked with clouds, and below the clouds Georgie could catch glimpses of great land masses, of dark continents and snow-covered ice caps and deep jungles and blue oceans and lofty mountain ranges—the Andes, the Alps, the Himalayas." Therefore, she now has a keener vision of the earth, of its lavish splendor, its vastness and complexity. She no longer needs the magic because she has dwelt in miracle all along.

The Scottish writer Mollie Hunter once told me that true fantasy could only be written by looking backward over centuries of history. It could only be composed by someone standing upon a countryside drenched in myth and folklore, in the immemorial memory of past heroes and tradition. I agree, of course, that fantasy of that kind is of enormous value and that our literature would be profoundly poorer without it—indeed, that it would hardly exist at all. I treasure the stories Mollie Hunter herself tells about the highlands of Scotland, about kelpies and walking stones, about the *sidhe* and the Great Grey Man of Ben MacDui. But I insist that nature taken pure, nature in its simplicity and silent grandeur, nature observed without thought of history—blades of grass in a farmer's field, cedars in a rocky pasture, spiders spinning webs in New England barns, dogs barking everywhere, clouds forming and dissolving, gaseous nebulae hundreds of light-years away—nature *alone* has a power that arouses the same reverence, the same marveling wonderment, the same sense of instruction and delight.

If we are lucky enough to behold it in Thoreau's way, we will thereafter see the world with altered attention and reach out buckets and nets for the fine seed of awe, "finer than the spores of fungi, floated from other atmospheres! finer than the dust caught in the sails of vessels a thousand miles from land!" And then the mystery of cactus and dandelion and maple tree, the magical hold upon us of sky and bird and snow and of woodchuck and puddle in the road will be strong enough to stimulate the kind of stories some of us love best, fantasies exalting the natural world, fantasies written for the young.

The Purposes of Fantasy

NATALIE BABBITT

I am going to start off by disagreeing with the poem "Ithaka." The poet tells us that you won't encounter Laistrygonians, Cyclops, wild Poseidon unless you bring them along inside your soul, unless your soul sets them up in front of you. Wrong—to my mind. Laistrygonians, Cyclops, and wild Poseidon are with us every step of the way, always and inevitably, and our souls have nothing to do with it.

When you say *fantasy fiction* to a group of average adults, you are apt to get reactions voiced in one of two ways: sniffily, as "that sort of thing is for children," or in a cooing tone, as "Oh, you mean nursery tales!" I'm not surprised by this phenomenon anymore, but it will always intrigue me that, considering the fundamental role fantasy plays in all of our lives, I find so little understanding of it.

Probably the difficulty lies partly in the fact that when most people think of fantasy, they think of Peter Rabbit, the pushmi-pullyu, Pinocchio, or Mrs. Doasyouwouldbedoneby. But in the classic sense these dear creatures, beloved though they may be, are not true fantasy figures. They were invented out of whole cloth expressly for the amusement or improvement of a very young audience, just as Dorian Gray and Frankenstein's monster and Paul Bunyan were invented out of whole cloth expressly for the amusement or improvement of an adult audience.

True fantasy is not so much invented as it is distilled and interpreted—from impressions that go far back into prehistory, impressions that, so far as we can tell from the study of folktales, are common to us all whatever our age and nationality. By no means does true fantasy always amuse, and it does not aim to improve an audience so much as it aims to define the universe.

This does not mean that we should talk about fantasy in hushed and sober tones—as inappropriate as talking about it in the wuzza-wuzza tones we use when speaking to infants and puppies. It is far too colorful and robust for either of these approaches, too ancient and universal, and it belongs to children no more than it does to the rest of us. In order to talk about it at all, however, we have to try to find out why there is such enormous appeal in the first place in the notion of half-human animals and half-animal humans and in witches, vampires, fairy godmothers, Laistry-gonians, Cyclops, and wild Poseidon—all of the presences that flap, stalk, creep, and flutter through our heads in darkness and daylight alike.

We adults need to admit without embarrassment that there is fantasy—many kinds of fantasy—in the sternest of us. Why else the cruel shock of one's reflection in the department store dressing-room mirror? Can this withered crone be me, who not five minutes back was tripping gaily as a girl through the sceptered aisles of Better Dresses? Why else the absence of thirteenth floors in tall buildings or the lift of the heart when our horoscope tells us that tomorrow will be a sensational day in which we will get money in the mail? Can anyone say without hesitation that he or she can hang an unprotected arm down over the edge of the mattress at night without a single moment's suspicion that something may grab it from under the bed?

Our fantasies are sometimes kinder than reality, sometimes more horrifying, and nearly always more interesting. It's hard to accept the idea, then, that they spring and have always sprung from ignorance, fear, and superstition; but that seems to be the case.

We look with indulgent amusement now at primitive religions. Imagine! People once actually believed that there were spirits living in trees. That kings had supernatural powers. That your soul might at any time escape through your nostrils unless you kept it inside by wearing a bone through your nose. That gods could inhabit the bodies of certain animals which became, by association, holy.

All this sort of thing is nonsense, of course. Trees the abode of spirits? Yet, we are encouraged to talk to our plants, and a lot of people, although I am not among them, have been touched by a book called *The Giving Tree*, in which a tree is the protector of and provider for a boy growing into manhood.

Kings with supernatural powers? Absurd. Yet, when John F. Kennedy was shot, many people feared that the assassination signaled the coming of Armageddon, and most of us felt that something magical had been lost forever. The symbolic significance of that particular murder was immense and still absorbs the interest of large numbers of people, even to the extent that the assassin's coffin was dug up a few years ago to make certain his remains were really in it. In an almost pathetic attempt to find reasons for the killing, a multitude of books have been written expounding seemingly endless theories about it, for we have a difficult time accepting the idea that events, good or bad, can actually be random. It is far more reassuring to believe they are part of a careful plan set in motion by forces either benign or malign but above all beyond our control.

Of course, we don't believe a person's soul can escape through his nose, but we do say "God bless you" when someone sneezes, don't we? And we do make sure a dead person's eyes are closed. I have not been able to verify this recently, but I seem to remember reading that the practice of putting coins on the dead one's closed eyelids came from a belief that evil spirits would be satisfied to take the money and leave the soul alone.

What about animals whose bodies are inhabited by gods? The idea of animals being part human—rather than the other way around—is familiar to us all. We are charmed by anything—be it a novel, a TV commercial, or the pet store down the street—that suggests that animals have human brains and on occasion can speak. Charmed. I have just said we are charmed by these ideas, and what partakes more of magic than the idea of a charm?

We are a very advanced civilization. We understand earth, and we understand the heavens. Some of us even understand molecular biology. But there is much inside our heads that, like the cockroach, has survived countless centuries of attack from common sense and the cold eye of science—vague stuff that breeds in dark corners and cannot be pinned down under microscope or through telescope—stuff that in spite of ourselves continues to influence much that we do. Nearly all of it has to do with the dismaying fact that we still don't know, after all this time, exactly where we came from or exactly where we're going. We are arguing still, again, and always, about creation. We are baffled, outraged, challenged, and humbled by death. For all our indoor plumbing and instant coffee and flu shots and permanent press, we are still, as we were at the beginning, creatures of ignorance, superstition, and fear.

If science has been unable to explain our beginnings to everyone's satisfaction, and if the world's religions disagree, as certainly they do, about our ends, we can turn to fantasy, just as we always have done. Fantasy doesn't exactly explain these things, but it does give us a variety of systems by which we can at least catch hold of them and examine them for possibilities. We would deny emphatically that we take our fantasies seriously. Yet, we cling to them because somehow there is comfort in them.

I find it interesting that of the two forces, good and evil, that we long ago took to personifying, the evil ones are surviving in the best condition. When things go wrong for us, as individuals or as a nation, we are quick to suspect there is a dark, malignant force at work. That force has been given many names down through the years, but even at its most general, when we call it simply Bad Luck or the Russians, we tend to believe it is always present, waiting offstage, ready to strike at us just when things are going our way at last. We delight in horror in our movies, books, plays, and on television. A new retelling of Bram Stoker's *Dracula* brings us out in droves. At movie houses across the land, we wait in line to see skyscrapers burn, ships sink, and airplanes crash.

There is, however, something more in our attraction to these dramas than a simple taste for blood and violence, more than a desire to see someone else get swallowed by the evil so that it won't be ready to swallow *us* for a little while longer. We are attracted by the hero, who faces the evil, who may even dance on its teeth and still survive. For the hero, of course, is us. These stories, however they are presented, act out encounters with disaster. Many characters will be mauled, burned, drowned, or drawn and quartered, but not the hero—not *us*—because the hero knows how to placate the evil, how to shame the devil, when to pour the libation, when to ring the bell. The hero knows the *rules*. He will not die.

This concept was badly eroded when Kennedy was shot, which accounts in part for the national confusion characteristic of us in the 1960s. It seemed as if the rules had broken down and there was nothing to depend on. But we are back again with new heroes. We need them too badly to stop constructing them.

The hero, because he is us, is not a fantasy. True fantasy figures representing good have not survived so well as the evil ones, at least not among adults. They have been left mostly to the youngest children. Fairy godmothers, brownies, the Easter bunny, and Santa Claus all have roots as old as Beelzebub's, but they seem to require too great a suspension of disbelief for adults. They do not battle evil directly but only stand behind the hero and cheer him on. They represent earthly rewards for good behavior: in ancient terms, courtesy to the hag on the road and soft answers to the cruel stepmother; in modern terms, the straight-A report card, the tidy room, the little sister left unmolested. In short, the kind heart and the stainless life, which will surely be rewarded. We like to think children are the only ones who need a system of learning and reward, and so, as we grow older, we abandon Santa Claus and the rest as pure make-believe. They are not useful and no longer stir our imaginations. As Alan Watts has said, "Heaven is rather static and glistering as compared with the riots of imagination that have gone into the depiction of the Inferno . . . In general it seems that, in artistic representation, hell is exuberant and heaven is not." However this may be, our heads are certainly full of the noise of wings and voices, but almost never the wings and voices of the angels. On the whole, we seem more prepared for punishment than for reward, more inclined to believe we totter always on the brink of disaster rather than on the doorsill of paradise.

In literature the battle against evil began at the beginning and has never stopped, and since one of the definitions of literature is that it is a system for interpreting the real world in symbolic terms, we can tell a good deal about concepts of evil down through the years by reading novels. The adversary changes his face continually, masquerading as everything from a white whale to a corporate executive. Evil, in fact, floats comfortably into any category, any scapegoat, that a new generation or a new dilemma can suggest. The modern novel for adults has moved far afield from the magic of the old tales. Only in stories unabashedly cranked out to curdle our blood do we still find devils, witches, and formless horrors lurking in hallways. John Updike's *The Witches of Eastwick* is too real to be scary, and the witches' powers, minor at best, are used very sparingly. These days, in what we call adult literature, evil is more apt to wear the mask of society itself. And to a very large extent, novels for teenagers have followed the same trend. So the old magic, for most of this century, has confined itself to stories for children, where its time at the conscious surface is brief. The stories it inhabits seem appropriate to perhaps no more than the second six years of life, and most of us seem to feel that children have a right to it.

Even so, both in and out of literature, it is interesting to observe how, for people of any age, the realm of fantasy can move itself about and shift its accessibility. It can exist across a prairie where it can only be reached via a cyclone. It can lie on the other side of a wardrobe or down a rabbit hole. It can be found somewhere between here and madness in a place called the Twilight Zone. It can be all around us in nature, daring us to trace its footprints in the snow of the Himalayas or to dive for it in the waters of Loch Ness, or it can come right into our kitchens and dress us for a ball or claim to be butter when what we thought we had was margarine.

For the most part, in literature, at least, fantasy exists elsewhere than in the real world, and we must make a great journey to get to it. Sometimes the journey takes the wink of an eye; sometimes much, much longer. We will need a guide, a little protective magic, and a lot of courage to get there. Sometimes a writer can successfully suggest, as Richard Adams did in *Watership Down*, that it is all around us but is simply not available to humans. On the other hand, Shakespeare brings the two worlds together on the same plane again and again and manages to maintain the credibility of both even while they are interacting as a single unit.

Erich Fromm has suggested that the acceptance and understanding of this other world is contained in the subconscious mind, which he calls the storehouse of a "forgotten language . . . the common origin of dreams, fairy tales, and myth." But whether inside our own heads, as he says, or "outside over there," as Maurice Sendak would say, the other world will always be somewhere, as it always has been, because no matter how we may try to deny it, our need for it is very great, and I think there are two reasons for that need.

The first and most obvious is that it suggests answers to questions for which there are no observable answers in our physical, observable world. I will tread carefully now and suggest that all religions other than the one a given individual subscribes to are defined by that individual as fantasies. It therefore follows that an individual who subscribes to *no* religion would see *all* religions as fantasies and would perhaps be free to observe that all have certain elements in common: a supreme creator in his or her place of residence, most often a mountaintop or far up in the sky; at least one character, and often many, who is half divine, the offspring of a god and a mortal; and a strict code of behavior for mortals, the violation of which will result in earthly misery and banishment after death to a place of darkness. Beyond these common elements, the variations and embellishments are as colorful and bizarre as subscribers care to make them, but they will all be embellishments that explain the otherwise unexplainable and that define standards of action. Human beings, it would seem, cannot live without codes and explanations. If none are provided in the natural world, we will certainly invent them.

There are, of course, other problems in life beside the large ones involving the dramas of creation and death. There is, for instance, all that time in between. Life—any individual life—can seem curiously long in the living of it and often remarkably flat and plodding. I think the other great reason for our need for fantasy is that it makes things more diverting.

The need for diversion being less crucial than the one for divine guidance, we create our fantasies of diversion with gusto and humor and then abandon them without a backward glance or else allow them to be absorbed or mutated into other forms to serve new needs. The church bells that clang so sweetly from our steeples were put there in the beginning to drive away demons, not to summon us to services, but nobody cares about that now. Cats have been honored, stoned, and honored again around the world in an ever-changing climate of opinion as to which realm—gods' or devils'—really claims their loyalty. Colors go in and out of favor, particularly white, red, and black, all of which are loaded with symbolic baggage both favorable and not so. When I was a child, I was scared to death of Jack Frost, but his place in the pantheon now seems to be gone altogether. Onions used to ward off the devil; now they only ward off potential lovers unless neutralized by breath mints.

Television commercials, by the way, are crammed with fantasies of diversion, contrived by seemingly rational bipeds to convince other seemingly rational bipeds to buy things. Remember the man in the rowboat floating in the toilet tank? Mother Nature materializing in the supermarket? What about the jolly Green Giant, the Pillsbury doughboy, and the Keebler elves who bake in a tree? What about Morris the cat? And my own favorite, the golden retriever puppy who wears a pacifier on a blue ribbon around its neck which it only lets go of to get more Kibbles 'n Bits.

These fantasies rise and fade, come and go. Some are memorable. All are diverting. I don't know whether they really sell any products, but at least they brighten our lives. It would be nice if they were real, but, alas, they are not.

The first great disillusionment is surely the discovery that there is no Santa Claus, but do we cast off all illusions forever with the loss of that first one? Do we put all fantasy away with other childish things when we become men? Not at all. We merely go on to others. My father used to say with patient confidence that someday his ship would come in. It never did, but he never gave up hoping it would. Hope, finally, is what fantasy is all about.

We live every day with hopes large and small, for few if any of us believe that our lives as we are living them are perfect—that we are as happy as we would be if things, at least in some fashion, were different. Perhaps the things we wish were different are large, important things; perhaps they aren't. Mostly, they are a combination. I think we can be full to the brim with hope that someone will discover a cure for cancer and at the same time feel the same degree of hope that our children will all get into Harvard and that the seat next to us on the bus will stay empty. Some hopes are pinned on trivialities, some on life-changing possibilities; but hope is a happy gas that expands to fit the space available. Without it there is nothing to keep us afloat.

Fantasy literature lets us share the hero's hopes and eventual triumph. In this century things haven't been very pleasant on this planet, but few of us are so deflated that we go out of our way to remind ourselves of that fact all the time, in spite of the thrust of much modern adult fiction. Most of us would rather read a book that ends on a note of hope—one of the special qualities of fantasy literature. It is not a sop for the terminally optimistic but an affirmation of one of the things that makes us, as a species, unique: the always present hope that something will happen to change everything for the better, once and for all.

I think there are signs that the forms of fantasy in literature are on the move again. Confined for decades to books for the very young, they are beginning to reappear in books for adults. They have already sprung full-blown into movies like *Star Wars* and *Close Encounters of the Third Kind*, always a few steps ahead of what science tells us is actually possible. No man in the moon? No Martians? Very well—we go on to reporting sightings of UFOs and visits from alien beings from planets far more remote than Mars and the moon. No matter how amazing our present realities, the future promises marvels still more marvelous. Something *is* going to happen—maybe—that will make everything different and better.

There are those who say that fantasy is bad for children. You might as well say that breathing is bad for them. If we don't give them classic fantasy—if we withhold folktales and fairy tales and myths and legends, whether translated straight from ages past or newly constructed on the old frameworks—it doesn't mean for a minute that children will have no fantasies. Deprived, they will merely construct their own, just as whole societies, races, and religions have done and continue blithely to do. For fantasy is a language we are born knowing, and its embellishments, interpretations, and casts of characters are fluid and adaptable to any life, any problem, any situation.

Fantasy is, finally, more than just a language like English or Spanish or Greek. It is universal. Its symbols are called up everywhere to speak volumes in a single reference. Didn't the Russians once call this country a pitiful, helpless giant? Don't we try to keep the wolf from the door? Don't we call an ill-tempered woman a harpy? Everyone in the world knows what a Cinderella is, and we add new characters all the time. My niece has a fish named Darth. A friend has a dog named Bilbo Baggins. There is a shop in New York City called The Flying Saucer News and Prosperity Clinic. I can say to you, "Open sesame" or "I think I can; I think I can" or even now "May the Force be with you," and your minds will instantly flood with impressions of fears overcome, evil vanquished, the indomitability of the human spirit reaffirmed.

Our days would be dull and hopeless without these images, the bad as well as the good. But, thank goodness, we will never be without them. We have never been without them. The real world is no more real than it ever was, which may seem like a strange thing to say in this atomic age. But the face of evil, no matter how its mask may shift, has always threatened the same thing—an end to our own personal existence. We deal with our Laistrygonians, our Cyclops, our wild Poseidons just as we always have— face to face when we must, and at other times symbolically. Fantasy offers a system of symbols that everyone of every age understands; it enriches and simplifies our lives and makes them bearable.

Another World?
A Sampling of Remarks on
Science Fiction and Fantasy

World Building

LAURENCE YEP

I'm going to talk about world building and how you build a world, because that's the important thing in science fiction. And I'm going to talk about science fiction and fantasy in interchangeable terms because I see science fiction as fantasy in new forms.

I think of fantasy and writing in general as a special way of seeing. It's a way of looking at the world more intensely and more sensitively and more sharply than we normally would.

Fantasy begins with the most ordinary kinds of things. One of my favorite adult fantasy stories is the story of a man who's sitting in his kitchen when all of a sudden the chair beneath him comes to life and falls in love with him. The chair follows him around all the time, wanting him to kiss it. The story doesn't end happily, and I won't go into it. But, at any rate, it's a very amusing story that comes out of the most ordinary thing you could find in your house—a kitchen chair. We could do similar things with a rug or with the lights overhead. Let's say the lights were alive and were a species of animal. They might signal to each other by a certain pitch of sound or by flashing different colors. What would they feed on? They might feed on neon signs, and they might swallow them up like worms, and they might sleep in the daytime like bats, on the ceilings. Fantasyland isn't some faraway special place. It's right around you, right now.

When we talk about reality, what we're talking about is a sense of reality. And that's a social consensus about what we see and what we don't see. I don't mean to imply that a sense of reality is bad; it's necessary. Our five senses are taking in information all the time, and unless we have some way of dividing that information, our minds will be overwhelmed.

But the real danger is in treating the sense of reality as an absolute. If you had gone among the classical experts a century ago and asked them about Troy, they would have laughed at you and said that Troy was an imaginary city; and so it's just as well that a certain seven-year-old German boy one Christmas day didn't talk to these classical experts. What happened was that he received a picture book, and in that picture book there was a picture of the burning of Troy. And that picture seemed so real to him that he believed Troy actually did exist. He still believed in it—even when he went to California from Germany and made one fortune in the California gold fields and then went on to the financial capitals of Europe and made another fortune. By then he was ready to look for Troy.

No matter how hard we looked, we would not find Narnia. But Heinrich Schliemann did find Troy—because he didn't have intellectual myopia telling him that this mound in Turkey could not be Troy. When the classical experts saw the mound or heard about it, they said it was just a mound; there was nothing underneath because Troy was imaginary. But Schliemann actually dug in that mound, and he found several cities. He missed the Troy that he wanted to find. The important thing, however, is that he laid the basis for a new kind of reality.

What happens is that our sense of reality reflects the world in which we live, and our world is more than just a collection of physical objects. It's also the meanings we give to those objects. We look around a room and see a table, chairs, lights; we look around us and see a room. But if by some magic we could take a caveman out of the Stone Age and bring him here, he would look around and see a very strange kind of cave. He would look above him and see these strange fires burning on the ceiling, with cold but intense light. And he might just wonder what the chairs were—maybe some new kind of animal. We look around, and there's a little voice inside our minds, deep within our unconscious, that says this is a room, those are lights, this is a table, and those are chairs. The caveman looks around and says this is a cave, those are fires, and these are just strange animal-like things. We're routinely reading the world in the way that we've been taught by our culture. Each moment that we exist, we are continually re-creating the universe that we inhabit. Like Aslan, each of us must sing our own Narnia into existence, and we do so each moment that we exist. Sometimes we assume our imagination is inferior at dealing with the external world; so critics sometimes assume that fantasy is inferior to realistic fiction because fantasy either deals with some suspension of a natural law or rewrites history, whereas a realistic novel supposedly mirrors everyday experience. But we expect more of realistic stories than we do of reality itself. And we encapsulate that truth in the saying "Truth is stranger than fiction."

We have to remember what Lloyd Alexander said—that the most

uncompromisingly realistic novel is still a manipulation of reality. When you talk about a realistic novel, what you're talking about is one or two aspects of that reality. So let's take *Huckleberry Finn,* one of the examples of realism. To a certain extent, compared to many novels at that time, it is realistic. The characters talk and act more like real people than do the sentimental heroes and heroines of the novels of the time. And yet, I doubt if any boy on the Mississippi frontier even in the 1840s could have found six bodies in just a few days and heard the tales of several other violent deaths. If you take a body count of *Huckleberry Finn,* it seems like a series of violent fantasies. Samuel Clemens had to be true not only to the physical reality around him, but also to an emotional reality. And the emotional reality was that Samuel Clemens lived in a violent universe, against which his cynicism and his sense of humor were his only defenses. What happens to the people whose society's sense of reality corresponds very poorly to their experience of the world? If society's sense of reality either doesn't explain enough about their experience or ignores too much, they have to seek alternate worlds. They become lovers of fantasy and science fiction.

The Story of the Golem

JAN MARK

The perspective through which we view heroes and villains has changed considerably, and the most obvious example of this fact, I think, is Charles Dickens. Dickens has survived because he was a superb writer, but a great deal of his subject material was very similar to that of his contemporaries, who sank without a trace. He was preoccupied, as most of them were, with a phenomenon we simply don't recognize anymore—that is, the hero as victim. Who cares what happens to Oliver Twist? He is a kind of hero-shaped hole in the middle of the narrative. Everything goes on around him. Oliver never does anything; he's simply there for people to be nasty to him while he wrings his pallid little flippers. The people we carry away from that narrative are Bill Sikes, who's a burglar and a murderer; Nancy, who's a whore; Fagin, who's a fence; and the Artful Dodger, who's a pickpocket—not the innocent and virtuous Oliver, who's a bore.

We now see and now admit what Stevenson was one of the first to have pointed out—that the real motive force behind any narrative is the villain. The hero reacts; that's all he's there for; it's the villain who makes things happen. But in contemporary fiction, especially in contemporary popular fiction, it's sometimes very difficult, if you are not told, to decide which of the main characters is the hero and which is the villain, because their behavior and attitudes are so morally dubious that—unless it is pointed out that the hero is of the right nationality or political persuasion—you'd never work it out for yourself. But we are taught that there are certain ways of recognizing a hero.

Inspiration is very nice when you get it. It's like being given a present you weren't expecting. You don't hand the present back and say, "My birthday's not till November." You take it and run. Inspiration comes similarly. You aren't expecting it, but you don't return it. You use it fast. I think Isaac in *The Ennead* was inspiration. I suddenly saw him. I tend to assemble my characters much as Frankenstein assembled his monster, using bits of people I've known.

I was thinking about *The Ennead* for a very long while before I began to write it, and when I began to write it, it changed shape dramatically. To begin with, I simply had Isaac on a planet, and the planet was floating footloose and gravity-free in space. I don't know much about physics or indeed astrophysics, but I do know that a planet needs a planetary system to anchor it. I had to give it a star; I had to give it fellow planets. This didn't all occur to me at once; it dawned on me bit by bit, as I began to assemble the story, that there were things missing. Isaac lived on this planet, and I didn't want to run the risk of the reader forming a background picture of my planet that was contrary to the one I'd formed. (Creating the background picture is always incumbent upon the writer.)

The whole purpose of the entire system was to show a colony that was being destroyed by its colonists. When I wrote the story, I was really thinking of Rhodesia as it was then—it became Zimbabwe subsequently—with a colonial government which had seceded from the parent nation in order to pursue its own way of life in direct contravention of the wishes of its neighbors. And this is what had happened on the planet I was writing about. The people who lived there had come from Earth; they colonized this planetary system because Earth was no longer habitable. They had moved remorselessly through the system, rendering derelict one planet after another. They were coming to the end of their resources. But wherever they went, however bad life was where they lived, there was always something worse to go back to. The one thing they feared more than anything else was being returned to the place from which they had come. Now, they came from all over the place—there was no real way of telling who any of them were or who any of them had been because they'd lost all sense of nationhood, racial distinction, nationality, religion, culture. They had no culture. It struck me as a particularly happy thought to name the nine planets I was writing about after the nine Muses, the tutelary goddesses of culture in ancient Greece, with their star named after the mother of the Muses, Mnemosyne, Memory. So there were these nine planets named after Art, Poetry, Music, and Dancing, circling a star called Memory and housing people who had no memory of anything—no religion, no art, no literature, no culture at all. They'd lost everything except for one particular person who, as it turned out—although I didn't intend this to begin with—was a Jew.

It seemed to me as I was finishing the book that, all things considered, he'd be the one most likely to retain some sense of cultural identity. But when I first wrote him into the manuscript, he was simply a name. The only way you could tell anything about the past histories of these people were their names. They might seem to have Greek, African, Scandinavian, British backgrounds by their names, but there's no other evidence at all. He was the Israeli contribution; his name was Moshe and in the first draft he had one line.

I think if you read *The Ennead* now, it would be very difficult to see where the story would be without Moshe. He seems to hold the whole thing together—and indeed he does—but he wasn't there to begin with. He was simply a name with one line. He was a prop character, but I began to see more and more possibilities in him, and as I was introducing themes of Greek and Roman mythology developed from the idea of the Muses, so I began to introduce Jewish mythology as well. But the knowledge of Greek and Roman mythology in England is considerably greater than the knowledge of Jewish mythology. I was taking a sizeable risk when I gave Moshe such a leading part. He tells a story which is misunderstood by the others, not because they don't know what he's talking about but because they don't know what a story is. They've lost even that form of communication. And when he tries to tell them a story, they shut him up. What he's saying upsets them. Not the gist of it, not the meaning of it, but the means he uses to tell it. They don't understand it. And it's the story of the golem.

It's very unfair to use literary allusion with small children because everything is so strange to them. They can't really differentiate between what is unknown and what is genuinely arcane. It's a sign of a developing mind to realize not only that one doesn't understand something but that there is a means of finding out. And I think an experienced reader would see that there is more in *The Ennead* than there appears to be. The use of literary allusion is a great pleasure to a writer; it's a shared secret, almost like a Masonic handshake, between the writer and the reader. By referring obliquely to other literary forms, if the reader can recognize the allusion, the writer is opening up another dimension behind the book that is actually being offered to the reader. You can't do that with children, and by doing it in *The Ennead*, I was really excluding children from getting very much out of it. The reason I wouldn't use the golem in a children's book is because the historical background to the story is so horrifying. It's not something that you can just offer; it needs to be explained.

The golem I was thinking of was the original Golem of Prague, made by the rabbi Löw in 1580 to protect the Jews in the ghetto from the Blood Libel at the time of Passover—from the curious belief that Jews needed Christian blood to make their matzos. This belief seems strange now, but it has broken out at various times throughout European history up to the 1930s. The rabbi made a golem, which was a clay figure; he made it out of the mud at the river, and there were two versions of how he brought it to life. One version says that he was a cabalist and that he conjured it to life through a ceremony involving himself, two of his pupils, and his son-in-law, who represented the signs of earth, air, fire, and water. But the version I like is the one that says he wrote upon the golem's forehead the *Shem*, the unpronounceable name of God, and that as soon as the name was written there, the golem stood up and was a man. In Hebrew the word *golem* simply means an unfinished clay figure; in Yiddish it's rather more insulting—someone whose mental processes are unfinished. And although he could walk and obey commands, the golem could not think, and he couldn't speak, and he obeyed the rabbi's commands and performed many acts of heroism, defending the Jews from the Christians in the ghetto. But ultimately he disobeyed the rabbi just once, and the rabbi, seeing how dangerous he might become, erased the *Shem* from his forehead, and he fell down dead.

Moshe tries to tell this story in the course of *The Ennead* because he sees it as an analogy to the way in which the people living on the planet Erato behave. They don't act rationally; they react; they are afraid. They're afraid of being sent back where they came from, and he says, "You've got the name of that place written on your foreheads; everything you do is because of the fear that you have." But they don't understand him; they don't understand his message or the way he's telling it, and they disregard it. *The Ennead* wasn't meant to be a book about religion; I don't think it is. If it's about anything, it's about the results of a particular political system.

It's a convention in science fiction, indeed in many kinds of fiction, that people led by a charismatic leader will band together and overcome tyranny. Experience leads us to suppose, I think, that the only people who are the least interested in overthrowing a tyrant are those with a worse tyrant to put in his place. And people support tyrannies by inertia, not by force. Most people will do anything for a quiet life, and this is how people lived in my book. They sold each other, they betrayed each other, and they would do anything in order to be left alone; this was what supported the tyranny that suppressed them.

The tyranny in *Divide and Rule* was of a rather different sort, but I want to touch on that to finish with. It involves a journey of a kind, but it really is a very symbolic one. It's a cyclical book: it deals with seasons, it ends chronologically where it began, and it deals at heart with the cyclical sacrifice. Again, initially I was writing about a political situation. This is the proof, I suppose, of the fact that although all fiction derives from a known constant, from a certain truth, the truth with which the writer begins may not be the one ultimately presented to the reader. And the certainty I began with was not the one that really informs the book I finished. At the time I wrote it, it seemed to me that one of the things we humans fear most is the unmarked grave, the unrecorded death. The fear of disappearing is what informs this book—the fear of dying and of no one knowing what became of us. We can suffer a great many things so long as people know we're suffering. I think this is why we are able to scream.

Traveling the Road to Ithaca

JANE YOLEN

Writing is a process, a journey on which the author goes hand in hand with her characters. If everything is written down in the author's mind before the journey is started, then (in the words of Truman Capote) you are not a writer but a typist. You have to be open to wonder as you go along, wonder and discovery, uncovery, and recovery. *Discovery:* the act of coming upon something that is unexpected. *Uncovery:* finding out all you can about your discovery. *Recovery:* using your discovery to tell more about character, setting, plot, and ultimately theme.

It is theme—that elusive word that literature teachers mangle (sending elementary school children home with the instructions to find the "author's intent" and high school students to discover the "thematic underpinnings" of a book)—that I want to deal with now. The theme of every quest story, every hero story, is—in Joseph Campbell's words, "fundamentally . . . inward." The hero seeks himself, seeks to mature, so that when he comes into his powers, he uses them for others, not himself. That is why the story of Jason is a quest but not a hero tale, for vainglorious, selfish, egotistical Jason wants all the honors and does not share. He is the earliest antihero. The heroes we pattern our children's books upon are most often the unlikely hero, the youngest son in the fairy tale, who goes forth like Tolkien's Frodo, although he does not know the way. It is Arthur pulling the sword for his foster brother Kay. And Taran discovering that he really does not need to know his name. And Morgon unriddling for the sake of the riddles themselves, not because he wants a kingdom. And, I hope, Jakkin, who tries to save the dragons of Austar and in so doing discovers and saves himself.

But to ask someone to offer the author's intent (friendship, loving-kindness, do not cry over spilt milk) and grade it as the correct answer is to overlook the simple fact that each reader reads a different book. The book is created between author and reader, re-created at each reading. William Blake wrote, "A fool sees not the same tree that a wise man sees."

Which is not to say that the tree the wise man sees is the correct one. Only what *he* sees. And again Blake, "The apple tree never asks the beech how he shall grow, nor the lion, the horse how he shall take his prey." When we discuss books, we are all like the blind men and the elephant, each describing a different thing, a different part, that which we hold in our own hands.

I am reminded of the child who described *The Tale of Peter Rabbit* as a sad story because poor Mr. McGregor had no lettuce. And so it is. The child's insight is added to my own. That is how we get to know books, layer upon layer, more layers than the author labored to put there, but there nonetheless because every reader brings his or her own background and baggage to the reading of the book. And that changes with every new reading.

When I go home from here, over the next few months I will be traveling with Jakkin and Akki across the harsh Austarian landscape and deep into the honeycombed caverns that run through the mountains. These journeys are uncharted until I get there, and then the book *is* the map. But what the chart will not show to the casual eye is that it is a sure mapping of the heart: Here the four chambers belong to Jakkin, Akki, the dragons—and me. And through some magical, mystical process—somewhat like the christian Trinity—we are four in one. For all the actors in a story belong to an author and are the author, yet they are uniquely themselves as well. And if the author's heart is, in reality, protected by the sturdy wall that is the breastbone, on the pages of the book it has no such bulwark. Anyone can read the story and—loving it—take it in in a kind of literary eucharist; cannibalism to its detractors, and the ultimate sharing to those of us who believe.

You are an invited guest on a literary journey. You think your load is light—the weight of a hardcover or a paperback book. But like Saint Christopher's burden—which he took without thinking and which grew heavier with each step through the water—a well-crafted book holds similar weight.

Alternate Worlds

ZILPHA KEATLEY SNYDER

My fascination with a world that seems ordinary and mundane but in which one cannot really be certain about boundaries and possibilities began, I think—as so many things do—in childhood. Growing up in a rather limited, narrow environment, I escaped through books and games into a much wider world. I loved almost any kind of story, any kind of imaginary world, but I loved best the kind that suggested that around any corner, no matter how unpromising, a free and boundless adventure might be waiting.

Rather than choosing to write about a totally diverse world, one set on another planet or in a different time span, I began by writing about a close, familiar world—the kind of world we wake up to every day of our repetitive, predictable lives—but about a day that somehow turns out to be transformed into something strange and new and magical. A reviewer once wrote about me that I was the kind of writer who tended to walk the boundaries between here and otherwhere with a foot on either side. An apt description, I think.

A long time ago Jean Karl told me that what an author must know about her story is like an iceberg—a huge pyramid only the tip of which appears in the written text but which is supported and authenticated by the underlying mass. I've found this to be true—and in the case of an alternate world, terribly true. One must work out every detail of the new society, every aspect of their domestic, social, educational, commercial, agricultural, governmental, and religious lives. It's a large order. I remember that when I was working in Green-sky, I amassed huge amounts of information about my new world—much of which never appeared in the books. I even knew, for instance, what the plumbing was like in Green-sky.

It's such a wonderful feeling to watch a child discover that reading is a marvelous adventure rather than a chore. I know that many writers for children say they do not write specifically with a child audience in mind. They write to please themselves, and what they have to say just happens to be right for children also. This isn't true for me. I am very aware of my audience. Sometimes I can almost see them out there reacting as I write. Sometimes I think, "Oh, you're going to like this part."

So, if I have a credo it is "I write for joy." For if there is no joy, what a book may have to say about significant issues matters very little, because its readers will be very few.

The Face of a Spider

H. M. HOOVER

A person's outlook on most voyages in literature is a matter of perspective, shaped by the passage of time; thus perspective is usually looking back, and doing so from a personal point of view. Also, everyone's perspective depends on the type of person he or she is.

I have always thought, for example, that Medea got a very bad press. When we consider the Princess and her voyage with Jason and the Argonauts, looking back from our point of view and from a woman's point of view of what we would now consider reality, we see that she's been tricked by the gods into falling in love with a total stranger. She leaves with him abruptly. She's on a ship with fifty men, all strangers. They claim to be kings and princes, and according to the myths, they talk nonstop. They tell stories of hunting and war. (I grew up with people who told hunting and war stories, and wouldn't want to be on a small ship with them.) Two of the men are really women in drag. Two others wear makeup, and a third claims that he's a centaur. There's absolutely no privacy. The ship is small enough to be beached at night. During the day the deck is cluttered with benches and oars because, of course, they're rowing. There's no bathroom, which is awkward. No one seems able to navigate, and according to some of the myths, they get lost in the Libyan desert—which is really lost when you're going from the Black Sea to the Greek islands. And Medea has to lead them home.

Then when she finally reaches Greece and helps Jason reclaim his throne, which he promptly gives away, Medea learns that this honeymoon voyage is going to be the highlight of her marriage. And people wonder that she turned mean!

Of course, this story that we call "Jason and the Argonauts" is primarily the work of storytellers and writers. The men who existed, if they did exist, were, in all probability, pirates or tradesmen trying to open commerce with

191

various cities along the Black Sea coast. They were the Bronze Age equivalent of traveling salesmen. But that doesn't make a very good story, so you need a myth, or you need storytellers and writers to create myths that come down through the years, and as time passes, those myths and stories become realities of their own.

The thing to remember is that there is no metaphor to real-life voyages so far as the people involved in them are concerned. There we are, just slogging along, trying to make our plane, trying to reach the destination that we've set out for. The trip has no psychological overtones, no mythic meanings. We're just too tired to worry about it until it's over, and then we start thinking about it, and the story gets better than the trip actually was, which is what good fiction is.

Adventures, when they occur, along with the growing and learning they may bring, also interfere with regular hours, getting to work, getting the kids to school, picking up the dry cleaning, and PTA meetings. And you really don't appreciate them at the time. Adventures are something that you try to avoid in daily life if you possibly can.

In science fiction, which is what I write, your perspective changes quite often from looking back to looking forward, but most other details of fiction basically remain the same. You're still trying to tell a good story. Most of my books entail an adventure; home and loving parents don't figure much because loving parents tend to view adventure as a very dangerous thing for children. And since the books have children as main characters and parents are notorious for wanting to deprive their children of a certain sort of thrill, I usually try to write parents out.

Like most fantasy writers, I read a lot of mythology. I read quite a bit of history, science, and sociology; I enjoy it. For example, I've always been excited by the views of an electron microscope for the perspective that they give. You see pollen grains that look just like sycamore burrs. You see human hairs that look like logs, and if the hair has been bleached, the logs look as though they're weathered and are stripping up in little pieces, which you'd never notice if you saw them without magnification.

The most fascinating thing I ever saw was a little gray spider. Looked at through the microscope, it was about the size of a little fingernail—you suddenly saw these bright blue eyes and a little gray, furry face. And it looked frightened. And that fascinated me, this tiny detail: the response that the little creature had was, for all intents and purposes, intelligent.

If you look at a pansy face, you see that it's a landing field for bees, with color code lines pointing toward the terminal for the unloading of freight, which is the pollen.

There's no real need for science fiction writers to sit down and invent a monster or a creature totally out of their imaginations. If you simply look around you, you will see the most wondrous creatures, and they're all of this Earth. All you have to do is enlarge them or adapt them to another world. And most of them will adapt if you are careful enough.

When I do create a different planet, I try to make up established laws for that world and stick to those laws, because I think it's more fun that way. I like to give stories a sense of place.

History keeps repeating itself. The space shuttle was designed to do what the Argonauts and the sailors of their time, the Bronze Age, used to do—keep the shore in sight. Our shuttle always stays close to Earth for this reason. It can't survive the depths of space any more than those small boats could survive the deep oceans.

The fact remains that no matter how science fictiony we get, the most glorious spacecraft we'll ever know is Earth, and it's probably the only ship floating in space on which we'll ever be able to stand and look out at the stars without any added breathing apparatus or anything between us and those stars. And yet we treat Earth as if it were disposable, as if when we thoroughly muck it up, we can journey to another world. And the fact is, I rather doubt that we can. I don't think we can ever put Earth in our past because while the term *man in space* evokes grand visions of man standing against a star-filled background, the reality is that when we go to space, we're going to take ourselves along. Once off Earth we will never be able to stand free, looking out at those stars. We'll always be enclosed in a very small container, comparatively speaking, and if we step out of that container, we'll be in a smaller container—either craft or spacesuit.

I think it's interesting to speculate on whether or not Earth-born minds could stand this sort of travel, whether we could endure the sort of disassociation from Earth that future space travel might allow. Of course, now we're very primitive; we're simply in the planning stages, and we're worrying about the technology. What I think we really should worry about, just as much as the equipment to get there, is the psychology and the physiology that's going to be involved, and whether we really can bear it. I'm not sure I could.

Any work of fiction is a form of fantasy, no matter how real it is. It's all imagined. But the difference between fantasy and realistic fiction is that fantasy has to make sense and realistic fiction doesn't. I had lunch today with a friend of mine, who is also a writer, and he said that in his latest book he had one incident that was taken from real life, and that was the one incident that the editor asked him to remove because nobody would believe it. And that is very true. You cannot use coincidence in fantasy and make people believe it. As much as possible I try to stick to established fact and theory, because as a child I was always confused by writers who ignored realism. I had a very literal mind, and I noticed when authors ignored facts; and I was *really* irritated when they ignored facts and created different facts, and then ignored those to make their plot work out. I just couldn't follow it.

In creating a fictional world, I try to make the world real, perhaps more real than I would if it was on Earth. We're very much influenced by place, or at least I am. I think it's definitely beneficial in writing to establish what the weather is like and whether or not there are birds in that world and what color the grass is and how the air smells, so that readers know where they are. They can feel where they are; they can know what life would be like if they walked there. And that's what a writer hopes for, to achieve the effect of realism no matter what the material.

The Perilous Realms: A Colloquy

EDITED BY BETTY LEVIN

Opening Statement

LLOYD ALEXANDER

Staying alive and relatively sane on the downhill slope of the twentieth century is a precarious occupation. The profession of literature is equally hazardous. Writers are running out of material as rapidly as we are running out of other natural resources. Sex and violence, inhumanity, the abuse and corruption of power—in short, most of our human proclivities which give writers their basic stock-in-trade—have been preempted by the six o'clock news. Science fiction has been outstripped by science; the popular song "Send in the Clowns" will have to be replaced by "Send in the Clones." Reality is more horrendous than realism. The monstrousness abroad in the real world makes the evil Sauron, in comparison, almost as benign as Colonel Sanders.

Writers who believe in what they do, however, will continue to write because they must; because to them, in a world seemingly bent on its own destruction, the act of creation is the only thing that makes any sense. But devotion to art does not confer immunity to risk. "The Perilous Realms" is a title well chosen. The perils are numerous, too numerous, and so I'll limit myself to only three: the perils to writers of fantasy, to writers of realism, and to readers of both.

First, let me suggest what I think is the essential formal difference between the two modes: If the work contains an element of the impossible (at least as we currently understand the word), we classify it as fantasy; if the work does not contain this element, if its events could indeed physically happen in the real world, we classify it as realism. I should add immediately that this is simply a categorical convenience. The difference is technical, not aesthetic.

The definition, however, hints at the dangers. The pitfall in writing fantasy is not adding enough realism. Fantasy deals with the impossible, not the illogical. Creating a secondary world where the impossible becomes ordinary does not carry with it a license to do as one pleases. In its conception and in its deep substructures, the fantasy world must, if anything, be more carefully rationalized than the real world.

The real world, as we all know, sometimes to our bewilderment, is often illogical, inconsistent, a kind of elaborate random walk. In fantasy, magical elements have to make sense in their own framework. The goal, of course, is to make fantasy seem absolutely real and convincing. This statement applies not only to setting but to characters as well. The writer may populate his imaginary world with all manner of imaginary creatures, human or otherwise. But within that world they must be as carefully observed as in any work of realism. They must have real weight, solidity, dimension. Their fantastic condition must speak to our real one.

Sheer inventiveness can be amusing, entertaining, even dazzling, and I don't mean to downgrade it. The danger is that too often it can turn into sheer gimmickry. Choosing the wrong form is, I think, probably the biggest risk in any kind of creation. Fantasy, however, seems to offer special temptations. To the unwary writer it promises such fun and freedom, great soaring flights of unbounded imagination. This promise can turn out to be a siren song. Before listening to it, the writer would be well advised to ask, Why fantasy instead of some other form? Unless fantasy is the best and only way the writer can express what is deepest in his mind and heart, the writer should consider some other mode and spare himself, and his readers, much labor and grief.

This is not to say that writers of realism have it any easier or are any less vulnerable to dangers. If a work of fantasy can fail through lack of realism, a work of realism can fail through lack of fantasy. In this case I use the word *fantasy* in the sense of transformative imagination. Realism is not reality. The magic of realism is that it can *seem* to be real life, more real even than life itself. But this marvelous illusion comes from the transformative imagination of the writer—imagination that shapes, manipulates, and illuminates. Without it the work is only a play of surfaces.

"True to life" may not always be true enough. The difficulty perhaps is in confusing truth with objectivity. By its very nature, art can never be objective. Try as we may, we can't "tell it like it is." We can only tell it the way it seems to us.

And this, of course, is what we must do—in realism or in fantasy—if we hope to create anything of durable value. If writers, in any mode, do less than their best, the reader is psychologically and emotionally short-changed. If literature follows the same process of erosion we see in our other natural resources, even in our language itself, the reader's taste and perceptions will be dulled and distorted.

We have always needed good art to sustain us, to strengthen us, even to console us for being born human. Where better can we learn to see through the eyes of others, to gain compassion, to try to make sense of the world outside ourselves and the world within ourselves? Certainly not by reading the labels on processed foods or the literary equivalents thereof.

With so many perils besetting us in the real world, it seems quixotic to worry about the world of literature. But the world of literature—which is the world of ideas, attitudes, and emotions—is no less real than this island planet we're obliged to live on. Like it or not, it's all we have, at least for the time being. Which is precisely why we must keep on and manage somehow to make the best of it—or make it as best we can.

Whichever road we follow, the perilous realms of realism and fantasy, at the end, turn out to be the same place.

Opening Statement

NATALIE BABBITT

As a child I read fairy tales and myths almost exclusively, while my sister, two years older, spent all her time reading *Oliver Twist* and things like that. Fairy tales gave me a great deal of confidence about life. Somehow or other, they helped to explain things to me in a way that *Little Women* couldn't. Within the last ten years I've come across two books which have helped me to understand why that kind of reading was so comforting.

The first is Joseph Campbell's *Hero with a Thousand Faces*. It was a revelation. What Campbell has to say, in simple terms, is that the hero is universal and the path he follows is universal—in myth, in fairy tale, in folktale. And so, at bottom, all fantasists are telling the same story.

Campbell says the pattern consists of separation, adventure, and return. The hero crosses some kind of threshold in order to be tested in the otherworld and then returns to the real world. I realized that this was something I had known all my life from reading fairy tales, because they take the hero on that path every time. And thinking about it more carefully, it seemed to me that a lot of realistic fiction does the same thing. But often the hero of realism will refuse the call to adventure. Or he will cross the threshold and become bogged down or fail at the trial, as we often do in life. Or he will succeed in the trial and then refuse the return, which is symbolic of withdrawal from reality or the waking state or life.

Fantasy, which covers things larger than life, must follow the complete round. The hero must return. The happy ending, according to Campbell, is not a denial of real life, but a going beyond, a superseding of the life we know. So, finally, viewed in this way, fantasy becomes a kind of religion.

The other book that has moved me very much is Carl Sagan's *The Dragons of Eden*. A lot of statements in that book support the things Campbell says, particularly about the imagined differences between myth and dream and fantasy. At one point he quotes Erich Fromm who has said that the images of fantasy may possibly come from the right side of the brain—the creative, intuitive side. Fromm calls those images the "forgotten language" of dream, myth, and fantasy. This concept fits in well with what Campbell is saying when he claims that the pattern the hero follows is one we all know and have always known—and that we were born knowing, whether we realize it or not.

I think that all of us who work in fantasy sometimes feel trapped by that pattern. We know what has to happen in order for the story to work properly. The pattern must be followed every time. We expect it, and the reader expects it (consciously or subconsciously). But at the same time, there is no satisfaction without it. I agree with a fifth-century philosopher quoted by Sagan: "Myths are things that never were, but always are." And that's what interests me.

Opening Statement

SUSAN COOPER

I always say, when I'm talking about my books, that I don't write children's books; I write books that are published for children. And when I began thinking about this colloquium, I realized that in the same way I never really thought of myself as writing fantasy. The books just come out as they come and are published for children.

I remember when I was first writing books, I was a reporter on a newspaper, writing in the evening, writing short stories, mostly autobiographical, as we all do at the beginning. And I remember one day looking down from the top of a double-decker bus and seeing a green horse walking across Piccadilly Circus. Well, in fact, it was an advertisement for a movie called *The Green Horse*.

The click that goes off in your head when you see something impossible starts you off in a new direction. It started me off, first of all, into a futuristic novel. And to my astonishment, when the book came out in paperback, there it said on the spine, "Penguin Science Fiction." And I thought, Good heavens! I've written a science fiction book. But the button that presses itself in your imagination—not necessarily by seeing a green horse but by finding the release of going beyond the bounds of possibility—tends to influence the direction you will take with all the books you write after that.

I think also I was retreating into a part of my imagination that was closely linked with a couple of books by John Masefield, *The Midnight Folk* and *The Box of Delights*, which are marvelous fantasies for children. My imagination possibly jumped back to those because I was in a strange country, homesick and rather unhappy. And out of that came these books called *The Dark Is Rising* sequence, perhaps going into the imaginative, looking-back part of one's head instead of into the more intensely focused world of the realistic novel.

We fantasy writers are not writing about things that happened to us in the way that Bob Cormier described when he said, "I am writing out of my own emotions." Maybe we hide all the emotion behind fantasy. Perhaps we are putting a protective layer between our naked souls and you, the reader. I think it's likely that fantasists need that filter. The things we write come out through the subconscious, not from looking at actual incidents and deciding that they are a great basis for a book. We don't work that way. Katherine Paterson said about the fantasy she took out, or left only hinted at, in *Terabithia*: "Why did I succeed only when I stopped trying?" I think that's the only way you *can* succeed with fantasy. The only way you're going to catch the butterfly is not by running around with a big net, but by waiting for it to alight.

When I was writing *Silver on the Tree*, I wrote a passage where two boys come to a door. They pushed the door and went through it, and I had no idea, having got to this point in the plot, what they were going to find on the other side. That was probably the point at which I stopped writing that day and went to bed. And the next time I sat down to write, they were through the door, and I started writing the way you do when you get stuck; you just write. It's almost an automatic process. I began to find myself describing in very precise detail a strange place that was a series of corridors and a mixture of a theater and a library. It was only when I got to the end that I realized what I had been describing was a recurring dream that I've had perhaps four times in the last twenty-five years. I'd forgotten it. I'd never written it down. Into the book it came.

But it seems to me you can't say that this is the way fantasy works and that realism doesn't work this way. This is what happens to everybody. Dreaming is a creative process, says one neurologist. Maybe that's what we are—creative dreamers.

Panel Discussions: The Perilous Realms

Two separate discussions followed these opening remarks. The first panel included Lloyd Alexander, Susan Cooper, and Natalie Babbitt, and was moderated by Betty Levin. In the second, these panelists, joined by M. E. Kerr and Katherine Paterson, responded to questions from the audience.

I

Betty Levin: My first question is about magic, about something Lloyd said
   in an interview: "I'm a very hardheaded realist. One of the driving ideas
   in all the Prydain chronicles is the uselessness of magic. Magic can't help
   us." I wonder, Lloyd, what then is its attraction for you? It's there all the
   time.

Lloyd Alexander: I know. There is no easy answer to that. The attraction is
   that magic elements, as devices, are indeed fascinating to me. They're
   fun, and they can be very profound, used as metaphor. On the other
   hand, as much as I enjoy magical things, I don't believe philosophically
   that we can count on them. Our own effort as human beings is far more
   powerful than any magic anybody could conceive.

Levin: In that same interview you speak of Alan Garner as being much
   more mystical than you are.

Alexander: He seems so to me, yes. But if you take the word *mysticism* to
   mean a direct knowledge of something without intellectual mediation, I
   think all writers are very likely mystics. I think we catch on to things
   directly.

Susan Cooper: I think fantasy writers are more like poets.

Levin: You have said, Lloyd, that you regard Alan Garner as one of the
   great masters in the field of fantasy. And his early books are certainly
   laden with magic. Is magic itself one of the great perils in this genre?

Alexander: It's a technical danger to the extent that you've got to be so
   careful not to let it get out of hand and drive you to an illogicality. For
   example, the worst danger that anybody can fall into is to have the
   unbeatable weapon, because if you have the unbeatable weapon, the
   story is over.

Levin: Ursula Le Guin has said, "In fantasy there is nothing but the
   writer's vision of the world. There is no borrowed reality of history, of
   current events. . . . There is no comfortable matrix of the commonplace
   to substitute for the imagination, to provide ready-made emotional
   response. . . . To create what Tolkien calls 'a secondary universe' is to
   make a new world. A world where no voice has ever spoken before."
   What have you to say to this, you who use the voices of faerie or myth
   or the epic tradition?

Natalie Babbitt: She's wrong!

Cooper: Well, maybe she's right for her kind of fantasy, which is making
   a whole other world. But our kind of fantasy starts off in this world.
   Extraordinary things happen within the framework of the real world.
   She's right in her sense, but wrong in ours.

Alexander: I think she's wrong even in her sense. It's a wonderful
   statement, a beautiful idea. I don't know if it holds up if you look at it

closely. It seems to me that no matter what form we're working in, there is no way that we—being born as human beings into this world—can possibly do something that is not relevant. We can't escape from the real world. We may disguise it or turn it into metaphor, but the real world is all we have. There is no way we can even express something ultra-normal; we don't have the raw material to do it. There may well be civilizations somewhere based on an entirely different something we can't even express; we don't have the vocabulary for it. Everything in our heads comes from the same raw material, the same place.

Levin: This leads me to the fantasist's sense of place. When you start to write, do you have a mental map—whether it is a real map of Wales or a made-up map of a house or of the woods around Winnie's house?

Babbitt: You have to know the place intimately, whether you made it up out of whole cloth or whether it's a real place. You have to know what it looks like, what it feels like, what it smells like, and how long it takes to get there.

Cooper: And that's the real world inside your head.

Babbitt: Yes. If you can draw a map of it afterward, that's fine. Maps in books are largely decorative. I think you need the maps in Tolkien because it's a very long story and they're helpful. But even without a map, you'd better be accurate.

Levin: Suppose you're working within a real place, as Susan sometimes does?

Cooper: It depends on what you mean by *real*. Once you conceive of a place you're writing about, it's real, although all the time I was writing *The Grey King* and *Silver on the Tree*, both of which are set in my part of Wales, I did have two ordnance survey maps on the inside of the closet door of my study. Largely, I expect, because looking at a certain bit of the map would send me back to this picture in my head.

Babbitt: I think the situation is the same for a fantasist as it is for a realist. I think it's how you view the world that determines the sense of place. If we're going to describe a room, it can't be just any room. In *Tuck Everlasting* the wood around Winnie's house has to be just here. In our own lives this placement is terribly important, so it comes out in our books.

Levin: I'd like to move from the geography of fantasy to the whole question of transition. There are two powerful opposing views (with many variations) on getting from the realistic situation to fantasy. W. H. Auden writes of one view in his afterword for George MacDonald's *The Golden Key*: "A fairy tale like *The Golden Key* . . . demands of the reader total surrender; so long as he is in its world, there must for him be no other. . . . The way, the only way, to read a fairy tale is the same as that prescribed for Tangle at one stage of her journey." And then Auden quotes MacDonald, who describes a great hole in the floor of a cave with no stairs leading down it.

Tangle is told, "You must throw yourself in. There is no other way." Another view is expressed by Roger Drury in a *Horn Book* article included in Paul Heins's *Crosscurrents of Criticism*. Drury says most combinations of realism and fantasy can be boiled down to two types: real people in fantastic situations and fantastic people in real situations. "In traveling away from the center of our experience, we make a gradual transition from the probable, to the unlikely, to the downright impossible. We get there by imperceptible stages. Do we cross a boundary? Perhaps. But where the boundary is drawn depends on the traveler." I wonder how you feel about this.

Babbitt: I think I differ a little from Lloyd and Susan and also from Joseph Campbell in *Hero with a Thousand Faces*. Campbell says the threshold between the real world and the other world is terribly important. And in most fairy tales you can find those thresholds. In the first of the Narnia books the children go into the wardrobe and then into the other world, and Alice goes down the rabbit hole. For me that other world is there all the time. And in my books one of the things I like to do is explore that threshold. There isn't really one world for me; the two exist simultaneously. If anything, in *Tuck Everlasting* it's the fantastic element moving into the real world. A great deal depends on how receptive you are, whether you are aware of the fantasy element, of the subconscious.

Cooper: That's right. It's a question of different levels of awareness. It's a little like being raised in Britain. There you are in a country that's had people living in it for God knows how many hundreds or thousands of years, especially in Wales. You walk those mountains and the awareness of the past is all around you. And I tend to write from that kind of awareness. The magic, if you like, is all around. There is no moment at which one slips down the rabbit hole or jumps into the pit.

Babbitt: But there are certain kinds of places that have this atmosphere, and certain places that don't. I get no sense of that otherworld in an apartment house in New York City or in my own house in upstate New York.

Cooper: I often think that is why there are so many more fantasy writers in Britain than in America.

Babbitt: That may be.

Levin: Can we move on to the question of formula in fantasy? Brian Aldiss has said: "One element that menaces literature is formula. Formula is the enemy within, the hardening of the arteries . . . The whole point of formula is that it first teases and then satisfies expectation. Anything else is bad business." I wonder how this stacks up with your view of the whole tradition of fantasy, which includes formula—except that it may be a dirty word to describe the sort of thing Tolkien and Lewis address in fantasy, the recognition and consolation.

Alexander: Perhaps the difference is that formula may be one thing or the other, although the monomyth might seem to be formula—what Natalie was talking about in Joseph Campbell. I don't call that formula any more than I would call the gestation of a child a formula.

Babbitt: It's like calling champagne a beverage.

Alexander: There's a qualitative difference.

Levin: Yet some critics of fantasy say the reason it is unreal and unsatisfying is that we know Winnie will not go to the spring and drink the water. We know that Arawn will be defeated in the end. We know that the Dark will be overcome by the Old Ones.

Alexander: We know these things, but the characters don't. We can go to *Hamlet* and see it a thousand times; we know exactly—word for word, motion for motion—what's going to happen. Hamlet doesn't know it. This is what gives the play perpetual, tremendous drama, and we are moved every time.

Babbitt: In fantasy you know that triumph is going to happen, because you know the basic pattern of life, and most philosophies and most religions tell us that death is a triumph. And the end of the story is a kind of death, and that is a triumphant thing. In realism expectations depend upon what decade you're in. For the last twenty or thirty years we have known when we pick up an adult realistic novel that the hero is going to be thwarted and will not succeed. But the pattern that now exists in fantasy crops up through all recorded literature in different genres. It's always there. The general attitude or degree of acceptance for it is what changes. During our lifetime, the only place you can find this pattern is in children's stories, the only place where it's acceptable.

Levin: But children are your audience, and they recognize the form, the pattern, even if they don't know that they do. Take the totemic power of names, for instance. Even though children aren't conscious of it, they recognize something when Merriman speaks of the power the Dark will have if it knows your name or when Gwydion tells about Hen Wen knowing the Horned King's name. What about this recognition?

Babbitt: We recognize these things without having to be told.

Cooper: It all goes very deep.

Babbitt: There is a theory—and I believe it—that we all know these things without realizing we know them. They are so ancient.

Cooper: It's part of our consciousness.

Babbitt: It's part of the way we deal with life. Over and over again I find that something I wrote that I thought was original was written decades ago by some philosopher. But in a sense that's what makes writing fantasy satisfying.

Levin: And it's also what makes people suspicious about fantasy.

Babbitt: My husband is suspicious about fantasy, but not for that reason.

He does not like those symbols and devices to come between him and the truth that the writer is talking about. And I think what Susan said at the outset is true. We writers of fantasy do speak through certain kinds of filters which make it more comfortable for us to talk about the things we talk about, which are often pretty basic and sometimes quite difficult and go beyond personal loss or personal problems. We are trying to deal with unanswerable questions.

Levin: Is there a double standard, then? Do we as readers and as critics have expectations of fantasy that are different from our expectations of realism?

Babbitt: I think so. I think fantasy is always the same and has always been the same since people started telling stories, but realism changes as the world changes. And the world needs that constant redefinition, but you have to redefine realism in ways that are understandable to the current reading population.

Cooper: You have a double standard the same way you have a double standard in the theater. When you go to a straight play, it is happening right there mostly as it would happen in real life. When you go to the opera, you know that these people are standing there, singing. Your children don't wake up in the morning and sing, "Dear Mother!" But you've stopped noticing because that's the convention in opera, and you're in it. It awakens other things in your head.

Levin: I think that's true for the kind of fantasy you write and for the kind of fantasy Lloyd writes. I wonder if it's true for the kind of fantasy—if it is fantasy—that Natalie writes.

Babbitt: I guess I have to confess that the main characters in all my stories are not people, but ideas. That's not to say that I'm not hampered in the same way that anybody is by my characters wanting to take over. My characters are very real to me.

Cooper: And that's why you put the prologue at the beginning each time.

Babbitt: In a sense, yes. Because it's really my voice. I don't set out to tell a story. I guess what I'm trying to do is answer unanswerable questions that trouble me. But I still get trapped with formula. I agree it is not a very attractive word, but I think formula exists.

Levin: I think children come to your books with different expectations. And as they go from page to page, even when the Man in the Yellow Suit doesn't get a name, they are brought into a world that is different from whenever-in-Prydain and twentieth-century wherever-Will-is. I think it's necessary to take this difference into account.

Babbitt: Yes, *Tuck Everlasting* doesn't have the trappings of fantasy to prepare you for what happens. I think it's too bad to violate the expectations of the reader. But if you start taking readers into account too much, you're just crippled; you can't do anything.

Levin: In Natalie's review of Susan's *Silver on the Tree*, Natalie writes: "In the final scene Cooper makes an important point clear. The Dark of these five books is not intended to represent the modern face of evil, which, to say the least, shows no sign of vulnerability. Rather, Cooper's Dark and her Light symbolize the lingering power of ancient superstition in religions buried in the subconscious of us all. The stuff of dreams and nightmares. And Cooper warns us through the Old One, Merriman, that the next threat will come not by the spilling of blood but through the coldness in the hearts of men." I want to ask you how you feel that kind of good and evil is divisible—the old from the current. And I want to ask Susan what happens when the old evil possesses somebody who is living and interacting with people in the present and who have to respond today.

Cooper: I don't think of evil as an abstraction. I just think of it as something that is inside all of us; it always has been, and it's old in that respect.

Babbitt: I think we call a lot of things evil today which aren't evil in the classic sense. The Man in the Yellow Suit has no name because if he were named, he would be diminished thereby into a simple evil figure, which he isn't. Not evil the way we think of the Nazi commandant in the prison camp. The kind of evil Susan is talking about is much greater than that; she means, finally, a moral choice dictated by very ancient things.

Levin: I'm still mystified by the separate concept of evil, evil that is set off and then exists in its own right, in a sort of existential way, and that occurs so often in this literature, whether in the Man in the Yellow Suit or in the Cauldron Born.

Babbitt: I think the difference is that on the one hand we're talking about good and evil, and on the other we're talking about order and chaos. And chaos is something much worse than any man-conceived or man-made evil. What Susan is talking about, and Lloyd, too, and I am also, is that difference—which is why the Man in the Yellow Suit has to die. He is not simply a bad man. He is a symbol of the release of chaos or the loss of order.

Alexander: With the Cauldron Born, it's not so much that they are evil in themselves as that they have been forced to become the slaves of evil. The worst evil that has been perpetrated on them is that they have lost all memory of themselves as ever having been human beings. So that the question at issue is the evil of dehumanization. That, I think, is an enormous current problem.

Levin: That's an essential realism.

Alexander: Yes.

Cooper: I'm thinking back to my mountains. Occasionally, you can be walking across them and you will get a great sense of evil or of something bad, and it always turns out to be somewhere somebody has lived. Never mind what happened there. It turns out to be the site of an old Iron Age hill fort or something. And I guess the evil I put into my books all comes from the mind of man. It comes from the same kind of inexplicable malice that Robert Cormier deals with in *The Chocolate War*.

II

M. E. Kerr: I think of myself as living entirely in a world of fantasy, even though there are no green horses in my books. I think that whether you are writing fantasy or realism, you can have a social conscience and a moral viewpoint in children's literature, in a way that you can't when you're writing for adults.

Natalie Babbitt: I think one of the ways of finding out your moral principles is through writing.

Audience: I'm wondering what it is about the Celtic ground that seems to be so fruitful for fantasy writers.

Susan Cooper: I've absolutely no answer to that question. I happen to have a part-Celtic imagination, so that's one good reason.

Betty Levin: Doesn't it have a lot to do with the English-speaking tradition? The Celts left their mark all over Europe, and it is certainly strong in our language and literature.

Lloyd Alexander: I'd like to push a little bit further on that. It seems to me that each mythology has its own particular flavor and attitudes. There's a difference, which I can't define too well, between the northwestern mythologies and the Mediterranean mythologies. It's not necessarily the surface features of the mythology that affect us; beneath the surface there is an attitude that interests us and attracts us. I'm almost ready to say maybe we need it; it answers an almost dietary deficiency. We tend to gravitate toward things that sustain and feed us.

Cooper: That's it. You go back to your own roots. I write about Buckinghamshire and Wales because that's where my roots are. Alan Garner writes about his particular place. Lloyd's got Welsh roots.

Audience: Earlier, Susan Cooper made a statement to the effect that fantasy hides or filters the author's real emotions. I would like to hear the other authors speak to that point.

Katherine Paterson: I think all writing is a kind of filter. There are very, very few people to whom I would lay open my naked emotions. And yet I do when I write. In fact, I guess that's why I half suspect that every book is going to be hated, because I think, I've really revealed what's inside of me, and others won't like me, the way they never did when I was a kid. So it's sort of a daring thing, but not as daring as if I were really laying myself open, because I've got this protective fictional layer between me and it. I don't think it's a matter only of fantasy. I think it's how we organize our lives so we can stand them, and I think we do it in any kind of fiction.

Audience: It seems to me that fantasy is the place where moral problems or dilemmas, or good and evil, can be worked out in a way that realism doesn't allow because our realism is so cynical.

Babbitt: I think that adult fiction in the last few decades has pictured no blacks and whites, but mainly grays, and everything is quite blurred, so that the choices the characters have to make are very different from the choices in children's fiction. Often there is a feeling at the end of an adult novel that there is no choice.

Audience: And do you feel that writing fantasy allows you to explore the black and the white?

Babbitt: I'm not sure fantasy deals with the kind of issues that are comparable to modern problems. I'm talking about a framework that is older and goes deeper.

Alexander: The topical issues change so quickly that by the time you've sorted out your own position on them, it doesn't apply anymore. Let's say Dickens sets out to write a certain type of novel, say *Nicholas Nickleby*. He's engaging the question of the cruelty of putting boys in those ghastly schools in Yorkshire. Not that he's only dealing with these issues; he's dealing with a lot of other things. But he could be pretty sure that the school problem would be around for a good long time, and his attitude would be valid for a good long time. Now if we try to do something like that today, all of a sudden those Yorkshire schools will be out of business or turned into rest homes for the elderly. We can't get much of a handle on things that are happening so quickly. The difficulty may lie with the times. In fantasy you have a distancing device that allows you to stretch out your time a little bit. Fantasy can deal with an appearance of permanence.

Levin: Can I extend that question and pass it along to Susan and Katherine? Just picking it up with that query in the Tolkien book *The Two Towers*: "The world is all grown strange. How shall a man judge in such times?" And the answer, from Gandalf: "As he has ever judged. Good and evil have not changed, nor are they one thing among elves and dwarves and another among men." And do you—Katherine especially— do you feel this way? Can a modern novel for children, which has a social-realistic base, deal with the same kinds of things by which we judge good and evil?

Paterson: Well, it's easier in fantasy. I find, even if I set out to make an evil character, I have to love him or her before I'm through. But that's *my* truth, you see; that is not necessarily another realist's truth.

Audience: Don't you think that those of us who admire Bob Cormier's books do so because he has—rare in an intensely realistic novel—attacked an almost abstract problem of good and evil and not simply a social issue?

Paterson: For me, the focus of *The Chocolate War* was the moment in which Jerry realized the evil within himself. I was very despairing when I finished the book, because it was almost archetypal warfare until that point when Jerry had to face himself. That's what makes the book different from a lot of books I see for young adults, which have total cynicism toward the evil of our day; that's what puts it on the level of fantasy, in a way. Jerry's self-confrontation reminded me of the moment in *A Wizard of Earthsea* when Ged meets his shadow. It's in a totally different language and a totally different setting, but it's equally archetypical. It's the confession of sin and knowledge of the Fall. It's what puts *The Chocolate War* on a different level from a lot of what's being written nowadays.

Cooper: I wonder whether publishers automatically put books that deal with moral questions on a children's or a young adults' list. Do they put them there because they think adults won't read that sort of book? It seems to me *The Chocolate War* could have gone either way. I think *Lord of the Flies* would, today, have been published as a children's book. I think publishers assume that people who feel strongly about some issue, as Dickens did about so many, no longer use the novel as a platform because they can so easily write what is called nonfiction instead. So you have somebody like Robert Coles instead of Dickens. Those two are more or less twentieth- and nineteenth-century equivalents. It's a pity that publishers put certain books on children's and young adults' lists and thereby cut them off from an awful lot of people.

Levin: It seems to me that in the realistic novel—at least in the ones we have been discussing—the choices are more complex. The protagonist has to find a way through a tangle of alternatives, whereas the fantasy hero has a more clear-cut view of choices facing him. Those choices may be difficult and they may cause great pain and suffering, but they are usually clearer. And the child reader sees this, even if the child feels the pain that accompanies the difficult choice.

Alexander: That does seem to be the case; the writer of fantasy can allow himself to deal with absolutes, to a large extent. My hunch is that probably a writer of fantasy would allow the existence, at least, of absolutes.

Cooper: Yes, it infuses everything we do, because we're dealing with the substance of myth, which really is good and evil.

Alexander: Whereas in real life there is very seldom any clear-cut thing; there are many more areas of gray.

Audience: You're saying then that fantasy writers are dealing with proto-types?

Cooper: No, that's not the same thing at all.

Alexander: No, not quite the same thing.

Babbitt: The problems are prototypical, perhaps.

Paterson: It seems to me important for the child to get both.

Cooper: Oh, sure.

Paterson: There is, underlying reality, such a thing as good and such a thing as evil. That seems important to me in the nourishing of a person's soul.

Cooper: I think so, too.

Audience: But in fantasy, good and evil are projected.

Paterson/Babbitt/Cooper: Yes.

Paterson: And the child can deal with them.

Cooper: You will get a rare child who will recognize what is happening. I had an extraordinary letter once from a girl of fourteen who wrote: "I want to thank you for writing your books. I think they're wonderful. They have helped me to see the good and evil in myself."

Paterson: But even if the child can't recognize that a book has done this and say so, the book can be helpful.

Cooper: Yes.

Babbitt: I think that with any storyteller, whether the story is realism or fantasy, the same pattern is there. What differs is how much of it the writer deals with.

Paterson: And I find it's like an unresolved musical chord. If I get to the end of the book, realistic or fantastic, and the chord hasn't been resolved, I'm left unsatisfied. I want to go the whole journey, no matter how realistic the book is. I don't mean that it has to be happy.

Audience: Natalie Babbitt referred to the structure of fantasy as being round, the hero having an eventual return and a happy ending. In realism is it necessary to resolve the story?

Paterson: Yes, I have to come to some resolution with the story.

Audience: Is there any age at which the child does not need the story resolved?

Paterson: Well, ninety-eight.

NOTE

This material is drawn from a colloquium called "The Perilous Realms of Realism and Fantasy," the title derived from J. R. R. Tolkien's reference to the perilous realm of faerie. The remarks presented here have been edited from many hours of discussion, and the informal nature of the exchanges has been retained.

IV

Realism:
More Perilous Realms

Drawing by F. O. C. Darley from *Yankee Doodle* (1865)
Logo for Simmons College Summer Institutes, 1975 and 1977

Introduction

GREGORY MAGUIRE

It is a measure of the vitality of children's literature that modern realistic fiction has kept up with the times. Lloyd Alexander has remarked, "The real world as we all know, and sometimes to our bewilderment, is often illogical, inconsistent, a kind of elaborate random walk." Modern realistic fiction for children has not shied away from the task of portraying the modern world, a place in which terror and despondency and hope and courage all make their home—uneasily, perhaps, but honestly.

At Simmons College, courses such as "Modern Realism: Vision and Voice," "The Adolescent in Fiction," and "Modern British Fiction" have approached the knotty problems of realistic fiction for children. Students, and the authors whose talks appear here, have considered the importance of place, the building of character, the pacing and plotting of realistic fiction, and the narrative forms and techniques through which the author may suggest a vision of the world—as varied as those of Ben Marchand and the voice of despair in Robert Cormier's *After the First Death* or of Esther Rudomin and the voice of trust in Hautzig's *The Endless Steppe*. The voice of the fantasist is not excluded from this chapter because the fantasist is as concerned as the realist with a central critical question posed by the essayist Annie Dillard: "Does fiction have meaning? Can fiction work to interpret the world?"

"Realism: More Perilous Realms" concerns itself with questions of daring and complacency, action and inaction, freedom and responsibility. As well as attending to questions of domestic tranquillity and violence, a number of the pieces in this chapter consider the wealth of material by writers of Holocaust and war literature for children. At programs given by Simmons College many authors have spoken on the topic of the child embattled and triumphant—authors such as Aranka Siegal, Ilse Koehn, Bette Greene, Doris Orgel, Johanna Reiss, Esther Hautzig, Erik Christian

Haugaard, and Milton Meltzer. In addition, publisher Dorothy Briley talked about the challenges she faced in publishing the Mildred Batchelder Award–winning *Hiroshima No Pika* by Toshi Maruki; and Ginny Moore Kruse, director of the Cooperative Children's Book Center in Madison, Wisconsin, gave a talk on the World War II resistance fighter Sophie Scholl.

In November 1984 Simmons College mounted an art exhibit— ". . . And Peace Attend Thee . . .," images of war and peace, nightmare and dream—by illustrators of books for children. The display reconvened themes and ideas expressed in the original exhibition held at the City Gallery of New York from March 12, 1984, through April 13, 1984, coordinated by the artist Nancy Ekholm Burkert and Joan Marie Cavanaugh. The images of despair included works by Steven Kellogg and Alan Cober and prompted individuals to reflect on the spiritual and physical destruction that war inevitably brings. The idyllic moments created by Maurice Sendak and Uri Shulevitz and the festive one by Vera Williams were reminders of the joy in simply being alive. And the contemplative moods prompted by the works of Blair Lent, Ed Young, and Marcia Sewall encouraged viewers to hurry the quest for peace and nuclear disarmament.

Modern realistic fiction for children has no greater or lesser charge than that to which all art responds: to help shuck off the appearance of things, to let reality stand in its nakedness. One is left with chilling questions, however. Are children in the twentieth century too blunted by nihilistic cultural tendencies to trust fiction? Are children in danger of becoming immune to the hardest questions that fiction asks? Will children, in time, dare to disturb the universe?

Do I Dare Disturb the Universe?

MADELEINE L'ENGLE

Do I? Do we? We'd better dare and help the children dare; otherwise, we won't be around long enough to do much disturbing.

How do we dare encourage young people to dare disturb the universe—when universe disturbers usually come to a bad end, like Jerry Renault in Robert Cormier's brilliant book *The Chocolate War*? But Jerry, as hero, isn't alone in being hurt by the fact that he dared. Anwar Sadat was very aware that by daring he was risking his life, and in the end he was assassinated. Gandhi could well have remained a snobbish Anglo-Indian, playing it safe as a lawyer. But he thoroughly disturbed the universe and got a bullet through the heart. Moses got the children of Israel through the Red Sea, but he himself never reached the Promised Land. Jesus was certainly a universe disturber, and he was hanged on a cross.

Those who dare disturb the universe have many things in common. They refuse to submit to the bullies. They will not tolerate phoniness and sham and pretense. They will not settle for the easy answer. They keep on asking questions—of themselves, of the world, of the universe—long after it is clear that people want answers, not questions; bread and circuses, not justice.

I come from a long line of women who were universe disturbers. My maternal great-grandmother, Susan Fatio, was a pioneer in northern Florida, constantly getting caught in other people's battles for that lovely land. She watched seven homes being burned to the ground. When the Indians who had been friends of the Fatio family turned against *all* white people, friend or foe, because of Andrew Jackson's brutally unfair treatment, she fled across the St. John's River in a small boat, arrows and bullets from the Indians spattering the water around her; and from the farther bank she watched her home go up in flames. But her sense of justice did not falter, and ultimately the Indians were once again her friends.

Susan had little formal education but was taught at home by her parents. She spoke French, Spanish, Italian, German; read Latin and Greek; knew philosophy and history; and from this knowledge, plus her life experience, she learned to do what she believed was right, and she wrote her memoirs in order to let her descendants know what disturbing the universe was like for her. Her passion for education was paramount, and her children were all reading and writing by the time they were five. Susan would have deplored limiting children by reading levels and vocabulary. She would have been horrified by the fact that few Americans bother to learn the language of other peoples. As she had a passion for education, so she had a passion for friendship. And she did what she believed to be right.

When a horrendous slave trader for some obscure reason married an African princess and brought her home with him, setting her up on a large plantation on Fort George Island, Susan was the princess's only friend—the only person to care that the strange and beautiful black woman was agonizingly lonely, and the only person to be outraged that the princess was ostracized by white and black people alike. Susan found this situation intolerable, and once a week she had herself rowed down the river, a parasol protecting her from the blazing sun, to spend the day with the princess. And together they told stories. When disturbing the universe meant that yet another house was burned down by the enemy—red, black, or white—she looked for the meaning in story, and she had a treasure trove of stories from all countries. My mother particularly remembered the one about Don Juan Cockroachie.

Susan's daughter-in-law, the Madeleine L'Engle after whom I am named, was equally forthright in her attitude towards life. Her father was ambassador to Spain, and she was his hostess. Her closest friend was the Princess Eugenie, later to become Empress. One day Madeleine and Eugenie were out riding with Eugenie's brothers, and to prove that they were as brave as men, the two girls followed the brothers' example, took hunting knives, and made deep cuts in their arms. Foolish—but I sympathize. Madeleine came back to the United States and married a young army surgeon and went all over the country with him. His specialty was breaking up yellow fever epidemics, and her first child was born in an adobe hut in Texas. They went through the Isthmus of Panama long before there was a canal. From the court of Spain to pioneering, she took it all in stride.

When war broke out between the states, Madeleine's husband resigned his commission in the United States Army and took one with the Confederate Army. He was murdered early in the war, and Madeleine then ran an army hospital, caring for Yankee and Southern boys with equal compassion and tenderness. After the war she was penniless. There was literally not enough to eat; her children's clothes were extraordinary, since they were cut out of her old ball gowns from the court of Spain. But she never lost her ability to laugh, her ability to enjoy. When she was dying, in her eighties, she asked for a bowl of ice cream, ate it with pleasure, and died.

Madeleine lived, as her mother-in-law Susan had lived, in a "both/and" world. The Indians were our friends, *and* when wronged, they will not hesitate to kill us. We Southerners are at war with the United States, *and* these wounded young enemies are to be loved and cherished. I don't understand this, *and* I will seek for meaning in story.

Story is played down nowadays. Lots of best sellers are "How-to" books. How to lose weight. How to gain weight. How to enjoy sex. How to enjoy celibacy. How to grow plants. How to fix your own septic tank. Stories are looked down on, not because they are less true than the how-to books but because they are more true. And that truth, which would set us free, usually runs counter to culture and so disturbs the universe. Have you ever come across someone reading a novel, who jumps guiltily when caught and explains that what she or he is *really* reading is a book on the family life of hamsters? Why do we feel guilty when caught with fiction?

In *The Dragonriders of Pern* Anne McCaffrey challenges many of our attitudes towards sexuality and women. Good. A lot of young people are reading the Dragon books. Patricia McKillip is equally challenging in *The Riddle-Master of Hed*. Hardness of heart and lack of willingness to believe are explored in the books about Thomas Covenant, the Unbeliever. Not long ago, the young man who introduced me to Thomas Covenant came to me in great excitement. He is a composer, but he majored in computers at Harvard, and he told me that ultimately the computer will stop being binary—yes/no, 0/1, either/or—and will become trinary: yes/no/MU. MU means that neither yes nor no is an appropriate answer; some questions cannot be answered in a binary manner.

This idea pleased me enormously because I have long believed in the "both/and" world. And then I flew off for eight days of very over-scheduled lecturing in the Pacific Northwest. I was being sponsored—and paid for—by four different groups, and each group wanted to get all the blood possible out of this poor turnip. So on the last day, in Spokane, Washington, I was exhausted. I called the airline to confirm my flight home the next day, the first of May, and was told that I was properly in the computer but that the flight would leave at 11:25—not, as my ticket said, at 11:35. No problem.

The next morning I was driven to the airport bright and early, ready to get on the plane and collapse. I handed my ticket over the counter, and the man said, "That flight was canceled April twenty-fourth." I said, "I reconfirmed it yesterday and was told I was in the computer and that there was a ten-minute change in time." He looked at me expressionlessly and then played for a long time with his binary computer. Finally, he said, "I think the computer thought you were leaving from Portland, Oregon." I said, "As you can see, I am in Spokane, Washington. What are you going to do?" He played with his binary computer again, and ultimately I was sent to Seattle, where I changed planes and airlines. One of the hostesses on the last plane said to me, "To err is human. To foul it up completely, it takes a computer."

I was by then so exhausted that I began to leaf through the airline magazine. There was a glowing article in praise of the binary world of the computer, which we are about to inherit. It said, "Computers give us more time to discover our own potential. It's either that or kill ourselves from boredom. What the automobile is to the legs, and the television is to the eyes, the computer will be to the mind." And I sat there and said, "O my God."

I refuse. I will not let the computer be to my mind what the automobile is to the legs or television to the eyes. I don't like what the automobile has done to the legs. I don't like what television has done to the eyes. I refuse to have my mind zotzed by computer chips. I'm all for technology, which is trinary, but I will not submit to technocracy, which is binary. The binary computer knows us only by number, and the binary computer is goofing. It not only makes travel more and more complicated and less and less pleasant, but by its goofs it has already come close to starting atomic warfare. And the binary computer does not know how to be afraid. It does not know how to say, "I'm sorry, I nearly blew it." It does not have a sense of humor, and it does not understand story—story that asks questions, that dares disturb the universe.

The binary computer cannot call us by name, and so it would like us to forget our names and accept numbers. *No.* I do not know my social security number. I have no intention of ever knowing my social security number. When I'm speaking at colleges or universities, I'm usually asked for this number, and I tell them that if they want it that badly, they can call Washington. I am not a number. I am a human being whose name is Madeleine.

I started my fight to be named, not numbered, when I was in an English boarding school and was given the number 97: 97 on my bed, my uniform, my desk, my locker, my napkin cubby hole. And I did not want to be 97. I'm glad I started early the fight to remain human. I've often had to pay for it; for instance, I lost Phi Beta Kappa at Smith on behavior. I was fighting for academic reform and thereby disturbing the universe.

Perhaps it is easier for women to be trinary than it is for men. Women have not been forced by society to repress their intuitive selves. The conscious and the subconscious minds have been allowed to be in touch, and so we have been able to live in a "both/and" way. Whereas men have largely been limited to the part of themselves that is above the eyebrows. They have been forced to live in the binary, either/or world, where you have to be either an intellectual or stupid, good or bad. Believe me, you can be both. Like it or not, I am an intellectual. I am also frequently stupid. When anything good comes out of my pen or my typewriter, my intellect and my intuition are working together, collaborating instead of denying each other, as happens in the binary world. When I have to make a decision in life and my intuition and intellect are in conflict, I have learned that I do well to listen to my intuition.

I heard a college-educated, supposedly intelligent man so threatened by the conscious-subconscious dilemma that he announced belligerently, "There is no conflict between my conscious and my subconscious mind. My conscious mind is completely in control of my subconscious." When we deny the conflict, the conscious mind loses out. We lose our ability to laugh, to ask questions, to tell stories. And we are thereby that much less alive.

To dare disturb the universe means to dare to be alive. If you are alive, you can be hurt; you can be killed. So a lot of people take refuge in being at least half-dead. If you are half-dead, you don't have to see that the African princess is dying of loneliness, and you don't have to do anything about it. If you are half-dead, you don't have to smell the stench of the *favelas* in South America, and you can pretend that the writers and teachers on that strange and brutal continent are not being tortured and exterminated. You don't have to hurt when a group of American nuns are raped and then murdered because they care what is happening to the poor people in El Salvador. If you're half-dead, you can leave the dying people on the streets of Calcutta, instead of joining Mother Teresa. And a lot of us might well not be here if Dr. Semmelweis hadn't decided it would be a good idea for doctors to wash their hands after dissecting a cadaver instead of going directly to deliver a woman in labor.

Perhaps we're not all called to go to El Salvador or Calcutta, to fight the rigidity of the medical profession or the church establishment or the legal or any other establishment, but none of us will escape the moment when we have to decide whether to withdraw or to act upon what we believe to be right, knowing that we will likely be punished by those who do not want universe disturbers to stand up and be counted.

To be alive hurts. It is dangerous. The increasing suicide rate is an alarming reminder that some people don't think it's worth it. In what we teach, in what we write, we are either helping children to make the decision to grow up alive, or we are encouraging them to diminish themselves, to submit to being numbers, to forget their names. Jerry Renault dares to disturb the universe, and he gets hurt, badly hurt, but being safe is never part of it. Hurt or not, he is still a hero, and we need heroes—Darers and Disturbers—to look up to, in order that we may dare and disturb rather than be half-dead.

When I was writing *The Arm of the Starfish*, I would read in the afternoon to my mother and ten-year-old son what I had written during the morning. When I came to the scene where Joshua, who dared disturb the universe, is shot and killed, my son said, "Change it."

"I can't," I replied. "That's what happened."

"You're the *author*. You can change it."

"But I can't," I repeated. "That's what happened."

And that's how it is with story. A story has its own life. I don't control, manipulate, or own it. And story has taught me that when someone is so bold as to dare disturb the universe, there's trouble ahead. But there's far worse trouble ahead if we don't. If we sit back and are indifferent, we're really in for disaster. I have a poet friend in Minneapolis who is married to a successful surgeon and who, rather to her surprise, found herself part of a peaceful demonstration in front of a factory which makes refrigerators and also bombs. There was no violence in this demonstration. Nevertheless, she spent a night in jail. And she accepted it as a result of her daring. We are finally rising up to demand that the folly of nuclear stockpiling stop, that war stop.

I was born shortly after the armistice which ended the war that was supposed to end all war. My father was gassed in the trenches in France. He would not let his men go where he had not led the way, and a large group of men were spared mustard gas because of his bravery. Mustard gas goes on eating the lungs, and it took until I was nearly eighteen for my father to finish coughing his lungs out. There is one ray of hope in this story. At the beginning of World War II everybody in England was given gas masks to protect against the mustard gas. But we have not used mustard gas again. We have used worse things, but we have not used mustard gas because we were so appalled by what it did to people. We have seen what the atomic bomb has done, what radiation sickness has done, so perhaps, just as we have never used mustard gas again, we will not use the bomb. We do still have an iota of free will.

"Is free will worth it?" someone at a university in Ohio asked me. "What about the Holocaust?"

"Free will is very expensive," I replied. "What is very precious is often very expensive. And I think one reason we pay so much attention to the Holocaust is that we can dump on the Germans and forget that we dropped two atom bombs."

Did I dare disturb the universe when I said that? Perhaps, but isn't that what it's all about? You cannot spend your childhood listening to your father cough his lungs out; you cannot graduate from college into the

Second World War without having acquired a profound antipathy towards war, any kind of war.

I received a letter from a twelve-year-old girl. "We're studying the Crusades in school. Can there ever be such a thing as a holy war? Is it ever right to kill?" No, although there are times, as with the Second World War, when there is no choice. It is always wrong to kill, *and* Hitler and the Nazis are doing something intolerable, so they have to be stopped, even if killing is involved. Perhaps we went into overkill, but that, too, is sometimes inevitable.

Another child wrote me, "I'm Jewish, and most of my friends are Christian, and they tell me that only Christians can be saved. What do you think? I'm asking you this because your books have made me trust you." That kind of responsibility is something I wasn't prepared for when I started writing stories. This particular child is now in college, having her junior year abroad, and we're still corresponding, and during her holidays we have had several lunches together.

Last winter another child wrote, "How can I stay a child forever and never grow up?" And I replied, "You can't. And it wouldn't be a good idea if you could. What you *can* do, what I hope you *will* do, is stay a child forever *and* grow up." It is likely that the child within each of us, in collaboration with the mature adult, helps us dare disturb the universe, helps us dare to stay alive.

To be alive means to be open, open to joy, open to pain. It means to be vulnerable, and that means we are likely to be hurt, and badly. It means to be hurt and betrayed by those we trust. It means to love and find out that we love more than we are loved. It means that if you refuse to sell those chocolates, you're going to get beaten up. It means that if you, like Joshua, care about the fall of the sparrow enough to do something about it, you're likely to get killed. But I still would not have Jerry Renault, or Joshua Archer, do anything different.

During the Second World War, the war of my young womanhood, I had an English friend who was married to an RAF pilot. To be a Royal Air Force pilot was to be daily in danger of death, and when he was out on a mission, she was in constant fear that his plane would be one of the planes shot down. One day, much to her delight, he came home on a surprise leave. She gathered together all their food coupons and left him at home with their three children while she set about to buy food for the most festive meal possible in war-torn London. While she was gone, there was an unexpected daytime air raid, and her house was hit. When she got home, the house was gone, and her husband and three children were dead.

She spent the rest of the war working very hard for other people and trying to heal from her terrible grief. After a while a man fell in love with her, and she with him, and he wanted her to marry him. And, she wrote me, this was the most terrible decision she had ever had to make. As long as she didn't let herself really love, as long as she didn't marry or have more children, she was safe; she could never be hurt again as she had been hurt. If she loved again, she would once more be vulnerable. She made the creative choice. She opened herself to vulnerability and to love. To being alive. Sometimes simply choosing to be alive is to dare disturb the universe. But it's not an either/or decision. It's "both/and."

My composer friend who told me about the trinary computer illustrated it with a Hasidic story. A young student said to a rabbi renowned for his wisdom, "Rabbi, in the old days there were men who saw the face of God. Why does nobody see God today?" And the rabbi replied, "My son, today nobody can stoop so low."

And then there's the Zen story of the student who went to Master Hakuin and asked, "What happens to the enlightened man after death? What happens to the unenlightened man?" Master Hakuin replied, "Why ask me?" "Because you're a famous Zen master," the man told him. "Yes, but not a dead one," said the master.

We all have our favorite stories which illustrate the trinary vs. the binary world, the "both/and" vs. the either/or world. In story we learn about people—people who are named, not numbered, who disturb the universe simply by their *being*, their being *who* they are. Stories help us to understand our *who*, help us to stay alive. No matter what we end up doing, no matter what our *what* is, it is our *who*, our being named and being alive, that is going to make a good doctor or a good teacher or a good parent or a good writer or a good lover of sunrises and first stars and the amazing complexity of other human beings.

One of my favorite *New Yorker* cartoons shows an enormous computer; three scientists are standing in front of it while all its lights flash on and off, and suddenly it spits out a piece of paper on which are the words *I think, therefore I am*. Those famous words of Descartes plunged us into a limited, binary world. Computers can think, binarily speaking, but they can't laugh; they can't cry. They may *be*, but they are not alive. To be alive is to be vulnerable, to be open to tears and laughter, to dare disturb when it has to be done. Let's not be like the two caterpillars who were crawling along the ground when a butterfly flew over them. One of them said to the other, "You'll never catch me going on one of those." To be alive means risk, vulnerability, and hurt, but it also means the beauty and freedom of the butterfly; and it's worth all the pain—I promise you that it's worth it.

Do we dare disturb the universe? We'd better dare, even if it means a night in jail and a possible longer jail term for my friend in Minneapolis; even if it means that we will be criticized, and possibly physically hurt, if we take an unpopular stand and go to visit that African princess, defying all current social mores. But we'd better not disturb it blindly, with a sentimental expectation that all fairy tales have a happy ending. We must dare disturb, knowing that everything truly important has a very high price, and we're going to be the ones to pay it. If we refuse, not only will we be half-dead, but there's a good chance that shortly we'll be all the way dead.

But I don't believe that has to happen. Not as long as there are enough of us to dare disturb the universe. Shall we?

Where Is Terabithia?

KATHERINE PATERSON

When I returned from Japan in 1962, I went to New York City to study at Union Seminary there. I had every intention of returning to Japan after my year at Union was over, but in February a young minister from a church in Buffalo came to Union for a continuing education program. In my weekly letter home, I made the mistake of mentioning the fact that I had met such a person. At this point I had had exactly one very public and—and far as I was concerned—very casual lunch with the fellow, but my mother at once leaped to the most drastic conclusion possible under the circumstances. She rushed to tell her best friend the dreadful thing that had occurred. Katherine had gotten herself involved with a preacher from Buffalo.

"Why, Mary," said Helen, "that's lovely. If Katherine marries him, she'll stay in this country. She won't be going back to Japan all by herself."

"But," replied my mother, "I've been to Japan. I've never been to Buffalo."

I share this story with you to indicate the weird brand of parochialism that existed, and perhaps still exists, in my family. We're forever put off by people who find exotic the places we call home, whether they are in upper Jiangsu province or northern Shikoku or southeast Virginia. But the idea of leaving home and heading for a place called Buffalo, New York, seems on a par with Columbus setting sail west for East India. Let me remind you that it was not the fact that John was either a Presbyterian or a pastor that bothered my mother. She herself had been married to a Presbyterian pastor for thirty-nine years. It wasn't even the actual city of Buffalo that she was objecting to. She'd never been to Buffalo. What was bothering her was the idea of Buffalo, which conjured up vague visions of snow and ice but which she couldn't actually picture. Buffalo was simply not real to her.

Flannery O'Connor, whose words about writing have meant a great deal to me, has said that fiction is incarnational. By *incarnational* we mean that somehow the word or the idea has taken on flesh, has become physical, actual, real. We mean that the abstract idea can be perceived by way of the senses. This immediately makes fiction different from other kinds of stories. The fairy tale begins, "Once upon a time," thus clearly signaling its intent to escape the actual and the everyday, but a novel takes its life from the petty details of its geography and history and culture.

This is one of the reasons why writers like Flannery O'Connor and Eudora Welty and William Faulkner move us so powerfully. Their roots are planted very deeply in a particular soil, and they grow up and reach out from that place with a strength unknown to most writers. It is also the reason why a writer like Pasternak would refuse the Nobel Prize rather than leave Russia. For Russia, despite her terror and oppression, was the soil from which his genius sprang, and he feared that if he left her, he would leave behind his ability to write.

What happens, then, to a writer without roots—who is not grounded in a particular place? When I was four years old, we left "home", and I've never been back since. Indeed, I couldn't go back if I wanted to because the house in which we lived was torn down so that a bus station could be built on the site. Since I was four, I've lived in three different countries and seven states at about thirty different addresses. I was once asked as part of an imaginative exercise to remember in detail the house I had grown up in. I nearly had a mental breakdown on the spot. But the fact that I have no one place to call home does not make me feel that place in fiction is unimportant. On the contrary, it convinces me that I must work harder than almost any writer I know to create or re-create the world in which a story is set and grows if I want to make the reader believe in it.

A writer friend once complained to me that a certain editor had asked her to make the setting of a story more explicit. "I don't know where your story is taking place," the editor had said. "But," said my friend, "it didn't matter where that story was taking place. It could have taken place anywhere." I have to argue with that point of view. A fairy tale might take place anywhere, but a novel has to take place somewhere, and, usually, the more definite the setting, the more convincing the novel.

Of course, that definite world of the novel is not necessarily an actual spot on the map. Nowadays, people in my part of the country will sidle up to me and say, "Will you settle an argument for us? Is Rass Island really Smith or Tangier?" naming two islands in the Chesapeake Bay. But Rass is deliberately a fictitious island. I chose to do it that way because Chesapeake islanders are notoriously protective of their privacy, and I didn't want anyone to feel that I had intruded. Besides, if I created a fictitious island, I did not have to be limited to the specific history or geography of an existing island. I did, in one sense, create my own Chesapeake world, but in another sense, I was strictly bound to the world that actually exists. I couldn't, for example, send Truitt Bradshaw out to crab in the winter months. If Rass had been a Virginia island rather than a Maryland one, he might have dredged for crab in winter, but in Maryland, because it is cooler, it would be impractical. (It is also, incidentally, against the law in Maryland.) I wanted people who knew the bay to see Rass as a true place, if not an actual one.

It is vital that the place in which the story takes place be a true one. Because the place will shape the story, just as place shapes lives in the actual world. Louise Bradshaw never became flesh; indeed, the poor girl didn't even have a name until I found out where she lived. When I discovered Rass, I discovered who Louise was and what would happen to her.

Place provides so many wonderful surprises for a writer. It almost seems sometimes that geography and history exist for the writer's benefit—so that she can write this particular book. Can you imagine the excitement that went through me the day I came upon that scrap of information telling me that the bay watermen believed you should sing to oysters? I nearly wept for the joy of it—the taciturn Mr. Bradshaw sprang into life. Picture this man, out on the bay in the freezing air of a Maryland winter, bent to one of the most exhausting physical tasks left in this modern world, his voice going out over the lonely water in a song for the oysters. If such an image had just come to me out of the blue, I'm not sure I would have had the courage to use it; but it was true—one of the glorious eccentricities of these stubbornly independent, literally red-necked men, who in so many other ways reminded me of my strong, inarticulate uncles who farmed the limestone hills in the Shenandoah Valley. And it makes me wonder, now that it's too late to ask, if they, too, had secret songs that none of us ever heard.

I look back on the books I have written, almost as though someone else had written them. There are things I love in them for which I take no credit. The waterman singing to the oysters is one of the nourishing images of my books—and it was the place of the novel that gave it to me, not I that gave it to the place.

Of course, place will limit as well as enlarge. In *Rebels of the Heavenly Kingdom*, it takes the entire book for Wang Lee to begin to grow beyond the prejudices of a nineteenth-century Chinese peasant. When he first meets Mei Lin, he cannot help but despise her unbound feet. As silly as it seems to us from our vantage point, everything in his nature demands that he think himself superior to her. He may be poor and illiterate, but he is, after all, the first son of an old family who own their own land. She is a former slave girl with big feet. You cannot write a book about nineteenth-century China and force the characters to think or behave as you would like them to. If you are not willing to let them act out of the context of their own place and time, then you are honor bound to leave them alone and devote yourself to a more congenial setting.

This means that the writer of historical fiction would be both dishonest and stupid to write what I've called at various times "bathrobe" fiction. Remember those Christmas pageants we used to do in Sunday School years ago, where all the characters wore bathrobes instead of costumes? Well, some people write historical fiction that way. They simply dress up modern characters in pseudoancient dress. Since the characters are therefore tamer and more like ourselves than the historical characters would have been, we, the readers, should be able to identify with them more readily. Right? Wrong. We're no more convinced and moved by this kind of writing than we were by the sixth-grade cutup wearing his father's bathrobe and trying to look holy, like Joseph. The truer a fictional character is to the time in which he or she lives, the more we are convinced by the reality of the character and the more we may be able to see ourselves in that character. The world of the book must be as accurate as the writer can make it, not only because the writer owes this much to history but also because she owes this much to fiction. (At precisely this point on the rough draft of this speech is penciled in my husband's handwriting, "and to the reader." Yes, John, and, of course, it is not only to history and to fiction that the debt is owed, but to the reader, perhaps, most of all.)

When I was writing *Of Nightingales That Weep*, in which Goro is a potter, I had to find out what kind of pottery wheel, if any, would have been used by a potter in twelfth-century Japan. I spent hours, days, as I remember it, researching this single detail without coming up with an absolute answer. Finally, I did some educated guessing, based on how long it seemed to take innovations from Chinese pottery and Korean pottery to get to Japan, and decided that the pottery wheel used by Goro was not a treadle wheel but one in which a stick is inserted in the wheel to make it spin. The fact that the wheel is marvelously balanced makes it possible to throw a pot on it. At that time at Crowell there was a very picky copy editor who wrote me a letter asking me if I were *sure* that that was the kind of wheel Goro would have used. Wouldn't treadle wheels have been in use in Japan by this time? Alas, of course, I wasn't sure. So I gathered my courage and called the Freer Gallery of Art in Washington. I explained my problem to the pleasant secretary who answered the phone. Was there anyone at the gallery who could help answer my question? She told me that everyone was out to lunch, but when they returned, she would ask one of the curators and call me back. About two hours later the phone rang. It was my friend the secretary who told me that Dr. So-and-so and Dr. So-and-so had leaned across her desk at each other and argued for nearly an hour as to what kind of wheel Goro would have used. And the conclusion was that although it was *possible* that he might have had a treadle wheel, it was more *likely* that

he would have used the wheel I had described. You can imagine my
delight when I called the copy editor to say that the experts at the Freer
Gallery said that "although it was *possible* for Goro to have used a treadle
wheel, it was more *likely* . . ."

At first, I was very shy about asking experts for help, but my courage
grew as I realized how useful they could be and how important it was to
get the details right. I have a friend in the Oriental section at the Library of
Congress whom I call to check things for me. I remember when I was
writing *The Master Puppeteer*, I was having the characters walk into an
eighteenth-century public bath, and I realized that I didn't know whether
they would be carrying soap or not. It was suddenly vital that I know
whether they had soap or something else to scrub with. It took two days
for Mr. Ohta to get back to me to say that it was probably a pumice stone
and not a piece of soap. Two days seemed a long time to wait while the
bathwater cooled, but that scrap of information made the scene more real
to me, and, therefore, I think I was able to picture it more effectively to the
reader.

The writer of historical fiction loves these bits of detail, not because she
is a teacher of facts but because she is responsible for creating a world into
which the reader is invited to enter. And that world must be rendered true
with bits of pumice stone.

Not only must the physical details of that world be as accurate as
possible, the sensibilities of that world must ring true. As you know, my
parents were missionaries, and then my father worked for many years as
a Presbyterian pastor in this country. My mother was always trying to push
my books and would send them to many of her friends. I am still a bit
surprised that my books sell without my mother here to advertise them.
Anyhow, she had sent my first two books to friends who were also former
missionaries, expecting them to rave. Instead, they told my mother they
were very disappointed to find that I had not mentioned the name of Christ
in either book. The fact that the books were set in twelfth-century Japan,
where, as far as anyone knows, the name of Christ had never been heard,
was beside the point. ("If Katherine were truly Christian, she would have
found some way to work it in.") Other critics are a bit more subtle. For
example, they decry the fact that my Oriental women of the twelfth,
eighteenth, and nineteenth centuries are not true feminists. But I am not
writing a tract advising girls of twentieth-century America how they *ought*
to act. I am writing a story set in a different world, and the girls of that story
are bound by the world in which they live. They are not totally bound, it's
true. The characters from history or fiction that we remember are those
who kicked against the walls of their societies. But the writer cannot
pretend for the sake of her own prejudices that those walls were so flimsy
that a character could demolish them with a single dramatic gesture. She

cannot even assume that her character would see all of those walls as evil. A woman in another century, living in another culture, will not look at her world from a twentieth-century American feminist viewpoint.

A basic task of any novelist is to create a world. For the historical novelist, the task is to re-create a world. The temptation is to throw so much information at the reader that the reader is overwhelmed by how much the writer seems to know. But the reader is in no way transported into the world of the book by multiplicity of detail. What the writer must do is select the details that will reveal—the details that make the reader experience this world for himself and forget all about the writer.

These details are invariably sensuous—that is, they are perceived by the senses. Because we know the physical world by means of our senses, we can only know a fictional world the same way. If someone tells us a place is beautiful, we have nothing but the author's word for it, and we are seldom convinced, much less transported. But let the writer say:

> From the station to the beach, and her footprints on it first, lonely, winding along the waves' edge. She takes off her shoes. She comes up the path, through the back gate, into the garden—a bird is singing—and walks across the grass barefoot. There is a gossamer web laden with shining dew strung between the handles of the french windows. To enter she must break it. She stands still. And turning, looks out to sea. The dawn has triumphed. The sun has risen out of the blurry wisps of restraining cloud; the sea is blue, blue, and breaks loudly white, and Godrevy has come out of the misty margin of the sky, and stands on the horizon, black rock, white lighthouse, the endless burst of surf at the foot of the rock frozen by distance.

The passage comes, as many of you recognize, from *Unleaving*, by Jill Paton Walsh. Jill could have said, "It was early morning as Madge walked from the station along the beach to the house." She could have, but she wouldn't have been Jill Paton Walsh if she had, and we wouldn't know the world of Goldengrove.

Now, by naming the place Goldengrove, the writer has given us more than an address; she has signaled to us the idea that the place embodies. The name, as you also probably know, is from Gerard Manley Hopkins's poem entitled "Spring and Fall: To a Young Child," which reads:

> Margaret, are you grieving
> Over Goldengrove unleaving?
> Leaves, like the things of man, you

With your fresh thoughts care for, can you?
Ah! as the heart grows older
It will come to such sights colder
By and by, nor spare a sigh
Though worlds of wanwood leafmeal lie;
And yet you will weep and know why.
Now no matter, child, the name:
Sorrow's springs are the same.
Nor mouth had, no nor mind, expressed
What heart heard of, ghost guessed:
It is the blight man was born for,
It is Margaret you mourn for.

Goldengrove is not only a place; it is an idea. It is the idea of life as too swift, too fragile. When the child mourns the falling of the leaves in autumn, she is, unknowingly, mourning the brevity, the frailty, of her own life in the world. The fact that Jill has constructed her fictional world so solidly gives this idea power. But will the children who read this book understand it? Perhaps not in intellectual, philosophical terms, but a novelist is not so concerned with that kind of understanding. What she is aiming for is a deep underground connection with the reader.

In Hopkins's poem, Margaret weeps for the falling leaves, not understanding quite why, but she does weep. As the poet says: "Ah! as the heart grows older / It will come to such sights colder."

Those of us who write for the young choose the passionate heart over the cold intellect every time.

About ten years ago when my family was on vacation, we stopped at a roadside table for lunch. The four children had been cooped up in the car, so of course they raced to explore the picnic area. At one point the boys spotted a snake which they assured their nervous parents was harmless. That particular mountain is famous for its rattlesnakes, so even though the boys urged that we examine the slant of the creature's eyes and the shape of its tiny head and see for ourselves that it was no rattler, we chose to give the little fellow a wide berth. It wasn't long before one of the four had disappeared. When you have four children, one is always disappearing. The rest of us went to the woods to find him and stumbled into a cathedral of pines. The trees were so tall that you could hardly see the sky, and the ground was a carpet of brown needles. All the running and yelling stopped. It was obviously a sacred place. For a while we stood silently in the cool shadows of the trees and then in a whisper signaled to each other that it was time to resume our trip.

Several years later when I was writing *Bridge to Terabithia*, I put this pine grove into my story. It seemed to belong there even though the actual grove was many miles away from the scene in my book. Not until I was in the final revisions of *Bridge* did it dawn on me that I had cheated. Maybe such a landscape would not occur in Virginia. With a sickening heart I sought out a botanist. Was the scene I'd described possible? Next to an ordinary Virginia woods, I had planted a pine grove. Was that possible? Yes, my expert said. There were certainly pine groves in Virginia. With cutting and regrowth it was possible that one might grow adjacent to a mixed woods—not usual, but certainly possible. Possible was all I needed. And now when people ask me, as they often do, if Terabithia is a real place, I say yes, because it seems rather complicated to explain that actually it is composed of at least three places, as that ordinary Virginia woods looks suspiciously like the ordinary North Carolina woods behind the house we lived in in 1946.

But when people ask me, "Where is Terabithia?" I don't think this is what they mean. They never ask me where Lark Creek, Virginia, is located—only Terabithia. I think it is the idea of the place that haunts them, not the place itself. I say this because the twin question is nearly always: "Where did you get the name Terabithia?" As though if the name were understood, the place could be found.

I thought I'd made up the name. I wasn't trying in the least to hide a philosophical secret in it. I was looking for a polysyllabic, rather romantic sounding word that gave the same feeling the name of a country might give. The word *Terabithia* occurred to me. I played around with the spelling. I know at one point it was spelled Terebithia. I chose the *a* spelling because I was trying to make it as easy to pronounce as I could. I'm sure no one believes me, but I spend a lot of time trying not to cause my readers undue trouble with pronunciation. Well, at about the time I was to check the final galleys for the book, I happened to reread *The Voyage of the Dawn Treader* in C. S. Lewis's Chronicles of Narnia. As you all know, there is an island in *The Voyage of the Dawn Treader* named Terebinthia. T-e-r-e-b-i-n-t-h-i-a. I was appalled. I had pinched my word right out of Narnia. At first, I thought I would have to change it. I didn't want everyone complaining that I was hanging on to Lewis's coattails. But the thought of finding a word of exactly that length and going through the galleys and making all those corrections spurred me to seek another solution. And my kindly brain supplied the needed justification. Leslie Burke had read the Narnia books, too. She would very probably come up with a name for her kingdom that closely resembled something she had seen in the Chronicles of Narnia and would think she had made it up out of the blue. Besides, Lewis obviously got the name for his island from the terebinth tree in the Old Testament. It wasn't really original with Lewis, either.

I think to find the true ancestry of Terabithia, however, you have to look elsewhere. To *The Secret Garden*, perhaps, or even to Eden. Or better yet, to the enchanted places of childhood, to the secret places of the heart.

I couldn't count the number of letters I've gotten over the years in which people describe for me their own Terabithias. A young man wrote of a huge live-oak tree into which he had climbed when he was a boy. It was his place to dream and to weep. Recently, he had returned to the town in which he had grown up, only to find that his tree had been cut down. He felt he had to write to me, that I would understand his grief, how that tree had been so much more to him than just a tree.

When children ask me now, "Where is Terabithia?," I try to explain that for most of us it starts out as a place outside ourselves—a tree, a hideout in the woods, a corner of our backyards, the springhouse on our uncle's farm. As we grow older, however, it becomes a place inside ourselves into which we may go. But the change from an outside Terabithia to an inner one doesn't happen accidentally, I remind the children. "If you want an inner Terabithia when you are fifty, you must begin to build it now." Some of them smile and nod. They know exactly what I mean. The world of the imagination must be cared for and nourished.

Fiction, as I said earlier, is an incarnational art. The word must become flesh. The idea must find shape in a physical form. The Sino-Japanese character for *idea* is made up of two other characters—the character for *sound* written above the character for *heart*. An idea is a sound in the heart. And fiction does not grow only out of place, it grows out of passion. If I am to write books for those who weep for falling leaves, not knowing why—whose hearts have not yet grown cold—I must write out of the heat of my own deepest feelings, the sounds of my own heart. I must struggle to capture in a story, as Hopkins said, "what heart heard of" and, at ten or twelve or fourteen, neither mouth nor mind could express.

It never fails to amaze me that when I listen to the sounds of my own heart, my own fears and desires and jealousies and angers and secret joys—the very things in my ordinary life that on social occasions I take care not to expose—when I write a novel out of these, I am somehow able to connect deeply with my readers.

I am often urged to set an example for my readers or taken to task because I have *not* set a proper example, but, with all due respect, I don't believe that is what I am called to do. I am called to listen to the sound of my own heart—to write the story within myself that demands to be told at that particular point in my life. And if I do this faithfully, clothing that idea in the flesh of human experience and setting it in a true place, the sound from my heart will resound in the reader's heart.

Not in every reader's heart, of course. I haven't the power to engage everyone deeply, and if I try, I will fail utterly. A novel designed to please everyone all the time will, in the end, affect no one very deeply. And when a child, sometimes one of my own four, is brave enough to say, "I didn't like that book so much," I try to comfort myself with the hope that my reluctant reader will give my book a second chance some other time. As readers we all can remember a book which, when we first tried to read it, took us nowhere, but then, coming to that same book at a different juncture of our lives, it became a cloud and fiery pillar leading us through some particular wilderness. I can always hope the same thing will happen to a book I've written. But as writers we must be content to let our readers come to our books from where they are at that moment in their lives and take from our books what they will. If we have listened to the sounds in our own hearts and served the work those sounds have called into being as faithfully and carefully as we know how, then that is all we can do. The rest is not in our hands.

My husband gave me this story to close with. Last July he was working in the craft shop at Silver Bay, New York, near where we vacation. At the same table where he was working on stained glass were an elderly woman friend of his and a girl of twelve or so whom he did not know and who seemed totally absorbed in her work. John and Elsie were chatting as they worked, catching up on each other's activities over the winter, when Elsie mentioned that she had read *Jacob Have I Loved*. Never shy, John asked her how she had liked it. "Oh," she said, "I loved it because I know the place." "I loved it," said the girl, without looking up from her glass work, "because I know the feeling."

Between the seventy-year-old friend and the twelve-year-old stranger, *Jacob* was given the review every writer longs for. If, when you finish a book, you know the place and share the feeling, not only has the writer succeeded, but the reader has as well. We have both done our work in bringing this story to life. I don't know that we could ask for more from each other.

"A Rattlin' Good Story"

ROBERT CORMIER,
WITH QUESTIONS FROM
BRUCE CLEMENTS

Writing is such a private thing that I'm always thrown a little bit when it becomes public, and I always have to do a lot of soul-searching when I move from the typewriter, which is so private, into a public forum like this one. And there's always an adjustment to make when I find myself having to address an abstract subject. I find that very difficult to do, but somehow I manage, although leanly at times.

I'm very aware that the people in my books are on journeys. In fact, there is a literal journey in *I Am the Cheese*. But I realize the journey my characters are on—and I myself am on, because they are a reflection of me, and I'm in all of them, even Archie Costello—is a journey toward identity. I think so often that's what kids are looking for.

I was fortunate in growing up because I came to know who I was quite early; it was in the seventh grade. I had nothing going for me. I didn't have long blond hair. I had this skinny face and scrawny build, and I was terrible at sports. I was filled with yearnings and longings and loneliness. I wanted the world to know I existed. And that's the thing that used to haunt me when I listened to all these famous people talking on the radio. It bothered me that they didn't know that I was here on the planet Earth. So few people did.

Anyway, I wrote a poem at recess—that shows you how much I was in with the group—and showed it to Sister Catherine, who was my nun in the sixth and seventh grades. She was a huge woman, and she wore a habit with a heart-shaped crown that made her look even taller. But I took my courage in my hands and showed her this poem, and she read it, and she didn't say whether she liked it or not; she didn't discourage me. She said, "Robert, you're a writer."

I've never deviated from that identity. I knew immediately and from that moment that I was a writer. I've always had this little secret deep inside of me, and I've had it for years and still have it and am still delighted with it. So many people I know, including my own youngsters, are always searching for their identities—who they are and why they are here in this great, big, terrifying world. And I'm still trying to solve on paper those mysteries about identities and journeys toward them and searches for them.

Until I wrote *The Chocolate War* I didn't realize what a great audience was out there, a very responsive, serious, and personal audience. I would like to give you an example of what I mean. Yesterday morning I was home writing when the phone rang. It was a long distance call from Imo, South Carolina, and a boy was on the phone. He asked if I was Robert Cormier, the writer, and when I said yes, he said, "We're having an argument in class about *The Chocolate War*, and the teacher has given us permission to call you." I could hear a hubbub in the background; he was in a phone booth or at a phone in the corridor. Apparently he had called the newspaper with which I was formerly affiliated and had gotten my home address and phone number. He wanted to know whether Jerry Renault died at the end of *The Chocolate War*. He said, "I don't believe he died, even though the first three words of the novel are, 'They murdered him.' However, there's a faction at my school that believes he died, and we figured, let's go straight to the author."

I told him that in my mind Jerry Renault was still alive, and that, in fact, I'd embarked on a sequel in which Jerry Renault was very much a presence, although the key word is *presence*. He said, "Great. However, would you mind repeating that to my witness here?" Another boy came on, and I repeated it to him. He was in the against category; he thought that Jerry Renault had died. I said, "Look, I'll put it in writing if you wish," and later in the morning I dashed off a letter so that he could present factual evidence to the class.

This type of thing just about knocks me out. I've never had an adult come up to me about my adult novels and say, Why did you do such and such on page 98? Or, Why did you introduce Tubs Casper and not bring him back? What happened with him and his girlfriend? These responses give me a sense of responsibility toward my audience. And I think this sense of responsibility stays with me at the typewriter.

Writing is always a matter of selection. When I write, although I don't feel that I'm writing exclusively for young adults, I do know they will be part of the audience. This sensitivity came to me before *The Chocolate War* was published, when I learned a lesson. It seems that I am always learning. In *The Chocolate War* I wanted to show how a character by the name of Archie got the idea for the big raffle at the end. But I didn't want him to suddenly snap his fingers and say, "I've got a great idea." I wanted to be very, very clever and realistic, and I devised a masturbation scene in which he would be alone in the house. Two climaxes would come together—the raffle and . . . I thought, My God, this is great!

When I was halfway through *The Chocolate War*, my agent said, "I think this is a young adult novel," which scared the daylights out of me because at the time I didn't know what a young adult novel was. So I consulted with my children. My son was great for telling me things like, "Dad, they don't say *broads* anymore. They say *chicks*." He read the book when it was completed, and I had a daughter thirteen going on fourteen, Chris, who wanted to read it, too. I said fine, because I was in a new realm and it was perilous. But I did a strange thing: I removed the chapter on masturbation. I said to her, "You know, toward the end you may notice a gap in motivation, but don't worry about it." She didn't notice any gap in motivation; she just liked the book. I put the chapter back in when I sent it off to the publisher.

Eventually it went to Pantheon, and a marvelous editor there by the name of Fabio Coen loved the book. It had been rejected four times by editors who thought the ending was too downbeat. One editor said there were too many characters for a young adult audience, which astounded me because the young adult audience is in a high school with thousands of kids every day. The editor asked if I would reduce the number of characters, but I wouldn't. Anyway, Fabio Coen called and said, "Fine, we'll accept the book, downbeat ending and all. However, there's a chapter I'd like to have you think about." You know, editors never tell you to take this out or to do this or that. He just said to think about it, and I knew immediately what chapter he meant. And I read the book and realized it didn't need that chapter.

From this experience I learned some things about cleverness and about what it means to be too clever. I also learned that I was willing to inflict a masturbation scene on other people's daughters but not on my own. And this was a great lesson. As I said, I am always learning. So again, I try to be realistic in my writing, but I understand that realism can be carried to a point where it can offend. I don't mind offending if it is true to the situation, but the cleverness of being too realistic when it is gratuitous is dangerous.

At the moment I've embarked on a new novel [*After the First Death*] which is nearing completion, and again there are perils and again it is a matter of selection. The story is sort of violent, psychologically violent more than anything else. There's a scene in which a girl has to be searched, because she could be hiding something. And she is exposed to a boy who is with a girl on a one-to-one basis for the first time. I thought, great, this boy has to search this girl; it opened up all kinds of possibilities to me. And yet I knew that the search should be carried out by this older person in the book, the way a blind man would search an object for defects—impersonally. I eventually had the older man search her, because that was more realistic, but here again I had to resist the great titillating scene of a boy having to search a girl thoroughly. Again—that sense of responsibility when you sit at the typewriter. It is always with the writer.

I think what we're all trying to do, at least what I am trying to do, is simply to tell a good story. If you don't tell a good story, no one will read it, and there won't be room for discussions about realism. First, I realize what I write has to work as a story, and I think all of us who write want to make people alive to what's going on in the pages. Really, when I sit down at the typewriter, I'm just trying to tell a rattlin' good story, the kind of story that I myself would like to read.

I think that young people absorb things more easily than we suspect. The controversy about *The Chocolate War* came from adults rather than from kids. In a town in Massachusetts there was an attempt to ban *The Chocolate War;* it came from a member of the school board who was also a parent. The kids started a petition in support of the book. More than that, when they decided on the petition, one student stood up at a meeting and said, "I think everyone should sign this petition." And then another student stood up and said, "Wait, that is exactly what happens in *The Chocolate War.*" The teacher said she had chills, that this one moment was worth the entire controversy—the threat to her job, the town hearing, the publicity, the phone calls—to know that the kids had gotten the message. The point is that I think we can trust the audience and not worry, Will they absorb this? I think they can take it all right.

Someone once asked me, "Do you like to write novels because you can sprawl around?" But I find that I can't sprawl around. I have to keep to the forward movement. The events of Chapter Three dictate the events of Chapter Four. Sometimes I'd love to sprawl and put in little sermons, but there is no need for it. Once you set things in motion, there is a sense of inevitability. This sense of inevitability about the people is what makes it impossible for *The Chocolate War* to have a happy ending, which is what one editor suggested. In *After the First Death* there is a situation where a certain person must die, and I resisted it. And yet I remember reading that when the *Titanic* was in trouble and hit the iceberg, they called in one of the engineers, who studied the amount of water pouring into certain chambers and said something that still haunts me. He said, "The ship must go down." It is not that it will go down or that it may go down. The ship *must* go down. The laws dictate it. And when I came upon an episode in *After the First Death* that involved a child, late at night I realized, through all the dictates of the plot I had set up, that the child must die: I had nothing to do with it.

The idea for *The Chocolate War* occurred to me when my son was attending a school much like the school in *The Chocolate War*. He was a freshman and wanted to play football. He also was not a top student; he had to work for his marks. We were glad to send him to this school and pay the tuition.

One day he alighted from the school bus with two shopping bags full of chocolates, and I said, "My God, what have we here?" I was appalled because back in the Depression when I was going to school—a Catholic school—we sold everything, raffles, greeting cards, and candy. I thought, We haven't come far in a generation—my son is doing the same thing in this school, where we're paying a pretty hefty tuition. We talked about it, at first sort of facetiously, but it developed into a serious discussion in which I came up with three options. I said, "We can buy the chocolates ourselves, twenty-five boxes at a dollar each." Frankly, I hoped he would not say yes to that idea. The second option was that he could go out and sell them—hit the neighbors, the relatives, and so on. The third option I sort of threw out quickly. I said, "You know, you don't have to sell the chocolates. There's a certain amount of freedom that we have, and you can exercise it." He said, "That sounds great." Then we really got serious and talked about it during the evening and decided he definitely wouldn't sell the chocolates.

To show the school that this wasn't just a defiant act or a frivolous one on his part, I wrote a letter to the headmaster, saying that Peter was not going to sell the chocolates, that we had talked it over as a family, that he had our approval. The next day when he set off to school, I didn't let him go by school bus. I drove him to school, and as he went up the walk, I thought, What have I done to my son? He's a freshman in this very active, very athletic-minded school . . . And that's where the guilt came in. You know, I write from emotions. He went in and presented the note to the headmaster, who didn't say anything, and nothing happened. Peter didn't sell the chocolates.

And then out of my emotions those great words came to me—I call them my crutches with wings: What if? I thought, What if there were an unscrupulous headmaster? What if there were a peer group applying pressure? And I began writing. That was the genesis of *The Chocolate War*. It was really rooted in reality, the only fantasy being the question, What if?

Although *I Am the Cheese* has nothing to do with my life, it's the most personal story I ever wrote. I went to the typewriter one day and I just placed a boy on a bicycle and wanted to see what would happen. I made it a Wednesday morning. I gave him a box to carry. Then I found that I was giving him my own idiosyncrasies. I'm claustrophobic and I made him claustrophobic. As a newsboy I was chased by every dog in existence; I fear dogs and I made him fear dogs. I gave him all these idiosyncrasies of my own and he became very close to me. And then he started living as a person.

I wrote the complete bike-ride sequence first. I was experimenting at the time with using first-person present tense to get a feeling of movement and thrust. I had about thirty thousand words of the boy on the bike, which I knew worked. But I knew I didn't have a novel because there was no . . . what I call friction: the irritant in the oyster that makes the pearl. I had to find a second level to provide the suspense and the plot, and that's when I came up with the witness-relocation idea, to explain why the boy was fleeing and where he was going. The problem was to work the explanation in without disturbing the bike ride. I thought I'd write it on another level, but then there was a problem of splicing in, and setting up a way for the flashbacks to come in, so I went into third person, and that meant a lot of juggling. I finished the book in a very deep depression because I didn't think it was working—there were so many elements. Until I sent it to my editor in New York, I was unsure about all of it.

The first indication I had that *I Am the Cheese* could be considered fantasy was when my publisher was sending it around for paperback sale, and someone suggested that it should be sent to a paperback editor who is noted for science fiction. I realized that probably some people would not, or would not want to, accept the book as reality. A few years ago, if we were talking on the phone and there was a click on the line, it was simply a click on the line. Now we're not quite sure. Maybe the book should be fantasy, if that makes people more comfortable.

Bruce Clements: How does a story begin for you?
Robert Cormier: Well, "The Bumblebee Flies Anyway" is a poster I've had on my wall for years. It's the old axiom about the law of aerodynamics that says the bumblebee—because of a heavy body and short wing-spread—is not supposed to be able to fly. The bumblebee, unaware of the law, flies anyway and manages to make a little honey every day. I knew someday I would use it as the theme of a novel, and I knew I would be writing about someone who defies the odds. I waited until a novel grew out of it.

There's another line that has been running around my mind for years and years, from Stevie Smith, the British poet: "I was much further out than you thought, and not waving but drowning." It intrigues me. I may never use the line, but these words constantly come into my mind. Someday a short story or a novel may emerge. Sometimes I start them prematurely; I have unfinished novels on the shelf, the ones that ran out of steam after fifty pages.

Clements: What do you do best? What do you do about as well as anybody
   does it?

Cormier: Oh, boy . . . eat peanuts, maybe. No, that's being funny. I think
   I'm pretty good at dialogue, dialogue that moves the story along. I can
   tell you the things I'm not good at; I'm terrible about movement, getting
   people from here to there. That is always a problem for me, and I really
   have to work at it. Characterization through dialogue and action through
   dialogue are probably my strongest assets. And expository dialogue. I've
   always admired writers like John O'Hara, who wrote so much dialogue.
   He had the ear, and I was influenced by him early on.

Clements: Are there things you just will not do?

Cormier: Yes. Thank goodness the readers can't see what I throw into the
   wastebasket. Thomas Wolfe said it so beautifully, and I think William
   Faulkner also echoed it, something like: "The reader does not see how
   much the writer failed by." You know, you get an idea for a story or an
   emotion, and it's up above you somewhere, and you probably don't
   even get close, but the reader doesn't know that. Sometimes you are so
   pleased with something you wrote. In fact, I'll get up and I'll say to my
   wife, "I just wrote something terrific." I don't mean it in a boastful kind
   of way, but it hit what I meant to do, and that doesn't always happen.
   When it does, it gives you a tingle. The last chapter of *After the First
   Death*, when Miro was sitting in the woods, waiting for the car, came
   right out. I don't think I touched it. It was beautiful. When I say that, it
   sounds like I'm boasting, but it was beautiful. I knew what I wanted to
   say, the scene I wanted to picture, the way I wanted the book to end; it
   had been cooking within for a while. I sat down at the typewriter and it
   came out, and I felt like yelling out a shout of joy, because it seldom
   happens that way. It's usually just hard work.

   Someone once accused me of trying to manipulate the reader. My
   goodness, that's what every writer does. I *am* trying. That wasn't an
   accusation, it was a congratulation. I'm trying to make that reader laugh,
   cry, be angry, react, and so it's all manipulation. I'm trying to reach that
   concept I have in mind.

   It's so hard to talk about that act. I always hesitate to say *the creative act*,
   because it sounds very high-blown. I know I have an instinct that tells
   me I've got to elongate this or I have to slow down the action, and so I
   use a different kind of sentence; or I have to speed it up, and so I chop
   the sentences. One part of me is ruthless, and has to be.

Clements: I was at a party once with W. H. Auden, and he said, "The poet
   is different from everybody else. Everybody else walks down the street
   and they see a truck coming—the truck hits this child. Everybody gasps
   except for the poet, who says, 'I can use that.' "

Cormier: I think we're all poets, then, because the great part about being a writer is that you use everything. You know you're robbing people all the time. Was it Thomas Wolfe whose father died, and in the midst of his grief Wolfe ran to the mirror and looked in it, so he could capture his expression for use later on? There's a terrible detachment that writers have.

Clements: Even if you write without a notion of this audience out there, do you think of one of your books as younger than the other two, or older?

Cormier: I never thought in those terms. Younger in the sense of the audience?

Clements: Well, accessible to younger people?

Cormier: On the surface, *The Chocolate War* can be read strictly as a school story. I've had letters from boys saying that this is the first book they have ever read, and asking me to write another one just like it. And they mention the nice short sentences and the short chapters. Teachers have told me that they've used it with their reluctant readers. I'm hoping there's another level—I know I tried to put in another level. I think *The Chocolate War* is the most accessible. The others have their complexities and ambiguities.

Clements: What is the hardest thing that you do? Or to put it another way, what gives you the most pain as a writer?

Cormier: In terms of the writing itself, or of what happens to the characters?

Clements: I could put it another way. What makes you cry?

Cormier: What happens to the people in the books. I really care for them. I said this to some people once, and they kind of scoffed. Later somebody in that group began writing and said, "Now I see what you mean when you say that what happens to your characters can affect you." And it's true. You don't run out of the house and go into a chaotic state because of what happens to your characters, but they do affect you.

Kate is a case in point. What happened to her really affected me. Little Raymond, too, I loved dearly. It's hard to write those scenes. I wrote the scene in *After the First Death* where Artkin came in and chose the boy before I knew who it would be. And then later—I did it as if I was holding the typewriter away from me—I wrote in Raymond's name. You'll notice the death was offstage. It was hard for me to face that child dying in cold blood, so I just set it up ahead of time out of context, and when I reached that scene I inserted Raymond and got rid of it quickly. That was one of the most painful things I have ever written.

Kate's death, too, was painful, for in my mind she died twice. The death of Kate was so abrupt—Kate and Miro are together near the end of the book, and the gun goes off, and she dies instantly, and so I had to write it instantly. And yet I thought, it doesn't satisfy; something is missing, to have her die so quickly. So I recapped the time she almost choked to death, and I brought her to the point where she was almost dying, but she was relieved that time—and then came into the death again. As a writer, I knew instinctively I had to do this. I had to do it. Hard writing. Painful writing. In fact, one of my phobias—and I'm loaded with them—is choking. I've always had a fear of choking, as my wife and family will testify, and yet I knew how it would feel to choke to death. That chapter was a tough thing to write. There are things you avoid even when you know they're coming.

I often say I write with a sense of joy because I love writing, but within that joy is all this hard work, and there is also a dark side to it that you don't often talk about.

NOTE

The remarks in "A Rattlin' Good Story" were made by Robert Cormier on three separate occasions from 1978 to 1985.

The Third Eye

MOLLIE HUNTER

The title above is also the title of one of my twenty-four books for young readers—in this case, for those who have the misfortune to be categorized as "young adults"—in my view an ugly and misleading phrase, since these same little unfortunates are usually around a mere twelve years old.

Be that as it may, however, the theme of this book is "perception," i.e., what the dictionary defines as "taking in with the mind and the senses." Hence the choice of its title in a phrase equating with that "Eye of Enlightenment" which, in some Eastern philosophies, refers to the phenomenon of the mind's ability to grasp the significance behind the outward appearance of the passing moment. Hence also the use of the same title for this article, since it is by telling something of how the book developed that I hope eventually to make some points about perception as this relates to the literary experience in childhood.

To indicate briefly, then, the practical basis of this development, the setting is a typical Lowland Scots village of the 1930s—the time and setting of my own childhood. The plot is woven around the lives of three sisters growing toward maturity in that setting, and the ways in which their lives have been intertwined with the facts behind the death of one man known to them all.

The facts in question, however, have roots that go far back into the past of all the adults concerned in the story. Also, the death has been a violent one; and under Scots law, this latter circumstance means that all the features which may have any bearing on it must be investigated by the chief law officer of the county—the Procurator Fiscal. Called for examination, therefore, is the last person to see and speak to the man before his death. This is the girl, Jinty Morrison, the youngest of the three sisters; and right from the book's opening it is clear to the reader that Jinty is not only afraid of the questioning she must face, but also that she fears it because she has something to hide. A mystery is thus implied; and the rest of the book is devoted to resolving that mystery.

The technique employed for this was that of extended flashback occurring while Jinty waits for her interview with the Fiscal; and the importance of that particular choice of technique will eventually emerge. But for the time being, it is the motivation for the story that must be explored, because this also has roots that go far back into the past—my own past, which holds an obsession that has persisted with me ever since early childhood.

The obsession was, and still is, with courage; the kind of courage that can nerve a person to die for an idea. I read much of this, as a child, perhaps because my home had so many books (mainly of a religious nature) centering around this theme; and very often the sight that haunted me behind eyelids closed desperately tight in the attempt to lose myself in sleep, was the figure of Joan of Arc or that of some other martyr burning at the stake. *Could I have endured so—for an idea?* That was the question that tormented me. And knowing myself to be one of Nature's cowards, the torment lay in the fact that the answer was always a resounding *No!*

Came my adolescent years in World War II, and the aftermath of war when story after story came out of Europe of men and women civilians who had resisted the evil ethos that had finally been defeated there. But too late, too late for them, came that victory, because they were the ones who had been dragged off to prison or to a concentration camp, never to be heard of again. And so they must be presumed to have died there; executed, perhaps, in a prison yard in a gray dawn with nobody, not even their executioners, to know or care who they were; nobody to know or care that the body which had slumped to the concrete had been a person who had died for an idea—surely the loneliest of all deaths? And courage, courage of this kind, *should* have witnesses!

The thought was like a cry in me, its existence adding a further and infinitely more tormenting dimension to my obsession. And far from fading as other matters faded from my mind with the progression of the postwar years, the obsession remained prominently there and grew to the point where, in some form or another, it has appeared to date in all my writing. Yet strangely enough, it seems to me, this has never been commented on by any of the critics who have reviewed my work although to do the critics justice, of course, this could be because the form in which the obsession has shown has always been more oblique than direct. Until, that is, I came to write *The Third Eye.*

I had by then reached the point when it seemed to me that, unless I *was* prepared to express myself openly over something that had so long haunted me, I would have failed the writing challenge implicit in such a situation. And simply because of that, I would also have failed all those for whom I had so long affected to care—all those voiceless ones, those pitiful, nameless dead of the prison yards. Yet even so, I was sadly aware, this was still a situation where willingness to accept a challenge was not enough. All that gave me was the theme of a book, leaving me still with a plot to find, a setting, and a format.

I struggled over this, struggled hard; but one can no more command the creation of a particular book than one can force growth from an infertile seed. And so, with my mind persistently remaining a blank on the book I really wanted to write, I turned to occupying my time with a project I had mentally named my "village book," writing scenes and sketches drawn from the Lowland village of my childhood, characterizing the people I had known there, and half-hoping as I did so that enough might emerge eventually to cohere into a book. Almost as if I were prescient, also, I wrote particularly of one person I had known in those childhood days, a man on whose family lay a very ancient doom. And the more I wrote of him the more he haunted my imagination until he had grown there to almost the proportions of a latter-day Lear.

Yet still this work was all meaningless because, of course, it had no motivation behind it. I was very conscious, indeed, that—having already used this village as the setting for an earlier book—I was doing no more than gathering up all the bits and pieces of observation and experience which that earlier book had left unused; acting, in fact, like the person I am in my non-writing life—the thrifty housewife who cobbles together the bright bits and scraps left over from some major job of sewing, and hopes to create from them "something useful." In the process, also, I was consistently being reminded of the leading character in that earlier book, which was one that had required her personality to dominate the entire story. And since I was still cherishing a rather forlorn hope that this present exercise might just eventually also become a book, I had to find a leading character who would *not* be a dominant one; who would, on the contrary, be the kind of person who stood aside observing events, someone who would be a witness . . .

Hold on! As if a shutter had clicked in my mind, I suddenly had the connection between the kind of leading character I wanted and the form I would give to my obsession. That Lear-like figure! There was one way in which the tragedy in his life could be resolved—by an act of lonely courage. And supposing I made that girl, the one I needed for my leading character, a witness to the *fact* of that courage. I would have found a voice then, would I not, to cry out *my* witness to the courage of all those other lonely deaths?

In a rush of triumph, I followed up this realization. I achieved a name for my girl, one that was typical of her background. Other characters began to assemble around her, the incidents I had earlier written of began to relate to them. Yet still the story did not take fire as I had thought it would—not until I found that format of young Jinty Morrison reliving these incidents in flashback; because then, I realized, I was telling of events *solely through Jinty's perception of them*—solely, in effect (as happens with that "third eye") *in the light of the significance she sensed for them at the moment of their happening*.

The story, in fact, not only took fire, came really alive, with this realization. It also took on a dimension different from that originally intended for it, because telling everything thus—through Jinty's perceptions—meant finally that I was writing not only about courage and witness to courage, but further, about the *significance of witness*.

I remember sitting back at this point, putting down my pen, and thinking about what was implied in this whole question of childhood perception. I became aware then that the experience had clarified for me a great deal of what had previously been no more than assumptions with regard to the part that perception plays in the literary experience of childhood; which brings me now to the point of sharing the conclusions derived from my thinking.

In the book, *The Third Eye,* I have drawn the girl Jinty as a person of peculiarly vivid perception; and lest this be used as an argument against what follows, I hasten to maintain that to make a leading character the personification of a book's theme is an allowable and perfectly acceptable literary device. Nevertheless, this is a device I have been able to use only because I have a strong capacity to recall the perceptions of my own childhood; and it could be said, therefore, that this personal situation had led me to overestimate the strength and incidence of perception as a general phenomenon in childhood.

On the contrary, I think it is one which is too often underestimated; and as an example of this, I give an actual experience which I have related to the plot of the story.

A minor character in this is a nine-year-old boy called Toby. He is a sickly child, and he is blind, lonely also, since he is the only offspring of a widowed father. Jinty has formed an older-sister relationship with him, very precious to Toby since she has found a way of describing colors to him so that he can "see" them. Realizing also how important to him is his sense of touch, she brings him flowers to feel, and she is about to set off to gather for him the first snowdrops of the year when she and the rest of the children in the village school are told of his death. She picks the snowdrops, nevertheless, but is in such a state of shock that it seems to her as if a stranger had taken possession of her body and is performing the actions for her. Her way home takes her past the village churchyard where Toby's funeral is in progress. As she lingers at the gate there, she is noticed and beckoned in, her original purpose with the snowdrops having been surmised by another character who has knowledge of the relationship between her and Toby.

In the churchyard, she does as indicated to her. She drops the flowers down onto the coffin in the open grave; and while she does so, her perceptions are making her acutely aware of the emotions surrounding her, the pathos emanating from the fact of the child's death, the bleakness of the father's grief, the inarticulate sympathy drawing together all the men around the grave.

Now, it is a fact that all the circumstances of "Toby's" life and death as I have described them in the book, actually occurred in the village of my childhood; and it is only for purposes of this story that I have transmuted the relationship that my three sisters and I had with him, to one in which it is Jinty alone who has this relationship. It is a fact also, that when we were told that school would close for a half day on the afternoon of his funeral, we did not rush out determined to enjoy our freedom, but went to the woods, instead, to gather snowdrops. From the woods, then, with our hands full of the flowers, we went to the village churchyard. There, with the shyness of country children, we did no more than stand dumbly at the gate, until we were noticed and beckoned in; and, obeying the gesture made to us, we dropped the flowers down onto the little boy's coffin.

Remember, we were four sisters ranging in age from nine to twelve; and normally, among ourselves, we were very talkative. But from first to last throughout this whole occasion there was no word spoken among us. None of us made any suggestion about going to the wood or about picking snowdrops. None of us mentioned the boy, or the fact that he was dead, or that his funeral was due to take place. None of us proposed going to the churchyard, or waiting at the gate there. Never once, either, in all the years that have passed since that occasion, has any of us ever so much as mentioned it.

And so what am I to conclude from all this? That my sisters, when it came to the pathos of that child's death, were *less* perceptive than I was? Why then, the undiscussed and combined gathering of the snowdrops? And why, once we had them, did we not take them home as we usually did, instead of going with them to the churchyard—so making the only gesture that *could* be made in those circumstances by children like ourselves?

Why also our later silence on the details of what took place in the churchyard, the appearance of the men at the funeral? And remember, in this connection, that funerals in the Scotland of our childhood were attended only by men, so that this one was, for us, a unique experience which therefore afforded also a unique opportunity for us four little gossips to chatter afterwards about the impressions gathered there. Can I say, then, that my sisters were also less perceptive than I in their witness to the bleak grief of the father, the silent sympathy of the rest of the men?

If I cannot say that—and I do not believe I justifiably can—then the only difference between my sisters and myself is that none of them was born with the writer's mind and thus with the desire to communicate in some way the significance behind the outward form of all that happened on that occasion. But I *was* so born, and thus I am justified also in attributing my perceptions of the occasion to the fictional character of my book. I would maintain, too, that I am further justified in assuming that the reader will be able to share fully in these perceptions—always providing, of course, that reader identification with the character has already been achieved. And so, it is with this proviso in mind that we must now approach the nub of what is involved in relating perception to the literary experience in childhood.

We are all aware, of course, of the ways in which reader identification can be achieved at the superficial level—either in terms of a character's age, or circumstances, or failing such obvious methods, through involving the character in events that create wishful thinking on the part of the reader. But to go more deeply than this into the process, means touching in some way the mind of one's character; and for a reader who has already identified at the superficial level, this means inevitably a touch also on that reader's own mind. To touch the mind of one's character at the level of perception is to reach the deepest level of all, the one in which all feeling is rooted; and thus, with the channel to this already opened to the reader, it can truly be said that one has reached the point where total reader identification is also rooted.

Bear in mind in all this, however, the definition of perception as one's awareness of the significance behind the outward form of the passing moment, and you will be reminded also that any real-life experience of it is therefore a very fleeting one, vanishing almost before it can be grasped. Perception, also, is a phenomenon that is unrelated to intelligence, or to age—except that, in the case of the latter, the very novelty of experiencing it in childhood can make this the time when its impact is most vivid. And so here, in this exception, we have a paradox, in that childhood is all too often also the time when there is neither a point of reference to which one can relate the phenomenon, nor the vocabulary to express its impact.

How to resolve that paradox, then, becomes the task of the children's writer who would touch the reader at that deepest of all levels; and all my experience in this regard has taught me that this is best done by keeping in mind an equation that can be expressed thus: *Perception plus Experience plus Understanding equals Insight.*

To define how the equation is built up I would say first that, from the very moment of birth, we are all capable of some degree of perception. To this, as we grow, is added a more or less amount of experience in various of life's aspects. Further growth gives us some understanding of our experience, including that part which involves perception. And when full adulthood is reached, the achievement of perspective on the cumulative effect all this has had on us, is expressed in the quality we call "insight."

To operate in the terms I have indicated, therefore, it is not enough to be writing simply from understanding of experience or recollection of perception, since all that would imply would be *hindsight*; and the cardinal sin brought about by writing from hindsight is, of course, that of "writing down" to children. To write from insight, on the other hand, is to hold the whole balance of the equation consistently in mind; and by doing so, to enable oneself to communicate directly from insight to perception.

Communication, however, is like blood, in the sense that it must flow at the impetus of a pumping heart, or else congeal; and if story is to be the medium of communication with children, the impetus of the writer's imagination has to be strongly behind it. Strong too, must be that grasp on technique that enables the writer to structure a story. *But*, beyond all these things, it seems to me now and always has seemed that one must also have a willingness to think deeply about one's own humanity, both on its own account and as it concerns the generality of humankind.

This, I hold, is the only way in which one can truly enable children to open the door of literary experience; the only way one can lead them, from that first opening, through all those other doors beyond which they have not yet had the chance to explore. In the case of the book on which I have based my argument, the first of these doors was the one marked "Courage." From this, to keep faith with the concepts I had worked out and thus, it seemed to me, with the children for whom I wrote the book, I traced a route that ran directly from my adult insight to my childhood perceptions. So I reached the door marked "Witness to Courage." And once this was opened for the reader, I felt that at long last I had kept faith also with my brave and voiceless ones, my nameless dead.

The final door in the book was marked "Perception"; and in *all* experience of literature, that of children as much as that of adults, the most profound of pleasures lies with encountering that door and discovering it to be the only one which always swings open of its own accord.

One Human Heart

A CONVERSATION BETWEEN
PAULA FOX AND
CATHIE MERCIER

Cathie Mercier: You write for both children and adults. As you write, are you aware of your audience? Do you decide to write an adult book, or do you make the decision during the process of writing?

Paula Fox: Well, once I've started, I don't think about whether I'm writing for children or for adults. Recently, at the American Library Association convention in Chicago, a man came to the booth where I was signing books and said, "Is this book good for a nine-year-old boy?" And I replied, "There is no such thing as a nine-year-old boy. There's Charles or Leslie or Lewis or Pierre, but there's no such thing as a nine-year-old boy. It's always a person." But I don't think about that person at all once I start to write a book.

I do have something in mind, however. It's very difficult to say exactly what—why something starts out one way and not another. When I sat down to write *A Servant's Tale,* for example, I didn't think about it as a book for children; but I didn't really think about it as a book for adults, either. As I begin to work, it's very clear that the direction of the book has already been determined. I'm really discovering the story that I've already thought of.

I think I've said before that I particularly love Coleridge's phrase "difference is not division," which goes with what Wordsworth said, "We have but one human heart." Clearly, there are children's books, and there are books for adults. Why would a child want to read Sartre's *The Words,* for example? On the other hand, my two sons spent six months in Greece many years ago when they were little. My husband had brought a number of Kafka's books with him, and my children, who had run out of comics and children's books, were so desperate that at ten and twelve they read *The Castle* and *The Metamorphosis.* I don't mean they liked them, but at least the books were something to read in English.

It's very complicated—and also very simple—the difference between children's books and adult books. Children have not been in the world as long as adults. They may have every kind of virtue, great wit, and imagination, but they don't have judgment. In fact, it takes a long time for any of us to have a little judgment. And there is something about where you are in time that determines the kind of book that will engage you and interest you. I really don't think most children would like *Edwin Drood* as much as *Great Expectations*.

Mercier: You once said that you started writing rather late. When did you begin, and what prompted you?

Fox: Actually, I started writing when I was seven, as many children do. I didn't need prompting; I wanted to write stories. I don't quite know what it means to say I wanted to write stories. I wonder if children who play the piano very early have strong musical feelings and say, "I want to be a pianist." I don't think they feel that way. I don't think writers do, either—people who tell stories. I always loved stories and was always explaining to myself what was happening. I think there's probably something nutty about a lot of writers, certainly about me, in that compulsion to explain, or that wish to form beginnings and middles and endings to what does not seem to have beginnings, middles, and endings. That is, to make some kind of coherence out of what isn't coherent about life.

That compulsion, that wish, started very early. In my twenties I was very busy earning a living, paying rent, and traveling around, but I always had the wish somewhere. At some point I let go of a job and swung out over open space; it was very frightening at first.

Mercier: I'm sure all would-be writers could sympathize with that plunge.

Fox: Yes, and without a net.

Mercier: You said that you enjoyed reading when you were young. What were some of the books that meant something to you as a child?

Fox: *The Little Lame Prince*, I remember. *Treasure Island*. When I was a child, which was a long time ago, children's books were quite different from what they are now. I read poetry. The first poem I learned by heart was "If," by Rudyard Kipling. I still remember memorizing it. I was taught to read when I was five by a minister who took care of me when I was a child, and he loved history and books and poetry. Edwin Markham, all kinds of American poets, Mark Twain, other writers—he read to me, and I wanted to learn to read. I did learn, very young, and I read Mark Twain and Dickens when I was ten or eleven. Then, of course, there was Thornton Burgess, who used to have a little serial that ran in the newspaper, and there were some wonderful animal books which I've forgotten now. I remember *The Wind in the Willows*, when I was a little older.

Mercier: What kinds of things do you read as an adult?

Fox: Well, now I'm rereading a lot. I read *Anna Karenina* again a couple of
years ago, and I couldn't bear it, it was so wonderful. It was as if I hadn't
read it before. I read *Middlemarch* again, several times. I read a lot of
nineteenth-centry and early twentieth-century writers. I think there are
some wonderful writers around—Elsa Morante for one, an Italian writer.
I don't want to go through a list, but, anyhow, I read all the time.

Mercier: Do you read contemporary children's books?

Fox: I read some. Not a lot.

Mercier: Many of your stories possess a firm sense of place, and some—
I'm thinking of *The Slave Dancer*—are set in a specific historic period. Do
you take physical trips to do research for some books, or do you take
journeys of the mind?

Fox: I've lived in a lot of places. I lived in New Orleans for a while, three
months. Most of the places I write about are places that I've been to.
Reading Thomas Hardy's *The Mayor of Casterbridge*, you could draw the
village because it was so specific. Hardy, obviously, always had a place
in mind. I always have a place in mind, but I change the furniture
around, as if the place were a dollhouse. I move the post office to the
other side of town, or whatever, but there is some kind of concrete sense
of the place always in my mind when I write. So when I was writing
about New Orleans, I recalled so much. I remembered its aroma and its
temperament, which had not changed then as it has changed in the last
twenty years. When I lived there, it was still close to its past; there was
the old French market, and you could still sit on the banks of the
Mississippi. It's all quite different now.

   You know, to imagine a place where you've been is just as complex as
imagining a place where you haven't been. For example, this room we
are in: To imagine and convey a sense of it after we have left would be
very complicated. All imagining is difficult. And almost everything in a
certain sense is imagined.

Mercier: For *The Slave Dancer* did you do research to verify the historical
accuracy?

Fox: Oh, yes, I did a year of that before I wrote it. I read. I had a
tremendous file of three-by-five cards, and I read primary sources,
secondary sources, diaries, logs, and testimony; and when I began to
write the book, I found that, with all I had learned, too much information
was getting in the way. I couldn't put down anything without thinking,
But was it so? For example, I remember very specifically that I wrote
something about a kerosene lamp; and then, because I had been doing
all of that research for a year, I thought, Well, were there kerosene lamps
in New Orleans? So I managed to track down the information that there
weren't any kerosene lamps in 1840. I had acquired a kind of sensitivity

by that reading, but it got in the way, so I had to get rid of some of the information before I could really write the book. By the end I was so nervous about the book that a historian of the period read it and checked it through because he also knew something about sailing and I knew nothing. I had sailing books in front of me with ships all laid out, and I couldn't understand anything. I couldn't understand how the wind took the sail, but I kept at it. I had a lot of trouble writing a storm in that book; that's why I had to know about sailing.

Mercier: Integral to your work is the theme of journeying, both in body and in mind. Many of your young journeyers, your heroes, suffer from a lack of being understood and are not communicative. Some are imprisoned in a cell of isolation. I think of Gus from *The Stone-Faced Boy*, whom you describe as having " 'a face made out of stone.' Then, too, it made him mysterious because no one knew how he did it. He didn't know himself. It was as though he shut a door. He could even hear a little click of the lock. Right after the click, he knew his face was without expression." What is it about the removed, the isolated, child that intrigues you, that moves you to write about him or her?

Fox: I think you started out by saying the children I write about very often are not understood. Well, I think most children are not understood. I think we know much less than our jargon leads us to think we know. There are all kinds of social sciences that have acquired enormous influence in the last thirty-five or forty years so that our understanding, instead of expanding, seems to be more constricted. When we speak of, for example, a "troubled child," it seems to me that our minds often shut off. The child no longer exists as a fascinating, complex, or not-so-fascinating, not-so-complex being—there's no longer a real child there.

Mercier: Instead, there's a category.

Fox: There's a "troubled child." All of this language, part of which we could blame Rousseau for, and all the ideas about environment and forces working upon the child have led us to terrible categories that imprison people. In fact, it is very hard for people to understand one another. Human history is surely a testament to that. And to go around cheerfully feeling as though we've solved everything because we've read a bit of Freud and we've read a little sociology here and there is very strange—when all around us are battlefields and slaughterhouses. But such a situation is very much part of the human condition—certainly the human condition in our country.

I don't think that the children I write about are as remote from ordinary life as people who write about my books are sometimes inclined to say. I think that it's too easy to dismiss a phenomenon which we could think about forever and which we might never really understand. To

think and to try to conceive of other people—especially young people—
is an extraordinary thing. Obviously, when you write a book, there's
always an emphasis, and something written about is thereby emphasized. So the children are larger than life and less than life. Gus is a very
private person, who is in the middle of his family and who is not
immediately categorizable. T. S. Eliot has a terrific phrase in which he
speaks of "formulating people and pinning them sprawling to the wall."
That is a tendency we all have because it's the easy way. Life is hard, and
it's easier to formulate people and not think about them. My tendency is
to write about children in a certain way rather than to write about a
certain kind of child.

Mercier: Were you an understood child?

Fox: No, I don't think so. I really don't know anybody who has been an
understood child. But I would like to meet one. Then I would stop
writing.

Mercier: Your books have demonstrated that you also have an interest in
varied relationships between children and adults. The adult-child relationship is particularly satisfying in *One-Eyed Cat*, where the boy Ned is
supported by loving parents who truly strive to understand him, who
are patient and pull away as he struggles internally with himself. *Is* there
an ideal child-adult relationship? Should there be?

Fox: Well, what I think about those two grown-ups is that they're both
people who have a strong sense of their own privacy. They are people
who are not trying to show that they're wonderful parents; they're not,
either of them, trying to show that they try to understand everything.
They seem to be people in their own right, and they're perhaps more
likely than others to give space to a child. In *A Likely Place* I wrote about
a babysitter who is not a parent but who is subtly aware without being
direct about it. When someone dropped a fork, she didn't say, "Oh, its
perfectly all right; it's all right." Nor did she smack the child nor do any
of the other things that we are all inclined to do. She just did a tango,
which is maybe the right thing to do.

Mercier: I'm also intrigued by the relationship in *One-Eyed Cat* between
Mr. Scully and Ned. Have you had a Mr. Scully in your life?

Fox: I'm practically Mr. Scully myself. I suppose with him I was more
conscious in a certain way than I usually am. I think I feel very
powerfully how removed children and old people are now, much more
than they used to be. We tend to have a lot of nostalgia about a past that
never existed. The idea of a traditional family: How long has there been
such a thing? Not for as many years as we think nor for as many years
as politicians would like us to think. In fact, when did all those happy
families appear—with Grandma and Grandpa living in the old Victorian

house? These generalizations we make are not true, but obviously there is an idea somewhere that *is* true. When I lived in Greece, for example, in a village by the sea, I saw how the very young children and the very old people were together, and I think I do have a certain ideology about that. I feel that they ought to be together more. When I was a child, as I said, I was taken care of by a minister. The people in the church, the people that I knew, were of all ages, from infants to people in their nineties. No one was called a senior citizen. It sounds like a mild disease. That's another category, you see—like the nine-year-old boy.

Mercier: You were speaking about extended families. I had a Mr. Scully. My grandparents living next door and my parents and my maternal grandmother living in our house with six children made quite an extended family. What you said about the need for young people to be with old people is something that I felt very strongly in my own life. I want to go on record saying it is very important, if possible, to have that happen. I wouldn't trade it for the world.

Fox: It's a way of measuring yourself in your own life.

Mercier: And it's a way of learning so much more about the world, what's out there, what you're in for, what you can do and what you can't do, and what you can do to put it all off a little bit.

Fox: Yes, and hide a little bit, too.

Mercier: Yes, and hide, and commiserate, maybe.

Back to your work. Often you use simple plot lines, very direct and straightforward without a lot of external action. I think of Lewis in *A Likely Place*. The action in the book is that he leaves his home, he walks to the park, he meets Mr. Madruga, he walks home, he walks back to the park, and he and Mr. Madruga form a friendship. Together they write a letter. This is not an action-packed narrative; this is not *Treasure Island*, for example. Yet, there's a great deal of growth, of internal action, in both those characters. Which comes first, the plot or the character?

Fox: Oh, the character is everything. I don't think about the plot very much. I read books that are wonderfully plotted, but my mind doesn't work with plot that way. One is stuck with the way one is, and everything comes to me from the way people are. I always think of the person before I think of what's going to happen to him or her.

Mercier: Although you don't always employ the first person as a narrative technique, you do use it sometimes, and many of your stories are told clearly and undeniably from the child's perspective. Perhaps your ability to see from a child's point of view makes the characters in your book so real that they stand up and say, "I am here. I have an identity. I am this person." For example, I think of Victoria in *A Place Apart*, Jessie in *The Slave Dancer*, Maurice in *Maurice's Room*, and Good Ethan himself. Do your characters maintain a persistent reality for you, even after their story has been told? Do you now care as much about Victoria as you did when you were writing about and working with her?

Fox: That's an interesting question. I've never been asked that before. I think so. When I think about them, I think of the way I thought about them when I was writing about them. I think about all those people in that way. They don't just sort of suddenly become paper dolls and lie down inside the book. They're very much still there for me, and I think about them.

Mercier: So back to Victoria: Is she growing up somewhere?

Fox: No, no, she sang her song and passed into the mist. But I do sometimes speculate about some of the people. No, I think that I have a very powerful sense of the difference between the apple in Cézanne's painting and the apple I pick up and eat. They are connected, but they haven't grown, those apples in that bowl.

Mercier: Have you ever thought about writing a sequel?

Fox: Yes, I have, and I haven't. I thought about writing a sequel, in fact, to *The Stone-Faced Boy*. But I don't think I will. I have something else in mind. I don't know; once it's done, it's done.

Mercier: Would you like to see any of your books made into movies, or none of them, or a specific one?

Fox: Well, I'm neutral about it. I did have a movie made from an adult book. The thing that was very nice about it was that they paid me enough to buy a little house in Brooklyn. That was a terrific surprise. It was a small-budget movie, but the payment was very pleasant. And the other very pleasant part was that I didn't have to do anything. So it's really not something I think about because it's just not there. The movie companies are always interested in children's books that get the Newbery Medal, for example, or honor books; they read them, and they think of television adaptations.

Oh, I did get a very funny letter once. *Portrait of Ivan* was sent to some producer, and he wrote to the agent who sent it and said it was a very nice book, but that they were into teenage pregnancy and diabetes right then. So, whatever they're into, it's not my books, I don't think.

Mercier: You say that when you write, you finish, and then it's done and removed, somewhat apart from you. After you are involved in the intensity of a particular story, what do you do to put that distance between you and the book? When you finish a book, what's your first reaction, what's the first thing you do?

Fox: "Oh, it's done! It's done!" A kind of tremendous relief. A day of not feeling guilty—the way I usually feel about one thing or another—for example, because I didn't work, I didn't do this, I didn't do that. A certain tremendous relief, sometimes a certain exhilaration. And then, a few days later, it all goes away, and I start thinking about another book. The book is finished—it finishes itself to the extent that anything is ever finished; and that's the end of it. Working is very hard. Anybody who writes knows that writing is terribly hard work; in fact, what people don't know is that it's like playing the violin.

My youngest son, when he was about seven or eight, said he wanted to play the violin. I waited a few months to see if he'd keep on wanting to, and he did; so I found a violin teacher and a very small violin. After about three weeks I went to see the violin teacher and asked, "Well, what do you think?" He said, "Well, he has the prerequisite for violin playing; he's physically strong." It's also true about writing. This tremendous amount of physical endurance. I know a few writers, not many, and they get so tired, so really tired. It's very hard work.

Mercier: I can't help but think of Virginia Woolf and her insistence that in order for women to write they need to have rooms of their own. Do you have a room of your own?

Fox: I certainly do. It took me a while to get it, but I did.

Mercier: Would you tell us about it?

Fox: Yes, it's at the top of a very narrow house, twelve-and-a-half feet wide. The house was advertised as being thirteen feet wide, but the bank put us right to that; I also went to the historical society, and they confirmed that it's only twelve-and-a-half feet wide. I'm on the top floor in a very quiet room overlooking a schoolyard, which is noisy at noon when the children come out to play, and beyond that is the bay, New York harbor opening up. It's a very small room and anything can distract me. I'm always hoping there will be things to distract me, so it's a very nice plain room, with a table and a typewriter. I go there every day when I'm working, even though I feel terrible and wish I could have some vodka in the morning, or anything to get out from under.

It's true. Oh, it's so hard. And then other days I just go to work, just like everybody; you go to your work—that's what you do. Sometimes children have asked me, "When you get your idea, those mysterious ideas, then you go to work?" And I say, "Oh, no. You have to go to work first." And I have to; some people don't have to, but I have to go every day to the same place. I find it very difficult now to work away from this place.

Mercier: What is the one question about writing that you've always wanted to be asked but have not yet been asked?

Fox: I have to think about that. I'll tell you the worst question. "Where do you get your ideas from?" That's the question I get from children all the time. It's as if you can go to Macy's and there's an Idea Department—I mean, as if an idea is *external*. It's a question I dread, and they always ask me when they write letters. Almost always.

Mercier: What is the most interesting question a child has asked you?

Fox: I saved one letter from a child who had read *The Slave Dancer*. A southern child, I think, South Carolina. She said, "I noticed in the summer a lot of white people lying around on the beach trying to get tanned, and then they're so mean to black people. Can you explain this to me?" I kept that letter.

Mercier: What did you reply?

Fox: That's a secret.

On Censorship

ALICE CHILDRESS

Book banning goes back a long way for me.

My great-grandmother was a slave in Charleston, South Carolina; she was bought and sold there. It was against the law, after slavery, for all Black people to learn to read and write. During slavery you could have your ears, or your nose, or even your life cut off, because knowledge was considered a very dangerous thing. For a person in bondage to be able to read and write meant that revolt would be on the way.

Drums were banned. African drums are instruments for messages, rather than for entertainment; people knew signals and messages so that drums were taken away, and in their place stringed instruments like banjos were substituted—as a happier sound, a different sort of sound. Then their languages, of course, were banned when the slaves were brought here; they were Mandingo, Ewe people, Ga people, Ashante, or Fante—they didn't understand each other. And what slavers did was take one Fante, one Ga, one Mandingo, one Ashante and make what they called a mixed lot so that the captives could not communicate with one another.

The descendants of Africans were the only people in America who had their languages abolished by law. Laws were established making it illegal to speak an African tongue. Out of this situation came a dialect of many different tongues—a sort of common Black speech for communication in English. The slaves did not learn it as one people but as a varied people.

Then, with freedom there came another kind of banning. As it became legal for Blacks to learn to read and write, school boards without Black members selected all the reading matter; even all-Black schools were not allowed to select their own books. Of course, reading material for Blacks was already banned in another way; the public libraries of South Carolina and of other Jim Crow states were closed to my people. We weren't allowed to draw books.

So banning is not new, but today we notice different forms of it. On the one hand, it's good to care about what our children read, but on the other hand, when banning starts, the first books knocked down are always books of social import that examine the condition of life around us. Pornography is the last to be banned. Bernard Malamud's *The Fixer* and Kurt Vonnegut's *Slaughterhouse-Five* were among those banned in the famous Island Trees case—which, as you know, went all the way to the Supreme Court—along with a disproportionate number of Black books— Langston Hughes's *Best Short Stories of Negro People*, and *A Hero Ain't Nothin' but a Sandwich*. Steven Pico and the American Civil Liberties Union in a court action challenged the banning of books.

By the time the case got to the Supreme Court, I was prepared for them to protest the four letter words in my book and to count how many times this word and that word were said. I was very much surprised that only one short paragraph was quoted in the presentation against the book. A Black schoolteacher in Harlem was talking about teaching a Black class, where on the wall in the front of the classroom there were only two pictures—one of George Washington and one of Abraham Lincoln. Two whites before an all-Black class as the only symbols of their country. This is the paragraph:

> Only two pictures on my wall when I came here . . . George Washington and Abraham Lincoln. Abe was, at least, involved with the Civil War and the Emancipation thing; but George was a slaveholder, and it is impossible to hang George over my front blackboard and not discuss him. When I discuss him, I don't go by what's in these history books or we'd be dealin in lies. George was a slaveholder, and he had it put in his will to free alla his slaves *after* his death, but he owned a slave woman whose cookin was so fine that he freed her while he was livin. She musta really known how to barbecue!

That was the paragraph. And the Island Trees school board charged that it showed a lack of respect for a founding father of the United States of America to tell children that he was a slaveholder, and also that it showed a flippant attitude toward him and that no founding father should be criticized in a children's book. Among the comments in the transcript was one by Justice Thurgood Marshall, who questioned what was wrong with discussing founding fathers who were slaveholders.

And all the other books were challenged on what seemed to be strange grounds; the school board said that Malamud's *The Fixer* was anti-Semitic. They quoted one little passage where someone called a prisoner a "dirty

Jew bastard." Of course, this remark was made by a jailer kicking and abusing a Jewish prisoner. So words were taken out of context, and it is my belief that people were after larger game, which is the content, the education, the opening up of the minds of children.

Discussed at other times was the question of dialect. I visited West Africa and Ghana and met many children of different tribal groups, which are still strong there—Ga people, Ashante people. They speak their own languages and also speak English and French. They do not speak dialect as we hear and know it in this country. They have a sort of flavor of their own—either Ewe language or Ga or Ashante. But here we have a commonality. If written in dialect, books are often charged with being backward or not teaching children proper English or not giving them a good education or just being difficult to read.

It so happens that there are millions of books written in quite "good English," and the choice is there in every library; why make a big fuss over a few dozen books written in dialect—almost another language—for children who were raised speaking that dialect? A few books that say to many children, Welcome, I hear what you hear and hear what you say, are not there to claim that this is the way to speak English. In Harlem I was given assignments—I had to read Sean O'Casey, for example. It never did any harm; it did a lot of good. I also read I. L. Peretz and Shalom Aleichem.

Some banned works are tough books, like Piri Thomas's *Down These Mean Streets*, and in my book *A Hero Ain't Nothin' but a Sandwich* Benjie's thoughts run on: "Walkin through dark, stinky hallways can be hard on anybody, man or chile, but a chile can get snatch in the dark and get his behind parts messed up by some weirdo; I'm talkin bout them sexuals." There are certain harsh realities of life that can be told honestly, and there are a lot of things we tell children that they already know; they just can't discuss them with us. Once these things are in books, the children feel freer to talk about them.

When these books got back on the shelf at Island Trees, they thought of something else. The next step taken by the board was to make *librarians* notify the parent by mail if a young adult had taken out one of the books in question. A notice was sent: Your child has drawn out such and such a book which you may find objectionable. Well, Steven Pico and the American Civil Liberties Union went back to court and found that there is a law in New York State that makes it illegal to report books drawn from the public library. It is an invasion of privacy.

There are other books banned all over this country. *Romeo and Juliet* was banned in the Midwest because the nurse is a poor role model. People said, Here she is hired by the parents to care for their daughter, and she's helping Romeo and Juliet to meet and warning them that their parents are coming, and so forth. Another school banned all of Shakespeare except

Romeo and Juliet. One censorship case involved the Song of Solomon in the Old Testament because it is sexually descriptive writing and might not be good for children.

There is no common Black dialect that all people speak. As the poet Paul Lawrence Dunbar said, there's a difference between dialect and minstrelsy. Minstrelsy has a different purpose and a different sound. It is mocking; it is ridiculing. But dialect is the speech as it comes out of the homes of Black children—or of Welsh coal miners, or other groups.

In *Rainbow Jordan*, Rainbow's mother explains something about her life. The book is about children having children and about those children sometimes having to raise their own parents. Her mother says:

> Fifteen was too young for me to have a child. Mother nature made me able to give birth from the age of twelve . . . but she didn't bother to turn my mind on in the same year; strange, weird, crazy. Leroy did not need to be a father at sixteen. When he took Rainbow out . . . somebody always ask, "Whose baby is that?" I told him he better learn to wipe that stupid, young, simple-ass look off his face and learn to act like a man. The two of us took Rainbow to the Baby Health Station for her checkup. The girl on the desk lookin dead at us, say, "Where are the child's parents?" Me, I stop wearin hair braids and made him get outta those funky-lookin sneakers and the T-shirt sayin "The Best in Town." I grew up fast while he was still playin stickball in the street. Playin stickball with his cap turn backwards. What kind-a simple-ass way is that? His folks didn't want us to get married and neither did mine . . . but Rainbow was a fact and we all got a thing bout "honor" and doin right by the unborn.

This is a sort of idiomatic speech, the speech of the people There is a feeling; there is a flow. There are many varieties of speech indigenous to different parts of America—different backgrounds, races, or peoples.

It is a matter of fact that I was born where I was born, under Jim Crow law at a certain time in history; and I went through restrictions and experienced Jim Crow until Martin Luther King and others changed the face of the entire country and made public transportation available on railroads and buses for everyone.

These are some of the reasons that I write what I write.

Only a Lamp-holder:
On Writing Historical Fiction

KATHERINE PATERSON

When I was a writer of historical fiction only, I used to be roundly taken to task for not writing stories that are true to life for today's children. It seemed to me then that in many instances historical fiction is much more realistic than a lot of today's realism. And I find it very strange when people separate realistic fiction from historical fiction, by which they seem to mean romantic and therefore unrealistic fiction. As my editor reminds me, nothing becomes dated more quickly than contemporary fiction, and for this reason it becomes very unrealistic to the young reader.

Often, then, we writers of contemporary fiction try to take out details that would date it. When you read these books, you discover that we writers have not revealed the date, we have not described clothing, we have not put slang into the mouths of our characters, because if we did, the book would immediately become dated and therefore unrealistic. But how can you call such a book even loosely true to the facts of observed life?

On the other hand, in historical novels we are quite free to anchor our characters with every fact of life at our command, being only limited by those facts that are going to delay our story and, therefore, drive off all but our most doggedly determined readers. When I first began to write historical fiction, I didn't even know I *was* writing historical fiction. I was just writing a story, and I was setting it back there somewhere; and when I was told that I was a historical novelist, I found it very interesting. I had never thought of myself as a historical novelist; I didn't know that historical fiction was a bastard child of letters, respectable neither as history nor as fiction.

Twelfth-century Japan torn apart by civil war and civil strife seemed very close to Washington of the late 1960s. I didn't think I was writing romantic literature; it seemed very realistic and terribly current. But there are perils and limitations. A friend who is a middle-aged American businessman came up to me after church one day to tell me how much he'd enjoyed *The Sign of the Chrysanthemum*. He hadn't expected to, not knowing anything about ancient Japan, but the thing that particularly appealed to him was how nearly the dreams and feelings of those ancient Japanese matched his own. And he concluded by saying to me, "People really haven't changed, have they?" I stammered for an answer because the dreams and feelings and fears of the Japanese as revealed in their own literature from the twelfth century are indeed recognizable to us as the dreams and feelings and fears of fellow human beings, but the dreams and feelings and fears in *The Sign of the Chrysanthemum* were those of the middle-aged American housewife who was speaking to him. I do not forget that it is my own Western twentieth-century mind that takes the ancient events and sifts them and creates the characters who allegedly took part in them. And, therefore, I become very nervous when people talk about my Japanese novels. If you've read Japanese novels, you know perfectly well that I have *not* written a Japanese novel. I've written quite a Western novel which happens to be set in Japan.

So I do try to be true as best I can to the times and feelings of feudal Japan. I may relate to the reader cruelties that may be absent from some contemporary fiction for children, but there are also details, events, attitudes—things that are quite true—that I will not write about when I write for children because I cannot do so within the boundaries of my own moral code.

ANN SCHLEE

At the beginning of *Middlemarch* George Eliot has Dorothea think: "To reconstruct a past world, doubtless with a view to the highest purposes of truth—what a work to be in any way present at, to assist in, though as only a lamp-holder!" I'm going to distort the meaning of what she was saying by seizing on this image of a lamp-holder. I like to imagine she was thinking of an oil lamp, which lights so well the things that are close to it but allows the corners of the room to recede into darkness. Lamplight has none of the impartial glare of electricity, and when you're writing, it gives you an immense power to concentrate on one issue.

The task of my fiction seems to be to suggest the past rather than to re-create it. What is not relevant can be left in the shadows because I'm dealing with a world I can never entirely reconstruct, and this gives me the power to concentrate. In writing about moral issues, you don't need to create an entire world. You need to shine a light on the specific thing you are talking about. I like writing about the past because it provides me with a special language. The material of letters and diaries and memoirs is strange; it's already fictionalized. It contains the fictions people project about themselves, giving it a quality of intensity. The thoughts and events have already been shaped and sharpened into words; the material already has a character of its own. In a short story by Elizabeth Bowen one of the characters is absolutely caught up in the past, and she cries out, "So much flowed through people then, so little flows through us now. All we can do is imitate love and sorrow." Perhaps this happens because we only meet them through the medium of language.

I'm talking exclusively about the Victorians. You cannot hear what the Victorians sounded like. You can explore and try to get closer and closer. You almost get it in stray bits of writing in odd letters, particularly from half-literate women, who had their eye so keenly on things. You sometimes get the actual inflection of the human voice, but you're never sure, as you are with contemporary speech, exactly what it sounded like. So what the past provides a writer is a slightly overarticulate language, because it's been written down, just as you when you write—even a letter to a friend— are a bit more articulate than when you talk to her.

Setting stories in the past also helps to solve one of the great difficulties of children's fiction—the invention of a child protagonist. It seems to me that children's literature—and here I'm thinking of it as a distinct form of literature—is about people who are small and not given all the facts, trying to cope in a world where the power belongs to big people who have more knowledge. In a way, almost all children's books are legends of power and weakness. One has to develop a child character who is, in a sense, a hero with power over the action in the story. Yet, in reality children don't have power in their situations. In the past children were far more exploited, but they also were much more caught up in the web of adult existence. In writing about the past, the writer has the chance to depict extraordinary adventures and seizures of power at an age that modern schoolchildren can identify with.

I will just mention a bloodcurdling tale in the history books of some Elizabethan boy sailors on a ship in the Mediterranean. They are mentioned as "young," so they were probably young teenagers. Their ship was captured by Barbary pirates. The English crew was imprisoned in the hold of the pirate ship, and a skeleton crew of pirates set aboard the English ship to sail her back to port. Very unwisely, misled by the youth of the four boys, the pirates left them on the English ship. Five days later a storm brewed. Every hand was needed on deck, and the boys were released from the hold. The captain said, "Do whatever you have to do!" Immediately, one of the boys pushed the captain overboard. Within minutes they had seized a number of arms that were lying about, killed two more Barbary pirates, thrown two others overboard, locked the rest in the hold, and sailed the ship back to a port in Spain.

This is a deeply immoral story! It could not possibly be told in modern terms because the boys' first move was to sell back into slavery the pirates who had captured them. It's a perfect example of the past letting you down: children taking action in the past that would be very difficult for them to take in modern times.

Finally, I want to make a very general point about approaching children's problems. We believe in books. Somehow we want to make childhood better, and we believe that a book given at the right moment can work magic in a child's life. I believe it profoundly. I question the idea that the only kind of book that can help a child through a problem is a book about that very problem. From my own experience I would say that many children in the grip of great trouble cannot face their problems and will reject books about those problems. But a book that is set in a parallel world—fairyland or wonderland or the future or the past, a parallel world in which things are happening on a rational basis—can sometimes be the way to acceptance.

I was talking to a woman my age, whose story I knew a little bit about, perhaps more than she realized I did. She's one of my students, and we were talking about children's books that have done this very thing in one's childhood, that have struck a shaft right into the center of one's life. Various students came up with various responses, and she came up with *John Halifax, Gentleman*. She said, "This book moved me beyond belief. I can remember weeping, and yet it made me so happy. I've read it again in recent years, and it's terrible. It's so boring, it's so sentimental, but I loved the father. He was so kind. He was so good."

Now, I know from things she let drop that she didn't have a father. And knowing that the child was from what we now call a one-parent family, nobody would give her *John Halifax, Gentleman*, to read. But she had found something in it. She still didn't know that was what she found, for she made no link to her own situation, but she derived great comfort from the book.

I will end by saying that I would like to place the kind of historical fiction I write firmly in this parallel world, where children—without immediately confronting their own situations, which can be too terrible to confront—can reach out and find what they need without having to name it too distinctly.

JILL PATON WALSH AND ANN SCHLEE

Jill Paton Walsh: Ann, there's a quotation from *Hamlet* that would clinch what you're saying: ". . . with assays of bias,/ By indirections find directions out."

I find the past much easier to discover, and more open to our view, than the present. You can find out more about the past. For example, you can read private letters and diaries, which would be intolerable conduct toward your contemporaries. It is nearly as intolerable to eavesdrop and certainly intolerable to put real people directly into your books. So, in the present we are isolated and must guess; whereas in the past we can diligently plod down to the library and find out.

Ann Schlee: Yes, you can delve into past intimacies, but this is the stuff of fiction, and E. M. Forster says somewhere—it's a cry of frustration—that you get to know the people in books better than you ever get to know the people in your life. He has some lovely phrase—searching for the friend who is always promised but never arrives in life, but in books you can find him; which is a slightly keyhole attitude to the past, but historical fiction is a rich field for that reason.

Audience: It seems to me that we often rob the past of its vitality and true strength by talking lightly about using it as a vehicle to view current problems.

Schlee: You mean we're cheating a bit? Yes. And I think it's a paradox that throws up the very problem revealed by the story about the Elizabethan boy sailors—that you want the vitality and the power of those boys. I mean, in an awful corner of one's mind, one thinks, What a rollicking good tale. And yet, to tell it in terms of our own morality would surely be impossible; it would be false. If you're going to rob the past of what you want, I think you have to hold faith with it. It would be dishonest to have one of those boy sailors say, "Oh, war is wrong; I should not shed blood; slavery is an abomination," because he would not have thought that.

Paton Walsh: It's often done, Ann, isn't it? You often get highly contemporary attitudes, especially about trendy subjects, coming from characters in historical novels.

Schlee: And yet, if one told that story in its own character, it would give offense, wouldn't it? It is a perfect example: If you're going to use the past, you must keep faith with it.

Paton Walsh: I think that what strikes us as interesting in the past—the selection we make from it—is always highly contemporary and subjective and differs from generation to generation and from person to person. But that type of subjectivity is involuntary, and we must be forgiven it, or we couldn't use any history at all. But there is another kind of subjectivity, in which we know darn well that we're leaving something out that ought to be in, or changing something to fit a modern view; using that deliberate bias is very wrong, and we shouldn't do it. Since neither Ann nor I has ever done it, we can be very hard on it!

Schlee: I will admit that I have done it once.

Paton Walsh: And I thought you were my friend!

Schlee: I'll confess that in a book that hasn't come out yet [*The Proprietor*], there's an episode taken from a known shipwreck, and, oh, it was so

Victorian. The ship was sinking, a boat had been rowed out, and a line had been cast, and who was to go down the line? In my book it's a tiny episode, but what actually happened was that they said, "Well, the women must go down the rope to safety," and amongst the women there was one "lady," so fifteen minutes were wasted while this "lady," who was only fifteen years old, clung weeping to her father, refusing to be separated from him. This episode is cited in every contemporary account as an example of filial piety and virtue. No one had anything but praise for her. Eventually, she was overpowered and put down the rope. There were left two stewardesses, and they were put down the rope next; then there was left a group "of the common sort" of women, one of whom was holding up a baby, and they were left to drown. Now, I have rescued the baby, who becomes the heroine of the book; this is a total cheat, but I couldn't resist it. I couldn't. It was rather nice to have this godlike power.

ERIK CHRISTIAN HAUGAARD

What preparations do I make before I commence writing a historical novel? First, it is necessary to choose the period of time I am going to write about. In my case this choice is often dictated by something that has happened in our own time. For instance, I chose to write about the civil war in England because I found the confusion in men's minds in the time of Cromwell not unlike the chaotic state our own poor brains are in today. A time of change, when the wind is blowing in all directions.

Before I wrote the first sentence, I studied anything which I could find from that time. Cromwell's letters were a great help in constructing this towering figure in my mind. Some sermons helped me as well, for ministers usually garble the philosophy of their day and are great for platitudes. I try to keep all my reading material as close as possible to the period I am describing, making copious notes all the time, naturally. You will use only a fraction of the material you collect, but the rest is not wasted. It is used indirectly. It is this knowledge that makes you able to create well-rounded characters. Information you don't use in your novel is still part of your imagination. It often forms the major substance, the backgrounds of your characters, without which they would not be believable to your readers or to yourself.

Naturally, you must be familiar with the countryside and the towns where your novel takes place. I knew Cambridge well before I wrote my Cromwell novels. I visited Greenland in order to write *Leif the Unlucky*. I walked the same paths the Vikings had trod and slept in the mountains under that great pale northern sky. When I woke, I thought, as I watched the eagles circle above me, "They too saw this." When I wrote *The Rider and His Horse*, in which I attempted to describe the fall of the Masada, the last Jewish stronghold in the war against the Romans, I walked from Jerusalem to Ein-Gedi. In that strange oasis, amid a world of rocks and sand, I bathed in the pool beneath the waterfall, just as the hero of my book did. From Ein-Gedi I walked along the shore of the Dead Sea until I came to the Masada. I climbed the "snakepath" to its top. By then it was noon, and when I reached the plateau, I was as thirsty, tired, and worn out as its defenders must have been when first they climbed that barren mountain.

The background for *The Samurai's Tale* was much more difficult for me to absorb. Together with my friends, without whose help it could not have been written, I visited the castles, temples, and battlefields mentioned in my novel. But I felt very much a stranger, not so much to the landscapes as to the background of my hero. I had jumped backward in time before, but here I landed in a culture almost utterly foreign to me. When I wrote about a Jewish boy who lived two thousand years ago, I was, after all, familiar with his religion. I, too, had been brought up on the story of Saul and David, as he had. Even before I saw Jerusalem, I could imagine it in my mind. The sound of its name echoed in my brain, which names like Kai, Mino, Iwamura, or Mikatagahara did not.

Naturally, I had made myself familiar with the history of Japan and read what I could find in English of its classical literature. My friends translated for me a great deal of invaluable material, such as the house laws of the Takeda family. Still my hero escaped me, and I had great difficulty becoming him. I was ready to give up when the turning point came.

My friends and I had been staying in a primitive inn. The innkeeper was very fat, his eyes mere slits; his wife and daughters did most of the work. His self-appointed job seems to have been to entertain the guests. He loved talking, airing his opinions. He knew, or rather thought he knew, everything. Listening to him arguing with my friends, I could imagine myself for the first time back in the sixteenth century. This man is eternal, I thought. He was here when Oda and Shingen fought. And then, as now, he held opinions which he enjoyed expressing. I had experienced a little bit of reality, and I drew comfort from it.

I wrote *The Untold Tale* while the war in Vietnam was still raging. In that unfortunate country a massacre had taken place, and the newspapers were filled with it. The name of the place and even the names of those involved were on everyone's tongue; I could not help but be interested. But how many cruel events like it had occurred without anyone noticing them? I knew little about Vietnam and could certainly not write a novel about it. One evening— just as I was ready to retire to bed—I recalled a similar massacre that had taken place long ago in a war between Denmark and Sweden. That very night I took down my history books and began studying.

By isolating my massacre from the opinions and political prejudices of the day, I hoped to describe such a crime more truthfully than I could have had I placed it in Vietnam. I called the book the *The Untold Tale*, for it is a story seldom or never told. I think one of the reasons why I have been attracted to the historical novel can be found here. When you write a story that takes place in times long past, you are more free. Your readers have less prejudice and will accept your tale with open minds. You and your reader have less at stake, and thus you might get nearer to the truth, possibly even to reality. For it is amazing how often sensitive, intelligent people can excuse or even condone the most despicable acts if perpetrated in the name of the politics they believe in or by the nation they belong to.

There is a reason why I have preferred not to write children's books that deal with the problems of our times. I do not think myself fit for it. You can write only from experience, and I am afraid I have lived with my back to the problems that cause us such fear and anxiety today. I was a happy child; my parents liked me well enough, and I liked them. If we did not always agree, I was allowed to disagree. I did not quarrel with their tastes, which were classical in both music and literature. My father read aloud to us in the winter evenings, mostly Dickens, whom he was fond of. I probably read too much Marryat, for I was caught early by the conception that the purpose of life is adventure. I had few friends but never felt lonely. When I was merely thirteen, I found in my parents' library a copy of Voltaire's *Candide*. I loved it. I used to sleep with that book under my pillow. I hated school; it was so dull. Outside the window of the classroom life was going by, and I was forced to sit still and not take part in it. When I was a child, I wanted more than anything to grow up as quickly as possible. The world belonged to adults, and I could hardly wait until it would belong to me as well. I left school the day after my fifteenth birthday; I wasn't really an adult. Although it was hard sometimes to manage to survive in the adult world, I have never regretted my decision. I searched for adventure and found it, and it did not disappoint me. It is strange that in our age you feel almost as if you have committed a sin by being happy. I was very happily married; my two children have given me few problems. I could not write about the unhappinesses that are peculiar to our times, for I have experienced few, if any, of them.

But I can write about emotions, fears, and feelings, which are eternal; so it was logical for me to place my stories in the past. Besides, I love history, the feeling that time stretches backward as well as forward. I wanted in my novels to give my readers a feeling of the nearness of the past, to make children realize that yesterday was once today. This can be done only if you succeed in making the past real to them. Your fictitious characters must breathe, their hearts must beat, and it must be blood, not printers' ink, that pulses in their veins.

For every author certain aspects of the human personality are more interesting than others. Courage, moral as well as physical, has always fascinated me. Moral courage is a virtue, but physical courage is not always so. As I consider all human beings unique, encompassing private worlds, the points at which their courage breaks are different. In order for their courage to be believable, there must be harmony between their actions and their personalities. Plot and actions in the novel must appear logical and not surprise the reader. The reader must think, "Yes, that is what would have happened."

Naturally, the historical background should always be correct. It is unwise to have—as a friend of mine did—a Jesuit priest appear a hundred years before the order was founded. Interestingly enough, in that particular case, not one critic pointed out the author's blunder. But even though everything has been carefully researched, a historical novel may still lack life. The feeling of having been transported back in time may be missing. I believe this happens when the author is totally out of sympathy with the period he or she is describing. The author becomes too conscious of the fact that what is being described happened long ago. Then, in desperation, he or she tries to explain the period, rather than making it come alive. Being unable to make the jump back in time—which is necessary to transform the past into the present—the author clutters the book with observations that belong to a historian.

You can have characters in your novel who hold opinions different from those of their time. But you must explain why they hold them, why they choose to swim against the current rather than with it. In your research you will come across persons who were out of step, who held unpopular views. I treasure these characters, for they allow me to criticize without sacrificing reality. While doing research for my Cromwell books, I discovered John Selden. Here was a mind I could warm to. In a world of bigots I found a reasonable man, someone who was above the petty battle of creeds that caused so much suffering at that time. This enabled me to allow opinions to be expressed which, while still historically correct, were entirely different from those most people adhered to.

Authors who hold strong views, whether philosophical, religious, or political, have great difficulty keeping their faith or their politics out of their books. In a historical novel this can become ludicrous. I recall a novel for children written by a Swedish author. It took place in the Bronze Age and had a slave as its hero. This youngster was remarkable for having a thorough knowledge of the theories of Karl Marx some thousands of years before they had been formulated. I half expected the slaves in the novel to break into "We Shall Overcome" or "The Internationale" at any moment. Books like this are of little interest as history or as literature, although often they have a great circulation among those who share the author's faith. The subject is fascinating enough. But in order to make slavery understandable, you must attempt to explain why, in most cases, both slaves and masters accepted it. We all know the twentieth-century opinion and morality, and we rightfully detest slavery. But why was it successful for so long? If you described the *reality* of the relationship between slave and master, it might be a useful book. Such a novel might even throw light upon why we, in our times, have seen nations bend submissively—even willingly—under the rods of tyrants.

It seems only fair that I should attempt to answer the question: Can we achieve reality in historical fiction? I doubt it. But it is still a goal worth striving for. I fear that it is becoming increasingly difficult to achieve, especially in books for young readers, because in our times the gap between what was and what is has become so wide that it is difficult to bridge. This, however, makes the attempt even more important. If the past is a total mystery to you, are you not even more liable to repeat its mistakes? In order to convince a young person that time did not start when he or she was born, the books of historical fiction must be of high quality. This means that they must contain reality, that they must make the past real. The reader must feel that the characters in the book have existed. Finishing the last page, the boy or girl should have this thought: "Yes, they have lived, as surely as I am living now."

I believe the same vices are flourishing today as in the past. Virtue now, as then, very often goes unrewarded. The lust for power, the wish to be master, has not disappeared because we have abolished slavery. The problems facing human beings have not changed. We still suffer in our loneliness—half animals, half gods. Cursed with the knowledge of our fate, we flounder on, just as our grandparents did, trying to find a bit of warmth in a cold world.

I consider my young readers reasonable beings who have as yet not experienced as much as I have. My hope is that from my books they might learn a little about life, which will prepare them for becoming adults. I do not believe for a moment that we are born good and become bad. I am afraid that I have Voltaire's contempt for Rousseau's theories. I admire civilization and the civilized person. It seems to me that humanity has suffered too much from savages, few of them noble. To attempt to understand is the creed that produces civilization. The process of growing up should last until your death. There is no graduation, no final examination. I have hoped by my books to help a little in that process—to expand a young person's world to include the past and thus make him or her capable of facing the future.

"Howl like the Wolves"

BARBARA HARRISON

Fifty miles east of Lyons, in the mountain village of Izieu, France, stands the stone schoolhouse which served as a refuge for Jewish children during World War II. Klaus Barbie, the SS henchman called the Butcher of Lyons, led the roundup of the children in April 1944, the arrest and deportation to Auschwitz of forty-one children between the ages of three and thirteen. In one incomprehensible act, they were swept like sacks of potatoes onto a truck and then into the ovens of Auschwitz. To this day Klaus Barbie claims, "I am a convinced Nazi . . . and if I had to be born a thousand times, I would be a thousand times what I have been."

Along with the literary critic and historian F. L. Lucas, who writes about the meaning of tragedy, we mutter as we hear these stories and read them, "How unbearable!" and Lucas's image of a girl frozen into a woman before his eyes becomes the image of the children of Izieu; the children of Terezin, Czechoslovakia; the children of Adana, Turkey; the children of Hiroshima, Japan — children deprived of innocence and of youth.

More than three hundred books have been published in this country for school-age readers, from six to eighteen, on World War II, the Holocaust, and war in general; they include memoirs, autobiographies and biographies, poetry, picture books, and fiction, much of it inspired by actual episodes. Many of the works are powerfully told and profoundly moving; they deal with a period in history when the world was rent asunder, when the Pied Pipers of death pounded on the doors of houses in villages and cities throughout Europe and stood on platforms in village squares, forcing hordes of human beings, among them hundreds of thousands of children, first to the ghettos and then to the killing fields — to the precipice of Babi Yar, to the fiery pits of Treblinka, and into the ovens of Auschwitz. These books provide piercing glimpses into the hearts of young people; they define the dangerous hours of youth encumbered and enslaved, when madness, oblivious to everything except itself, terrorizes, threatens, and snatches hope from its victims. In these portraits of Holocaust and war, children are forced to come to grips with the limits of their own sanity and mortality — and their wounded souls rise before us like lonely and abandoned gods.

The books are important documents for historians and for social and political scientists; they are worthy of close critical attention as both art and literature and can be assessed from the many perspectives of literary criticism. But we must acknowledge at the outset of any scrutiny the quintessentially moral nature of these books. They instruct; they seek to make people better than they are. And they raise questions of morality that many consider irrelevant to literary criticism. In approaching these books, the critic cannot, in John Gardner's words, count the "left-side hairs on an elephant's trunk" while the elephant is "standing on the baby." In *On Moral Fiction* Gardner makes a persuasive case for the necessity of moral art and moral criticism, reminding readers of Tolstoy's axiom that the highest purpose of art is to make people good by choice. This is the clear intention of the authors of these books.

In a literary sense a tragic work of art deals with human aspiration and suffering and examines with profound seriousness the place of the individual in the universe. Tragedy speaks to what it means to be thwarted by circumstance and what it means to have circumstance as an ally; it speaks to the depths to which human beings can plummet and the heights to which they can rise; it has elements of exaltation and elements of despair.

During World War II over a million children were murdered only because they were Jewish, and close to five million Jewish adults were murdered, among them the parents of the children; such facts challenge our capacity to find an appropriate literary form to express what took place. The facts are imbued with the spirit of tragedy, but at the same time they challenge the very limits of literary tragedy. Literary tragedy requires heroic conflict and heroic possibility. Many individuals fought, many rebelled, many resisted. Courageous actions were taken, both witnessed and unwitnessed. Yet the Holocaust informs us that on some level all vestiges of heroic conflict and heroic possibility were stolen from the victims — the young and the old — among them the most virtuous and high-spirited, the most chaste and courageous. They could abhor the situation; they could desperately want to alter it; but unlike the heroes and heroines of ancient Greek tragedy — Ajax, Antigone, and Iphigenia — they were rendered helpless.

Angelos Terzákis in *Homage to the Tragic Muse* tells us that youth, even in normal circumstances, is the tragic age, characterized by naïveté, generosity, innocence, rebelliousness, a pioneering spirit, and daring. Older tragic heroes like Lear and Othello also have these youthful qualities, but these very attributes, so essential to the idea of literary tragedy, were bent and thwarted and torn away during the Holocaust without an echo of any chorus to say, "Sing sorrow, sorrow, but good win out in the end."

Heroic prototypes do emerge — the non-Jew Sophie Scholl, her story recounted in the biography of Hermann Vinke, *The Short Life of Sophie Scholl*, and the Jew Hannah Senesh in the biography *In Kindling Flame*, by Linda Atkinson. Both of these high-spirited young women had nobility of soul, and fiction will reverberate and re-create their stories in infinite variety; but an even greater challenge — requiring more perspective and aesthetic distance — is the interpolation of heroism apparently wasted or rendered meaningless.

During the Holocaust, for many people hope was transformed into Edvard Munch's scream of primal terror, with its blood-red sky and deformed landscapes and roads zigzagging at the edge of the precipice — Munch's Everyman on the bridge, his hands clutching his head. How do the authors of books published for young people deal with a reality so devastating and debasing? Children's literature is a reflection of the times in which it is written; the literature mirrors the times. Most of these books were published in the 1970s and 1980s, and although there is now greater candor than ever before in books for the young, the one characteristic that adults are reluctant to see diminished in any way is hope, which has traditionally been the animating force in children's literature. Many adults cannot endure the thought that during the Holocaust hope, along with the children of Izieu, was swept into the ovens.

In "Beyond Anne Frank: Children and the Literature of the Holocaust," professors Lawrence Langer and Sondra Langer observe that *Anne Frank: The Diary of a Young Girl*, published in 1952, one of the earliest and most important World War II books written from a child's point of view — along with the play and the movie based on it — "have played a disproportionately large role in shaping the attitude of children and adults (who read no further) toward the experience of the Holocaust." They believe that Anne Frank's diary is perhaps too bearable and that when Anne proclaims, "In spite of everything I still believe that people are really good at heart," she has some hope that the liberation of Holland is at hand. After all, it was July 1944. The Langers caution that the young reader, any reader for that matter, would be making a mistake "if he is led to believe that the relationship between idealism and the prospect of extermination was the same in the Frank family hiding place as it was in the vicinity of the gas chambers of Auschwitz." They call for books, like Marietta Moskin's *I Am Rosemarie*, that "move beyond the comfortable reflections of Anne Frank without indulging in the horrors of an adult masterpiece like *The Painted Bird*." Of course, the tension created by Anne's idealism and subsequent death in Bergen-Belsen contributes to the power of her autobiography and to its assurance as a literary classic as well as a seminal document of Holocaust literature. Readers are with her, hiding in the secret annex in Amsterdam, and with her in Auschwitz — shaven, starving, frozen, and sick with typhoid fever. And although on some level the diary might be too bearable, our awareness of Anne's love of life and buoyancy of spirit in conjunction with our knowledge of her fate — her death one month before the liberation in the gas chambers of Bergen-Belsen — is both untenable and shattering.

On what level of truth telling, then, do the books function? How many disguises do the authors use to mask the passivity, the indifference, and the calculated cruelty; the screams, the stench of burning bodies, the sight of smoke rising from the crematoriums, the humiliation and death? How far into the reaches of the rank and sinister in the human spirit do we choose to take our children? "Is mass murder a subject for a children's book?" is the question posed by Eric Kimmel in "Confronting the Ovens: The Holocaust in Juvenile Fiction." But the central and exacting question is, what does it mean to comprehend mass humiliation and mass atrocity? And what does it mean to comprehend a world without hope, stone-cold and silent? How is truth perceived and interpreted by authors of a few of the best books for the young? How determined are these authors — and how successful — at cornering truth and calling it by name?

The author Aranka Siegal is a survivor of Auschwitz. She and her sister were among the children liberated in 1945, yet she chooses not to write about her experience in Auschwitz in her autobiographical book *Upon the Head of the Goat: A Childhood in Hungary 1939–1944*. Aranka Siegal said that her purpose in writing the book was "to bring children the lesson of the Holocaust without the horror," and she ends the book as the family is being herded onto the death train. In a painfully wrought scene her mother struggles to protect her three young daughters from the menacing hands of soldiers searching the prisoners. Siegal writes:

> They laughed at her, and as we came into the first line position, Iboya, Mother, and I were pulled apart by three of the leering Germans. The back of my neck was suddenly in an iron grip, and a coarse, rough hand brushed down my chest and over each of my breasts, bursting the buttons of my blouse. Bending over me so close that I could smell his sausagy breath and see the tobacco stains on his teeth, the soldier reached into my bloomers and felt inside my private parts. I couldn't tell if the stinging in my eyes was more from hurt or shame.

In this passage the humiliation and the violation of the innocent fore-shadow and stand for the ultimate obscenity of the death camp.

In *Upon the Head of the Goat* Aranka Siegal introduces readers to 1939 by recalling an incident which takes place while she is visiting her grand-mother in the Ukrainian village of Komjaty, not far from her home in Beregszász, Hungary, shortly after a fierce border confrontation between Hungarians and Ukrainians. The nine-year-old is gathering wildflowers in the woods near her grandmother's house on the banks of the Rika River, full and almost overflowing with melting snow. Distracted by a log shunted about in the wild currents of the river, she walks to the edge, holding freshly picked yellow crocuses in her hands. As the log ap-proaches, it is transformed before her eyes into the body of a young soldier, his face bloated in death. The child is stunned. She drops the crocuses, and they scatter over the young man's body as it continues its collision course with one rock, and then another, in the rushing waters. The child sees more bodies, stiff and distended and driven by the current in the mournful waters of the Rika. Recollections like Aranka Siegal's leap from the deep well of memory and crouch on the pages of the books.

Many of the authors repeat the mythical pattern of loss and banishment; one recurring theme is the loss of a beloved and idyllic place — a garden, a countryside, a home. In her autobiography *Mischling, Second Degree: My Childhood in Nazi Germany*, Ilse Koehn takes readers from the lilac bushes and hazelnut trees in the garden of her home in Berlin to the shattered, confused world of a divided family, thinking "I don't understand, I don't understand." For Esther Hautzig in *The Endless Steppe*, a privileged childhood ends in a nightmare journey from the "woodland capital" of Vilna, Poland, to the "enormous, unrippled sea of parched and lifeless grass" in Siberia. Her journey begins in June 1941, six months before the massacre in Vilna of thirty-two thousand people, when Esther is ten years old and still believes that the garden of her very own home is the invulnerable center of her universe. After six weeks of "sinister twilight" in a sealed cattle car with a hole in the floor for a toilet, a pail of water for both drinking and washing, and a bucket of cabbage soup for food, she is "like a little old woman."

The archetypal contrast of the garden and the wilderness is echoed again in David Kherdian's *The Road from Home: The Story of an Armenian Girl*, a memoir of the Armenian Holocaust 1915–1923 — which foreshadowed the calculated destruction of European Jews. David Kherdian's stirring memo-rial to his mother, Veron Dumehjian, is written in the first person from her point of view. Kherdian begins: "For as long as I knew the sky and the clouds, we lived in our white stucco house in the Armenian quarter of Azizya, in Turkey, but when the great dome of Heaven cracked and shattered over our lives, and we were abandoned by the sun and blown like scattered seed across the Arabian desert, none returned but me, and my Azizya, my precious home, was made to crumble and fall and forever disappear from my life." The images in this passage — the crashing and shattering of a pure and ordered world, the powerlessness before forces greater than oneself, the sense of loss and abandonment, and the loneliness of survival — recur again and again in such literature. Kherdian identifies the Armenian genocide with the Jewish Holocaust as he quotes Adolf Hitler's call in 1939 for the mass murder of the Polish people: "After all, who remembers today the extermination of the Armenians?"

The impact of Hans Richter's *Friedrich* lies in vignettes of experience rendered in quick, almost abbreviated prose. The book begins in 1925 with the births only one week apart of Friedrich Schneider, a Jew, and of the narrator, a Christian; it ends in 1942 with the death of Friedrich Schneider, when the boys are seventeen. With disarming candor Richter describes the rise in economic security of the narrator's family and the decline of the Schneiders; he relates one incident after another in the lives of the two families, who live in the same apartment building in Germany.

Like so many of the young people in the books, both Jews and non-Jews, Friedrich is attracted by the pomp and circumstance, songs and banners, costumes and parades of the Hitler Youth. Innocently, his friend invites him to a meeting of the *Jungvolk*. Proudly, Friedrich brings to the meeting a neck scarf and a leather scarf ring with a swastika stamped on it, and he grows paler by the second, almost unable to breathe, as he hears the blistering words of the party speaker: " 'One sentence, one sentence only I want to hammer into your brains; I will repeat it until it comes out of your ears, and repeat it: The Jews are our affliction! And again: The Jews are our affliction. And another time: The Jews are our affliction!' " It is 1933. The boys are only eight years old.

In another episode the narrator's father, though a loyal Nazi party member, cautiously warns Herr Schneider to leave Germany. " 'Everything points to your going today rather than tomorrow. Why can't you grasp that, Herr Schneider?' " Herr Schneider rebuffs this well-intentioned warning: " 'I am German, my wife is German, my son is German, all our relatives are German. What could we do abroad? How would we be received? Do you seriously think they like us Jews better elsewhere? And anyway, it will all quiet down eventually. Now that the year of the Olympics has begun, we're hardly bothered. Don't you agree?' " The incident takes place in 1936. The boys are eleven years old.

The book is understated, almost cryptic — so little included, so much left out — and it prompts the reader to live the events along with the two boys, to witness how evasive, how deceitful, reality can be. Illusion holds sway here as in Elie Wiesel's Sighet ghetto and in villages and towns all over

Europe during World War II. Death holds sway as well. Although the menacing reality is as close to the Schneiders as the fingers on their hands, it evades them; and one of the recurring themes in this terrifying epoch, and also in literary tragedy, is struck — the confusion between illusion and reality, between what seems to be and what is.

The action in *Friedrich* is developed through a succession of incidents that culminates in the return of a broken and dispirited Friedrich to his friend's apartment, seeking an old photograph of his parents. He is given food and refuge but is ultimately turned away from the neighborhood air-raid shelter by the narrator's family and others because of the air-raid warden's threat to tell the authorities. Friedrich dies alone on a doorstep, and the book ends. Friedrich's innocence and death are without meaning. Any notion of hope, so implicit in children's literature, vanishes; and heroic action, so necessary to any classical conception of tragedy is impossible in the context of this story, which precludes any possibility of transcendence or retributive justice. The immense power of evil prevails. Hans Richter reminds readers that there is ample to tell about the Holocaust short of the shattering world of the death camps — countless agonies of loss, betrayal, and death.

These worlds of literature offer little comfort. Children witness the arrest of parents and siblings; they themselves are arrested. They see their parents abused, humiliated, and brutally beaten. They observe the gathering anguish in the faces of parents, grandparents, aunts, and uncles, and along with their parents, they begin to question the very existence of God. They return home from school to find their parents and siblings lying in pools of blood.

In a poignant scene in Esther Hautzig's *The Endless Steppe* Esther Rudomin's grandparents are torn from each other by soldiers at the train station; the grandmother is ordered to the second train, the grandfather to the first. "Never have I heard a more dreadful scream," writes Esther, "not even in a nightmare." The child is overwhelmed by compassion and fear; with one hand she gently strokes her grandmother's arm in an effort to console her, and with the other she clings desperately to her father.

The terror of seeing parents powerless and bereft is made very real by David Kherdian in *The Road from Home*. The only child in the family to survive the cholera epidemic that strikes down her brother and two sisters during the family's forced exodus, Veron follows her mother to find out where she goes each day for hours on end. Kherdian writes:

> She [the mother] walked in the direction of the river until
> she came to a clearing near some stunted trees. It seemed
> a strange place to go alone because there wasn't anything
> there. She suddenly stopped walking, and after standing

still for a moment, she slowly sat down against one of the
trees and began crying. At first only her body shook, and
I could hear her sobs, but then she started wailing. I had
never heard Mama cry like this before. I was frightened
deep, deep inside, and I began running back toward the
the tents. As I ran, all I could see was a picture of her in my
mind as she was at that moment — seated on her legs, her
body heaving, lurching away from the tree, and in front of
her, three large, evenly spaced stones.

Kherdian's simple description evokes tragic Niobe, all her children struck
down by the gods and she herself turned to stone; or tragic Hecuba, her
children, too, struck down in war — the loss of one's children an anguish
too loud for words. And the surviving child, Veron, is frightened out of her
wits, indelibly marked.

For some, physical survival meant only a slower and crueler death.
Among the novels that bring such exiles to the United States is *Alan and
Naomi*, whose author, Myron Levoy, takes as his theme the madness of
young Naomi Kirschenbaum, a war refugee from France. When the Nazis
uncover the resistance work of Naomi's father — mapping escape routes
through the sewers of Paris — and are about to apprehend him, he enlists
Naomi's help in tearing the maps into shreds. They are not fast enough.
Seconds before the Gestapo break down the door, he shoves Naomi under
the bed, and from this vantage point she witnesses her father's death, a
warm stream of his blood reaching her on the floor. When her mother
returns home shortly after the incident, she finds the eight-year-old child
covered with blood, trying to wipe it from the face and body of her dead
father. It takes the Kirschenbaums three years to find their way through
the escape routes of Paris to the safety of their family in the New World;
there, Naomi, with her doll, sits for hours on her bed in her relatives' New
York apartment, tearing paper into bits, the bits growing into mounds
around her.

The boy Alan Silverman, at first reluctantly and then energetically and
lovingly, uses his tattered Charlie McCarthy dummy to coax Naomi back to
health. Finally, Naomi turns her doll toward his Charlie McCarthy and
introduces herself. "I am Yvette," she says. Communicating through dolls,
the two twelve-year-olds become close friends, and Alan leads Naomi back
toward sanity, even encouraging her to go to school. But Naomi's hold on
sanity is fragile. When the girl sees Alan covered with blood in a street
fight, she plunges back into hideous memory; she becomes "a mechanical
girl. A broken toy," and one suspects she will never recover. With the pain
and longing that come from knowing that he has suffered an irretrievable
loss, Alan howls Naomi's name into the wind and then throws himself

down and cries "into the ground until the ground itself seemed to be
crying, caking his lips with mud." Levoy makes no compromise with truth
in using the theme of madness. The destruction of a mind is as wrenching,
as final, a loss as death in the ovens; any slim hope of the future is
abandoned. In offering Naomi comfort and friendship, Alan rises higher
than he himself expected to rise; and if anything makes Naomi's plight
endurable, it is this heroism. Although we are under no illusion that
Naomi will ever recover, she continues to live in Alan.

For many, the Holocaust experience was not a catastrophic confrontation
with madness but a gradual loss of trust in the reasonableness of the world.
With their sixth sense children often know there is trouble; they overhear
bits and pieces of adult conversations, whisperings in the night. "When I
sat at the top of the stairs, I could hear a great deal," says the young
protagonist in Johanna Reiss's *The Upstairs Room*. Doris Orgel, author of the
autobiographical novel *The Devil in Vienna*, has said that her parents
thought she should know as little as possible:

> My parents thought it very important that I shouldn't
> know certain things, for instance, that my grandfather
> went to jail and that there were various moves underfoot —
> illegal ways of trying to get out and buying visas. They felt
> it was very important to tell me as little as possible because
> they felt that I might inadvertently tell the wrong person.
> It would get around, and it is not paranoia to say that
> people — what they called security department people —
> were informers. In every neighborhood there were what
> they called block wardens whose job it was to receive
> complaints from people.

In many cases parents, fearing the impact of horror on the minds of their
children, were in conflict about how much to share, if anything. Ilse Koehn
simply did not know she was a *"Mischling*, second degree," a child with
one Jewish grandparent who was to die at Treblinka. The author has said,
"I was blissfully ignorant of my status, although I could not ignore the fact
that my usually happy mother started crying a lot . . . and that my
mother's parents put enormous pressure on her to divorce my father, this
sudden noncitizen and non-Aryan, so much pressure that my mother had
a nervous breakdown. Only after the war could Ilse Koehn's family unite
and face these truths.

The adults in these books are torn between protecting their children and
sharing information with them in order to insure their survival. At one
point Ilse Koehn's father admonished her to stop crying over a burst
balloon because, he told her mother, " 'We must bring her up to see real

life, life as it is, not as we would like it to be. It's never too early to learn that!' " The father's warning prompts us to examine the political and moral truths of our decade and to ask, What is real? What is illusion? What should we tell our children about the past, and at what age? How do we prepare them for the many ambiguities of contemporary existence — the promise of long life signaled by medical technology in the face of the threat of life aborted by nuclear war? At what age do we discuss with them the precariousness of hope as we approach the year 2000?

One of the striking commonalities in the books is the outpouring of questions by the young heroes and heroines. In *The Endless Steppe* Esther Rudomin asks, " 'How could we be arrested without having done anything wrong? . . . Why are we under arrest?' " " 'Why us? . . . Why us?' " " 'What have I done wrong?' " In Marietta Moskin's *Rosemarie* the twelve-year-old protagonist with her newly issued identity card in hand looks into the mirror and wonders, "Did I look different? Had I changed over-night? . . . 'Can people tell I am Jewish just by looking at me?' " In Johanna Reiss's *The Upstairs Room* Annie asks, " 'Father . . . why would he [Hitler] let Jews buy food only at certain hours? . . . Father, what does *Kristallnacht* mean?' " Johanna Reiss has commented, "What did I do? I was simply born at the wrong time, in a wrong place, and into the wrong religion, and mind you my family was not even religious." Such questions demand complex responses today, just as they did then.

Two works, one on the effects of the A-bomb and one on the Holocaust, point to the power of the picture book to depict reality and raise once again the difficult issue of adult response — Toshi Maruki's *Hiroshima No Pika*, translated from the Japanese, and Roberto Innocenti's *Rose Blanche*, translated from the Italian. *Hiroshima No Pika* is the account of seven-year-old Mii and her parents, who are having a breakfast of sweet potatoes on the morning of August 6, 1945, when the United States Air Force bomber *Enola Gay* dropped the bomb on Hiroshima. Mii is briefly knocked unconscious; her father is enveloped in flames and pulled from the fire by her mother, who wraps her badly burned husband in a kimono sash, lifts him onto her shoulders, grabs her child's hand, and races for the river. As they run to escape the fireball at their backs, they see children physically mutilated, "heaps of people everywhere," the body of a man floating in the river, a dead cat, a swallow with wings so badly burned it can no longer fly. Fire leaps across the pages; the dead and dying are elongated, arms and hands beckon and beseech; and there is the repeated image of the child Mii, clutching two red sticks from the morning meal, unable to open her hand. Four days after the giant mushroom fills the sky, Mii's mother pries open her child's hand to release the chopsticks. The dreamlike and fantastical paintings enact a nightmare — grief and loss amidst the rubble, the devastation, and the mountains of dead and dying.

Dorothy Briley, the publisher of *Hiroshima No Pika*, has compared her experience on first seeing the book with her experience on first seeing Picasso's *Guernica*. Both works overwhelmed her — the *Guernica* with the horror of war and *Hiroshima No Pika* with the fear of nuclear war. In considering whether the book should be published for children, Briley began thinking about her own childhood during World War II. She was seven when the United States entered the war and eleven when it was over; she grew up in a small rural town outside Nashville, Tennessee. She recalled the air-raid drills; the daily accounts of battles and bombings; the death tolls reported on radio, in newspapers, and on newsreels; and the weekly larger-than-life pictorial coverage in *Life* magazine. "Thinking about myself at that age heightened my conviction that this book really needed to be published," said Briley.

"The genius of Toshi Maruki's book," commented Briley, "is its utter simplicity. Without anger, without trying to induce either collective or individual guilt, without asking anything of us except to listen, it reminds us of why some way other than war must be found to resolve international differences." Her respect for the book derived from her desire to speak out on behalf of nuclear disarmament, her recognition of the need for children to talk about the threat of nuclear war, and her belief that knowledge of the devastation wrought by the bomb could help prevent it from being used again.

The 1982 publication in the United States of *Hiroshima No Pika* paved the way for *Rose Blanche*, published in 1985 and set in Germany, which recounts in words and in pictures the loving act of a child who sees people in need and reaches out to help them. The title, which is also the name of the protagonist, is taken from the White Rose, the World War II resistance movement led by Sophie Scholl and her brother Hans Scholl — both executed for high treason in Munich when they were barely twenty years old. In Roberto Innocenti's tale Rose Blanche is perhaps ten years old when she sees a young boy trying to escape from a Nazi van crammed full of prisoners. On foot she follows the slow-moving vehicle as it makes its way to a prisoner-of-war camp, where she sees cold and starving people behind barbed wire. Daily the young girl scavenges for food and takes it to the prisoners; it is not much food, for she obviously hasn't much. Her mood is one of bewilderment rather than of fear. One foggy day as she arrives at the camp, soldiers shoot at the moving figure in the distance and kill her. As in *Hiroshima No Pika* the artist has particularized history, singling out one child, one place, one tragedy.

At the beginning of the book we see a gathering in the town square, a festive arrangement of adults and children waving small Nazi flags. Nazi banners hang from windows. It is a crisp day with a hint of chill in the air, a hint of cruel winter; some people are wearing overcoats. As the story progresses, the sharpness of the opening becomes muted and blurred. Windows are broken, shutters are closed against the devastation, and reflections of the self — the scars, the truth — can be seen in the city's windows, rivers, and puddles. In the paintings the viewer is riveted by the opposition between the life of the swastika, with its black-and-white symbol on a bright red field and the life of the resistance movement, symbolized by the red ribbon in the child's hair; in the final painting the red ribbon is transfigured into a field of bright red poppies. The jacket painting, not repeated in the book, portrays Rose Blanche with straggling blond hair, wrapped in sackcloth, staring through a window, and surrounded by wounded soldiers; she herself has waged a war.

The technical ability in both *Hiroshima No Pika* and *Rose Blanche* is exceptional, yet both books present problems to critics. Although acknowledging the beauty and power of *Hiroshima No Pika*, Jo Carr, an instructor of children's literature, says that it "borders on sensationalism. . . . it shocks without informing." Carr claims, "Children should be asked to face the horror of Hiroshima only after they are old enough — and informed enough — to understand the event in its historical context." The critic Patricia Campbell, too, although quick to acknowledge Innocenti's skill, claims that for children *Rose Blanche* is "a deeply problematic work. . . . Without a grounding of fact, this is a story full of puzzles and intimations of unusual horrors." Campbell also says, "A young child has no orientation in time, place or reality for this book, no frame of reference for understanding its broader implications. Without historical perspective such a reader sees only the literal events and senses an implied horror too large and too vague for the fragmentary story."

Yet, with or without a grounding in fact, readers of each book observe one individual taking compassionate and courageous action, heroic to the core. The mother in *Hiroshima No Pika* pulls her husband from the flames, lifts him onto her shoulders, grabs her child's hand, and rushes in search of safety. The child in *Rose Blanche* feeds starving people. Rose Blanche's action is reminiscent of Laura's in Ann Schlee's important book for children, *Ask Me No Questions*, in which young Laura sees starving children eating from a pig trough during the nineteenth-century cholera epidemic in England and begins to steal food from the kitchen pantry to feed them. "Ask me no questions" is the repeated refrain that Laura hears from adults around her when she asks about the starving children.

On one level the criticism of *Hiroshima No Pika* and of *Rose Blanche* has the familiar ring of the words *ask me no questions*. The criticism seems to say, ask me no questions about the bombing of Hiroshima and about the suffering of Jews, Poles, Gypsies, and thousands of other innocent people in death camps and on the streets during World War II. Someday when you are old enough, you will study these events in their historical context. Ask me no questions now. Ask me later. Or, please, don't ask me at all. Find out for yourself. But in postponing discussion, we must be careful that we are not also saying, ask me no questions about compassion, about responsibility, about indifference, about cowering before circumstance, and about acting when life demands action.

Max von der Grün makes plain in *Howl like the Wolves* that to answer such questions honestly may also deny our most cherished ideals. In presenting readers with both autobiography and document to explain his own survival, von der Grün effectively reveals the tension between the individual and circumstance and unsparingly confronts the death camps. He gives us firsthand accounts of the murder of writer and pacifist Erich Müsham; the torture of the resistance fighter Jakob Boulanger, who was forced for four years to stand sixteen-and-a-half hours a day in a tomblike bunker; the diaries of children — young David Rubinowitsch, for example, who at the age of fourteen died in a gas chamber at Treblinka; and horrific eyewitness accounts of the massacres and executions of Jews, which took place in Rovno in the Ukraine and in the gas chambers of Belzec and Minsk.

At seventeen von der Grün was drafted into the German army and witnessed the court martial of a soldier no older than himself, who had been accused of "undermining German morale" for writing a letter home, complaining about the lack of food, the brutality of his superiors, and the futility of war. The youth was sentenced to death, and the execution carried out. As von der Grün ponders this event with disbelief, he wishes that the young man had been given the advice his own mother gave him, which was never to write home any news that was less than good. " 'If you're all right, then say, "I'm fine," ' she told him, 'but if you're having a hard time, then write, "I'm feeling very well." ' " Unlike Rose Blanche, von der Grün learns how to avoid trouble and thus to be a survivor but not a hero. After his father's arrest for resistance activities on October 1, 1938, von der Grün joins the Hitler Youth, not by choice but for self-preservation; and as Hitler passes through von der Grün's hometown, he recalls raising his hand in salute. "But I no longer remember whether I too cried 'Heil'. Quite possibly I did, for my mother had made it clear to me that in certain situations one had to howl along with the wolves if one were not to be devoured by them." Later in the book his mother again calls out to him, " 'And don't forget: Howl like the wolves, but not too loudly, because that would attract attention. Now the only important thing is to survive.' "

On some level, to howl like the wolves if life demands it is the advice that all of us must give to our children if we are to bring them up to see life as it really is and to survive; but we are reluctant conveyers of such advice, and we are diminished by it. We tend to be angry at circumstances that make cunning and shrewdness requisites for survival and to reject advice that works so blatantly against idealism and heroic possibility.

In "Only a Lamp-holder," Erik Christian Haugaard says, "Courage, moral as well as physical, has always fascinated me. Moral courage I suppose to be a virtue, which physical courage is not always." In Haugaard's *The Little Fishes*, published in 1967, twenty-two years after the end of World War II, the twelve-year-old philosopher Guido, an orphan informed by need and want, is wise beyond his years; he has a big heart and an empty belly. On the streets of Naples — as in the ghettos — Guido and the other orphans " 'have grownup eyes and children's hearts. . . . Even the tiny ones on their mothers' arms have the eyes of old people.' " Early in this undervalued masterpiece of war literature, Haugaard establishes the essential polemic. *El vecchio*, the priest, sees human beings as fundamentally good, while his friend Old Sack of Bones sees them as evil; for him only the devil lives: " 'men, they will eat each other. They are sacks of bones that the devil has blown life into.' " The story of Guido and of Anna and Mario, the two children he takes under his wing, and their trek on foot through the ravaged countryside of Italy in 1943 is a work characterized by restraint and control, similar in style and tone to Hemingway's *The Old Man and the Sea*.

Although Haugaard reaffirms *el vecchio*'s view of life and claims that understanding is the key to the transcendence of suffering — reminiscent of the versions of survival of Bruno Bettelheim and Viktor Frankl — there is some ambiguity in the final passage in which Guido and Anna strike out on their own as war refugees; and even more in the epilogue, in which Haugaard states that although we would like to think that Anna and Guido find happiness, "a kind wish is like a summer cloud, it brings no rain to the parched earth." The courage that makes tragic heroes and heroines is fully present in this work, for like Rose Blanche the characters are able to act for themselves and are given a stage where heroic action is possible, however minimal the chance of survival. Starvation and deprivation, and not the Holocaust itself, are the overwhelming protagonists in *The Little Fishes*.

Hope is on no firmer footing for Jan and Regine, the young lovers in Irina Korschunow's novel *A Night in Distant Motion*. The Polish Holocaust described in the book is one of the little-told tales of World War II — Hitler's calculated decision to exterminate the entire Polish people and to resettle Poland with German citizens. Taking her title from the Rilke poem "A Night in Distant Motion" and telling the story in the first person, Korschunow describes with understatement and sensitivity the young protagonist's first sexual encounters in war-torn Germany and her first encounters with truth. The central episode is the affair of Regine Martens, a German girl barely seventeen, and Jan, a twenty-one-year-old Polish laborer — neither of them Jews.

In their propaganda campaign and in official documentation, the Nazis aligned Poles and Gypsies with Jews. Jan was simply a nonperson, an inferior breed less than human, to be eradicated or used as slave labor. And along with one-and-a-half million Poles conscripted into the German labor force, Jan was forced to wear on his breast a blue-purple P, like the yellow star worn by the Jews. Regine and Jan both know they are walking a precarious path. The risk is great — for her, jail or a concentration camp, and for him, sure death.

When the affair is discovered, Regine, like the younger Annie in Reiss's *The Upstairs Room*, is given refuge in the attic of a farm family in a small village. The novel is told as a reminiscence, a "rememory," of "a night in distant motion" — a time not to be relived — and of Regine's relationship with Jan; and of the toll of war on schoolmates, on the farm family who is giving her refuge, and on her parents — a coalescence of memory and imagination, a piecing together of the past, a mixture of dream and reality. The farmer's wife has lost her husband and four sons to the war; yet it is this towering woman, a colossal figure in black, whose compassion is touched by the young Regine and who is Korschunow's major accomplishment in the book.

Many books for adults, like those for children, use a child's point of view to force us to grapple with the impact of the Holocaust on hope — so synonymous with our conception of childhood. Despite their child protagonists, however, certain works make sense primarily to older readers. The major difference between a child reader and an adult reader may simply be that the adult has lived longer, has assimilated more of life's maledictions and beneficences, and can draw on experience in piecing together reality. The sheer primordial bestiality and sexual violence unleashed in Jerzy Kosinski's *The Painted Bird* — the macabre odyssey of a child between the ages of six and ten as he moves from village to village in Eastern Europe — place it beyond the pale of books for the young. The unrelenting intensity of Elie Wiesel's *Night* and the mythopoeic dimension of Stratis Haviaras's *When the Tree Sings*, which describes the victimization of a young Greek Orthodox village boy during the occupation of Greece by Axis forces, mark these as books for adults. Both might be read by high-school students experienced at reading and at life, but the authors make very complicated linguistic demands on their readers, both experiential and perceptual — demands of irony, surrealism, and gallows humor.

Many people have worried about the limits of language, its failure to capture the intricacies of human experience and the prismlike quality of emotion. Isaac Bashevis Singer feels that language is too limited to interpret the monumental cruelties of the Holocaust; yet, to a child's eyes the lesser cruelties and the greater can be all one. Most of the children's books about the Holocaust work on a simple and profound level of truth telling; the voices of children come through — clear and emphatic and fiercely moving. Through the unguarded eyes of childhood the authors under discussion show paratroopers dropping from the sky like pellets of hail; they tell how it feels for your best friend suddenly to refuse to sit next to you anymore, to hear the incantation " 'Jew, Jew, ugly mole, / Stick your face in a dirty hole. / Stick your face in a mustard pot, / By tomorrow Jew will rot!' " And how unwittingly you may play on the piano in your home the tune you keep hearing over and over again, identified by your mother as the Nazi anthem with its recurring theme, "When Jewish blood spurts from the knife / Then things will go twice as well." Along with young Alex in Uri Orlev's *The Island on Bird Street*, you are tempted to believe with old Boruch "that there are times when even children must be taught to bear arms." From the speechless depths of the mind rise recurring motifs of deceptions and enclosures, small and restrained spaces, small suffocations in the context of large suffocation, reflections in windows and mirrors — broken and unbroken — ("Who am I?"). And you hide within your mind, withdrawing into a shell to protect sanity: "By shutting out the worst details I was able to bear it," says Rosemarie.

But the image that recurs in the books like a death knell is one of ungraceful aging, anguished and illogical aging. Children of war walk side by side with the old people in the riddle of the sphinx, but it is not only the young who grow older; parents and grandparents grow older, and no one is spared — all are old and bent and as ancient as the sphinx itself. "Within a single morning, on a perfect June day, my young father had become an old man," says Esther Hautzig. Aranka Siegal says, "I looked at Mother; her face seemed old and tired, her green eyes sunk deep and black." Rosemarie says, "Through my tears I looked at Grannie. She seemed to have aged by ten years that afternoon and she looked so fragile that a gust of wind might have blown her away." Elie Wiesel says, "From the depths of the mirror, a corpse gazed back at me." It is as if each person experiences the five ages of creation, from the golden Azizya of Veron Dumehjian's childhood to the Age of Iron, which Hesiod describes as "cruel, unjust, unfilial, and treacherous."

For most of these authors World War II and the Holocaust was the central experience of their lives; they have been in its grip for more than four decades. Over and over, they strive with urgency to convey the basic belief that infuses tragic literature with its passion and meaning: that we are humane only if, as a people, we are able to maintain the capacity to be another, to imagine each other person in ourselves. Only then can we conceive of justice and the classical Greek concept of *aidos*, which demands mutuality, reverence for life, and a feeling of self-consciousness and embarrassment at wrongdoing. "I was ashamed that I was not Jewish myself," said Anna Simaite, the Lithuanian resistance fighter.

Tolstoy embodies this knowledge in "Esarhaddon, King of Assyria," an antiwar fable which he wrote at the request of Shalom Aleichem, the popular Yiddish author, to benefit the battered Jews of Kishinev as they suffered through the Russian pogroms. Translated by Shalom Aleichem, the fable appeared first in Yiddish in 1903, then in Russian in the same year. Every person is every other person, says Tolstoy; Esarhaddon is his archenemy Lailie, and Lailie is his archenemy Esarhaddon. " 'You have seen that in doing evil to others you have done it to yourself as well. . . . You can make life better within yourself only by destroying the barriers that divide your life from that of other beings, and by regarding others as yourself and loving them.' " But for W. H. Auden the primary weakness of evil is "a lack of imagination, for, while Good can imagine what it would be like to be Evil, Evil cannot imagine what it would be like to be Good." Those who know the good, choose the good, says Socrates, but if no one can discern the good or if it is lost or unrecognizable or masquerading as something else, what will become of us? And what will become of our children?

The great fear that haunts us in this nuclear age is summed up by the author and critic Eleanor Cameron. "The idea of the ethical is what we are losing in our time, and without it we cannot survive as a people, as a nation." Without this call of the imagination to the ethical, the Orwellian prophecy is fulfilled; passivity lies like a plague upon the people. In our world, as in *1984*, love disappears, and there is "no dignity of emotion, or deep or complex sorrows." Individuals in Orwell's prophecy become walking automatons, in which all traces of individuality — of particularity — all vestiges of the emotions so fiercely a part of the origins and preoccupations of Greek tragedy are gone. The tragic impulse is gone. The heroic possibility is gone. Literature is destroyed, and memories become dimmer and dimmer as the call to the ethical fades from the human mind.

It is this great and very real fear that prompts a simple answer to the question, Is the truth, so devastating and debasing, literary material for children and adolescents? Many people are convinced that few subjects are more closely related to the concepts of justice and injustice, freedom and responsibility, indifference and compassion as well as to the Socratic conception of the good than the subjects of World War II and the Holocaust. Most of the authors under discussion write from their childhood memories with spirited sympathy for the children who read. They do little in their writing to mask the reaches of human cruelty; indeed, they have spent their lives cornering truth and calling it by name.

A striking maturity is evident in the works — years of sifting through memory, emotions tempered through time, agony examined through endless hours of reflection. These authors have implicit trust in the young reader. Marietta Moskin says, "I wanted young readers to know that these things did happen and can happen again; in fact, are happening now in some parts of the world. Prejudice exists, genocide exists, slaughter of the innocents continues."

Time magazine journalist Roger Rosenblatt reminds us that in the decade of the 1980s war is a very real circumstance for children; we who can choose to keep our children ignorant are a minority. On September 14, 1981, Rosenblatt began his forty-thousand-mile journey to the war zones of the world — among them, Israel and Lebanon, Belfast, and Cambodia — where he interviewed children, asking questions "about death, hate, revenge, and forgiveness," an account recorded in *Children of War*. Rosenblatt was convinced that if he gathered together all these children in a neutral zone, they would recognize each other instantly: the eight-year-old Cambodian boy who buried his mother; the five-year-old who woke up in a dark and bloody room, the sole survivor of the massacre of her father, brothers, and sisters at Tel Zaatar; the teenage Vietnamese boy whose very life was threatened when he was wrapped in a sack and dealt a harsh blow with intent to kill so that others could eat his flesh and survive. And we suspect that if the adults who were once children of war were brought together, they, too, would recognize one another — among them adults who remember the war as if it were yesterday and are now writing about the experience in books for the young. "But for me it is still all too real," says Ilse Koehn. "It was a time when fear was my twenty-four-hour companion." And, says Johanna Reiss, "War leaves scars. A couple of years ago in the middle of the night I had an intruder in my apartment — I live in Manhattan — and my first thought was I came three thousand miles away from there, and they found me." Through the voice of his great-grandmother, David Kherdian reminds us that " 'what you learn in childhood is carved on stone.' "

That literature of this kind requires great skill is axiomatic. Some measure of the success of the authors is that they catapult readers into the realm of self-examination, prodding them to try to understand the diabolical nightmare at the very center of the maelstrom, the death camp itself; they caution readers that to prevent such atrocity from ever happening again they must be able to recognize in the mirror the face of Klaus Barbie as well as their own. On some very real level they persuade us that to understand mass murder and mass humiliation we must be able to understand a single murder and a single humiliation; to understand the loss of the children of Izieu, we must be able to comprehend the loss of one child. In endowing the child victims with life, the authors particularize the loss of millions of people and protect them from the menacing cloak of anonymity and invisibility. Clearly, the best literature apprehends individual experience in the context of the larger horror; it convinces us of the truth of the experience it tells and rediscovers for us, in John Gardner's words, "what is necessary to humanness."

In these books the survival of hope is not an idealistic illusion but an existential act. Although the authors come close to it, few of them make the statement that Elie Wiesel has made again and again in writing about the Holocaust: "Wherever one starts, one reaches darkness." Hope was ravaged by war and Holocaust; it became Nikos Kazantzakis's wandering god in *The Odyssey: A Modern Sequel*, all bent and crooked, stumbling, abandoned, and within death's reach. For their own survival, many of the authors of these books, like Odysseus, exiles from home, struggle to reanimate the idea of hope — an idea that during the war, like Odysseus's god, had become old and lonely and all but forsaken.

We suspect that authors writing about this despairing period for young people are able to take hope by the hand and to coax it back to life because they hold closely to Erik Haugaard's belief that "every time a child is born the world is re-created." For these authors, the context is not only yesterday but tomorrow, when time, place, and memory are new, and hope again is a song of promise. "We cannot change yesterday's history," says Aranka Siegal, "but tomorrow is yet to be experienced, its history is yet to be written."

Truth, the Child, and Literature

ERIK CHRISTIAN HAUGAARD

One of the prime virtues that we drill into the minds of our children is truth. Even politicians and people who work in advertising tell their children always to speak truthfully and admonish them if they do not. The unforgivable wickedness of lying is not a matter the grown-up leaves much doubt about. Father and Mother are always explicit when the subject is brought up.

If the child's relationship to his or her parents is such that common sense dictates discipline, the child need not succumb to the evil of lying more than a few times a week. But I have known parents with whom no sensible child could share a house without becoming an accomplished liar. Children from such homes very quickly find out that the real crime is not to utter an untruth but to do it so clumsily that they are found out.

Every child knows that lies come in various sizes and that they are not equally reprehensible. There are lies to get one out of trouble, and their seriousness depends upon the nature of the trouble. Then there is bragging; these untruths, after all, hurt only the teller. There are many kinds of lies, and a child knows them all; but, strangely enough, children often believe that only children lie.

At a very early stage the youngster also learns that although lying may be dangerous, it can be even more perilous to life and limb to speak the truth. He or she need say only once in a crowded bus, "Look at the funny red nose that man has" or "Isn't that lady ugly?" to understand the tragedy in the fate of Cassandra and the importance of not letting truth loose except at appropriate moments.

For teachers and parents to discuss the whole matter of truth and lies with children more honestly would be an interesting experiment. Sometimes the kindest act can be the telling of a lie, and the most cruel, the revealing of the truth. Adults could point out, too, that lies usually dress up in truth's wardrobe and that words like *reliable, pure, sterling,* and *genuine* are often used to camouflage the grossest trickery. I do not think that such education would make children into cynics, but it would make them less gullible.

There is little chance, however, of this happening. Truth is the most positive word in our vocabulary. The paradox is that all of us think we know what truth is and, therefore, very few of us have ever tried to define it. This deification of truth is an inheritance from science, a by-product of the technical age we live in. The child is brought up to believe that all statements are either true or false. Other periods have had other values: goodness, beauty, courage were contrasted with evil, ugliness, and cowardice. The resulting societies were entirely different from ours; but we all have in common the idea that if we carry our guiding principle to an extreme, it is at the cost of all other virtues.

The modern child is nourished on the belief that all questions can be answered, and that even the most complicated problems have an easy solution if only we could find it. The nineteenth-century mind did not take kindly to the idea of the unsolvable mystery, so the only honorable and worthwhile task became the search for truth. Soon literature itself became suspect; it was, after all, a fabrication. It never really happened. It was fictitious, and wasn't that the same as untrue or false? If many grown-ups were uncertain, could you blame a child for thinking the two synonymous?

No one likes to be classified as a liar, and since the middle of the last century authors have been trying to reestablish themselves: realism became the rage. True-to-life, factual, unflattering, faithful, down-to-earth, unromantic novels flooded the market. It is interesting to note that realism became identified with suffering and unhappiness — a kind of Horatio Alger story turned upside down.

But no matter how unvarnished and undisguised the background was, the story itself was still thought up, imagined. This bond with former literature, however, could be cut. One could get one notch nearer to reality — to the truth — by telling about the life of a man who had really lived, preferably one you had known yourself. A murder story in which the murder has really taken place is bound to be more truthful — especially if you have interviewed the murderer in the death cell — than, say, Dostoyevski's *Crime and Punishment.* You could also construct your novels out of historical facts; like a modern Gradgrind, you could pile them one on top of another and call the result "Faction."

Poor old fiction! Will no one come to its aid? Must I alone, without even a Sancho Panza to protect me from my foolishness, take up the lance? It is fitting that an author who writes for children should attempt it. We are — or at least we ought to want to be — related to the child who pointed out to the world that the emperor had no clothes on. There are other reasons as well, the most important being that never before has it been so essential that our children be introduced to literature as early as possible.

When children, like little savages, were left to their own devices and Nature was their nursery-school teacher, they made their own literature by telling stories and playing games of make-believe. But the children of today are not left to themselves; they are bombarded with messages, most of which were not originally meant for them. As for Nature, modern suburbia does not have space enough for her. For all our wealth, we may end up producing a generation of slum children. The mark of such children has been their combination of worldly wisdom and ignorance. They are exposed to too much and experience too little — a deadly combination. And country children are exposed to too little and experience much. As slum children have been forced, in a crowded world, to witness every aspect of life, so are our children staring at a glass screen, watching a world they cannot participate in. For the whole point of television is that you must accept it; it becomes your imagination. Literature, on the other hand, is meaningful only when the reader's imagination is working almost as hard as the author's.

The fairy tale used to be the first literature the child came into contact with. It made some demands on the youngster's credulity, for the stories are filled with strange and wondrous creatures — giants, witches, fairies, trolls, and gnomes. But the very young child accepts the world of faerie, for it explains much and is not unlike his own world. Little children are constantly at the mercy of forces they cannot control or even understand. Even the kindest mother can all of a sudden turn into, if not a witch, then a stepmother. As for giants they are common enough, and if they are not capable of tearing up trees with their hands, they can do it with their machines, and yet they are often simpletons like the ones in the stories. Children depend upon their wits, and so do the heroes and heroines in the world of faerie.

The fairy tale claims to be a true story, to have actually happened; for "once upon a time" was a real time. Often the storyteller declared at the end of a tale that he or she had attended the prince and princess's wedding and had worn out a pair of shoes dancing at the festivities. Fairy tales were not created by children or for children. They belonged to the lowest classes; try once, for fun, to read them with this fact in mind. Imagine yourself bound to a master and to his land, or to a mistress, to Turgenev's mother, that witch of all witches. Then you will understand that the fairy tale attempts to create a bit of justice in an unjust world. It is because the tale told the truth that the evil characters had to be disguised. The storyteller had to be careful when he told his audience that kings and masters could be evil, cruel, and stupid, while asserting that goodness and kindness were the highest of all virtues.

The age of the storyteller is gone and with him the classical fairy tale disappeared. The world of magic is still attractive to us, but those who claim ownership of it belong to a different class; they are intellectuals. There are now many forms of the fairy tale, from the sophisticated and complex, like the Lord of the Rings books, to crude science fiction. I must admit that I am not particularly attracted to science fiction. I prefer foolish kings and evil queens to mad dictators from outer space, and wishing rings to the mock paraphernalia of spaceships.

I have another good reason for disliking science fiction; I find its message is usually as banal as its literary style. It pictures human beings plaguing one another ad infinitum. Unfortunately, I think it is now the favorite reading of teenagers; maybe the sophisticated cynicism appeals to them. The truth of the matter is that very evil people are very boring. Most authors and storytellers of old knew this fact. They never bothered to draw a detailed picture of the ogre in the castle. Science fiction seems to take for granted that a kind of horrible fascism is humankind's fate and that the object of science is the destruction of the human. Little humor relieves this depressing view of life.

The giants, the kings, and the queens from the world of faerie were human; their ambitions were at times ridiculously so. When you are queen, to wish to be the most beautiful woman in the realm seems rather silly; and to be willing to murder your stepdaughter to retain the title, even more so. But knowing something about human nature, we must admit that such absurdities are not beyond us. If it were possible to create the inner life — the very soul — of a two-headed, green-skinned monster, with antennae instead of ears, from the faraway planet, we would probably not be very interested because we would be incapable of understanding it.

The truth is that we cannot imagine anything beyond the possibility of our own experience. Even Homer could not really conceive of what it would be like to have eternal life, eternal youth, and unlimited powers; therefore, when the gods appear in the *Iliad*, they are filled with human weaknesses and human vices. Zeus is merely an earthly king, a little more powerful, yes — but godlike, no. When Phidias created his giant sculpture of Pallas Athene, he portrayed a woman. Did he really believe that by enlarging a mortal shape a hundredfold, he could create the figure of a goddess? I don't think he did, any more than Homer thought he was drawing accurate portraits of the gods. Our measuring stick has been formed from our experiences. All art and literature are concerned with human values and with human knowledge, and I really don't see how it can be otherwise. That this knowledge is often not well founded is another matter.

The message, the knowledge, which the author wants to bring to his audience cannot be separate from the style or the story. If a piece of fiction is to be successful as literature, the three must harmonize. If the message overpowers the story, the whole thing becomes a diatribe. If, on the other hand, the style becomes an end in itself, the story will be esoteric and precious. When the three — story, style, and message — become one so that the reader is not aware of them as separate entities, the author has succeeded. This harmony can be very difficult to achieve, especially for a writer who holds strong opinions; at times authors like D. H. Lawrence and Thomas Hardy were unable to keep in check their passionate beliefs, thus marring their books. In Joseph Conrad the balance is perfect; nothing intrudes. The result is that you almost refuse to believe that you have read fiction, make-believe. The people must have lived; the events must have happened — just exactly as the author wrote them down. What results is a higher knowledge, a truth that is accepted on several levels of realization: intellectually, emotionally, and even sensuously, as if you had experienced it yourself and were now recalling it.

This result can only be achieved by fiction. Yet many people approach fiction as if they were entering a sideshow at the circus, absolutely convinced that they are about to be cheated. But if their attitude toward fiction is one of mistrust, they make up for it by a total credulity when they are faced with nonfiction. Under that guise you can make them believe almost anything.

In the sixteenth and seventeenth centuries many a traveler returned from a visit to the Americas with marvelous tales of what he had seen: people with no heads who spoke and ate through holes in their stomachs, riverbeds of diamonds and rubies, talking fish, and many other weird sights. They published these tales under the heading "True Descriptions of the New World" and were immediately believed.

Consider for a moment the present state of the world, and recall all the memoirs of politicians. Did you ever read one that admitted to any faults in policy? Did any of the writers ever confess to questioning his abilities as a leader? Without doubt, we have been governed by sages; I wonder what the world would be like had we allowed ourselves to be ruled by fools? Maybe we should give it a try; we could hardly be in a worse state.

Our faith in the accuracy of nonfiction is not only foolish; it is also dangerous. You will notice that when the written word is used in the most negative way, it is hardly ever fiction that is subjected to this shame. Books that are meant to entice hatred belong on the nonfiction shelf. They are usually made up of confessions and genuine eyewitness accounts: filth like *The Protocols of Zion* is an excellent example. Nonfiction must bear the brunt of the guilt for such crimes, partly because the credulity of the public makes it a desirable medium and also because to utilize fiction successfully for the "big lie" would be nearly impossible. Even though the propaganda machines of governments and commercial companies use nonfiction to bait their hooks, such books are still readily believed, and fiction is still mistrusted.

My house stands on a pier in the ocean; at the base of the stone quay live innumerable crabs. The children of the village spend many a lovely summer day catching them. They tie a piece of bacon on a string, using a small stone for an anchor; then they let the bait down to the bottom of the sea. The crabs fight to grab the fatty bacon, and so greedy are these little animals that once they get a claw into it, they will not let go, and the children can pull them out of the water onto the pier. Here, they are deposited into buckets, trapped by their own stupidity. When evening comes, the children empty the buckets into the sea. The crabs crawl into their hollows between the stones, and both children and crabs are ready for the next day. You see, the crabs learn nothing; every day throughout the hot summer months they are captured and put into buckets. The pier has been there for two hundred years, so for two centuries these crabs and their ancestors have been caught and let loose without ever becoming wiser. The process is depressing, especially because it reminds me of the history of the human race.

I am sure that this little speech will not stem the flood of books by politicians, movie stars, generals, and other public and would-be public personalities who are suddenly overwhelmed by a desire to reveal the truth in print, either personally or by telling it to someone else.

I remember clearly my first realization that history books were not always truthful; it came as a great shock. I was skimming through my cousin's schoolbooks. My cousin was Norwegian. His history book was concerned with Norwegian truth about our joint history, while mine had been rather oriented toward Danish truth; the two did not resemble each other.

Children are often naive enough to believe that grown-ups are habitually more truthful than they are. Being weak, they need to have faith in their parents and the grown-up world to which their parents belong. Although I think it is very important to sow in the minds of youth some seeds of doubt about nonfiction's claim to veracity, I think it is even more important to make young people understand that fiction is concerned with truth, that it is not merely tall tales to be enjoyed in moments of leisure.

Why do authors write fiction? I think that because we wish to get as near the truth as possible, we choose the imaginary tale. We can only write from our own experiences, but we create from a composite of them. Ten incidents from our lives become one imaginary one. But an even more crucial motive is the realization that it is far too difficult to write the truth about ourselves. By using a fictive person, we are free to use all the knowledge we have acquired through life. God may have created Adam in His own image, but even He did not attempt a duplication.

I have become aware of this fact because there are certain incidents in the book I am working on that actually happened to me in my youth. The novel takes place in Nazi Germany in 1937, and its protagonist is a young Danish boy who is on a week's excursion with his school. I did go on such a trip and recall clearly what happened during those seven days. But the hero of my book is not a portrait of myself. Much of what happens to him is constructed out of incidents that happened to me; and sometimes he even reacts in the same way I did. But he is not me. If he had been, I would have had to write accurately not only about myself but about my parents, my brothers, and my friends. Could I have done it? I am certain I couldn't; and I am even more certain that what I would have written, had I tried, would have been a very poor book and a very untruthful one.

For I can never write the truth about my parents. Not only because my feelings would interfere with my memory but because their past is not my past. If in a novel I draw a portrait of a father, it has two sources — myself as a child, recalling my father and other grown-ups, and myself as a grown-up, relating to my own and others' children. The truth is never two-dimensional, but the picture most of us have of our own parents is so. Try to think of one of the autobiographies you have read. Are not the portraits of the author's parents missing the shadings that the pictures of the other people have? In our relationship to our progenitors we seem incapable of growing up — partly because of our awe of them when we were small and they were giants, but also because as far as we are concerned, they have never been children. Ask any child to imagine his or her parents as children, and you will find that the child will appear confused and will have difficulty understanding the task. Try to visualize your parents as five-year-olds. It is difficult, if not impossible.

Moreover, why should one write self-portraits when there is a whole mass of humanity to draw upon? You need to reflect your face in a mirror in order to see it, and that reflection is not a true image. Writers and poets are too introspective as it is. Don't let them indulge themselves; like Narcissus, they are bound to suffer the consequences.

I have spoken of truth without really defining what I mean. Certainly, I mean a great deal more than facts. Facts are useful, as scaffolding is to someone who wants to build a house; but the truth of a story does not depend on factual accuracy. *War and Peace* is, no doubt, correct in its dates, military weapons, costumes, and what-have-you. I have never bothered to check. But that is not what makes Tolstoy's book believable. Pierre's fate does not move you because of historical accuracy; it is another kind of fidelity that has convinced you.

To make my point clearer, I might take as an example *The Wind in the Willows*. It has a few factual idiosyncrasies. To begin with, Toad seems marvelously adept at changing his size. But I shan't make a list of the absurdities, for they don't matter at all. Toad is very real, and when my daughter says that I am a bit "toady" at times, I know exactly what she means — without agreeing with her.

If you wish to create literature, this accuracy, this fidelity to your characters' emotional makeup, is a necessity. In order to achieve it, you must submit your own personality to theirs. It is they who are important, not you. You may have created them, but they are not your slaves. They have their own fate to fulfill; you merely have to write it down. True, you have given them their souls, but once given, these souls cannot change or be taken away. By the time you have written the fourth chapter, the last chapter of the book is inevitable.

It may come as a surprise to you, but the Ten Commandments do not prohibit lying; they do not even mention it. What the Ninth Commandment is concerned with is the wrongness of bearing false witness against your neighbors. I agree with this most wholeheartedly, and I am as indignant as anyone can be when I read a bad book in which the author has borne false witness against his own characters. But — and this is the crucial point — you cannot do it unpunished. This crime carries the death penalty, not for the author but for his or her book. Oh, it might sell just because the author has borne false witness against his own characters; he has filled them with the cant of his time. But they will not survive when new slogans are invented and new fashions become the order of the day.

We are so used to truth being contained in a mathematical formula or precept, it is extremely difficult to explain and understand that truth in literature involves the whole book, not a part of it. A book may contain opinions which you favor or morality which you are in sympathy with, but these are not its truth. After all, propaganda is written for good causes as well as for bad. The truth of a book lies in the beating of its heart — if it is alive, it is true.

The author constructs his book from knowledge, from memory of things and events past. I sometimes think that an ability to recall with accuracy an emotional state — your reaction to something that happened as far back as the early years of childhood — is what is usually called talent in a writer. Your memory may not harbor dates or names, but it must be able to recall the whole spectrum of joys and fears that you have experienced.

Your readers' memories are rekindled as they examine their own experiences in the light of what they are reading, and it is from these memories that they decide whether the book is true. This is why children — no matter how intelligent they may be — cannot appreciate all literature written for adults. They lack memories; that which they are reading about has not yet happened to them, and they have no measure for judgment. As often as not, they will call an adult book "boring," which it may not be, except to them. I recall that when I was a youngster reading an adult book,

I would skip a great deal — even whole sections — but it had nothing to do with vocabulary. I didn't do this when I read *Mr. Midshipman Easy* even though Captain Marryat, especially in this book, had a fondness for polysyllables. No, it is simply that there was nothing in the book which did not, in one way or other, fall within the experience of an adventurous boy.

I believe that children's literature of quality is more important today than ever before. It must counteract the enormous force of the media with their pop-music mentality, their stupid banalities, their noise, and their violence. Somewhere in Tolstoy's *War and Peace,* Prince Andrei asks what would happen if everyone were given his leisure without the culture to endure it. In the West we are well on the way to knowing what happens. In the woods near my former home in Denmark, a retired eighty-year-old man had a lovely seventeenth-century cottage. One day when he was in Copenhagen, a group of Boy Scouts camping in the forest broke all the windows in his house. Astonished, because these were well-to-do middle-class children, the old man asked them why they had done it. The boys answered almost in unison, "We were bored!"

At the present moment, half the Western world is jogging. At all hours of the day you can see people out running; the expressions on their faces tell you that it is a serious matter. Exercise is good for the body; it is important to keep in shape. I would love some day to see reading become as fashionable. I agree that a potbelly is not an object of beauty, but a mind that has long since lost its flexibility is not admirable, either.

I believe that books will be here as long as humankind is. I know you can microfilm them and project the pages onto a screen. But there is no pleasure in holding a microfilm in your hand; books are beautiful in themselves, and like the faces of human beings, they develop character as they age. Is there a more pleasant room in a house than a library, a jungle more filled with adventure than a secondhand bookstore? Those who have not read a book since they left school will never know the joys of the book lover.

I was fortunate to be brought up in a home where books were as natural a part of the furnishings as tables and chairs. The bookcases were in my father's room, but we children were allowed to go there as much as we pleased. My parents did not attempt any censorship, and I borrowed many a book that I returned after reading only a few pages. As I have mentioned before, a book is re-created by the reader from his or her own experiences. That which the child cannot understand because he or she cannot imagine it as yet, the child will reject. Therefore, it would be very difficult to corrupt the mind of the young via literature, and one need not forbid a child to read anything. Let me emphasize the word *read,* for I believe that pictorial pornography can be very harmful.

I never associated books with lack of masculinity or with ill health. I never heard of the sickly bookworm on whom the sun never shone. Where in the world did this concept come from, and why? Book lovers there are, and there must be book haters as well. Strangely enough, some of them have even written books, for in children's books I have come across ludicrous caricatures of book lovers. I am sure that there are boys and girls who are sickly and who also read books, but I hardly believe that their ill health is caused by their habit of reading. Yet, I am afraid that the number of people who find it slightly suspect if their children read a great deal is not a minority. Is this a relic from the Dark Ages, when only the village priest could read and write, and reading, in the minds of the superstitious peasants, was connected with witchcraft? You can find book haters everywhere; I have met them among young librarians in Denmark. They speak a new language and would like to change libraries into communications centers. Such a place is merely a kind of playroom, a pop-cultural amusement arcade.

Real culture is a love affair, one that lasts your whole life. But, unfortunately, if you are introduced to literature by someone who thinks it tastes like cod-liver oil, there is a chance that you will never voluntarily open a book. The cod-liver oil syndrome has another unfortunate aspect: those who adhere to it love to analyze and can find meanings of the most incredible obscurity in the most plainly written verse and prose.

Recently, in an Irish schoolbook, I came across an interpretation of Robert Frost's "Stopping by Woods on a Snowy Evening." It is such a lovely, simple poem. By the time I had finished reading the elaborate explanation of it, my head was swimming. How had I missed so much of the poem? There was layer upon layer, depth beneath depth. One of us, either the commentator or myself, must be a perfect idiot. Well, I have reached an age when my own limitations do not upset me, even if they are pointed out to me by a schoolteacher. But this was not always so. As a child I was insecure and would have believed that the teacher's interpretation was the only possible one; and I might have turned against the poem and the poet. Literature is written for our enjoyment, for our pleasure; and this is the message I wish teachers and schools would bring to our children — but not by making obscure that which was meant to be plain and by inventing complications to make a book into a mental obstacle course.

For myself I cannot imagine life without literature, without books. The fate of the human being is to be born mortal with a knowledge of eternity. Lost in such a void of time, our own measured years are not long. But because we have literature, art, and music, our great past can become the present. We can span the gaps of generations and establish an intimate friendship with someone dead for hundreds of years. The life of the human being is a lonely life, but the lives of those who have denied themselves a knowledge of our common culture are doubly lonely.

The gods have given us a lump of clay and a period of years, the length of which is unknown to us, in which to play with it. Our own glory lies in what we do with this lump of clay — this soul of ours. We could with pride and good sense create something beautiful, something valuable enough for us to deserve to own the earth. But we could also create monsters, and anyone who has studied the history of humanity knows that we have done this often enough.

We have in our cultural heritage, of which literature is not the lesser part, something to give our children — a tool that may make them capable of being better and greater human beings than we are. I am certain of one thing; if we deny literature to them by showing no respect for it ourselves, we will have stunted them, made them incapable of becoming what they could have become.

I have spoken of children, and I am fond of them. I have spoken of literature, which I love. Has what I have said made any sense? I am an author, a poet; and they, like the March Hare, are slightly mad, even in the middle of the summer, and should be treated gently.

V

Motion and Rest: The Art of Illustration

Drawing by Uri Shulevitz from *The Magician* (1973)
Logo for Simmons College Summer Program, 1982

Introduction

E T H E L   H E I N S

In defense of language and literature it has become fashionable in recent years to invoke — out of context, of course — the opening line of Saint John's Gospel: "In the beginning was the Word." But in the first of his Charles Eliot Norton Lectures at Harvard University, gathered together into a book known as *Icon and Idea*, the critic Herbert Read set forth an interesting hypothesis: that art has been the "means by which man was able step by step to comprehend the nature of things" — a gradual recognition, in other words, of what is significant in human experience. No written records were left by the prehistoric era, which might even have stretched back beyond the invention of language. "Before the word," says Read, "was the image, and the first recorded attempts of man to define the real are pictorial attempts, images scratched or pecked or painted on the surfaces of rocks or caves."

Thus, it is not illogical to declare that vision is a vital aspect of our creative response to the world; to perceive an image is to engage in an act of constructive imagination. From a myriad of sensory impressions the child articulates forms, patterns, ideas, things, events. But we are living in a noisily pictorial age — a time of ever-increasing infatuation with graphics. From all sides children are bludgeoned with debasing influences: the clichés of television, the gimmickry of advertising, the frenetic violence and vulgarity of animated cartoons, which are repeated in tasteless, mass-produced books. The child's natural curiosity and flair for excitement are exploited while his or her sensibilities are corrupted. Clearly, visual education should no longer be left to happenstance.

The picture book — a combination of art and literature — is essentially a dynamic form with its ebb and flow, its thrusting movement counterbalanced by reflection. For young children picture books are a vigorous form of communication, satisfying their hunger for story and providing an accessible means of heightening their perceptions of the world and of themselves. For older children such books can be both an aesthetic experience and a source of unexpected enjoyment. But all children approach the picture book with uncritical eyes; they are unaware of style or the elements of composition and are unimpressed by sheer color, elaborate artwork, or pretentious effects.

Liberated by the wizardry of modern printing techniques, illustrators are now limited only by their own talent, imagination, and judgment. Yet, many picture books seem to be brilliant but empty vessels. Illustrations often lack coherence, readability, and narrative direction, as though the artist were using the book as a portfolio or an art gallery, creating a complex graphic orchestration that obscures what should be clear and comprehensible. All good illustrations must emanate from the mind, and the quality of the illustration reflects the intensity of the imaginative experience. As Uri Shulevitz states in his excellent book *Writing with Pictures*, "The main function of illustration is to illuminate the text, to throw light on words"; and, "The range of illustration thus extends from its modest role as mere explanation of text to its highest possible achievement, when it enlightens spiritually and mentally."

The picture book in all its abundance and variety may well be the richest form of children's literature. And it is a literature blessed with brave new talent as well as with seasoned artists who are still adventurous innovators freshening their work by refining their art and constantly renewing the sources of their inspiration.

The papers and interviews in Part V are enormously diverse, forming a patchwork of miscellaneous offerings rather than a collage held together with unifying ideas. All of the contributors are unique in their devotion to art in the context of books for the young.

From her deep wellsprings of imagination and wit, Ellen Raskin, a remarkable, gifted woman, talks of the ambiguity of Blake: "Innocence and experience are part of the same soul. One starts out in innocence, has to go through experience to regain innocence and adulthood." Fritz Eichenberg remarks that for him "art is not a means of making a living. It is a means of walking on clouds; it's a dream world . . . a lonely battle." Tom Feelings speaks with dignified joy of his African heritage and the conflicts of its juxtaposition with his role as an artist in America. Robert McCloskey, a laconic Down-Mainer, re-creates some of the little-known stages in the artistic and literary journey of his many-faceted creative life. And Maurice Sendak expresses his passionate preoccupations: Mozart and the eighteenth century, the Grimm fairy tales, the works of Randall Jarrell, and *Outside Over There* — the third book in a trilogy bound together by an insistent theme. Bringing all of the ideas down to earth, Dorothy Butler, with her combination of wisdom, idealism, and good common sense, offers her own persuasive, logical, humanistic apologia for books in the lives of young children.

Early Friendships

DOROTHY BUTLER

I am not sure what the organizers of this gathering meant me to talk about, despite their most faithful supply of advance information; one never is, really. But I feel invited to mount my favorite hobbyhorses and canter all over the field. And so I'm going to tell you how I feel about very small children and their books, unashamedly repeating things said and written elsewhere, in the long-held belief that if a thing is worth saying, it's usually worth repeating.

I believe that this particular proposition — that babies need books to become truly human — must be said and resaid until the world at large starts to take notice. I believe that this fact is becoming, by the day, a more and more urgent duty for those of us who believe it. For I constantly meet people — professional, even academic people — who say, "But you don't really mean babies, do you? Three- and four-year-olds, perhaps."

Three and four years old can be too late, in the world we find about us. For children will attend to something in their search for stimulation and diversion, and most of them find the flashing light and strident sound of the television screen on hand from the very beginning.

Words are finely tuned instruments of communication, which must be encountered early if their shades of meaning are to serve the emerging intelligence. The daily offerings of the media, even programs ostensibly aimed at young children, are uncertain, to say the least. Because they must grab for the child's attention, they are usually loud and often crude. Subtlety has no place in a program which must involve the child without benefit of an intermediary; humor must be obvious, action predictable. Because looking requires less intellectual energy than listening, language is relegated to an inferior position. All too often, stereotyped, sentimentalized characters utter fragmentary, staccato, and mundane comments which, even if attended to, have nothing to offer the searching minds and imaginations of the children watching.

For it is precision that children need: a step-by-step accumulation of concepts, the opportunity to look again, to listen again, the inducement to wonder long before they can ask why and how, and the assurance that answers will be there when it is time to frame the questions.

It would be convenient for society if there were some piece of equipment which could provide these essentials for children, but there is not. Has anyone wondered what happened to the prediction of thirty years ago that closed-circuit television would replace teachers in schools? In the apparent wealth and wonder of new predictions about life as it may be lived in the twenty-first century, few of us think of calling earlier prophets to account.

For the campaign to replace teachers with television screens quite simply did not work. If one teacher lecturing thirty children has a hopeless task, an inanimate box has an even more impossible one. It seems likely that the only children who can benefit at all from a group situation are those who have their own personal sources of nourishment in the background. As society is currently constituted, this means a parent. All children need at least one person apiece who is prepared — preferably delighted — to present the world to them, to show, to tell, to involve. That this must be a loving person almost goes without saying. Babies and small children need at least one loving adult each, to weld them to the world.

And this process, of course, means the invocation of language. There can be no doubt at all that language is the strongest of all humanizing forces. Only the most rudimentary thought is possible without language. And communication, the lifeblood of relationship, is rooted in language. A chronic inability to communicate bedevils our society at every level from the domestic to the political, from the local to the international. A first-things-first campaign that accords language a central place on the early — and later — educational stage is drastically overdue. If we abandon language — and we do, to the extent that we glorify facts over wisdom, machines over books — we retreat suicidally from the possibility of ever understanding ourselves and other people, our motives, and the likely effects of our actions. We reduce our capacity to communicate, at our own and our children's peril.

Language means listening. It is the child's ear we must attend to first, and, fortunately, this is not difficult. Children are born already loving rhythm and the sound of the human voice. It seems likely, indeed, that children become addicted to the regular beat of their mothers' hearts, and the other sounds of their bodies, before birth. And what a strength this is! The lullaby must surely be as old as humanity itself.

The plight of the totally deaf child demonstrates dramatically the supremacy of the ear over the eye in human learning. Among deaf children one sees a tragic inability to harness the resources of potentially normal minds. Blind children, by contrast, have very little intellectual impairment. Deprived of the sense of sight, they are nonetheless able to learn because they can hear. The compensations of extreme aural sensitivity in the blind child is well recognized and documented. No comparative increase in visual acumen occurs in the deaf child — and would scarcely compensate, if available. The task of reaching and enriching the mind of the deaf child is, in our current state of knowledge, dauntingly difficult. Language — heard, when spoken; read, when written — is the indispensable tool of intelligence.

But surely, many will reply, the visual is important, too. Of course it is — enormously important. But our world is overwhelmingly geared to the visual; in this field, our task is to sift the honest from the banal. And where do we find the best visual nourishment for young children — the most colorful, the most delicate, the most vigorous, the most peaceful, the funniest, the most evocative pictures? Why, in picture books of course!

In the best picture books we find word and picture so well balanced that one is unimaginable without the other; the support is total and reciprocal. But, at the risk of laboring the issue, I must point out that the blind child hearing the text of such a book is in a better situation than the deaf child viewing the pictures. For pictures state and define, whereas language suggests. The words, the ideas proceeding from a story, make an infinite number of connections in the listener's mind, depending on a number of factors: the nature and effectiveness of the story itself, the texture of its language, and, of course, the existing and unknowable state of the receiving mind.

Although the course of a particular story cannot be charted through the million convoluted channels of a child's mind nor the impact of a particular character or event be assessed, we nonetheless discern in a child's conversation and play fascinating flashes of evidence of the effect of books on mind and imagination. ("Drat the boy!" and "Stuff and nonsense!" are among my grandson Oliver's responses to the daily dosage of Ardizzone which he currently demands as sustenance.) We can only guess at the ramifications of another person's mind, child's or adult's. Our own, after all, defy our understanding. But in the presence of well-read-to children, we sense an abundant flow of ideas, an expectation of understanding, a wide repertoire of responses, and early predilections for the work of particular authors or artists that imply the beginnings of taste, of personal preference.

Recently, I witnessed under my roof the capitulation of a small child to the magic of Little Tim, Lucy, Ginger, Charlotte, and their seagoing friends. I have been through this before; in essentials the generations don't change much. I might have expected this child to be caught up and carried away by Ardizzone's wordy documentation of the trials and triumphs of this self-reliant, venturesome band! During his lifetime Edward Ardizzone seemed to keep an uncanny memory for the concerns of childhood: the need to feel capable; to remain intact, however buffeted by adults or by circumstances; to venture bravely and to come home safely.

And how my small grandson loved (to the extent of squeezing out of the adults in his life nine readings in two days) an Ardizzone title which is outside the Little Tim series — *Johnny the Clockmaker!* There is evidence that the author's style, both literary and artistic, speaks to Oliver with startling and satisfying directness. I had all but forgotten *Johnny* and find myself astonished, all over again, by the sheer weight of information provided by text and picture, quite apart from the wonder of Johnny's own competence and resilience, Susannah's spirited and unselfish efforts on his behalf, Joe the Blacksmith's kindness, and the overall satisfaction of child success in the face of adult skepticism and stuffiness. Cog wheels, weights, chains, pendulums, and the working details of a blacksmith's forge have invaded our lives.

Tim and Johnny have become part of one small boy's inner landscape. They are friends who will stand by him in adversity, whose spirit and example will remain long after the details of their stories have been submerged by the concerns of passing years.

I am reminded of one of my own children, now well established as an adult. "Hey!" he said recently, catching sight of a copy of *The Story of Ferdinand* on my shelves. "I remember this!" (As well he might. When he was four, five, and six, and a very gentle though large and strongly built child, it had been one of his favorite books.) Now, he read it through again, smiling. *Ferdinand* makes good reading at any age. Then:

"It doesn't seem to have that 'sniffing' bit in this version."

"Well," I said. "It never did. You invented that."

"Did I?" in astonishment.

"Yes. Don't you remember? 'All the other little bulls . . . would run and jump and butt their heads together, but not Ferdinand. He liked to sit just quietly and smell the flowers.' " We did the sniffing bit in nostalgic unison — the long, appreciative inhale through the nose, the equally satisfying exhale through the mouth; and we beamed at one another. "I do believe," said this boy-turned-man, "that Ferdinand was a formative influence on my life!"

I believe so, too, and I could add a whole string of early and late friends, from Mike Mulligan and Madeline to Prince Prigio and Bilbo Baggins, all of whom provided color, action, and humor in the lives of this child, his sisters, and his brother.

What is it about books?

Well, to begin with, there is nothing else like a book. If a visitor from another planet arrived and asked, "What is a book?" one could not say that it was like anything except its derivative, a magazine. If you happen to have built or altered a house lately and have been obliged to wrestle with a set of architect's plans, neatly rolled, you will have some appreciation of the genius that first secured successive pages by a spine on the left-hand side and bound them together within stiffened covers. Only the invention of the wheel can be mentioned in the same breath. And just as the wheel has never changed in roundness, so the book has never changed in bookishness. It doesn't need to change. It is perfect.

And have you noticed the love the book engenders in the breasts of its supporters? They are a fierce, devoted, and passionate lot, the book lovers! Intoxicated, most of them, by the feel and the smell of books, fanatically dedicated to the cause of preserving the lives of dusty and battered old volumes which they have had ever since they can remember (although they may never open most of them again), and constantly acquiring more books, even though their houses may be shabby and their cars elderly.

These people seem to be less concerned about the weather than others, and I have it from the young that they make good parents because they are inclined to be abstracted. Although they are usually still awake when you get home, they have not been watching the clock, even though they may have meant to do so. You frequently find them chuckling away to themselves, too, and this helps if you are about to tell them that you just backed the family car into the letterbox or have failed yet another math exam. Their own tendency to have their noses in novels when they should be mowing the lawn or cleaning the windows probably predisposes them to let you down lightly, anyway. There is even quite a strong chance that they flunked math themselves.

At the other end of the scale are the people who use books for functional purposes only — they read newspapers and occasionally magazines and consult directories, cookery books, and car manuals, as necessary. These people often have very tidy houses that are innocent of the litter of books, papers, and periodicals. They can never be heard shouting at their children to help search for mislaid and overdue library books, but they can be heard nightly demanding that their children start on their homework immediately (usually while they themselves watch television).

These parents sooner or later almost certainly fall victim to the blandishments of an encyclopedia salesman. The set, in fine bindings, is out-of-bounds to the children, in effect if not by edict. It cost a great deal of money and may be consulted only after parental permission has been granted and extensive hand-washing entered into. Strangely and unfairly, the kids next door (whose parents may not even believe in homework and are certainly too lazy to police its performance) seem to do better at school, anyway. But then, life is not fair.

In between these two extremes, the ranks grow thinner by the year. Does anyone know any people who read voraciously *sometimes*? Even more crucially for our present purposes: Does anyone know of even a few late conversions — people who came to books at fifteen or eighteen or twenty-five and thereafter became real readers with all the symptoms of the cheerful addiction that the term implies? Sadly, I do not expect affirmative answers. In my experience readers are made early, or not at all.

The implication of this likelihood is profound. It means that those adults who have daily contact with very young children have a power in the lives of these children that is sobering in its significance. The chances are that we can turn at least a few of them into committed and responsive readers.

Mind you, the path is fraught with danger for teachers. Parents and librarians have all the fun. No need for them to grit their teeth, reading manual in hand. They can busy themselves with the product — the book — and with their own presentation of it and to the child's reception as an experience. It goes without saying that the book has to be a good one — a real book with flesh-and-blood characters — a far cry from the passionless early reader or primer with which the teacher is all too often demonstrating the bleak and boring nature of the task at hand.

It is hardly surprising that most children who learn to read easily, who become involved and responsive readers, come from homes where books are enjoyed at all levels and read aloud regularly to children. For the children who emerge from these homes expect a page of print to produce meaning smoothly. They know, unconsciously, that the resources of the mind have more to do with the reading process than the panicky attempt of the eye to translate successive symbols into single words.

In real reading, the eye must swing along the line while the meaning pours into the mind, and the mind, in its turn, responds. For responsive reading is quite different from word-by-word decoding. It involves a process described in 1924 by J. H. Jagger as "thinking under the stimulus of the printed page." Even earlier, in 1916, J. B. Kerfoot asserted that "no story is ever told by the author of a book; the telling is done by the reader, who takes the text for his scenario and produces it on the stage of his own imagination, with resources furnished by his own experiences of life." And of literature, I would add, in the case of a child.

Children with well-nourished minds, who have been talked to, listened to, and read to from earliest days, have built up a huge store of information about the way people behave, the alternatives available in a host of situations, and how action determines result. They have been warmed within by contact with hundreds of diverse and colorful characters. They feel the assurance of their own humanity with all its fallibility — but with its courage and humor, too.

For it is through books and from books that the well-equipped child gathers a great deal of experience of life and people. This is, after all, one of the basic functions of fiction: a function which is seen as clearly in the two-year-old, enjoying *Mr. Gumpy's Outing* on her parent's knee, as in the adult engrossed in a new novel. It should be obvious that such a child, listening to the patterns of language in the service of a well-rounded, satisfying story, is already learning to read. Slipping into "doing it yourself" is simply the next, barely separable step.

Experience with children in their early teens who read falteringly, if at all, invariably reveals a poverty of resources. These children usually have more than adequate phonic skills (the so-called basics), but these avail them very little unless they have the confidence and expertise to swing their eye along a line of print, with expectation of meaning. Such expectation is simply not present if the child's own language is immature, if his listening powers are underdeveloped, if his contact with books and their contents has been minimal.

In the course of my work, I am often obliged to listen to a child struggling to decode one word after another, a necessary diagnostic torture applied once only, with the greatest reluctance and with repeated reassurance to the child that as this procedure isn't really reading, it doesn't matter. We merely need to know how he or she approaches the printed page. Better things are on the way.

The plight of these children suggests an analogy with that of a person ostensibly being taught to drive but actually being prevented from taking the car onto the road. Gear and clutch operation, braking, steering — all have been taught; but until the driver can synchronize all these while the car bowls along the road, his skills will avail him nothing.

And so it is with reading. The fortunate child draws on a deep well of language and experience to inform an eye which requires only minimum detail from the page for the extraction of meaning. It is surely everyone's good fortune that exactly the same joyful procedure, undertaken early in children's lives, will equip them simultaneously for mastery of the reading process and for active membership in the human race, with all its strengths and frailties, its hopes and sorrows, its joys and passions. One suspects that for some people the sheer simplicity of the suggestion is against it. Reading to children? Education has to be harder than that!

I am constantly overawed by the ponderous findings of reading research. One is obliged to believe that the ultimate revelation of the intricate physical and neurological processes by which the human being derives meaning from a page of print will avail us valuable insights into the teaching of reading. This may well be so; although the evidence is not impressive that scientists are much closer to the resolution of the mystery of reading than they were sixty years ago. Jagger's "thinking under the stimulus of the printed page" is still, for me, the definition that reveals the nature of the process as I experience it.

The earnest search must go on; but, in the meanwhile, why should we not be using in the practical field the truth that is unassailable: that reading cannot be taught, but must be learned, and that it emerges naturally against a background of books and language, with committed and caring adults as intermediaries?

As a child I learned that I could disappear into a book and find myself entirely in another world. I know now that my experience is crucial in the production of a committed reader. If we can give this experience to children in their earliest years, they will want to take the same route, time and time again; they will know that familiar landscapes and old friends are waiting for them there, as well as unimagined wonders, and new and different people. If we can ensure that these children will later slip into reading themselves, hardly noting the transition (as we can, if we attend lovingly to minds rather than overearnestly to mechanics), we will have the satisfaction of knowing that we have given these children a priceless gift.

"I am a deep-sea diver, and Kit is my fairy godmother," said a five-year-old grandson recently, in explanation of the game he and his younger brother were playing. A world in which deep-sea divers can have fairy godmothers suits me very well indeed.

Picture Books as Literature

SONIA LANDES

One role of pictures in a picture book is to enhance the meaning of a story by illustrating the words. But good picture book artists go well beyond mere illustrating, by inventing and developing additional story material. A study of picture books should begin with Randolph Caldecott, the illustrator whose name on the medal stands for the best in illustration. Aside from his robust style and freedom of line, his greatest contribution to illustration lay in his ability to enlarge the dimensions of the text and enhance its meaning. He did this by inventing characters and by adding to the plot.

Let us take the well-known nonsense rhyme "Hey Diddle Diddle," discussed by Maurice Sendak in his essay in Elizabeth T. Billington's *The Randolph Caldecott Treasury*. The words are a sequence of non sequiturs. They tell about a cat and a fiddle, about a cow jumping over the moon, about a dog that laughs, and about a dish running off with a spoon. Caldecott manages to extract meaning from these words by joining the non sequiturs together. Giving the fiddle to the cat starts a merry round of strange happenings, the last and most interesting of which is a love story. Caldecott first hints at the romance by having the dish and the spoon sit out a dance; then they elope. "The dish ran away with the spoon" may be the last words of the song, but not of Caldecott's story. An additional page, with no words at all, shows the irate parents, the knife and the fork, dragging their errant daughter, the spoon, away from her love, who lies shattered upon the floor.

"Sing a Song of Sixpence" is a mixture of nonsense and plot. Once again Caldecott invents meaning. He changes the *of* in the title to *for* — "Sing a Song for Sixpence" — and begins to put the pieces of the puzzle together. A little rich girl kindly gives a poor man sixpence for his song. He runs to buy a pocket full of rye, which he scatters around a trap to catch the blackbirds to bake in a pie. As the ragged family, sitting eagerly around the table, cuts open the pie, the birds begin to sing. (As early as 1549, an Italian cookbook speaks of a pie of live birds. The birds are placed in a ten-inch-high, very thick pastry, which is covered with a lattice crust so the birds can breathe. The pie is then rushed to the table.) "Was not that a dainty dish to set before the king?" Dainty meaning delicious? Dainty meaning worthy?

And who are the king and queen? They are the children Caldecott wrote for. He fills their world with their favorite characters. The proper decor for this queen's parlor is Little Red Riding Hood, Hansel and Gretel, and Little Bo-Peep. In the king's room are heroes for boys: Jack, the giant killer (the Victorian two-headed variety of giant) and Robinson Crusoe. There is something for the grown-ups, too. The maid has a handsome and affectionate soldier ready to console her — after the loss and return of her nose.

There are other additions to the rhymes. A cat in "The Queen of Hearts" tattles on the knave of hearts who stole the tarts; this all-knowing cat points a paw in the direction of the thief. The daddy "gone a-hunting" in "Baby Bunting" has a bad day and *buys* the rabbit skin at a store. Later, a bunch of rabbits stare in utter amazement at the little girl wrapped in fur.

Caldecott created books a hundred years ago. Today's illustrators are still following in his footsteps, inventing characters and stories while substantially increasing the art and devices of the picture book.

"Charlie Needs a Cloak" is actually a how-to book, with instructions from a narrator who pretends to be as blind as Charlie is. But the reader isn't. The pictures reveal two dramatic and parallel stories. In one story the sheep eats Charlie's cloak, and Charlie shears the wool of the same sheep to make his new cloak. In the other story a mouse, never cited in the text, brazenly steals some of the things Charlie needs and uses. The mouse even steals the scene. Once the child readers spot the mouse, their eyes immediately go to the bottom of the page (this is literally a subplot) to find out what unbelievable object it is now carting off.

Or take *The Story of Ferdinand*. This is the story of a peaceful bull, but a supporting cast is revealed in Robert Lawson's pictures. An ominous scavenger, a vulture, whom Munro Leaf never introduces to the reader, sits patiently waiting for Ferdinand. Ferdinand is, of course, as unaware of this vulture as Charlie is of his diminishing cloak. (The unaware hero suits children's stories very well, for unawareness symbolizes innocence and purity.) The robin in *The Tale of Peter Rabbit* is a different kind of "other." I've always imagined that the robin is Beatrix Potter's signature bird — a solitary warbler, a teller of tales. Its role, like hers, is that of the sympathetic observer, ever-present but outside the story and never referred to in the text.

One last, modern example. Rosemary Wells, following Caldecott's dish and spoon, takes the story in *Benjamin & Tulip* past the end of the text. After physical attacks on Benjamin by Tulip, Benjamin finally wins out and has the last word — " 'There!' " But the story doesn't end with that word. Turn the page and see another fight between them, a watermelon-seed–spitting fight, in which the watermelons serve as shields and the seeds fall safely between them. *Ptui!* No words needed.

Today's illustrators have clearly gone far beyond Caldecott with their book jackets. Caldecott's covers are announcements of the contents, a montage of pieces of the stories to come. Illustrators now often want the jacket to do more — to develop character, to set a mood, to anticipate a theme.

Doctor De Soto, framed between the title and the author of William Steig's *Doctor De Soto*, poses for a picture, surrounded by all the equipment that pronounces him a dentist of great importance. He holds the drill so dear to him, so terrifying to all his patients, and leans comfortably on the chair so distasteful to them. His professional stance tells us he is ready for all comers. The flame is burning, the water drips, the drill is in his hand, and the chair is waiting. The reader is ready for a parade of patients, but the surprise visitor, a wily fox, is saved for what lies between the covers.

The cover of *Where the Wild Things Are* makes a true wrapping around the book, which is symbolically rapt in a dream. It is thus the first double-spread in the book, anticipating the climactic point when three double-spreads picture the rumpus. The stage is set. The trees on the cover stand clear and tall in the light of the moon; the boat is docked in the moving water. Although the wild thing is dozing, his raised foot waits for the story to begin — for Max's imagination to dream him awake and for Max to journey in the boat to the land where the wild things are.

In contrast, the wraparound cover of *Anno's Journey* is almost a medieval anticipation of aerial photography, showing from above the crisscrossing paths, the farms and fields, the people and their artifacts. Anno's book pictures a journey we see and recognize. Max's journey is the night journey of his mind.

The use of these covers as wrappers for their stories is not only symbolic but also a technique for preserving detail, which demands room — two pages are more than one. It is the artist's claim to space. Sendak uses both covers as an expression of the spaciousness of his fantasy. (When we dream, there are no boundaries.) Anno's is the spaciousness of reality. (There are more things in our own small world than we dream of.)

What today's illustrators understand is that picture books really deal with two story lines, the visual and the verbal; and they can be separately phased so as to reinforce, counterpoise, anticipate, or expand one another.

Caldecott and Wells, as we have seen, used the duality at the end —
pictures without words to hold the reader to the story. Artists like Steig
and Sendak use the same device at the beginning to lure the reader into the
story.

Sometimes the whole traditional configuration — cover, frontispiece,
and title page — is changed in new and creative ways. Take Tomie de
Paola's *Big Anthony and the Magic Ring*. The story actually begins with the
title and cover illustration. Big Anthony, stool in hand, is on his way to
milk the cow. The title page shows him sitting on the stool milking the cow
and introduces a second important character coming up over the hills. By
the time the text begins and the author identifies his characters, Big
Anthony has already managed, with the legs of his stool, to knock over the
pail and spill the milk. That tells us immediately that Big Anthony means
well but is not very successful.

In de Paola's *"Charlie Needs a Cloak"* the story also begins on the cover.
One sheep, the black-nosed one, has singled out Charlie for his affection
and attention. This story thus begins with a "leader," as do many of
today's films, and it continues on the title page, as the sheep prances
toward Charlie, and then on the verso of the title page — again a cinematic
device — to the text proper. By that time the sheep is practically kissing
"Poor Charlie."

Several years ago at the Boston Public Library, John Ciardi spoke about
endings. He said that the ending of a book must use up all of the story. He
used the metaphor of a fire so carefully laid that the ashes are equally
distributed — with no uneven lumps. One of the most effective ways a
good story does this is to come full circle by relating the beginning to the
end.

This circle technique is particularly effective in a picture book. For
example, the sheep is eating Charlie's tattered cloak at the beginning of
"Charlie Needs a Cloak." At the end when Charlie sports his newly woven
cloak, the sheep renews the never-ending cycle as he takes a fresh bite of
his own wool from Charlie's cloak. And at the start of *The Story of Ferdinand*,
the bull, minuscule and silhouetted, sits under his favorite cork tree,
imperceptible, though almost in the center of the page. At the end, free
from civilization and its threats, he rests on the other side of the tree, to
show that he has left and returned, and sits in total peace and contentment.

Likewise, when we meet Peter Rabbit on the first page of the book, we
see him only tail-side. He is finally completed at the end when we see,
drawn to exactly the same scale, his head peering over the covers. Sendak's
Wild Things opens with "The night Max wore his wolf suit" and ends with
the removal of the wolf cap and the emergence of the real boy. In *Anno's
Journey* Anno shows us first a tiny view of the scene we are about to enter
and closes with a mirror image of the same.

One reason beginnings come full circle is that this completes the logic. A good story is a tight story, which begins with a problem and derives the resolution from it. Start-and-finish pictures are the visual expression of this closure. The classic, archetypal closure theme is the quest — home-adventure-home. Schoolchildren understand this sequence almost instinctively. It is the story of their lives, the essence of growing up. The child's quest consists of repeated sorties from the love and safety of the home into the uncertainty of the outside world. Going to school is part of this quest; the child returns each time to the safety of home, a bit wiser and better prepared for the next encounter.

The presentation of home at the outset and the return to the caring home both figure strongly in picture books. Think of the loosely connected pictures of the characters at home at the start of such books as Steig's *Sylvester and the Magic Pebble*, Gág's *Millions of Cats*, and *"Charlie Needs a Cloak."* Then look at the cozy, comfortable circles of home at the end of these books.

Today's picture books are equally powerful in conveying metaphor. Pictures, even more than words, communicate symbolism and contribute a language of their own. By way of framing the issue, take the age-old battle of good and evil — innocence and experience — and look first at the chart called Literary Imagery in *The Child as Critic*, by Glenna Davis Sloan. Such items as blossoming tree, butterflies, dove, and new baby surround innocence, along with comedy and romance and the accompanying seasons of spring and summer. But experience — with irony, satire, tragedy, and the seasons of fall and winter — is surrounded by vulture, sword, haughty beauty, and leafless tree. This is the critic's dictionary of symbolism.

Now to a picture book. In *Ferdinand* the newborn bull, still unsteady on his gangly legs, sniffs a flower — a daisy, symbol of love — and a butterfly. His full-blossomed tree behind him, the safety of a fence, the warm spring day, and the sun high in the sky, casting its shadow directly beneath him, all attest to his innocence. The images of experience are just as marked, beginning with the vulture, the unmentioned character, and then the patched matador — haughty beauty surrounded by cut and embroidered flowers. The matador's sword is carried by a youth who hopes in turn to become a haughty beauty. Finally, in the happy ending, goodness triumphs, and the vulture who sat on the dead tree stump on Ferdinand's way to the bullring is replaced by birds of peace who herald him home.

It is, of course, unlikely that first and second graders or even younger children will understand innocence and experience as abstract ideas. Blake understood, however, that children do know the difference between the lamb and the tiger. If, therefore, you ask children what pleases or frightens them in a picture, what makes them feel happy, sad, friendly, safe, or in danger, you will have led them into reading and understanding ideas through symbols. In *"Charlie Needs a Cloak,"* for example, the children's happy-feeling answers to a picture of Charlie in his garden included a newborn lamb, the sunshine, pink clouds, flowers, a puddle of rain, green grass, and a fence to protect the sheep. With luck these images might even appear in their own stories.

Imagery is only one device for depicting mood and theme. More subtle is manipulating size and perspective. Here, we are still in the realm of metaphor: Big equals strong but sometimes stupid; small equals weak or frightened but sometimes happy. The context tells the meaning. When the duck decides to take his spanking — his point of recognition — in Marjorie Flack's *The Story About Ping*, Kurt Wiese's illustration shows him rising up out of the water, larger by far than in any other illustration. In contrast, he is smallest when he is trapped under the basket waiting to be served for dinner. Peter Rabbit suddenly shrinks, from the biggest and the only happy picture of him — when he is eating in the forbidden garden — to a small rabbit confronted by Mr. McGregor, his very large enemy. Max is large when he is king of the royal parade and again when he is a boy — no longer a wild thing — in his very own room. Ferdinand, on the other hand, is different from most heroes; he does not want to be seen or noticed, as we realize from the first page of the book. The biggest and most unhappy picture of him, therefore, shows one huge flank of the poor beast when he is about to be stung.

A somewhat different example is the artist's manipulation of size and shape in the total illustration. Once again, the picture contains metaphor. Tight bounds imply constraint — Peter trapped in the gooseberry net. Open borders imply freedom and fantasy — Max's walls dissolve to become the world all around. *Wild Things* is the most spectacular example of a book that uses the size and shape of illustrations to tell the story. Watch the first six illustrations explode from the confined world of Max's make-believe to the full world of his imagination. No borders, no limitations.

It is clear, then, that modern authors of picture book texts are free to choose their language as one part of a two-part invention or convention. There are things they do not have to say in words because the artist (who is often the author) will show them. It is one line of counterpoint against another; neither one crowds out the other. The result is great efficiency in communicating meaning — or to use the new language of contemporary discipline, high semantic or semiotic capacity. This is crucial with children, who have keen receptivity but limited reading endurance. Novelists can't work this way; they must spend a lot of time showing in words what a picture book shows through images.

Although language in picture books can be characterized by extreme economy, it is not exempt from the usual canons of style. Good writing is good writing at any level. Picture books are judged by their words as well as by their pictures.

I once asked Maurice Sendak whether the first line of *Wild Things* came naturally or whether he had to hammer it out. He said, "I'm sure it didn't come naturally. It had to be shaped and shaped. I think if there is any model I used, it's a kind of rough model of how children sound. I've listened to children playing, and that breathless pacing is what is so wonderful, and I'm trying to catch it." In that sentence he does. Sendak has also caught the alliteration and the caesura that characterize the verse of *Beowulf* or *Sir Gawain and the Green Knight*. Listen. "The night Max wore his wolf suit and made mischief of one kind" is an incomplete line that pushes you on to the next page; the open long *i* sound of *night* resonates on the word *kind* and holds you there for a moment. In that moment the reader rushes to see what mischief Max is making. In this remarkable opening line there is both stopping and going, tension and flow.

Suppose Sendak had written "A forest grew that very night in Max's room" instead of "That very night in Max's room a forest grew." Not only does he connect these three rhythmic phrases, which comprise six iambs, with assonance (that and Max, room and grew), but by inverting the normal word order, he saves the fantastic surprise for the end and turns prose into poetry. In addition, the use of the word *night* has "layers and layers of meaning" — a favorite Sendak phrase. Sendak begins the story, as we have just seen, with "The night Max made mischief." The mischief that night is made in a make-believe place, but the reality of that place is his very own room. (Note that all of these excerpts consist almost exclusively of one-syllable words.)

Beatrix Potter is another great writer-illustrator of the twentieth century. She once said that she chastened her style by reading the unrevised Old Testament. (She also memorized half the psalms and entire Shakespeare plays.) Compare Mr. McGregor's words when he goes to fetch a sieve "to pop upon the top of Peter" with the low style of a supermarket adaptation, "to pop a sieve over his head." Ask children which sounds better — "the tip of her tail twitched as if it were alive" or "the end of her tail waved back and forth." They will not only choose the right one, but they will tell you why.

How can we encourage children, for whom picture books are written, to dwell on a book, to select and choose, to enjoy the thrill of discovery that so many of them miss? Reading aloud to children is, of course, the primary requirement. But equally important is talking about books. Two simple questions can be asked over and over again and seem to open the book to them and to their imaginations. The first is simply "What do you see?" The child will look closely at the picture and point to things and see what he or she had not seen before. The second is "What does the picture tell that the text does not?" and vice versa. These questions send the children back and forth between picture and text, responding all the while to the wholeness of the story.

Picture books bring, as Robert Frost has said about poetry, "delight and wisdom" to the young reader. In this case, the wisdom is the initiation into literature. This is the way children become "readers" before they can read.

How I Found The Treasure

URI SHULEVITZ

I found *The Treasure* unexpectedly. At first, I didn't even know I was looking for it. But then, one can sometimes find better when not searching.

The Treasure is the story of Isaac, who dreams of a treasure in a distant land, of his journey there, and how he finds the treasure when he returns home. Similarities between Isaac's story and my own life contributed, no doubt, to my interest in it. The way I found the story and developed the right technique for the pictures seems in itself to me a kind of reenactment of Isaac's journey, and makes for a little tale all its own.

When I was a teenager in Israel, I read in a French novel by Romain Rolland, *The Enchanted Soul*, a retelling of an old Indian parable. The parable impressed me so much that, over ten years later, I still remembered it. At the time I was living in New York City, and I painted a series of small watercolors inspired by it. Occasionally, I even toyed with the idea of making a book out of it, and it was this idea that led me to search for its source. I made a number of trips to the New York Public Library, where I looked for the parable in ancient Indian scriptures, a literature I was totally unfamiliar with. Soon, I became convinced that it would be a very long search, and, furthermore, the chances of finding the parable were slim. Discouraged, I gave up.

Some time later, while browsing in a bookstore, I came across *Indian Myths and Symbols in Indian Art and Civilization,* by a German scholar, Heinrich Zimmer, and there, unexpectedly, I found the Indian parable. I bought the book at once. After a lengthy exploration of Indian culture, the author, to my surprise, closed his book with a Hasidic parable from eastern Europe. It was a retelling by Martin Buber of Rabbi Isaac and his dream.

A couple of years later I submitted the Indian parable to Clare Costello, then my editor at Farrar, Straus and Giroux. In a subsequent meeting she told me her reservations about it. As it turned out, she, too, was familiar with the story of Isaac and, as if reading my mind, suggested the Hasidic tale instead. In the meantime my interest in the Indian parable was declining, and now its sole purpose seemed to me to have been to lead me to the Hasidic tale and *The Treasure*. Having "traveled" through many books, I had found, quite unexpectedly, a tale from eastern Europe — my place of birth.

I plunged into the new project. The work was flowing and after a couple of months I had done the dummy and final sketches for *The Treasure*. In the meantime Clare Costello left Farrar, Straus. I stopped work on the book until Sandra Jordan became my new editor about a year later.

During this time I had been studying painting with Peter Hopkins, who taught me the techniques of the Old Masters of the Renaissance. Under his guidance I mixed my own oil paints from color pigments and made field trips to the Metropolitan Museum of Art to study the old paintings. Feeling enthusiastic about the Old Masters, I decided to try the oil painting techniques in illustrating *The Treasure*. After many attempts I was getting nowhere. These were followed by experiments with egg tempera, colored inks, opaque watercolors — but with the same results. I spent three months searching for the right technique until, finally, I came back to an old favorite of mine — transparent watercolors — a technique I felt at home with. Now the work was on the right track, and it took me another three months or so to complete the final illustrations.

Although I didn't use oil paints, and while painting the watercolors, I didn't think about the techniques of the Old Masters — at least not consciously — my experiments with the oil paints for the picture studies were coming through and enhancing the watercolors. It seemed to me that the illustrations were in the spirit of the Old Masters, something I hadn't seen in my work before. Nothing was wasted after all. The studies in various techniques that seemed to lead nowhere had actually enriched my work. The watercolors for *The Treasure* seemed to me a high point toward which I had been traveling for a long time.

When *The Treasure* became a book, I felt as if I were standing on top of a hill from which I could view some artistic and everyday occurrences, as well as some coincidences from my past, that converged and culminated with the book's completion. Like Isaac, I, too, had experienced years of hunger. When I was a child, for a period of over four years there wasn't a single night I didn't go to bed hungry. I, too, had dreams — dreams that helped me ease my hunger pains. But unlike Isaac's dreams, mine were of a humbler nature; no angels promising treasures, merely visions of enough bread to eat, which at the time seemed to me more fantastic than fairy tales. In fact, the story I asked to hear from my mother again and again was how after the war there would be as many rolls and as much butter as one could eat. I never got tired of hearing that story.

As a child, I also traveled a lot. We kept moving from one country to another. Ever since, I have been puzzled and fascinated by the idea of travel and what it means. It seemed to me that traveling *from* was not the same as traveling *to,* and that travel didn't necessarily lead somewhere, and that it could also be a waste of time. Therefore, when Isaac's dream turns out to be true, and when the purpose of his journey to another land turns out to be a way to discover what has been at home all along, it struck a deep chord in me. The story's eastern European background, identical to mine, only added to my emotional response. It was the combination of all these, rather than one single element in the story, that resonated with my own life.

Bothering to Look

A CONVERSATION BETWEEN
ROBERT McCLOSKEY AND
ETHEL HEINS

Ethel Heins: I am hoping that Robert McCloskey will re-create some of the stages in the artistic and literary journey of his remarkably creative life, a life that has added immeasurably to the reading and aesthetic development of children. But I must open by speaking of another journey, too, the journey of a young children's librarian — obviously me. It began in a large library many, many years ago in the Bronx, in New York, where I had arranged with the Viking Press to have Robert McCloskey come to speak to my reading club. It all happened so many years ago that some of the details have gone a bit fuzzy, but others are remarkably sharp. We had about three hundred children that evening, in absolutely breathless anticipation — when to my astonishment there arrived not only this already famous young man but his wife, Peggy; another children's librarian; his mother-in-law, Ruth Sawyer; and his noted editor, May Massee. It was a star-studded cast, which a young and inexperienced children's librarian could scarcely cope with, and I almost fainted. The year was 1942, and Bob McCloskey started by telling the boys and girls that he had just completed a new book of stories. And he proposed to read one of these stories aloud to the children because he really wanted them to tell him what incidents should be illustrated and because he also wanted their advice about exactly how to illustrate them. The story was "The Case of the Cosmic Comic." And you chose some children from the library — do you remember? — because you needed some models.
Robert McCloskey: I remember. I was also illustrating a textbook at the time, and I needed models. So I jumped at the opportunity of finding some children. I came away with four of your audience — four of my audience — two boys and also two girls, to come in several times a week and pose for me.

326

Heins: And, of course, by coming in, he means traipsing all the way down from the Bronx to Greenwich Village, where Bob was then living; so it was quite a journey — but, needless to say, their parents were quite pleased about it. One thing I remember very distinctly was his saying to this great group of children, "Now, the story is about some boys who come home from school, and they read the comics in the local newspaper; and how do you think this picture should look? Where do you read the comics?" And they all shouted, as in one voice, "On the floor!" So if you look in *Homer Price*, you will see that the boys have indeed come home from school and are reading the comics on the floor.

Freckles, upturned nose, ingenuity, a bit of mischief. Is this immortal boy Tom Sawyer? Or is he Homer Price? Or is he Bob McCloskey himself? This terribly real boy romps with devastating humor through two books of dilemmas involving radio robbers, Superman, musical mousetraps, an implacable doughnut machine, mass production, a mad scientist, a wild jukebox, all these and more in books that have been called tremendous pieces of Americana. This is the kind of local Americana, however, that encompasses the whole world of boyhood; it really is universal boyhood. And, Bob, would you tell us how much of you is Homer? How much of you is Lentil? And how much of Hamilton, Ohio, is in both books?

McCloskey: That's a large order. There has to be a little bit of me in all of it, I guess. To begin with, every artist, when he starts out to make a drawing, has a little bit of himself in it; I don't know if you've ever noticed it, but Fritz Eichenberg's lions look a little bit like Fritz. And Jimmy Daugherty's Abraham Lincoln looks a little bit like Jimmy Daugherty; his Daniel Boone is Jimmy Daugherty again. And not so much now, but back when I had a crew cut years ago, even my ducks looked a little bit like me. Of course, Homer looked a lot like me. We started out to say how much of me is in the books. I was a counselor at a boys' camp, and I made drawings, drawings, and drawings of boys, and there are a lot of composite pictures of lots and lots of boys.

Heins: Well, Homer is frequently sitting in front of a huge pile of gadgetry and work-in-progress, I would call it. Weren't you an inveterate mechanical inventor?

McCloskey: That's part of my growing up, those scenes in the bedroom with all the gadgets and things: "Pick up your room, pick up your room."

Heins: Didn't you invent a contraption for your mother, a mechanical whipping-cream device or something?

McCloskey: After seeing this sugar candy — cotton candy — being made at the circus, I tried to make one of those machines. And the basis of it was a vacuum cleaner motor and a dishpan and a few pieces of my

Meccano. I tried it; I poured on the sugar, and, of course, nothing happened; the sugar just went dribbling like sand. Being a gourmet candy cook, I knew that you had to melt sugar to make it sticky, so I knew this wheel had to be hot to melt it and make it into a molasseslike mixture. And I had no know-how at that time; I didn't know how to make the wheel hot. So I figured, well, why not take a shortcut and pour molasses on it, which I did. And the molasses hit the wheel, and it made a band of molasses that went right across me; and right around the kitchen wall, the curtains, the sink, the refrigerator, there was a band of molasses. It wouldn't have been so bad if it had been light molasses, but it was dark molasses. Well, anyway, it was a band of icky stuff that took a long time to scrub off.

Heins: Oh, I'll bet. But the thing that fascinated me, Bob, is that your mechanical ingenuity and dexterity are combined with a good deal of interest in and talent for music. This combination of interests is not at all uncommon; in fact, it is a very common combination, and it appeared in *Lentil* with the harmonica, and with Michael Murphy and that glorious musical mousetrap contraption.

McCloskey: I sold the mousetrap story to Weston Woods, because they were going to make it into a movie. They got as far as having a car to build a mousetrap on, but at the same time they were working on the script for the "Cosmic Comic," and they dropped the mousetrap project and concentrated on the "Cosmic Comic." They had someone working there, one of the young fellows, who was interested in gadgets and movie effects, but he was more interested in trying the spaceship and the rockets and things in "Cosmic Comic" than the mechanical mousetrap in the musical mousetrap story.

Heins: I think the mousetrap story would have made a movie easily as good as the doughnut one because this contraption is absolutely Rube Goldberg — a marvelous gadget. And there's also a lovely literary allusion. The children's librarian — she's Peggy, and she's right there in the book — runs in near the end of the story, shouting, "It's not *Rip Van Winkle*, it's *The Pied Piper of Hamelin!*"

McCloskey: That was, I think, the first time Peggy had ever posed for me, that particular drawing. I used her as a model for *Blueberries for Sal,* but she wasn't very cooperative when I was doing that book. She was pregnant with Jane at the time and pretty cranky about it, I remember.

Heins: She doesn't look very pregnant to me; here, in the book, is Peggy Durand McCloskey as I knew her. When this book came out, I was astounded at the wonderful likeness.

Speaking of mechanical inventiveness and ingenuity, Peggy said in 1958, when you got your second Caldecott Medal, that you claimed your "greatest contribution to the war effort was inventing a machine to enable short second lieutenants to flip over large charts in a high breeze." By that time even Peggy had picked up this predilection for tall tales.

McCloskey: Well, you know, that wasn't a tall tale; it's true — I invented it, and I didn't get any medal for it. I came out of the army along with a boy who'd gotten a medal for boning chicken for a general. He had this knack of removing all the bones and keeping the skin on and making the chicken look exactly as it had. Well, he got a medal, but I didn't get any medal for making this chart turner. I think that was equally deserving.

Heins: Absolutely. Unfortunately, Bob, I have no pull with the Pentagon, so I think we'll have to let the matter rest, once and for all.

Homer Price! What an incredible Greek revival took place in Centerburg. You begin the book with that wonderful, wonderful drawing of the bust of Homer — the Greek Homer — with the head toppled off, lying on the floor, and this twentieth-century all-American boy lounging over the pedestal. What prompted you to have Uncle Ulysses as the chief character — Uncle Ulysses, who runs around constantly saying, "Zeus!" Nowadays, of course, he'd say something quite different. As if that weren't enough, there is Uncle Ulysses' brother with the astonishing name of Telemachus; and then in the story called "Mystery Yarn," that crafty Miss Terwilliger with her suitors and her pink knitted dress and her blue knitted dress and her secret unraveling — what can she be but another Penelope?

McCloskey: No, that hadn't occurred to me, it really hadn't.

Heins: Oh, I had it all figured out, you see, because the dress was curiously unraveled.

McCloskey: No, I just had to pick a name. I was probably like the man in New York — he had to be interested in the classics, that surveyor who went across upstate New York and named everything after classic towns. I started with the name Homer, and the others just sort of fell into place.

Heins: You even stopped up the boys' and girls' ears with cotton so they wouldn't be able to hear the music of the musical mouse-trapping machine, as in the episode of the Sirens in the *Odyssey*.

McCloskey: Nowadays, anything goes, but those were the days in children's books when I had May Massee as my editor. Someone asked me recently what May Massee was like, and I said she was sort of like a velvet hammer.

Heins: Yes, that sounds right.

McCloskey: Nice silver-haired little old lady with glasses, and hard as nails. And she called up right before *Homer Price* was going to go to press, and she said, "Bob, we cannot have 'Mystery Yarn' — can't you just write another one or something?" And I said, "No, I can't write another one." Marian Rous was there at the time, and Marian said, "Oh, we can't have that story because Miss Terwilliger cheated." She cheated by unraveling her dress, and that was underhanded. That was a really sneaky thing for her to do.

Heins: She *was* crafty. How did you get around it?

McCloskey: Well, I got around it by adding one paragraph, and Marian was the one who came along with the idea for it, saying, "Look, we solved it." I had Miss Terwilliger really save the yarn that she was unraveling, so it wasn't cheating. By a technicality it was saved yarn. She kept knitting the dress longer and shorter as the styles changed, and she kept it on the shelf, you see, so when she unraveled her dress, she didn't unravel it past the —

Heins: Past the knees —

McCloskey: Past the critical point. So it was all saved yarn. It wasn't cheating.

Heins: Don't you love our 1940s reticence?

McCloskey: Well, it wasn't reticence in that respect. The yarn could not be just any old yarn that was on a dress, even if it was the same color; it had to be yarn that had been saved — same as being wound on a ball. And after the explanation May grudgingly said, "All right," so there was the story.

Heins: Somebody still has to write a whole book of May Massee anecdotes. Is it any sort of coincidence — I'm sure you were a reading child because you certainly were not a television child even though you were a radio child — is it a coincidence that you injected one story with a Pied Piper and lots of stories with the *Odyssey?* And the doughnut machine sort of reverberates with echoes of "Why the Sea Is Salt" and other stories of that type. Were these maybe implanted in you as a reading child?

McCloskey: Well, yes, but then "nothing new under the sun." Or hardly.

Heins: It's very interesting because we hope that modern children growing up to be writers might have similar things implanted in them from having been reading children, too; we don't know.

You mentioned James Daughtery before, who was lovingly known in my tender years as Jimmy, a most magnificent draftsman and a wonderful critic, too. And this is what he said about the drawing in *Homer Price:* "The satire is warm and genial and tolerant, so you feel the pictures are the product of a warm and generous mind as well as a shrewd and witty recording of familiar scenes — the true comedy of democracy in a great American tradition." And then he said the book "is America laughing at itself . . . without bitterness or sourness or sophistication." Now that's a long mouthful, probably guaranteed to make you clam up and be silent, but I wonder if you could comment on it, because this book has been called a genuine piece of Americana with its midwestern Ohio ambience, and thoroughly democratic and terribly American in every sense of the word. Did it come naturally? Of course it did, but were you aware of it as you were doing the work?

McCloskey: Well, I guess I was aware of it to some extent, because if you remember back in the thirties in the Depression days, Americana was the big theme of American art; we were just beginning to discover ourselves. If you remember the days of the WPA and the rest, there was a lot of Americana in all the art; we were very saturated with it back in those days.

Heins: That's right, and, of course, we were catapulted from the Depression into the war, which emphasized it even more.

McCloskey: We were sort of tossing out a lot of artiness that had come over from abroad, and I think that a lot of this feeling came naturally, and some of it I acquired; the two are inseparable in some ways. The French can't seem to stand my books; they don't touch them — they're too American for the French taste.

Heins: And yet, the French are terribly fond of the Laura Ingalls Wilder books, for instance; they adore them and love them for the openness and the freedom, which are precisely what I think they would find in your books.

McCloskey: Well, I don't know.

Heins: Of course, you really began as an illustrator, and May Massee was a genius, no question about it; she may have been a velvet hammer, but it was the hammering that produced the result.

McCloskey: You have said that I had this sort of big rush of creative things, and you have given a few dates, but dates don't really mean anything to me, and I can't remember them; but there was a big rush of material from me at one time, although not all of it was thought up or done at that particular time. May was just a crafty sort of person — she was a really knowledgeable dame. She ran a pretty tight ship at Viking Press, and she had her stable of authors, and if you remember children's publishing back in those days, you know there weren't all that many publishers, and they didn't do all that many books every year. And she had a list of maybe eight, ten books and sometimes fewer, and other publishers would have about the same, about half a dozen — some a few more, maybe a hundred or so books published every year, maybe two hundred.

Heins: Surely, by that time, there were more than that.

McCloskey: Anyway, not too many for her to keep tabs on what people were doing and what was coming up. I think she sort of placed these books and timed them a little bit like a poker game. She was going to put this book out on the table and balance her list, and I think she did very well at it.

Heins: She was a very powerful influence.

McCloskey: Yes, she was a powerful influence, and I have a feeling that she may have sat on something I was doing for a year or two until she got something else out of the way, and then she cleared the slates and said, "O.K.; now it's time for you to get to work on this."

Heins: Didn't you say somewhere that she told you to get rid of all the dragons and the limpid pools and learn how to do your own kind of thing?

McCloskey: That was true. There was a lot of that influence on me in Boston at that time.

Heins: Well, I'm afraid that some of the dragons and the limpid pools, the black drama and the high art, have crept back into some of the work for children. Was there, outside of May Massee, a definite inspiration behind the style of art that you chose, or something on which you more or less looked as a model? I somehow feel there was not; I feel as though it was just absolutely yourself being expressed in the best possible way, but maybe I'm wrong.

McCloskey: I don't know. I guess things creep in. I tried as best I could to draw as well as I could at any given time, and I tried as best I could to pick something and put a line around it, to the best of my ability. I tried not to think too much of style; and I think that I'm enough of a craftsman and a graphic artist and a printmaker that a lot of the way my things look was dictated by the medium I was using at the moment — whether it was lithography or brush-and-ink or pen-and-ink, or whether later on it was gouache or watercolor.

Heins: I think we all know by now that a great deal of your work was essentially autobiographical. Obviously, *Lentil* was, which came out in 1940.

McCloskey: That book has a lot of me in it. I did play the harmonica as a boy, but I did not go barefoot every day because I didn't dare do that; my mother wouldn't allow it.

Heins: By the way, you came to Boston to do murals, and I actually have never known where those murals are.

McCloskey: Well, it wasn't my commission; I was working as an assistant. There were two assistants — Marc Simont was the other — and the two of us were working on those murals; we were working for a painter by the name of Bradford. And the murals are in what is now the M.I.T. Faculty Club on Memorial Drive. They're still there. They were painted for Lever Brothers — that building was their headquarters — and they were to be a sort of monument to an English gentleman who was head of Lever Brothers. He was about to retire and wanted to leave this big memorial. And he did, and Mr. Luckman came in immediately afterward, moved the whole company to New York, sold off the building, and built that tremendous thing full of glass in New York that became the Lever Brothers Building.

Heins: But it was while you were here, I think, working on the murals, that you read the story of the peripatetic ducks — is that right?

McCloskey: Well, I saw them here in the Public Garden. We had a studio on Otis Place, a nice little sort of a back-corner street.

Heins: If there are any people who don't know the story of the ducks in the bathtub in Greenwich Village, I think it would be lovely if you told them a bit about it. Obviously, you found your inspiration in Boston, but you did your work in New York.

McCloskey: Well, back then I was so full of myself, and there I was with a book to do and the illustrations, too. Today if I were doing this book, I would find a spot in the country next to the mallards, and we would live together happily. But then I had to be in the center, where the action was, and so I brought the ducks to New York, and they lived in my studio on Twelfth Street, along with Marc and me, and I made all of my duckling — and duck — drawings there.

Heins: What happened to the ducks when the book was finished?

McCloskey: They went to — I like to think that they all — well, actually, there were two sets of ducks. I like to think that they all went to the country and ended their lives happily. Some of them did go to Connecticut and live in the brook in Cornwall; some of them fell by the wayside in New York. I remember, though, feeding mother and father mallards wine to slow them down so they would be more accommodating and I could draw them more easily.

Heins: The thing that astonished me years ago and astonishes me still is that you started out to be an artist. And whether it was May Massee literally pulling the writing out of you or whether you would have done it anyway, I don't know. But you certainly turned into a very fine writer, because obviously most of the books are yours. Some of them you only illustrated — a few by other authors — but *Homer* and *Centerburg Tales* are, or are said to be, Mark Twain almost reconstituted; they're remarkably well done, and they endure. Here, for instance, is a tiny example of cadenced, economical storytelling in *Blueberries for Sal:* "Little Sal's mother slowly backed away. (She was old enough to be shy of bears, even very small bears like Little Bear.)" And just before that, "Little Bear's mother turned around to see what on earth could make a noise like *kuplunk! 'Garumpf!'* she cried, choking on a mouthful of berries. 'This is not my child! Where is Little Bear?' She took one good look and backed away. (She was old enough to be shy of people, even a very small person like Little Sal.)" That's not only compact and elegant picture-book writing, but it's also very beautifully balanced writing. Did you ever really know, when you were tinkering with arts and crafts and teaching boys how to do little soap sculptures, that you were going to be a writer as well as an artist?

McCloskey: No.

Heins: It just sort of came spontaneously, or did May —?

McCloskey: May liked my drawings, and she said, "I haven't anything for you to illustrate, and why don't you go home and write something?" And, well, that was it. Of course, she did that not only with me; I suspect she did the same with Jimmy Daugherty, and I know she did it with Ludwig Bemelmans. She went to Bemelmans's restaurant one night and saw some things that he'd painted on the wall, and suddenly he was no longer a cook and a maître d', but an artist and a writer.

Heins: That happened before my time in New York, but it was a legend even then. The elegant simplicity of your books, I think, is one of the great reasons why they have lived and lived and lived — *Ducklings* and *One Morning in Maine,* still with that marvelous firm line and the lack of any pretense. In *Blueberries for Sal* we have another journey, of course, and although it's only on one small mountain in Maine, for a four-year-old child it was a great journey, and certainly for a small bear it was a great journey. And in *One Morning in Maine* you have a small odyssey over the water, along with the symbolism of the lost tooth.

McCloskey: I guess, come to think of it, that's the form that a lot of my books took — a sort of walk, such as Lentil's or the ducklings'; it hadn't occurred to me. I guess the book that would be different from that would be *Time of Wonder.* Even *Burt Dow* is, I think, a sort of adventure that moves, from here to there.

Heins: And a marvelous journey in a text Ruth Sawyer did for you to illustrate, *Journey Cake, Ho! Journey Cake, Ho!* is of course a wonderful Southern-Mountain-sounding version of the famous johnnycake story — "The Bun" in the Russian folklore — it's universal. Did Ruth Sawyer make it up, or did she actually find this version in Appalachia?

McCloskey: She may have found this story in Appalachia — it's a universal tale that she adapted for recitation with orchestra, on the order of *Peter and the Wolf.* She and a composer from Philadelphia, Isadore Fried, collaborated on an opera — I guess you'd call it an opera — something done on some sort of grant from the Hartt School of Music in Hartford; but along with that collaboration grew this idea of doing a *Peter and the Wolf* type of thing with *Journey Cake.* Isadore composed the music for this, and it was going to have some songs in it as well as some orchestral background. I remember hearing years ago a rare recording that they'd made of some of the songs, but I don't remember any orchestral background. Whether it ever got as far as any full orchestration, I don't know; but I do know that was the original idea. One day it occurred to

her that the story might make a good picture book. May Massee agreed,
and I produced the pictures.

Heins: This all comes as a total revelation to me — it's a book I've known
ever since it came out, but I don't think it is nearly as well known as the
books you have done yourself. It was out of print for a while, but Viking
brought it back, and as far as I know it's in print now.

McCloskey: Originally, the book was printed on a cream-colored stock.
Back in the May Massee days no effort was too great in order to do a book
exactly the way you wanted to do it. I picked this particular shade of
cream-colored paper, and it was going to have to be made to order. And
that, of course, meant that you go to the paper mill and order the paper
made for this particular book. So it occurred to them that they could
never again get the same shade of cream-colored paper, so they took
white sheets of paper and ran them through the press one time, printing
them all-over cream color before printing the book. That was the way the
book started: a first printing of just plain cream color on the paper — you
can see that process wouldn't last long in these days of conglomerates
and cost-cutting.

Heins: Obviously not.

McCloskey: The paper got less and less creamy, and now I think it is
almost white.

Heins: Those of us who are somewhat advanced in years know all this to
be true; it is simply one more indication of what was considered in those
days — what you did when you created a book for children. There was
no limit to the pains taken and to the care expended, because a children's
book was considered a terribly important thing — particularly, of course,
by publishers like Viking, but there were other publishers, too, that
worked in the same way.

Now let's talk about *Time of Wonder*. It's quite obvious it had to be in
color. The book is a perfect example of using color only because nothing
but color could have conveyed the full visual effect of what you were
doing. The violent moods of weather, the undulating landscape, the
modulating color of things in sunshine and in storm. I have two
questions about the book. Was it a great hump to get over, deciding you
were going to work in full color, or did it come as a natural evolvement?

McCloskey: Well, I wanted to work in full color long before, but they
couldn't afford it.

Heins: By the fifties they could.

McCloskey: If I'd had the technical know-how, I might have done
Ducklings in color.

Heins: I'm so glad you didn't; it's perfect as it is.

McCloskey: Back then, I wanted to do it in full color, but if I had done that,

I would have had to do it on lithographic plates and make separations. I would have had to make four plates for each page, and as it is, the drawings are lithographs, but they're done on zinc, and only one drawing was done per page. And, of course, a layman would think that I made those drawings with brown chalk on a piece of paper, but, no, I made them with black lithographic crayon on the gray plates, and then in the printing process they ended up with the color of ink that we used and then the color of the paper — which is something you have to keep in mind when you make your sketches. You must think in terms of what the finished thing is going to look like instead of what's here in front of you, which often just hasn't a feel of the drawing that finally ends up in the book. You have to translate that in your mind. The same way with *Journey Cake, Ho!*; for that book there were several drawings made for each finished picture, and the color was all added on from the thought in my head and from the sketches I made beforehand. The plates that I made, the separations I made for each drawing, don't look like the finished product at all until they finally went through the press with the colors of ink that I chose. And, of course, one thing about the cream-colored background — it changes the character entirely; if they change that cream to white, it takes the umph, the everything, right out of all those drawings. It irritates me; I can barely stand to look at it printed on white paper. But we got off *Time of Wonder*.

Heins: I know, but let's go back a bit. I have said for about seven years in my course called "Art and Text" that *Make Way for Ducklings* is an absolutely perfect book; it doesn't require color. This book and books like *Millions of Cats* and Tom Robinson's *Buttons* — these are books that show it isn't color alone that attracts children; it's many other factors.

McCloskey: I feel that you're right. I think *Ducklings* is better without color. I have been approached by people who have said, "Why don't you redo it in color," and I have resisted.

Heins: Well, thank you for resisting. The other thing about *Time of Wonder* — getting back to that, which *is* in color, and beautiful, glorious color — is the fascinating use of the second-person pronoun throughout. "You" did this, and "you" did that. It's very effective, but what made you decide to do it?

McCloskey: I don't know. It's probably something you would make a very definite decision about if your training were all as a writer. I would perhaps make a decision like that about a color or a way of doing something as an artist or a craftsman or a printmaker. But I wouldn't make it as a writer.

Heins: It just came out that way, then?

McCloskey: It just came out that way. There are people who know all about writing, who make unconscious or arbitrary decisions about their drawings to go with it; you ask them why, and they don't know.

Heins: I suppose instinct does it.

McCloskey: Yes, I guess it's instinct.

Heins: I said before that your work is so autobiographical that after the army, when you and your family went to live in Maine, the books switched from *Lentil, Homer Price,* and *Centerburg Tales,* all set in Ohio, to the ones with the Maine backgrounds. Eleanor Cameron, a novelist and critic, has spoken of her love of the sea, the sea at the other end of this continent (she's a Californian), and of the "somber facade of blackish green" forest that can be seen from the shore, which, of course, is exactly what had such a profound and pervasive effect on your work. I would love to talk for a moment about what I call that most magnificent piece of American hyperbole, which is *Burt Dow: Deep-Water Man.* Is Burt Dow a real person and still up there in Deer Isle?

McCloskey: No, not now; he died.

Heins: But he was a real person?

McCloskey: He's buried up there.

Heins: It's a marvelous book, and I love it.

McCloskey: Oh, Burt was a great friend of ours. My children, too, adored Burt.

Heins: What was he like?

McCloskey: Oh, really a very shy fellow, a wonderful guy. He loved children, and when we were off on a picnic — he often used to come on picnics with us — he would end up by entertaining the children. He didn't have a lot of words, not much to say, but he would tie knots for them. And he would keep them busy for hours just watching him tie those amazing knots.

Heins: What did this gentleman called Burt Dow think of the paces you put him through? I mean, here we have a story that starts with the biblical tradition and then sweeps in (talk about heroic tales) with references perhaps to *Moby Dick.* It's pure Jackson Pollock inside the whale's tummy; and there's that marvelous line, "It was the first time he'd ever had a chance really to express his personality in paint." Oh, what a wonderful thing.

McCloskey: Oh, well, I think all that Jackson Pollock part went over Burt's head, but he liked the story. When I finished the dummy, I was down in New York; so I got in the car, drove up to Maine, took the story in, and showed it to Burt. It was the middle of winter, as a matter of fact, and there was snow, but Burt was there next to the stove in the kitchen. He read the story, and on the back of the dummy he wrote, "I like this story, and you can use my name in it." He gave me written permission to use it. Of course, it took me over a year after that, making the final drawings — watercolor, they were, casein paintings — and Burt used to drop by occasionally to look over my shoulder and see what was happening, how they were going along.

Heins: And poor Ginny Poor does have a pantry, I assume.

McCloskey: Ginny Poor is her maiden name, and she still lives there in Deer Isle; she has a pantry — it isn't pink — and Doc Walton isn't really the local doctor's name; but I used Doc Walton, which is Ginny's husband's name. She's really Ginny Walton. So, here are two friends of Burt's, and I have used them; the trim wasn't green and the pantry wasn't pink; I just picked those colors because they clashed well together.

Heins: Was Leela really Burt's sister?

McCloskey: Leela really was Burt's sister.

Heins: Oh, poor Burt.

McCloskey: Unfortunately, Leela died right before I managed to get under way with the final version of this book, so she didn't see it, but Burt agreed that I could use her. Burt also had a brother named Frank, and Frank sort of got left out. He wasn't such a good friend of ours, and he took this in stride. Burt seemed to get mixed up in things more than Frank, somehow. Frank's biggest claim to fame was that he was captain of the boat that the movie actor fellow, Leslie Howard, chartered the time he spent the summer on Deer Isle.

Heins: I wonder if I could just sneak in one or two more or less philosophical questions about picture books, based on things that you yourself have said. Way back in 1942 when you accepted your first Caldecott Medal, you hinted that children's taste could indeed be formed by good books and that children, in your own words, I think, "could be turned into art appreciators if they were given fine books at the right moments in their lives." Now, do you still feel that way? This was a very long time ago.

McCloskey: Yes, I still feel that way.

Heins: Well, so do we; that's fine.

McCloskey: I remember one time — I think it was in Milwaukee; maybe it was St. Paul — they were trying to get people who were artists to have lunch with me, and they had a person who had a job in the art school there; and he indeed felt that children's taste could be molded by picture books, and he looked me up and down and said, "Of course." Obviously, he didn't include me or my work in the things that were going to improve their tastes at all. "You have to get them with the right stuff early," he said, and mine very definitely wasn't the right stuff.

Heins: It leaves me speechless because, of course, we all think it *is* the right stuff.

McCloskey: Well, that's the way. Win a few, lose a few.

Heins: I'd like to bring in something you said which was incredibly trenchant and at the same time prophetic. It was years ago, 1958, sixteen years after the first statement, and I'm going to read one or two things that you said then because I am really quite stunned by the analogies to what we think nowadays. You said, "With everyone clamoring for more sciences, I should like to clamor for more artists and designers. I should like to clamor for the teaching of drawing and design with every child, right along with reading and writing. I think it is most important for everyone to see and evaluate pictures and to see and evaluate surroundings." And you were talking about a course of study to develop a visual sense, not the kind of art that, as you pointed out, children are encouraged to do — a vague kind of self-expression. You said this was fine and very important, but that children also should literally be taught to read pictures and to have their own built-in sense of design. I wonder if you could comment on this far more serious topic we've arrived at.

McCloskey: I think what I feel is lacking is the ability to look at something and evaluate it and know what you're seeing. And I think so many people just don't look at something and take it in; they really have to run it through a computer before they believe it, and even then they won't believe it. Acid rain, for instance. You can look around you and see what's happening from acid rain and show it to people, and they still want to run some more tests and get some more figures. They won't believe it; they won't believe it. They've never really looked at a tree, and they don't know the difference between a healthy tree and an unhealthy tree. It's just such a simple basic thing, not bothering to look, and they don't even see what they're seeing when they're looking at the television set. They're being fooled all the time.

Heins: And this is a lack of perception.

McCloskey: A lack of perception. Their eyes are not trained. They just don't register.

Heins: Certainly one's perception is not trained by looking at the television screen; that's about the last place perception could be sensitized or trained. You also said that nature is going to be designed right out of our own environment because everything is being machine-designed, machine-made — new fabrics, new design, new man-made materials. You talked about shopping centers and gas stations, overpasses, and underpasses (this was 1958, you see), and then ended up a long list of uglifications with houses with picture windows looking right out on the highway — such an abomination. And it's true; it's a question of people's not learning how to see and not realizing what they are seeing.

Remember the marvelous story at the end of *Homer Price* called "Wheels of Progress," which is devastating in its irony, and yet the irony is not over the heads of children, not in the least. Remember that illustration showing all the houses, all looking exactly alike, and because the man who put up the street signs had gone on strike for more pay, everybody got lost. This is the reductio ad absurdum — no one could find his or her way home, there were no street signs, every house looked exactly the same; it's a wonderful story that, I think, is apropos not only now but probably for the next century as well.

I'll just end with something I think you said. "It has been said a picture is worth a thousand words, but it's not worth *anything* unless the person who made the picture had something really to say." You said that, didn't you?

McCloskey: Yes, I did, yes. Well, you can't get anything more out of it than what's put into it.

A Strange Balance of Joy and Pain

TOM FEELINGS

When I heard Maurice Sendak speak, one of the things that went through my mind was the parallels between us. We were both born in Brooklyn; both exposed to American popular art — comic books, Mickey Mouse — as a matter of fact, I started off as a cartoonist. And we are both American. But at some point I think the parallels stop. He refers to his influences, and the influences that seem to have the strongest hold on him are what I would consider high art influences, which are mostly European. He refers to painters, the opera, musicians, and though I've been influenced by the same music, I suppose because I've lived here all my life, I think it's secondhand. My major musical influence, I believe, was blues, jazz — the music that comes from Black people, which in this society was always considered, I suppose, maybe not American and not African but from a subculture.

It took me about twenty-five or twenty-six years to realize that influence and what it meant to me. That's when I started drawing exclusively in the Black community. At that point I began to pull away from the things that I was taught in art school; the only artist I remember connecting with very closely was Goya — and those artists who seemed to me to have an emotional impact in their work. The kind of things that are now called *timeless, eternal,* and *everlasting* — to me that means things that are grounded in the past but also are linked to the present, even if they are linked only in that you get an emotional rush from them when you see the paintings or hear the music.

People ask me why I still concentrate on Black subject matter exclusively. I'd like to tell you a story about something that happened in 1968. A writer wanted to do a book called "On the Spot Drawing." He was an artist who drew from life because he felt there were so many artists working from photographs that they were somehow losing touch with the community.

341

He got in touch with me because he'd seen some drawings of mine in a magazine. We met, he said he hadn't known I was Black. He had seen my drawings and liked them and wanted to include me in this book of twelve different artists. As it happened, I was the only Black artist. When he said he was going to write the text, I insisted that he make it clear that I am Black. He responded with, "Well, I don't know why you would want that. I mean, we're all just artists and you don't need to be seen as Black. You know we're all the same, basically." I said, "No, based on my history and what I understand, and also knowing where this book will be going and hoping that there will be Black children who'll see it, I want you to make it very clear that I'm Black." We argued about it for a couple of days, and he wrote something and read it to me over the telephone, and I said, "No, that's not what I want said." Finally, he came over with his little girl — she was about three years old — and he sat and talked to me: Why did I want to be included as a Black? The same kind of thing. And I said, "Look at your little girl watching TV. Suppose every time she turned on the television she had only Black images to relate to in terms of her own identity. After a while, she'd begin to question who she was." He sat and thought about it, and then he went back and wrote something that ended up saying we all know how we have been affected by great art and how it has affected us and changed the world. But what about the art that was never allowed to be? All those Black children who were artists but who were not given the chance to be artists, for one, and, more important, were not even encouraged to draw the things that were around them, the things they saw that were important — their mothers, their fathers, their communities. . . . Well, I think he understood what I meant only when I focused on his child.

I don't mean to say that that was the direct reason for my drawing children; it might have been an indirect reason. I went out in the streets to draw. When I asked adults if I could draw them, there were women who said, "Let me comb my hair." There were men who said, "I'm too busy." I was kind of shy anyway. Then there were the children. I found out — when I went over to a child and asked to do a drawing — that children, if they see you like them, give it right back. And sometimes they don't even ask to see the drawing. That activity is enough for them. I spent most of my time, then, drawing from life — drawing from life, which connected me with the community, because I had to talk to people, listen to what was being said, and even when I didn't say anything, absorb what was going on. When I went back into the studio, which was my mother's small kitchen, and painted the pictures, I really was connecting two things: my need to be a part of the community and attach my art to the community, and also, my need to put in what I felt — if I could.

As I said, while I was in art school, I directed a lot of my feelings toward those artists who had an emotional content to their work. At that time it was said that Black people had always been considered very emotional, in some cases too emotional, but I consider that to be a part of my heritage now. If being very emotional had anything to do with keeping me from becoming cold and indifferent to the things that went on around me, I think that's a plus. And if I can transfer emotion to my artwork, that's even more of a plus. There's a quote from Aaron Douglas, a Black painter who came out of the Atlanta School: "The technique itself is not enough. It is more important for the artist to develop the power to convey emotion. The artist's technique, no matter how brilliant it is, should never obscure his vision."

For most of my life I've worked to develop an emotional content in my artwork. I make no distinction between illustration and fine art, except that as a Black illustrator I am a storyteller in picture form. I'm expected to reflect and interpret Black life as honestly as I can. For me this is a natural extension of the African oral tradition of storytelling and therefore a functional art growing out of a direct need of mine to communicate on a large scale to the massive group of Black people, young and old. This pinpoints for me my particular responsibility as an artist and a book illustrator. The last twenty years of my life I have sometimes chosen to live outside of America, and at those times I sat, thought, and questioned America's values in a relatively free atmosphere without being surrounded, bombarded, or exposed to them daily in the media of the U.S.A. Now I've already spoken about that little girl standing in front of the television set. If she were to see Black images every day, how she would look at herself? So when I speak to you about being bombarded with images, that's what I mean. In the last two decades I think I've found the kind of personal clarity and understanding that come out of my own life's experiences and the experiences of people who came before me and left some important guides for me and others to pick up on.

What is an illustrator? A storyteller in picture form. A good illustrator both reflects and interprets life. Illustrated books are important in shaping images in positive and negative ways. At their worst they can teach racism, reinforce self-hatred and stereotypes — and they can lie. At their best, by exposing the viewer to the finest work an artist can produce, they can stretch the child's mind and strengthen his or her spirit, preparing the child to face reality by rejecting the shallow and slick and by helping to develop a sharp creative mind ready to accept the truth. If painting is supposed to change or intensify our perception of reality, thereby producing a lasting effect on the beholder, then book illustration can be a high form of functional art, for it can communicate on a large scale and to a large group of people and in a very personal way. You have to sit down, shut out everything else, and *read* a book and *read* the pictures. It's hard to do that with the television on.

Now, what do Black illustrators have that is different and unique to bring to this world of book illustration? I believe Black artists can bring a quality that is grounded in the culture of Africa and expanded on by the experience of being Black in the Americas — a quality already steeped in Black tradition rooted in Africa. Before slavery and after, the oral tradition brought from Africa was carried on — telling tales and singing songs that provided entertainment, passed on messages, and communicated our fears, hopes, dreams, and fantasies, our explanation of the world, our vision of reality, and our sense of truth. This oral tradition was a vital educational tool for Black children; now it is less strong. Today our direct links between generations are being broken. Illustrated books and picture books, which are natural extensions of the African storyteller, can help fill in the place of folk memory. The Black artist can awaken in the viewer a sense of awe, wonder, and participation in the beautiful mystery of life, its pain and joys. For Black people in particular, pain and joy seem to be the two strongest opposing forces that affect our lives.

In the sixties in America — a time of much turmoil — I experienced much pain, and I wondered if any joy showed in my artwork. So I searched for joy in the original homeland of all Black people, Africa. Living in Africa heightened my feelings of identity and reaffirmed all the positives I felt deep inside. I found the joy, and I think that's reflected in the books I illustrated for Black children years later when I came back to America. But it was back in America that I realized that pain and struggle are unavoidable conditions, especially in the lives of Blacks in America.

Our lives contain a strange balance of joy and pain, shown in our beautiful rhythmic movements and in our clear dance-consciousness. There is a definite duality going on here — the two elements joy and pain never just exist side by side, but they interact with each other and they build on each other. For the pain of the Black experience has always been tempered by the strength of the Black people, and the joy has always been tempered by the pain. Sometimes what comes out is a bittersweet image. Because even within a restricted form, we have learned to improvise. We celebrate life. We hear it, feel it, accept it in Black music — the spirituals, the blues — where the lyrics are sometimes mournful but the rhythm is jubilant and even joyful, so joyful that one is moved to dance.

But it is very important to understand that the joy of the rhythm is not an evasion of the pain and sorrow but an affirmation of the presence of life. A noted Black historian calls this our heritage of celebration, coming from our roots in Africa. He says: "To understand the totality of our art, we have to understand that in Africa we created a society where everything is celebrated — even death is celebrated as a continuation of life." There is a tendency to think that many times the Black artist is without form, but really he or she is moving within a restricted form dictated by mood and circumstance. In America, *America* is our restricted form, and we improvise within that form. Listen to the music of Duke Ellington, Charlie Parker, Miles Davis, or John Coltrane. Look at the dance movements of Mo-hammed Ali, or of Dr. J in basketball. This is an artistic way of surviving, drawing on resources that are unknown to us because we cannot identify them but that nonetheless belong to us, that have been the basis of the art of celebration. That is part of our survival — not to celebrate oppression, but to celebrate survival in spite of oppression. I, therefore, believe that Black artists going into any art form, including book illustration — because of our unique ancestral background and because of our historical relation-ship to the Americas and the world (the constant struggle, for freedom and liberation at its best) — give to that art form a humanism that is sometimes exactly the opposite of Western society's pessimistic and cynical attitude. The attitude is based on the belief that it is impossible for an individual or the group to change for the better, that all men are inherently greedy, self-centered, and in constant battle to conquer each other or nature. For the most part I believe that our ability to endure and to survive with dignity the worst kind of antihuman oppression in American history points to the fact that all human beings can hold on to their souls, through anything, and therefore can change themselves and the society they live in for the better. In my own work I now try to reflect this dual heritage.

I work to intensify the reality. To tell the truth even when it hurts, now, in the present. To magnify the beauty. To show strength and dignity, because I know they're there. To affirm, to justify the constant hope, sometimes even in the face of overwhelming, staggering odds. In visual terms I work to incorporate that rhythmic motion, that dance-consciousness, that underlying joy, and even those things that speak to the harsh reality of a painful situation. For I know that even within this sorrow is still the affirmation of the presence of life, a tremendous ingrained quality of hope, and finally the unconquerable strength and dignity of a people who have gone through all this and survived and are still trying to pass this knowledge on to their children.

There's a quote by Toni Morrison in which she talks about essentially the same thing but then says: "I don't want to be misunderstood, to suggest that oppression is good for you, but what one gleans out of life's experiences can be transmitted in its better, nobler, and finer form as an enhancement of your life rather than a narrowing down of it. I am not celebrating oppression." She said, and I also believe this sincerely: "I believe that art can be both uncompromisingly beautiful and socially responsible." That is one of the reasons why I always, in some way, in any kind of way, connect what I do with the community. Moreover, I understand that in this society people tend to pay a lot of attention to someone who produces a product without paying any attention to the people who produced the person who produces the product — which always seemed kind of strange to me until I went to Africa and investigated my heritage. Once you understand and believe that what you do is connected to the person who went before you, then you understand that what you're doing is what you *should* be doing and not something you're doing for money. I have to say that because sometimes it's hard, not having money. But my concentration is not on money; it never has been. I concentrate my energy on work and sometimes what happens is that the money comes, the money comes. My style of living has never changed, so I have never had a credit card. I have never driven a car, so I have no license. I am not saying these things are virtues — I'm just saying my style of life hasn't changed, so it's not very easy to buy me off . . . not with material things.

Me and Blake, Blake and Me

E L L E N R A S K I N

At first I was going to call this speech "Me and Blake." I decided that was a bit presumptuous of me. Then I was going to call it "Blake and Me," and I decided that sounded as if I was too intimate with Blake. I've been very close to Blake on and off through many years, so I now title my speech "Me and Blake, Blake and Me, or From the Sublime to the Ridiculous."

To make this easier I'll read my outline, and then I'll go through it point by point. Now, the outline reveals similarities between me and Blake and Blake and me.

     I. We are both famous.
    II. We both published a book called *Songs of Innocence*.
   III. Blake entertained biblical prophets and angels in his
           home. Me too. I did.
    IV. We are both crazy, Blake and me.
     V. We are both creative cheaters.
    VI. We do not write fantasy.
   VII. We are both artists who write.

As I said, I'll go through this point by point.

I. We are both famous. Well, this year I am famous with the Newbery Medal, and I decided I might as well make the most of it; it's my one and only year. I remember as an adolescent discussing very seriously with my girlfriends the question "Would we rather be famous alive or dead?" It was a very romantic period in our lives, and somehow we thought we couldn't be famous both ways, so we always chose we'd rather be famous dead. Somehow, I guess, we couldn't cope with death and thought we'd still be around to hear the applause. I've changed my mind; I'm very happy with the Newbery Medal.

Blake, however, was never famous while he was alive. He published his own books and did not receive any acclaim, and even since his death there have been times when he was completely ignored and other times when his art has been appreciated but his writing not understood. I don't know exactly where he stands now; I think his art is becoming appreciated but not necessarily his writing. Not much Blake is read other than *Songs of Innocence* and *Songs of Experience*.

II. We both published a book called *Songs of Innocence*. Blake finished it and printed it himself in 1789, and my *Songs of Innocence* came out in 1966. I would not have thought of reillustrating Blake. I think his illustrations for *Songs of Innocence* and *Songs of Experience* are some of the greatest engravings and book illustrations ever done. But at that time I was a free-lance illustrator doing book jackets, and I'd just done a jacket for a book called *Improvisation in Music*, by a woman from Boston named Gertrude Price Wollner. I played the piano as a child and play the harpsichord as an adult, but I never, never thought of improvising. I was one of those very good students as a young child who always played only the notes I read from the page. In her book Mrs. Wollner said you can improvise as long as you choose two things and stick to them. One is a scale (you can choose your own); the other is a tempo.

Well, I thought I'd try it, and wondering what to do, I picked up *Songs of Innocence* and thought I'd set it to music. Now, Blake had sung *Songs of Innocence* to a friend, and the friend had transcribed the melodies, but the music has been lost. But the poems themselves are very musical. So I started writing the music, and I told the art director at Doubleday, for whom I had done the jacket for Mrs. Wollner's book, what I was up to. He told the children's book editor, who asked to see one of the songs and an illustration to go with it. I thought about it, and I did show him most of the songs I had already done and one illustration. I decided not to try to recreate Blake's own *Songs of Innocence* in any way; the words are almost unreadable, and the colored illustrations are so subtle that they would be very costly to reproduce. I would just reillustrate the poems in my own way and have one volume with the music and the other with just the poetry and my illustrations.

And so that is what I did. When I finished the songs, I called up Mrs. Wollner in Boston and went to see her; she looked over the songs and helped me. She gave me some very good criticism, and the book was published. After that I never played the piano again. (The finance company had taken the piano out of my home when I was young, and I didn't play again until I was grown up. Somehow I never got over the feeling that maybe I could have been a musician.)

I have my own copies of Blake's *Songs of Innocence* and *Songs of Experience*. They are the Trianon Press reproductions of the original editions, very expensive because they were done in a limited edition with fine paper and excellent bindings. And the number of colors needed to reproduce Blake's pages was so large that the books would be prohibitively expensive if anyone tried to do the same thing. I bought them when I was doing *Songs of Innocence* and then I decided I had to see the originals. I compared my editions with the originals they were reproduced from, which are in the Rosenwald collection in Philadelphia, and they are so close I could not tell the difference. (Maurice Sendak once called me and said he was looking for copies of the Trianon Press edition and had tried every book collector he knew of. One of them said, yes, he had had one, but he'd sold it. Maurice asked to whom he'd sold it and found out it was me. At that point I almost lost a very good friend. Maurice called me repeatedly trying to get the book, until we decided to trade. He did have books I wanted, for example first editions of Henry James, and so I traded the Blake. Then I couldn't sleep for a week; I'd lost my book. Finally I called Maurice and said I wanted my book back. He did give it back, and of course I gave him back his books. Then he would call me and tell me he'd found another copy of the Blake without the original cardboard slip cover, and how much did I want for my slip cover? We didn't speak for a year after that. There's a Blake line, "I was angry with my friend.")

III. Blake entertained biblical prophets and angels in his home. He did not conjure up these prophets. He and his wife Catherine had Elijah to tea, Isaiah to tea, Ezekiel to tea, John Milton and God to tea. It was totally natural to them. It was almost as if I had had Sydelle Pulaski — one of my characters in *The Westing Game* — to tea. A writer lives so closely with the characters he or she creates that they become real people. Blake was so involved with the prophets, and he himself was writing prophetic books, that it just seemed natural. The prophets did not prophesy when they were with Blake; they never said anything they had not said in the Bible. And when Blake wrote about them, he set down the whole conversation; when he asked them a crucial question, they always referred him to the Bible.

Well, I said to myself, "Me too." A childhood experience of mine made me understand that it is not crazy to have Elijah to tea because I've sat with a might-have-been Elijah at a table. My great-grandmother lived in Sheboygan, Wisconsin. (I specify Wisconsin because someone once asked me what part of Russia Sheboygan is in.) And my family — my mother, father, sister, grandmother, grandfather — and I went to my great-grandmother's house for Passover. Now, my great-grandmother was one of the very few Jews who lived in Sheboygan, a small town with maybe two or three Jewish families. The time was the Depression, and every tramp knew about Jewish houses on Passover night. During the Passover ceremony there is one point at which one of the men leaves the table and opens the door to let in God's messenger, who is going to announce the

Messiah. At our Passovers every time a tramp would come in and sit down at the place set for the prophet at the table. Well, as a child, who was I to say he was not Elijah? I certainly wouldn't have expected him to come in a business suit, you know; he came in poverty. So it's an image that has stayed with me all my life — accepting the wondrous, just as Blake did.

IV. Blake and I are both crazy. Well, Blake's contemporaries Wordsworth and Coleridge thought he was crazy. Blake was paranoid; there's no doubt about it. And with very good reason. At fourteen Blake chose to be an engraver; it was his life's ambition, which stayed with him through all his years of writing. Since he was an engraver, he engraved what he wrote. When you read his prophetic books, remember that everything had to be written in reverse for engraving. He spent seven years as an apprentice. He worked and worked at his art and was nearly forty before in 1796 he received his first long assignment: to do a book of his own designs and engravings to accompany Edward Young's *Night Thoughts*. It was an expensive edition, and it came out at a very bad time; no one bought it. Blake was very poor, so he had to do hack work for patrons.

Blake lived during the Industrial Revolution, when skilled workers were no longer valued. The factories were using unskilled labor, including child labor, and they belched smoke. Blake became more and more upset at the factories, the mills; he found himself unable to work. Maybe he did go a bit crazy.

I have this paranoia too, though not because I haven't been recognized or because I haven't been able to work. I think criticism has got to me. I am very sensitive to what anyone says, and somehow no matter what the critics say I always think they're right. I don't know why. So I always have with me the question, can I get away with this, can I really do this, or should I change it? I could never rhyme "eye" with "symmetry," as Blake did in "The Tiger."

V. Blake and I are both creative cheaters. Blake did not draw his illustrations from life. He said natural objects deaden imagination — as they do for me. Parts of Blake's drawings are taken from standard prints of the time. Any symbol he found useful he would use; for him the procedure was part of the creative process. I do draw from life when I have a chance, but like many other artists I have a large "swipe file" of magazine pictures I've cut out. I use them not only in my art work but also in my writing. Before I did *The Westing Game* I knew I needed sixteen characters. I went through my swipe file of people, picking out pictures to be my sixteen people, and then I wrote about them. Not all writers or artists go as far as Blake did in taking from engravings of the time, even from Michelangelo, but we all build on one another's work. There is no such thing as something that springs from the soil without nourishment. It comes out of tradition, out of experience.

I can write about images from my childhood for children today. I wasn't sure I could do this, but there was no way out; I had to use the images from my own childhood, because the child I was is the only child I really know. I didn't understand my own daughter when she was a child because she was different from the child I was. I raised her differently from the way I was raised. She was brought up in New York City; she had a great deal of freedom, a big mouth, and skill at sports — none of which I had had. So I could never write for my daughter. Once she grew up we became more alike, not in the way we look but in our personalities, our work habits. But writing of the child I was for the children of today is not difficult.

Some of the images from my childhood I use quite unchanged. How can a child of today understand who Frankenstein's monster was or what is so funny about Abbott and Costello's routine "Who's on First"? The reason I can refer to such things and get away with it is that most of the other writers writing today — writing movies, television scripts, or songs — are members of my generation. We are all building from the same images of American childhood and recreating them for the children of today.

VI. Blake and I do not write fantasy. I don't like to see people and things put in categories; I think it's difficult and at times a bit dangerous. I was on a panel in Berkeley, California — a panel on the creative spirit. That was the theme, and we all hated it; all of us talked against the idea of a creative spirit. We didn't believe in it. But it was a fascinating panel because everyone had been put in a category except me; I wasn't sure what category I was supposed to be in. I finally ended up in one because of how the discussion was going and because of the questions from the audience and my reaction to them. I'll tell you who was there. One was my editor, Ann Durell, who ended up completely on the other side. We even started out sitting in definite positions, and she was way over on the other end by the time we finished — my own editor! The others were Marcia Brown, for book illustration; Julia Cunningham, who is now writing gothics; Ursula Le Guin, for science fiction; and June Jordan, for poetry and ethnic realism. So I said, if it's humor you want me for, I'm not coming because I refuse to speak on humor — there's nothing as deadly as speaking about what's funny. And I was told, no, just talk about whatever you want to talk about. So I wasn't sure who I was. I knew I wasn't fantasy. Some people were starting with fantasy, I realized quickly, because both Ursula Le Guin and Marcia Brown, through fairy tales, got onto fantasy with the idea of good versus evil. I didn't understand what that meant, and neither did June Jordan; so we wound up at one end of the table and decided we were the ethnics and the cigarette smokers. We were the smoking ethnic realists. And we truly did not understand this fight of good versus evil because it seemed the more they talked about it, the more they were getting to the notion that both were present within one person, and that idea was even stranger to us.

Now, you would think the realists would surely understand evil, but the evil I know, the evil that Blake knew, and the evil that June Jordan knows are so outside of us that they are all way off in the distance and don't personally concern us; they concern all of society but not us as individuals. To Blake, evil was the Industrial Revolution and organized religion. The evil in my early years was the Depression and Hitler and the war. The only thing I could think of to talk about was surrealism. To me surrealism is the inertia of the waking nightmare. It's being powerless before the threat or temptation of the irrational, the ignoble, the insurmountable force.

Now, it doesn't have to be that heavy; it can be even funny, and there have been some funny surrealists — for example Márquez, in *One Hundred Years of Solitude*, can be very funny. Certainly the Irish writer Flann O'Brien is a very funny surrealist. It's just something recognizable and strange to us because there is a logic in the illogic; it's something we know and yet can't fight. It's like when you have a dream of something happening and you can't move. You know it's never going to happen really, but there you are, and the frightening thing is the fact that you can't fight against it. Sometimes it's even as silly as knowing that you have an exam in class and haven't studied for it or can't find your locker. Such back-to-school dreams are horrible, and it's the same sort of inertia that Blake is getting at. Blake wrote, "I awake but my soul is in dreams." Now, I don't know if you're interested in surrealism. The inertia can also be movement that never stops but grows and grows. That to me is the child: the inertia before a stronger, unknowable, irrational force, which is the adult. This is innocence versus experience. I don't think it's any deeper than that, nor did Blake.

If Blake thought that innocence and experience, the two forces, were so far apart, he would not have switched poems when he put them together in *Songs of Innocence* and *Songs of Experience*. He did — he took one poem from one book and put it in the other. Blake, who came before Hegel, was a Hegelian; good and evil are the same thing. Innocence and experience are part of the same soul. A person starts out in innocence and has to go through experience to regain innocence and adulthood; that's all Blake is saying.

As a child I came to Blake in a very unusual way. I remember a nightmare that I had over and over again. It started because I was standing next to my mother in the backyard while she was hanging up the wash, talking to a neighbor woman and whispering about "the tiger lady." All of a sudden the neighbor pointed to me, and they stopped talking. I don't even know if I remember that they were actually talking about it or if there *was* a tiger lady and I was the only one who had seen her, but somehow she ended up behind the green sofa in our living room, and it reached the point where I was afraid to enter the house. Although I wasn't more than six years old, I would dream about the tiger lady, who was half tiger, half lady, in an almost sexual way. There was something forbidding and very tempting and very frightening in the tiger lady. A few years ago I was reading the obituaries in the *Times*, and it said "Tiger Lady Dies." I wish I could tell you more. I can't even tell you her name; she was a woman who had been arrested years before, during my childhood — a nurse who poisoned people in order to get their money. Perhaps she had a tiger-skin coat, but who she actually was is not important. What is important is the strange, forbidden, frightening woman of my nightmare.

Then when I came to Blake in school, they gave us "The Lamb," which I thought was sappy, and "The Tiger," which made a profound impression. First of all, it instantly reminded me of the tiger lady, and second, no matter how I read "symmetry" and "eye," the rhyme wasn't right. I read the lines so many times to see how they worked that they always stayed with me.

VII. Blake and I are artists who write. There's a difference between an artist who writes and a writer who writes. An artist is someone who has a different eye. People who read Blake are always trying to read his symbols as definite things. An artist never sees a symbol as one thing. In illustration, yes; a symbol has to be definite when pictures, instead of words, are telling a story. But Blake was not an illustrator; he was an artist. His engravings for *Songs of Innocence* and *Songs of Experience* are art, and the artist does not want somebody to explain in words what the picture means. There should be a deeper meaning — and almost all art is in that sense surrealistic — that is received through the eyes, something you cannot explain. And if you look at great art, you'll find you wonder why it's done. The artist asks why, and the writer asks what; but you never ask what in front of the painting. If you ask, what is it?, and answer the question, it's not a painting that stands up as a true graphic statement.

And that is why Blake is so difficult in his symbolic and his prophetic books. Not because he's writing in code, as some people have said, because he was afraid of being arrested; he writes as an artist, obscurely and graphically.

What is Blake saying? He's just saying, don't pick my work apart, and if you do have to take it apart, you're going to lose the whole message and feeling. And the fact that I have been doing just this is the enigma.

NOTE

In honor of Ellen Raskin's major contributions to the field of literature for children, the Center awarded an Ellen Raskin Scholarship in her memory during the summer of 1985.

The Lotus Blossom—Or Whodunit?

MARCIA BROWN

"We betray our children when we fail to take a long view of their lives."
—*Lotus Seeds*

I live with a friend who reads Ngaio Marsh, P. D. James, Dorothy Sayers, and Agatha Christie, with the greatest relish, for relaxation. My trouble is that I can't relax or even sleep if I do so. My whodunits have to be of other deeds.

I'm first going to talk to you about an ugly subject, one that we all know about, perhaps have been part of, either as perpetrator or victim, but one that we can do something about. The subject is common to whodunits—betrayal.

The advantage of climbing is often the view one gets as one pauses on the way. The same might be said for sticking with a career over several decades. I don't have to tell you that this is a discouraging period. City library budgets allow an annual purchase of maybe two hundred books. The closing down of children's literature classes or library schools themselves indicates that with all our educational effort that has attained a high rate of literacy in the country, a huge number of Americans are not reading. They have been given the name of *aliterates*—those who can but won't read, who will turn quickly to the pictures. It might seem odd to you that this upsets an illustrator. But, of course, we are going to feel the effects of this aliteracy, even though the technology in part responsible can inform us, can entertain us, can even help us to earn a living with scant attention paid to reading. People who seldom read or write lose respect for precision of language. You have heard the mumbles and grunts as some otherwise attractive soul tried desperately to verbalize a thought. But ultimately one wonders if not reading may not come to mean not thinking clearly.

Townsend Hoopes, president of the Association of American Publishers, was quoted in the *New York Times,* speaking of the dangers this problem poses for the nation. We are not a verbal culture with fabulous oral histories. "The inevitable consequence," he said, "is that such people [referring to aliterates] seem satisfied with their own initial, shallow interpretations of what they do read, and deeply resist requests or instructions to explain or defend their points of view with any reasoned analysis or cogency."

Ahead of us may lie a clearer than ever division in the country, a narrow elite of informed people and a large majority who cannot be bothered to read. You could take that further into the cruder designation of an almost feudal culture and call the divisions the exploiters and the exploited, or even, eventually, the knaves and the fools.

Three million young people get high-school diplomas in a year, but how many read? More than 98 percent of American homes have television, and here come Pac-Man, his wife, and all his friends.

There are many encouraging experiments being tried out in various parts of the country. In Connecticut, schools are aware that children spend enormous numbers of hours looking at television, absorbing—along with much information—values, mores, points of view that have been manipulated for the sake of viewer ratings. They have conducted experiments, asking children not to look at any television at all for set periods of time— say, two weeks. The results—no one can say how long the effects will last—were surprising. Instead of missing the programs, the children found that they had more time for after-school outdoor play, for their own hobbies, and, miraculously enough, for reading. Library circulation went up.

The shadow of the nuclear conflict is bringing about a more and more narrow fundamentalism. To be secure about fundamentals is to live intact in a cocoonlike safety. Other arguments are closed out of the mind. But when all things are certain, does not mental rigor mortis set in? We are seeing a worldwide outbreak of fundamentalism—religious and political— as people yearn for certainties. Some paths lead to Jonestowns. Some paths lead to a courageous summoning of strengths, a sorting out of gear, to a determination not to be seduced by terror and hatred or to fall into a acquiescence that ends in self-betrayal.

In our local newspaper the plans for mass evacuation to Vermont are discussed, ludicrous as the evacuation of a megalopolis that is crippled by a four-inch snowfall may be, instead of plans that have the courage to say, "No! This must not be."

Are ideas worth more than life? If there is no life, what chance has the idea? If you do not know the book *Silence* by the contemporary Japanese author, Shusaku Endu, I strongly recommend it. Its message: What can be the real test of faith? What is the ultimate moral act?

Another book has been called by Julian Symons of the London *Sunday Times*, "The most successful book yet written about the greatest single horror inflicted by one group of men upon another." It is *Black Rain*, by an elderly, unsentimental, and unsparing novelist, Masuji Ibuse. We are just beginning to get information about the long-term effects of the bombs dropped on Japan that were a fraction of the power of the bombs that could be used today.

In our town we have a book fair to benefit the library, which has always received its major funding from the interest and labors of the townspeople. Books are donated, sorted, and priced throughout the year and offered for sale Labor Day weekend. There is a Collector's Corner, an auction, the plum of which last year was a first edition of *Moby Dick*. The idea of books living many lives in many homes is delightful. The sight of booklovers going out hugging their boxes of purchases, often at prices below current paperback prices, is heartwarming. We happen to be a rather bookish community.

On Sunday afternoon, after three days of work on the fair, my friends and I knocked off and went on a picnic to a lovely pond in a local park. (Why do parks so often commemorate warlike encounters?) The pond is full of Chinese lotus, great creamy white cups and huge leaves, that are changing form constantly, flopping this way and that in every breeze. The leaves, like many other things, are most interesting when they are nearing the ends of their lives, torn by winds, battered by autumn rains. Brown and ragged, they curl and droop over their now empty seedpods until they slip back into the mire to store up strength for next summer's blooming once more of that startling beauty and purity. Once can understand why the Oriental civilizations revered the lotus as a symbol of spiritual power and rebirth. When the flower has finished blooming, the seedpods form— looking like medieval Venetian chimney pots—and the stalks lose their sinuousness and dry, eventually bending over and dropping the seeds into the mud.

That Sunday afternoon I took many photographs to which I can refer while painting. For some time I have been studying the Chinese technique of painting, learning the basic strokes derived from Chinese calligraphy, learning from observation of master paintings, trying to incorporate into a painting the opposites—yang and yin—that so long ago the Chinese were aware made up the richness of life, the smooth and scratchy, the sensuous flow and the rasping, dragged brush textures. The subject matter is modest, a slug swinging on a blade of grass, a flower half hidden in leaves. But whatever one paints, it is the end of a contemplative process that began with looking, with feeling, associating the ephemeral with something more durable in the spirit, with thinking, with, again, minute observation. A painting that is vital, vibrant with spontaneity, may be the last in a group of many that were not. The means are the simplest: ink from soot rubbed on stone, a brush of hair, paper from natural fibers. The very materials are part of one's feeling about the pictures. Like the daily practice of music, the daily practice of painting enables one to do the painting when the time comes, to perform as one would like.

As a people we often shy away from tackling the difficulties of learning an art or how to judge it. It is depressing to witness the floundering of reviewers who often do not seem to realize that a finished work is but the tip of an iceberg. What is not seen may be the months or years of thought and feeling from which the final work was distilled.

I have a young friend with an eagerness to draw who spends all her time making more or less accurate copies of Snoopy. She is no longer content with the expressionist paintings of her early childhood. In school she is encouraged into a facile, colorful design demanding neither imagination nor observation nor feeling, certainly very little muscular control. And so those muscles that helped so gaily to delineate her pleasures as a small child, go unused. Snoopy is safe and won't show up the wobbles and naïveté she now sees in her early pictures. He is blessedly the same, and so are her pictures; and a door is slowly closing, possibly forever, because a teacher refuses to, or doesn't know enough, to recognize the need for training muscles to respond to brain impulses. If my young friend is very strong in her determination, perhaps she can bridge the period when her critical sense has outstripped her skill. But I can't help feeling that she has been betrayed, as so many of our children are betrayed.

Muscles untrained are very hard to bring under control later on. But worse, a period when the foundations for skills that will enrich adult life are laid down, has been neglected.

I am finding this out daily as I practice the flute, trying to get muscles to respond allegro or presto.

We take it for granted that a surgeon's scalpel will be guided by a mind trained for years before the knife descends to make an incision.

Yet in spite of a wide interest in art, there is still an ingenuous faith that new work springs forth from an artist's hand with little or no preparation. When someone asks me what new book I am working on, and I reply that I am painting, a look of disappointment usually comes to the person's face because he had expected a factory production of bright new images and, in my case, usually a different technique and superficial style from any other of my books. I have always thought books are as individual, or should be, as the people who make them. We all work differently. I have often wondered how an artist can keep on applying the same technique year after year to a vast number of different subjects. Is it laziness? Is it a habit of wishing to please that set in when he was young and was shepherded through his first books by a strong-minded editor? Is it simply an imperviousness to boredom that some of us feel if we do the same thing over and over? I don't know. Illustrators are a diverse lot! But after a few books we are apt to know ourselves well enough to know what we need in the way of a long period, without pressure, in which to grow and, more important, be receptive to ideas that spring up, as it were, from nowhere but in truth from the whole well of impressions and associations that we are feeding on every day. Some illustrators work under the closest direction from editors. If I feel one snuffling at the back of my neck, I go to pieces. We all know that publishing and distribution of books are different from what they were thirty years ago. Publishers quite frankly ask authors today not only to write the book, but to sell it, and often push farther into the future or out of the window altogether the chance for the author to work undisturbed on his next. There are two sides to this question. Most of us welcome the opportunity to meet the people who use our books with children and always return from some jaunt of speaking somewhat enriched from new human contacts. But we often wonder, also, if that is the best way to spend energy that as we get older is less, and more precious. In this situation, someone is sure to betray himself or someone else.

We betray our children when we fail to take a long view of their lives. Interest in the arts grows, yet in some schools children laboriously construct huge oilcloth hamburgers because some adult artist had success creating one. Swimming pools and arenas get built. The funds the libraries had got are now cut. When art is so accessible in the museums of our large cities, perhaps the reaction is, "The children can always be taken." Are they?

In some towns where art is not readily accessible, much more effort is made to teach children that art is something to live with, to make if you can, but a sustaining food for mind and imagination and spirit. Recently I visited a library in Oklahoma where valuable prints and sculpture circulated to the children along with their books, just to make sure they got that nourishment.

"Isn't gaiety one of the most important feelings to have in life?"

"No, joy."

Every time we opt for shallowness, every time we fail to exercise the muscles of deeper feelings, we betray our children.

Like many college students, I worked in the summer to help with my expenses. I got a job at a country inn, expensive for the time, to which came many people whose names were known to me from the art, music, and theater worlds. Exposure to strong individual personalities when one is young is priceless as a means of growth.

I wanted art lessons; so I offered to work for my training, sweeping studios, setting up huge still lifes from which we would select smaller groups on our canvases, timing the model's poses, all the chores necessary in an art studio that leave plenty of time to paint and learn.

I was blessed to be able to study under a gifted painter, Judson Smith, who was also a wise and compassionate man. Like many children I was brought up trusting in many certainties that, as I came to mature, I saw as illusions. The artist told me, "Try to be absolutely honest in your thinking for one minute." Can you?

He told me, "The only thing you can depend on is change."

Rather than deal in recipe methods that have to be discarded, he tried to bring out the fragment of uniqueness in each one of us.

"Find your grandfathers." Seek your own counterpoints of personality, cast of mind, in painters of the past. Learn from them, study them.

"The means, not the end." The daily practice, the hairbreadth progress that adds up in time to an inch, to a foot. The habit of taking responsibility for one's own slow growth. "Don't worry about a personal style. None of you is just like another." The caution about believing praise. The long view.

Young people can easily betray themselves. More easily are they betrayed by people who ask too little of them. When I am asked by a young person what he should do to prepare himself for a career in illustration, I am reluctant to suggest that he study with a fashionably successful illustrator. We all know what can be the result—as year after year the copies of the illustrator's style proliferate. A good foundation in felt drawing, painting with a painter who emphasizes observation and feeling for life, cultivation of a habit of drawing feelings, familiarity with as much great art as possible, analysis of composition, exposure to the other arts— music, dance, theater—all these added to a familiarity with outstanding illustrated books to get a sense of how to handle a dramatic line, how to create and maintain characterization, the importance of extended research and the honest use of it as stimulus, not traceable model. . . . The preparation will take years—many of them while practicing illustration. One is always preparing.

Techniques that fit the manner of the subject can be learned, invented as one goes along, if you are first convinced that such changes are necessary to your own growth.

An actor who used exactly the same voice and mannerisms for every character would be a sorry example of the breed, yet we happily look at endless pastel renderings, no matter what the country, the place, the period. Are we being betrayed? Are we betraying ourselves by asking too little?

Illustrators of my generation have been through many battles, have seen many styles come and go. In the forties, perhaps as a backwash from the grief and horror of World War II, there was a wash of sugary sentimentality akin to that of popular greeting cards. You know the style. You know the commercial success of such a style. You also know how pallid is such a view of childhood.

In the fifties some of the rigor of abstract expressionism exploded in our books. In spite of almost constant war someplace in the world, it was a time of expansion, exploration, and discovery. Then in the sixties, someone—perhaps because he had seen the Art Nouveau show and exhibition of Tiffany glass at the Museum of Modern Art—rediscovered the sinuous line. But the snakeskin was empty. The living creature was gone, in spite of a hundred Magic Markers. In the seventies, many wanderers returned to safety, and the safety was someone else's.

From the confusion of growing up in the fifties, when drawing from life was not thought necessary and self-expression was all, young illustrators shot in the other direction, copying photographs in a deadly imitation of the look of things; and the spirit again was somehow missing. Antlike attention to every stitch in his pants does not a lively little boy portray. Illustrations become symbols, shorthand. Two chevrons were smiling eyes, one inverted chevron a smiling mouth. The nose was often lost in the shuffle. These facile symbols may be amusing but are utterly incapable of expressing a deep response to life. Who is betraying whom?

It isn't enough to complain or nod to the vocal complainers. What are we going to do? We can almost always do something. We can choose. If we only can buy two hundred books, let them be strong ones that will live in the memory. We can ask publishers to retain some of the strong books of the past rather than let them go out of print for a weaker new version.

There has been a spate, a flood, of individual folktale and fairy-tale books. Rather than yet another flossy, glossy overdecorated edition, why not reorder Wanda Gág? Evaluate and reevaluate.

When authors and editors who have devoted lifetimes of application of talent and integrity of spirit to their work are treated by publishers as commodities and therefore expendable, who is betraying whom?

Publishers are in business. Many of the ills besetting business are theirs. It seems that finally they are beginning to realize that a passion for black figures and an MBA are not the only qualifications necessary. They embrace the Peter Principle passionately, and the perfectly competent secretary becomes a third-rate editor.

As Jean Karl wrote in *Advocate,* the criticism of many issues by parents' groups first shocked sturdy New Yorkers, used to endless variety in people and books. To act positively, she decided to be even more critical herself, and ask, "What is gratuitous, what is honestly necessary to characterization? What words are so necessary that the book is less without them? Are we going to betray children's need for diversity by settling for blandness?"

> Willie, in the best of sashes,
> Fell in the fire and burned to ashes.
> After a while the room grew chilly.
> But no one cared to stir up Willie.

A teacher in Arkansas told me recently that someone had stirred up Willie, having lost a sense of humor, and demanded that the anthology containing the offending verse be withdrawn from the library shelves.

Examples of loss of perspective and a sense of balance, even humor, abound, and I'm sure each of us has a tale to tell.

The leading characters change, but the play goes on, under a different name—*Huckleberry Finn*, *The Catcher in the Rye*, and now *Shadow*. You can name in your own minds the title for the next scene. Who will betray whom?

Reviewers of books sometimes measure the book in front of them against the book they had thought it would be or should be. They often don't even see the book in their hands for what it is. When we heed the words of critics who have looked at too much and felt too little, whom do we betray?

We can't pretend that 1980s children live in a Kate Greenaway world, charming as that may be to have on our library shelves. Does anyone have to say again that unless we corrupt their taste by sugar or Strawberry Shortcake, children are not sentimental creatures?

We betray children every time we act as if there is one way to do things, one way of feeling, one religion, one road to enlightenment. Experience, if we have learned anything at all, should have taught us otherwise.

One of the serendipities of that golden Sunday afternoon spent in contemplating the lotus was meeting Mitchell. Mitchell was three and had come to the park with his father and sister to fish. The sister and a young friend of mine went off to catch frogs. Mitchell felt his fish were taking too long to bite and walked around in search of company and conversation. But his conversation was measured in an original way. It all came out of his pocket.

"Where do you live?"

Deep delving into his shorts pocket, a sidelong glance at the palm of his hand. "Bridgeport."

Every word he answered was brought forth from that pocket, examined, and then uttered with finality, like a card being slapped on a table.

"I have some surprise words," he finally offered.

"What are they?"

Deep into the pocket again. "Strawberry pie!"

Mitchell didn't know it, but in that pond he was a lotus seed.

Enamored of the Mystery

MAURICE SENDAK,
WITH QUESTIONS FROM THE AUDIENCE

The only thing that really interests me especially at the moment is the new book I'm working on [*Outside Over There*, 1981]. This is the obsession that occurs during the creation of a new work. Children ask where my ideas come from, and of course I make up answers because you can't tell children you don't know; they really cannot accept that. But the answer is, of course, I don't know.

It's fun to trace what happens.

This book has been in my mind for seven years or more, and actually the main character has been in my life since I was a child. However incoherent it may sound, let me tell you this is what's known as the creative process: It is indescribable; and the artist fails and is triumphant at the same time.

As a writer and an illustrator of books, I really have only one theme. I've been doing books that are variations on that theme ever since I've been writing. I always write about a kid who tries to find an answer to a problem and who manages to do so in one way or another.

What are the things—ingredients—that are going into this book? What's it all about?

When I was very young, I was an avid reader, and I lived next door to a little girl who was also an avid reader. She was more fortunate than I, for she was given more books. We used to meet in the hall, Selma and I, and exchange books.

I don't recall any of the stories we read, except *The Big Little Book of David Copperfield* with Freddie Bartholomew's pictures in it. The only other book that comes to mind is a mysterious book; I have no recollection of the title, no recollection of the plot. I recall only that it had a character who is a girl, and that for some reason she is in the rain, a lot of rain, and that she's wearing a very oversized coat. Perhaps the artist didn't draw it well, or

362

perhaps it was planned that way; I don't know. She has an umbrella pressed against her, and the rain is forcing itself on her. And for some reason that I will never know, she was imprinted on my brain when I was about six or seven years old. There she sits in my head all these long years; obviously, she touches off something deep and unconscious. I don't know what it is, nor am I terribly concerned with finding out. I simply have to use her—in some way to get rid of her, exorcise her. She has never fit into previous books; I've never found a place for a little girl in a raincoat.

There is something else. When I was about four, there occurred the terrible kidnapping of the baby of Colonel Lindbergh. It was a very traumatic event for children in the early 1930s; we all thought we could be kidnapped. I recall that for a brief period of time, perhaps for only one night, my father slept on the floor of our room with a big club. My sister was in one bed, and my brother and I in the other. My father was very disillusioned when some mean relative said, What a fool you are; who wants them? It had never occurred to him that we weren't good enough to be kidnapped. It had never occurred to us, either; being kidnapped was always the lingering nightmare of my life. When I was about six or seven, the man was captured, and then I went through the whole court case, the electrocution. All of it left an indelible mark on my life. I've met many people my age who lived through the Lindbergh case and call it the most frightening experience of their lives.

So I have a kidnapping, which has obsessed me; I have a girl in the rain, who has obsessed me; I have a few feelings about my own childhood, which always obsessed me; and now I want to make a book and bring all these things together. They seem to be very disparate elements, but somehow as an artist you have a funny kind of faith that they *will* come together. The unconscious has such a need to make an artistic whole out of these disparate elements that it's going to happen. You just have to wait.

Somehow I always knew that I would achieve three major picture books—there might be more, but there would be a trilogy. *Wild Things* was the first, *Night Kitchen* was the second, and this new one will be the third. I always knew this one would be the third, that the third would be about the little girl in the rain. I didn't know if I'd pull it off, or how. I tried writing the story about five years ago. I made my first attempts, and they were terrible. And then two years ago in the spring—I don't know what happened at that particular point—I began writing it again, and it began to happen.

What *did* happen, I realized later, was that I'd illustrated *The Juniper Tree*, a collection of tales from Grimm. While I'd always loved the tales, I never loved them more than after I'd worked on them for a number of years. So they became, aesthetically, a kind of model; they showed what a story should be, how a story should be constructed, on so many fantastic levels. And so, I guess mostly unconsciously, I began constructing my story about this girl in the rain based on what I'd learned from Grimm. And about two years after I finished *The Juniper Tree,* I wrote the first draft of this story.

I'm not going to tell the story, not because of coyness but only because I'm still trying to solve it. Although I've written it, it keeps getting rewritten, and as I draw pictures, the story begins to change and fall into images. The creative process is a very organic process; it starts this way and turns into a book. A lot of it I'm in control of, and a lot of it I'm not in control of. It's as though the unconscious offers up certain terrific information that excites me, and I put it down on paper. Other information I don't like at all, so I have to discriminate. I am really like a typewriter—someone is dictating, and I am putting down information that I receive. Now it's all being put together like a great big meal, and I just hope it's a good meal. It could be a bad meal. As an artist, you never know until you're finished.

I often use the image of having a baby—we men are all so jealous of birthing—and making a book becomes having a baby. I talk about it endlessly, and my friends have taken up the habit. They ask, "How's the baby coming? What month are you in?" Well, I am now deep into pregnancy. I'm definitely going to have a full-term child, but whether it'll be alive or dead, I don't know yet. And that's the state I am in with the book.

Audience: Do you have regular hours of work?

Sendak: Lord Byron did unimaginable damage to the creative process. And I happen to like Lord Byron. But creative work is not sporadic; it is not the great sprees of drunken free-for-alls and high living that he described. It is a very Kafkaesque, pedantic going to the office every morning, even if your office is in your own home; sitting at the drawing table the prescribed number of hours and getting up and taking the dogs out at the prescribed time. My dogs move at exactly 11:30; they know that's the time, and I mustn't be five minutes late, or they berate me. Then there's the walk, there's lunch and the soap opera with lunch, and then back to work; there's the dogs at 4:00, the nap at 5:00—it could be quite boring if work isn't going well. If work is going well, it's the only way you can work. You simply must get in a lot of hours, allowing for no socializing, which I don't miss when I'm happily working but which I miss terribly when I'm not happily working. I recommend dogs if you're living alone because they make you fit into their routine. They're creatures of habit; everything is prescribed.

Audience: When you're revising, do you keep your drafts?

Sendak: I throw nothing away. The first drafts are almost always surplus and messy, but the first drafts also have some of the best words you're ever going to find, because they're spontaneous. The end of the story I'm working on now, the last quarter of the story, is exactly as it was in the first draft; it hasn't changed at all. The first sentence of the story is as it was five years ago. I've always had the first sentence. I just didn't have the second.

Audience: You have said that you always search for the right music to play while you're working. What are you listening to now?

Sendak: When I was doing *Wild Things* and other books, I listened endlessly to music. It solved the problem of cutting out city street noise and also kept my temperature at a normal level. When you're working, you get overexcited, and the more overexcited you are the less time you can give to your work because you wear yourself out. So music acts as a tranquilizer.

This new book is very related to Mozart. I don't mean to make a mystery out of that, but it is related to Mozart, and I don't know why. Because of him and because of Grimm, I have set the book in the eighteenth century, one of my favorite periods in history. The story takes place between 1790, the year before the death of Mozart, and about 1810. I could say that's because it's the time setting of Grimm, but I think the reason goes deeper than that. Mozart is, in my opinion, the greatest of all artists. So in working through this book, to keep up my courage I listen to him all the time. More than that, when I take breaks, I do drawings to his music. I build a kind of relationship with him. Don't forget that when you're doing a work, you're alone; it isn't a cooperative job. One of the things I miss is working with other people. (That happens only at the very end, when you're in the publishing house, and then you regret having wished for it.) So you have to invent relationships, one of which is with artists you admire. Mozart is a guiding spirit.

Audience: What illustrators have influenced you?

Sendak: I have ripped off so many illustrators I wouldn't know where to begin. But, of course, that's what artists are there for. People call me on the phone, my "friends" from New York, who never call to tell me something good but always call to tell me about a new book that looks like mine—just to ruin my day. There's really no such thing as ripping off; there's only ripping off badly or well. Bad imitations are sad, deplorable, and shouldn't be published. But when you steal from another artist, you learn a lot. They're the best teachers in the world. Schools don't teach you how to draw, how to be creative; it's only the examples of great artists that inspire you.

My favorite illustrator is Randolph Caldecott. I have constantly said that; I think he's the king. The people who are esteemed in our profession—like Caldecott and Walter Crane—you use endlessly. In Germany I've ripped off Wilhelm Busch and any number of the German Romantic artists. In working on this new book, I've learned a whole slew of new names I never heard of before. It's wonderful to steal from new people; it's charming to incorporate them into my own work. I don't mean to be so facetious about stealing, because it's much more important than that.

It is my belief that no one has done the organization of a picture book so well as Caldecott. You can analyze it till you're blue in the face, but you're never going to understand how he did it so well. I've studied his books, and I teach a class of my own, and we take Caldecott and examine it page by page; we breathlessly follow every detail and come out at the end and say, What happened? Well, that's how you should come out at the end. You should never find an answer; you should only be enamored of the mystery and some of the tricks of the trade.

Audience: What do you think of Edward Ardizzone?

Sendak: I think he's superb. Ardizzone comes from the land of Caldecott, and he has a beautiful, sensational graphic ease; he draws so wonderfully; he composes a page as though there were no difficulty at all. Yet, I know Mr. Ardizzone, and I know how hard he works on a book to make it look as easy as it does. I think Caldecott probably worked this way, too. In my opinion, Ardizzone is one of the very few brilliant people in the world of picture books. Who really knows what a picture book is? Very few people who produce them know what they're doing.

Audience: What drove you to write?

Sendak: I always wanted to write, but I didn't have the confidence I had in my illustrating; that talent was much more definite. I drew better than I wrote. Why was I an illustrator? Apparently I was hooked on words, not pictures. But illustrators are very strange birds. They're not designers, which is what makes graphic shows of children's book illustrations a little bit strange. Illustrations are so linked to words that they should be inseparable from them. I'm not a painter; you put a canvas in front of me, and I don't know what to do with it. I need a springboard, and my springboard is language. So it's not odd that I became a writer but only that I was as timid for as long as I was. And rightly so; you don't jump into print.

I earned a reputation as an illustrator, which was a pretty good reputation, and by 1957 I felt I could try my wings. I had my great friend at Harper's, Ursula Nordstrom, encouraging me. My first book was a typical first book in that it goes running off at the mouth. It's still good; I mean it's an honest work. It desperately needs cutting, but it's all there, every theme I've ever used. Every story I've written since then is in my first book. You worry you're going to die two months later, and you have to get it all in—that's one of the frantic qualities of first books. After that, experience gives you more confidence.

Audience: What is the motivation for illustrating another author's work?

Sendak: Very simple: I love to work, and my own books are very, very slow in developing. We're talking about a period of seven years for this new book. I have to be working during that time, not so much for financial gain but because I feel the need to work. I've been illustrating since 1948. That's a long time, and I've illustrated over seventy-five books. Only ten or eleven of them are books that I wrote.

Audience: On what basis do you choose another author's book to illustrate?

Sendak: Only by what relationship I have to the writing. If it's something I feel a kinship with, then obviously I'm going to do it. I was very fortunate in the early days of my career in being matched up with good books—not because I knew they were good, since I didn't have much taste in the beginning. To my editor at Harper's, I was like a hothouse flower. In the old days it was possible to nurture a youngster like me in the world of publishing. You watered him, you gave him work to do, and even if he didn't sell tremendously well, he might eventually. But Ursula Nordstrom had a good deal of faith in me, and only gradually did I learn, with her help and my own insight, what kinds of books I was best suited for. I made terrible mistakes. I illustrated very bad books. I don't mean the books were bad but that my pictures were bad. But how else do you learn, except by trial and error?

I'll give you an example. A favorite book of mine was *Childhood* by Tolstoy, his first successful story, which became part of the trilogy *Childhood, Boyhood* and *Youth*. It's a wonderful story, and I wanted to illustrate it. I peddled it around, and I finally succeeded in having it published by Pantheon in the late 1950s. It was a disaster. The pictures look perfectly all right, except that there's no need for them whatsoever. I was illustrating a man who was an incomparable writer. He was also an incomparable illustrator; I mean, Tolstoy does not need an illustrator. I fell into the trap of being so enamored of the pictures he conjured up that I wanted to draw them. And it was only when I drew them that I realized I was competing with a genius. There was no winning. The book absolutely fails because I can't draw as well as he writes. So by trial and error you learn whom you may or may not illustrate.

I'm much more selective now than I was at twenty-five or thirty-five or even forty-five. There are now, I think, very few things I do well. My horizons have not expanded; in my opinion, they've narrowed, oddly, so that I will illustrate only those things I really feel I have a special affinity for. Otherwise, who needs another book that is expensive to produce, hard to do, and takes a year? Life is going swiftly, so you become superselective. I could always do one of the Grimm tales because I have an affinity for them, but for about five years I've not seen anything contemporary that I might illustrate. The last contemporary work I illustrated is *Fly by Night,* by Randall Jarrell.

Audience: Is there a particular kind of writing that needs illustration?

Sendak: No. I think very few books need an illustrator. As the reader grows up from childhood into adulthood, why are books illustrated at all? It's hard for me to say this because there are people I'd love to illustrate, but a part of me says, Why? Because a book needs an illustrator—or because you want to illustrate it? I could rationalize myself into doing it, but I think most books don't need to be illustrated.

Audience: What about books for children?

Sendak: The whole rationale for picture books is that children are just learning to read and the pictures make it easier. I really think children are going to read anyway; if they're encouraged to read and helped to read, they'll read. Maybe pictures do make it easier, but I don't think they're absolutely necessary.

Audience: In the twentieth century we tend to think of the illustrated novel as being for children. And yet novels for adults were often illustrated in the Victorian period.

Sendak: All the illustrations in Dickens's novels are beautiful. Charles Dickens is a wonderful example of someone always on the verge of being a brilliant children's book writer. There are endless episodes in Dickens that have the ingredients of ingenious writing for children, like pots that move and chairs that creak—the quality that allows, I think, for illustration. But book illustration is, for the most part, a lost art.

I think the trend toward illustrating books for adults is reviving now. Some part of me says, Terrific, it's nice to see it revived. And another part of me says, But what's the reason? A publisher recently said, Why don't we do adult books illustrated as they used to be in the old days? I said, Wonderful idea, what did you have in mind? And the answer was, Well, would you like to illustrate *David Copperfield?* I said the usual thing: I don't think you need me. If you're going to do that, why not pick somebody who wants to illustrate it—but then who is there?

I have a great dislike for the Heritage Press editions. *Moby Dick* was illustrated; *Madame Bovary* was illustrated; and they look terrible. And yet the illustrators are all good artists; what happened was no wedding at all. They were simply putting a name artist with a name author. What's the point of that? To have a library of illustrated books? There are very few books that represent marriages like Tenniel and Carroll—very few in the whole world. It happens maybe once or twice in a generation.

Audience: Whether the book you illustrate is for adults or children, it *is* art. And a book like *Wild Things* isn't just for children. The art is there for all of us.

Sendak: Well, there you're getting into another subject entirely. You're talking about breaking out of the category called Kiddie-Book-Land—where a lot of us serious practitioners have been buried for a very long time. It's only been in the last ten years that people are not embarrassed to admit that they read books for children. It's great fun to speak at colleges because the young people there love to talk about reading books for children—reading them with the same generous pleasure that they get from reading anything good. In the old days I can't tell you how many embarrassing parties I went to where only the women talked to me because I was the man who wrote the book that put little Jane to sleep. The macho daddies didn't know what to make of a man who did that for a livelihood. I've been through it a thousand times.

But now I think our time has come. Our work is coming into its own as an art form, a very serious art form. It's an art form that is thoroughly practical—children use illustrated books. And the picture book form is one of the most beautiful forms to work with; pictures and words are married as they are in no other form.

So I agree with you wholeheartedly. And I would love to see the day when our art really is taken as seriously as we're taking it right now.

Audience: If there's a film adaptation of one of your books, should children read the book first and then see the film? Does it make any difference?

Sendak: Not to me. It makes no difference to me, and it makes no difference to the child. I think you'll only get a child uptight if you give him or her the option—would you like to see the film of this first and then read the book, or read the book and then see the film? Already the child smells a rat. Already there's something educational about the whole thing, which takes away from any personal pleasure he might have had if he had just been left alone in a corner with the book. So I would say, if you have to, trick him; show him the film later.

Audience: Have you considered working on an original film production, rather than on a book to be adapted?

Sendak: No. I would like to do more films, although *Really Rosie* was discouraging in many ways. But I believe, after much misadventure and all kinds of feelings, that my life is in books. The time I gave to *Rosie* was two years of great pleasure; but I was anxious all the time that I wasn't doing a book. This was after much carrying on and grumpiness about being in a rut and feeling that there must be more to life than doing books. As it turns out, for me there isn't. It's as much as I want to do, and it's the best I have to offer.

I'm so determined to produce those books that are still in my head, and I'm worried about how long it takes me to work. I'm more and more aware of how slow I am. I have the incredible faculty of dragging. I have to keep eliminating work from my life to allow for getting on with the books.

Audience: What magazines and reviewers do you look for?

Sendak: I don't look for reviews; I usually get a package of them from my publisher. Occasionally, someone will extricate the most venomous of them, so that my day won't be entirely ruined. I don't look to any particular person to say something about my work. I take reviews seriously; I wish I didn't. Being human, of course, we suffer terribly from bad reviews. And almost always we feel they're undeserved.

Audience: Have you spent time in Germany?

Sendak: Yes, I have. In preparing Grimm, I went on what is called a "Grimm *Reise*" with some very good friends; I spent some months in Germany just traveling through parts of the country where the tales are set. I was going to be superauthentic. I got a look at Grimm illustrations that have never crossed the Atlantic. The most famous ones we know are those by George Cruikshank and Arthur Rackham; there may be a handful of others. For Arthur Rackham I have a very special bad feeling, but George Cruikshank's pictures are superb, and I think maybe the best. The Grimm brothers loved them. In the Grimm Museum in Kassel, West Germany, there are many other versions, some of them just as interesting as Cruikshank's. There is a very different attitude toward the tales in Kassel. A popular illustrator of Grimm is someone I dare you to tell me you've heard of; his name is Otto Ubbelohde; I dare you to spell it. He is very Art Nouveau-ish. The Germans love him, and most Germans know his work better than they know Cruikshank's. And the Ubbelohde Grimm is a beautiful version—a robust, healthy, outdoors kind of Grimm, the kind of Grimm I could never achieve. But that was the great fun of being in Germany, seeing how many artists had done Grimm and how valid most of their work remains.

I also followed the Mozart trail, the various places he visited. At a small party in Paris with people I didn't know terribly well, I made a faux pas, saying, Just think, Mozart was in this city, and he had such a terrible time; he hated it so much, and he complained to his father how expensive it was to go from the Left Bank to the Right. Now I can see why this remark was so disastrous, because you daren't ever tell Parisians that there's anything wrong with their city; and to remind them that Mozart loathed Paris and that Paris treated him miserably was dreadful. It was a long time before I got served that evening.

Mozart's mother died in Paris perhaps because of bad French doctors. It was a terrible experience. There, a total flop at twenty-one, he had been with her in a lousy hotel on the Right Bank. When his mother died, he had to deal with the problem all by himself. There's a famous letter to his father and his sister—he wrote it while his mother was lying dead in the next room. "Our mother is very ill. But you must be prepared for the worst, and may it not happen, but if it does, take courage and pray and hope." He was preparing them for what he knew had already happened. And oddly enough—critics are so incredible—they blamed him for being coldhearted; how could he have written that letter?

Audience: You said you hated school. A number of children feel the same way. Have you ever considered putting that into a book?

Sendak: I don't know, quite honestly, whether it's a subject I could deal with. It's a realistic rendering of a problem. I would much rather go around the situation and show how a child deals with revolutionary, tumultuous feelings that have no place in a given setting, like the classroom or his mother's apartment or whatever.

I wouldn't ever write a book about how I hated to be in school. I couldn't do that. But I would write a book that would intimate that it's all right to hate being in school—it's perfectly normal to be unhappy in school, occasionally. I can't remember ever having liked being in school, but I would guess there must have been a day or two. I did have a wretched time. I'm not saying it was the school's fault particularly; it may have been my parents' fault, or it may have been a general problem. I just know that it was a form of implacable misery, since I had to go every day. I felt very alone; I'm the youngest of three, and unhappily I had two very bright siblings who loved school. So I had the example of my sister, a large girl who was always skipping grades; I hated her for that with a passion.

Audience: Have any of your relationships with authors been important in your work?

Sendak: If only Randall Jarrell had been alive when I was doing Grimm! He was one of the greatest writers to work with, excepting Ruth Krauss, one of the few writers—if not the only writer—who had a tremendously original graphic sense of bookmaking. He knew how to talk about pictures, and in his books that I illustrated, he contributed tremendously to what they looked like. It's tragic I didn't have him for Grimm—it would have been one of the great collaborations of my life.

Audience: Is color preferable to black and white in a picture book?

Sendak: I think children can appreciate black and white very easily. I would say eight out of ten books could be in black and white. It is so rare that a book *must* be in color. Think of some of the books we've mentioned today, some of our favorite books: The perennial example is *Alice in Wonderland*—it's never suffered from being in black and white. I think it is an adult idea about what children like—color does this or stimulates that. Real art stimulates children. Something genuine, something honest, something captivating stimulates children, whether it's black and white or color. Not having color in every book is no loss at all. If anything, the economic pressures are good in that they make publishers think twice about whether a book should be in color.

Audience: How do you approach a book like *Fly by Night?* Do you start off in pen and ink or do you start off with flashes of color?

Sendak: A book almost always dictates its needs very quickly. If I have any rapport with the book I'm illustrating, it gives off its messages rapidly. *Fly by Night* was black and white after I read the first two sentences.

The clues are easy, as far as I'm concerned—you just have to read the story. Randall mentioned light and shadows that are black and white and gray; he told the illustrator. Randall has always told every one of his illustrators, if they would just read him carefully, what they were supposed to do. It was like a blueprint.

The book took ten years to produce, and there was one quite nasty review that said, "No wonder it took ten years. They must really have had grave doubts about doing this book." The real problem, of course, was that everyone was stunned for a very long time after Randall died. It just seemed impossible that he was dead. And it was easier simply to shift away from his book and do something else. When enough time had elapsed, guilt began to creep in and say, How dare we keep a work of his away from the public? Only then did I begin.

Audience: How do you feel about *The Bat-Poet?*

Sendak: I love it. It was the first of Randall's books that I illustrated, and I still think it's one of the great fables about the life of the artist; a self-portrait of Randall. I think the mockingbird in that story is the traditional hack who makes a big noise but has none of the quiet perfection of the bat-poet. Randall was making fun of his enemies, mocking them, and talking about real artists.

Audience: Aside from William Blake, do you have a special feeling for any of the eighteenth-century British writers?

Sendak: I'll tell you—I will make the confession here—I have great, great difficulty reading poetry. It's one of the banes of my life. I have tried over and over and over again.

I have just read a biography of Lord Byron. Well, I was in the Romantic period, which was early nineteenth century. My other passion is Charlotte Brontë. She had nothing to do with that period—she's 1850—

but who is Charlotte Brontë's great passion? Lord Byron. So I started to read Byron's poems; I could not read them. I wish somebody would work on me and solve the problem I have about reading poetry. Instead, I took up the biography of Byron by Leslie Marchand, which I recommend. It is a three-volume work which he condensed into one. It's superb. And it brought me to the point where I am now reading a little book *about* Byron's poems, and I'm actually enjoying it.

Byron had a passion for Pope; he put down every poet of that time as schlock—corrupt and commercial—except Pope. And I finally read Pope. I have read half of *The Rape of the Lock* because it has illustrations by Aubrey Beardsley, which sort of helped to ease me in. And I'm actually enjoying it. I feel very sophisticated and intelligent because I'm reading a long, difficult poem by Alexander Pope. It's not easy, but little by little I'm learning.

I can't think of any other eighteenth-century English work except for Richardson's *Pamela*. I have read *Pamela* because of Mozart. Mozart has forced me to read many eighteenth-century books that are related to *Don Giovanni* and to *The Marriage of Figaro* and to what was going on socially in his time.

Audience: Do you like Jane Austen?

Sendak: No. I love Jane Austen. The one disappointment in Charlotte Brontë, the one thing I have against her, is her put-down of Jane Austen. It's the one major flaw in her character, and it's hard to find a flaw in Charlotte's character. But she wouldn't take on Jane Austen, and that was a great mistake.

Audience: What about George MacDonald?

Sendak: You're asking me about all my heroes. George MacDonald comes out of the tradition of German fairy tales, Novalis, Grimm. He loved German stories. But he is an uneven writer. He's a strange artist in that he walks a very fine line. If you read the collected short tales—and I'd like to illustrate many more of them before I die—you find some that are simply so poor they can't be illustrated.

When MacDonald is great, he combines all the best elements of Grimms' fairy tales. His writing is on those various levels where the surface is smooth and Victorian and unruffled, but you feel some strange business going on, and you're lured into it like being lured into a witch's net. You cannot get out of a MacDonald book, which is just what he intends, of course. You are stunned by the smoothness and ease of the surface, and you find yourself bogged down in a brew that you don't want to come out of. He's the most magical fairy tale writer I've ever read.

His appeal on one level at least is that he deals with human feelings. Since human feelings and people are what interest me most in life, the charm of MacDonald is the endless varieties of human nature that appear in his stories, the fascination with people. The Light Princess is one of the most charming young women in all of literature, and yet the tale is very brief, and he brings her from shallowness to gravity in the most original way. George MacDonald is an excellent model for us all to follow.

With a Jeweler's Eye: On Creating Picture Books

CHARLES MIKOLAYCAK

One of the things in life that annoys me is the difference between an author and an illustrator handing his book to a friend. When an author offers a book to a friend, the person says, "Thank you. I can't wait to read it." The author waits, and eventually the person reads it, usually providing an enthusiastic response. However, when an illustrator hands a picture book to a friend, that friend usually flips it, often from back to front, and says, "Oh, it's lovely." And that's usually the only response!

A picture book is almost 80 percent visuals and 20 percent text. And while the text can be read in a brief time, there's a great deal going on in the pictures. Certainly, pictures can be scanned instantly, but if the reader is going to "read" a picture book, he's going to have to learn how to "read" pictures. Because we see many things instantaneously, we don't usually stop to consider the corners of pictures, the juxtapositions of spaces, or other visual details that are at work.

To explain more fully what I mean, I'm going to take you on a journey—the evolution of a picture book by me, *Peter and the Wolf*, from a narrative by the Russian composer, Sergei Prokofiev. I will try to convey a bit of the work that went into this particular picture book—*my* kind of picture book.

Since I am not always the author, I often have to depend on another person's text, which usually comes from an editor, who telephones, "Hey, Chuck, we've got the perfect story for you! [It's always the perfect story.] And we think you're the only one who can do full justice to it." So it begins with the editor who suggests the text, to which I say yes or no, depending on how much I like it.

Linda Zuckerman, then my editor at Viking, called one day and said, "Do *Peter and the Wolf!*" And I thought, "Wow! I haven't listened to or seen *Peter and the Wolf* since I saw the Walt Disney version as a kid." Well, I got out two recordings—one the Walt Disney version, which is rhapsodized and bowdlerized, and then a real version narrated in French by Gerard Philippe, which I liked. I sat down and reflected, really to get a philosophy going. It was at this point I wrote Linda a letter. It read:

> My *Peter and the Wolf:* I love the Russian-ness of Warren Chappell's version. It's right. I dislike the primitiveness of the newest version. It looks like a meadow in Bavaria by a Yugoslavian primitive, populated by people in Russian— or what the illustrator thinks are Russian—clothes. The others—an English version I found and the Disney version—are not even worth mentioning.
>
> My *Peter and the Wolf* will be placed in a Russia that maybe existed—maybe still exists—if only in my mind. It's a prerevolutionary Russia, about 1907 or so, where my grandparents came from. The book will be pretty; it will involve people other than those the narrative dictates. I hope that this way the pictures will create a world that was—or wasn't. But it is a real world, in that I've listened to many versions and been captivated by the tellings. If I'm to interpret the music, this is not to my thinking. A composition should live on its own as a picture book should live on *its* own. I shall listen again to the music over and over, but when I return to the text which I'm supporting and elaborating, my pictures will live. If I can create a Peter, perhaps me as a boy, and a wolf—how I observe things in animals I love—and a plausible world, in part of my imagination, combined with lots of hearsay and some visual truths, I will be happy. That's a big order. The milieu, the world, is very important to me here. It shall be very bright Russian—and me. I guess I'm wanting to make this a piece about me, and not the illustrated version of the music. I want it to be a happy book—no demons; I've been working on a lot of books, mythology and Bible stories, that summoned up demons in me. I want flowers, fields, blue skies, silliness which isn't really silly, fathers and mothers who aren't so stern they don't understand, houses that are loving, churches that are imposing. I want to create—or re-create—a memorable day for a boy. I want the reader to come away from the book needing to listen to a recording of *Peter and the Wolf,* carrying in his or her mind my pictures, which, I hope, will be true enough to help make Mr. Prokofiev's music live.

So that was the note. Then, for the first time in creating a picture book, I made a map—a map of Peter's Russian country—one that shows the town, the zoo, the field, his house, the meadow, the woods, the pond. It was just on a tiny piece of paper, a veritable sketch. And my editor called back and said, "OK, go ahead with your version of *Peter and the Wolf*."

And I worked on this book for about ten months. At some point, someone sent me a tape of Alec Guinness reading the story, and I listened to it. I had two other tapes, and this recent gift started an obsession in me. Soon I started getting tapes from all over the world; I called late at night, everywhere from Radio Hungary to friends in Poland—begging friends who were going on vacation. No one escaped. I now have one hundred and nine versions. One of the most marvelous of all was one I'd lusted after—one I'd heard of that was recorded by Eleanor Roosevelt. It is long, long out of print. I mentioned it at a conference, and someone apparently made a note of my desire for it. About three weeks later, to my surprise, there came in the mail a cassette of Eleanor Roosevelt reading *Peter and the Wolf* that someone had made from the recording. Now, if you have any rare recordings of *Peter and the Wolf*, please write me in care of my publisher. For although the book may be behind me, my obsession with it is not.

EVE RICE

The books I had as a very small child—like *Peter Rabbit*, Marie Hall Ets's *In the Forest*, and *The Quiet Noisy Book*—in some ways made me who I am; the books molded me and shaped me and became part of my very being. And I am sure I am not alone in feeling their influence.

What can you do once you discover that picture books have such incredible power in the lives of young children? If one had any sense, one would be terrified of the responsibility this places on any person who might attempt to write or illustrate them. But there is another side—an irresistible challenge that beckons many of us to try nonetheless: the challenge of creating something that will have the power to stay on in memory and, one may also hope, of creating a work truly *worthy* of lasting so long. For worthy or not, we persist in loving many of our childhood books—even some very mediocre ones—because of the special meaning they once had for us. Of course, there is more to the challenge of picture books than mere longevity. They also demand absolute simplicity: an ability to be totally direct without being heavy-handed, to be clear without being transparent and obvious, and to be aesthetic without entering the realm of the aesthete.

And so, I find myself both awed by picture books and drawn to them. The third ingredient is the great pleasure I derive from creating them. Although I have written for readers of various ages, I still feel that picture books offer the greatest reward: I get a satisfaction out of shaping a picture book that I simply do not get from working on books for older children.

There are, to be sure, many different sorts of picture books, for example, those for the very young and the moderately young and those for children just learning to read on their own. But what I'm referring to is that neglected area after the age of board books. Board books are mostly collections of single words—*ball, seal, pencil,* and so forth. To me they are not really books at all but three-dimensional objects masquerading in two dimensions masquerading as books. By contrast, in picture books for the very young we discover the first real stories. They are the simplest of true books, the most pared down, and yet, they are deceptively simple. Creating one is a process of distillation: it's like gathering millions and millions of rose petals to make a tiny amount of a fine perfume. In a picture book you are left with the essence, oblivious to all that was discarded to make one very simple statement. Such a book is a place in which every single word, and even every *syllable,* has to be absolutely correct. As an artist, I often do "simple" line drawings. One might think it would take me far less time to put down unadorned lines than to cover a page with intricate crosshatching. However, if I make a mistake in that simple line, everyone sees it; but if I make a mistake in the crosshatched version, the wayward mark is easily disguised. It's the same sort of thing with the words in a picture book: there's no room for error. I think that very young picture books are the hardest books to do, and this is one of the reasons I keep coming back to them again and again.

I accept it as a truism that children who start with books are the ones most likely to stay with books. As a creator of that kind of very first book, I have the opportunity to draw a child into the world of literature and art. I am fond of saying that children are "tasteless," which is not to say that they have bad taste, but rather no taste at all—and that they will like what you give them, good or bad. It's a question then of fighting TV and glossy advertising and a lot of other artifacts of late twentieth-century culture. I tend to think that the visual pollutants we offer do more harm at this early age than the verbal pollutants, and that long after a child has forgotten what Big Bird said, Big Bird's neon features will still be burning in his or her memory. In our society we do make a real effort to teach children how to *hear* and how to use language, but we are sadly neglectful in teaching them how to *see.* We just assume that the visual side of life will take care of itself. However, one look at the billboards along any highway should convince us of the perils of leaving our visual education to chance. Despite our daily dose of pictorial "mush," we can take some real comfort in knowing that there is good art—and there are good picture books— available. But no picture book, no matter how worthy, can reach off the shelf and grab the child passing by; a book, unassisted, won't get to a child.

It remains to teachers and parents, or to any of us in similar roles, to bring a child to books. And it is those same adults who must take a gentle hand and turn off the TV set if we wish to have anything other than neon gloss.

There is another lesson that TV seems to have forgotten: Children are not less intelligent than adults, they are merely less experienced. And because of this, they are often interested in very different things than we are as adults. Aspects of daily life which long ago became commonplace, banal, or beneath our notice are still deeply significant and satisfying to a small child. In some ways childhood is a place where fantasy is no more fantastic than reality, because to the very young child everything is new and different and wonderful—and the great stories of childhood are, more often than not, the ones that are lying right on the doorstep.

ROSEMARY WELLS

Characters are the essence and the starting point of every book I have written. They can come from the present or from my past life. They bend and weave themselves around neutral objects like telephones or watermelons, and around neutral circumstances like boarding schools or tennis matches. It doesn't really matter whether the book is a ten-page board book for the youngest child or a novel for teenagers, whether it is about human beings or animals. The activity of the character in a bathtub or a babysitting job gives me the plot of my story. The individuals are like a private cast of actors, who change costume, sex, and age many times, but remain always themselves. Among my favorite circumstances or objects are those things that have always been basically mysterious to me, such as cooking or any type of mechanical device.

When I was a little girl, we had a telephone with no dial on it, as I'm sure everyone over a certain age remembers. There were two important things about that phone. One was, we didn't have a party line and I dearly wanted one; I was sure these lines tapped into an ongoing party, day and night, that never stopped. Peopled by strange adults, unmarried men who needed a shave and loosened their ties, unmarried women who drank martinis and took off their shoes and gossiped on the phone, preventing decent people from making important calls. (I begged my mother for a party line but she wouldn't have one because you could never get through to the doctor when you needed to.) The other important thing about the phone was the operator. I had seen her picture in the *Saturday Evening Post*, wearing a headset, a white uniform, and red pumps. She said, "Number, please," every time I picked up the receiver. I was a sensibly brought-up child, who knew the difference between magic and facts. Therefore, I rejected out of hand all those silly stories about electricity coming through the wall invisibly from distant generators, and radio waves in the air that no one could see or hear. The explanation of the telephone was much simpler. Operators lived in phones, and we had a nice one about seven-eighths of an inch tall.

In 1981 Dial Press published a picture book of mine called *Good-Night, Fred*. Alas, children today know little about operators, but Fred has a grandmother who he is sure is in the phone and of course she *is* in the phone. After she comes out, she walks around on his hand and goes for a ride in his windup bathtub boat. *Good-Night, Fred* is about sixty lines long. It took over a year to write. A novel, *When No One Was Looking*, also took a year to write, so you can see that the differences between producing picture books and novels begin to blur. They blur still further because characters can be interchangeable among books for all ages. There is another important person in *Good-Night, Fred*, Fred's older brother, Arthur. Arthur, when confronted with the telephone that does not work, takes the phone apart. Soon the living room is littered with thousands of bits of telephone innards. Arthur is new as a male character, but he is not new. The same insouciant personality is present in my novel *Leave Well Enough Alone*. Dorothy, the heroine, is a mother's helper who hates children. She is up to her ears in a murder mystery and moral dilemmas of several kinds. She is also trying to help her employer write a cookbook over the summer. Her employer has no scruples whatever. She simply copies recipes out of other cookbooks and rewords them after arduous trials in the kitchen. She is nearly defeated by a turkey galantine, which calls for every bone in the turkey's body to be removed without cutting the meat and disturbing the shape. But Dorothy is undeterred. She takes matters in hand. If the bones won't come out from the meat, the meat can be cut from the bones and then all sewed back together again to form a turkeylike object. She makes a note on the recipe card to use all light-colored thread in the future.

This character is too valuable to be used only once. This kind of scene is too valuable to be restricted to one or another kind of book. Dorothy is very much a part of myself, as she is a girl, but she is also part Christopher, our neighbor's son.

One boiling day in August I asked Christopher to come and get rid of a bees' nest in the rock garden. Half an hour later he showed up with a motorcycle helmet, a ski mask, his father's heavy rubber fireman's coat and boots, and a pair of telephone lineman's gloves. He also had a Luger, which he called a BB gun, and five baby-food jars stuck with nails and filled with gasoline. The jars had cotton wicks leading out of holes in the tops. He showed me a Marine Corps survival manual with a section on grenade making in the wilderness. His plan was to light each wick and to throw each jar just so and blow up the bees' nest like a land mine. If the jars failed to explode, he would shoot the bees with his pistol. My older daughter was holding the baby in the back of the kitchen, vigorously shaking her head and mouthing the word no, over and over. I dissuaded Christopher, disappointing him horribly because I wouldn't take the responsibility for him losing an arm or an eye on our property from a Molotov cocktail. He finally agreed to light a simple fire over the bees' nest, but not without putting on all his protective gear and asking me for two-and-a-half glasses of water and a cooking timer set for fifty seconds. He had figured out the loss of body fluids in ninety-eight-degree heat to be at this rate and amount. In the end he burned the nest out nicely, but not before he threw one of his little lighted jars at it as a final gesture.

Many times Christopher has offered to babysit for our children. I know that if I allowed him to watch the children and something went wrong with the telephone, he would take the telephone apart all over the rug, as Arthur does in *Good-Night, Fred*. I know if I allowed him to watch the children and something went wrong with the stove, he would seal the children's dinner in tinfoil and cook it in the dishwasher, as Pinky Levy does in my next novel [*The Man in the Woods*]. I know if I asked him to babysit for us, he would read my youngest daughter a bedtime story out of Edgar Allan Poe, which Dorothy would have done to a three-year-old and which I did.

Christopher is an author's gold mine.

I have another one of these people, from my own past this time. A completely different and much less lovable person, who, nonetheless, like a variation on a symphonic melody, will be even better the second time around. The person appears as Claude in *Timothy Goes to School*. *Timothy* is the story of a very happy-go-lucky little character, who happens to be, in this case, what reviewers call one of my "furry little animals." He's a raccoon. He goes charging off to school in his brand new sunsuit. There he encounters Claude, who is slightly bigger, very self-assured, and dressed in a jacket and tie. Claude tells Timothy in no uncertain terms that nobody wears a sunsuit on the first day of school. Timothy goes home in tears. All week long thereafter he manages to wear just the wrong thing for Claude's eagle-eye approval. All week long he hopes that at least Claude will show himself to be clumsy, stupid, or unpopular. Claude, being the class big shot, is none of these. He is, instead, a whiz at everything and admired by all. Just before Timothy gives up in the end, out of the blue comes Violet, who has been in the background all along. She is in just the same predicament with Grace, who sings, dances, counts up to a thousand, and sits right next to her in class. Timothy and Violet become instant friends and go home, laughing about Claude and Grace all the way. This book came about because Victoria, my own first grader, came home in tears after the school Christmas concert. But I never could have written it properly without a girl I haven't seen in twenty years. Her name was Marion Airs. It really was.

When I was in school, I was neither inept, ugly, badly dressed, nor despised. However, I didn't know this because for twelve years, on and off, I was plagued with Marion Airs. In grade school Marion could hit a softball two hundred feet. Her product maps always got the hemp and coffee in the right sections of Brazil. As we grew older she developed a terrific figure, and she got it early. When she was fifteen, she went steady with a senior who resembled a young Jack Kennedy. When she was sixteen, she was given a powder-blue convertible. I remember that convertible because whenever she came tooling by with a carful of friends, I would always hide behind the nearest shrubbery. I never hid fast enough though because eagle-eye Marion would always wave airily, like Grace Kelly, to the rhododendron bush in front of me as she swirled on by. After the senior prom, to which I was not invited, she smashed up the blue convertible totally, but God smiled on Marion and her date and she emerged umblemished to become class valedictorian. A generation has passed since I have seen or heard of this person, and yet I still have occasional dreams about her. I dream that she has been abandoned by three husbands, has a cellulite problem, and is now personnel manager for Midas Muffler. In my heart I know better. I know that she is either *the* real estate dealer to see for the whole south of France, or else she is happily married to Thor Heyerdahl's son and takes pictures of underwater treasures in the Caribbean.

My own daughter, Victoria, started school with some advantages I did not have. She is a much more attentive and better student than I was. She has lovely, wavy blond hair and small feet; she is allowed, within reason, to pick out her own clothes, a thing I was not permitted to do until I was married. Still, Victoria's start in the first grade was inauspicious; she ran into Melissa almost immediately. Victoria never mentioned Melissa until the school Christmas concert. As it happened, by her own choice Victoria wore her favorite Scottish kilt to the concert because she hated the dress I had picked for her. She came home in tears; after several hours of cheerful prying on my part, she finally told me that Melissa had said that nobody wears school clothes to the class Christmas concert. This was true. I had been in the audience watching all six elementary grades perform, in turn, thirty-eight Christmas favorites from all over the world. And every girl had been there in a dress. I pointed out to Victoria that no one had noticed and that she'd looked splendid in her kilt. Naturally, this did no good as I'm thirty-plus years old and Melissa, who gave Victoria the word just before they went on stage, is seven-and-a-half.

I told Victoria that Melissa was just plain mean and that she shouldn't pay attention to people who were mean. I told her that Melissa had worn an ugly dress and was probably jealous. I told her Melissa's parents probably didn't love her very much and as a result poor Melissa had to pick on other people. I told her Melissa would never do well in this world.

Victoria answered that Melissa was in the top reading group, the top spelling group, the top math group, had three best friends, her own pony, and been chosen to play the wisdom tooth in the class musical about dental decay, whereas Victoria had been given a minor role as a food particle.

I could then see eleven more years of Melissa looming on the horizon. It is unlikely that Victoria will suddenly start playing the violin like Isaac Stern or playing tennis like Tracey Austin. It is even less likely, given her inheritance, that she will develop a reasonably mature figure at a reasonable age, like thirteen or fourteen. The worst of it is that with all my up-to-date ideas of motherhood I am no better equipped to deal with Melissa than my mother was with Marion. And that is because the Claudes and Marions are placed in this world to test us.

When I was little, I was sure that very beautiful, rich, and famous people—and this included teachers—never ever went to the bathroom. It took me years to be sure this was untrue. I know now also that everyone has a Claude in his or her life, somewhere. I'm sure even Nancy Reagan has a Claude.

Using these examples, I am really trying to make a very serious point. I have been asked to speak here today about how it is that I write such totally disparate things as young adult novels and illustrated picture books for the very young. To me the writing is all the same, whether there are three words or three hundred words on the page. They must be just the right words and no more or less than are needed. Whether I write a picture book or a novel depends on two things: what is happening in my life at the time, and how much I need a break from the last kind of book. When five-year-old Victoria was dragging one-year-old Meg around the kitchen like a sack of meal, pointing out objects and shouting their names to increase Meg's vocabulary, I sat down and wrote the four Max and Ruby board books. This was such an enormous project, done in such a short period of time, that I could not give up a single day over the winter for anything else. Needless to say, I was nearly blind and catatonic by the time March rolled around and the books were due. It was time for a vacation. I took one. It was time for my annual tennis lesson. I took it. It was time for a change, and playing a little tennis reminded me of a time when I was fourteen and nearly took the game very seriously. This was the beginning of the novel *When No One Was Looking*.

All stories, adult novels, plays, or books for the youngest children must have solid emotional content. They must have characters who are good or bad but never indifferent, who jump right out of the pages into the life of the reader. Probably the greatest writer for young children of all time, Margaret Wise Brown, or Golden MacDonald as she sometimes called herself, did this sort of thing so well that she could even make a main character out of a little island and get away with it. I came to my own career in children's books as an illustrator of other people's words. After a few years of doing this, I began to write, but having children of my own and reading to them did more to change the course of my work than anything else. Margaret Wise Brown wrote many books under many names. Above all, hers were the most asked for of the hundreds of children's books that I amassed for my girls. I loved reading Brown's books aloud dozens of times; since these are classics it took me a long time to admit it, but they are not all of them brilliantly illustrated—at least by today's standards. I began to realize that this didn't matter so much. What did matter was the story and the rhythm of the words. What did matter was that no matter how many times I read *Goodnight Moon* or *The Little Lost Lamb,* I never got bored. The jokes never paled, and I didn't look forward to the end of the book. And, of course, neither did the children.

Reading to my children has taught me to write for children. There does exist the best of both worlds, where the illustrations are so magical and the text such poetry that they are a pleasure to read aloud the requisite two hundred times. My children, husband, and I never tire of *Little Bear* or *Owl at Home* or *Goldie the Dollmaker*, but not all picture books are this good. I have found that the best stories can carry along out-of-date pictures, colorless pictures, even mediocre pictures and be asked for again and again, but that Rembrandt himself couldn't illustrate a boring story or a vehicle for nice paintings that would be read twice by a mother or listened to twice by a child on her lap. I mentioned that I started out as an illustrator. As you know, I still am one. I love to draw; I've done it all my conscious life. Drawing, alone, has saved my sanity during years of school when I was a daydreaming, poor student, who failed algebra three times and secretly despised "American Bandstand." I don't mean to denigrate in any way the importance of illustration; I just mean to emphasize the huge importance of stories in picture books, because sometimes—in the rush to admire large and impressive picture books—the little ones, the black-and-white ones, the ones with the stories, can be trampled upon.

There is a part of me that still feels the awe I did thirty years ago when every four or five weeks the *Saturday Evening Post* carried a Norman Rockwell cover. In each of these were expressions so exquisite, and props so appropriate, that a whole long story was told in a single painting. I will remember, in detail, the tremendous laughter a Sid Caesar-Imogene Coca skit generated. These five-minute plays were deceptively simple, yet works of comic genius. My memory of many of them is very valuable to me because I tend to organize my picture book dummies as small one-act plays.

Once the words are right, the pictures take on a life of their own. Then I will sit down with my inks, and glasses fit for a jeweler, and try to put the proverbial thousand words that are not in the text into the face of one worried raccoon.

From Our Correspondent in Utopia

FRITZ EICHENBERG

We are all dreamers of some sort—without dreams there is no hope for making the world a little better.

Shortly after the First World War, I became an apprentice in a print shop in Cologne, in order to learn a trade. I think a guardian angel pushed me into doing it, and at the age of seventeen I learned how to make a lithograph on stone. When I came to this country, I was completely unknown here; I had a reputation in Germany by that time. But I believe that in 1933 my guardian angel whispered in my ear, "Get out easily while you can." At that time it was still possible for me to travel on my German passport to any part of the world; so I set out to find for my little family, which I had left in Berlin, a place where we could live in dignity and where I could make an honest living. I confess I love this country—the most hospitable on earth.

I never had any illusions about the fact that art is not a means of making a living. It is a means of walking on clouds; it's a dream world, for what you are creating is not reality. At best, working in art can be described as a lonely battle, regardless of the cash that comes in. And I have never been interested in money. If you do anything, the greatest satisfaction is actually that you believe in what you're doing—that it is love in the widest sense that pushes you on to touch other people, to touch their hearts and their minds. For I believe that whatever we can do with love succeeds. I have followed this very simple principle all my life. And it has worked; it has carried me through everything. I love my work now as much as I did fifty years ago.

Books have been my life. They have surrounded me since childhood. They have been my friends, my teachers, my inspiration and have made me a better artist. We all owe them a debt of gratitude, but how do we reward them in return? I have always dreamed of The Perfect Book, and I haven't yet abandoned hope of meeting up with it some day. But I am getting worried.

For more than forty years I have labored with young people interested in art and literature to merge their talents and aspirations in what I call, for lack of a better definition, The Perfect Book. And I think it's very important to convey to them the idea of integrity—that you don't get intoxicated with success.

I have raised some children of my own with love and the help of books, and I am watching with undiminished suspense their children grow up— with love and books. Now these inestimable blessings have become the playground of national or international conglomerates, a massive army of investors bent on digging gold. The big questions are: Have books become better representative agents of our culture? Have they improved the quality of our lives, raised our taste for fine things higher than their dividends on the stock market?

I am still searching to find the reason for the alarming decline of good taste, of good craftsmanship on all levels of the art of the book, and for the lack of an informed sense of design fitting our time. Why has our young generation gone back with a vengeance to the days of Art Nouveau, the worst period of art in twentieth-century history? I know of what I speak because I grew up with it; I had to live with overstuffed furniture, with fringes and tassels on dresses and curtains, with sentimental salon art, with books bound in encrusted linoleum. When the Werkbund and the Bauhaus began to clear the air, these things vanished into attics, only to be resurrected seventy-five years later as the rage—the Tiffany lamps, the cast-iron gnomes, the fake chinoiseries are fetching prices at Sotheby auctions that would make a Rembrandt blush!

To come back to books: This trend includes the new veneration of Walter Crane, Edmund Dulac and Arthur Rackham as well as the born-again William Morris and his school—good craftsmen all; yet the trend is a puzzling phenomenon in our era of technology which invites and defies analysis.

The relentless Utopian investigator, bearing down hard on many young and successful illustrators and others of their generation intensely interested in books, finds perhaps a partial reason for this astonishing throwback. It may be nostalgia, plain and simple—the lure of more secure, romantic, carefree days which seem to have gone forever, except when we resurrect them in the harmless sudden craze for collecting antique Coca-Cola bottles or old comic books fetching astronomic prices. There must be some hidden magic to it, calming us down in our world of sinister, creeping forebodings, which makes even Dracula seem benign and familiar to us.

To bring us back to our theme, the decline of The Book as a valid expression of *our* time. There is no doubt in my mind that this strange nostalgia is partly responsible. Can it be stopped, and where can we begin to stop it? One might start at the top. But where is the publisher, the president, the chairman of the board willing to accept the premise that the pen and the brush are mightier than the dollar? And how about the editor-in-chief, the production person, the designer—not to speak of the lowly author and artist? Have they given up the search for perfection that makes for books to be proud of?

My secret Utopian source assures me that all this is a pipe dream. But I refuse to accept that idea. I am certain that there must be a publisher (not yet swallowed up by the communications industry or some multinational corporation) who is willing to pick up the torch, eager to be initiated into the secrets of those certain ingredients that make for The Perfect Book. This means the selection of the right typeface to express the spirit of the book, a happy relationship between text and illustration, perfect craftsmanship in binding and printing, reproductions which do justice to the quality of the original artwork, and a tasteful jacket that doesn't try to compete with a garish movie poster. To sum it up: A harmonious orchestration of all these elements working together will produce a fine book.

Hoping against hope for a sympathetic response in editorial offices, we should be deeply concerned, as incorrigible Utopians, with the neglect of the book's aesthetics: the decline of taste, the lack of craftsmanship, and the absence of good design. If people in publishing would honestly look at their productions with an educated eye and search their hearts, a change would come quickly enough. The yearly crop of well-designed and well-produced books is appallingly meager, but close scrutiny would reveal that they cost no more to be put on the market than books poorly done.

Even if there is a deficit, it cannot be figured in dollars and cents—an especially ticklish matter right now, says my Utopian spokesman. It is a cultural and educational deficit we are facing. In developing a sense of quality in our children—and in their parents—the book is our most valuable ally. It should be a joy not only to read, but also to feel, to handle, and to establish a personal relationship with. It should become part of our heritage, to be cherished and to be passed on to the next generation as proof of our quest for perfection on many levels of our daily lives.

You can't read a book without thinking about the origin of those little characters we call type. They were designed to express a thought, an idea; and placed next to each other, they might change the thinking of a whole generation, might change the world—as they often have. The typeface chosen should reflect the book's content, contribute to the clarity of the ideas expressed, and be read with ease. Like notes in a musical score, those letters should cling to you, continue to grow in your mind, and develop understanding and sensitivity—a sense of the quality of life. A fine book is a memorable symposium of art, literature, and aesthetics not easily forgotten, especially when it is put into the hands of a child at his or her most impressionable stage, with mind and heart wide open.

This is not the place to debate the literary trends and qualities of contemporary children's books and their subject matter. Harassed reviewers have often enough complained about the unending avalanche of adorable mice and rabbits, cats and teddy bears that proliferate between book covers in various disguises season after season.

I seem to remember a motto that the founding fathers of Dartmouth College chose as befitting their time: *"Vox Clamantis in Deserto"*—a voice crying in the wilderness. I seem to be one of the criers, but I am not weeping; there is still hope for the future. No Utopian could exist without it.

In many conversations with young people I have found an amazing new interest in the revival of craftsmanship—working with the hands and the mind, creating things of beauty but admittedly not making big waves. Despite or because of the almighty computer, there seems to be an almost universal yearning among the young to get away from pushing buttons, to use their talents in a less mechanized, more creative fashion.

During the last decade many small private presses have sprung up all over the country—in barns, garages, and basements. One could have laughed them off a short while ago but not any more. The new movement may not amount to much in terms of our GNP or on the bulletin board of the stock exchange. But it certainly makes one hope that out of all these tenderly treated "obsolete" presses will come a renaissance of a sense of quality, of thoughtful selection of the right typeface on the right paper, of searching for some neglected literature worthy of noble treatment, of the joy of orchestrating all these elements between the covers of a well-bound book and sending it out hopefully into the world. Some of these little presses will remain amateur, while others will become professional. It has happened before but never with such urgency: the will to create a thing well done, with hands and thoughts, with loving care.

Who knows? This message may even reach the ear of a captain of the publishing industry, and he may start setting cold type in his own basement—just for the fun of it. And, our Utopian correspondent thinks, one enlightened publisher may even want to produce (among the many best-selling titles on his list) one Perfect Book a year, which would set an example for the rest of this mighty industry, the purveyor of culture.

VI

The Primacy of Poetry

Drawing by Ellen Raskin from *William Blake: Songs of Innocence* (1966)
Logo for "The Child in Literature: Songs of Innocence, Songs of Experience"
Simmons College Summer Institute, 1979

Introduction

BARBARA HARRISON

Bernard Evslin, a reteller of Greek myth, recounts an early childhood experience: When he was very young, no more than four years old, at bedtime his uncle would read Homer to him in Greek, and sometimes Ovid or Virgil in Latin. The bedroom was unlighted; the house was still; and as the boy drifted off to sleep, he heard only the haunting sound of his beloved uncle's voice speaking a strange, exotic tongue. Much later, when Evslin as a young adult studied Greek and Latin, he observed, "I'd been bitten by poetry in the dark and didn't know it."

Evslin's childhood memory signals the current that moves through the essays in Part VI like the flow of the ocean tide, beginning with Norma Farber's charge to adults in "Bilingual Children" to share "armfuls of poems" with children. "The light of common speech is not enough," says Farber. Our mission is to begin early, while children are devouring their world, to encourage their deep and unqualified seeing, their new and naked seeing, brought as it is from the very center of the earth.

Young children are in the most poetic time of their lives, stretching and inventing words and creating curious and intriguing metaphors and rhymes. Indeed, they are children of the Muses, kindred spirits of Orpheus, players of the lyre and the pipe, endowed at birth with the sacred crown of laurel. But somewhere along the way, for most, the crown of laurel goes askew. Eventually, it falls from their heads. And when they notice it is gone, many spend the rest of their lives searching for the poet and the poem, for life magnified and beatific. This does not have to be the case. We have a growing heritage of poetry to transmit to our children that will support, sustain, and embellish their universe of strangeness and wonder.

The primacy of poetry—"its affinity with childhood and its affinity with ritual and myth"—resounds in the essays like the pealing of a bell. As many have said, the making of poetry is governed by the laws of the imagination; it has the capacity to startle and to unveil; it has the promise to transcend the verbal and the temporal, to humor and to console. In Coleridge's words, "the poet described in ideal perfection brings the whole soul of man into activity." The call of the poet is to dream and to memory.

In "The Dream Voyage" Gregory Maguire reminds readers of Homer's two gateways to dream, one made of horn and one of ivory; and Nancy Willard in "The Watcher" tells of dream watchers and visitors to the phantasmal *demios oneiron,* or village of dreams. In "Sing Together Children" Ashley Bryan encourages the revival of poetry as a spoken art. Children are mesmerized by sound and by rhythm. John Langstaff claims that children are saviors of the oral tradition, as he describes the chanting on street corners of rhymes, games, and songs. The oral tradition "is alive, alive-oh, just like the cockles and mussels of Molly Malone," exclaims Langstaff.

Yes, poetry is the birthright of the child, a legacy from towering Parnassus. "Let us keep that birthright vital in the mind and memory and in the mouth and ear of our children—even though, for whatever reason, we have let it die in ourselves," pleads Farber. Our work is to secure the crown of laurel on their heads so that their eyes will not become unseeing, their ears unhearing. Our charge is to be sure our children are "bitten by poetry in the dark."

Bilingual Children

NORMA FARBER

Let our children learn to speak two languages from birth—the two languages of their mother tongue.

Let them become as fluent in the exercise of poetry as in the use of prose. For both modes are available to them from the start. In the beginning, as the most natural way in the world, we practice with our children the meters and dynamics of simple poems. We are gladdened by each answering syllable, however strange, however awkward its shape. They are enhanced sounds, these earliest utterances. For children master their first phrases with a pulse, an intensity, a brio closer to song than to common speech. Children tell us small poems long before they command the technique and habit of prose. And we recognize those young sounds as coming from the distant country of our own childhood. Our greatest asset in responding to children is that each of us has been a child. The language of poetry, so natural to the voice of childhood, has simply been overtaken in most of us by the daily usurpations of prose.

Bilingual parents sometimes express the intention of raising their children to be doubly fluent. Why limit our young, they ask, to learning only English? Let them master French, for instance, en même temps. A good intention. And so often a failed one. The second language becomes dissipated in the powerful thrust of the first. Maybe later, much later, the children will study that second language—out of grammar books. By then it will truly be a foreign language.

But there is a sadder defection, the loss of our own tongue, that "other" tongue we practice with our children simply and spontaneously, when they are still too young, too new, to resist it. They seem quite at ease with it. Rhyme and rhythm and sound-color and musical abundance and mystery do not embarrass them. And because we can mask our own delight by pointing to the child's delight, we manage to avoid the look, even the experience, of self-consciousness. Songs and game-poems and Mother Goose are early childhood's daily fare of natural food. In that pristine, all-possible time, we may believe that children will be talking poetry, poetry, poetry all their lives, Molière to the contrary.

In due course normal attrition sets in. Our children are more and more on their own. They begin to read by themselves. Increasingly, we are excused, dismissed—if we consent to be. This freedom tempts us. We readily convince ourselves not to interfere with the child's independence, not to delay the child's growth.

We need to be reminded that a certain growth still requires our active engagement. Children may resist the incitements of new, more difficult poems. They may turn away from the challenge. A cleavage may develop between useful, real speech and the language of vivid images, of intense emotion. Alienation may follow. The children will grow beyond the claims and attractions of Mother Goose. They have no patience for more demanding forms. Their daily instrument has become prose: an excellent tool, engaging enough. Adequate medium for the stories they love to read and hear. They discard the old plaything, that musical toy—poetry. They have outgrown it. Ordinary speech and its custom will presently lie upon them with a convincing weight.

Let us intervene. Let us pretend, if we must, that we ourselves, prosaic adults, feel a greater need, a wilder enthusiasm for that fugitive other language than we may rightly claim. Let us keep that birthright vital in the mind and memory and in the mouth and ear of our children—even though, for whatever reason, we have let it die in ourselves. Let us take up armfuls of poems signaling the years from the Queen of Hearts to King Lear—anthologies furnish us abundantly. Let us speak poems aloud at home, in the school, in the library, in the open, wherever they may resound. Let us ourselves memorize them, or at least their memorable lines, so that readily and ear to ear we may share them with young listeners, swiftly, urgently, on any pretext, at the drop of a reminder.

For the light of common speech is not enough. There are further glories to be witnessed in all our noisy years. They must be sought out, claimed, hailed in their rich complexity. Sense and the senses must become prepared, line by line and poem by poem, for the great master-sounds and master-images yet to be heard. Let the children grow sensitive and strong to receive the poems that still await them. Let them become fluent of imagination to fathom meters and meanings. Let them grow agile of tongue to taste the most sonorous cadences. Let them listen.

"And hear the mighty waters rolling evermore."

NOTE

Norma Farber served as honorary chairperson of the Endowed Scholarship Fund for children's literature at Simmons College; she also provided a number of scholarships and grants before her death in 1984.

A Mother Goose Portfolio

INTRODUCED BY GREGORY MAGUIRE

The historical identity of Mother Goose is elusive. She is French. She is German. She is American. She is Bertha, the mother of Charlemagne. She is the Queen of Sheba. She is given homage in the title of Perrault's classic collection of fairy tales. She is the muse for past and contemporary poets, whose own works, if loved enough, may become part of the oral tradition, part of the Mother Goose legacy.

Mother Goose herself has been an ambassador to children through the ages and across cultures. The twelve drawings and prints by twelve artists reflect the richness and variety of her legendary past. A stalwart band, this company of Mother Goose—and they are shown here in temptation and battle, loss and gain, trauma and resolution. (Half of the characters are concerned at least in part with the perils and pleasures of hearty eating.) These are timeless rhymes.

The rhymes, selected by the artists and by me, are represented in a variety of texts: *The Annotated Mother Goose, A Family Book of Nursery Rhymes, The Oxford Dictionary of Nursery Rhymes,* and *The Oxford Nursery Rhyme Book.* "Bobby Shaftoe" is printed here in the version recited by my grandmother, Mary McAuliff—no scholar she, but an exemplary grandmother.

The illustrations were contributed to the portfolio by the artists; the portfolio was originally made available for sale in 1983 to raise scholarship money for children's literature studies. The reprinting of the portfolio here helps to highlight the scope of Mother Goose rhymes, often a child's earliest exposure to poetry. Full of sense and nonsense, the rhymes can become a springboard to fuller and richer experiences of poetry later on in childhood.

Little King Pippin

PORTRAIT BY ARNOLD LOBEL

Little King Pippin he built a fine hall,
Pie-crust and pastry-crust that was the wall;
The windows were made of black pudding and white,
And slated with pancakes, you ne'er saw the like.

Tom Tom the Piper's Son

PORTRAIT BY MARCIA SEWALL

Tom, Tom, the piper's son,
Stole a pig and away he run;
The pig was eat, and Tom was beat,
And Tom went howling down the street.

Bobby Shaftoe

PORTRAIT BY ASHLEY BRYAN

Bobby Shaftoe's gone to sea,
Silver buckles on his knee;
He'll come back and marry me,
Pretty Bobby Shaftoe.
Bobby Shaftoe's bright and fair,
Combing down his yellow hair,
He's my own forevermore,
Pretty Bobby Shaftoe.

Robin and Bobbin

PORTRAIT BY DAVID MACAULAY

Robin and Bobbin, two big-bellied men,
They ate more victuals than three-score and ten;
They ate a cow, they ate a calf,
They ate a butcher and a half,
They ate a church, they ate a steeple,
They ate the priest and all the people,
And still complained they were not full.

Simple Simon and the Pieman

PORTRAIT BY URI SHULEVITZ

Simple Simon met a pieman,
Going to the fair;
Says Simple Simon to the pieman,
Let me taste your ware.
Says the pieman to Simple Simon,
Show me first your penny;
Says Simple Simon to the pieman,
Indeed I have not any.

Little Miss Muffet

PORTRAIT BY ERIK BLEGVAD

Little Miss Muffet
Sat on a tuffet,
Eating her curds and whey;
There came a big spider,
Who sat down beside her
And frightened Miss Muffet away.

Two Lovers

PORTRAIT BY MARCIA BROWN

He loves me,
He don't,
He'll have me,
He won't,
He would if he could,
But he can't
So he don't.

Peter Peter Pumpkin Eater

PORTRAIT BY CHRIS VAN ALLSBURG

Peter, Peter, pumpkin eater
Had a wife and couldn't keep her;
He put her in a pumpkin shell
And there he kept her very well.

Nothing-at-All

ILLUSTRATION BY BLAIR LENT

There was an old woman called Nothing-at-all,
Who lived in a dwelling exceedingly small;
A man stretched his mouth to its utmost extent,
And down at one gulp house and old woman went.

Saint Dunstan and the Devil

PORTRAIT BY FRITZ EICHENBERG

Saint Dunstan, as the story goes,
Once pulled the devil by the nose,
With red hot tongs, which made him roar,
That could be heard ten miles or more.

Doctor Fell

PORTRAIT BY TRINA SCHART HYMAN

I do not like thee, Doctor Fell,
The reason why I cannot tell;
But this I know, and know full well,
I do not like thee, Doctor Fell.

Old Mother Hubbard and Her Dog

PORTRAIT BY NANCY EKHOLM BURKERT

Old Mother Hubbard, she went to the cupboard
To fetch her poor dog a bone,
But when she got there, the cupboard was bare,
And so the poor dog had none.

"Sing Together Children"

ASHLEY BRYAN

On Black American Spirituals

I searched at length for introductory collections of spirituals for children, because the spirituals are the greatest and most distinctive musical gift that America has given to the world. These songs are recognized and sung throughout the world. They are *our* music—belonging to all of us—but although one would expect these songs to appear again and again in editions for children, they just don't. After I had talked about the spirituals for a long time, and after I had lamented that no edition existed for children, a friend of mine in Milwaukee, a librarian whom I cared for very much and who had been urging me on, sent me a Christmas card with the proverb "God admires me when I work, but He loves me when I sing." My friend asked, "Where is that book, Ashley?" So I took the year off from teaching and worked on the block prints for *Walk Together Children*.

People have taken these spirituals for their own because they relate directly to the experiences of individuals throughout the world. They strike common roots of feeling that stir the soul. There's a song, "I got shoes, you got shoes, / All a God's children got shoes." Well, you know, they didn't have shoes, but they were singing, "When I get to Heaven gonna put on my shoes." I always loved that song, but it wasn't until my grandmother used the phrase that it took on new meaning. Her husband died after her seventh child was born; she had to raise the children herself, and she saw to it that they all learned trades through the English custom of apprenticeship. Now, one day, in talking about her husband and trying to make clear to me his deep love and respect for her, she said to me, "He first put shoes on me." She meant he was the first person to give her shoes, and that spiritual then came to me with tremendous force: "I got shoes, you got shoes, / All a God's children got shoes." I knew that would be one of the spirituals I would include in my collection.

On Collecting and Retelling African Folktales

I love retelling African stories because the forms from which I work are very brief and give only the story ideas. They are the forms that were recorded by anthropologists, missionaries, and explorers in the nineteenth and twentieth centuries; these individuals generally wrote down the stories to document the language and to translate other material into the language of the tribe. (A phonetic code transcription of the African language is used in some of the texts along with an English translation. From these I am able to get a hint of the sound of the African words.) The story is not recorded the way it is told. In Africa a story is a very dramatic event; it involves everything theatrical, and not only the teller but the audience participates in song. In retelling the stories into written prose, I wanted to get the feeling of the spoken voice; my source of inspiration in this work has always been poetry.

A lot of material, including books, photographs, and background information, I find in the New York Public Library in the Schomburg Collection in Harlem, which is a rich reference collection of Black life and literature. And I am very familiar with an extensive bibliography of African folktales and other materials through work that I did in the forties with Professor Paul Radin. I make copies of stories that I feel I would like to work with. For example, the story "Frog and His Two Wives," in my collection *The Ox of the Wonderful Horns and Other African Folktales*, was recorded by Heli Chatelain in the late 1800s and published in 1894 in his *Folk Tales of Angola*. Of course, my love of poetry and the spoken word inspires much of what I do. These folktales are like a tender bridge linking the past and the present, and I hope that they prompt all of our children to travel back and forth eagerly and often to the beautiful dark mother, Africa.

On Illustrating the Books

When I worked on *The Dancing Granny*, I knew that the story needed brush drawings to carry the rhythm and movement of the figure. So I did hundreds of drawings. These brush drawings come directly from oriental art; I love the Japanese artist Hokusai and his work. I studied his Manga drawings done from daily life; these influenced me in getting that dancing figure to keep moving. After I did hundreds of brush drawings, I made selections and then made the compositions for the pages, from which the plates of the book were done.

In *Walk Together Children*, I did block prints, which are the same size as those in the book. I tried to give it something of the spirit of early hand-printed books. I used linoleum blocks because in coming and going from the coast of Maine, where I was working at the time, I could carry twenty-four linoleum blocks—whereas wood blocks would have been far too heavy.

I worked with pencil drawings when I did Susan Cooper's story *Jethro and the Jumbie*. I wanted to capture the character of the child Jethro and the spirit of the jumbies, who are sort of bogeymen. The story has a certain fantasy quality—it is real and it is not real—and I wanted the drawings to complement the subtlety that Susan Cooper achieved in words.

For *The Adventures of Aku*, I worked from certain influences, basically African—masks, sculpture, bushmen rock paintings. Of course, African art has had a significant influence on Western art. With each text, with each book, I try to find the medium that will be most sympathetic to the story.

On Personal Experiences and Personal Reflections

The Dancing Granny is an African story, but it is a Caribbean version collected in Antigua, the West Indian island from which my family came. To me the granny in *The Dancing Granny* is my grandmother, whom I used to write letters to as a child. She couldn't read or write, but all the children would sit around the table, and we would start off our letters, "Dear Granny, I am fine. How are you?" And we would write to Granny each month. Finally, at the age of sixty-eight, my granny came to New York to visit. She spent five years visiting each of her four children; that is, she spent five years with each child. She was eighty-eight when she went back to Antigua, and she died when she was about ninety-three or ninety-four. While she was in New York, my grandmother followed baseball; she knew everything about baseball. And she figured out the bus system—how to get from where we lived in the Bronx to Harlem to visit her friends. Everywhere she went, she sat down and talked to the person next to her. She even picked up all the dance steps from the great-grandchildren. They would do the latest things, and Granny would watch them; she would figure out what they were doing, and she would do it and outdance them. When I came across the story motif about the dancing granny, I said to myself, "That's my grandma, and I'm going to do that story!"

Old Man Mad About Drawing

There's an anecdote I have always shared with my students in drawing and painting at Dartmouth College about the Japanese painter and graphic artist Hokusai. He was born in 1760 and died in 1849. The story has a lot to do with the nature and quality of journeys and journeying, and I tell it to students early in the semester in order to add a little levity and humor at the beginning of their voyages in the world of art:

> From the age of six I had a mania for drawing the forms of things. By the time I was fifty I had published an infinity of designs, but all I produced before the age of seventy is not worth taking into account. At seventy-three I learned a little about the real structure of nature, of animals, plants, trees, birds, fishes, and insects. In consequence, when I am eighty I shall have made still more progress; at ninety I shall penetrate the mystery of things, at a hundred I shall certainly have reached a marvelous stage; and when I am a hundred and ten everything I do, be it a dot or a line, will be alive. I beg those who live as long as I to see if I do not keep my word.

He signed it "Old Man Mad about Drawing." On his deathbed at the age of ninety, he cried out in anguish to his daughter, "If heaven would grant me ten more years! Only five more, and I would become a real painter." This story should indicate a sense of balance and a sense of humor. It underscores that what one is journeying toward is always ahead. You must maintain that quality of freshness, of youthfulness, of excitement in the enterprise—not exhaustion, not frustration. When have you earned enough to be frustrated? When have you given enough to be exhausted?

On Black American Poets

I focus on Black poets because of the beautiful sound and spirit of their poems and because the poets are often not as well known as they should be. One of these wonderful poets is Gwendolyn Brooks. In *Bronzeville Boys and Girls* she captures the richness in the voices of the children and their freshness and innocence. In the title of each poem is the name of a child. There is "Cynthia in the Snow," "Beulah at Church," and "Michael Is Afraid of the Storm." Little Marie Lucille is quite a philosopher:

> That clock is ticking
> Me away!
> The me that only
> Yesterday
> Ate peanuts, jam and
> Licorice
> Is gone already.

And this is
'Cause nothing's putting
Back, each day,
The me that clock is
Ticking away.

In *I Greet the Dawn*, a collection I compiled of the poems of Paul Lawrence
Dunbar, I wanted to include in the book poems in both dialect and the
standard English that he spoke. He was one of America's most popular
poets at the turn of the twentieth century, and he died very young at the
age of thirty-three. Two-thirds of his poetry was written in standard
English and one-third in dialect. Both groups of poems are quite beautiful,
and what I tried to do in *I Greet the Dawn* was to reveal this proportion and
to give readers a chance to evaluate Dunbar's full range and tremendous
gifts. Here is "We Wear the Mask":

We wear the mask that grins and lies,
It hides our cheeks and shades our eyes,—
This debt we pay to human guile;
With torn and bleeding hearts we smile,
And mouth with myriad subtleties.

Why should the world be overwise,
In counting all our tears and sighs?
Nay, let them only see us, while
　We wear the mask.

We smile, but, O great Christ, our cries
To thee from tortured souls arise.
We sing, but oh the clay is vile
Beneath our feet, and long the mile;
But let the world dream otherwise,
　We wear the mask!

Robert Hayden is one of America's really fine poets, a lovely man, a
wonderful person who died at the age of sixty-seven in 1980. I would like
to share his touching "Those Winter Sundays."

Sundays too my father got up early
and put his clothes on in the blueblack cold,
then with cracked hands that ached
from labor in the weekday weather made
banked fires blaze. No one ever thanked him.

I'd wake and hear the cold splintering, breaking.
When the rooms were warm, he'd call,
and slowly I would rise and dress,
fearing the chronic angers of that house,

Speaking indifferently to him,
who had driven out the cold
and polished my good shoes as well.
What did I know, what did I know
of love's austere and lonely offices?

Langston Hughes loved the work of the jazz musicians and used some of their forms in his poetry. He also enjoyed reading his poems to the accompaniment of jazz. Dreams were close to his heart, too, and he has written many dream poems, including "Dream Variation," "The Dream Keeper," and "Montage of a Dream Deferred." There is a group of twelve poems called "Madam to You," about a woman in his Harlem neighborhood. He often wrote about the people around him and always with feeling and insight. In reading the poems, I work to make his messages felt and the presence of the people felt. This one is called "Mother to Son":

Well, son, I'll tell you:
Life for me ain't been no crystal stair.
It's had tacks in it,
And splinters,
And boards torn up,
And places with no carpet on the floor—
Bare.
But all the time
I'se been a-climbin' on,
And reachin' landin's,
And turnin' corners,
And sometimes goin' in the dark
Where there ain't been no light.
So boy, don't you turn back.
Don't you set down on the steps
'Cause you finds it's kinder hard.
Don't you fall now—
For I'se still goin', honey,
I'se still climbin',
And life for me ain't been no crystal stair.

I always like to share with others the excitement of what happens when these poems are heard rather than seen on the printed page. We become so accustomed to looking at the poem on the page that we forget that poetry is an oral art, that it is meant to be heard in the same way that songs are meant to be heard. You can be as good a sight singer as you like, but if you have never heard songs sung, you have not touched the essence or the life of the song.

So often White people feel that because a poem is by a Black person and about Black people, they can't read it well because they are White. But art knows no boundaries. What I am trying to say is that anything you love in art, you can make your own. Marian Anderson, loving the classical songs of the world, learned them and sang them—"You must first possess a song yourself before you can give it to another"—and her singing of German lieder in German was loved. It's the same with Black classical singers today. They do not think: I'm not German or I'm not White or I'm not Italian. They give themselves to the music, and they find a way to offer it to others. And that's what I ask of you—in your own style, with your own voice, and with your own kind of rhythm. Everyone comes from a heritage that is unique and special.

Walk together children! It is this beautiful heritage that you must proudly share.

> Sing together children,
> Don't you get weary,
> There's a great camp meeting
> In the Promised Land.

The Dream Voyage

GREGORY MAGUIRE

Moving.

Floating, coasting, drifting, flying.

The thin screen of light that describes "day" or "night" is run up somewhere, lifted out of the way, and the world has the grainy particularity of biology and geology seen underwater.

Now and then something is brightly colored, serving as flag or marker.

Sometimes someone speaks, although the words often come muted.

On and off, there is earnest bustle. The bush shakes loose its flowers which go rolling away. People meet and say and do, with an uncommon commonplace ability, an unnatural natural talent.

Alighting, arising, embarking. The screen descends.

There is something extraordinary in a dream, but it is as elusive as it is ineluctable. We may yearn toward the dream's fruit, or meaning, or code, but dreams work with a focus that is not the clarity of our waking lives, and we may fumble, dim and slow-witted, before a dream's hazy effects. At heart, we continue to want to learn, regardless of any philosophical allegiances we might have with Nietzschean apprehensions, Kafkaesque remonstrations, or the excoriating fears of the futility of the human life as played upon by the six o'clock news and other cultural agencies. We do not lose our childhood sense of "Why?" even though our waking lives suggest that the answer is no longer even "Because"—that there simply is no answer. If we are kept sane nowadays, it is because we have our questions answered in the most unorthodox of routine media, in our dreams and shades and waking visions.

> In dreams a dark chateau
> Stands ever open to me,

In far ravines dream-waters flow,
  Descending soundlessly;
Above its peaks the eagle floats,
  Lone in a sunless sky;
Mute are the golden woodland throats
  Of the birds flitting by.

No voice is audible. The wind
  Sleeps in its peace.
No flower of the light can find
  Refuge beneath its trees;
Only the darkening ivy climbs
  Mingled with wilding rose,
And cypress, morn and evening, time's
  Black shadow throws.

All vacant, and unknown;
  Only the dreamer steps
From stone to hollow stone,
  Where the green moss sleeps,
Peers at the river in its deeps,
  The eagle lone in the sky,
While the dew of evening drips,
  Coldly and silently.

Would that I could steal in!—
  Into each secret room;
Would that my sleep-bright eyes could win
  To the inner gloom;
Gaze from its high windows,
  Far down its mouldering walls,
Where amber-clear still Lethe flows,
  And foaming falls.

But ever as I gaze,
  From slumber soft doth come
Some touch my stagnant sense to raise
  To its old earthly home;
Fades then that sky serene;
  And peak of ageless snow;
Fades to a paling dawn-lit green,
  My dark chateau.

I think that Walter de la Mare's "sleep-bright eyes" *did* "win to the inner gloom." But some treasures are not to be taken from their home without the threat of fatal peril. In his poem "The Dark Chateau" de la Mare describes a ringing up of the curtain, and a dream voyage into a country laden with uninterpretable meaning, and a reluctant retreat. Of what value is this excursion to de la Mare or to us, when he ruefully admits the country—and the experience—is "all vacant, and unknown"?

Homer sets us straight—as always. In the *Odyssey* Penelope reminds us:

> "Friend,
> many and many a dream is mere confusion,
> a cobweb of no consequence at all.
> Two gates for ghostly dreams there are: one gateway
> of honest horn, and one of ivory.
> Issuing by the ivory gate are dreams
> of glimmering illusion, fantasies,
> but those that come through solid polished horn
> may be borne out, if mortals only know them."

Dreams "may be borne out, if mortals only know them." I risk collapsing two ephemeral subjects into a single lumbering cliché, I know, but it seems to me that there are two kinds of dream experience. From the one nothing can be gleaned, or harvested, or stolen. From the other, at great risk, can be had only one crop, and that is not prophecy come true, as Penelope suggests, but poetry itself.

This is not necessarily to set to work all dreams that issue through the gates of "solid polished horn." All dreams are adolescents in that sense: they refuse to follow direction. And well they should. But Walt Whitman, who once wrote of a dreamlike trance in which he saw trees promenading about him for his express enjoyment and delight, can claim thus to know trees on an intimate basis and then can write:

I saw in Louisiana a live-oak growing,
All alone stood it and the moss hung down from the branches,
Without any companion it grew there uttering joyous leaves of dark green,
And its look, rude, unbending, lusty, made me think of myself,
But I wonder'd how it could utter joyous leaves standing alone there
  without its friend near, for I knew I could not, . . .

Those dreams of inspiration which seem most direct have long achieved a sort of celebrity status in their own right. Most famous, probably, is Coleridge's dream voyage to Xanadu:

> In Xanadu did Kubla Khan
> A stately pleasure-dome decree:
> Where Alph, the sacred river, ran

> Through caverns measureless to man
>   Down to a sunless sea.
> So twice five miles of fertile ground
> With walls and towers were girdled round:
> And there were gardens bright with sinuous rills,
> Where blossomed many an incense-bearing tree;
> And here were forests ancient as the hills,
> Enfolding sunny spots of greenery.

Coleridge has written (with cautionary note that any "supposed *poetic* merits" are of less interest to him than its curiosity from a psychological perspective):

> In the summer of the year 1797, the Author, then in ill health, had retired to a lonely farm-house between Porlock and Linton, on the Exmoor confines of Somerset and Devonshire. In consequence of a slight indisposition, an anodyne had been prescribed, from the effects of which he fell asleep in his chair at the moment he was reading the following sentence, or words of the same substance, in "Purchas's Pilgrimage": "Here the Kahn Kubla commanded a palace to be built, and a stately garden thereunto. And thus ten miles of fertile ground were inclosed with a wall." The Author continued for about three hours in a profound sleep, at least of the external senses, during which time he has the most vivid confidence, that he could not have composed less than from two to three hundred lines; if that indeed can be called composition in which all the images rose up before him as *things*, with a parallel production of the correspondent expressions, without any sensation or consciousness of effort. On awaking he appeared to himself to have a distinct recollection of the whole, and taking his pen, ink, and paper, instantly and eagerly wrote down the lines that are here preserved. At this moment he was unfortunately called out by a person on business from Porlock, and detained by him above an hour, and on his return to his room, found, to his no small surprise and mortification, that though he still retained some vague and dim recollection of the general purport of the vision, yet, with the exception of some eight or ten scattered lines and images, all the rest had passed away like the images on the surface of a stream into which a stone has been cast, but, alas! without the restoration of the latter!

In poetry the experience of having a dream is echoed. Poetry concentrates more devoutly than science, diffuses more compassionately than faith. It requires both "the eye of the hawk, the ear of the dolphin," as David McCord has said—the loving scrutiny of an exacting and informed mind—and, I am tempted to add, the dream of the human soul. John Keats, in "The Fall of Hyperion," reminds us that "fanatics have their dreams," but "bare of [the poet's] laurel they live, dream, and die":

> For Poesy alone can tell her dreams,—
> With the fine spell of words alone can save
> Imagination from the sable chain
> And dumb enchantment. Who alive can say,
> "Thou art no Poet—may'st not tell thy dreams"?
> Since every man whose soul is not a clod
> Hath visions, and would speak, if he had lov'd
> And been well nurtured in his mother tongue.

We are all capable of dreams. The mother tongue speaks in its images and emblems—a mug shattering on a brick sidewalk, a face with honest light in it, a dark chateau, trees bending in friendly obeisance—and we mimic the mother tongue as best we can. Perhaps we are all capable of poetry as well, of making the dream voyage and returning, not through the gates of ivory but through the gates of horn, and yielding up a sheet of directions, a map, a list of coordinates suggesting where we have been and what we have learned. Learned, yes. However dim, redundant, or ineffable, something is learned.

For like Emily Dickinson, we know to

> Tell all the truth but tell it slant—
> Success in Circuit lies
> Too bright for our infirm Delight
> The Truth's superb surprise
> As Lightning to the Children eased
> With explanation kind
> The Truth must dazzle gradually
> Or every man be blind—

And poems are the word of the mother tongue made flesh. They are the end result of the dream, which may be a waking dream as well as a sleeping one. Maybe when we do write poems, we are awake and dreaming at once.

One never knows when one will be going on a dream voyage. It's useless to keep the knapsack packed, the photograph in the passport up-to-date, the bus schedules stuck with magnetized plastic fruit to the refrigerator door. We may dream, says Jorge Luis Borges, but we may not command.

> Out of what country ballad of green England,
> or Persian etching, out of what secret region
> of nights and days enclosed in our lost past
> came the white deer I dreamed of in the dawn?
> A moment's flash. I saw it cross the meadow
> and vanish in the golden afternoon,
> a lithe, illusory creature, half-remembered
> and half-imagined, deer with a single side.
> The presences which rule this curious world
> have let me dream of you but not command you.
> Perhaps in a recess of the umplumbed future,
> again I will find you, white deer from my dream.
> I too am dream, lasting a few days longer
> than that bright dream of whiteness and green fields.

We can only hope that the voyages will be many—and perhaps it is not too much to remember Cavafy's "Pray that your journey be long." We can revel that so many dreamers come back through the gates of polished horn, bearing poetry in their capacious holds, perhaps having "drunk the milk of Paradise." We can take poems of all sorts to our hearts, thereby learning something in a world that rebukes the importance of such learning. We can enter into the poem, which is the only preparation possible for the event in which we, too, are called, suddenly and without reason, to make the dream voyage ourselves.

> How many miles to Babylon?
> Three score miles and ten, sir.
> Can I get there by candle-light?
> Yes, and back again, sir.

The Watcher

NANCY WILLARD

If I could gather together all the lies I told as a child, I think none of them would equal the lie I was told at the funeral of Professor Rubel, a colleague of my father's. Before I tell you the lie, I have to tell you the truth. Like my father, Professor Rubel was a scientist. Unlike my father, he was dying of cancer. He was also very fond of children and had none of his own. When my father visited Professor Rubel for the last time, he took me with him.

Entering the hospital room, I thought the professor must have fallen on hard times, for he did not wear a suit like other men, nor even a lab coat like my father. Professor Rubel greeted us in a gown which barely reached to his knees; he looked like an angel who had been issued the wrong robe. It was October and a flock of wild geese wrote a ragged V on the overcast sky.

"It is wonderful what I can see from this window," remarked Professor Rubel.

A week later I saw him again, in his coffin. Professor Rubel appeared to be sleeping. I do not remember the details of the funeral, which I attended only because the babysitter failed to appear. But I do remember the minister's message on that occasion. And this was the message: Professor Rubel was not dead but sleeping. He had fallen asleep in the Lord.

I waited for him to step out of the coffin, and when he did not, I asked my mother why he did not jump up at once, before the coffin was lowered into the earth.

"He's not going to wake *here*," explained my mother. "He will wake in heaven."

"But how will he get out of the ground?"

"When you wake in heaven," said my mother, "you leave your body behind, like baggage."

Why didn't I ask how the soul got to heaven? Because the word baggage gave me an answer. I had once seen a coffin being loaded into the baggage car of a train, like the case of a gigantic musical instrument. No doubt, people got to heaven by train, a special train for sleepers who woke in a different place and a different condition. Did other sleepers ride it also when they embarked for the less perilous countries of their dreams? And did the conductors ever make mistakes and send to heaven those whose time had not yet come? Surely this was the danger to which the prayer I said every night made a veiled reference:

> Now I lay me down to sleep.
> I pray the Lord my soul to keep.
> If I should die before I wake . . .

From that night on, I fought sleep like a deadly enemy, giving in only when I was too tired to keep my eyes open. I needed a higher authority than my mother to set my mind at rest on this matter, and I found it in Miss Brandenburger, the elderly lady who taught the Monday after-school Bible class in the basement of the Presbyterian church. Five other little girls and I were coloring maps of the Holy Land when, between the taking of a red crayon and the putting away of a blue one, I slipped Miss Brandenburger my question.

"Miss Brandenburger, if I forget to say my prayers, will I die before I wake?"

"Certainly not!" she exclaimed.

"The prayer says it could happen: 'If I should die before I wake.' "

The four other girls glanced up in alarm. Miss Brandenburger, determined to quash an epidemic of difficult questions, said, "There is One who watches over you. You know that. The fall of a single sparrow does not escape His loving eye."

She did not say that the one who watched was God, so I supposed it was some heavenly being whom God had assigned to be the watcher. Probably there were many watchers on the train of sleepers, who separated the living and the dead at a crucial juncture, like Albany or Chicago, when the conductor's voice booms over the loudspeaker: "All those passengers going to points west will please move to the head cars. Those cars will be taken off this train."

Indeed, I had heard mention of these watchers in a Christmas carol that my uncle liked to sing at family gatherings, "Green Grow the Rushes, Ho!" My uncle liked the pagan carols best. The heavenly rest and calm of "Silent Night" bored him. He liked the yule log, the holly and the ivy, the rising of the sun and the running of the deer, and the partridge in a pear tree. Nearly all his favorite carols could be found in our big Christmas carol book. But his version of "Green Grow the Rushes, Ho!" did not come from a book. He sang it the way he'd heard it as a child,

> Twelve for the twelve apostles,
> Eleven for the eleven that went to heaven,
> Ten for the ten commandments,
> Nine for nine bright shiners,
> Eight for the April rainers,
> Seven for the seven stars in the skies,
> Six for the secret watchers,
> Five for the symbols at your door,
> Four for the Gospel makers,
> Three, three, the rivals,
> Two, two, the lily-white boys
> Clothed all in green-o,
> One is one and all alone
> And evermore shall be so!

"Six for the secret watchers." Now, let me tell you about the time I saw one of the watchers on a train bound for New York. Although I alone saw him, I was not traveling alone. My sister, my mother, two aunts, one uncle, two cousins, and my grandmother boarded the train late one evening in Ann Arbor. We traveled coach. We reclined the seats as far as they would go and dozed fitfully under our coats.

In the middle of the night I climbed over my sleeping family and set out for the bathroom. Every single soul in the car was asleep but me, and the universe felt chilly, the way it must feel to a kitten that has been separated from its littermates.

Every soul? No, not every soul. As I pattered down the aisle, I saw a white hand resting on a coloring book. By a single beam from the reading light overhead, it was coloring a picture of the man in the moon. The moon was purple, the sky around it was green. I glanced at the face above the hand and saw not a child but a grown man in shirtsleeves. He was nearly bald, but he had a heavy black beard. The seat next to him was empty.

The next morning I was afraid I had dreamed him, and I hurried down to see him again. Ah, how changed! The purple moon in the green sky had disappeared. My watcher was swathed in an overcoat and reading the *Wall Street Journal*. But perhaps this was his daytime disguise, as the constellations are hidden from us at noon. Perhaps like the thirty-six secret saints in Jewish folklore, he was both a watcher and an ordinary man, even a foolish one, who only came into the fullness of his wisdom when no one was awake or aware of him. For if he was indeed the watcher, where else could I meet him except in a dream? Dreams are the guardians of sleep, Freud tells us, and not its disturbers. And what was the coloring book but his dream book, the book of our journeys and destinations, of which the dream books sold at newsstands and smoke shops were only a pale reflection?

Many years have passed since I saw that hand secretly coloring the moon, among the nighttime travelers. I never again saw a watcher, yet I would be glad for the chance to thank him for the gifts he brings me from time to time. I am in no hurry to join those passengers who no longer dream because, like Professor Rubel, they have awakened out of this life. What is a watcher but a latter-day Hermes, that wise and crafty messenger who traveled so freely between the countries of the living and the dead, and who led the souls of the ancient Greeks to Hades? The route he took led past the *demios oneiron,* the village of dreams, located between those who live in the present and those whose present has become the past. Only the living dream. The dream is the language through which our past speaks to us.

When a character in my book *The Highest Hit* rejoices that he has met his dead wife in a dream, I hope my readers will understand why the dream is important. The dream is a place where the dead are alive.

> "We lose sight of each other, but we find each other again. . . . How lucky I am to have dreams! After she died I thought I'd never see her again. Last night we were walking on the road to our village in Poland, the way it used to be. The fields, all wheat and poppies. . . . And then Rachel and I had an argument. You know, she was always a heavy woman. She died of a heart attack, talking on the telephone. Just dropped right over. Two hours before she died, she wanted a chocolate pudding for lunch. I told her, 'You can't have that pudding. You got to watch your weight.' Now every time I see her, she yells at me, 'Why didn't you let me eat that pudding, seeing as I only had two hours left to go?' "

But if dreams teach us anything, it is this: that our past is much broader than we can ever imagine. In an article called "Finding Celie's Voice" (*Ms.,* December 1985), Alice Walker describes the dream visitors who came to her from places far beyond her immediate experience:

> After I had finished *The Color Purple* and it was winning prizes and being attacked, I had several extraordinary dream-visits from people I knew before they died and from people who died before I was born, but whose names and

sometimes partial histories I knew. This seemed logical and right. But then, at my most troubled, I started to dream of people I'd never heard of and never knew anything about, except, perhaps, in a general way. These people sometimes brought advice, always excellent and upbeat, sometimes just a hug. Once a dark, heavy-set woman who worked in the fields and had somehow lost the two middle fingers of her right hand took hold of my hand lovingly, called me "daughter," and commented supportively on my work. She was only one of a long line of ancestors who came to visit and take my hand that night, all apparently slaves, fieldworkers, and domestics, who seemed to care about and want to reassure me. I remembered her distinctly next morning because I could still feel her plump hand with its missing fingers gently but firmly holding my own.

Since I am not white and not a man and not really Western and not a psychiatrist, I get to keep these dreams for what they mean to me. . . . Since this dream I have come to believe that only if I am banned from the presence of ancestors will I know true grief.

We all have said, "I had an extraordinary dream," when perhaps we should have said, "An extraordinary dream visited me." Extraordinary because of the comfort and wisdom dreams can bring us. For the sake of these gifts, the ancient Babylonians had a special ritual called incubation, or temple sleep. Those who sought inspired dreams visited the temples of the dream deities and, after offering prayers and sacrifice, slept in these sacred places. Even the insomniac might go to a professional dreamer for help. When Alexander the Great became fatally ill in Babylon, it is said that his generals slept for him in the temple of the god Marduk, hoping for a revelation which would show a cure. When I stay up late to finish a poem or a story, I like to think that writers are the spiritual descendants of those who practiced the nocturnal craft of dreaming.

Dreamers are travelers. Consider the Senoi, a group of people who live in the jungles of the central highlands of Malaysia. Each morning a family gathers to discuss the dreams its members have brought back from the night before. When a Senoi boy, for example, describes a dream of falling (quoted in *Dreams,* by David Coxhead and Susan Hiller), he is greeted with questions that start in wonder and end in poetry, questions that we might ask ourselves and that I will certainly ask Professor Rubel if I meet him in a dream.

"Where did you fall to? What did you discover?"

The Oral Tradition: Alive, Alive-oh

JOHN LANGSTAFF

Ballads are among the most ancient forms of traditional music. Many of our ballads are rich narratives as well. Over the years many of these—all of the Robin Hood ballads and many of the great epic ballads—have been retold as stories in prose, and they are still being put into books today.

I remember hearing as a young boy some of the traditional singers, like Horton Barker, *sing* some of these ballads. Jean Ritchie, from Kentucky, is still singing them today, but the tradition is dying out; unfortunately, the oral tradition of ballad singing is not being passed on. The same thing happened to storytelling, which died out for a long time; but now it has been revived, and people are going back to telling stories. We'll go on singing the ballads, but we'll sing them as we learn them from books.

So what is going to happen to the oral tradition? Where do we find the oral tradition today? Is there such a tradition anymore, and—because everything is now available in print and in other media—will there continue to be one?

Of course, there are always jokes, superstitions, and riddles. You probably know Alvin Schwartz; he is marvelous, and he's doing a lot of very interesting work, talking to people who are eighty and ninety years old and gathering material from them. It's a fascinating development, for us and for children, to go and talk with older people and learn from them.

I, too, have found some sources of a living oral tradition. When I was a teacher, the parents of my young students would sometimes say that my music teaching wasn't always about *music*. Sometimes I would use material that wasn't strictly musical. Poetry, of course, is very much a part of song, and I always used it; but what about the nonsense rhymes that can be such an integral part of childhood? Like this:

> Rain, rain, come down dashing,
> Put my mother in a passion.
> Rain, rain, go away,
> Come again on washing day.

Or this:

> Ahem, ahem, my mother's gone to church,
> She told me not to play with you because you're in the dirt,
> It isn't because you're dirty, it isn't because you're clean,
> It's because you have the whooping cough from eating margarine.

Or:

> Paddy on the railway, picking up stones,
> Along came an engine and broke Paddy's nose,
> Oh, says Paddy, that's not fair,
> Oh, says the engine, I don't care.

Now, what kind of doggerel is that? It's for jumping rope or bouncing a ball, something functional. I was curious about the fact that a lot of parents said, "Well, 'London Bridge' and all those things, that's sort of old-fashioned—that's all from the past and not really relevant to children today."

So we went out, my daughter and I, to collect street rhymes. She had just become a student in the Boston area, so she did the legwork of collecting in the streets, playing with children all over Boston and Cambridge. I even got her to go down to New York and try to find street chants among some of the American Indian people; I thought they might be in New York, having come to work on the skyscrapers. She went with a photographer and played games with the children, teaching them games that she knew until they began to include her in their games. There were Portuguese, Armenian, Italian, Black, Irish—children from all kinds of backgrounds. She found street rhymes still very much alive, tremendously alive, an oral tradition being carried on—by children.

It's an incredible phenomenon because adults have no connection with it at all. Neither parents nor teachers are teaching the children these chants; in fact, we wondered, frankly, whether we should publish them in a book. For example, since I put "Frog Went A-Courtin' " into a book, children have thought it is *the* "Frog Went A-Courtin'." That's so wrong. I have to keep explaining that to children all the time. I say that there are many ways of singing "Frog Went A-Courtin' " and that their great-grandfathers and great-grandmothers might have known it very differently. There's no right way. I simply collect variants of traditional material.

I can't remember who wrote these words, but I have them in my notes: "For the children of big cities, the city sidewalk is where the action is and from the secret society of city children come these songs, rhymes, and games with their primitive vitality. In them lives the American city child's world. Their origins stretch all over the world of Europe, Africa, and Asia. Some are very old, and some strictly contemporary." Whooping cough? Children hardly know what it is today. "You have the whooping cough from eating margarine"; but in the North End of Boston you have it "because you kissed the boy behind the magazines"—or something like that.

We found a little six-year-old singing:

> Ringo, Ringo, Ringo Starr,
> How I wonder what you are.
> Underneath that mop of hair,
> Ringo, are you really there?
> Ringo, Ringo, Ringo Starr,
> How I wonder what you are.

I said to this child, "Do you know who Ringo Starr is?" He had never heard of Ringo Starr. Maybe a fourteen-year-old brother or sister would have known, but the child didn't know who Ringo Starr was; the name just had a wonderful sound. In years to come it's going to be fascinating when people, reading a book by collectors like the Opies, may say, "Hmmm, what is this about? 'Underneath that mop of hair'?" Perhaps in 1999 everybody will be wearing crew cuts again. People may say, "That's an interesting thing; way back in the seventies men had long hair."

We found that there were a lot of things going on in the street among these children, aged five to ten. You talk about people handing on the traditional ballads from generation to generation, but what is a generation? To a grown-up, twenty-five or fifty years, but to children, five to ten years. And these children were learning chants in the way the oral tradition has always been passed along, the way I've seen the American Indians learn their long dances: the older men in the front, the strong young men in the middle, and then at the very back the tiny children trying to get the feel of it. They're not being taught anything; they're just trying to get the step, and eventually they're going to move up toward the front. And that's what I think happens to the little city children. They don't learn a thing from anybody except by hanging around and listening.

They pick up name-calling:

> Eddie Spaghetti with meatball eyes,
> Put in the oven and make French fries.

And all kinds of strange nonsense:

> Sam, Sam, the dirty man,
> Washed his face in a frying pan,
> Combed his hair with the back of a chair,
> And danced with a toothache in the air.

Now, that's interesting; I wonder, do they know "Old Dan Tucker"? Those lines are straight out of "Old Dan Tucker." And this one, with an adult overtone:

> Mary made a dumpling, she made it so sweet,
> She cut it up in pieces and gave us all a treat,
> Saying, "Take this, take this, and don't be slow,
> For tomorrow is my wedding day and I must go!"

And for ball-bouncing:

> Down by the river where the green grass grows,
> Where little Mary washes her clothes,
> She sang, she sang, she sang so sweet,
> That she sang Patrick across the street.

What a great line: "That she sang Patrick across the street."

And then near Boston we came across some children singing the identical tune to these words:

> Down in the valley where the green grass grows,
> There sits Kennedy as sweet as a rose,
> Along came Nixon and kissed him on the cheek,
> How many kisses did he receive?
> One, two, three, four, five. . . .

These children didn't know who Kennedy and Nixon were, not at that age.

In Boston we came upon a group of Black children playing a very interesting game with a lot of pantomime in it, on the four corners of a sidewalk. We took notes and taped what they said, but I couldn't make anything out of it, I couldn't understand what the words were. The photographer said, "Oh, that's a Chuck Berry tune the kids have picked up, and if you know the Chuck Berry tune, you know what those words are." Yet there was something about those words we couldn't understand, so we went back and saw the Black children and said to them, "Where did this game come from?" And they told us they had learned it from the Chinese children over in Chinatown. They had learned it just as they heard it! Here was the oral tradition being passed on without any knowledge of its significance.

We found a lovely tune in Harlem in New York City. The children were all sitting around in a circle singing something that sounded like "Duck, Duck, Goose, Goose." One child got up and walked around and tapped three children, and then those three children got up and moved around; later on, a few more children got up and moved around, till they were all moving around. Then all of them bowed to the king of the mountain while they sang, "And we'll all sing glory to the mountain, and we'll all bow to the mountain." I said in my unguarded, foolish way, "Oh, what is that tune you're singing; do you know what tune it is?" It was, of course, "Go Tell It on the Mountain," note for note. But the children in their wonderful way said, "No, no, it's not 'Go Tell It on the Mountain'; it's 'Glory to the Mountain.' " It was different to them. One tune was a carol, and one was a game, and they didn't want me telling them that both tunes were the same. They were right. This was their game. It was different, and that's right; the innocence of the child is quite vast and wonderful.

About counting rhymes: I don't know how you count off with children but there are many rhymes besides "eeny, meeny, miney-mo." Here is one of them:

> My mother and your mother live across the bay,
> Every time they have a fight, this is what they say:
> "Ichabocka, ichabocka, ichabocka boo,
> Ichabocka soda cracker, out goes you!"

And that means *you*; that means you're *it*; but for what? A game of tag? Or was it something else far, far back in ancient times when people needed to choose a victim? This sort of ritual comes from adults, somewhere back in the distant past.

And there are other wonderful counting rhymes; one rather lyrical one begins, "Intree, mintree, cutree corn." This rhyme is from New England, with lots of apples and pears in it, not just McIntosh and Delicious apples but the really old ones.

It is good to bring these traditional folk rhymes into the lives of modern children.

> Eskimo, Eskimo, Eskimo pie,
> Turn around and touch the sky.

Or this:

> Rinsel, tinsel, the ordinary soap,
> Judy is a dope, dope, dope.

"Rinsel, tinsel" might have been something out of a television jingle, I don't know.

> I'm on the king's land, the king's not at home,
> The king's gone to Boston to buy his wife a comb.

I love that one—even though when I say to children, "Do you know what a comb is?" they say, "Ice cream comb."

All of this is the true oral tradition, and I have told you one real way to find it. I've known graduate students in Boston who go out and do their own collecting and research. And they corroborate my belief. The oral tradition isn't dead; it's not even hiding. It's alive, alive-oh, just like the cockles and mussels of Molly Malone. Go out and find yourself some.

VII

A Myriad Eyes

Illustration by Bernarda Bryson from *Gilgamesh: Man's First Story* (1967)
Logo for "Do I Dare Disturb the Universe?"
Simmons College Summer Institute, 1983

Introduction

BARBARA HARRISON

Children's books have vital sociological, historical, and psychological implications in this country and in the world and justifiably attract the attention of scholars and nonscholars. Many people look to the books as a reflection of the times in which they are written. The enterprising collector of children's books A. S. W. Rosenbach claimed, "Not only do they [the books] have as much scholarly and bibliographical interest as books in other fields, but more than any class of literature they reflect the minds of the generation that produced them." On one level the history of children's literature is fascinating social history, providing valuable information on how society informs youth and on how it inculcates values. In addition, the books reveal attitudes about and insights into minority groups, the roles of women and of men, the evolution of family life, and concepts of childhood and adolescence. In its literature the soul of a nation can be laid bare.

During the first year of its existence, the Center for the Study of Children's Literature received five thousand inquiries representing an amazing cross section of interest in children's books. The inquiries included questions from individuals wanting to study children's literature as literature and as art; professors all over the world wanting to spend a sabbatical semester studying at the Center in order to develop courses in children's literature; collectors wanting to buy and to sell books; parents, teachers, and librarians seeking sources of information; psychiatrists and psychologists examining the use of children's books in therapy; school administrators seeking programs on the teaching of literature to children; individuals doing research on such topics as feminism in children's literature; aspiring authors and illustrators wanting an apprenticeship with courses in their craft; people interested in toys and childhood memorabilia cited in children's books; individuals seeking courses in comparative children's literature and in film adaptations of children's books; film directors and producers seeking books for film adaptation; radio producers seeking books to adapt for radio dramatization; educators wanting to pursue in colloquy the relationship between literacy and literature—the connection between the child's early experiences with literature and his or her ability to learn how to read. Of course, of the myriad eyes that focus on the literature, none are more important than those of children.

The nature of the inquiries represents extraordinary interest in this new and growing academic discipline, and it also suggests a certain fundamental vulnerability, which takes many forms. Among the myriad eyes are those of people who see the value of children's literature only as utilitarian. Like archaeologists at a valuable dig, they pick away at the literature. As they scrutinize, they often totally disregard aesthetic concerns. The list of nonliterary uses and abuses of children's books is long and at times interesting, at times tedious. Many people think that it is easier to write a children's book than to write a book for adults. There is much evidence to the contrary—a year of Dr. Seuss's life and a thousand pages of manuscript for *The Cat in the Hat* and three years of E. B. White's life for *Charlotte's Web*. It took White two years to write the book. Dissatisfied with it, he set it aside for a year and then spent another year rewriting it. In White's words it took him "an unconscionable time to do it." On writing for children, White states that his fears "are great—one can so easily slip into a cheap sort of whimsy or cuteness. I don't trust myself in this treacherous field unless I am running a degree of fever." Lesser writers fall prey to what White calls the "cheap sort of whimsy or cuteness." It is a "treacherous field." In children's books proportions and emphases, by intention, may vary, but the work to be successful must have unity and the ring of truth. Children sense and reject condescension.

The vulnerability manifests itself in still other ways. Among the myriad eyes are those of people who set themselves up as watchdogs of morality and social consciousness, grappling with what is and isn't appropriate reading for children. For example, over time there has been a shifting attitude toward fairy tales as stories appropriate for the young. As early as 1802 an article appeared in Sarah Trimmer's periodical *Guardian of Education*, stating that " 'Cinderella' paints some of the worst passions that can enter the human breast." As late as 1971 an article in the *Plain Truth* warned readers, "belief in fairy creatures replaces belief in God." More recently, Bruno Bettelheim in *The Uses of Enchantment* gives the tales rousing support.

In 1975, before the Center for the Study of Children's Literature was established, a three-week pilot program was held, in which participants examined children's literature through the eyes of the literary critic, art critic, musical folklorist, author, illustrator, literary historian, librarian, sociologist, teacher, and child. One of the following essays, "A Common

Humanity," by the author Milton Meltzer, was presented at this institute. "A Myriad Eyes: The Many Perspectives" points to the multiplicity of personal points of view reflected in the essays that follow. One common feeling links all of them; it is best stated by C. S. Lewis, to whom we are indebted for the title of Part VII:

> Literary experience heals the wound, without undermining the privilege, of individuality. There are mass emotions which heal the wound; but they destroy the privilege. In them our separate selves are pooled and we sink back into sub-individuality. But in reading great literature I become a thousand men and yet remain myself. Like the night sky in the Greek poem, I see with a myriad eyes, but it is still I who see. Here, as in worship, in love, in moral action, and in knowing, I transcend myself; and am never more myself than when I do.

A Myriad Eyes:
The Many Perspectives

On Being a Parent

FRANCES V. SEDNEY

Books and children, I love them!

Sometimes I love the worst of them and always, I hope, the best of them.

Professionally, as a longtime children's librarian, and personally, as the mother of nine children and the grandmother of eight, I know that as one man's meat is another man's poison, so, too, one child's "It's the best book I ever read" is another child's "Yuk, I'm not going to read *that!*"

I love what some literary critics call trash, and I love Newbery and Caldecott winners—well, sometimes I do. It's a sometimes-yes, sometimes-no situation with both. But only the thinnest of critical lines divides the two. That's something we, as adults interested in children's books, don't always want to admit, but it's true. That critical line is one that most of us, in our roles as parents, teachers, librarians, walk gingerly along, mentally tossing books to the right (accepted) and to the left (rejected). But the children, thank God, cross that critical line. They hang trapezelike from it, and they dip or dive into the bounty of books on both sides. And that's good.

Children question the decisions of adults on everything else; why should our judgments in the book world be sacrosanct?

Any book can be the best if it's being read and enjoyed by the right child at the right time. Or the worst if some judgmental adult has determined that now is the right time. As librarians, teachers, or parents, and as adult readers, reviewers, or selectors of children's books, we must never allow a judgmental line to become a barrier between any of our children and any book.

On Writing Poetry

DAVID McCORD

I write totally and absolutely for myself. I learned instinctively that the author, man or woman, writes for himself or herself, and to please himself

438

or herself, and if that isn't achieved, he or she is not going to have any audience worth having. You've got to do something to the best of your ability and be as satisfied as you can be with it yourself. I can't look at a fifth grade audience and say I know what's going on in their minds. I was a fifth grader once, but I don't know what I thought about or how I thought or what the approach to other people's minds was. I haven't any idea of that, so all I can do is write out of my own experience, imagination. (I think I'm making up in my case for a childhood that was spent so much alone. I was solitary, no brothers or sisters, and I think in a way I'm atoning for that.) I just let my mind go and I level with the kid, and then I know never to write down, never to talk down, never to anybody, because there isn't a soul you will talk to with the intelligence of a medium-sized rabbit who doesn't know something more than you do about something, always. You have to remember that in life.

Most poems grow by heat lightning; that faint glow of lightning over the mountains that you don't hear any thunder with, other than the *flash bam*—and that's the poem that comes all of a sudden. One of my poems is called "The Walnut Tree." When I was about high school age, I guess, I was out at my grandmother's in Washington, Pennsylvania, twenty miles from the West Virginia line, and my mother and my grandmother and my Uncle Nye were looking over an abandoned farm. I found right by the house and by the edge of the hill a swing hung from the very tall limb of a walnut tree. The ropes were very tall, as I remember; you always adumbrate things in childhood, but I think I'm right. I got in the swing and had a swing. The land sloped right away, so when I went out I seemed to fly—I went right out over the landscape.

Well, I wanted to write a poem, but I didn't want to make it like Stevenson's. I didn't want it sentimental; I wanted it to be an experience of life. It took me fifty-seven years, trying every year, before I saw that, and I saw it in a red light as I was coming by myself over from Route 1 through the mill town of Lynn, Massachusetts. (Maybe some of you live in Lynn, and I'm not running it down, but Lynn is not the most romantic town in America.) Right in the middle district at the red light—*bam*—I saw the poem and I wrote two lines, and I pulled through the red light to the curb and I wrote all of it. It was published on the cover of the *New York Times Book Review*.

This is an example of how something lies with you. Somehow I had gone over that experience in my mind enough so that it came out as though it was already made. Once in a while, if you think for a long time about something you wanted to write, a poem will do that. Usually it doesn't.

On Being Published

OUIDA SEBESTYEN

Sometimes writing fiction is a struggle, sometimes a joy. Most of the time it's like a chronic backache or a ringing in the ears that won't go away. I get the feeling, looking back, that I began to write not long after I began to read, trying in some half-understood way to pass on some of the pleasure that reading had given me. It seemed like reasonable work for a shy, delicate type, a loner lost in a sturdy clan of farmers and teachers. I wrote little half-baked stories, and plays in blank verse. No one clamored for them. I wrote my first novel when I was twenty. Off it went, with my heart and soul in it. Back it came. Off again. Back again. Over and over. It happened that Little, Brown and Company was the first publisher I ever sent a manuscript to. They told me, "Sorry—but keep trying us." Thirty-five years later they published me. I guess they figured I'd finally got the hang of it.

For years I wrote hopefully. Success was coming. I told myself that, every five years, when I sold a story. Naturally I had days—what am I saying, I had *years*—when I thought of giving up. But there was nothing else in the world that I wanted so badly to do. Writing incorporated all my other enthusiasms. And that was a big order because I was an artsy-craftsy amateur at everything. I knew I was a one-thing-at-a-time person. I could never be all the things I wanted to be if I lived to be a hundred, but the people in my fiction could. I knew writing was a career I could carry anywhere in the world and tuck into the spaces around two other activities that were beginning to appeal to me very much—being a homemaker and a mother. I liked working alone, maybe not speaking to a soul all day. Doing exactly what seemed right for me. I wanted the freedom of being my own boss. I wasn't about to give up just because I couldn't write!

If all this sounds impractical, if not downright arrogant, it was. It made for years of frustration and teetering along the poverty line. In those years I began to tack quotations on the bulletin board behind my desk to keep my spirits up. One—the only line I remember from Will Durant's *The Story of Civilization*—I took as my aim: "To seek, beneath the universal strife, the hidden harmony of things." And because writing was a lonely, self-revealing business, I needed another quotation from Longfellow to help the words come: "Give what you have. To some one it may be better than you dare to think." And a little one by Emerson: "Do the thing, and ye shall have the power."

I did my thing. I wrote and wrote. And I didn't have the power. I wrote and married and had a son, and still no one would buy my fiction. Or my plays or poetry or articles or true confessions. My son was born when I was thirty-seven, and I comforted myself by thinking maybe I was going to be late-blooming in everything I did. The years went by and the dream got dimmer. Somehow I found myself middle-aged, divorced, with a young son, no skills, no home. And if that sounds like the mother in *IOU's*, it's a ridiculous coincidence.

My recently widowed mother and I set up a three-generation household in Colorado, and I decided to give writing one more chance—Pikes Peak or bust—before I laid the dream away forever and got a job, like real people. Between odd jobs—I called everything odd jobs because my real job was writing—I wrote my fourth novel. Nobody wanted it. I did sell three short stories, but I sold them over a period of ten years. A lot of months my mother's Social Security checks paid the rent. But we were rich. I know it, looking back, and what is even better, I knew it then; we were rich in everything but money. I had two people who never gave up on me. And it was one of the joys of my life to dedicate my first two books to them.

Because, yes, it happened. One of those three stories I'd sold had been an enlargement of a little incident my aunt had told me—how as a child she had won a contest and got a prize that obviously had been meant for the boy everyone had expected to win. During an especially low period in my writing, I remembered the story I'd made of it, and since I'd tried and failed at everything *but* children's stories, and since the main character was young, I sent it to the children's editor at Atlantic Monthly Press. I think I started with the A's, planning to go right through every publisher in the alphabet. I asked if it had any possibilities as a book. I didn't know. I thought maybe they could add lots of pictures or something. The editor said if I'd like to try to enlarge the story and make a novel about that spunky little girl and her family, she would like to see the results. It wasn't a promise of anything. It would all be on speculation. But that letter of encouragement after all the years of rejection slips absolutely electrified me. If she had asked me to write a sequel to *War and Peace*, I would have tried. I looked at my bulletin board. It said: Do the thing, and ye shall have the power. And I did. Three months later I sent her *Words by Heart*.

Then I waited. Weeks went by. I read in the paper that our post office had been robbed. I could picture my manuscript lying discarded in a ditch. Finally the phone rang. A soft voice said, "Did you know you've written a beautiful book?" At that moment I didn't know *anything*. The voice said, "I sobbed when I read it. The assistant editor sobbed. That doesn't happen very often in this business. And we want your book."

I don't know whether I had finally learned how to put a story together, very simply and, I hope, truly, or whether speaking to children released something natural and idealistic and naive that I had been trying to camouflage as I wrote for adults. Or whether I was taken over, in the

strange process that writers sometimes feel. Or whether it was a massive
stroke of luck. But something went right. *Words by Heart* was published.
The generous reviews took my breath away. It was honored and translated
and paperbacked and condensed and dramatized. Everyone was so kind.
And, of course, all the friends and relatives who gave up on me years ago
told me they knew all along I could do it.

So here I am—Cinderella. The oldest promising young writer ever to
become an overnight success. I'm so thankful. I'm so glad it worked, after
all those years, and that in *IOU's* I could let the mother say something that
was true for me, too: Somehow money never seemed as important as living
our days the way we liked. I've been so lucky—I'll never have to say I
wished I'd lived them differently.

On Telling Stories

EILEEN COLWELL

From the earliest days of history, men have told stories and through them
kept alive the deeds of mighty heroes and explained natural wonders. The
position of the storyteller used to be an honorable one, and in the Middle
Ages he could demand as his due a harp from the king and a ring from the
queen. Listening to tales was the favorite pastime of the people, and for
centuries the professional storyteller gave pleasure to untold multitudes.
Gradually the status of the storyteller declined, until today storytelling is
no longer a living art and the old tales, handed down orally for so many
centuries, have become the preserve of the scholar.

Yet children still love to listen to stories the world over, and I believe that
they need them from infancy. Because I feel this so deeply, I have told
stories as often and in as many places as possible. Storytelling not only
gives delight, but there can be no better way of introducing literature to
children and of encouraging them to listen to the music of words.

I have *told* stories always, not read them. For both the audience and the
storyteller this is more enjoyable and memorable. The children receive
the story as a living experience; the storyteller is helped and stimulated
by the response of the listeners.

There are two essentials in choosing stories to tell. First, the story, if it is
to be told with enthusiasm and sincerity, must appeal strongly to the
storyteller himself. Second, it must be remembered that the story that
reads well does not necessarily tell well. For this reason, for instance, I
have reluctantly omitted Walter de la Mare's beautiful stories from my
repertoire, for he is essentially a contemplative and descriptive poet. To
abridge his stories sufficiently for telling would demand such skill and
perception that I hesitate to suggest it.

Let no one imagine that storytelling is easy. There is no shortcut to perfection. Much reading must be done before the right story is found; much preparation is needed for the story to be so thoroughly absorbed that it can be told effortlessly and freely. But at last the time comes when we are able to say with Walter de la Mare:

> Quiet your faces; be crossed every thumb;
> Fix on me deep your eyes;
> And out of my mind a story shall come,
> Old, and lovely, and wise.

As we see the expectancy on our children's faces and know that we have a story worthy of that eager anticipation, we have our reward.

On Teaching

JOAN M. TIEMAN

If teachers are convinced that literature is "the stuff" that makes the act of reading worthwhile, then their classrooms will reflect this conviction. In my classroom good books are strewn around, and children share their latest favorites with one another. Part of each day is devoted to reading aloud and to talking about books. Silent reading is also an important activity.

Unfortunately, the study of literature is given little, if any, serious attention in elementary schools across the country. However, reading instruction is an integral part of every day, but this instruction tends to focus on the mechanics of reading. Many teachers have done specialized course work in the teaching of reading, but few have studied literature in any depth. Teaching literature to children requires knowledge of the literature. Only through sober, rigorous study in this field, so long neglected in the classroom and yet so vital to our literacy, will strides be made in improving literature education in schools.

When children begin school, it is the teacher's task to assess the nature of their previous experiences with literature. If they were fortunate enough to be read to and thus are familiar with the world of Max, Babar, and Curious George, then it falls to the teacher to extend that knowledge. If they were not read to and have never met Humpty Dumpty or Horton, then the teacher must begin at the very roots to help them tap into this rich world. Children's preferences in reading are profoundly influenced by their teachers.

It is of the greatest importance that the quality of the literary experience children receive in school be outstanding. Because of this, our role as teachers is vital and, in fact, basic to the perpetuation of a literate society. The poet Sam Cornish hits the mark when he says, "A little boy wanted to fly, so his teacher taught him to read."

On Studying

THERESE BIGELOW

A person would have to be crazy to take a leave of absence, pack up an entire household, one husband, and two children, and move to Boston for a year to study. That's just what I did in September of 1978, the second year that the Center for the Study of Children's Literature at Simmons College offered a master's degree. Why I even contemplated that insane act goes back to my childhood.

I learned to read in kindergarten and quickly discovered the solace, entertainment, and joy that a good book could be. Fortunately, my family lived just a bus ride away from the main branch of the Omaha Public Library, with its excellent collection of children's books and its Supervisor of Work with Boys and Girls, Adeline Proulx. I was the third oldest of eight children. My mother was a very smart lady who enjoyed a break from the first four. She provided us with nickels for the bus and quarters for egg salad sandwiches at Kresge's lunch counter and sent us off to the library each Saturday.

By fourth grade six books a week could not keep me busy, so I added another trip during the week. The summer between fifth and sixth grade I discovered the exquisite pleasure of staying up all night to read. I cried over Charlie's death in *Rose in Bloom* and still hold that experience close. I can safely say that I learned as a child the excitement of escaping with a book.

My senior year in college, when career opportunities for women were still limited and I had chosen to major in history—a pleasure to study but not a useful transition to the business world—I remembered the pleasure I had found in books as a child and decided to become a children's librarian. I applied to and was accepted at Drexel University. My avocation and vocation became one.

In the spring of 1975 I read an announcement in *The Horn Book Magazine* about a three-week institute in children's literature to be held at Simmons College. Wow! Three weeks studying children's literature with other crazies who cared about children's books! The experience was so satisfying that I returned in 1977. At that institute, the first master's candidates for the fall were introduced. A sense of excitement stirred my soul. I wanted that degree. My husband was supportive and my children willing, and all said they too wanted to move. I applied to Simmons and was accepted, and arranged for a leave of absence from the Hampton, Virginia, Public

Library. The experiences of that year are some of the best of my life. The academic atmosphere was stimulating, the in-depth study of the books invigorating, and the new friends rewarding. I returned to my position in Hampton with a new degree and a renewed excitement about children and their books.

On Not Teaching Creative Writing

NANCY BOND

You can't teach creative writing. I remember, before I undertook the job, talking it over with a friend and being earnestly advised *never* to admit to the class that I thought the subject unteachable. "Make them believe not just that it's possible, but that you know the secret," he said. For myself, never having formally taught anyone anything before, confessing my doubts at the first meeting seemed not only the most honest approach, but also the safest. I would, among other things, be covering myself if I were a dismal failure. So, although I didn't argue with my friend at the time, I did indeed begin that first year, and every subsequent one, with my original disclaimer.

How much of a success I am at *leading* (much better word!) a creative-writing class is for others to say, but I find it a new challenge each time and I have learned a great deal from it about the craft of writing in general, about my own approach, and about people.

There is no secret, at least none that I know, to teach people that will make writing fiction easier or more accessible, no neat little key that unlocks all the doors. Writing is hard work; the trick—if you can call it that—lies in wanting badly enough to write to be willing to undertake the hard work. If you don't want badly enough to do it, believe me, there are hundreds of other things clamoring to be done instead. Even when you do have the desire, it's perilously easy to become distracted by almost anything.

It seems to me that a certain amount of learning to write stories comes, by osmosis, through reading them. As I look back at my own writing, I find it hard to say where, exactly, I learned the structure of a novel or the function of dialogue or such details as making chapters and paragraphing speech. I'm certain that most of it came from familiarity with novels, with absorbing the way other writers had done these things. If someone asks me about paragraphing dialogue now, that's where I send her or him—to books. You don't need a teacher for that, just common sense; you can find it on your own, the resources are all around. These details aren't designed to be tricky; they're used to help the reader to understand what the writer is writing about—to make communication possible. It always surprises me to come across a student who has *not* absorbed this kind of information from years of reading. Sometimes it simply takes a little push in that direction. And the encouragement always to figure out why. If you like a book you've read, *why?* If you don't like it, *why?* What can you learn from it?

If reading is invaluable to a writer, writing is, of course, essential. The chief excuse my writing course has for existing—any writing course, for that matter—is that it compels its members to write regularly and often. If you want to write, there's no substitute for doing it. Every year in class I point out the difference between people who want to be writers (a wonderfully vague possibility that usually depends upon staying vague) and people who want to write (a lot of hard work and frustration compensated for by the occasional euphoric feeling of accomplishment). As most people who have tried writing know, one of the most difficult hurdles to surmount is that of making yourself sit down and *write*. There are suddenly thousands of other things that urgently require attention.

The point is to try all kinds of things, not to be afraid of failing, and probably to learn more from those pieces that dissatisfy than from those that feel good. If a piece doesn't work, the trick is to figure out why. *Why* is a potent question in writing.

Students brave enough to plunge in and try the process of writing, especially those without much experience, are often extremely good critics and are good at accepting criticism, probably because they feel they have less to lose. To be told your writing is no good (which, I hasten to say, we do not say to one another, but I'm sure there's always that fear) is less devastating if you've already told everyone you don't want to be a writer. A basic part of the class is criticism. The class is a small seminar: no more than ten, ideally about eight, students, who share their work and make oral and written comments on each other's. The structure of the course depends largely upon what the students want. Some years we've spent part of each session discussing the books on the reading list; other years we have never gotten to them, using our weekly three hours to discuss the written assignments. How well I remember the first year I taught, worrying and worrying over how I was going to fill the time! Every year since, it's become harder and harder to keep up with my plans.

Initially, I asked each student to read aloud her or his piece in class, then we would discuss it. Now, although it leads to a certain amount of confusion, each person makes Xeroxes for the others (oh, the proliferation of paper—but you can always write first drafts, as I did for this article, on the backs of Xeroxes), passes them out, and eventually gets them back with comments. It's a little like a second-grade Valentine's Day. But it's much more satisfactory to discuss a piece you've had time to read to yourself, probably several times, and think about, than to try to respond to something you've only heard once. It's also useful to practice analyzing and making critical comments on other people's work; it sharpens your editorial faculties, which you will call upon again and again in looking at your own writing. One of the pitfalls of our society is believing that a piece must be right as written if it appears in print, whether you agree with it or not. Part of being a writer is learning to question whether it's right. (By *right* I mean most effective, successful.)

If I pass on little else, I try to demonstrate to students that the process of writing is largely that of asking questions and solving problems. If one thing doesn't work, you try another; you go back to the point at which things began to fall apart, and then to the last piece of good solid ground, and you try another solution. It's like solving a puzzle. It isn't a bolt of lightning that strikes the top of your head and runs down your arm onto the paper, coming out exactly as it was meant to. That's what I mean about hard work and frustration. And, oh, the joy of finding the *right* answer to your puzzle! That's the euphoria.

On Literary Criticism

PAUL HEINS

In *An Experiment in Criticism* C. S. Lewis made an interestingly paradoxical statement: "The truth is not that we need the critics in order to enjoy the authors, but that we need the authors in order to enjoy the critics." But being a reasonable man, he went on to admit that "criticism normally casts a retrospective light on what we have already read. It may sometimes correct an over-emphasis or a neglect in our previous reading and thus improve a future rereading." Since C. S. Lewis was trying to distinguish in his experiment "between readers or types of reading," it might also be important to remember what Georg Brandes wrote to Hans Christian Andersen regarding critics: "A literary critic is someone WHO KNOWS HOW TO READ, and who teaches the art of reading." Of course, if one knows how to read—in Brandes's sense of the word—one does not need critics, although what they have to say may prove interesting. Obviously, if one is seeking "a retrospective light" on what has already been read, criticism may be not only valuable but important.

The problem with children's books and with the criticism of children's books is that the endeavor is beset with ambiguities. For obviously the criticism of children's books can be meaningful to adult readers acquainted with such books; but what about people who are not extensively acquainted with them but who make audacious snap judgments about them? To cite a single example: Although Bruno Bettelheim in *The Uses of Enchantment* gave his imprimatur to the meaning and importance of fairy tales, he dismissed "the rest of so-called 'children's literature' " because "most of these books are so shallow in substance that little of significance can be gained from them." The term *most* is a strange word to apply to a body of literature which in recent years has produced such works as *The Owl Service, Carrie's War, Unleaving, Petros' War, Bridge to Terabithia,* and *The Slave Dancer.* In a sense, of course, C. S. Lewis was right. The criticism of children's books will scarcely mean anything to people completely unacquainted or—at most—only somewhat acquainted with them. At this juncture the critic can only be an apologist and suggest, "Read extensively and judiciously; discover for yourselves the children's books worthy of reading and worthy of critical scrutiny."

On Editing

JEAN KARL

When someone asks me how important book reviews are in the editorial process, one of the first things that comes to mind is a comment made by Bertha Gunterman many years ago. Bertha Gunterman was one of the early editors of children's books. She was at Longmans Green, or Longmans as it was later called, for many, many years. She must have begun editing books sometime in the mid to late 1920s. Years ago I had dinner with her, and we got to talking about reviewing. She said, "Oh, you know, I've come to the place where I don't pay much attention to reviews. I find that most of the books that get really good reviews don't sell very well. And the books that reviewers don't like at all seem to be the books that sell the best. So I just don't pay much attention anymore. I just publish what I want to publish."

I think that in any given situation editors do tend to publish the books that they want to publish. Editors are, in a sense, the primary reviewers of written material: not of the two thousand five hundred published books each year, but of two or three thousand or more manuscripts, all of which must be read and "reviewed," and most of them returned to the authors.

Editors, like reviewers, are looking for literary merit and for child appeal, but they often consider a number of other things as well. For example, an editor may have published two or three books by an author very successfully, and along comes that author's next book, and it's an utter dog. The author is convinced that this is the greatest book ever written, but the editor knows it's *not* the greatest book ever written, and everybody else who reads it is going to think the same. This may be a good author and a person the editor wants to continue to publish. So what does the editor do? He or she is probably honest enough to try to tactfully point out to the author that this is not one of the world's great books and that it is not going to do his or her reputation a great deal of good to have it published. But if the author still feels that it is a monumental work, the book will be published. In other words, sometimes lesser books get published, not over the editor's dead body but over the editor's knowledge that the book is not a magnificent volume. The publisher goes ahead simply because he believes that this author's next book is going to be really worth publishing, and it seems necessary to get this one out of the way so everyone can go on to something better.

Editors also take a look at the needs of the marketplace. They travel around and talk with people. If people say they desperately need books for third grade to fifth grade, they begin looking for books that fit readers of that level. Some publishers will commission books. I do not ever commission books, because I think that's one of the best ways of getting really bad books—which I would then have to publish, or at least in some ways would feel honor-bound to publish. But if a book is submitted that seems to fill an expressed need, I will look at it very carefully. And perhaps, even if it is not of the caliber that I normally want, I will try to work with the author to get the book up to a level that makes it publishable, simply because there seems to be a demand for the kind of book it represents.

Publishers, after all, do publish books to sell. There is no point in publishing books that will remain in a warehouse. Publishers can't invest all of their money in books—even great literary works—that are not likely to reach very many people out there. You all know the classic cartoon: the writer says to the editor, "Yes, but if one person is reached by this book, it will have achieved its objective." Well, if a publisher sells only one copy and the rest sit in the warehouse, that publisher's capital is tied up there, and he can't publish some other book that might be equally good and would reach a far wider audience.

So, editors must consider what they can sell, although they do not necessarily believe that everything they publish must be a great best-seller. I do not anticipate that every book I publish is going to sell a hundred thousand copies. With some books I'm content if the first printing sells out. Other books I expect to do more than that.

I also believe that we must do a wide variety of books. Children are not all alike. Different children have different interests. Some of them read fantasy. Some of them read very literary books, thank goodness. Some of them prefer nonfiction. And some need to be lured into reading with sports books or mysteries or light school-stories or, when they get a little older, those dreadful romances. All of us, as adults, at times read books that are not up to our intelligence level or our normal level of reading. We do it to relax, to be entertained. And children need to be allowed the same kind of opportunity. So there must be many kinds of books for children.

No matter what an editor thinks about a book, or what he or she thinks is going to happen to it, there is absolutely no way to know in advance how well a given book is going to sell. I always think that publishers don't need to go to the racetrack or the casino, because they gamble every day in a much more substantial fashion. They're gambling all of the publishing costs of a book on the chance that a given book will find an audience.

The salesman's motto is "If it sells, it's good." To some extent I think that this may be a publishing criterion, but it certainly is not the ultimate criterion. In other words, if a book does not sell very well, this doesn't mean that the next book by that particular author will not be published. Maybe the first book was published with the knowledge that the author was very young or inexperienced but someone with great potential, and with the hope that the next book would be better and the book beyond that even better. The editor is trying to build up someone in the belief that eventually that author will write a very great book. And so the editor may see that author through a number of books until the author has either realized his or her potential or the editor has decided it's never going to happen and the first evaluation was wrong.

So what the reviews say is often not the most important consideration. And what Bertha Gunterman said is often true. Books that are not well reviewed or widely reviewed sometimes do sell well, and books that are heavily reviewed and well reviewed sometimes do *not* sell well. What we must be concerned with, ultimately, is getting books we believe are worth reading to the children, because they are the people for whom the books were intended.

On Publishing

MARGARET K. McELDERRY

Looking back on the decades in which I have worked in the field of books for children—and they are a fair number by now—I see clearly that there have always been times of great difficulty, uncertainty, and stress. In between these dismal valleys, there have been periods when pressures have eased up a bit and the tamped-down-but-never-quite lost optimism, shared by most adults who care about children and their books, burns bright—tempered by caution, of course, learned in the process of survival.

Over the past weeks as I have been thinking about these remarks which concern the perspective of editor and publisher, I have felt at times that *perspective* has been replaced by *kaleidoscope*. There are so many elements fragmenting the publishing scene today that it is not easy to predict, even in broad terms, quite where we may be going. The elements shift and re-form. One alternates between hope and despair.

Let's look first at the negative side of the picture. Costs of book materials and manufacturing have risen and continue to do so with uncomfortable regularity. For instance, just this month there's an increase in paper costs going through. If the market for books were expanding as rapidly as the costs, there would be no particular problem. Larger editions could be printed over which to amortize the higher costs, so the unit costs for books would not increase drastically. However, the exact opposite has happened and is still happening. Our traditional market, the institutional one, has shrunk greatly due to lack of funding. Fewer copies per title can be printed than formerly, and because of the smaller printings the retail price of the books goes up even more.

The reduced institutional market does not affect picture books quite as much as it does reading books. Picture books have an increasing outlet in bookstores—a subject I'll touch upon soon when we look at the positive side of the picture—but reading books must be read by an interested and knowledgeable adult before they can reach young readers, and few bookstores can afford a children's book specialist.

In the last ten years the publishing industry—for industry it has become—has undergone vast changes, many of which can be considered negative. In the seventies, when federal funds were available and books were selling well, a number of publishers were bought out by huge communication corporations or conglomerates. When the bloom quickly faded, the large corporations just as quickly divested themselves of their publishing interests. More and more mergers among publishers have taken place as they struggle to survive. This process tends to diminish the individuality of the field, although more recently within a merged situation, individual editors are being given their own imprints and editorial autonomy. Only a small handful of totally independent publishers is left (you can, I think, count them on one hand), although small, new publishing houses are developing, especially on the West Coast.

Another phenomenon that has tended to further depress the market for individual and more creative writing for older readers is the commercially successful young romance series. Series of romance and career books for girls have been successful in the past, but none were as expertly tailored for the market as the current ones are. The colors used on the covers, the size of type and margins inside, the degree of intimacy between the sexes, all these factors and many more tiny details are analyzed and developed for the optimum appeal to an exact age. This is formula writing in the nth degree. Electronic devices and computer software also undoubtedly draw some young readers away from books, and some young people may never come to books at all.

To offset these negatives, what positives are there? First of all, the country's economy has begun slowly to improve. The improvement is noticeable in better bookstore sales. Some libraries, public and school, are getting a bit more money for books and staff. Then, there is the proliferation of small bookstores, stores that deal only in children's books. This is one of the most exciting and promising developments, for in this kind of shop there is interest in and room for reading books as well as picture books.

Most of these shops are owned and run by women, often former teachers or librarians. They are in the business because they want to be, because they know and like what they are selling, because they believe they are performing an important community service while making a modest living in an independent fashion.

Another positive piece of the kaleidoscope is the resiliency of publishing. Sometimes it has been counted as almost down and out, but it always manages to climb back. At present, many publishers are retooling, so to speak, to direct their children's book departments toward bookstore sales with books for babies—"baby lit." That's where the larger sales are. If this redirection is done in moderation, it is healthy and good. Like most things, if it is done in excess, it's a little bit shortsighted. It narrows the field too much, making more difficult the way of those writers who have something to say to older readers and who need to find publishers.

There are encouraging signs that the field of technology will not be the kiss of death for young readers. You know, television was supposed to finish books off forever, and you just have to look around to see how untrue that was. Or home computers—the ones that you were supposed to have in your home so your child's education could go forward properly, and to ease your own burdens, and for entertainment. I read that sales of these computers were 40 percent short of what had been projected for them. Possibly the novelty has worn off. In schools computers are now a part of instructional materials, because computers are part of the world and will remain so, and they are wonderful in many respects. But I'm told that there is a move away from using computers to teach specific subjects toward teaching basic computer literacy—which, of course, children must have.

What has always run through the fabric of the decades, like a tough, bright thread, has been the belief in and concern for and dedication to children and books on the part of certain individuals with imagination, force, and determination. Always, there have been enough writers and artists, librarians, educators, parents, editors, booksellers, and publishers with these qualities to keep good books—real books—alive, to provide new and exciting books, to skirt whatever the pitfalls and stumbling blocks of their decades have been. Just as children, given half a chance, are naturally optimistic—looking ahead—so these adults have continued to push for excellence whether older or new, giving a bit of ground here when necessary, gaining a bit or a lot there, at propitious moments. This thread is still very strong. We must see to it that no one snaps the thread but that it is protected and cherished in every possible way by precept and example.

I recently saw a sign in a printer's office that I like. It reads:

> This is a printing office and crossroads of civilization. Refuge
> of all the arts against the ravages of time, armory of fearless

> truth against whispering rumor, incessant trumpet of trade.
> From this place words may fly abroad, not to perish on
> waves of sound, not to vary with the writer's hand, but fixed
> in time, having been verified in proof. Friend, you stand on
> sacred ground. This is a printing office.

Well, that really says it. I believe—and I have, as yet, found no one who
disagrees—that books, good books, will continue to play a crucial role in
our society.

NOTE

These remarks were made in 1984.

On Awards and Prizes

GINNY MOORE KRUSE

I have done no formal research on awards and distinctions; however, I will
lay claim to being a certified award-watcher, and I have been one
throughout my career as a teacher and as a librarian. Actually, my life as an
award-watcher began as a child, when books that won the Newbery Medal
and then the Caldecott Medal were called to my attention. And, frankly, I
didn't know about any other children's book awards until I heard about
and began to observe the Boston Globe–Horn Book Awards that were
established in 1967. It was then that I began to realize that there could be
many ways for books to be cited and to be appreciated. A book that
accelerated my career as an award-watcher is the Children's Book Council's
Children's Books: Awards and Prizes. Through this publication I came to see
even more ways in which children's books are valued by groups of people,
and the many ways in which books achieve prominence.

My most recent experience with awards has been as a member of the
Newbery-Caldecott Committee and then subsequently as the Chairperson
of the Newbery Committee. The major annual award given in the United
States for distinguished writing for children is the Newbery Medal, given
by the Association for Library Service to Children of the American Library
Association "to the author of the most distinguished contribution to
American literature for children published in the United States during the
preceding year."

Another prominent award is the ALA Mildred L. Batchelder Award,
given each year to the publisher of the best translated children's book
published in the United States in the preceding year. Among the Batchelder Award-winning publishers are Holt, for *Friedrich* by Hans Richter,
translated from the German by Edite Kroll, and Dutton, for *Petros' War* by

Alki Zei, translated from the Greek by Edward Fenton. Annual awards for illustration include the Caldecott Medal and the American Institute of Graphic Arts Award. Publisher Phyllis Fogelman has said that the only exposure to art for most children comes through picture books, and it is essential that we are aware of citations of distinguished picture books.

A number of awards are given for special content, among them the National Council of Teachers of English Award for excellence in poetry for children, presented annually to a living American poet for an aggregate body of poetry. David McCord, Eve Merriam, and Karla Kuskin are among the poets who have received this award.

The Children's Book Guild of Washington, D.C., established in 1977, gives an award for an author of nonfiction, and authors and illustrators who have received the award are David Macaulay, Millicent Selsam, Jean Fritz, and Shirley Glubok.

Each year the Women's International League for Peace and Freedom collaborates on an award called the Jane Addams Children's Book Award, given to a book with literary merit that stresses themes of dignity, equality, peace, and social justice. Books winning that award include Milton Meltzer's *Never to Forget: The Jews of the Holocaust* and David Kherdian's *The Road from Home: The Story of An Armenian Girl.* An award such as this gives us a window into another kind of excellence.

The Child Study Children's Book Award given by Bank Street College of Education each year is for a distinguished book for children or young people that deals honestly and courageously with the problems of their world. One of the award-winning books is *The Devil in Vienna,* by Doris Orgel.

The Coretta Scott King Awards are given annually to a Black author and a Black artist for outstanding inspirational and educational contributions designed to promote better understanding and appreciation of the culture and contribution of all peoples to the American dream. Eloise Greenfield has been honored for her *Africa Dream,* Walter Dean Myers for *The Young Landlords,* and Ashley Bryan for *Beat the Story-Drum, Pum-Pum.*

The Christopher Awards annually cite books for various age levels reflecting a high level of human and spiritual values. An outstanding book overlooked by the other award processes received this award—*What Happened in Hamelin,* by Gloria Skurzynski. *Gentlehands,* by M. E. Kerr, and *The Great Gilly Hopkins,* by Katherine Paterson, also have received the Christopher Award.

I want to mention a short-lived attempt by adults to give awards called the "Newcott-Caldeberry" for several years, beginning in the late sixties, for books that children were simply reading and telling each other about, regardless of awards, adults, bibliographies, and reviews. They were given each year at a kind of alternative Newbery-Caldecott banquet called the

Newcott-Caldeberry Picnic at ALA. In the year I participated in the selection, the process was purely personal and individual and not very complicated. The book that received the Caldeberry, as I remember, was *Stevie*, by John Steptoe, and the one that received the Newcott was *The Outsiders*, by S. E. Hinton.

There are awards for a body of work. The ALA/ALSC Laura Ingalls Wilder Award cites distinguished work as well as substantial contribution, which has to involve acceptance by children over the long span of a career. The International Board on Books for Young People's Hans Christian Andersen Award recognizes a body of work internationally.

The International Reading Association annually gives an award to a book whose author shows unusual promise in the children's book field, and some very fine books have been cited: T. Degens's *Transport 7-41-R* and Laurence Yep's *Dragonwings*, for example, and Nancy Bond's *A String in the Harp*.

In *Children and Literature: Views and Reviews*, Virginia Haviland says, "In countries with a large and competitive book production, awards are needed less for the purpose of stimulating publishing than to call attention to distinguished work." To this I add, attention to the variety of ways books are formally appreciated is essential.

On Being a Librarian

CAROLINE WARD

As a librarian you have to be an astute administrator, a budget analyst, a master puppeteer, a storyteller, an articulate book talker, and an infallible book selector. You have to have a photographic memory, for the person who comes up and says, "My grandmother told me this story; it was a little blue book; I don't remember the title, but let me tell you the plot." A background in mechanics so you can fix the furnace, the Xerox machine, the video monitor, and the computer also would not hurt. It sounds like I'm being facetious, but actually most librarians do all of those things very well. But I'm going to place one more challenge on librarians: be belligerent. I use that phrase right out of Frances Clarke Sayers's speech. (She's another one of those ladies with three names who ran the New York Public Library.) In 1949 she gave a very moving speech entitled "The Belligerent Profession." You can find it in a collection of her marvelous essays called *Summoned by Books*. I'd like to quote just a bit from that speech.

> The quality of belligerency was never more greatly needed
> in the library profession than it is at this moment. We have
> been called many things in our time. Gentle, and genteel,
> modest and mousy, learned and lame, dedicated and

dowdy, unprepossessing and underpaid. I hope for the
day when we shall be called the belligerent profession. A
profession that is informed, illuminated, radiated, by a
fierce and beautiful love of books. A love so overwhelming
that it engulfs community after community and makes the
culture of our time distinctive, individual, creative and
truly of the spirit.

Journeying

JEAN FRITZ

One day several years ago, as I was looking around at the pictures on our walls, I noticed that they were all serene pictures. The reflection of a boathouse in a pond, an embroidered Chinese crane, a quiet mountain landscape. I loved them, but I knew there was something missing. I went right out and, luckily, I found and bought just what I wanted: a collagelike painting of a busy harbor, full sails, tall masts, and flying bridges interrupting each other in haste. It is a picture with a get-up-and-go quality to it which speaks to my own need to get up and go. I may like coming home, but when it comes right down to it, I prefer going away.

Yet, look at the two books I've written about myself: *Homesick* and *China Homecoming*. You would think from the titles that journeying was only of incidental importance to me. But as a lonely, homesick child in China, I may have longed for the security and sense of belonging I thought I would find in America. But I also longed for the unknown on the other side of the world. Moreover, although it may not be obvious, most of my books— certainly all my biographies—have been motivated by a need for journeying. The journeys are backward in time. They are journeys to different worlds, for it is the business of exploring the otherness of different times and different places that is so exhilarating.

Indeed, every book is for me an excuse to travel, a chance to incorporate more places, more times, more people into a sense of home, which, over the years, if you're addicted enough to journeying, becomes indistinguishable from a sense of self.

C. P. Cavafy eulogizes journeying in his poem "Ithaka": "Pray that your journey be long, / Filled with adventures, filled with wisdom." But narrative writing and poetry are two very different things. Poems exist to set the blood racing, to shake you out of old, worn patterns, to force you to face life afresh. And it is wonderful to carry with you Cavafy's assurance that you will never meet the Laistrygonians on your journey "if your soul does not raise them up before you," and you will not see "the Cyclops / And raging Poseidon." But if you are writing narrative, whether fantasy or realistic fiction, you had better meet the Cyclops or you will have no story.

Besides, how many of us get through life without entertaining the ghost of some Poseidon hidden within the soul? Indeed, life itself throws islands of evil across our paths. It surprises us with seemingly insurmountable storms, and it gives us giants that we have to cope with. Realistic fiction makes the obstacles familiar, within the scope of known experience, but if less picturesque, they are no less hazardous to deal with. If Ulysses were to appear in a twentieth-century novel, his story might well begin, rather than end, with his arrival home. How, after the long separation, are he and Penelope going to make it?

In realistic fiction for children, how does the journey figure? As I reviewed what I thought of as journey books, I found most of them to be survival stories in which courage and persistence are pushed to their limits before a safe harbor is sometimes reached and, since they are realistic, sometimes not reached.

Think of a few of the titles: *The House of Sixty Fathers, North of Danger, Transport 7-41-R, North to Freedom, The Slave Dancer*. These are struggles for life—grim journeys, abounding with emotion, ringing with truth. But they are not the journeys of joy that Cavafy would have us take, stopping at Phoenician markets to buy amber, visiting Egyptian cities to learn and learn.

Our whole American history is one of journeying. We have romanticized our westward movement until it lies at the root of what we choose to call "the American Dream." And yet, although some of our pioneers and many of our naturalists have left joyous accounts of the American landscape, seldom is this joy reflected in realistic fiction for young people. Excitement? Danger? Yes, for the pioneer movement was again a story of survival, although over the years Hollywood has monkeyed with the starkness as well as the wonder of it all.

On the other hand, in our most famous and beloved series for children about the westward movement—the Little House books—the predominant mood is one of snug simplicity, a warm, loving family existing on a kind of island of safety or near-safety, in the midst of wilderness. After reading this series, a young girl wrote me that she, too, would like a nice, neat prairie to live on.

Another giant in the field of pioneer books for children is James Daugherty's *Daniel Boone*, always more popular with librarians, I expect, than with children. Yet Daugherty's westward movement is certainly a heroic one, a trip bigger than life through a countryside made lush by language so rich you come away reeling. His battles are tropical forests of prose, unmistakably American prose, as Carl Sandburg's prose is, but so heavy with glory a reader is slowed up on the journey by the growth on the path. So in the end, how real is it?

I'm not belittling Laura Ingalls Wilder or James Daugherty. They are masters in the field. But I have asked myself, are there books of joyous journeying that are also realistic?

And there is one that stands high above all others, so joyous, so real, that one comes away from each reading with a sense of renewal. *Huckleberry Finn*, of course. What might be made to seem frightening is a splendid adventure to Huck. Listen to him talk about a storm:

> It was one of those regular summer storms. It would get so dark that it looked all blue-black outside and lovely; and the rain would thrash along by so thick that the trees off a little ways looked dim and spider-webby; and here would come a blast of wind that would bend the trees down and turn up the pale underside of the leaves, and then a perfect ripper of a gust would follow along and set the branches to tossing their arms as if they was just wild; . . . and now you'd hear the thunder let go with an awful crash and go rumbling, grumbling, tumbling down the sky towards the underside of the world, like rolling empty barrels down-stairs. . . . "Jim, this is nice," I says. "I wouldn't want to be nowhere else but here."

Huck's summer mornings are as long as Cavafy could imagine a summer morning to be. Moreover, Huck enters each port with more pleasure, more joy, than Ulysses ever did. Ulysses never cared for storms. What he liked were the occasional domestic little gardens he came across, something that would remind him of home. Narrow escapes abound for Huck, as they did for Ulysses, but Huck is an adventurer, pure and simple. "There weren't a home like a raft," he says. "Other places do seem cramped-up and smothery, but a raft don't. You'd feel mighty free and easy and comfortable on a raft."

There may be many current books that catch this sense of joy in journeying, but I think particularly of one—Cynthia Voigt's *Homecoming*. Four children who are abandoned by their mother make their way without money to an unknown aunt in a distant and strange city. Of course, their survival is at stake, but the journey itself is laced with joy. Listen to the author:

> Dicey thought about the word "home." If you took home to mean where you rested content and never wanted

to go anywhere else, then Dicey had never had a home. The ocean always made her restless; even their own remembered kitchen wasn't home. Nobody could see home really until he was in his grave. Nobody could rest really until then. It was a cold, hard thought, but maybe true. But what did it matter where they were going, as long as they were going? Dicey didn't feel like finding a harbor. She would rather just sail along dreaming, not caring where they were going or when they would get there. Couldn't you live your whole life without going into harbor? The land would catch you in the end, but until then, you could keep free.

In my four books of historical fiction, I've often paused in my plot to take pleasure in place. Not in the journey, for none of these books were journeys, but just pleasure in place. When it comes to biographies, I select people whose lives make a good story. Many have been journeyers and have gloried in their journeys—Columbus particularly. I love to picture him standing on the deck all night, oblivious to danger, staring at the sky, "drunk with the stars," a sailor said. From newly discovered island to newly discovered island, he stretched his vocabulary to meet the wonders. "Trees so tall," he said, "they scraped the sky." At last he gave up on words. "It would take a thousand tongues," he said, "to list all the marvels."

When I visit the Caribbean in the winter, I feel close to Columbus. Time and again on a particularly beautiful day, I find myself repeating Columbus's favorite expression. "Oh, it's like April in Andalusia." I've never been to Andalusia, but "April in Andalusia" is such a voluptuous phrase, it reverberates with joy.

The travel that I myself do in the process of research is more than a fringe benefit of my particular occupation. I sometimes suspect that travel may motivate much of my work. This kind of exploratory, purposeful travel gives me a kind of delirious sense of *now*, of operating at full tilt from present moment to present moment, while at the same time being delivered on a path where I feel, miraculously, a participant in history. Often the findings I make may come to a dead end as far as a specific book is concerned, yet they are part of the journey, and sometimes the most memorable part.

This year, on a research trip to Texas, my husband and I were going through New Orleans and stopped at Chalmette, the site of the Battle of New Orleans. What interested me, however, had nothing to do with the battle. My attention was attracted by two men digging at the site. They turned out to be archaeologists who had come across the foundations of a house that was not known to have been there. The date, they figured, was about 1790. They showed me where the kitchen had probably been, about eight feet underground, and they were sifting through the mud for artifacts. They would toss a shovelful of mud onto a net and then go through it all by hand. And they let me help! All afternoon I fingered through mud, coming upon artifact after artifact. Handles of cups, broken pieces of Wedgewood saucers—all indicating that this had been a wealthy family. And from the position of the artifacts, the supposition was that the inhabitants had left in a hurry. At the end of the afternoon, when I went back to our car, I was, of course, covered with mud. But it was 1790 mud. When had our 1980 Honda been exposed to 1790 mud before? I doubt if that mysterious 1790 house will ever appear in a book, yet I wouldn't part with the memory.

Again and again I have found in my journeys that the real joy invariably takes you by surprise. Always, you must be alert to possible diversions, be ready for spontaneous interruptions, be willing to step aside without inhibition.

On this same Texas trip in search of Sam Houston, I decided on impulse to look for the creek where Sam had been baptized. I knew this had been a big day for Sam. He had wrestled with the question of baptism all through his marriage and was in his sixties before his wife, Margaret, finally persuaded him to take the step at the Baptist church in Independence, Texas. But what could a creek tell me? Yet, it was while talking to the minister in Independence that the scene became alive suddenly. The minister showed me a letter written by a young Baylor College student who had been baptized along with Sam. "And when General Houston was baptized," he wrote to his mother, "Mrs. Houston, who was standing on the bank of the creek, was so happy she shouted like a Methodist." Later, when I stood on the bank of the creek, I was glad that I had not been content to transfer the baptism from printed page to printed page without letting that creek and Mrs. Houston have their full say.

When it came time, however, to write about my own two most important journeys—the journey to America and the journey back to China—I faced the problem of story. In a biography I feel how a life falls into a form before I commit myself to the writing. I enjoy finding the shape in my material in much the same way as a sculptor sees his subject embedded in a particular rock. The trouble with *Homesick*, my first book, was that I had too much material, too many crises. To tell it all in proper sequence would have resulted in a long string of anecdotes without form. Whereas the kind of book I like to write must be like a spiral, curling back on itself, going ahead but carrying echoes as it goes. Eventually, I decided to let go of the literal time sequence.

But if I had to cut down on material to make *Homesick* into a story, I worried about having enough material for *China Homecoming*, which would stand as nonfiction. Everything went so well. I would often remark to my husband, Michael, "If we could only be kidnapped"—just briefly, of course, just a small cliff-hanger. In the end I had to get along without a cliff-hanger, but the journey itself provided a theme which gradually unfolded as we went along and was climaxed by an experience which for me was so emotional that I could begin to see the shape of the whole book. It was the day that I asked our interpreter if he knew what had happened to the international cemetery where my sister Miriam had been buried in Hankow. I knew the cemetery would no longer be there, but I asked if he could show us where it had been. Oh, yes, he said, he knew exactly where it had been, and he took us to a playground.

It was a lovely playground, and I was pleased that the cemetery had been turned over to children. But after we got back to the hotel, Michael said, "Are you sure that was the right place?" That made me wonder, so one afternoon we both walked back to the playground. I don't know what I thought I would find, but I began walking around the edges, looking down at the ground. Not looking for anything; just looking.

Then, off in a far corner of the playground, I found a broken piece of stone, and on it in English was the name Sears. There was a date. This was obviously part of a gravestone. As I looked around the park, I saw that the benches were all the same shape. So I went up to one, leaned down, and rubbed my hand under it. Yes, I could feel letters. By this time the Chinese were very curious and were crowding around to see what I was doing. In my limited Chinese I explained to a woman that this used to be a cemetery, that I had a little sister who was buried here, and I thought these were gravestones.

She understood immediately, and with no other suggestion from me, she called three young men, and with Michael's help the four men turned over each one of these benches. Just as I had expected, they were gravestones. The oldest went back to 1896. As we turned them over, the Chinese would ask: Who was this? And I would say: This was a Russian; this was an Italian; this was an Irishman. I didn't find my sister's gravestone, but it didn't matter to me any longer because on my own I had uncovered that portion of history, the colonial portion, through which I was tied to China. That gave me what I had been looking for.

There was a sequel to this story that I didn't include in the book for fear it would get some people in trouble. The caretaker of the playground came out and said there were more stones in another place. I took out my map of Hankow and asked him to mark where the place was and write the address in Chinese, which he did. The next day I told our interpreter and asked to go there. There was no such place, he said. There was no address like that at all. Forget about the stones because the Red Guards smashed them all and threw them into the Yangtze River. I dropped the subject.

But the next-to-last day of our stay, we had a different interpreter. As we got into the car I handed the map to the driver and asked him to take us to that address. And he did. It was a building supply yard filled with bricks. But there were also old gravestones waiting to be put to use. Some already were in place holding up little huts. One stone was under a tap of water and was used as a base for washtubs. The young woman who was our interpreter worried about how I was going to take this. Didn't I feel this was a desecration? No, I said, I didn't feel that. The land is for the living, I told her. That is what history is all about. Gravestones have been put to use all through time.

As far as joy is concerned, I have never had a journey so filled with joy as that one was. I was eager to find an excuse for another joyful journey. After finishing Sam Houston, I began playing with the idea of writing about Robert Louis Stevenson. Born in Edinburgh, he once went by donkey-back through France, lived for a while in Hawaii, then in Tahiti, and died in Samoa. I couldn't ask for a better journey than that. The longer I read his letters, the more perfect he seemed as a subject. A joyous traveler, just the kind that Cavafy extols.

"Happiness," Stevenson writes, "is not the reward man seeks. His soul is in the journey. He was born for the struggle, and only tastes his life in effort and on the condition that he is opposed." Sick all his life, Stevenson would not let anything deflect him from his pleasure. "The worst sin," he said, "is sloth. Turning away from the glories of life, sulking at dawn, eating without relish." Stevenson didn't always manage to be joyous, but he seldom forgot what joy was.

Of course, I fell in love with Robert Louis Stevenson and longed to follow in his footsteps. From the South Seas he wrote, "These voyagings, these landfalls at dawn, new islands peeking from the morning bank, new forested harbors, new passing alarms of squalls and surfs, the whole tale of my life is better to me than any poem." Yet, on closer examination I felt that his life was really a poem. In spite of all the voyaging, his life did not have the makings of a true tale. His struggle was for health, and he made a long, gallant struggle in many places, celebrating life all the while. But whatever real action there was, whatever adventures, they went into the books he wrote. At the moment I can only love Stevenson. I can't write a book about him. But I do have a journey in mind.

You won't be surprised to hear that it will take me back to China, to out-of-the-way places I've never seen. It's the story of the long march, the Red Army's 6,000-mile journey on foot over snow-covered mountains, treacherous rivers, uninhabited grasslands and swamps, fighting the enemy all the way. I want to talk to survivors, many who were teenage boys and girls at the time. I want to see the land. It is time for me to get up and go again.

Between a Peach and the Universe

E. L. KONIGSBURG

When I was a sophomore at Carnegie-Mellon University, I studied T. S. Eliot, and I studied calculus.

Well, T. S. Eliot has made it to Broadway, and calculus hasn't.

But I must confess that when I was in college, I would not have been surprised if calculus had made it instead. For at that time I thought that the poetry of Mr. Eliot was every bit as arcane as calculus.

Upon returning home from seeing a performance of *Cats*, I opened my sophomore textbook *Chief Modern Poets of England and America*, and I saw, written in the margins of those pages, notes that make no sense at all, in a hand I do not recognize.

> The Rum Tum Tugger is a curious beast:
> His disobliging ways are a matter of habit.
> If you offer him a fish then he always wants a feast;
> When there isn't any fish then he won't eat rabbit.

Here are my notes: "Rum Tum Tugger" and "beast" are underlined and in the margin beside that line I wrote *Lion of Judah*. Beside the line "If you offer him a fish then he always wants a feast" I have written *Miracle of loaves and fishes*. And scribbled in the margin beside the line "When there isn't any fish then he won't eat rabbit" there is a note to the effect that Catholics don't eat meat on Fridays.

On Broadway T. S. Eliot's *Cats* appeared to be pretty uncomplicated. I wondered if at Carnegie-Mellon I or my teacher, Dr. John Hart, had been reading a bit too much between the lines. Dr. Hart was one of a group of professors who met once a week and read and discussed a single page of *Ulysses*, by James Joyce, and I was, God forgive me, a sophomore.

After finishing "Rum Tum Tugger," I continued reading the textbook

section on T. S. Eliot and found "The Love Song of J. Alfred Prufrock." I
remembered liking that poem for its rhythm.

> Let us go then, you and I,
> When the evening is spread out against the sky
> Like a patient etherised upon a table;

I will spare you what I had written in the margin beside "etherised upon
a table." As I continued reading, I stopped trying to decipher my notes—
which were marginal in both the literal and figurative senses of the word—
and I began to read the poem straight through. And I found myself saying
yes, I understand—and yes, I don't. Not, *no, I don't understand*, but *yes, I
don't*. Saying *yes, I don't understand* is a privilege that comes either with
religious faith or with old age.

At last I came to these lines:

> And indeed there will be time
> To wonder, 'Do I dare?' and 'Do I dare?'
> . . . .
> Do I dare
> Disturb the universe?

A little later in the poem these haunting lines appear:

> I grow old . . . I grow old . . .
> I shall wear the bottoms of my trousers rolled.
>
> Shall I part my hair behind? Do I dare to eat a peach?
> I shall wear white flannel trousers, and walk upon the beach.

In South Florida, the trousers may be polyester, but I have seen them
walk upon the beach. In South Florida, those trousers may have an elastic
waistband and be part of a lady's three-piece pant suit, but I have seen
those trousers rolled. I have seen them on tired women and on retired
men. And I have seen old men with their hair parted just behind the ear
with a few thin strands stretched across their pate. I have seen them—men
and women—walk along the beach and not dare to eat a peach. Or a slice
of red roast beef. Or drink a cup of undecaffeinated coffee after 4:00 p.m.,
and I wonder—oh! I wonder—when does caution become reason? And I
wonder, did any of these men, did any of these women ever ask, Do I dare
disturb the universe?

Who does ask, Do I dare disturb the universe?

And who does disturb the universe?

Kings did and politicians do. The Wright brothers did, and NASA does. Martin Luther did, and John Paul does. Sigmund Freud did, and Dr. Ruth tries to. Rachel Carson did. Ralph Nader did. Betty Friedan did. Shakespeare did, and so did Michelangelo. Mozart did, and so did Picasso. Any creative act in some way disturbs the universe. A few great works change all the works that follow. No one who paints cannot not know the Sistine Chapel ceiling, and no one who composes music cannot not know Beethoven—even if that person has never heard Beethoven's Fifth. Michelangelo and Beethoven are there, somewhere; they tore up the ground they walked on, and they changed its contours, and even if we do not know whose footsteps we are following, we are walking over prepared soil.

We are beyond having a universe in which there is no Shakespeare.

If we are to discover what it takes to plow up the universe, let us examine the lives of some men who did. Let us track the lives of three men who disturbed the universe so profoundly that none of us can conceive of our universe without thinking of their disturbances. The three are men of science, and their work has dealt directly with our physical universe. All three are "megamen" of science, and they are—in order of appearance— Galileo, Newton, and Einstein. I have chosen them for two reasons: one, their disturbances are so profound that they are beyond value judgments. That is, we need not question the merit of what they have done as some might question the merit of the work of Sigmund Freud or Karl Marx or even—in the Florida legislature at least—the work of Charles Darwin. And two, their accomplishments are so large that they allow us to examine, in blow-up, details that we might miss in lesser lives.

Let's us go then, you and I, and examine the steps between a peach and the universe.

First, Galileo.

Galileo was born in 1564, also the year that Shakespeare was born and the year that Michelangelo died. When Galileo made himself a telescope— one which is on display to this very day in Florence—he discovered the moons of Jupiter. When he published his findings in a book to which he gave a beautiful title, *The Starry Messenger*, a Florentine astronomer proved in the following way that satellites of Jupiter could not exist:

> There are seven windows given to animals through which the air is admitted to the tabernacle of the body. Two nostrils, two eyes, two ears, and a mouth . . . From this and many similarities in nature, such as seven metals, et cetera, we gather that the number of planets is necessarily seven. Moreover, these satellites of Jupiter are invisible to

> the naked eye and therefore would be useless and there-
> fore do not exist.

That was the mind-set that existed in Florence when Galileo lived there.

Galileo again turned his telescope toward the heavens and discovered something worse: Copernicus was right. The earth, by damn! revolved around the sun, not vice versa.

And here, his real troubles began.

The pope, Urban VIII, said that Galileo left no room for miracles. Monsignor Riccardi, the chief censor of the Roman Catholic Church, said that Galileo was being blasphemous. Had not Solomon written:

> . . . the earth abideth for ever. The sun also ariseth, and
> the sun goeth down, and hasteth to his place where he
> ariseth.

And wasn't Solomon writing God's words? And Hemingway's future titles?

Galileo had an answer. He said, "The Bible shows the way to go to Heaven, not the way the heavens go." But that answer was too wonderful, too witty, and it only made things worse.

Remember, at this time the Catholic church was still reeling from the effects of the Reformation. It was the time of the Inquisition, and no one, especially the chief censor, could be accused of having a sense of humor in church matters.

But Galileo desperately wanted to publish, so he and the chief censor worked out a compromise. The chief censor said that Galileo could publish his findings if he agreed to write a preface that he would submit to Riccardi for approval. In this preface Galileo must qualify his theories as "dreams, nullities, paralogisms, and chimera."

In 1632, *A Dialogue on the Two Chief World Systems* was published, the two world systems being the Ptolemaic, that the sun revolved, and the Copernican, that the earth did. Galileo lived up to his part of the agreement, and he published his work with the disclaimer as advised and as approved by the censor.

But he did two other things wrong. First of all, he published in Italian, not in erudite Latin, and thus made his work accessible to all; and, second, he wrote beautifully. He was a gifted writer of exposition—we call it nonfiction. And then, on top of all this, the quality of the research was so powerful that it proved Copernicanism beyond a doubt. It was like publishing a paper with a preface saying that the color red does not exist and then printing the entire text in red ink.

So Galileo was called before the tribunal and forced to deny—first weakly and then more and more vehemently—the principles of Copernicus. Finally, the judges said that he could not be absolved unless he declared that he "abjured, cursed, and detested" his past errors. And Galileo did.

The normal sentence for such heresy was imprisonment, but the pope commuted this to house arrest on the condition that Galileo "repeat once a week the seven penitential psalms," and Galileo did; and never talk to any Protestants, and Galileo did not.

And that is what happened to you in the year 1633 if you dared to disturb the universe.

But was it really disturbing the universe that mattered so much? Was it really troubles with the universe that caused such profound troubles for the man Galileo?

Please remember that he was born in the same year that Shakespeare was. We all know that in 1633, when Galileo got into trouble, England had been Protestant for a hundred years. But Galileo wanted to publish in his neighborhood, not Shakespeare's. If he had chosen to publish in a country just a little farther north, say Germany or Holland, he would have met with far fewer problems. Even Venice, an Italian city but one with a freer and looser society, would never have troubled him the way that his own neighborhood did. For between a peach and the universe there is the neighborhood, and those who dare disturb the universe must first have the courage to dare disturb the neighborhood.

It takes more courage to disturb the neighborhood than it takes to disturb the universe. And the price is often higher.

So, between a peach and the universe we have the lesson of Galileo—that it takes more courage to disturb the neighborhood than it does to disturb the universe.

In the very year that Galileo died, Isaac Newton was born into Protestant England, where the neighborhood was friendly to science. It is here in the person of Newton that Galileo's work would be extended, and it is from the person of Isaac Newton that we can see what, besides daring to disturb the neighborhood, it takes to disturb the universe.

The year in which Newton was born was important, not only because his work started where Galileo's left off—it did—but also because having been born in 1642 meant that in 1665 Newton was ready to start graduate school at Cambridge University. And that year is significant because 1665 was a plague year. By August of 1665 one-tenth of the population of London had died of the plague. So, in September Cambridge called off all its classes. School was closed, and its students were sent home—Isaac Newton among them.

Home to Isaac Newton was a small stone house in Woolsthorpe, where his mother lived, and where it is supposed there was an apple tree. Newton was devoted to his mother, and she to him, but there was no one at Woolsthorpe with whom he could discuss his intellectual achievements.

There, in those two plague years, 1665 and 1666, Newton formulated his three great laws of motion—inertia, gravitational attraction, and action-reaction; developed the laws of pendulum motion, worked out the inverse square law, proved Kepler's laws of planetary motion, developed the mathematical treatment of wave motion, worked out the main irregularities of the moon's motion, explained the tides, showed that comets are members of the solar system, showed that the density of the Earth is between five and six times that of water, and figured out the precession of the equinoxes. He also conducted experiments that led to important discoveries about the refraction of light and the nature of color.

Not bad. But wait, there is more.

As a mathematical tool to help himself solve the problems he was working on, Newton invented differential and integral calculus. He called his invention *fluxions*.

He invented something else as a tool. Just as Galileo was witty, Newton was handy. When he was studying light, he ground his own prisms; and when he was studying the stars, he invented the reflecting telescope. The reflecting telescope—and Newton along with it—came to the attention of the Royal Society of London for the Promotion of Natural Knowledge, known as the Royal Society, and it was at the urging of its president that in 1687 his major work, *Principia*, was published. The *People* magazine part of me makes me need to tell you that the president of the Royal Society at that time was none other than Samuel Pepys, the diarist, and the book itself was financed by Edmund Halley of Halley's Comet fame. The travel guide part of me makes me need to tell you that *his* telescope is on display at the Royal Observatory in Greenwich.

Most of us would have been proud to have claimed the invention of the reflecting telescope or the invention of calculus in those two plague years. I, for one, would have considered it an accomplishment to have mastered the *use* of calculus in two years. I certainly didn't do it in two semesters at college.

There is an awful lot about Sir Isaac Newton that *People* magazine could have feasted upon. He was petty and mean, wise and generous, a mystic and a civil servant—but the aspect that I want now to emphasize, the aspect that I think all who are interested in disturbing the universe must know about, is his ability to profitably survive a plague year. I don't mean physical ability. I mean mental ability. I mean mental *agility*. I mean that those who would disturb the universe have a need for solitude. And that,

I think, is the second step between a peach and the universe: the ability to be alone profitably—to enjoy solitude with vigor.

Like Newton, Einstein was isolated from other physicists at the time he published his first paper on relativity. He was working as a technical expert third class in the patent office in Bern, Switzerland.

And like Galileo, Einstein also disturbed his neighborhood.

In 1933 Philipp Lenard wrote in the Nazi paper:

> The most important example of the dangerous influence of Jewish circles on the study of nature has been provided by Herr Einstein with his mathematically botched theories consisting of some ancient knowledge and a few arbitrary additions. . . . Even scientists who have otherwise done solid work . . . allowed the relativity theory to get a foothold in Germany because they did not see . . . how wrong it is . . . to regard this Jew as a good German. . . . It is unworthy of a German to be the intellectual follower of a Jew. Natural science . . . is of completely Aryan origin, and Germans must . . . find their own way into the unknown. Heil Hitler.

By 1933, Einstein had disturbed his neighborhood to the point of personal danger, so he left his native Germany and moved to Princeton. Shortly after moving there, he wrote to a friend:

> Princeton is a wonderful little spot, a quaint and ceremonious village of puny demigods on stilts. Yet by ignoring certain social conventions I have been able to create for myself an atmosphere conducive to study and free of distraction. Here the people who compose what is called "society" enjoy even less freedom than their counterparts in Europe. Yet, they seem unaware of this restriction, since their way of life tends to inhibit personality development from childhood.

In that single statement Einstein summarizes for us that courage to disturb the neighborhood and a need for solitude, points one and two between a peach and the universe, feed each other.

Do I dare ignore the neighborhood, and do I dare demand solitude?

It is Einstein who directly reveals the third ingredient that is necessary if a person dares to disturb the universe. He said:

When I examine myself and my methods of thought, I
come to the conclusion that the gift of fantasy has meant
more to me than my talent for absorbing positive knowledge.

Einstein made that comment in a conversation with Janos Plesch about
the similarities between writing fiction and working mathematics. And
thus, this man of genius kindly makes a perfect transition for me, speaking
to you about the creative process, applied—as I know it best—to writing
fiction. For the third ingredient between a peach and the universe is the gift
of fantasy.

As a writer of novels for middle-aged children—kids between the ages of
eight and twelve—I have been concerned with each of these steps between
a peach and the universe. For neighborhoods, solitude, and fantasy are not
only what it takes to make me write, but they are also what I write about,
for neighborhoods, solitude, and fantasy are the concerns of children from
ages eight to twelve.

Let me start with fantasy.

Even if you are a writer of realistic fiction for children, fantasy enters into
the *process* of writing. The writing itself is the result of fantasy. I tell my
children, when they ask, that when I sit down to write, I start the movie in
my head.

But fantasy often enters into the actual story I am telling. From my very
first book—*Jennifer, Hecate, Macbeth, William McKinley, and Me, Elizabeth*—
there has been at least one element of "Let's Pretend" in each of my books.
My book *Up from Jericho Tel* begins:

There was a time when I was eleven years old—between
the start of a new school year and Midwinter's Night—
when I was invisible. I was never invisible for long, and I
always returned to plain sight, but all my life has been
affected by the people I met and the time I spent in a world
where I could see and not be seen.

I indulged a favorite fantasy—being invisible—when I wrote that book,
but beyond that I hope that I give my reader a sense of suspending
disbelief, a sense of fantasy.

Every now and then I get a letter that tells me that I have done that.
Here's one such letter. It is dated September 18, 1970:

Dear Mrs. Konigsburg,
    My name is Lorraine Piotrowski, and I am 11 years old,
(I think thats a sensible age, don't you)   I live in Ontario

and have read your books called: About the Bnai Bagels
and From the Mixed up Files of Mrs. Basil E. Frankweiler.
I thought both of them were delicious, and I ate them up in
my mind, and now and then the taste comes back to
me. . . .

When I get a letter like that I know that even the most realistic fiction not
only fills a need for fantasy in the reader but also feeds solitude. As
Lorraine Piotrowski puts it, "I ate them up in my mind, and now and then
the taste comes back to me." Fiction makes solitude rich. Fiction makes
solitude taste good.

The need for solitude has also been one of the concerns about which I
write. It was a concern with the need of a suburban child to have time alone
that most directly prompted my writing *About the B'nai Bagels*, one of the
books that Lorraine Piotrowski mentioned. *About the B'nai Bagels* is the
story of a young boy, Mark Setzer, who is middle-class suburban and
whose time not spent at school is spent preparing for his Bar Mitzvah or at
Little League. When his mother becomes manager of his Little League
team, even his play time is invaded, and when she appoints his big
brother, Spencer, as his coach, poor Mark cannot escape his family at all.
I think that we would say that his family had invaded his space.

I close that book with my young hero solving a moral dilemma, having
his Bar Mitzvah, and then this last paragraph. Mark is speaking:

> According to Hebrew Law, now I am a man. That is, I can
> participate fully in all religious services. But I figure that
> you don't become a man overnight. Because it is a becom-
> ing: becoming more yourself, your own kind of tone deaf,
> center-fielder, son, brother, friend, Bagel. And only some
> of it happens on official time plus family time. A lot of it
> happens being alone. And it doesn't happen overnight.
> Sometimes it takes a guy a whole Little League season.

Even if you do appreciate solitude, as Mark Setzer comes to, it is not
always easy to come by. The need for solitude gets no respect. Especially
if you are a woman experiencing that need. An American woman. An
American suburban woman. A married American suburban woman. A
married American suburban woman with children.

Do you ever wonder—as I do—where it is written that a wife is instantly
available to find the second section of the newspaper even if she was not
the last one to read it? Do you ever believe—as I do—that children come
with a gene that says that it is mothers and not fathers who are instantly
interruptible to unstick zippers? Do you ever think—as I do—that a plague

year would be welcome if it meant a year without a call from the aluminum-siding lady?

Aside from these interruptions, there are forces acting on us women over which we have no control. I think of a study done several years ago on nurses living in a dormitory in Denver. Within a year of their living together, all their menstrual periods—which initially had been weeks apart—fell to within a few days of each other. When I mentioned the remarkable implications of this to a young friend who was in college, living in a coed dormitory, she said, "That's strange. The same thing happened to me and my friends."

I don't know if it also happened when I lived in a college dormitory, because I went to college in an age when no one ever dreamed that tampon commercials would appear on TV, and cigarette commercials would not. Periods were mentioned in public only as full stops at the end of sentences. But do you wonder—as I do—if women were not meant to have solitude but were meant to be part of a pack for some communal, territorial, arena-stomping male selection process?

But if given a choice, I would rather have an unsatisfied need for solitude than have no need for it at all. Einstein once said:

> Perhaps, some day solitude will come to be properly
> recognized and appreciated as the teacher of personality.
> The Orientals have long known this. The individual who
> has experienced solitude will not easily become a victim of
> mass suggestion.

The art of being alone with vigor is a talent. Like all talent, it must be developed, and if the Orientals develop it more, some cultures develop it less.

That this is so became apparent to me a couple of years ago when I was in Texas and met a retired navy man who was seriously indulging his love of history, particularly Texas history. There is no history in the United States more wound up with that of Mexico than that of Texas. Long after the evening was mellow, the man asked me a question that I could not answer then and have difficulty answering now. His question to me was this: Why since the sixties whence has developed a broad acceptance of minority cultures in the United States, why since there has been a body of children's literature produced by Oriental Americans, by Black Americans, by Native American Americans, why has there been no work, let alone a *body* of work, produced by Mexican Americans? There are books *about* them, but there are no books *by* them.

At that time I pleaded with him that although I write books for children,

I am not and I have never claimed to be an authority on them. But when I asked an authority, she came up with one. Aurora Labastida coauthored with Marie Hall Ets the picture book *Nine Days to Christmas*, published in 1959.

I have given a lot of thought to his question since he asked it, and I have asked around, and I have learned that life in the Mexican-American United States is life in the neighborhood. And life of the neighborhood. Life with a kind of togetherness that is almost unknown outside the barrio. A kind of life where living is done in groups. Women visit while shopping. Watching television. Going to the Laundromat. Eating. The child never has a chance to develop a talent for being alone. The barrio is protection, but it is also a prison. It is as sweet as a marshmallow and as hard to punch out of.

How can a person disturb the neighborhood if it is always upon you? How can a person disturb the neighborhood if a person never learns to be solitary? How can a culture produce disturbers of the universe if it never unleashes its members from the neighborhood? How can a person think about disturbing the universe if that universe is always, always filled with talk and with doing and with playing? There must be solitude, and there must be something to feed that solitude, and I believe that books should. Certainly, books are a more alone—a more one-to-one—activity than television.

Thus, books enrich fantasy, and books enrich solitude. But by one of those wonderful organic paradoxes, it is equally true that fantasy and solitude enrich books—and make possible the writing of them.

Writers need to dream, and writers need to be alone. For I'm convinced there can be no creative process without fantasy and without solitude. And I'm equally convinced that a writer—even if he is not writing about the earth encircling the sun, even if he is writing fiction, must have the courage to disturb the neighborhood. Thomas Wolfe could not go home to Asheville again after writing *Look Homeward, Angel*. I know people in New Jersey who still will not speak to Philip Roth, and I know a town in Vermont where a Nobel laureate lives because he found out that it is easier to disturb Mother Nature than to disturb Mother Russia.

As a writer of fiction for middle-aged children, I have often addressed the need to disturb the neighborhood. There is no time in a child's life when the question Do I dare disturb the neighborhood? is ever more pressing than when he is in grades five through eight, for that is the time when children are being pulled by their peers on one hand and by their core selves on the other.

It is in the short story "With Bert and Ray" from my book *Throwing Shadows* that I deal most directly with my belief that it takes more courage to disturb the neighborhood than to disturb the universe. In this story

William tells how his widowed mother began a career in managing house sales. After a lengthy apprenticeship under Bert and Ray plus some serious self-directed study coupled with a deep understanding of quality, Ma—as William calls her—buys a Chinese silk screen from an estate sale for $125. Bert and Ray make fun of it, saying that it's a piece of junk. Ma, however, becomes increasingly convinced that it is something special, and with the courage of her convictions and encouragement from William, she eventually sells it to the Freer Gallery in Washington, D.C., for $20,000. The local paper publishes a story about the sale. I'll let William finish telling it:

> We must have got a hundred phone calls the day the story come out in the paper. I told Ma that what I couldn't understand was why Bert and Ray hadn't called us up to congratulate us. A lot of other dealers had. Ma said that she understood why they had not, and she was feeling pretty sad about it.
>
> I asked Ma if she thought that they was jealous about the money. Ma said that the money was just a little bit of it. "What do you suppose is the big part of it then, Ma?" I asked.
>
> "It's hard for me to know the words for saying it, William," she said. "I know what it is that's bothering them . . . but I don't know the psychological words for it."
>
> Bert and Ray finally called the next day, and I heard Ma say, "It seems like I got took pretty good, Bert. I found out that that there screen I sold to the Museum for twenty thousand dollars was really worth twenty-five. Guess I just still got a lot to learn."
>
> Well, that was it.
>
> Bert and Ray come on over to the house that night and teased Ma about how she got took and Ma just laughed at herself right along with them.
>
> Well, that was it.
>
> Bert and Ray just couldn't stand being beat out by Ma, who had been their student just a few years ago. Bert and Ray couldn't stand it that Ma already knowed more about antiques than they did, not only because she studies on them, but also because she's got all these delicate feelings about things that you can't hardly help but notice when you watch her looking at something or touching it so gentle.
>
> But Ma's been so wore down by everything, including living all them years with Pa, that she figures won't

nobody love her if she shows that she knows one thing more than they do.

But I look back on how good she stuck by her guns with that screen, and I figure that if she can stand by her guns with strangers, she soon will be able to with people who have us over to tea. And I figure that I got six more years before I finish school and have to go off and leave her, and I'm going to work on her . . . I'm sure that I can help her to find out how being grateful to Bert and Ray is something she should always be, but outgrown them is something she already is. By the time I leave home, she's going to be ready to face the fact and live with it. She'll need it, being's she won't have me around to push her here and there any more.

This story was sparked from my reading an account of how the Metropolitan Museum of Art acquired its polychrome statue of Saint John the Baptist by the Spanish master Juan Martínez Montañés. It appears that there was an antique dealer who could not sell the the piece out of her shop, so she packed it into her station wagon and took it to New York City, and the museum bought it; it is a beauty, and if you happen to have the 1981 Metropolitan calendar, look at the picture facing the week of February 1, and you will see the statue that Mildred Centers sold to the museum.

Mildred Centers lives in Jacksonville, Florida.

So you see, my immediate neighborhood is in the background of this story about disturbing the neighborhood . . . step one between a peach and the universe.

Before my time to ask, Do I dare to eat a peach? I want to ask, Do I dare to dream? Do I dare enjoy my solitude? Do I dare disturb the neighborhood?
And

> If I do,
> And if I dare,
> I may write a book about someone who does.
> Or
> I may write a book that does.
> Or
> I may disturb the universe.

Whatever Happened to the "All-White" World of Children's Books?

RUDINE SIMS

The Supreme Court outlawed segregated schools in 1954, but a decade later the world of children's books had not even arrived at "separate but equal." In a survey of 5,206 children's trade books published between 1962 and 1964, Nancy Larrick discovered that only 6.7 percent of these books included even one Black character in the text or the illustrations. Moreover, among the Black characters that did appear, many portrayed blatant stereotypes and laughable images.

This situation damages Black and white children alike, since literature is one of the important vehicles through which we socialize children and transmit our cultural values to them. White children, finding in the pages of books only others like themselves, come to believe in an inherent "rightness of whiteness" that grants to other races no important place or function in society. Exposed only to ludicrous or pathetic images of Blacks, white children absorb even more deeply the poison of racism—and grow to perpetuate this evil for yet another generation.

The negative effects of stereotypic, laughable, or pathetic Black characters in children's literature on the self-concepts of Black children are clear. Almost any U.S. Black over the age of thirty who attended integrated schools still carries vivid, embarrassing, and often painful memories of having white schoolmates call him or her Little Black Sambo or some equally demeaning epithet derived from classroom story hours. The effect of such experiences was particularly devastating because other images of Blacks were not available as counterpoint.

For Black children the absence of positive images in children's books was a clear signal that they themselves had little worth in the society that these books reflected. All-white books do not permit Black children to develop a strong sense of self-worth or to discover their own identity within a group;

thus, Black children lose out on some of the major benefits of exposure to children's literature.

Therefore, it was good news when Jeanne Chall and her colleagues reported that 14.4 percent of all children's books published between 1973 and 1975 included at least one Black character. However, a literary census, no matter how useful a gauge, cannot shed light on the deeper issues involved in the effort to add color to the all-white world of children's books. Understanding how the newer books handle these deeper issues requires that we analyze and evaluate the contents of the books.

The National Council of Teachers of English published my report of just such a study. The information that I present here comes from that monograph. I analyzed the contents of 150 books of contemporary realistic fiction about Blacks, published since 1965 and appropriate for children ranging in age from preschool through eighth grade. The sample was not random; the books came largely from the James Weldon Johnson Collection of the Countee Cullen Branch of the New York Public Library. However, the sample is representative, since it includes a substantial portion of the contemporary children's fiction about Afro-Americans published during the fifteen years (1965–1980) that my survey covered.

The emergence of a body of Afro-American children's literature was not without controversy. During the seventies accusations of racism and stereotyping continued, and additional issues surfaced. My analysis focused on three of these newer issues.

The first issue is the matter of audience. Being talked *about* is different from being talked *to,* and the choice of Black or white readers as the primary audience has a clear effect on the way an author presents characters and events.

The second issue is the author's interpretation of the term *Afro-American experience.* The extent to which a reader can find his or her own life experiences mirrored in a book may depend in large measure on whether the author has attempted to reflect a distinctive cultural experience (and how positively or negatively that experience is portrayed) or whether the author has simply presumed that the United States is characterized by cultural homogeneity.

The third issue is the author's perspective as an *insider* or an *outsider* in relation to the cultural group that the book portrays. This perspective determines the author's focus (for example, does he or she see the fictional character's life as a half-full cup or a half-empty one?) and the authenticity of the details by which the author convinces a reader of the truth of his or her vision.

By analyzing the books in terms of these three issues, I was able to place the books into three categories: (1) the social conscience books, (2) the melting pot books, and (3) the culturally conscious books.

The social conscience books seem well intentioned. The major goal of their authors seems to have been to create social consciences among white children—to encourage them to develop empathy, sympathy, and tolerance for Black children. However, one subgroup of books in this category bears the message—probably intended for a Black audience—that empathy and sympathy should flow two ways.

My sample contained 21 social conscience books but only four basic stories, each involving some type of Black-white conflict. The first plot involves school desegregation. A Black child or children enroll in a formerly all-white school. All hell breaks loose, often stirred up by "outside agitators." Violence occurs, the white citizens come to their senses, and peace is restored. The second plot is the guess-who's-coming-to-dinner story, in which a Black child or family moves into a neighborhood and is befriended by the white protagonist, who defends the Blacks against neighbors and his or her own family, eventually managing to win acceptance for them. In the third story, Blacks—usually supported by white friends—fight discrimination by working within the system, using such means as peaceful demonstrations, marches, and petitions. The fourth plot focuses on Black children learning to get along with whites. The Black children expect hostility, but they come to realize that if hostility exists, it is because the white children have problems of their own.

These four plots reflect the social climate in which these books were created; by the mid-seventies social conscience books had begun to disappear. In terms of the development of an Afro-American children's literature, it is just as well. Some of these books perpetuate old stereotypes (the shuffling, flat-footed, shiny-faced servant) or help to create new ones (the super-Negro or the fatherless Black family). The Black character sometimes serves as merely an instrument for the moral salvation of the white protagonist. But probably the most common characteristic of the social conscience books is a paternalistic or patronizing attitude toward the Black characters. For example, in *A New Home for Theresa*, by Betty Baum, a fat, white social worker, who "fills up a room with friendliness," comments: "I think that being born Negro in this country does something harmful to a child. He feels inferior and because he feels this way, he can't work as well as the child who feels good about himself."

However, a few of the social conscience books dealt sensitively and honestly with some of the important social issues of the day. And the books in this category, as a whole, made the Black child more visible in children's literature. Despite some serious flaws, the images of Blacks that these books presented were also generally more positive than those contained in earlier books. On the whole, however, the social conscience books may "mean good, but they do so doggone poor."

A second category, the melting pot books, began to appear in the 1940s and are still being published today. These books seem to have been created out of a desire to recognize that people are people are people; however, they tend to suggest that all Americans share middle-class values and life experiences. The melting pot books are usually picture books, and only the illustrations indicate the racial or ethnic identities of the characters. The authors make no mention of racial or ethnic traits in the text. In fact, the ethnicity or race of the characters could be changed without rewriting the text at all. Unlike the social conscience books, the melting pot books contain no racial conflict. Instead, they focus on integration. There were 40 such books in my survey, and I was able to divide them into three subcategories.

The first subgroup consists of stories told from the perspective of a white child, although a Black child also plays a significant role. But the fact that the second child is Black is irrelevant to the plot, which usually involves the two youngsters in some joint venture. The second subgroup of melting pot books focuses on interracial friendships. Generally told from the point of view of the Black child, these are simple stories about ordinary childhood experiences. The third subgroup features a cast of characters that is predominantly, if not exclusively, Black. However, the text does not indicate that fact, and the Black families are solidly cast in a middle-class American mold—if not economically, then certainly in terms of the values they espouse.

The melting pot books are, in many ways, a positive contribution to children's fiction about Afro-Americans. Aside from some early illustrations of characters with Caucasian features and decidedly brown skin or characters who were ambiguously shaded, the Black characters are usually depicted both realistically and attractively. Objectionable stereotypes are almost totally absent. When Black families are presented, they are frequently intact, nuclear families—in conformity with the American ideal. Interracial friendship is shown as both positive and possible. The stories are typically described as *universal*. In other words, middle-class American children will find their own life experiences reflected to some degree in these books.

On the other hand, "You can hide the fire, but what are you going to do with the smoke?" The fact that the melting pot books insist on an American cultural homogeneity means that they also ignore important aspects of Afro-American life experiences. Afro-Americans share in the culture of the larger society, but they also belong to a distinctive cultural group; this is a both/and phenomenon, not a case of either/or.

I labeled the third and largest group of books in my survey the culturally conscious books. These stories are always told from the point of view of the Black characters, and they always deal with a Black family or neighborhood. My sample contained 89 such books, which I divided into seven subgroups.

One subgroup focuses on the African or southern American heritage, within a contemporary setting. For example, *Cornrows*, by Camille Yarbrough, relates the African origins and history of that braided hairstyle, through the story of a girl and her family. Along the way Yarbrough also weaves into her tale rhymes, song lyrics, and references to such Afro-American heroes as Malcolm X and Lena Horne.

A second subgroup of culturally conscious books focuses on battling racism and discrimination—though not on desegregation, as do some social conscience books. For instance, Mildred Taylor's *Roll of Thunder, Hear My Cry*, set in Mississippi at least a generation ago, tells of the love and strength that enable the Logan family to hang onto their land and their dignity despite oppressive white neighbors, who are determined to have both the land and the subservience of the Logans.

The other five subgroups in this category feature themes that are common in all realistic fiction for children: everyday experiences, urban living, friendships, family relationships, and stories about growing up. The subgroup that deals with everyday experiences includes such picture books as John Steptoe's *Stevie*, in which Robert reminisces about Stevie, the little boy who used to stay with Robert's family while his own mother worked. As he talks about some of the experiences they shared and about his not-always-positive attitudes toward them, Robert realizes how much he misses Stevie now that he is gone. One of the features that distinguishes *Stevie* from the melting pot books is Robert's use of Black vernacular speech patterns. Robert is not an ethnically interchangeable character; to depict him as white would require a considerable alteration of the text.

In the culturally conscious books that deal with urban living, the city seems almost to take on a life of its own and to impose itself on the lives of the characters. *The Soul Brothers and Sister Lou*, by Kristin Hunter, details everyday life in an inner-city ghetto. This book touches on such grim realities as lack of money, lack of adequate housing, police hostility, and lack of recreational facilities for young people. In this harsh environment Louretta Hawkins searches for her own sense of self, for the meaning of *soul*.

The culturally conscious books about friendship focus on relationships outside the immediate family circle. In *Three Wishes*, a picture book written by Lucille Clifton, Zenobia loses and then regains the valued friendship of her neighbor Victorius. What sets such books apart from other realistic children's fiction on the same theme is that, in their presentations of the specifics of living in Black communities, they incorporate such culturally distinctive features as Black English and references to Afro-American traditions, values, and beliefs.

The culturally conscious books about family life focus on relationships among siblings, experiences across generations, or conflicts within the family unit, such as impending divorce. Clifton's *My Brother Fine with Me*, for example, features eight-year-old Johnetta, who decides that she could readily do without her younger brother Baggy—until he runs away for a brief interval. *The Hundred Penny Box*, by Sharon Bell Mathis, describes the very special relationship between eight-year-old Michael and his one-hundred-year-old Aunt Dew. In Eloise Greenfield's *Sister*, a book for older readers, Doretha copes with her sister's withdrawal and hostility after the untimely death of their father.

The largest subgroup of culturally conscious books features youngsters taking steps toward maturity—achieving some personal goal, acquiring some insight into themselves as individuals, recognizing their own growth over time, or some combination of these. Most of the books on achieving personal goals are picture books that feature male protagonists. Donny, in *I Can Do It by Myself*, by Lessie Little and Eloise Greenfield, is a good example of such a protagonist: he successfully negotiates an encounter with a bulldog so that he can get to the store in order to buy his mother a birthday gift with money that he has saved—all by himself. Most of the books on self-insight, by contrast, feature young girls. Bette Greene's heroine Beth Lambert is typical; she learns that she can compete freely with "cute" Philip Hall and still retain his friendship. *Growin'*, by Nikki Grimes, is one example of a book dealing with personal growth; here Yolanda comes to realize that, "when hard times come, good feeling people stick together."

The most complex books in the subgroup combine elements of the three types of books I have just described. Predictably, these books are written for older children; thus, the authors develop their themes in greater depth and on more than one level. For example, the hero in Virginia Hamilton's *M. C. Higgins, the Great* surveys his world from atop a forty-foot-pole—and tries to figure out how to save his home and family from the strip-mining spoil heap that threatens to crush them. He learns to take responsibility for making decisions and for taking personal action to help them all survive.

Like the culturally conscious books on friendship, those dealing with family relationships and with budding maturity are similar to general realistic fiction for children on the same themes. What sets these books apart from the rest is the fact that they employ culturally distinctive language or portray typical activities, values, attitudes, and perspectives of U.S. Blacks.

Indeed, the culturally conscious books that deal with everyday experiences, urban living, friendships, family relationships, and growing up could probably be further subdivided by the perspectives from which they are written. An author's perspective is revealed through his or her decisions regarding which Afro-American life experiences to emphasize, as well as through the accuracy and authenticity of specific details related to those life experiences. Books set in the city, for instance, can focus on such negative factors as poverty, drugs, gangs, crime, and their effects. Or, with those factors as givens, such books can emphasize the strength and support to be found in human relationships, especially within the family or between close friends.

An author's perspective is sometimes identifiable, too, through details that are inaccurate or lacking in credibility. For example, an Afro-American writer would be highly unlikely to write as Louise Fitzhugh did in *Nobody's Family Is Going to Change:* "Emma couldn't say 'Daddy.' It made her feel like a pickaninny in a bad movie running across a cotton field yelling 'Daddy, Daddy!' " If "pickaninny" ever crossed the mind of an Afro-American writer, he or she would not have a young Afro-American girl utter the word—and certainly not in relation to the use of "daddy" as a term of address, a context that seems totally irrelevant.

An author with an outsider's perspective sometimes describes incidents or behaviors without helping readers to understand their motivation, origin, or significance. Thus, in Michele Murray's *Nellie Cameron,* the reader finds an African Methodist Episcopal (AME) church service presided over by "Preacher Evans," in which "Nellie liked standing up and hollering out the words about Jesus and heaven and the Precious Lord," and "all the fat ladies like Mama sighed and sweated," and Mama shouted: "Amen. Say it. That's surely the way it is." Those descriptive phrases carry no sense of the power of music, of words well spoken, and of participation in a traditional call-and-response communication pattern to generate sincere expressions of religious feeling. Nor do they carry any sense of the rhythms, the highs and lows, of an AME church service. Thus the behavior of the women seems only strange and exotic.

Culturally conscious books that have been written from an Afro-American cultural perspective display features and themes not often found in social conscience or melting pot books—relationships between the very old and the young, the inclusion of Afro-American historical and cultural traditions, extended families, a strong sense of community, psychological survival. The most easily identifiable feature of culturally conscious books is the use of Black linguistic and rhetorical styles, although these styles may not appear in all such books.

Among the books in my sample that were published from the mid-seventies on, the vast majority fell into the culturally conscious category. (Such books appeared throughout the sample, however; a few had even been published prior to 1965.) These are the books most clearly intended primarily for an Afro-American audience, most determinedly mirroring—or even celebrating—a distinct Afro-American culture, and most frequently reflecting an Afro-American cultural perspective. As with all good fiction, the best of these culturally conscious books also touch on human universals that have meaning for readers of other ethnic or racial backgrounds. These books have become the core of an emergent Afro-American children's fiction.

However, if only 14.4 percent of children's books include at least one Black character, then 85.6 percent do not. The world of children's fiction remains largely white in terms of the characters, the authors, and the audiences for whom the books are written. Even within my own survey, which was limited to contemporary realistic fiction about Blacks, white authors had written 100 percent of the social conscience books, 87.5 percent of the melting pot books, and 28 percent of the culturally conscious books. With the emergence of a small group of fairly prolific Black writers, however, a new dimension has been added to the previously all-white world of children's books. We are no longer where we once were, but we are not yet where we ought to be.

A Chinese Sense of Reality

LAURENCE YEP

It's difficult to hear the songs of more than one world at any one time. And yet sometimes it's necessary to forget the songs of one world and learn the songs of another, especially if you're a Chinese-American.

When I was going into Chinese-American research and digging into history, one of the most important books to me was Ralph Ellison's *Invisible Man*. I felt very much like the Invisible Man, without form and without shape. It was as if all the features on my face had been erased and I was just a blank mirror reflecting other people's hopes and fears. And if I wanted to see any features on my face, I would have to go through a Hollywood prop room and go digging around for masks.

So, for instance, I could be pompously wise like Charlie Chan; I could be inscrutable like Kane in *Kung Fu*; I could be the dependable sidekick like Peter, the houseboy, in *Bachelor Father*; I could be one of the howling fanatics in *Fifty-Five Days at Peking* or *Sand Pebbles*; I could be sadistic, cruel, and cunning like Fu Manchu. The best thing I could hope for would have involved going from Hollywood to literature; then I could be the intelligent dependable sidekick like Lee in *East of Eden*.

Replacing those stereotypes with actual historical models created another difficulty. And I think I might make that clear by setting up an analogy. Let's suppose a faraway future for America, one in which its resources have all been used up, and its technology has become outmoded. In order to make a living, its men and women have to emigrate to other countries. Let's say specifically that men and women leave Mississippi, one of the hardest hit areas, and they settle down in Iran. They raise children, and their children raise children. And then one of their descendants decides that he wants to write about his ancestors. He goes to the library in Tehran (and, of course, he can't speak English; he can only speak Persian). So he goes to the history shelves, and he takes down several volumes of American history, written in Persian. He finds that they deal mainly with the development of the Northeast and Midwest. So instead he goes to the literature section, and he takes down some American classics that have been translated into Persian. He finds some sermons by Jonathan Edwards, some fantasy tales by Washington Irving, some essays by Emerson, some poetry by Whitman, and he finds Theodore Dreiser's *Sister Carrie*. (This is a very forward-looking library.) But it's from these scanty materials that he has to reconstruct a picture of what life was like in Mississippi three generations ago.

I faced similar problems when I first began trying to understand the background that shaped me. It took six years of research in libraries in different cities and universities to find the little bits and pieces of information. It took longer to assemble them into a mosaic. I don't have time to go into any in-depth explanation of that history, but I will present a broad outline just to make the background of my books comprehensible.

Most of the Chinese who came to America in the nineteenth and early twentieth centuries came from south China, and the southern Chinese are culturally and linguistically distinct from the northern Chinese. (A correspondent who went for a tour of China—his name is Ross Terrill—had a northern Chinese interpreter and a southern Chinese interpreter, and when the southern Chinese went off to take a nap, the northern Chinese leaned over to Ross Terrill and whispered, "You know you really have to be careful what you eat down here." There's a long history of stereotypes that northern Chinese have had about southern Chinese. But anyway, these southern Chinese had to come to America because of immense troubles at home. Another writer has compared the lot of the average Chinese farmer to a man standing up to his neck in a pool of water; a ripple in that pool would be likely to drown that farmer. Of course, a ripple would happen every three years because there would be floods. There could be a flood or a drought; there could be a human epidemic or disease, a plant disease, bandits, government troops, extra taxes to pay for government projects like the building of the great canals and the Great Wall, although the Great Wall had been built much earlier. But still it had been built with labor levies and with tax levies on the average little farmer.

After decades of trouble in southern China, many of the Chinese had no choice but to go off on a wild-goose chase to America to work in the gold fields and send money home—assuming that they survived the trip over to America. One investigating American committee said that the conditions on many of the ships that carried the Chinese would make even a slaver look good. Many of the owners brought derelict ships and assumed that they would be confiscated and condemned in San Francisco. Because they wanted to make as much money as possible, ship owners would cram as many Chinese as they could into the holds. It was a very long, hot journey in those days, of course.

For a variety of reasons, including prejudice and fear, it was mostly men who came over. Even though they had families, including wives and children, they lived most of their lives away from them, so to all intents and purposes they were bachelors. And Chinese society in America remained like that from the 1850s to the 1930s, for eighty years. When the first men grew old, they sent for their sons and cousins and brothers and nephews to replace them, to keep on sending money home.

Now, there were a small number of determined men who brought their wives over, and they did try to start families. They created a family society within the shell of the larger and older bachelor society. That family society was determined to sink its roots in America. It survived psychologically by forgetting about the bitter past and the violent confrontations between Chinese and Americans. It ignored many of the acts of discrimination that happened. And Chinese-Americans still maintain a discreet distance between themselves and whites, choosing to imitate their white counterparts within the confines of Chinatown—so you have Chinese basketball leagues, Chinese tennis leagues, and even Chinese Olympics. Dances were held in Chinatown: my dentist used to be a bandleader and that's how he put himself through college, playing American tunes at Chinese dances.

By the time they reached the third and fourth generations—my generation—many Chinese-Americans were growing up in households in which little Chinese was spoken. And the Chinese myths and legends were so much embarrassing superstition. If you went to the older people, and—at least this was my experience—if they knew English, they were often reluctant to talk about what they knew because they might have seemed superstitious, or because they had been laughed at by others. This happened when I went to visit an uncle who runs one of the last active temples in northern California outside of San Francisco. He would catch himself every few moments and say, "Am I boring you, or am I talking too much?" Of course he wasn't at all. By and large, even if older Chinese-Americans do overcome that fear, sometimes they've learned the information wrong, or they know a variation of what you know is true for the majority.

So I had to rely heavily on research material. Even when I found material about my ancestors, I realized that the writers treated them largely as a faceless crowd. They were statistical fodder for historians or abstractions for sociologists. So, for instance, I could give you the populations for each of California's counties for a fifty-year period, but I couldn't have told you what any of those Chinese hoped and feared. Or I could tell you about the acculturation process as exemplified by the Mississippi Chinese, but I couldn't have told you what their loneliness was like.

But I did manage to find two articles about a Chinese aviator who flew an airplane in 1909 in or near Oakland. It was very easy to visualize that flight and put it down on paper. But I found it was hard to explain how he got up there, on top of that hill, and why he ever built that airplane in the first place. And so I saw that if that scene was to have any meaning, it would have to be integrated into a larger whole. And what *that* meant was that I had to recreate the time of that bachelor society.

Now, I have to ask you to imagine what it was like then, trying to reconstruct that universe, and not as you know it in the already published *Dragonwings*. It's as if I asked you to build a house of toothpicks, and I gave you a little bottle of glue, but I took the box of toothpicks and I scattered them all around this room and around this building, so before you could even begin building that house you had to go and pick up the toothpicks. You had to find them first. And then, as a further complication, I told you it couldn't be built like an American house, it had to be built like a Chinese one.

That is similar to my own situation. I had no real guidelines for assembling that Chinatown of the 1900s; ironically, it would have been easier for me to write about a young boy growing up in New England in the 1600s. There would have been a great deal of source material, and I would have had writers like Hawthorne telling me how people dressed, what they hoped and feared, how they spoke. But the nature of the problem suggested its own solution. Because I'd grown up as an American child in the 1950s, I had to grow up again as a Chinese child in the 1900s. And that meant I had to develop a special sense of reality, a Chinese sense rather than an American sense.

As a writer, I also had to adopt the perspective of a child when I was using these research materials. So, for instance, if I saw a picture of a god on the wall, I had to be told that it was a kitchen god and I had to be taught how I was supposed to act toward it and especially at what times of the year I was supposed to be respectful. Or if I saw a piece of meat on a plate, I had to be told that it was duck and that it had been prepared and roasted in a special way. Milk and cheese had to seem exotic to me. An American chessboard had to seem strange to me because it lacked a river down the middle. And the turning point really came when I was in a friend's apartment, working on the novel, and I looked at a checkered tablecloth on her table, and the tablecloth suddenly seemed very strange and alien to me, as if I truly were accustomed to designs that weren't cold and abstract and geometrical but actually filled up space, fluidly. So it was more than a narrative device when I chose to describe this story from the viewpoint of an eight-year-old boy. It was close to my own process of self-discovery.

Now, what about the specific story of the aviator? I could have said he was trying to compensate for feelings of inadequacy: he wanted to show that a Chinese could do whatever a white man could do. Or I could make it the story of progress on the march—you know, the story of a farsighted person among shortsighted people. But the invention I was dealing with was more than just a better mousetrap or a bottle opener. I was dealing with a *flying machine.* Years after Kitty Hawk, people still didn't believe that men had flown. They thought the Wright Brothers had made up that story and the newspapers had been conned. So, with that early biplane I was dealing with the reach of imagination itself, that ability to grasp with the heart and mind what you can't grasp with the hand. And that imagination sleeps within each of us like a dragon waiting to wake and rise and fly and view a much larger part of the universe than we normally would. And it's that same dragonlike power that lets the writer pass from the world of the present into the world of the past. And once there, if the writer remains quiet, he can hear the voices of the dead, singing as they maintain and create their world which has long since vanished.

Whatever I write, I'm always aware that I'm not quite alone. If I listen long enough and hard enough, I just may be able to hear a few fragments of a chord of music or a few broken notes, and I know that if I wait long enough those few broken notes or those few fragments of a chord will regenerate themselves within my own unconscious and they'll grow until the song is once again made whole. And I think the deepest pleasure of writing is joining my own voice with the voices of the past as they sing their world into existence once again.

A Common Humanity

MILTON MELTZER

The first reading I can remember enjoying was "Gasoline Alley." I must have been about five when the comic strip—more than fifty years old today—began appearing in our local paper, the only thing to read in our house. My folks were immigrants with no time or money for books. As soon as I was big enough to carry a paper route, I bought dime-novel paperbacks at the candy store and followed the doings of Frank Merriwell, the eternal student at Yale, and Nick Carter, the detective snooping on the sinful streets of New York.

Then I found out about the public library, a jumble of old red brick downtown, full of books you could take out for nothing. Saturdays became a double delight. I began them at the library, yanking books off the shelves at random, sampling everything. Then I lugged the books the long blocks down to the movie theater we called The Dump, where I'd see the latest Charlie Chaplin, Tarzan, and Pearl White while I ate a hot dog and swigged down chocolate milk. At home at last, to hole up in the bedroom and read myself into a daze.

What I liked most were adventure stories that took me out of my skin. And biographies. I was always trying on a new hero for size—explorer, quarterback, reporter, detective. One day I looked up from a book and realized that what I was feeling inside, in my own private world, was astonishingly like what people everywhere felt—whether they lived yesterday or a hundred or a thousand years ago. This fear, hope, shame, love, it wasn't happening only to me. Maybe there was something of me in everyone, and something of everyone in me.

I know reading had much to do with shaping my picture of the world when I was growing up. Perhaps as much as the real world itself. It was junk one day and literature the next, but gradually I came to realize which said more to me. Often the world in my books was more real to me than the life around our kitchen table or on our street. The family and the neighborhood you took for granted. Great writers somehow managed to make life in the worlds they created far more intense. Between covers I encountered events as terrifying as a nightmare, characters more extraordinary than any I saw on my block, and frustrations and fulfillments on a scale that put my own into a new perspective.

It isn't just any book, mind you, that does that. "Few books have more than one thought; the generality indeed have not quite so many." The Hare brothers pointed that out long ago. Nor, even when a truly good book is at hand, can it be just any reader. Lichtenberg warned us of that when he wrote, "A book is a mirror: if an ass peers into it, you can't expect an apostle to look out."

But we like to think that we are neither such writers nor such readers. For us good readers, Thoreau holds out hope that we may one day encounter a good book. "There are probably words addressed to our condition exactly," he says in *Walden*, "which, if we could really hear and understand, would be more salutary than the morning or the spring to our lives, and possibly put a new aspect on the face of things for us. How many a man has dated a new era in his life from the reading of a book!"

I try to remember which books, read in youth, gave me the sense of awakening Thoreau speaks of. There were *Leaves of Grass*, *Spoon River Anthology*, and the short stories of Sherwood Anderson, *An American Tragedy*, Sandburg's *Abraham Lincoln*, the autobiographies of Clarence Darrow and Lincoln Steffens. I stumbled across them or someone told me to try them. I spent no time analyzing or weighing them. It was enough that they spoke directly to me. Here were words that I could use to shape my own experience.

There are other books of that time I can recall, which had a powerful, but different, meaning for me. They made me conscious of the world's blind hatred. They made me wonder why my existence was such a problem for those who were not like me. And what was that "me"? What was it about me that they would not accept? Was there any truth in the negative images held up to me by those writers? And here I speak as the particular kind of American I am, a Jewish American.

We are only a tiny minority compared with other ethnic groups, but what happens to any such group has echoes in the experience of the others. One's ethnic background—straight, mixed, or truncated as mine happened to be—leaves marks that cannot be missed. Like any plant, we grow from particular roots.

I grew up in an industrial town in central Massachusetts. We lived in a mixed neighborhood of working-class and lower middle-class families. They were of many different origins—Irish, Italian, Polish, Lithuanian, Slovak, Swedish, Armenian. Most were Catholic, some Protestant, and a small number Jewish. Most of their parents, like mine, had come from Europe around the turn of the century. The children I went to school with were the first generation to be born in America.

The public schools were dedicated to Americanizing us. The major task of the schools, said a leading educator of those times, was "to break up those [immigrant] groups of settlements, to assimilate and amalgamate these people as part of our American race, and to implant in their children, so far as can be done, the Anglo-Saxon conception of righteousness, law and order, and popular government."

You can make it here, he was saying, if you will only become *real* Americans. Drop what makes you different. Forget where your parents came from, what they brought with them, their own feelings and experiences, their own beliefs and values.

As immigrants continued to pour in from eastern and southern Europe the magazine *Scientific American* urged them to "assimilate" quickly or face "a quiet but sure extermination." If you keep your alien ways, it warned, you "will share the fate of the native Indian."

Jane Addams, founder of Hull House in the Chicago slums, was one of the few who understood how wrong this was. The public school, she said, "too often separates the child from his parents and widens the old gulf between fathers and sons which is never so cruel and so wide as it is between the immigrants who come to this country and their children who have gone to the public school and feel that they have there learned it all." The parents, she went on, "are thereafter subjected to certain judgment, the judgment of the young which is always harsh and in this instance founded upon the most superficial standard of Americanism." As far back as 1908 she urged the schools "to do more to connect these children with the best things of the past, to make them realize something of the beauty and charm of the language, the history and the traditions which their parents represent. . . . It is the business of the school to give to each child the beginnings of a culture so wide and deep and universal that he can interpret his own parents and countrymen by a standard which is worldwide and not provincial."

My parents, allowed only the most rudimentary schooling in the old country, were in a grand rush to become Americans. My mother had come to this Garden of Eden at fourteen, my father at eighteen, each traveling alone from remote villages of eastern Europe. They did not want to be ridiculed as greenhorns, and as Yiddish was the badge of foreignness, they spoke so little of their own tongue that I learned scarcely a word of it. They did not observe the ancient religious code and gave us no training in it. They told us nothing about their own years in eastern Europe. Was it because they wanted to forget the world they had left behind? Or because they knew I had no interest in their culture? For I did not realize their early life would have so much meaning to me. When, at last, I had the sense to want to know about it, it was too late. They were gone.

Whatever being Jewish meant to my mother and father, they took for granted. It was passed on unself-consciously to their children. They could not articulate it. Still, their behavior—the way they moved, walked, laughed, cried, talked—their attitudes, the way our family functioned, imprinted upon us something of the social history they brought with them.

If they did not tell me what a Jew was and why I was one, did the world outside? Only in the negative sense: the cost of being a Jew, the insults voiced, the jobs denied, the housing restricted, the club doors closed, the colleges on quotas. And that history . . . the very calendar that hung in Jewish homes marking the anniversaries, most of which were catastrophes, followed only sometimes by salvation. Passover, to celebrate the escape from ancient enslavement under the Pharaohs. Purim, the time when Haman's plan to exterminate all the Jews of Persia had been foiled by Esther. Hanukkah, which marks the victory of the guerrilla fighters led by the Maccabees over the ruthless despot, Antiochus, who tried to suppress the religion and culture of the Jews. And the Ninth of Ab, which is the fast day for remembering, and mourning, the destruction of the Temple in Jerusalem, the first time by the Babylonians, the second time by the Romans. But so many were the national disasters that followed, the fast day became a reservoir into which have been poured all the misfortunes of the Jews down through Hitler's Holocaust.

No wonder, then, an alarm bell rang whenever I heard or saw the word *Jew* in an unexpected setting. It might have been the sound of that word slashing into my ears while I played basketball in the gym. Or the sight of those three letters on the page of a book I was reading. Two novels especially, which I read as a youngster, stick in my mind. One was *Ivanhoe*, and the other *Oliver Twist*. Harmless in appearance, but poisonous in effect, as I now see them. I would guess that most readers, asked to recall whether there was anything about Jews in *Ivanhoe*, would remember Scott's sympathetic portrayal of Rebecca. What they forget are the innumerable references to Jews as usurers, liars, hypocrites, as covetous, contemptible, inhuman. The marvelous story Scott told captivated me; I tried to ignore everything in the novel that nourished anti-Semitism. But how can the young reader, Jew or non-Jew, escape the insidious influence of such a book?

And then there was Charles Dickens. I was drawn at once into the wanderings of Oliver Twist, the lost child, the rejected child, full of fear and hope, daydreaming of discovery in the dark places of London. My child's sense of justice was enraged by Dickens's exposure of the vast cruelty and greed, the indifference to humankind which birthed the slums and the haunts of crime the novel moves through. But over everything in the story fell the shadow of Fagin, that "villainous-looking," "repulsive," "greasy," "old shrivelled Jew," to use Dickens's opening description of the master criminal into whose hands the tender and innocent little Oliver comes. In the dark, monstrous visage and the wicked, staring eyes of Fagin, I saw the devil himself. The power of Dickens to draw characters by an intense poetic simplification made the anti-Semitic caricature all the more horrifying. I remember hurrying my eyes over those pages in which he appeared, anxious to get on to passages less painful to me as a Jewish child.

Of course, I encountered Christians in the novel who were vicious, like the brutal Bill Sikes. But my hero and all the other good people were Christians. They more than overbalanced a Sikes. And the fact that Sikes was a villain had nothing to do with his being a Christian. In the case of Fagin, his villainy was made identical with his Jewishness. To be a Jew, one could only conclude, is to be a villain.

If additional force was needed to confirm that image of oneself, there was *The Merchant of Venice*. Shakespeare's play was used in my high school English classes. We read it aloud and discussed it. That the characterization of Shylock disturbed me goes without saying. Years later, I found Professor Mark Van Doren putting his finger on how it was done. Shakespeare, he said, had not made the "least inch" of Shylock "lovely." "He would seem in fact to have attempted a monster, one whose question whether a Jew hath eyes, hands, organs, dimensions, senses, affections, and passions would reveal its rhetorical form, the answer being no . . . Shylock . . . is a man thrust into a world bound not to endure him. In such a world he necessarily looks and sounds ugly." Whoever reads or sees the play, he added, "should have no difficulty in recognizing Shylock as the alien element in a world of love and friendship, of nightingales and moonlight sleeping sweetly on a bank."

My teacher reveled in the superb lines; she talked of imagery and rhythm, of dramatic structure, of the position of the play in the body of Shakespeare's work. She said nothing of Shylock as Jew. It was not explained to us how church and state cooperated in the medieval centuries to make the Jews outcasts, shut them off from the land, excluded them from the Christian guilds so they could no longer practice their crafts and trades, and forced them to become merchants and moneylenders. As soon as the economy of each European country advanced, such Jews were restricted to smaller and smaller roles. And when they were no longer considered essential, their Christian rivals called them avaricious and heartless—the image perpetuated by Shakespeare's Shylock—and then took over their functions.

It is not only from the medieval mind that such abuse and contempt springs. We encounter it in many national literatures of later times, at least those I have some knowledge of. Take the Russians, whose novels, short stories, and plays I began reading in college years. Some of the young Jews of eastern Europe who took part in the revolutionary ferment of the nineteenth and early twentieth centuries were hostile to everything Jewish. They feared their Jewishness would block them from reaching the Russian people. They often came from families that had assimilated. They thought fighting for a revolutionary overturn of czarist society would mean creating a world in which all religions would disappear. There would then be no Jews, no distinction between themselves and everyone else.

Why did they feel so inferior? Why should they hope that a change in the social system would eliminate their own people? In part, it is due to the Russian literature they were raised on, rooted as it was in the ancient anti-Semitic tradition of the church. Pushkin, Gogol, Lermontov, Dostoyevski, Turgenev, all depicted Jews as vile creatures. Russian fiction, drama, and poetry portrayed the Jew as dirty, dishonest, contemptible; as parasite, opportunist, fiend. Their Jewish characters would do anything for money, betray anyone for their own advantage. The Russian writers who were respected for their sensitivity to the human soul could not see in the Jew anything human.

English literature is not much different, with some honorable exceptions such as George Eliot. To the writers I named earlier one could add many more. The French? The same. And the Germans? In the early nineteenth century Germany became the fountainhead of modern anti-Semitism. An endless stream of anti-Semitic books and pamphlets polluted the culture. Some of the most distinguished philosophers and poets contributed to it, among them Fichte and Goethe. It was reflected, of course, in children's literature. The brothers Grimm, whose collection of folktales has delighted children for generations, are also known for their devotion to the study of the German language. They produced the classic *Deutsches Wörterbuch*, which, under the term *Jew*, broadcasts an appalling variety of offensive definitions culled from German literature.

A Jewish stereotype was shaped in widely read German novels. The Jew was puny and cowardly, his eyes gleamed with the "calculated cunning of his race," his foreignness was evidenced in the jumble of Yiddish and German he was made to speak. He was inherently bad, this villain, and few readers would lament the violently cruel death the author invariably sentenced him to. Down deep into the twentieth century this caricature of the Jew appeared and reappeared in popular culture. Entrenched as an article of German faith, it would have the power of an atomic arsenal when Hitler triggered it.

And what of American writers? Not until the past few decades have Jewish characters become major figures in American literature. Earlier there were too few Jews in America to write about. The literary artists of the American Renaissance—Emerson, Thoreau, Hawthorne, Melville, Dickinson, Whitman—made glancing references, if any, to the contemporary Jew. But most Americans, then as now, were not paying attention to our major writers. They were reading popular novels and seeing popular plays created by hack writers who rang endless changes upon the Shylock theme. These writers, like their betters, had little or no connections with Jews and when they wrote about them, fell back on the stereotype. If Jews were present in this cheap fiction, it was usually as ugly, unscrupulous members of that money-obsessed tribe of Israel. As soon as I began reading dime novels, I became painfully aware of how common this portrait was.

Later, in high school, I read *The Education of Henry Adams*. In Massachusetts we were expected to venerate the native Adams clan which had given so much to American political and intellectual life. Yet here was Henry Adams writing of a "furtive Jacoob or Ysaac still reeking of the Ghetto, snarling a weird Yiddish." Traveling abroad, Mr. Adams looked out his train window and saw "a Polish Jew . . . in all his weird horror." The Jew, he wrote, "makes me creep." I soon discovered that nearly all the Boston Brahmins displayed the same contempt, although Henry Adams earns first rank for the intensity of his feeling.

Less possessed and more conventional was the antipathy found in the novelists I began reading in those years—Edith Wharton, Henry James, Theodore Dreiser, Scott Fitzgerald, Thomas Wolfe; and the poets—Ezra Pound, T. S. Eliot, E. E. Cummings. Anti-Jewish attitudes were widespread and even fashionable in that era. Not until Hitler's Holocaust did they go out of style.

I do not know if a sketch of my early readings helps to explain why it took me so long to explore this aspect of my self. Growing up Jewish in a non-Jewish world evidently produced conflicts I could not openly face. What happened to me is anything but unique. What child without an Anglo-Saxon name or skin has not felt himself an outsider? Given nothing to make him sure of himself and proud of his heritage, he may, in Peter Ognibene's words, turn into "a monomaniacal American, a compulsive imitator of WASP styles, an illiterate of the history of his own forebears."

Perhaps that is why I found it easier to be distressed on behalf of others who were underdogs. I am only now learning the lesson Albert Memmi has pronounced: "If everyone is ready to denounce oppression, no one is willing to recognize himself as oppressed." So while I remained ignorant of my own, I steeped myself in the history of other oppressed minorities. What I learned in writing about them was not a waste of effort. Exploring the experience of other peoples brings us up against the crises they encountered and gives us the chance to find in their lives the courage to face up to our own.

It has been only a few years since I began to study Jewish history and culture and to write about it. I hope to go on, glad to know that I have thousands of years of my people's history to deal with, if only an infinitesimal fraction of that time in which to discover myself in that collective memory.

Is it narrowing, is it limiting, to be intensely concerned with one's own ethnic group? I do not find it so. True ethnic consciousness can be a creative force. It is something larger than the self. It provides a bridge to the past and between the generations. It celebrates the beauty of the differences among the incredible variety of ethnic groups I think our country is lucky to embrace. It counters the feeling of alienation. To gain more insight into our cultural distinctions can only strengthen our national life. For differences do not mean inferiority. We do not have to give up our uniqueness to share a common humanity.

And the Whole Earth Was of One Language

MARIANNE CARUS

Thousands of mutually incomprehensible tongues are spoken on this small planet. People have long wondered about this, and every civilization has its own mythology of the primal scattering of languages. According to Genesis, this happened some time after Noah's flood:

> And the whole earth was of one language, and of one speech. And it came to pass, as they journeyed from the east, that they found a plain in the land of Shinar, and they dwelt there. . . . And they said Go to, let us build us a city and a tower, whose top may reach unto heaven. . . . And the Lord came down to see the city and the tower which the children of men builded. And the Lord said, Behold, the people is one and they have all one language . . . and now nothing will be restrained from them, which they have imagined to do. Go to, let us go down, and there confound their language, that they may not understand one another's speech. So the Lord scattered them abroad from thence upon the face of all the earth: and they left off to build the city. Therefore is the name of it called Babel; because the Lord did there confound the language of all the earth.

This, then, is one conjecture, to solve the riddle with a metaphor: The Lord punished his people for raising a lunatic tower, for having one language and becoming too powerful. The primal tongue had been scattered into fragments. "Thus Babel was a second Fall," writes George Steiner in *After Babel*. "The tongue of Eden was like a flawless glass; a light of total understanding streamed through it." But had the *Ur-Sprache*—the primal language—been irretrievably lost? And what had been the nature of Adam's tongue anyway? Had it been Hebrew or an even earlier version of Chaldean? "Jewish gnostics argued that the Hebrew of the Torah was God's undoubted idiom," says Steiner, "though man no longer understood its full esoteric meaning."

Throughout the ages poets have tried to understand, to interpret, to speculate on this second fall, on this alienation from the Ur-tongue. Kafka, in one of his notebook entries, says: "Had it been possible to build the Tower of Babel without ascending it, that would have been allowed." In other words, man would still be speaking an undivided tongue had he not gone to the forbidden height. And the Argentine poet Jorge Luis Borges wrote:

> All things are words of some strange tongue, in thrall
> To Someone, Something, who both days and night
> Proceeds in endless gibberish to write
> The history of the world. In that dark scrawl
>
> Rome is set down, and Carthage, I, you, all,
> And this my being which escapes me quite,
> My anguished life that's cryptic, recondite,
> And garbled as the tongues of Babel's fall.

Returning to the metaphor that Genesis suggests: this rubble of the smashed tower of Babel, the scattered shards of the original tongue, can be pieced together again—not to lead men back to Adam's language, but to free him of his alienation from other men. Translation, with its transfer of meaning from one language to another, becomes the great liberator.

The exquisite art of translators has not only created a link with our past, but has also perpetuated a closeness and familiarity with most of the great literary events throughout the ages. Most of the translations of these literary classics are an important part of our children's and our own cultural heritage, and we never think of them as not having originated in our own language. First, of course, there is the Bible, then the Greek and Norse and Asian myths and legends, Aesop's fables, the *Iliad* and *Odyssey*, Grimm's and Perrault's fairy tales and all the other European folktales, the *Arabian Nights*, the *Kalevala*, *The Cid*, the *Song of Roland*, the *Ramayana*, and the hero epics of ancient Persia. All these classics are read by children and adults alike. In our own time there are a number of children's book translations that already have become classics. For example, Johanna Spyri's *Heidi* was translated into English in 1884, four years after it appeared in German. Then there are others: *Pinocchio*, *Bambi*, Selma Lagerlöf's *The Wonderful Adventures of Nils*, Erich Kästner's *Emil and the Detectives*, Antoine de Saint

Exupéry's *The Little Prince,* Jean de Brunhoff's Babar books. And, of course, there is Astrid Lindgren's inimitable *Pippi Longstocking.*

The end of the Second World War brought about a great desire for international sharing, and children's books such as *Babar* and *Pippi,* which have already become classics, began to be translated in unprecedented numbers soon after the terrible postwar years. Jella Lepman, a German-born Jew who left Germany to work in England but returned after the war, began her work for children's books as a humanitarian project. She saw children's books as a means to international understanding and, therefore, peace among nations. In her book *Die Kinderbrücke,* translated as *A Bridge of Children's Books,* she described her efforts, the difficulties and frustrations, and the final triumphs. One of Jella Lepman's many ideas was to start a traveling exhibit of children's books for the German children. In a letter she sent at that time to publishers from twenty countries, she wrote,

> Dear Sir:
>
> This letter contains an unusual request. May we ask for your most special understanding?
>
> We are searching for ways to acquaint the children of Germany with children's books from all nations. German children are practically without any books at all, once their literature from the Nazi period has been removed from circulation. Also, educators and publishers need books from the free world to orient and guide them. These children carry no responsibility for this war, and that is why books for them should be the first messengers of peace. They are to be collected in an exhibition which will tour Germany and then, perhaps, other countries as well. We are asking particularly for picture books, or at least heavily illustrated ones, to help overcome the language barrier. But we also hope to make available the literature that just tells a good story for the group work we plan to do. We hope German publishers will be able to obtain the translation rights for many of these books.

From the traveling exhibit of children's books that resulted from this appeal, Ms. Lepman later established the International Youth Library in Munich, and this library now has the largest individual collection of children's books from many countries. Not long thereafter, the interest in internationalism and in translation of children's books, both of which were stimulated by Ms. Lepman and her efforts, led to the formation of the International Board on Books for Young People (IBBY). The new association had its first general assembly in 1953 and now meets every other year, celebrating its twenty-fifth anniversary at the 1978 meeting in Würzburg, Germany. IBBY brings together publishers, librarians, educators, critics, authors, and editors—anyone working with children's books. In 1956 IBBY's first Hans Christian Andersen Medal (also called the little Nobel Prize) was awarded to Eleanor Farjeon; and in 1958 the medal was awarded to Astrid Lindgren. In 1966 the first Hans Christian Andersen Medal for an artist was awarded to Alois Carigiet of Switzerland; Tove Jansson received the companion author's medal for her Moomin stories. *Bookbird,* the official magazine of IBBY, is written in English and published four times a year. It is edited in Vienna, printed in Germany, and has associate editors in each of IBBY's member countries.

When we first started *Cricket* magazine, one of our purposes was to give our readers a sense of the whole world, to strengthen the bridge of understanding that Jella Lepman had constructed so carefully. To achieve this end, Clifton Fadiman and I wrote to nearly three hundred authors all over the world. But why appeal to foreign authors? Aren't American writers good enough for our American children? Of course they are! But why should a language barrier deny our children the books and stories of brilliant authors in other parts of the world?

There are two important considerations here. First, we want our children to have the very best literature we can find, no matter where it comes from—the best stories, the best poems, the best illustrations. Often at *Cricket* we consider translating a story or poem simply because of its excellence in its genre. Second, now, more than ever, there is a great need for a cultural exchange between the countries of the world: why not start with books or stories for the very young? We see foreign-language children's books and poems and stories in the larger context of the cultural climate they transmit to our American children.

The earlier in life young children are exposed to one or several foreign cultures—either through books, stories, music, art exhibits, toys, games, or films—the more open-minded they will be later on. They may even acquire an interest and taste for history, travel, foreign customs, habits, and foods. Ten seems to be a crucial age. Before age ten, children seem to be eager and ready for many new experiences. They love, for example, to imitate and have fun with new sounds, and it seems easy for many under-ten-year-olds to learn a foreign language—especially its pronunciation and intonation—perfectly and without accent. After the age of ten it is much more difficult to start a foreign language, and although the child may learn the grammar and vocabulary, an accent will remain. (I am a good example of this, having learned English in a German school, *beginning* at the age of ten.)

But growing up in Europe had its advantages. I was able to read a great variety of books, some translated, some not, about the many different nationalities in that crowded continent. I remember being especially interested in the stories about the Germans who had been settled by Catherine the Great, empress of Russia, in the valley of the Volga. I read everything I could find about Russia, the czars, the revolution. Then, when Hitler gained more power in Germany, books about other countries disappeared. Only when I came to the United States could I read all the marvelous and wonderful British and American classics.

Probably my own experience in Nazi Germany has a lot to do with my insistence on having in *Cricket* translated stories from as many countries and about as many different cultures as possible. The earlier in life we lay the foundation for international understanding and tolerance, the sounder will be the bridges built later and the more ready for peaceful traffic and exchange back and forth. Paul Hazard says in his *Books, Children and Men*:

> Yes, children's books keep alive a sense of nationality, but they also keep alive a sense of humanity. They describe their native land lovingly, but they also describe faraway lands where unknown brothers live. They understand the essential quality of their own race, but each of them is a messenger that goes beyond mountains and rivers, beyond the seas, to the very ends of the world in search of new friendships. Every country gives and every country receives—innumerable are the exchanges—and so it comes about that *in our first impressionable years the universal republic of childhood is born.*

"Every country gives and every country receives" was an excellent slogan for 1979, the International Year of the Child, when special efforts were being made by all Western and Eastern nations to include the countries of the Third World in the give-and-take. I cannot think of any other project as important as that of making good books available to the children in these countries and to encourage authors from the Third World to write and to have their works translated, so that our children may become aware of these other cultures. It was encouraging to see several representatives of African countries—Ghana, Liberia, Nigeria, and Sierra Leone—at the IBBY Congress in Würzburg in 1978.

In 1978 we published in *Cricket* a story by a Mr. William Riziki Riwa, who is a gatekeeper for the path up to Mount Kilimanjaro. Mr. Riwa wrote and illustrated "The Honey Guide," about his childhood in Africa. Daniel Pinkwater edited the story and sent it to us; he also wrote us about Mr. Riwa's delighted response to the fee he received from *Cricket*. He bought a cow! And, because Mr. Riwa will need a shed for the cow, Mr. Pinkwater thinks that we'll receive another story from Africa.

We have not been able to present many stories by African writers in *Cricket*, but we have translated stories from many other countries. Sometimes we are able to pick them up from already translated books; in many other instances we have had to start from scratch. Often the first problem arises with the selection of the story we want to translate. It is easy for me to read German and French manuscripts in their original languages; difficulties begin with the arrival of stories in other tongues, such as Italian, Czech, Swedish, Dutch, and others still more exotic. Sometimes we get German translations of Swedish, Danish, Czech, or Russian books, and then it is easy for me again. But what do we do with manuscripts written in languages we cannot understand? There are several highly recommended people or consultants we can send these stories to. How can we be sure that they will make the right judgment in our case? Is the style good enough? The story worthwhile? Not only do these people have to master two languages, but also they have to be able to judge the book or story as a whole, including its style, plot, characterization, and so forth. Anthea Bell has said in one of her articles about translation that "it is quite a responsibility to recommend a book to a publisher who may not be able to read a word of it himself or herself." You have to use your best judgment when you get a synopsis of the story from your reader and perhaps a few translated paragraphs or a rough translation. Sometimes it's almost impossible to make a decision from the little you get to go by, but there are happy exceptions. When I received the reader's report for Sauro Marianelli's *A School for Robots*, I knew right away that I wanted to see this story in *Cricket*. It was wonderfully refreshing.

Often the translator of a book or story is not the same person as its first reader at *Cricket*. Sometimes we get a rough translation from the author or from the author's spouse or friend; in some cases we have accepted these and then put in a lot of editorial work. Of course, this is time-consuming. We are fortunate when we find an accomplished translator in whom we have confidence and to whom we can turn over the manuscript.

Translators have a very delicate task: to interpret and to transfer the meaning from one language to another. Ideally they will be writers or creators, not just language experts.

Some of the most famous writer-translators (for example Dryden and Goethe) have thought and written much about the theory of translation, and one could go on at great length about the differences in their theories. The most important theories seem to see translation as a three-step process. The first step comprises a strictly literal translation, word for word, done with the help of a dictionary. In the second step the translator restates the foreign text in his or her own idiom and gives it the form of his or her native tongue. The third and most creative effort is the highest and last mode of translation. It is really a synthesis of the first two steps: reproducing the original but at the same time recreating it; reinterpreting it faithfully but at the same time producing, as it were, a new and autonomous work.

Carmen Bravo-Villasante, who has translated Hölderlin, Heine, Goethe, and also Otfried Preussler's *The Satanic Mill* into Spanish, says that it is important to maintain the idiomatic balance and the literary tension. And Anthea Bell says:

> Any conscientious translator will of course stay as close to both letter and spirit of the original as possible, but especially in translating for children. I feel that if a clash should arise, then the spirit of the work must take precedence, or children will not read it. But one cannot lay down hard and fast rules; the whole matter is fraught with complexity. The translator is constantly adjusting, putting out mental feelers, so to speak, before making that little leap of the imagination with which one hopes to convey the author's meaning as faithfully as possible in the language of translation.

For the translator there is always this haunting conflict: Do I translate literally, following each word, staying as close as possible to the text, or do I follow the spirit of the story? How far can I go in legitimately adapting without hurting the original idea put forth by the author?

There is often the temptation to adapt too much, with the unspoken but nevertheless reassuring excuse that children will not understand the story otherwise. So, I am sorry to say, many translators transform the Champs Élysées or the Place de la Concorde into Park Avenue or Times Square, an eiderdown into a quilt, and similarly obscure many other such delicious small items which give foreign stories atmosphere, milieu, detail. On the other hand, the stories should not have too foreign a flavor and become insurmountably difficult; there is a very fine line here. It is the excellent translators who find it intuitively.

One of my German professors at the University of Chicago once made a statement that I have never forgotten; he said that there is no better way to find out about the national character of any country than to search for the untranslatable words in its language—as, for example, the words Weltanschauung, Gestalt, milieu. But there are three other untranslatable German words I can think of right away, and they are *Geist, Gemüt,* and *Bildung.* Each one needs to be qualified in translation and described with several different words. In her article "An Adventure in Translation," Elizabeth Shub describes her frantic search for the English equivalent of the German term *Raspelbrot,* a kind of bread that in English can't be described in one word. Some stories are nearly impossible to translate; for example, those of the Grimms' fairy tales that are written in *Plattdeutsch* (or lower German). This is so different from standard German that even German children may have trouble understanding all of it. After reading *The Stone Book*, however, I have a feeling that if anyone could translate these stories, it would have to be Alan Garner.

Poetry is especially difficult to translate and perhaps can be translated only by poets. Certainly, throughout the ages many famous poets have translated poetry from other countries: Dryden, Goethe, Rilke, Paul Valéry, Hölderlin, Pasternak, André Gide, Nabokov, Ezra Pound, to name only a few. Heinrich Heine once said about his German poems that, translated into French, they were "moonlight stuffed with straw." And Nabokov wrote a short poem entitled "On Translating Eugene Onegin":

> What is translation? On a platter
> A poet's pale and glaring head,
> A parrot's screech, a monkey's chatter,
> And profanation of the dead.

Yet the argument is not one-sided. Despite these attacks on the translation of poetry, there are other important voices raised for its support. Goethe wrote to Carlyle in 1827: "Say what one will of the inadequacy of translation, it remains one of the most important and valuable concerns in the whole of world affairs." And Pushkin once defined the translator as the "courier of the human spirit."

To me, well-translated poems don't sound like translations, but like genuine English verse. And isn't this the final test for story, poem, or book? The plot, story, characters, milieu, atmosphere, all should mirror the character of the foreign author. But the style, the *tone* of the book has to be credible, inevitable, and at ease in the language in which we find it. Schlegel and Thiek's translation of Shakespeare's works into German is such a masterpiece that I believe Shakespeare is read more in Germany than here in the States because of this masterly executed translation.

Although nations have become isolated and alienated from one another through the Fall from Grace that I described at the beginning, the barriers between languages and human understanding are slowly becoming smaller and less formidable. Translators all over the world are picking up the shards of this broken Tower of Babel and fitting them together into a new and colorful mosaic. The more pieces they can find and resurrect, the more inspiring and powerful the new masterpiece will be. The tower will not reach to heaven, but as a work of art it may eventually reunite the speakers of this earth's different tongues.

It is a matter of concern and importance that the children be included in this effort: they are, theirs is, the future.

For and Against Rubbish

ETHEL HEINS

We're here to speak for and against rubbish. But what *is* rubbish? Historically, one age's rubbish may well become another age's classics. We know that in the eighteenth century children defended themselves with their own underground literature—prodigious quantities of chapbooks that kept alive the legends and fairy tales that were to become the classics of the nursery. In those days fiction and fantasy were held to be malicious influences. For as the Puritans earlier were horrified by folktales, which they considered irreligious and immoral, the Age of Reason dismissed them as unrealistic and dangerous. Again children resisted, and the nineteenth century saw the proliferation of the penny dreadfuls—cheap, sensational serials that proved to be distant predecessors of the twentieth century's ubiquitous comics and endless sets of manufactured adventure series.

In modern times, starting with Caroline M. Hewins, virtually an army of idealistic, high-minded children's librarians, not to mention editors and publishers, have fought mediocrity and have tried to bring children the best in books. Walter de la Mare, a sort of patron saint of children's literature, has been quoted times without number: "Only the rarest kind of best in anything can be good enough for the young." In 1980 Barbara Tuchman wrote a long piece in the *New York Times* called "The Decline of Quality" in which she decried the deterioration of standards in all aspects of craftsmanship in the arts, ascribing the trend to commercialism directed toward popular consumption rather than toward people of discerning taste.

But now hear this: "Nobody who has not spent a whole sunny afternoon reading a pile of comics has any idea of the meaning of intellectual freedom. Nobody who has not written comic strips can really understand the phrase 'economy of words.' It's like trying to write *Paradise Lost* in haiku.'' Those statements were made some years ago by a writer of such excellence that he has just become the first author to win two Carnegie Medals in a row—Peter Dickinson. He was half serious, half not. He defined rubbish as all reading matter that contains to the adult eye no value, either aesthetic or educational. But he was forced to defend himself, and he offered some interesting propositions. One, that the child should experience a whole culture, not just a part; two, that the child should belong—or feel that he belongs—to the group in which he finds himself; and three, that there is importance for children in self-discovery—the ''treasure-trove'' value of books found almost by accident. Peter Dickinson made a firm point, however, that the child should not be *encouraged* to read rubbish, and in tackling the sticky question of a child whose reading diet seems to consist wholly of rubbish, he agrees with those who feel that it is better for the child to read something than nothing. Dr. Johnson said, ''I would like a child first to read any book which happens to engage his attention, because you have done a great deal when you have brought him entertainment from a book. He'll get to better things afterward.''

Will he? That's one of our questions. Is it pointless to worry about rubbish? Maurice Sendak admitted he wouldn't let his child, if he had one, read comics, as *he* did years ago. But there's always the possibility that under certain conditions we might be worrying in vain.

When our son was young, he was a voracious reader. I was a children's librarian and, of course, excessively smug about his reading. He never asked for comics. They were never seen in our house. This was also the time, I might add, when little boys frequently went to the barbershop to have nice short haircuts.

We had some people at our house, and someone said, ''Peter doesn't read comics? How have you avoided them?'' Remember, this was the fifties, when we had books like *Seduction of the Innocent*, by Frederic Wertham. And I said, ''Oh, no,'' in a holier-than-thou voice. ''He doesn't want comics; he doesn't need them. He's been exposed to all the really good stuff, and he's surrounded by so many good books because . . . ''Et cetera, et cetera. I didn't know he was listening, but he piped up and said, ''I *do* read comics. I read them in the barbershop.''

So much for me. Now we'll hear from Carolyn W. Field, longtime coordinator of work with children at the Free Library of Philadelphia, and then from Frances V. Sedney, coordinator of children's services of the Harford County (Maryland) Public Library.

CAROLYN W. FIELD

First of all, I wish to give tribute to the New York Public Library because it was one of the great training institutions. I started out in 1938 when Anne

Carroll Moore was head of children's work, and I worked with a number of the great among children's librarians. So I've had a long, glorious experience in the field of children's services in public libraries.

> Books are fun. Books are wonderful. They make me feel at home in the world. They tell me things I want to know, and then I ask more questions. The more curious I am, the more they tell me. They make me want to do, to be. They let me be myself and someone else at the same time. They make me laugh. They make me cry. They make me sing with joy, with loving, with living.
> Books   Wonder   Dreams
> Design   Understanding

These are the words that Mildred Batchelder, executive secretary of the Children's Services Division of the American Library Association, wrote to explain exactly what a children's library should be. She was writing to the architect who was to design the Children's World in Library 21 at the Seattle World's Fair in 1962. The words were so beautiful, so well prepared, that one of the exhibitors at the American Library Association made a broadside of these words and had the decorations done by Barbara Cooney. To me these words express exactly what books can do for an individual.

Some years ago Orville Prescott, a book critic, wrote an article in which he ridiculed librarians for making a fuss over the reading of series books. He was talking specifically about the Bobbsey Twins, Nancy Drew, the Hardy Boys, and so on. I know that Orville Prescott was a voracious reader, just as I was. I started reading before I went to school, and I read every single Nancy Drew and Uncle Wiggily story—all the series books. I read everything I could lay my hands on.

Since that time even more books for children have poured from the presses: good books that children would enjoy, books on every subject in the world. And today a child's leisure time has to be divided among many forms of recreation. When the child does read, he or she should be encouraged to read not only books that are fun and enjoyable but books that can contribute something to his or her development as an intelligent human being. Children are not born with innate standards of good taste, and they need adult guidance. Beginning with a book of nursery rhymes and the ABC's, adults can help to develop in the child an appreciation of the beauty of words, the beauty of illustration, and the fine craftsmanship of bookmaking. Exposure to good writing, original plots, and character development from the picture book stage through the junior high school years will help the child to appreciate the importance of cultural activities, even though he or she may not become a reader of literature or a devotee of the arts, music, or dance.

Constant exposure to the cheap, the tawdry, and the slick will contribute nothing to the child's development or appreciation of artistic things. The child who reads only the Bobbsey Twins, Nancy Drew, or the Hardy Boys experiences nothing except trite situations with cardboard figures, the same things repeated over and over again. I would also question Orville Prescott's statement that "a child's sense of loyalty to family, his capacity for friendship, and desire for law and order are fostered in warmth and adventure through these books." I believe that a child reads a series book in the same way that I read a mystery story: It goes in one eye and out the other. I pick up the same book six years later and read it over again and don't know that I've read it before.

A delightful book for an adult to read on the subject of series is Arthur Prager's *Rascals at Large: or, the Clue and the Old Nostalgia,* published by Doubleday in 1971. It discusses the series books that were currently being published or had been published, taking up each series in a chapter. Prager talks about the themes, plots, literary style (if you want to call it that), characterization, background of the author or authors, and virtues of each series.

In support of his enthusiasm for series books, he offers his own experience as a reader of these books and that of his daughter, who was young at the time. He also points out, however—and I don't think he does it consciously—that he himself had been a reader, a voracious reader, as a young man and that as his child was growing up, he read to her all the great children's books and showed her all the good picture books, so that although she became a devoted reader of series books, she still had this marvelous background. Toward the end of the book he says, "I'm glad to say that I walked into her room the other day and she was reading *The Wind in the Willows.*"

From time to time, I have to defend the Free Library's policy of not buying Nancy Drew and the Hardy Boys. Some parents become belligerent on the subject, and they argue that their tax dollars should buy what they want. Well, as a first defense, a librarian has to have a written book-selection policy. I'd like to quote from the "General Statement of Objectives" for selecting children's books at the Free Library of Philadelphia:

> The library's primary objective is to develop in children the enjoyment and appreciation of reading for reading's sake, and to provide books of literary quality as well as other materials—films, records, et cetera—which will satisfy a child's recreational needs and natural curiosity, thus contributing to his growth as an intelligent world citizen.

General policies for print materials are to meet the varied
reading abilities and interests of children. The library
strives to purchase titles covering a wide range of knowledge, from the earliest rhythmic poetry, such as Mother
Goose, to the latest book on space or drugs suitable to a
child's understanding. In the field of purely recreational
reading, stress is laid upon those books which develop the
imaginative faculties, promote understanding, and cultivate worthwhile ideals and values.

But just quoting policies and objectives to a belligerent patron is not
enough. The librarian should be prepared to recommend books that
children will enjoy as much as the series books. Some years ago several
members of our staff prepared a list of authors and titles called "What to Do
When They Ask for Nancy Drew and Other Series Books." (We revise this
list from time to time.) For example, replace the Bobbsey Twins with
Beverly Cleary—*Henry Huggins, Ellen Tebbits,* and the Ramona books. Or
Carolyn Haywood's Betsy and Eddie books. Or Hazel Wilson's Herbert
books. Instead of the Hardy Boys, give Scott Corbett's books, Clifford
Hicks's Alvin Fernald stories, or E. W. Hildick's detective stories. Or
Donald Sobol's Encyclopedia Brown.

In 1960 at a conference of the Association for Childhood Education
International, May Hill Arbuthnot said:

What children admire they emulate. Children need to be
guided in the kind of heroes that they emulate. Through
good books and the characters met in them, children may
learn patterns of kindness and gentleness, realize that they
can be courageous and strong without violence, identify
themselves with independence and achievement, feel a
desire to cherish and protect, which is the greatest element
of love. Therefore in my opinion, librarians have a responsibility to provide for children the books that will do just
this.

Many years ago I ran across the following statement, which expresses
my feeling about good books and children:

If at just the right moment, we present to the child just the
right food for his curiosity and eagerness, folklore, fairy
tale and fable, song, science, adventure, handcrafts and
games, each when the appropriate faculty is unfolding,

then we can keep him curious and eager all through his childhood. Nothing better can happen to a child.

FRANCES V. SEDNEY

I couldn't agree more with everything Carolyn said, but I like the song "I Love Trash." It happens to be the record I listen to when I'm doing my book selection—you know, with earphones. When I'm feeling idealistic, I listen to "The Rainbow Connection," which is on the same record.

I have a short statement which I'm going to deviate from because I can't wait to leap on Carolyn and the idea of all those children in Philadelphia who don't get to read series books. Maybe we can convert her. Wouldn't it be wonderful if she went back and said, "I've changed my mind and we're going to buy Nancy Drew?" Actually, I don't think of Nancy Drew as rubbish. I think of it as trash, and I love good trash.

Now, I want to say that I was formed from the same mold, the New York Public Library, that formed Ethel Heins and Carolyn Field. We were shaped by the older children's librarians and the administrative staff of that library, guided and molded by Anne Carroll Moore or, later, by Frances Clarke Sayers. None of us, as young librarians, had any doubt that they knew exactly what we were reading, what we were doing, where we were headed, and what they saw as our potentialities.

At that time I never would have thought of stocking the Nancy Drew stories. Much as I loved those books in my youth, there was no doubt in my mind when I came forth from beneath Frances Clarke Sayers's wing that the popular trash was not anything I would think of putting into a library. But now the time is many years and many children later; those books have long been shelved and circulated to the children of our country.

When I first agreed to take part in this interchange—defending the right of children to a steady supply of the trash they hold so dear, supplied from public funds, that is, from their parents' tax dollars, and available freely from their public library—I wandered through *my* public library, identifying those popular materials. And as I poked and probed, I gradually came to the realization that we have a supply of things I never would have bought when I first became coordinator of a library system. First of all, rag books. We have lots of books for the very early readers—we have the *Pat the Bunny* kind of book—and we package the rag books in little plastic envelopes. We also have board books for small children. We have object books shaped like telephones or like a can of Popeye's spinach because Popeye is the new thing. We even have a book that represents the Lone Ranger on Silver; it's shaped like a horse, and it rocks back and forth. We have spiral-bound books of all kinds and shapes—from the Sesame Street ones, with which you make funny faces by flipping things back and forth,

to Helen Oxenbury's books, which do precisely the same thing on a
different literary level. We have some of the Nancy Drew and the Hardy
Boys books. We have Alfred Hitchcock and the Three Investigators. We
have "Choose Your Own Adventures." We have the paperback Raggedy
Ann. We have all the Oz books in every conceivable edition that we can
buy or find. We have the Tintin comics. We do not have the ubiquitous
comics because I'm really not experienced enough to judge them. We do
have some other things in comic book format—for instance, *Dracula*,
Frankenstein, and *Around the World in Eighty Days*.

We have, of course, all sorts of magazines, such as *Mad* magazine, *Tiger
Beat*, motorcycle and skateboard magazines. We have shelves and shelves
of books about flying saucers, which are no longer being read so much
because there hasn't been a sighting recently; as soon as there is one,
the books will all go out. We have the Bermuda Triangle on every reading level, from hardly-able-to-turn-a-page to ready-to-go-and-get-your-
advanced-degree-in-physics. We have Sasquatch, Yeti, and all other types
of monsters—sea-bound, land-bound, and air-bound. We even have all
the Wildfire and the Key romances. The point is that we have everything
that anybody wants, as long as it is acceptable under our adult selection
policy.

We do not have a separate selection policy for juvenile books. What we
promise for our adults, we promise for our children. Everything in our
adult collection is available to children. I believe in children's rights. I
firmly believe that a child has the right to read anything he or she wants to
read, and the child has the right to find it at the public library.

But here is where discretion works. I believe the child should have the
best of the genre that he or she happens to be interested in. Some of you
may ask me questions that I have not, after all my years of thinking, been
able to answer. But we've been able to defend everything that we have put
in the hands of a child. We have had no difficulty in defending all kinds of
things we shelve, before the tax authorities and the school and religious
authorities. We're probably one of the few libraries in the country that put
Freddie's Book in the children's section and have managed to keep it there.

I truly take issue with many of the statements Carolyn made, even
though I will stand up and cheer for the ideology behind them. Although
I firmly believe that we are, in effect, molding children's lives and minds by
what we give them, I also believe that children love trash and can consume
vast amounts of it without harm. Trash does not replace all the other
books. The child who walks out with five Star Trek books and three Star
Wars books may also be carrying *Gulliver's Travels* and *Around the World in
Eighty Days* in the unabridged versions. And I'm not going to presume to
make the value judgment as to which one of these books is going to make
the most profound, the most lasting, impression. All I want to do is make

sure that a child can grow, in any way at all; to make sure I have whatever is going to engage that child so that he or she will keep coming back to me. Eventually, I'll get that child to read what I want him or her to read because I'm very persuasive.

FRANCES V. SEDNEY AND CAROLYN W. FIELD

Frances V. Sedney: Now, I want to ask you, Carolyn, about your book-selection policy. I have two questions. I want to know whether there is the same book-selection policy for adults as for children, or does the Free Library do something for adults that isn't done for children? And did you have a hand in writing that book-selection policy?

Carolyn W. Field: I'll answer the last first. Yes. Actually, the book-selection policy was stolen from the Enoch Pratt Free Library. In 1953 when I went to Philadelphia, we had so many things to do at once, we couldn't do everything thoroughly, so we borrowed a book-selection policy. But it has been revised and changed over the years so that now it's really our own. In our general selection policy for the Free Library of Philadelphia, the principles and objectives are the same for adults and children. Our special children's policy goes into details about our procedure in the selection of materials and our stand on certain matters. There are many books that are not bought for children, for reasons which we outline in our policy. For instance, we don't buy books on karate or on ventriloquism.

Frances, does your system have both a children's library card and an adult card, or only one kind?

Sedney: We have the same library card for adults and for children. We do identify a library card for a child under the age of eighteen by having the parents sign the card. This procedure is only because of fiscal responsibility, and it is required by our financial officer.

Field: Well, we have two cards—one for children and one for adults. "Children's Services" goes through the eighth grade or up to the age of fourteen. As of last April I finally got through what we call *open access*. Now, it's not complete open access according to the American Library Association Intellectual Freedom Committee—which I don't agree with at all, but I don't agree with them on most things. The child fills out an application, and the parent signs it. If the parent wishes the child to be allowed to take out anything in the library, there is a special little paragraph that says something like "I give my child permission to have anything in the Free Library of Philadelphia," and the parent has to come into the library and sign that line in front of a librarian or a library assistant. Then the child is given an adult card. But we do put the child's age on the card, so that if an eight-year-old has an adult card, the person at the desk knows that fact. And I need that information for statistical purposes. If the child does not have an adult card, we have what we call an adult material request slip, which the librarian fills out and the child takes to the desk with the adult book; so it's the librarian's decision as to whether or not a child can take out something that's in the adult department.

Sedney: I think that's just plain wrong because it seems to me a child is, first and foremost, a person, and a person has certain rights no matter what his or her age is—such as the right to have his or her reading free and uncensored. If somebody behind a desk had decided whether I, as a child of ten, eleven, or twelve, had a right to read certain things, I wouldn't have read some of the books that had the most profound impact on me. At that age I was reading in the adult department of the Boston Public Library, and no one ever questioned what I was reading. And I think that your procedure is tantamount to insisting that somebody fit into your preconceived idea of what a child should be allowed to read; I find this thought extremely difficult.

Field: Well, I don't. I said in the beginning that I feel very firmly that children need to be guided in their intellectual pursuits and in their reading, just as they need to be guided in their physical development. Children do not always know exactly what they need at a given moment. Chronologically, they're ready at certain times to receive certain ideas, but environmental influences also affect their development. There are many materials that a child may not be ready for; but if the subject matter is available in a form in which the child can absorb it, that book should be made accessible in the children's section. If you're going to have open shelves for the children and the adults all together as readers, however, then I really see no reason why the collections shouldn't be combined. I do admit that in certain places the situation is different. Remember that I'm talking from the point of view of a large, varied, metropolitan area; a smaller, homogeneous community would be an entirely different situation.

Sedney: I don't agree. It seems to me that the question is philosophical. The implication here is that the library can make the decision that a child has reached the psychological or intellectual time when he or she is able to receive certain ideas. I feel that if this decision is anybody's right, it is the parents' right, but I don't necessarily believe that it *is* the parents' right. I also think that it's the parents' responsibility to see what book the child is taking out, because the parent knows the child and can decide if a book is inflammatory educationally, intellectually, politically, or whatever. The parent could then say to the child, "I'd rather you didn't read this until you are fourteen, or sixteen, or eighteen." But I think you make too much of this guidance. And I'm speaking as a mother and as a librarian. I think that we certainly have a duty to mold the young, and we should put everything before them.

Field: I don't like the term *mold*. *Guide*, I think, is better.

Sedney: I think I was molded, and I think you and Ethel were molded. I think that's why we're similar but different. We are three jugs sitting in a row, each cast in a somewhat different mold.

The Impact of Controversy on Popularity

ISABELLE HOLLAND

The more I thought about this title, the more I realized that to write at all is to be controversial. When you write, you put yourself, what you think, and your underlying attitudes, both conscious and unconscious, on the line. To write now, at this particular period, is to write at a time when opinions, discussions, and arguments over and about children's literature are reported bountifully, noisily, and frequently. And no matter what viewpoint your books reflect, you can be certain you'll displease someone.

Twenty-five years ago, when I first entered publishing on the staff of a book publishing house, children's books were mostly decorous, closely bounded by well-defined rules and parameters, and were reviewed with equal decorum in the trade and other media. It was also a time when there was a much wider chasm between the world of children's books and the world of adult books. The term *young adult* (YA) was in existence, but it did not denote a separate category of book published by the children's book department. Three books, now young adult classics though still considered controversial in some areas—*To Kill a Mockingbird*, *The Catcher in the Rye*, and *A Separate Peace*—were published as adult books. I sat in on many an editorial or promotion meeting where such-and-such a title being presented to the sales and promotion staff was touted as one that would have good YA interest but was nevertheless discussed primarily as an adult book. The obvious advantage of this was that books that dealt in such controversial areas as sex, violence, and death—to name three obvious areas of dispute— if published for adults, would not raise the storm of protest and indignation that, today, greets so many books issued specifically for young adults. *A Separate Peace* contained more than a hint of homosexuality, and *The Catcher in the Rye*'s Holden Caulfield became the paradigm of the sensitive, misunderstood, alienated adolescent in an adult world. But because these novels were published for adults, they were greeted and reviewed—

516

favorably or unfavorably—as pieces of fiction, not as tracts to guide the young and growing mind.

Then a combination of librarians' needs and marketing focus created the genre young adult literature, to be published by children's book departments, and the watch-and-ward societies of both the right and the left started to draw up their guide and battle lines.

To write into this atmosphere is, to put it mildly, a challenge. Speaking for myself, I feel that challenge most deeply within my writer's self-confidence and self-esteem. A bad review is never pleasant. I've heard writers make the statement, "Bad reviews don't bother me," but I've never been entirely sure I believed them. I think a modicum of pride and defiance goes into that statement, plus a fair amount of creditable whistling in the dark. But I've learned to distinguish between a review that is bad, and a review that is simply mean or hostile. Sometimes, as I know all too well, a review can be both. But there are other times when I've realized—on careful rereading of the review—that a given critique, while certainly not laudatory, is not attacking my book on the grounds of its writing, its structure, its character motivation, its interest, or its overall competence as a piece of fiction. What I am being attacked for is some basic worldview or underlying attitude to which the reviewer is hostile.

This was true of a prominent and early review of *The Man Without a Face*. The book was attacked on the grounds that the only scene in which there was a homosexual element was not graphic enough, that I was not presenting the homosexual alternative in an attractive light, and that I killed off the teacher as punishment for his sexual orientation. The gay liberation movement was gaining strength about then, and I have every reason to believe that my book was judged solely from that standpoint.

In my book *Journey for Three*, a denigrating review in one of the trade magazines ended with the slap that the young teacher who appeared in the book as a sympathetic character was "of course described as 'pretty' "— with the implied comment, "How banal can one get?" And I had the strong feeling that I had run into an angry feminist. I have been told also that there has been feminist criticism of *The Man Without a Face* because, of the three female characters, Charles's mother and his two sisters, two of them, the mother and the older sister, are unpleasant.

In *Now Is Not Too Late*—my novel about an eleven-year-old girl coming to know the mother from whom she had been separated since before she could remember—I created a sympathetic, if somewhat acerbic, grandmother to whom the child turned for comfort and advice, and I was rebuked for being too moralistic. And another book has been criticized on the grounds that the parents are too articulate.

Well, what can I say? They're no more articulate than my own parents were. One writes from one's own experience, and that was mine. My parents and I had our problems, but one thing for which I will always be grateful is that they were highly articulate. Shoddy speech patterns and poor pronunciation were not tolerated, even casually. Of the variety of things I occasionally resented about my parents, lack of skill with words was not among them. And I suppose I assumed that most other people's parents were the same.

Cecily, my first book, published as an adult book but praised most gratifyingly in young adult columns, was pounced on in a Jesuit magazine for the sin of being about pleasant, middle-class people. And the reviewer poured his scorn on the unhappy Cecily with her inferiority complex about being overweight, unpopular, and a failure. This was in 1967, just before the storms of the sixties mounted to their peak, and I was slow to figure out why this good priest was so hostile. I realize now that, being a Jesuit, he was probably in the avant garde of those who wrote and reviewed in the last of the sixties and the early seventies and for whom legitimate objects of sympathy had to come with one of the approved labels of recognized oppression—a minority among the majority, a Black among whites, a Jew among Christians, a female in a male-tyrannized world, a homosexual among heterosexuals, an all-innocent adolescent among all-vicious adults—to be worthy of the attention of a novel. To be fat, unsuccessful, and unloved didn't count.

Probably the two most consistently praised books I have written are *Of Love and Death and Other Journeys* and *Alan and the Animal Kingdom*. Yet, in the first of these two, I was criticized in the journal of the Council on Interracial Books on the grounds of ageism. A character who did not appear in the novel but who was recalled by the mother in a conversation with her daughter was described as both old and senile. The criticism in the journal was aimed at me because I did not have another person of equal age but better mental health to balance her.

I hasten to add that this is not my only experience of being reviewed. I have received reviews on all the books I have mentioned which were either laudatory or, if they were critical, were critical on the grounds that, however painful for the author, are a critic's prerogative. That is, they discussed the book under review in terms of what it set out to do, whether it lived up to its own purpose, and whether it was credible as a piece of fiction.

I have gone into all of the above because, curiously, as a writer in an age of controversy, the brickbats that have assaulted me most have come from what is generally thought of as the left.

From the right, what I have received is the thundering silence of no sales or no placement on library shelves. I am quite certain that there are libraries, both public and school, in certain parts of the country that do not stock *The Man Without a Face*—to mention the most obvious one—on the grounds that the subject of homosexuality is offensive and that my own view on the matter, implicit in that book, does not support the judgment prevalent in a given area.

But the writers who are being singled out by the Moral Majority as subject to censorship are running into a different—and more widely publicized—version of the same thing. The author whose work offends the political and/or sociological views of a prominent reviewer in a leading journal pays the price of neglect by libraries whose overworked staff simply order titles from laudatory reviews and approved lists. In other words, the impact of controversy on popularity in this case can deprive a book of its chance to survive. Who will know whether it is good or not if no one orders it? The writer who offends the Moral Majority may very well make it onto the library shelf, only to get pulled off by irate parents. Either way, in this day of rampant controversy, the writer finds him- or herself defending not the quality of a book, but the inside of his or her own mind. Because there is no question: All writers, good, bad, and indifferent, project outward the perceptions and assumptions that make up their myths. Every individual, from the humblest to the most brilliant, has a myth that he or she lives by. It can be a formal religion or an informal, eclectic set of spiritual or ethical concepts. It can be a philosophy or simply a belief system summed up in phrases such as "On the whole, most people are decent," and, "On the whole, most people will rip you off," and, "The enemy is out there waiting to get you." But whatever the belief is, it is within a writer's system that the action of the novel takes place.

As a nonreviewer I have the right, along with everyone else in the world, of choosing to read books for pleasure. This means that there are a number of writers whose styles I admire, whose literary ability I applaud, but whose works I cannot stand. They may be the recipients of distinguished awards, but I'm not going to take their books off library or bookstore shelves. Conversely, there are writers whose values I share, but whose writing is so poor I cannot read their novels. Most of us do this kind of selecting to one degree or another. I have friends to whom the writing—the language itself— is preeminently important, and who will willingly put up with poor characterization, no plot, and repulsive people because the writer who records their lives is so magnificently gifted at stringing words together. I find this baffling. I like good writing. But I'm more interested in content.

I am not, however, a critic, a librarian, or a teacher. I do not have to choose a book for anyone else, although I am sympathetic with anyone who carries this burden and who does his or her best to provide a fair and just guide. But to choose a book for other people when that book is ultimately for children is to walk a thin line between advising and evangelizing. There are libraries and librarians who refuse to spend public funds on books of no recognized literary merit. Yet those are often books beloved by streams of children looking for the children's version of a "good read." Nancy Drew leaps to the mind. Growing up in England, I never read Nancy Drew. But I read countless versions of the English equivalent, usually with a title like *Erica of the Upper Fourth,* and my father, who disapproved of my taste, would certainly have agreed with those who believe that libraries are for teaching children to read good books.

But I worry about that attitude. Libraries, paid for out of the public purse, should have books for all the people, not just for those who want to read Willa Cather. I was a slow beginner. I read rapidly, but for years my choice of reading matter was the despair of my intellectual father, whose idea of the perfect book for the young child was Oliver Goldsmith's *The Vicar of Wakefield*—a choice he kept pushing at me as I kept reading about the adventures of Erica or Monica or Pamela, to his continuing despair.

His fixation on Goldsmith arose because that was the book that was given to him at the age of twelve when he was allowed to have his first library card. I'm sure he would rule out Nancy Drew as he did Monica and her brothers and cousins—my favorites back in England when I was twelve. But if his method had prevailed, I might never have become a reader. Because I think that first you learn to read at your own level, then, perhaps later than some, you read at the level other people approve of. That doesn't mean that I don't think children's and young people's minds should not be stretched. But I think they should have some of what they like to read, at least in modest doses. To this day I prefer a good mystery to many of the serious pieces of fiction reviewed at length on the front page of the *New York Times Book Review.* Which, of course, makes me the compleat middlebrow. But there's room for us, too. And if somebody cuts out my neighboring writer's book as unworthy, who knows when the same censoring eye will fall on mine? Furthermore, I want to be able to find books in the library that I enjoy, as well as those someone else thinks are good for me.

In days gone by, the world of children's books did not, as far as I know, enjoy much controversy. There are obvious exceptions—like that integrationist landmark *The Rabbits' Wedding.* And this does not mean that there were not serious books of depth and worth. But the great middle ground of children's books did not attract much national attention and, being for children and not young adults, did not deal with controversial subjects.

But the children of the past did not have television, newsmagazines, movies, or sex education (except for whatever they got at home). And even today not all children want books about current problems such as racism, prejudice, abortion, teenage pregnancy, and unwed motherhood. The popularity of fantasy and science fiction attest to that. But the environment bombards us and our children with all of this. And if it's there, in the airwaves, hammering at us for attention, then we, the writers, who are not more immune than anyone else to public preoccupations, will write about such things. And we will write about them in the way that we see them, adapting them to our individual myths, with the assorted roles of hero, heroine, villain, and victim allotted differently in the case of each individual writer.

I therefore find it more than just controversial, I find it outrageous when a critic writes a review slamming my book because he or she doesn't like the way I see things—rather than because of the way I write, structure, plot, or portray characters. And I am equally outraged when parents reject my books on the same grounds, not only for their own children, but for other children as well.

Having said that, I must, in honesty, add something that I have discussed elsewhere: To a degree, we are all guilty of judging a book on something other than its literary merit. To use an obvious example most people would not quarrel with: Any book espousing racist views and using, with apparent approval, racial slurs would not be fit for human beings who are still in the stage of growing and learning what the world is like. But it's a far cry from banning this sort of book to banning the majority of books that seem now to be endangered, from either side of the political spectrum. I have come across young adult books, well-written books, that I, personally, would not choose for a thirteen-year-old. I am not, however, prepared to say that therefore no one would choose them.

And finally, let us, for a moment, look at controversy itself. Is it such a bad thing? To live in a world without controversy one of two conditions has to prevail: Either the contents of books are controlled, as in a state where all print is censored, or, if the society is free, the people are so homogeneous as to race, religion, and ethnic makeup that much of the dissent we know does not arise.

Well, our society is both free and—more than any other society in the free, literate world—heterogeneous. When we rail at the Moral Majority on one side and the leading edge of the free thinkers on the other, let us remember this. We cannot have freedom and diversity without controversy. When parents in Tennessee try to remove books they see as a threat to their way of life, this is experienced in New York—and in Tennessee—as censorship. But that does not mean that the parents there or in Kansas or in Island Trees have no right to express their opinions. They do. Just as I have a right to fight them tooth and nail.

If I had the power, would I remove those who don't agree with me? Who hasn't had that fantasy from time to time, particularly when faced with a surly review by a disgruntled representative of an opposing philosophy? But no, although I retain the right to yell and scream, I would not remove them.

So, since I like writing books in a society that is both plural and free, I must accept the controversy. Because to be without controversy is to be silent, or afraid, or dead.

"Go, and Catch a Falling Star": What Is a Good Children's Book?

ETHEL HEINS

"Enduring Elements of Good Children's Books" was the assigned title for this essay, but the questions raised by this deceptively simple, yet hopelessly comprehensive, topic seemed overwhelming. After all, haven't critics since Aristotle been struggling with the problem of what constitutes a good book? I decided I could live peacefully only with a point of view less vague and confusing and, at the same time, less absolute. Borrowing an ironical line from John Donne, I chose, instead, as my title, " 'Go, and Catch a Falling Star': What *Is* a Good Children's Book?" Only in this less courageous way do I dare come to grips with such terms as *enduring elements* and *good children's books*.

It's not that a search for a definition of good children's books or a discussion of literary elements is unworthy of the attempt, but that the idea is almost terrifying in its ambiguity. For if one considers good children's books, one should logically try to find a common denominator for such diverse forms as fiction, nonfiction, poetry, folklore, and picture books—a futile task. And dividing groups into smaller units, how is one to establish a common goodness for, let's say, realistic fiction, historical fiction, and fantasy? True, these genres may exhibit excellences of storytelling, characterization, or style; but the goodness of each form must reside in its own characteristic nature. Nevertheless, to simplify our search for what may well turn out to be an unattainable definition, it would be wise to refer chiefly to the novel for children.

A good children's book, like any kind of good book, is not dependent on *enduring* elements but on *appropriate* elements. Focusing on the significance of the appropriate is the wonderfully inventive picture-storybook *Lion* by William Pène du Bois. In an animal factory, a workshop high in the sky, an angelic artist thought of a new word, *lion,* and worked hard to create an image and a sound to fit the word. At first, he unfortunately chose "peep

peep" as the sound and made preposterous animal figures, blatantly colored and decked out with feathers, fur, and fish scales, but he finally succeeded in capturing the essence of the king of beasts, including his roar. Feathers, fish scales, and a rainbow of colors were ludicrous on a lion, even though they could be appropriate for another sort of creature; and a good book, like a well-made lion, is a unique creation.

One can decide, for one reason or another, why a particular children's book is good. One can discuss the merits of, say, *The Secret Garden*, *From the Mixed-up Files of Mrs. Basil E. Frankweiler*, or *Tuck Everlasting*. But it is practically impossible to generalize and talk abstractly about a good children's book as such. Furthermore, attempts to define the very notion of a children's book in the first place have been ultimately fruitless, though interesting. Some authors—and I think they were being perfectly honest— have shrugged off the whole concept, maintaining that in their own minds no clear difference exists between a work for children and one intended for adults, and that the dividing line separating the two is largely an artificial, albeit a pragmatic, one. For a variety of reasons I cannot agree with those authors, but we must admit that occasional books enormously read by children—for instance, T. H. White's *Mistress Masham's Repose* and Sheila Burnford's *The Incredible Journey*—were first published in this country as adult books. And reviewers and critics wrestled with the perplexing dilemma presented by Alan Garner's *Red Shift*, surely as unyielding and recondite a book as anything that has ever appeared on a juvenile list, a book not surprisingly reviewed by the *New York Times* as an adult book, yet one about which the percipient English critic Margery Fisher wrote, "It would be equally insulting to children and to Alan Garner to treat *Red Shift* as anything but a superbly exciting piece of literature."

Moreover, to become even more analytical, what, precisely, *is* a child? What has happened to the very definition of childhood? What about the social convulsions of the past twenty years, garishly reflected and animated on the television screen, which have masked our children with cynicism and false sophistication? What about the lamented lost innocence of youth and the altered image of the child in contemporary culture?

Now we have reached the ultimate word, *good*, and it's time to return to the idea of good children's books. Once again renouncing both the vague and the absolute, I shall probably raise more questions than I shall answer. What does *good* actually mean here? Good for whom? How? When? In what way? First, we must acknowledge the power of fashion, taste, convention, and prejudice.

The Search for Quality

The search for quality in children's books is an adult preoccupation, of course; it began more than three hundred years ago. During the Puritan age, books written for children were so drenched in dogma and didacticism, they could scarcely seem childlike to us. But the authors meant those books—Harvey Darton called them "good Godly books"—to make children ultimately happy and to give them pleasure, pleasure being that of discovering and obeying the will of God. Of course, the Puritan dream of happiness is rather foreign to us today. But the spirit of this writing infused the majority of English and American children's books for the next one hundred and fifty years: a stern, rigid, vehement ideal of training up the child the way he should go, without any consideration of his nature, his environment, or his capabilities.

When the passionately religious books gave way to the moral, uplifting tales of the nineteenth century, the search for good children's books lost none of its momentum. Just as the Puritans judged folktales frivolous and immoral, the eighteenth-century Age of Reason found them irrational, unhealthy, and positively dangerous. In France the pedagogical Madame de Genlis (governess to the children of the Duke of Orléans) said that even if fairy tales *were* moral—and she didn't think they were—it was "not the moral of the story that the children would remember, but the descriptions of enchanted gardens and diamond palaces—as if diamond palaces really existed in our lives! Such fantastic imaginings could give them only false ideas, retard the progress of their minds, and inspire them with disgust for really instructive reading."

In England the redoubtable Sarah Trimmer founded a magazine called the *Guardian of Education*, early in the nineteenth century. Its main purpose was "to contribute to the preservation of the young and innocent from the dangers which threaten them in the form of infantile and juvenile literature." (And doesn't it all sound like the pious pronouncements of the Moral Majority?) One of her correspondents bristled over *Cinderella:* "perhaps one of the most exceptionable books that was ever written for children. . . . It paints some of the worst passions that can enter into the human breast, and of which little children should, if possible, be totally ignorant; such as envy, jealousy, a dislike to mothers-in-law and half-sisters, vanity, a love of dress, etc., etc." I feel a curious empathy with Sarah Trimmer, for she was often roused to editorialize, as I am, although I'm afraid her concerns are not *precisely* mine: "Formerly children's reading, whether for instruction or amusement, was confined to a very small number of volumes; of late years they have multiplied to an astonishing and alarming degree, and much mischief lies hid in many of them. The utmost circumspection is therefore requisite in making a proper selection; and children should not be permitted to make their own choice." Of John Newbery's edition of *The History of Little Goody Two Shoes*, Trimmer said: "This Book is a great favorite with us on account of the simplicity of style in which it is written, yet we wish some parts to be altered, or omitted . . . However, with all its faults, we wish to see this Book continue in circulation, as some of these faults *a pair of scissors* can rectify."

Wordsworth, with his newborn children trailing clouds of glory, probably helped to set the tonality of the literature of childhood in the nineteenth century. Not only the tonality of children's literature, but also of the changing attitude toward the child, for he stood—along with Charles Lamb and Coleridge—in fiery opposition to the moralizing books of the time. Later on, with Dickens, Mark Twain, and George MacDonald, to name only a few writers, the child became a symbol of the Romantic protest against a utilitarian society, and the imagination—at long last!—came out of exile.

I am galloping somewhat roughshod over a great deal of literary and social history; but the eighteenth-century doctrine of original sin turned into the nineteenth-century cult of original virtue—or innocence—in the child. And now the search for good children's books took a new direction.

Admittedly, it is a rather long leap from Sarah Trimmer to the pioneering zeal of Caroline M. Hewins, that New England herald of library service to children. She firmly thrust aside the notion that books for children were nothing but instructional tools, and she based her conception of library work on a pure love for books; for her this meant careful selection of the *best*, a selection rooted in an intimate knowledge of children themselves and based on an acquaintance with the so-called best of world literature.

In 1875 Caroline Hewins became the librarian of a private subscription library in Hartford, Connecticut, called the Young Men's Institute, and she promptly began to examine its collection to find what might be suitable for the few children whose families could afford to subscribe. To her satisfaction she discovered the Grimm brothers, Andersen, Hawthorne, Scott, Dickens, and Thackeray; but to her dismay she also found they were read much less frequently than those authors she called "the immortal four: Oliver Optic, Horatio Alger, Harry Castlemon, and Martha Finley of *Elsie Dinsmore* fame." When the older girls began to ask for the novels of Ouìda, Miss Hewins took them home, read them, and was *not* favorably impressed. Writing a letter to the local newspaper, she asked mothers and fathers if they knew what their daughters were reading, and she told them of a story "in which are men who have broken every one of the Ten Commandments, and yet are the petted idols of London society." Then she called in the president of the institute and showed him some of the books for older boys, which were full of "profanity and vulgarity. She was given permission to discard these and substituted better books as soon as possible."

It was exactly a century ago that Miss Hewins published the first edition of her famous pamphlet *Books for the Young: A Guide for Parents and Children*. Her guide opened with a rather spirited preface, followed by rules for parents on how to teach the right use of books. Here are a few:

> Do not let them [the children] read anything that you have not read yourself.
>
> Read to them, and teach them to look for the explanation of allusions in books. Do not count time lost in going to the library with them to see a portrait of Queen Elizabeth, or a picture of a Roman chariot, or to find out why mince-pies are eaten at Thanksgiving.
>
> Do not let them depend on school "speakers" and the "Hundred choice selections" for poetry which they must learn. Find it for them in Shakespeare or Scott, or whatever poet you love, and arrange a scene from the "Midsummer night's dream," the "Tempest," or "As you like it," and let them act it at Christmas or on a birthday.
>
> Remember Jacob Abbott's sensible rule, to give children something that they are growing up to, not away from, and keep down their stock of children's books to the very best.

The third edition of the Hewins book list, published in 1915 by the American Library Association, contains a fuller preface and even more definitive ideas. Still urging parents to obtain for their children the best books money could buy, she told them "best books" were those which enlarge the child's world and enrich his or her life: poetry; prints from great artists; an edition of Shakespeare to be handled "as freely as the Mother Goose which a child should know by heart at six"; fairy tales and myths; absurd fun like Carroll and Lear; and books about nature and the out-of-doors.

> A few stories of modern life that have become general favorites, even though they have faults of style like "Little Women," or a sensational plot like "Little Lord Fauntleroy," are on the list, for the sake of the happy, useful homelife of the one and the sunshiny friendliness of the other. Most of the tales of home and school are those in which children lead simple, sheltered lives. Stories of the present day in which children die, are cruelly treated, or offer advice to their fathers and mothers, and take charge of the finances and love affairs of their elders, are not good reading for boys and girls in happy homes, and the

> favorite books of less fortunate children are fairy-tales or
> histories rather than stories of life like their own.

I find this last statement fascinating—even though a mite patronizing—
because right now, after nearly seventy years, all the right-minded,
nondidactic writers I know—like Nina Bawden, Isabelle Holland,
Penelope Lively, and Katherine Paterson—agree with Miss Hewins that to
offer children only books that reflect their own background and circumstances is preposterous and regressive, and nothing but a throwback to our
puritanical forefathers.

Speaking of *Little Women*, as Caroline Hewins just did, it interested me
to note that Edith Wharton in her autobiography, *A Backward Glance*, says:

> I was never allowed to read the popular American chil-
> dren's books of my day because, as my mother said, the
> children spoke bad English *without the author's knowing it*
> . . . I remember it was only with reluctance, and because
> "all the other children read them," that my mother con-
> sented to my reading *Little Women* and *Little Men;* and my
> ears trained to the fresh racy English of *Alice in Wonderland,*
> *The Water Babies,* and *The Princess and the Goblin,* were
> exasperated by the laxities of the great Louisa.

(It should be recalled that when Edith Wharton was a child, *Little Women*
was still a new book and a best-seller.)

But the quest for good children's books went on. Caroline Hewins was
a close friend of Anne Carroll Moore's, who in New York was building a
powerful career on a relentless search for and a celebration of good
children's literature. But was the very term *good children's literature* only a
vague generality depending for its meaning on the cultivation, the taste,
and the purpose of its user?

In the 1920s the idea of good books for children spread like a rising tide:
there were the high-minded new editors of publishers' juvenile departments, the establishment of the Newbery Medal, and in 1924—part and
parcel of the same impulse—the founding of *The Horn Book Magazine,*
whose first editorial announced the aim of the fledgling journal, "to blow
the horn for fine books for boys and girls." It was in the 1930s that the
eminent French scholar-historian Paul Hazard wrote his unique treatise,
which was eventually translated as *Books, Children and Men.* Perhaps the
most often-quoted bit of the book is his four-page credo entitled "What Are
Good Books?"

After the war Lillian Smith of Toronto wrote her enormously influential
The Unreluctant Years, in which she raised, and convincingly answered,

some time-honored critical questions, thus injecting status into the field of children's literature by proving that the creative energy going into it is no different from that going into other kinds of writing. This was the period when Walter de la Mare was the patron saint of children's books, and his spirit hovered over most of the writing about them. Indeed, from his introduction to *Bells and Grass*, a single sentence was emblazoned in the hearts of children's book people: "I know well that only the rarest kind of best in anything can be good enough for the young." But how many are aware of the interesting words that follow? "I *know* too that in later life it is just (if only just) possible now and again to recover fleetingly the intense delight, the untellable joy and happiness and fear and grief and pain of our early years, of an all but forgotten childhood." I contend that here he is very close to the mind and soul of Maurice Sendak.

There have been myriads of book lists, like the thick volumes of compilations of recommended books from the *Bulletin* of the Center for Children's Books of the University of Chicago—volumes called *Good Books for Children*, whose introductions used terms like *noteworthy* and *best* books and reaffirmed the now traditional criteria of literary quality, quality of content, and suitability of style and subject matter for the intended age. Zena Sutherland, in her introduction to the *Bulletin*'s volume entitled *The Best in Children's Books, 1973–1978*, said, "It is incumbent on adults who are concerned with children's reading to select and counsel wisely" and, among other things, "to comprehend what the elements of good children's books are. In many ways the literary criteria that apply to adult books and children's books are the same," and she enumerated, "that most elusive component, a distinctive literary style" as well as a well-constructed plot, sound characterization without stereotypes, appropriate dialogue, and a pervasive theme.

Now, you who are criticizing the critics are undoubtedly thinking we are given to somewhat lofty generalizations; but if we *have* been a bit vague about what actually constitutes a good book, we have been quite definite about the bad ones, pretty sure of ourselves in identifying the tawdry and the trivial. At least we were until fifteen or twenty years ago.

The past one hundred years of intellectual, scientific, and technological expansion have brought not merely undreamed-of blessings but excruciating problems and unbearable burdens as well. But children's books did not keep pace with the breathtaking changes in the world and, for a long time, did not reflect these problems and burdens. By the 1950s sex and violence in explicit terms were still unthinkable in children's books, and although the dark side of life was not ignored, didacticism was abhorred, and the emphasis remained on traditional good taste and literary quality. Children's writers were not yet concerning themselves with the exceptional child, the abused or the retarded child, or the deeply troubled child. Nor was the imbalance of society's views of certain ethnic and racial groups a major theme, as yet. Thus, although a good deal of naturalism had been injected into adult fiction almost a century before, children's books were still comparatively unaffected.

Then we plunged into the 1960s, and as Ann Durell of E. P. Dutton said: "Indian summer was over . . . the winds of change were about to rise to gale force . . . the social upheavals were already being ushered in to the sonic boom of an amplified electric guitar." The adolescent, or teenager—said to be an American invention, just as the child had been a Victorian one—came to a new independence, and younger brothers and sisters soon began to demand equal freedom. Supported by Freudian theories, authors brought barriers crashing down. And the problem novel arrived, with topics that sounded (and this is Sheila Egoff in her Arbuthnot Honor Lecture) "like chapter titles from a textbook on social pathology." Moreover, the so-called issues approach to children's literature cast away traditional literary and aesthetic standards, and grimly determined adults linked the new view to the practice of bibliotherapy; the use of books to solve personal problems. Social and educational reformers, with their nonliterary assaults on children's books, might lead one to assume that the ancient tales of poets and storytellers as well as the whole body of creative writing for children were to blame for the injustice and inequality that plague us, and not society itself. Yet, over the heads of children the strident voices of adults continue to rage, particularly in the mass media. And latter-day Sarah Trimmers are romping through children's books, scissors in hand.

The Problem with "Enduring Elements"

But let us turn away from the great quest for the good, for I am still haunted by the notion of enduring elements of good books. If we consider elements as simply the component parts of a book, the questions that then obtrude are: Why should the elements of one good book correspond to the elements of another good book? Why should the elements which make one book effective and unique serve the same purpose for another unique book, which is, at its best, one of a kind? In a literary work elements are neither good nor bad in themselves, but merely descriptive. They only serve to indicate the boundaries, and ultimately the form, of the work in question. Certainly in Katherine Paterson's *Jacob Have I Loved* there is a biblical element of quotation and allusion. Critically, we can go beyond the mere identification of this element to indicate how the structure of the book, the very conduct of the story, develops from the context of specific quotations and allusions, and their relationship to the story may be the very key to its meaning.

We are convinced of the goodness or greatness of any book only when we perceive the peculiarly successful combination and interrelationship of its elements, even as a glance at such disparate examples as Jane Gardam's *A Long Way from Verona* or *The Slave Dancer*, by Paula Fox, or *Tom's Midnight Garden*, by Philippa Pearce, or *Sylvester and the Magic Pebble*, by William Steig, will suggest. Even when two distinct works offer analogies—such as *Hamlet* and the Orestes story or the tale of Brünnehilde surrounded by flames and that of the Sleeping Beauty encircled by thorns—the quality of each composition remains individual. One tunes in to a performance, the simultaneous existence of separate elements creating a unity, even as harmony, counterpoint, and instrumentation can coexist in a given measure of music by Bach.

In *The Rhetoric of Fiction* Wayne Booth states approvingly that Henry James, in his essay "The Art of Fiction," explicitly repudiated any effort to say " 'definitely beforehand what sort of an affair the good novel will be.' For him the only absolute requirement is that 'it be interesting.' He will praise a novel like *Treasure Island* because it succeeds 'wonderfully in what it attempts.' " Two months after the publication of James's famous essay, Stevenson published one on the same subject—"A Humble Remonstrance"—in which he stated the following cogent qualifications: "With each new subject . . . the true artist will vary his method and change the point of attack. That which was in one case an excellence, will become a defect in another; what was the making of one book, will in the next be impertinent or dull." So much for enduring elements!

Let me illustrate Stevenson's perception by referring to a work by a children's novelist who has recently used a former "excellence" quite unsuccessfully. I refer to two novels of Penelope Lively, both of which employ situations in which historical time intrudes into the present: her Carnegie Medal book, *The Ghost of Thomas Kempe*, and *The Revenge of Samuel Stokes*, which is reminiscent of the other one in theme, plot, and character. The events seem frustrating to both the characters and the reader; and while in the first book the element of the supernatural intimately penetrates into the life of the young protagonist, in the second one the effect is dissipated and trivialized so that the book unintentionally becomes a parody of its predecessor.

It is by now fairly obvious, I'm afraid, that the more one talks about good children's books, the more one must push back the frontiers of the subject. At the risk of being repetitious, I must stress again the inherent ambiguity in the term *good children's books*. For instance, if one adopts Louise Rosenblatt's concept of a tripartite relationship linking author, book, and reader, the "good" of the book is not necessarily the same for the author and the reader—one being concerned with creation and the other with response; while the book studied objectively as a literary work may be considered in terms of its construction or of its organic nature. Is it enough to say that a children's book is good in its own right, as a work of literature? Or should it be called good because of its lasting influence or because of what it can do to or for the reader?

If the goodness of a children's book should depend upon both its literary merit and its ultimate significance for children, there still remain a number of troublesome conclusions to be faced. One can immediately eliminate the book that seems to be an impeccable literary production but fails to reach an audience. It reminds me of Polonius saying to Hamlet, "What do you read, my lord?" and Hamlet says, "Words, words, words." What about the book of outstanding merit that is accessible only to a few? Do you know that vast, panoramic novel, Fritz Mühlenweg's *Big Tiger and Christian?* One of our children swallowed it in great joyous gulps when he was ten, scarcely eight years after he went through elaborate nightly rituals with *Goodnight Moon*, a mysterious subtle book to which he, like so many other babies, was compulsively attached.

What about the positive quality of an inferior book that appeals to many? Not really a futile question when asked in the light of these statements by Louise Rosenblatt in *The Reader, the Text, the Poem: The Transactional Theory of the Literary Work.* "Absorption in the quality and structure of the experience engendered by the text can happen whether the reader is enthralled by the adventures of the Hardy Boys, or by the anguish of *King Lear*. In either case, in my view, the text has given rise to a literary work of art." Lest we be unduly impressed by the term *literary work of art*, it must be noted that these statements concerned with the reading experience are capped by the astute conclusion: "How to decide whether it is good, bad, or indifferent art is another question."

If we are concerned with the child's responsive act in reading the book—his own contribution to the creative process, if you will—shouldn't we, as adults, play a part in making it comprehensible? Since more than three fourths of my working life was spent introducing books to children, I am naturally convinced of the frequent necessity for an intermediary—what Dorothy Butler calls the human link between the child and the book. Rosenblatt makes the following analogy: "The reader of a text who evokes a literary work of art is, above all, a performer, in the same sense that a pianist performs a sonata, reading it from the text before him." Since I belong to a musical family, the analogy is especially appealing to me; in fact, I would extend it to a double analogy and say that the pianist is not only a performer, he is an intermediary as well. For a listener may need a pianist in order to apprehend the music, just as a child often needs an intermediary to become aware of the existence of a book as well as of its imaginative and emotional force.

As judges or critics, adults are, of course, fallible. Perhaps the most egregious slip occurred when the Newbery Medal was bestowed on the worthiness of *Secret of the Andes* instead of on the perfection of *Charlotte's Web*, thus endowing the award book with a kind of negative fame. One of my predecessors, Ruth Hill Viguers, unfortunately put herself on record with an opinion of *Harriet the Spy:* "Many adult readers appreciating the sophistication of the book will find it funny and penetrating. Children, however, do not enjoy cynicism. I doubt its appeal to many of them."

I know that I have not only despaired of my subject but have actually failed to state in ringing terms what makes a children's book *good*. It would be comforting to be able to do so, but comfort cannot take the place of precision and exactitude; and if the subject does not submit to being encapsulated in a formula or a theorem, its very elusiveness may prove to be its glory. On the other hand, if this discussion has succeeded in arousing logical and pragmatic objections, I am sure that it has answered its purpose—to elicit varying points of view that will help to modulate your beliefs and opinions—and also mine. To tighten my closing thought, may I remind you of three lines from T. S. Eliot's "Little Gidding":

> What we call the beginning is often the end
> And to make an end is to make a beginning.
> The end is where we start from.

APPENDIX I
Chronology of Programs

APPENDIX II
Ithaka

C. P. CAVAFY

TRANSLATED BY BARBARA HARRISON
AND PAUL HEINS

As you set out on the voyage to Ithaka
Pray that your journey be long,
Filled with adventures, filled with wisdom.
Do not fear the Laistrygonians and the Cyclops
And furious Poseidon.
Such creatures you will never find
As long as your thoughts remain lofty,
As long as a rare emotion
Stirs your spirit and your body.
You will not meet the Laistrygonians and the Cyclops
And raging Poseidon
If you do not carry them in your soul,
If your soul does not raise them up before you.

Pray that your journey be long.
May there be many summer mornings
When with pleasure and joy
You will come upon harbors seen for the first time.
May you linger at Phoenician trading posts
And get precious things —
Mother of pearl and coral, amber and ebony,
And exotic perfumes of all kinds,
As many exotic perfumes as you can.
May you go to many Egyptian cities,
To learn and learn from their sages.

Always have Ithaka in your mind.
Your arrival there is your destiny,

But do not hurry the journey;
Better if it lasts for years
And you are old when you anchor at the island.
Wealthy with all you have acquired on the way.
Do not expect further riches from Ithaka.
Ithaka gave you the splendid journey;
Without her you would not have set forth.
She has nothing more to give you.

And if you find her unprepossessing, Ithaka has not deceived you.
So wise have you become, so full of experience,
You will understand by then the meaning of Ithakas.

Children's Books Referred To

Adams, Richard. *Watership Down*. Macmillan, 1974.

Aiken, Joan. *Midnight Is a Place*. Viking, 1974.

———. *The Wolves of Willoughby Chase*, ill. by Pat Marriott. Doubleday, 1963.

Alcott, Louisa May. *Little Women*. Roberts Brothers, 1868.

———. *Rose in Bloom*. Roberts Brothers, 1876.

Alexander, Lloyd. *The Book of Three*. Holt, 1964.

———. *The First Two Lives of Lukas-Kasha*. Dutton, 1978.

———. *The High King*. Holt, 1968.

———. *The Kestrel*. Dutton, 1982.

———. *Taran Wanderer*. Holt, 1967.

———. *Westmark*. Dutton, 1981.

Anno, Mitsumasa. *Anno's Journey*. World, 1978.

Ardizzone, Edward. *Johnny the Clockmaker*. Walck, 1960.

Atkinson, Linda. *In Kindling Flame: The Story of Hannah Senesh, 1921–1944*. Lothrop, 1985.

Babbitt, Natalie. *Tuck Everlasting*. Farrar, 1975.

Barrie, James. *Peter Pan*, ill. by Nora S. Unwin. Scribner's, 1911.

Baum, Betty. *A New Home for Theresa*, ill. by James Barkley. Knopf, 1968.

Bawden, Nina. *Carrie's War*. Lippincott, 1973.

———. *The Robbers*. Lothrop, 1979.

———. *The Runaway Summer*. Lippincott, 1969.

———. *Squib*. Lippincott, 1971.

———. *The Witch's Daughter*. Lippincott, 1966.

Bemelmans, Ludwig. *Madeline*. Viking, 1939.

Bond, Nancy. *A String in the Harp*. Atheneum, 1976.

Boston, Lucy. *The Children of Green Knowe*, ill. by Peter Boston. Harcourt, 1955.

———. *A Stranger at Green Knowe*, ill. by Peter Boston. Harcourt, 1961.

Brooks, Gwendolyn. *Bronzeville Boys and Girls*, ill. by Ronni Solbert. Harper, 1956.

Brown, Margaret Wise. *Goodnight Moon*, ill. by Clement Hurd. Harper, 1947.

Bryan, Ashley. *The Adventures of Aku*. Atheneum, 1976.
———. *The Dancing Granny*. Atheneum, 1977.
———. *The Ox of the Wonderful Horns, and Other African Folktales*. Atheneum, 1971.
———. *Walk Together Children: Black American Spirituals*. Atheneum, 1974.
Bryson, Brenda. *Gilgamesh: Man's First Story*. Holt, 1967.
Burnett, Frances Hodgson. *Little Lord Fauntleroy*, ill. by Harry Toothill. Scribner's, 1886.
———. *The Secret Garden*. F. A. Stokes, 1911.
Burningham, John. *Mr. Gumpy's Outing*. Holt, 1971.

Cameron, Eleanor. *Beyond Silence*. Dutton, 1980.
———. *The Court of the Stone Children*. Dutton, 1973.
———. *The Green and Burning Tree: On the Writing and Enjoyment of Children's Books*. Little, Brown, 1969.
———. *Julia and the Hand of God*, ill. by Gail Owens. Dutton, 1977.
———. *A Room Made of Windows*, ill. by Trina Schart Hyman. Atlantic, 1971.
———. *To the Green Mountains*. Dutton, 1975.
———. *The Unheard Music*. Little, Brown, 1950.
Carroll, Lewis. *Alice's Adventures in Wonderland*, ill. by John Tenniel. Scribner's, 1865.
Cendrars, Blaise. *Shadow*, ill. by Marcia Brown. Scribner's, 1982.
Childress, Alice. *A Hero Ain't Nothin' but a Sandwich*. Coward, 1973.
———. *Rainbow Jordan*. Coward, 1981.
Church, Alfred. *The Odyssey for Boys and Girls*. Macmillan, 1906.
———. *Stories from Homer*. Crowell, 1901.
Clark, Ann Nolan. *Secret of the Andes*, ill. by Jean Charlot. Viking, 1952.
Cleary, Beverly. *Ellen Tebbits*, ill. by Louis Darling. Morrow, 1951.
———. *Henry Huggins*, ill. by Louis Darling. Morrow, 1950.
Cleaver, Vera and Bill. *Where the Lilies Bloom*, ill. by Jim Spanfeller. Lippincott, 1969.
Clifton, Lucille. *My Brother Fine with Me*, ill. by Moneta Barnett. Holt, 1975.
———. *Three Wishes*. Viking, 1976.
Colum, Padraic. *The Children's Homer*, ill. by Willy Pogany. Macmillan, 1925.
Cooper, Susan. *The Dark Is Rising*, ill. by Alan E. Cober. Atheneum, 1973.
———. *Greenwitch*. Atheneum, 1974.
———. *The Grey King*, ill. by Michael Heslop. Atheneum, 1975.
———. *Jethro and the Jumbie*, ill. by Ashley Bryan. Atheneum, 1979.
———. *Silver on the Tree*. Atheneum, 1977.
Cormier, Robert. *After the First Death*. Pantheon, 1979.
———. *The Bumblebee Flies Anyway*. Pantheon, 1983.
———. *The Chocolate War*. Pantheon, 1974.
———. *I Am the Cheese*. Pantheon, 1977.
Crossley-Holland, Kevin. *Beowulf*, ill. by Charles Keeping. Merrimack Publishing Circle, 1984.

Dahl, Roald. *Charlie and the Chocolate Factory*, ill. by Joseph Schindelman. Knopf, 1964.

————. *James and the Giant Peach*, ill. by Nancy Ekholm Burkert. Knopf, 1961.

Daugherty, James. *Daniel Boone*. Viking, 1939.

Degens, T. *Transport 7-41-R*. Viking, 1974.

DeJong, Meindert. *The House of Sixty Fathers*, ill. by Maurice Sendak. Harper, 1956.

de la Mare, Walter. *Come Hither*. Knopf, 1923.

————. *Peacock Pie*, ill. by W. Heath Robinson. Constable, 1913.

dePaola, Tomie. *Big Anthony and the Magic Ring*. Harcourt, 1979.

————. *"Charlie Needs a Cloak."* Prentice-Hall, 1973.

du Bois, William Pène. *Lion*. Viking, 1956.

Dunbar, Paul Laurence. *I Greet the Dawn*, ill. by Ashley Bryan. Atheneum, 1978.

Ets, Marie Hall. *In the Forest*. Viking, 1944.

Ets, Marie Hall, with Aurora Labastida. *Nine Days to Christmas*, ill. by Marie Hall Ets. Viking, 1957.

Ewing, Juliana. *Mary's Meadow*. Little, Brown, 1900.

————. *The Story of a Short Life*. Joseph Knight Company, 1894.

Fife, Dale. *North of Danger*. Dutton, 1978.

Fitzhugh, Louise. *Harriet the Spy*. Harper, 1964.

————. *Nobody's Family Is Going to Change*. Farrar, 1974.

Flack, Marjorie. *The Story About Ping*, ill. by Kurt Wiese. Viking, 1933.

Fox, Paula. *A Likely Place*, ill. by Edward Ardizzone. Macmillan, 1967.

————. *Maurice's Room*, ill. by Ingrid Fetz. Macmillan, 1966.

————. *One-Eyed Cat*. Bradbury, 1984.

————. *A Place Apart*. Farrar, 1980.

————. *Portrait of Ivan*, ill. by Saul Lambert. Bradbury, 1969.

————. *The Slave Dancer*, ill. by Eros Keith. Bradbury, 1973.

————. *The Stone-Faced Boy*, ill. by Donald Mackay. Bradbury, 1968.

Frank, Anne. *Anne Frank: The Diary of a Young Girl*. Doubleday, 1952.

Fritz, Jean. *China Homecoming*. Putnam, 1985.

————. *Homesick: My Own Story*, ill. by Margot Tomes. Putnam, 1982.

Gág, Wanda. *Millions of Cats*. Coward, 1928.

————. *Tales from Grimm*. Coward, 1936.

Gardam, Jane. *A Long Way from Verona*. Macmillan, 1971.

Garner, Alan. *The Aimer Gate*, ill. by Michael Foreman. World, 1979.

————. *Granny Reardun*, ill. by Michael Foreman. World, 1978.

————. *The Owl Service*. Walck, 1968.

————. *Red Shift*. Macmillan, 1973.

————. *The Stone Book*, ill. by Michael Foreman. World, 1978.

Geisel, Theodor Seuss [Dr. Seuss]. *The Cat in the Hat*. Random, 1957.

————. *Horton Hatches the Egg*. Random, 1940.

Goffstein, M. B. *Goldie the Dollmaker*. Farrar, 1969.

Goudge, Elizabeth. *Henrietta's House*. University of London Press, 1942.

Grahame, Kenneth. *The Wind in the Willows*. Scribner's, 1908.

Greene, Bette. *Philip Hall Likes Me, I Reckon Maybe*, ill. by Charles Lilly. Dial, 1974.

Greenfield, Eloise. *Africa Dream,* ill. by Carole Bayard. Harper, 1977.
————. *Sister,* ill. by Moneta Barnett. Crowell, 1974.
Grimes, Nikki. *Growin',* ill. by Charles Lilly. Dial, 1977.
Grimm, Jacob Ludwig Karl. *Grimm's Fairy Tales,* ill. by George Cruikshank and Ludwig Grimm. G. Bell, 1908.
Grimm, Jacob and Wilhelm. *Fairy Tales of the Brothers Grimm,* ill. by Arthur Rackham. Lippincott, 1902.
————. *The Juniper Tree,* ill. by Maurice Sendak. Farrar, 1973.

Hamilton, Virginia. *Arilla Sun Down.* Greenwillow, 1976.
————. *Dustland.* Greenwillow, 1980.
————. *The Gathering.* Greenwillow, 1981.
————. *The House of Dies Drear,* ill. by Eros Keith. Macmillan, 1968.
————. *Justice and Her Brothers.* Greenwillow, 1978.
————. *M. C. Higgins, the Great.* Macmillan, 1974.
————. *The Planet of Junior Brown.* Macmillan, 1971.
————. *Jahdu,* ill. by Jerry Pinkney. Greenwillow, 1980.
Haugaard, Erik Christian. *Leif the Unlucky.* Houghton, 1982.
————. *The Little Fishes,* ill. by Milton Johnson. Houghton, 1967.
————. *The Rider and His Horse,* ill. by Leo and Diane Dillon. Houghton, 1969.
————. *The Samurai's Tale.* Houghton, 1984.
————. *The Untold Tale,* ill. by Leo and Diane Dillon. Houghton, 1971.
Hautzig, Esther. *The Endless Steppe.* Crowell, 1968.
Hinton, S. E. *The Outsiders.* Viking, 1967.
Holland, Isabelle. *Alan and the Animal Kingdom.* Lippincott, 1971.
————. *Cecily, A Novel.* Lippincott, 1967.
————. *Journey for Three.* Houghton, 1975.
————. *The Man Without a Face.* Lippincott, 1972.
————. *Now Is Not Too Late.* Lothrop, 1980.
————. *Of Love and Death and Other Journeys.* Lippincott, 1975.
Holm, Anne. *North to Freedom.* Harcourt, 1965.
Hunter, Kristin. *The Soul Brothers and Sister Lou.* Scribner's, 1968.
Hunter, Mollie. *A Sound of Chariots.* Harper, 1972.
————. *The Third Eye.* Harper, 1979.

Innocenti, Roberto, and Christopher Gallaz. *Rose Blanche,* ill. by Roberto Innocenti. Creative Education, 1985.

Jarrell, Randall. *The Bat-Poet,* ill. by Maurice Sendak. Macmillan, 1964.
————. *Fly by Night,* ill. by Maurice Sendak. Farrar, 1976.
Jones, Hettie. *The Trees Stand Shining: Poetry of the North American Indians,* ill. by Robert Andrew Parker. Dial, 1971.
Kästner, Erich. *Emil and the Detectives,* ill. by Walter Trier. Doubleday, Doran & Company, 1930.
Kerr, M. E. *Gentlehands.* Harper, 1978.

Kherdian, David. *The Road from Home: The Story of an Armenian Girl*. Greenwillow, 1979.

Koehn, Ilse. *Mischling, Second Degree: My Childhood in Nazi Germany*. Greenwillow, 1977.

Konigsburg, E. L. *About the B'nai Bagels*. Atheneum, 1969.

———. *The Dragon in the Ghetto Caper*. Atheneum, 1974.

———. *From the Mixed-up Files of Mrs. Basil E. Frankweiler*. Atheneum, 1967.

———. *Jennifer, Hecate, Macbeth, William McKinley, and Me, Elizabeth*. Atheneum, 1967.

———. *Journey to an 800 Number*. Atheneum, 1982.

———. *Throwing Shadows*. Atheneum, 1981.

———. *Up from Jericho Tel*. Atheneum, 1986.

Korschunow, Irina. *A Night in Distant Motion*. Godine, 1983.

Lagerlöf, Selma. *The Wonderful Adventures of Nils*, with decorations by Harold Heartt. Doubleday, Page & Company, 1907.

Langstaff, John. *Frog Went A-Courtin'*, ill. by Feodor Rojankovsky. Harcourt, 1955.

Langton, Jane. *The Diamond in the Window*, ill. by Eric Blegvad. Harper, 1962.

———. *The Fledgling*. Harper, 1980.

———. *The Fragile Flag*. Harper, 1984.

Leaf, Munro. *The Story of Ferdinand*, ill. by Robert Lawson. Viking, 1936.

Lear, Edward. *The Complete Nonsense Book*. Dodd, Mead, 1912.

Le Guin, Ursula K. *The Farthest Shore*, ill. by Gail Garraty. Atheneum, 1972.

———. *The Tombs of Atuan*, ill. by Gail Garraty. Atheneum, 1971.

———. *A Wizard of Earthsea*, ill. by Ruth Robbins. Parnassus, 1968.

L'Engle, Madeleine. *The Arm of the Starfish*. Farrar, 1965.

Levoy, Myron. *Alan and Naomi*. Harper, 1977.

Lewis, C. S. *The Voyage of the Dawn Treader*. Macmillan, 1952.

Lindgren, Astrid. *Pippi Longstocking*, ill. by Louis S. Glanzman. Viking, 1950.

Little, Lessie Jones, and Eloise Greenfield. *I Can Do It by Myself*, ill. by Carole Bayard. Crowell, 1978.

Lively, Penelope. *The Ghost of Thomas Kempe*, ill. by Anthony Maitland. Dutton, 1973.

———. *Going Back*. Dutton, 1975.

———. *The House in Norham Gardens*. Dutton, 1974.

———. *The Revenge of Samuel Stokes*. Dutton, 1981.

———. *A Stitch in Time*. Dutton, 1976.

Lobel, Arnold. *Owl at Home*. Harper, 1975.

MacDonald, George. *The Golden Key*, ill. by Maurice Sendak. Farrar, 1967.

Maruki, Toshi. *Hiroshima No Pika*. Lothrop, 1982.

Mark, Jan. *Divide and Rule*. Crowell, 1980.

———. *The Ennead*. Crowell, 1978.

Marryat, Frederick. *The Children of the New Forest*, ill. by Stafford Good. Scribner's, 1955.

———. *The Little Savage*. Dutton, 1907.

———. *Mr. Midshipman Easy*, ill. by Jo Polseno. Platt & Munk, 1967.

Masefield, John. *The Box of Delights, or When the Wolves Were Running*. Macmillan, 1935.

———. *The Midnight Folk*. Macmillan, 1927.

Mathis, Sharon Bell. *The Hundred Penny Box*, ill. by Leo and Diane Dillon. Viking, 1975.

Mayne, William. *Earthfasts*. Dutton, 1966.

———. *A Year and a Day*. Dutton, 1976.

McCaffrey, Anne. *Dragondrums*. Atheneum, 1979.

———. *Dragonsinger*. Atheneum, 1977.

———. *Dragonsong*. Atheneum, 1976.

McCloskey, Robert. *Blueberries for Sal*. Viking, 1948.

———. *Burt Dow, Deep-Water Man, A Tale of the Sea in the Classic Tradition*. Viking, 1963.

———. *Centerburg Tales*. Viking, 1951.

———. *Homer Price*. Viking, 1943.

———. *Lentil*. Viking, 1940.

———. *Make Way for Ducklings*. Viking, 1941.

———. *One Morning in Maine*. Viking, 1952.

———. *Time of Wonder*. Viking, 1957.

McKillip, Patricia. *The Riddle-Master of Hed*. Macmillan, 1976.

Meltzer, Milton. *Never to Forget: The Jews of the Holocaust*. Harper, 1976.

Minarik, Else Homelund. *Little Bear*, ill. by Maurice Sendak. Harper, 1957.

Moskin, Marietta. *I Am Rosemarie*. John Day, 1972.

Mühlenweg, Fritz. *Big Tiger and Christian*, ill. by Rafaello Busoni. Pantheon, 1952.

Murray, Michele. *Nellie Cameron*, ill. by Leonora Prince. Seabury, 1971.

Myers, Walter Dean. *The Young Landlords*. Viking, 1979.

Norton, Mary. *Bed-Knob and Broomstick*, ill. by Erik Blegvad. Harcourt, 1967.

———. *The Borrowers*, ill. by Beth and Joe Krush. Harcourt, 1953.

———. *The Borrowers Afield*, ill. by Beth and Joe Krush. Harcourt, 1955.

———. *The Borrowers Afloat*, ill. by Beth and Joe Krush. Harcourt, 1959.

———. *The Borrowers Aloft*, ill. by Beth and Joe Krush. Harcourt, 1961.

———. *The Borrowers Avenged*, ill. by Beth and Joe Krush. Harcourt, 1982.

Orgel, Doris. *The Devil in Vienna*. Dial, 1978.

Orlev, Uri. *The Island on Bird Street*. Houghton, 1983.

Paterson, Katherine. *Bridge to Terabithia*, ill. by Donna Diamond. Crowell, 1977.

———. *The Great Gilly Hopkins*. Crowell, 1978.

———. *Jacob Have I Loved*. Crowell, 1980.

———. *The Master Puppeteer*, ill. by Haru Wells. Crowell, 1975.

———. *Of Nightingales That Weep*, ill. by Haru Wells. Crowell, 1974.

———. *Rebels of the Heavenly Kingdom*, ill. by Kinuko Craft. Dutton, 1983.

———. *The Sign of the Chrysanthemum*, ill. by Peter Landa. Crowell, 1973.

Paton Walsh, Jill. *Goldengrove*. Farrar, 1972.

————. *Unleaving.* Farrar, 1976.

Pearce, Philippa. *Tom's Midnight Garden*, ill. by Susan Einzig. Lippincott, 1959.

Potter, Beatrix. *The Tale of Peter Rabbit.* Warne, 1903.

Prokofiev, Serge. *Peter and the Wolf*, ill. by Charles Mikolaycak. Viking, 1982.

Raskin, Ellen. *William Blake: Songs of Innocence.* Doubleday, 1966.

————. *The Westing Game.* Dutton, 1978.

Reiss, Johanna. *The Upstairs Room.* Crowell, 1972.

Richter, Hans Peter. *Friedrich.* Holt, 1970.

Saint-Exupéry, Antoine de. *The Little Prince.* Harcourt, 1943.

Sawyer, Ruth. *Journey-Cake, Ho!*, ill. by Robert McCloskey. Viking, 1953.

Schlee, Ann. *Ask Me No Questions.* Holt, 1982.

Sebestyen, Ouida. *IOU's.* Atlantic, 1982.

————. *Words by Heart.* Atlantic, 1979.

Sendak, Maurice. *In the Night Kitchen.* Harper, 1970.

————. *Outside over There.* Harper, 1981.

————. *Really Rosie.* Harper, 1975.

————. *Where the Wild Things Are.* Harper, 1963.

Shulevitz, Uri. *The Treasure.* Farrar, 1979.

Siegel, Aranka. *Upon the Head of the Goat: A Childhood in Hungary 1939–1944.* Farrar, 1981.

Silverstein, Shel. *The Giving Tree.* Harper, 1964.

Singer, Isaac Bashevis. *A Day of Pleasure; Stories of a Boy Growing Up in Warsaw*, photos by Roman Vishniac. Farrar, 1969.

Skurzynski, Gloria. *What Happened in Hamelin.* Four Winds, 1979.

Snyder, Zilpha Keatley. *And All Between*, ill. by Alton Raible. Atheneum, 1976.

————. *Below the Root*, ill. by Alton Raible. Atheneum, 1975.

————. *Until the Celebration*, ill. by Alton Raible. Atheneum, 1977.

Southall, Ivan. *Josh.* Macmillan, 1972.

————. *What About Tomorrow.* Macmillan, 1977.

Spyri, Johanna. *Heidi; A Story for Girls*, ill. by J. Watson Davis. A. L. Burt, 1901.

Steig, William. *Doctor De Soto.* Farrar, 1982.

————. *Sylvester and the Magic Pebble.* Simon & Schuster, 1969.

Steptoe, John. *Stevie.* Harper, 1969.

Sutcliff, Rosemary. *Warrior Scarlet.* Walck, 1958.

Taylor, Mildred. *Roll of Thunder, Hear My Cry*, ill. by Jerry Pinkney. Dial, 1976.

Thomas, Piri. *Down These Mean Streets.* Knopf, 1978.

Tolkien, J. R. R. *The Fellowship of the Ring.* Houghton, 1967.

————. *The Hobbit.* Houghton, 1938.

————. *The Lord of the Rings.* Houghton, 1974.

————. *The Return of the King.* Houghton, 1967.

Townsend, John Rowe. *The Summer People.* Lippincott, 1972.

von der Grün, Max. *Howl like the Wolves: Growing Up in Nazi Germany.* Morrow, 1980.

Wells, Rosemary, *Benjamin & Tulip*. Dial, 1973.

――. *Good-Night, Fred*. Dial, 1984.

――. *Leave Well Enough Alone*. Dial, 1977.

――. *Timothy Goes to School*. Dial, 1981.

――. *When No One Was Looking*. Dial, 1980.

White, E. B. *Charlotte's Web*, ill. by Garth Williams. Harper, 1952.

――. *Stuart Little*, ill. by Garth Williams. Harper, 1945.

White, T. H. *The Sword in the Stone*, with decorations by the author and endpapers by Robert Lawson. Putnam, 1939.

Wilder, Laura Ingalls. *Little House in the Big Woods*, ill. by Garth Williams. Harper, 1932.

Willard, Nancy. *The Highest Hit*, ill. by Emily McCully. Harcourt, 1978.

Williams, Garth. *The Rabbits' Wedding*. Harper, 1958.

Yarbrough, Camille. *Cornrows*, ill. by Carole Bayard. Coward, 1979.

Yep, Laurence. *Dragonwings*. Harper, 1975.

Zei, Alki. *Petros' War*. Dutton, 1972.

About the Contributors

JOAN AIKEN, born in Sussex, England, is the daughter of the American poet Conrad Aiken. She is known as a poet, a playwright, and an author of highly imaginative novels and short stories for adults and children. Her books include *The Wolves of Willoughby Chase, Nightbirds on Nantucket, The Whispering Mountain,* and *Bridle the Wind.* She is the winner of the Lewis Carroll Shelf Award, the Manchester Guardian Award, and the Mystery Writers of America Edgar Allan Poe Award.

LLOYD ALEXANDER is a violinist, a translator, and an author whose works include *The Marvelous Misadventures of Sebastian,* the Westmark trilogy, and the Prydain cycle, which begins with *The Book of Three* and ends with *The High King.* He has been awarded the Newbery Medal, the American Book Award, and the National Book Award.

NATALIE BABBITT is a poet, an illustrator, and a writer of children's books, among which are *The Search for Delicious, Kneeknock Rise, The Eyes of the Amaryllis,* and the contemporary classic *Tuck Everlasting.* She teaches writing for children, at Brown University.

NINA BAWDEN, a British writer, is an accomplished novelist for both children and adults. Her children's books include *Squib, Carrie's War,* and *The Peppermint Pig;* among her adult books are *Anna Apparent, Afternoon of a Good Woman,* and *Walking Naked.* She has received the Guardian Award and is a Fellow of the Royal Society of Literature.

THERESE BIGELOW is coordinator of children's and young adult services at the Charles Taylor Library in Hampton, Virginia. An active member of the

Virginia State Library Association and the American Library Association, she has served on award committees and has been a judge for the Boston Globe–Horn Book Awards.

ERIK BLEGVAD, born in Copenhagen, Denmark, is the illustrator of Mary Norton's *Bed-knob and Broomstick*, Carol Kendall's *The Gammage Cup*, and some of Jane Langton's fantasies about the Hall family. With Lenore Blegvad he has created many books, including *Mr. Jensen and Cat* and *Hark! Hark! The Dogs Do Bark*. He talks about his life and work in *Self-Portrait: Erik Blegvad*.

NANCY BOND is the author of *A String in the Harp*, a Newbery Honor Book and winner of the Welsh Arts Council's Tir na n-Og Award. Her subsequent works include *The Voyage Begun*, a Boston Globe–Horn Book Honor Book, and *A Place To Come Back To*, a Junior Literary Guild selection. She is on the faculty of Radcliffe College and has taught at Simmons College.

MARCIA BROWN is the distinguished illustrator of three Caldecott Medal books—*Cinderella*, *Once a Mouse*, and *Shadow*—whose talent and versatility are also evident in other picture books, such as *Stone Soup*, *The Three Billy Goats Gruff*, and *Dick Whittington and His Cat*. *The Lotus Seeds* is a collection of her talks and essays.

ASHLEY BRYAN is the reteller, compiler, and illustrator of a variety of children's books—for example, *Walk Together Children: Black American Spirituals; Beat the Story-Drum, Pum-Pum; The Adventures of Aku;* and *Lion and the Ostrich Chicks and Other African Folk Tales*. He has taught art at Dartmouth College and is the winner of the 1981 Coretta Scott King Award for illustration.

NANCY EKHOLM BURKERT is a studio artist and an illustrator of numerous children's books, including *The Nightingale*, *The Scroobious Pip*, *The Fir Tree*, and *Snow White and the Seven Dwarfs*, a Caldecott Honor Book. Her drawings and paintings accompany poems of Emily Dickinson in *Acts of Light*, edited and with an appreciative essay by Jane Langton.

DOROTHY BUTLER, author, educator, and owner of a children's bookshop in Auckland, New Zealand, received the Eleanor Farjeon Award for her contributions to children's literature. Her study of the impact of books on the development of a handicapped child was the basis of *Cushla and Her Books;* she has also written *Babies Need Books* and its sequel *Five to Eight*. Dorothy Butler has given the Arbuthnot Honor Lecture.

ELEANOR CAMERON, novelist and critic, established her reputation with *The Wonderful Flight to the Mushroom Planet* and has also written *A Room Made of Windows*, winner of the Boston Globe–Horn Book Award, *The Court of the Stone Children*, recipient of the National Book Award, and *Beyond Silence*. She is the author of *The Green and Burning Tree: On the Writing and Enjoyment of Children's Books*.

MARIANNE CARUS, born and educated in Germany, is the founder and editor-in-chief of *Cricket* magazine and a proponent of translated books and stories that transcend cultural and geographic barriers. *Cricket* was a National Magazine Award finalist in the category of General Excellence and received the Distinguished Achievement Award from the Educational Press Association of America.

ALICE CHILDRESS, actress, writer, and lecturer, has been the director of the American Negro Theater in New York and has written several plays, including the Obie Award winner *Trouble in Mind*. She has also written two novels for young people—*A Hero Ain't Nothin' But a Sandwich* and *Rainbow Jordan*.

BRUCE CLEMENTS, an ordained minister and a college teacher of English, is the author of *I Tell a Lie Every So Often; Prison Window, Jerusalem Blue;* and—with Hanna Clements—*Coming Home to a Place You've Never Been Before*.

EILEEN COLWELL, widely known as a storyteller and a pioneer in children's library service in England, is the editor of many collections of stories, including *A Storyteller's Choice* and *Humblepuppy and Other Stories for Telling*. She was named by the Queen of England a Member of the British Empire and was awarded the honorary degree of Doctor of Letters by Loughborough University.

SUSAN COOPER, born in England, is the winner of the Newbery Medal for *The Grey King*, the fourth of five fantasy novels known as *The Dark Is Rising* series. A playwright, the biographer of J. B. Priestley, and a former journalist for the London *Sunday Times*, she lives in Cambridge, Massachusetts.

ROBERT CORMIER, a New Englander, is a writer of contemporary realism, whose children's books include *The Chocolate War*, *I Am the Cheese*, and *After the First Death*. An award-winning journalist, Robert Cormier has also written for adults *A Little Raw on Monday Mornings* and *Now and at the Hour*.

PETER DICKINSON is a British novelist and a former editor and reviewer for *Punch*. His fiction for children includes *The Dancing Bear*, *The Blue Hawk*, *Tulku*, and *The Seventh Raven*; among his novels for adults are *Sleep and His Brother*, *One Foot in the Grave*, and *Tefuga*. He is the recipient of the Guardian Award, the Boston Globe–Horn Book Award, and the Carnegie Medal.

FRITZ EICHENBERG is distinguished as teacher, graphic artist, and illustrator of literary classics, such as works by the Brontës, Dostoyevski, Tolstoy, Goethe, and Shakespeare. His work for children is represented by the picture books *Ape in a Cape*—a Caldecott Honor Book—and *Dancing in the Moon*, and he has also been a prolific illustrator of books for older children. Fritz Eichenberg's wood engravings and lithographs are published in his book *The Wood and the Graver*.

NORMA FARBER was a Boston poet, whose many books for children include *As I Was Crossing Boston Common*, *Six Impossible Things Before Breakfast*, *How Does It Feel to Be Old?* and *There Once Was a Woman Who Married a Man*. Just before her death in 1984, her first novel was published—*Mercy Short: A Winter Journal, North Boston, 1692–1693*.

TOM FEELINGS is the illustrator of several award-winning books. *Moja Means One: Swahili Counting Book* and *Jambo Means Hello: Swahili Alphabet Book*, both written by Muriel Feelings, were Caldecott Honor Books. Tom Feelings is the illustrator of Julius Lester's Newbery Honor Book *To Be a Slave; Something on My Mind*, written by Nikki Grimes, earned the artist the Coretta Scott King Award.

CAROLYN W. FIELD, vigorous advocate for children and books, has served as coordinator of work with children in the Free Library of Philadelphia and as president of the Children's Services Division of the American Library Association. Carolyn Field has been a member of the Newbery-Caldecott Committee and was a judge for the Boston Globe–Horn Book Awards. She was the editor of *Subject Collections in Children's Literature*.

PAULA FOX is an author of novels for both children and adults. For children she has written *The Stone-Faced Boy*, *The Slave Dancer*—for which she received the Newbery Medal—*A Place Apart*, *How Many Miles to Babylon?* and *One-Eyed Cat*, a Newbery Honor Book; in 1978 she received the coveted Hans Christian Andersen Medal. Her novels for adults include *Desperate Characters*, *The Widow's Children*, and *A Servant's Tale*.

JEAN FRITZ is a versatile writer of fiction and nonfiction for younger children as well as for older children. Her short, spirited biographies include *And Then What Happened, Paul Revere?* and *What's the Big Idea, Ben Franklin?* Among her other works are historical fiction and the autobiographical novels *Homesick: My Own Story* and *China Homecoming.* Jean Fritz is the winner of the Laura Ingalls Wilder Award for her lasting and memorable contribution to children's literature.

ALAN GARNER, British playwright, novelist, and reteller of folklore, has earned distinction for *Elidor, Red Shift,* and the Stone Book quartet. For *The Owl Service* he was awarded both the Carnegie Medal and the Guardian Award.

VIRGINIA HAMILTON is the celebrated author of both fiction and nonfiction. For *M. C. Higgins, the Great* she received three major honors: the Newbery Medal, the National Book Award, and the Boston Globe–Horn Book Award. Virginia Hamilton is also the author of *The Planet of Junior Brown, Arilla Sun Down,* and *The People Could Fly: American Black Folktales,* for which she was given the Coretta Scott King Award.

BARBARA HARRISON was the founding director of the Center for the Study of Children's Literature at Simmons College. She has taught in the public schools of Washington, D.C., and of Newton, Massachusetts, and is the author of reviews and essays on reading, literature, and contemporary society published in *Commonweal, The Horn Book Magazine,* and *The Quarterly Journal of the Library of Congress.*

ERIK CHRISTIAN HAUGAARD, born in Copenhagen, Denmark, is the author of such historical novels for children as *Hakon of Rogen's Saga, Orphans of the Wind,* and *The Rider and His Horse;* his novel about World War II, *The Little Fishes,* is a modern classic. Erik Haugaard has received several awards, including the Boston Globe–Horn Book Award, the Jane Addams Award, and the Chapelbrook Foundation Award. He is the translator of *Hans Christian Andersen: The Complete Fairy Tales and Stories.*

ETHEL HEINS is a lecturer, an essayist, and a critic of children's literature, who has been on the faculty of the Center for the Study of Children's Literature at Simmons College. Formerly children's librarian at the New York Public Library and the Boston Public Library and school librarian in Lexington, Massachusetts, she is also former editor of *The Horn Book Magazine,* has been cited "for distinguished achievement" by Douglass College, and has received an honorary doctorate from Simmons College.

PAUL HEINS, a critic, an essayist, and a reviewer of children's literature, has been on the faculty of the Center for the Study of Children's Literature at Simmons College. He has taught English in the Boston English High School and is former editor of *The Horn Book Magazine*. The translator of *Snow White* from the German, Paul Heins was also the editor of *Crosscurrents of Criticism: Horn Book Essays 1968–1977* and is the recipient of an honorary doctorate from Simmons College.

ISABELLE HOLLAND writes for both children and adults. Among her children's novels are *Amanda's Choice; Heads You Win, Tails I Lose;* and *Of Love and Death and Other Journeys. The Man Without a Face* established her as an uncommonly fine writer for young people. For adults she has written *The Marchington Inheritance, Counterpoint, The Lost Madonna,* and other novels.

H. M. HOOVER, a leading writer of science fiction for young people, is the author of such books as *The Delikon, The Bell Tree, The Rains of Eridan,* and *Another Heaven, Another Earth.*

MOLLIE HUNTER, born in East Lothian, Scotland, is a writer whose many books for children include the autobiographical novel *A Sound of Chariots,* the fantasies *The Kelpie's Pearls* and *The Haunted Mountain,* and the historical novels *The Third Eye* and *The Stronghold,* winner of the Carnegie Medal. *Talent Is Not Enough* is a collection of her essays and lectures.

TRINA SCHART HYMAN, talented illustrator of numerous children's books, has used folktales in such picture books as *Snow White, Rapunzel,* and *Little Red Riding Hood,* and her artwork is also seen in biographies, novels, and books of poetry for young readers. Trina Hyman was awarded the Caldecott Medal for *Saint George and the Dragon,* retold by Margaret Hodges.

JEAN KARL, former vice president and director of the children's book department at Atheneum, has written science fiction novels for children— *But We Are Not of Earth, The Turning Place,* and *Strange Tomorrow. From Childhood to Childhood: Children's Books and Their Creators* contains some of the convictions gathered during her years of publishing experience.

M. E. KERR is an award-winning author of young adult novels, such as *Dinky Hocker Shoots Smack; Gentlehands; Is That You, Miss Blue?; Little, Little;* and *Night Kites. Me, Me, Me, Me, Me: Not a Novel* is a collection of memoirs.

E. L. KONIGSBURG is a novelist whose first two books, *From the Mixed-up Files of Mrs. Basil E. Frankweiler* and *Jennifer, Hecate, Macbeth, William McKinley, and Me, Elizabeth* were published in the same year and earned her respectively the Newbery Medal and a Newbery Honor Book citation. A former teacher of chemistry and a student of art and art history, she has continued to be well received by critics for such works as *Father's Arcane Daughter, Journey to an 800 Number,* and *Up from Jericho Tel.*

GINNY MOORE KRUSE, a lecturer, a consultant, and the director of the Cooperative Children's Book Center, University of Wisconsin—Madison, is a regular children's book reviewer on Wisconsin public radio and a regional adviser of the Society of Children's Book Writers. She has been a teacher, a school and a public librarian, and an active member of the American Library Association, having served on the Newbery and the Caldecott committees, both as member and as chairperson.

SONIA LANDES is an educator and an author of educational materials, such as the Weston Woods sound filmstrip *A Closer Look at Peter Rabbit.* She has taught courses in children's literature at Simmons College and Brandeis University and works closely with teachers at the Buckingham Browne & Nichols School in Cambridge, Massachusetts. Sonia Landes is coauthor with Alison Landes of *Pariswalks: Close-ups of the Left Bank.*

JOHN LANGSTAFF has retold folklore for children in such books as the Caldecott Medal winner *Frog Went A-Courtin',* illustrated by Feodor Rojankovsky, and *The Two Magicians,* illustrated by Fritz Eichenberg; he has also made several recordings for children and adults. The creator and artistic director of the Christmas Revels and the Spring Revels, John Langstaff is an inspired actor, singer, musician, and impresario.

JANE LANGTON, illustrator and author of books for children, is well known for *The Diamond in the Window, The Swing in the Summerhouse, The Fragile Flag,* and the Newbery Honor Book *The Fledgling.* For adults she has written several mystery novels, among them *Dark Nantucket Noon, Emily Dickinson Is Dead,* and *Good and Dead.* Jean Langton has taught writing for children, at Simmons College and at Radcliffe College.

MADELEINE L'ENGLE wrote *Meet the Austins* and its sequels *The Moon by Night* and *The Young Unicorns* as well as the perennially popular *A Wrinkle in Time,* which earned her a Newbery Medal and the passionate allegiance of young readers; she is also known for her books for adults. Madeleine L'Engle has served on faculties of colleges and universities across the country and has taught children in New York City, where she is librarian of the Cathedral of Saint John the Divine.

BLAIR LENT illustrated the Caldecott Medal book *The Funny Little Woman* by Arlene Mosel. His interest in architecture is evidenced in his exquisite illustrations for Andersen's *The Little Match Girl*, and his concern for the relationship of words to pictures in such books as *John Tabor's Ride*, *Why the Sun and the Moon Live in the Sky*, and *Tikki Tikki Tembo*.

BETTY LEVIN is a sheep farmer, a teacher, and a writer—often of fantasy—whose children's novels include *The Sword of Culann*, *The Keeping-Room*, *A Binding Spell*, *Put on My Crown*, and *The Ice Bear*. Having taught at Pine Manor Open College and the Simmons College Center for the Study of Children's Literature, she is a former Fellow of the Mary Ingraham Bunting Institute of Radcliffe College and is currently on the faculty of Radcliffe.

PENELOPE LIVELY received the Carnegie Medal for *The Ghost of Thomas Kempe* and the Whitbread Literary Award for *A Stitch in Time* and has written many other books for children. Her novels for adults include *Judgement Day*, *The Road to Lichfield*, and *Treasures of Time*, for which she received the first National Book Award given by the Arts Council of Britain.

ARNOLD LOBEL, a prolific and successful illustrator of picture books, is the author and illustrator of the much-loved Frog and Toad books for beginning readers. He received the first Irma Simonton Black Award from the Bank Street College of Education for *Mouse Tales* and the Caldecott Medal for his own book of verse, *Fables*.

DAVID MACAULAY is both author and illustrator of several books with architectural themes and drawings. *Cathedral: The Story of Its Construction*, a Caldecott Honor Book, was the winner of the Deutscher Jugendbuchpreis, a German award given yearly to the best nonfiction picture book. His other books include *City: A Story of Roman Planning and Construction*, *Pyramid*, and *Unbuilding*.

GREGORY MAGUIRE has writen several children's books—*The Lightning Time*, *The Daughter of the Moon*, *Lights on the Lake*, and *The Dream Stealer*, cited as a Teacher's Choice by the National Council of Teachers of English. He has taught elementary school and has been associate director of the Center for the Study of Children's Literature at Simmons College.

JAN MARK is the author of short stories and novels for children, including *Aquarius*, *The Ennead*, and *Nothing to Be Afraid Of*, and was awarded the Carnegie Medal twice—for *Thunder and Lightnings* and for *Handles*. A former teacher, she is currently Arts Council Writer Fellow in Residence at Oxford Polytechnic, Oxford, England.

ROBERT MCCLOSKEY is the renowned author and illustrator of two Caldecott Medal books—*Make Way for Ducklings* and *Time of Wonder*—and also of *Blueberries for Sal* and *One Morning in Maine*. Other books by McCloskey, reflecting his characteristic American humor, are *Lentil*, *Homer Price*, and *Centerburg Tales*, all of which reveal aspects of his childhood in Hamilton, Ohio.

DAVID MCCORD is a poet and an essayist whose collections include *Every Time I Climb a Tree*, *Far and Few*, *Take Sky*, and *One at a Time: Collected Poems for the Young*. He was the winner of the first National Council of Teachers of English Award for Excellence in Poetry for Children. He is a Benjamin Franklin Fellow of the Royal Society of England and the recipient of the Harvard Medal for committed service to Harvard University.

MARGARET K. MCELDERRY is the director of Margaret K. McElderry Books, an imprint of Macmillan. Before entering publishing, she was a children's librarian at the New York Public Library. For her impressive contributions to the world of children's books, she was awarded the honorary degree of Doctor of Humane Letters by Mount Holyoke College.

MILTON MELTZER, a leading author of nonfiction for children, has written such books as *The Black American: A History in Their Own Words* and *Never to Forget: The Jews of the Holocaust*. Chiefly writing political and social history and biography, he is deeply concerned with human rights, peace, and social justice.

CATHIE MERCIER, lecturer, book reviewer, and assistant director of the Center for the Study of Children's Literature at Simmons College, teaches courses at Northeastern University and is a leader of community workshops on aspects of children's literature.

CHARLES MIKOLAYCAK is the illustrator of such books as Barbara Cohen's *I Am Joseph* and *The Binding of Isaac*, Eve Bunting's *The Man Who Could Call Down Owls*, and Prokofiev's *Peter and the Wolf*, and reteller-illustrator of *Babushka: An Old Russian Folktale*. Several of his books have been American Library Association Notable Books and Children's Book Council Showcase Selections.

KATHERINE PATERSON, the widely acclaimed author of historical novels and contemporary fiction for children, has written *The Sign of the Chrysanthemum* and *The Master Puppeteer* as well as *Bridge to Terabithia, Jacob Have I Loved,* and *The Great Gilly Hopkins.* She has been honored with two Newbery Medals, two National Book Awards, and the Lewis Carroll Shelf Award. *Gates of Excellence: On Reading and Writing Books for Children* is a collection of her essays and speeches.

JILL PATON WALSH is a lecturer, a professor of children's literature, and a novelist, whose works for children include *Fireweed, A Chance Child, The Emperor's Winding Sheet, A Parcel of Patterns,* and *Gaffer Samson's Luck.* She is the recipient of several awards, including the Whitbread Literary Award, the Boston Globe–Horn Book Award, and the lucrative first annual Smarties prize. Highly admired as a speaker, she has given many lectures at the Center for the Study of Children's Literature at Simmons College and presented the prestigious Gertrude Clarke Whittall Lecture at the Library of Congress.

ELLEN RASKIN, who died in 1984, was the author and illustrator of humorous and eccentric works, such as the picture books *Spectacles* and *Nothing Ever Happens on My Block.* She also wrote the novels *Figgs & Phantoms* and *The Westing Game,* winner of the Newbery Medal.

EVE RICE is the author and illustrator of many books for the very young, including *Goodnight, Goodnight; Benny Bakes a Cake;* and *Once in a Wood: Ten Tales from Aesop,* all selected by *School Library Journal* for inclusion in its Best Books of the Year list. *Sam Who Never Forgets,* another of her many well-received books, appeared in the International Reading Association's Children's Choices.

ANN SCHLEE, a British author, has written several novels for children, among them *Guns of Darkness, The Vandal,* winner of the Guardian Award, and *Ask Me No Questions,* a Boston Globe–Horn Book Honor Book. Her novels for adults include *The Rhine Journey* and *The Proprietor.*

OUIDA SEBESTYEN is well known for her first children's novel *Words by Heart,* which was included in the *New York Times* Best Books, the *School Library Journal* Best Books of the Year, and the annual Library of Congress list *Children's Books.* She has also written *Far from Home* and *IOU's.*

FRANCES V. SEDNEY, coordinator of children's services at the Harford County Library in Maryland, is an active member of the American Library Association, serving on various administrative committees. She has been a lecturer and a core faculty member at the Center for the Study of Children's Literature at Simmons College and is recognized for her commitment to the child and the book.

MAURICE SENDAK, the internationally celebrated artist, created both text and illustrations for such works as *Where the Wild Things Are, In the Night Kitchen, Higglety Pigglety Pop!* and *Outside Over There.* He has received many honors, among them the Caldecott Medal, the Hans Christian Andersen Medal, and the Laura Ingalls Wilder Medal, and holds honorary doctorates from Boston University and from Princeton University.

MARCIA SEWALL has done both text and illustrations for several books for children—among them *The Little Wee Tyke: An English Folktale, The Cobbler's Song, The World Turned Upside Down,* and *The Pilgrims of Plimoth.* In addition, she has done the artwork for *Song of the Horse, Ridin' That Strawberry Roan,* and *The Squire's Bride.* Marcia Sewall's work has been cited twice among the *New York Times* Best Illustrated Books of the Year.

URI SHULEVITZ won the Caldecott Medal for *The Fool of the World and the Flying Ship,* a Russian tale retold by Arthur Ransome; he wrote and illustrated such books as *One Monday Morning,* *The Treasure*—a Caldecott Honor Book—and *Dawn,* winner of the Christopher Medal. He synthesizes years of experience as artist, illustrator, and teacher, and explains the process of creating a picture book, in his *Writing with Pictures.*

RUDINE SIMS, now Rudine Sims Bishop, is professor of education at the Ohio State University College of Education. An admired lecturer, she has also published articles and book reviews in scholarly and professional journals and is the author of *Shadow and Substance: Afro-American Experience in Contemporary Children's Fiction.*

ZILPHA KEATLEY SNYDER is the author of books of fantasy for children, among them *The Egypt Game, The Headless Cupid, The Changeling, Below the Root,* and *The Birds of Summer.* Her many awards include the *New York Herald Tribune* Spring Book Festival Award, the Christopher Award, and the George G. Stone Center for Children's Books Award.

JOAN M. TIEMAN, an educator and a master teacher in the public schools of Brookline, Massachusetts, recently held a distinguished Lucretia Crocker Fellowship awarded by the Commonwealth of Massachusetts. She has taught courses in children's literature at Simmons College and has done considerable work in teacher education.

JOHN ROWE TOWNSEND is an author, a critic, and a professor of children's literature, whose works for children include *Trouble in the Jungle; Good Night, Prof, Dear; Noah's Castle; The Islanders;* and *The Intruder,* which received the Boston Globe–Horn Book Award. He is respected for his critical works—*A Sense of Story, Written for Children,* and *A Sounding of Storytellers.* Among his distinguished lectures are the Arbuthnot Honor Lecture, the Anne Carroll Moore Lecture, and the Gertrude Clarke Whittall Lecture at the Library of Congress.

NANCY WILLARD is a poet, an author of children's books, and a Newbery Medal winner for *A Visit to William Blake's Inn: Poems for Innocent and Experienced Travelers.* She also wrote *Sailing to Cythera* and *The Island of the Grass King,* each of which won a Lewis Carroll Shelf Award. Nancy Willard teaches English at Vassar College.

CHRIS VAN ALLSBURG is the much-honored author and illustrator of such picture books as *The Wreck of the Zephyr* and *The Garden of Abdul Gasazi,* which was given the Boston Globe–Horn Book Award. For *Jumanji* and *The Polar Express* he was twice the recipient of the Caldecott Medal.

CAROLINE WARD has been assistant director of library promotion and advertising at Harper & Row Publishers, Inc., and is the former children's services consultant for the Vermont Department of Libraries. She is active in the American Library Association, especially on various committees of the Association of Library Services to Children.

ROSEMARY WELLS writes and illustrates picture books and is the author of novels for older children, including *The Fog Comes on Little Pig Feet, None of the Above,* and *When No One Was Looking.* Among her picture books are the Max series, *Benjamin & Tulip, Noisy Nora,* and *Unfortunately Harriet.*

LAURENCE YEP is the author of *Child of the Owl,* winner of the Boston Globe–Horn Book Award; *Dragonwings,* a Newbery Honor Book; and *Dragon of the Lost Sea.* He is highly admired for his use of Chinese folk elements in children's fiction and for his deft portrayal of the Chinese-American experience.

JANE YOLEN, a prolific writer, won the Christopher Award for *The Seeing Stick* and was a finalist in the National Book Awards with *The Girl Who Cried Flowers and Other Tales.* She has also written numerous fairy tales and picture book texts, including *The Emperor and the Kite,* a Caldecott Honor Book, illustrated by Ed Young.

Index

Boldface numbers indicate an individual's contribution(s) to this volume.

557